Tom Lodge

Black Politics
in South Africa since 1945

Longman London and New York

Longman Group UK Limited
Longman House, Burnt Mill,
Harlow, Essex CM20 2JE England
and Associated Companies throughout the world

*Published in the United States of America
by Longman Inc, New York*

© Longman Group Ltd 1983

First published 1983
Second Impression 1984
Third Impression 1986

British Library Cataloguing in Publication Data
Lodge, Tom
　　Black politics in South Africa since 1945.
　　1. Black nationalism – South Africa – History
　　I. Title
　　322.4′4′0968　　DT763

ISBN 0-582-64327-9

Library of Congress Cataloging in Publication Data
Lodge, Tom, fl. 1979–
　　Black politics in South Africa since 1945.
　　Includes index.
　　1. Blacks — South Africa – Politics and government.
　　2. Civil rights movements – South Africa.
　　3. Civil rights demonstrations – South Africa.
　　4. South Africa – Politics and government.
　　5. South Africa – Race relations.
　　I. Title.
　　DT763.6.L62　1983　　968′.00496　　82-14897
　　ISBN 0-582-64328-7
　　ISBN 0-582-64327-9 (pbk.)

Produced by Longman Singapore Publishers (Pte) Ltd.
Printed in Singapore

Contents

List of figures

Abbreviations

AAC	All-African Convention
AEM	African Education Movement
ALC	African Liberation Committee (of OAU)
AMU	African Mineworkers' Union
ANC	African National Congress
APLA	Azanian People's Liberation Army (PAC)
APTC	Alexandra People's Transport Committee
AZAPO	Azanian People's Organisation
BAWU	Black Allied Workers' Union
BPA	Black Parents' Association
BPC	Black People's Convention
CATA	Cape African Teachers' Association
CNETU	Council for Non-European Trades Unions
COSAS	Congress of South African Students
CPSA	Communist Party of South Africa
CUSA	Confederation of Unions of South Africa
CYL	Congress Youth League
EPC	Evaton Passenger Company
EPTC	Evaton People's Transport Council
FCWU	Food and Canning Workers' Union
FNLA	Frente Naçional de Libertaçao de Angola
FOFATUSA	Federation of Free African Trade Unions of South Africa
FOSATU	Federation of South African Trade Unions
FRAC	Franchise Action Committee
FSAW	Federation of South African Women
ICU	Industrial and Commercial Workers' Union
MDC	Movement for Democracy of Content
NEUM	Non-European Unity Movement
NUSAS	National Union of South African Students
OAU	Organisation of African Unity
PAC	Pan-Africanist Congress
PUTCO	The Public Utility Transport Company
SACOD	South African Congress of Democrats
SACPO	South African Coloured People's Organisation
SACTU	South African Congress of Trade Unions
SAIC	South African Indian Congress
SANNC	South African Native National Congress (later ANC)
SASM	South African Students' Movement
SASO	South African Students' Organisation

SAT&LC	South African Trades and Labour Council
SAUF	South African United Front
SCA	Soweto Civic Association
SSRC	Soweto Students' Representative Council
TATA	Transvaal African Teachers' Association
WRAB	West Rand Administration Board
ZAPU	Zimbabwe African People's Union

To Carla and Kim

Preface

This book is about the history of resistance movements within the black population of South Africa, from the end of the Second World War until the present. The period it is concerned with can be divided into four historical phases, each of which coincides with a different decade. The first, the 1940s, was a time when the proletarianisation and industrialisation which resulted from a socio-ecological crisis in the countryside and the demands of a wartime economy created a vast new urban political constituency. The established political movements came to terms with it only hesitantly and in the meantime this new army of the urban poor dealt spontaneously with the immediate problems which confronted it: the cost of food, the price of transport, the shortage of shelter and the lack of money. These new conditions combined to create a forcing-house for a new political ideology; a fresh assertive nationalism which drew on two separate sources of inspiration, ethnic romanticism and working-class radicalism.

The second phase, the phase of mass political campaigning, was to develop as the result of the incorporation by political organisations of the new social forces released in the previous decade. The new nationalist movement contained within it several different tensions, between ethno-nationalists and social radicals, between both these on the one hand and the older generation of liberal civil rights campaigners on the other, and, finally, between the movement's working-class base and its largely petty-bourgeois leadership. The fashion in which these inner contradictions expressed themselves and the extent to which they were resolved provide an important theme of this book, especially in Chapters 2–9 which described this second phase.

The 1960s, the third phase, witnessed the painful and sometimes clumsy process of transformation from a loosely structured mass organisation to a clandestine insurgent revolutionary élite. The 1960s were years of massive social engineering with the state's brutal efforts to reconstruct the social landscape produced by Africa's greatest industrial revolution.

The final chapter is about the 1970s and after, the fourth and present phase of resistance. This has taken place in a context of crisis for the South African state and the society it is designed to preserve. The elements in this crisis were originally economic but lately they have included the black resistance movements themselves, some of which appear to have set the country irrevocably on a course towards civil war.

This book is about resistance movements, by which I mean the groups, some of them structured by deliberate organisation but others not, which take action to oppose or frustrate the implementation of political or economic measures by those who administer, own or employ. In South Africa the resistance movement is usually predominantly black though the authorities it resists are not always white. Sometimes the resistance with which we are concerned takes the form of a self-conscious political body, for example the Communist Party or the African National Congress. On occasions, though, the resistance movement can consist of an urban crowd united only momentarily in its opposition to higher bus fares, or peasants, determined to destroy a barbed-wire fence erected without their consent.

The history of formal political organisations and the more inchoate resistance groups in South Africa is not easy to understand without some familiarity with local situations and the conditions arising from them. One of my main preoccupations, therefore, has been to set the events I describe firmly in their particular local context. This has been at the risk of losing sight of the overall picture for the sake of concentrating on details, but without taking the risk the variations and inconsistencies in black responses to political repression and social injustice would be incomprehensible.

The book is about black resistance; it does not claim to describe and document the totality of black politics. In using a concept of resistance I have limited myself to looking at forms of action which fall outside the legally sanctioned outlets of political expression for black South Africans. I have largely neglected the history of those who for one reason or another have chosen 'to work within the system': for instance there are very few references to the activities of 'homeland'-based political parties. Less justifiably perhaps, I have concentrated on explicit types of resistance which have directly confronted the authorities or the employers of labour. The story of the more introverted kinds of resistance – those offered by cultural conservatism or religious separatism for example – deserve and have received separate and extended treatment of their own.[1]

In the text I have usually adhered to what has become conventional South African terminology for describing the different people inhabiting this country, i.e. 'white' for European settlers or their descendants, 'African' for members of the Bantu-speaking groups, 'coloured' for those people who are legally categorised as being of mixed descent, and 'Indian' for the descendants of the Asian indentured labourers and traders who arrived in South Africa in the nineteenth century. When referring collectively to the African, coloured and Indian sections of the population, I have used the term 'black', following what is today popular usage within these communities. On the whole I have tried to avoid the suggestion that these social categories each encapsulate a homogenous group. In emphasising the social cleavages within each group and the bonds that exist between them I have used class-related concepts rather than those drawn from the study of ethnicity. One of the implicit arguments of this book is that the former are the more useful for the analysis of the resistance movements under consideration here.

For the sake of convenience I have also used the words 'reserve', 'homeland' and 'squatter' without using inverted commas throughout. All three words came to acquire particular meanings and connotations as a result of their use, at different times, in governing circles in South Africa; they became, in effect, part of the language of government. Rather than adopting the somewhat clumsy expedient of adorning the words with inverted commas throughout, I have allowed them to stand: it should become clear in the course of the book that this in no way implies an acceptance of the ideology that is expressed in their use in official government statements and documents.

I owe a great deal to the many people who have helped me with information, documentation, hospitality, encouragement, criticism and the various laborious tasks associated with preparing a manuscript for publication. I would like to acknowledge my debt to: Frances Baard, Brian Bunting, Marion Friedman, Peter Hjul, Helen Joseph, William Letlalo, Don Mattera, Tommy Mohajane, Dr Nthatho Motlana, Professor Es'kia Mphahlele, Jean Naidoo, A. B. Ngcobo, Matthew Nkoana, Peter Rodda, Albie Sachs, Rose Schlacter, David Sibeko, Ben Turok, Randolph Vigne, Ernie and Jill Wentzel, and M. B. Yengwa; without the insights drawn from the interviews they so generously gave me, this book would have many more gaps in its narrative and analysis than it has. In this respect I was also fortunate in having two perceptive and helpful correspondents in Philip Kgosana and Joe Nkatlo. I owe much to the advice, encouragement and stimulation provided by colleagues and students at the University of the Witwatersrand: Philip Bonner, Belinda Bozzoli, Jonathan Clegg, Tim Couzens, Peter Kallaway, Glen Moss, Bruce Murray, Patrick Pearson, Noam Pines, Charles van Onselen, Alf Stadler, David Webster, Eddie Webster and David Yudelman. In the same fashion, Christopher Hill of the University of York's Centre for Southern African Studies has been a valued source of imaginative comment. I am grateful to Joanne Yawich for allowing me access to her unpublished research work on women's protest movements, to Helen de Jager for supplying me with her research findings, and to Vusi Nkumane for his skilful translations from the Xhosa-language press. Anna Cunningham and Teresa Yudaken of the University of the Witwatersrand library helped me enormously by suggesting and locating potential sources of documentation as did Reuben Denge of the South African Institute of Race Relations. I am also very grateful to Pat Barkhuizen, Sue Ellis, Glynn Holton and Mary Pollard for their help with the typing and to Carla Grootenboer who drew the maps. My thanks are due to the Council of the University of the Witwatersrand for their research grant. Finally I must attribute my major source of inspiration to the exiled South African historian, Baruch Hirson. His compassionate intelligence and moral commitment have been profound influences on the shaping of this work.

Johannesburg, January 1982

Notes

1   See: Philip Mayer, *Black Villagers in an Industrial Society*, Oxford University Press, Cape Town, 1980, Chapter 1; Bengt Sundkler, *Bantu Prophets in South Africa*, Oxford University Press, London, 1961; David Coplan, 'The African performer and the Johannesburg entertainment industry: the struggle for African culture on the Witwatersrand', in Belinda Bozzoli (ed.), *Labour, Townships and Protest*, Ravan, Johannesburg, 1979.

CHAPTER I

Black protest before 1950

The 1940s were a watershed in the development of African politics in South Africa, a period in which a massive expansion of the black urban labour force, its increasing deployment in manufacturing industry, the revival of trade unionism and the stimulation of class consciousness, all had a radicalising effect on African political organisations, and in particular the African National Congress (ANC). In an environment of developing popular militancy manifested by industrial action and informal community protest, the frustrated aspirations of an African middle class assumed a fresh significance within the context of formal political movements. This chapter will examine these processes in some detail. Before doing this though, in order to set these developments in their proper historical context, African political responses from the founding of the first African national political organisation until the beginning of the Second World War will be summarised.

On 8 January 1912 there assembled in Bloemfontein several hundred of South Africa's most prominent African citizens: professional men, chieftains, ministers, teachers, clerks, interpreters, landholders, businessmen, journalists, estate agents, building contractors and labour agents. These men, after singing Tiyo Soga's Xhosa hymn 'Fulfil thy promise, God of truth', unanimously resolved to form the South African Native National Congress. Though not the first African political association in South Africa, its formation did mark a clear break with the past. Previously the focus of African politics had centred on electoral activity in the Cape Colony where blacks with the required property and educational qualifications could vote and stand for office. Their voice in Cape politics was significant. At the turn of the century African voters constituted nearly half the electorate in five constituencies, and some men believed that the most effective way of accelerating African political advancement was to use their vote to influence the election of men who would be sympathetic to African aspirations. The years succeeding the Peace of Vereeniging in 1902 witnessed the declining force of this argument. The founding of the Native National Congress marked the ascendency in middle-class African circles of the contention that African interests could best be promoted not through sympathetic intermediaries but rather by action by Africans themselves.

There were several reasons for this change in opinion. Among some members of the African élite hopes raised initially by the defeat of the republics in the Anglo-Boer war had been swiftly disappointed. Despite African expressions of imperial loyalty intermingled with politely phrased reproach at the prevalent discrimination against black men of 'training, character and ability',[1] the British government made it clear that its paramount concern was with the question of white unity in South Africa. African hopes that the

1

non-racial Cape franchise would be extended to the defeated republics were rapidly disappointed, and preparations for the Act of Union indicated that existing rights would not be respected in future. The Act not only removed the theoretical right of enfranchised blacks to be elected to parliamentary seats (which had existed in the Cape) but also provided for the removal of the franchise from African voters through a two-thirds majority vote of both houses of parliament in joint session. Nor, by 1912, was African concern limited to constitutional issues. The first post-Union administration, responding to the mining industry's labour demands and the disquiet of white farmers squeezed between capitalist agricultural companies on the one hand and competitive African peasants on the other, moved quickly to safeguard its position with these groups. Breaking contract was made a criminal offence under the Native Labour Regulation Act, the exclusion of Africans from skilled industrial jobs was for the first time given legal sanction in the Mines and Works Act, and in 1911 the Natives' Land Bill was drafted: it prohibited rural land ownership by Africans or occupation outside the 'reserves' (which comprised nearly eight per cent of the area of the country), dispossessing many landowners and outlawing leasing or tenant-farming relationships between blacks and whites. Obviously there was more at stake here than the interests of that small group who through their education at mission institutions had come to form an identifiable petty bourgeoisie. The Land Act of 1913 and complementary labour legislation were the legal tools employed to destroy a whole class of peasant producers, forcing them into already crowded reserves or driving them into new and arduous social relationships – as farm workers, as mine labourers, and later in the least skilled and most badly paid positions in urban industrial, municipal and domestic employment. The group of men assembled at Bloemfontein in 1912 were well aware of the wider dimensions of the social tragedy being enacted around them. But they had a particular concern, the fear of any petty bourgeoisie at a time of crisis, of being thrust back into the ranks of the urban and rural poor. It was a fear which was eloquently expressed by one John Makue in his testimony to the South African Native Affairs Commission in 1904:

> Our earning power is very small. I think when we are forced to work there ought to be big pay. There is no decent black man that can manage to exist on £8 a month, pay all the taxes, and the upkeep of his house in the proper manner – I mean a civilised native. I do not mean the raw man who comes from the kraals . . . now we are all blacks and measured with the same measure . . . I am measured with the same measure as the man who cannot look after himself and who is not in the same position as I am.[2]

The same anxiety underlay an early Congress civil disobedience campaign in Pretoria to gain for African railway passengers access to first class carriages.[3] Their exclusion from such facilities was sharply resented by African leaders. As D. D. T. Jabavu, a prominent political figure in the Cape, pointed out at a Natal mission conference in 1920:

> [Railway] waiting rooms are made to accommodate the rawest blanketed

heathen; and the more decent native has either to use them and annex vermin or to do without shelter in biting wintry weather.[4]

Above all the South African Native National Congress was to represent the concerns and anxieties of the small professional middle class which was mainly responsible for convening the Bloemfontein meeting. Its first president was John Dube, headmaster of the Ohlange Institute in Natal; its secretary was Solomon Plaatje, one-time court interpreter and editor of a Kimberley newspaper, and its treasurer Pixley ka Izaka Seme, a London-trained advocate. These were men who retained close ties with the African aristocracy, the rural chieftaincy, who, while anxious to promote the general advancement and 'upliftment of the race',[5] were also conservatives, concerned with protecting a moral and social order they correctly perceived to be under attack. Congress was intended to function first as a national forum to discuss the issues which affected 'the dark races of the subcontinent',[6] and second as an organised pressure group. It planned to agitate for changes through 'peaceful propaganda',[7] the election to legislative bodies of Congress sympathisers, through protests and enquiries, and finally, through 'passive action or continued movement' – a clear reference to the tactics which were being employed by Gandhi and his followers in the South African Indian community.[8]

In the first six years of its existence, however, Congress contented itself with less dramatic forms of response. African leaders were keen to demonstrate their loyalty for the duration of the First World War. The leadership was dominated by Cape-educated and influenced men, who tended to take a less confrontationist line than their Transvaal colleagues. John Dube, born in Natal and educated in America, thought in much the same terms as his Cape-based colleagues, announcing his intention as president to place 'hopeful reliance in the sense of common justice and love of freedom so innate in the British character'.[9] Two delegations were sent to Britain in 1914 and 1919 to request Imperial intervention in South Africa and Sol Plaatje remained in Britain for much of the war, writing his *Native Life in South Africa* and occasionally being received with some sympathy by Liberal politicians.

In 1918 there was a discernible shift in the apparent position of the Native National Congress. Still a very small and weak body (with not more than a couple of thousand subscribing members), on the Witwatersrand Congress leaders were nevertheless supporting striking municipal workers, by 1919 they were involved in a militant anti-pass campaign, and in early 1920 some Congress organisers were addressing public meetings of mineworkers just before the great African mineworkers' strike that year.[10] Sol Plaatje attended a stormy meeting of the executive committee of the SANNC in August 1918 and came away very disturbed. As he put it in a letter to De Beers in Kimberley:

> The ten Transvaal delegates came to the Congress with a concord and a determination that was perfectly astounding to our customary native demeanor at conferences. They spoke almost in unison, in short sentences, nearly all of which began and ended with the word 'strike'.[11]

What had happened? First of all, wartime industrialisation had expanded the black urban population and industrial labour force, especially in the Transvaal. With black wages pegged at 1914 levels, sharp inflation, and a reluctance on the part of the municipal authorities to provide adequate services and housing for this population, there had been a dramatic deterioration in standards of living within the black proletariat and the lower strata of the black petty bourgeoisie. The less affluent members of the African middle class shared many of the experiences of African workers: their incomes were not appreciably higher, their wives had to resort to informal sector activity and they lived in the same miserable urban slums.[12] With the expansion of the manufacturing workforce (easier to organise than the mineworkers who were isolated in their compounds) and the example of white labour unrest in the immediate post-war period, African workers were becoming increasingly class-conscious. At the political level this situation was reflected in the growing interest taken in blacks by white socialist groups, still yet to coalesce into the Communist Party, and in the success these groups had in attracting limited black support, especially for the syndicalist Industrial Workers of Africa, the trade union movement started by the International Socialist League.[13] It was also expressed politically in the leadership change within Congress. In 1917 the executive was taken over by Transvaal men, under the presidency of the Pretoria estate agent S. M. Makgatho. Though hardly revolutionaries, these men were nevertheless less immune to the stresses provoked and stimulated by wartime industrial and social developments than the Cape leaders. And in 1918, this leadership, prompted from below, and especially from the SANNC rank and file, itself drawn from the economically vulnerable layers of the lower middle classes, was to articulate the one shilling a day demand which accompanied the wave of African strikes in Johannesburg that year.[14] When, in the years which followed, the emphasis switched to passes rather than wages *per se*, it was partly because the experience gained in strikes had demonstrated how important the whole system of labour controls, of which passes were such an indispensable part, was in keeping wages down.

Nevertheless, though the apparent radicalism of Congress in the immediate post-First World War period reflected common interests between working-class and petty-bourgeois blacks, Congress hardly represented a class alliance. There was considerable unease among African political spokesmen at the direction Congress appeared to be taking in the Transvaal. Plaatje's misgivings were shared also by D. D. T. Jabavu: 'Bolshevism and its nihilistic doctrines [were] enlisting many natives up country. Socialism of the worst calibre [was] claiming our people.'[15] Plaatje and Jabavu were members of a group who had for years considered themselves as authentic representatives and spokesmen of the African community; now, suddenly, their role was being questioned. More conservative African politicians were being publicly denounced and shouted down at meetings when they counselled caution and moderation. Such people would help to guide Congress along smoother paths in the following decade. But by themselves they could not have accomplished the de-radicalisation of the movement. There were other more powerful forces at work. From 1920 onwards, until the accession of the Pact government in 1924, the authorities produced a series of measures which, though generally incorporating features that offended the integrationist and meritocratic principles of leading Congressmen, nevertheless mollified some of the immediate resentment of petty-bourgeois Africans and detached them from the movement set off by the popular classes.

The Native Housing Act of 1920 was a measure of this nature. So too was the provision of first class railway accommodation for blacks. In 1923 the Natives (Urban Areas) Act provided for housing programmes executed by municipalities, leasehold in townships and it afforded trading opportunities within the new townships for aspirant African businessmen. There were plenty of objections to the new arrangements: particularly disliked were the municipal brewing monopolies enshrined in the Act, but nevertheless they went some way towards meeting the Congress demand for 'some differentiation of treatment . . . between those who were educated and civilised and those who had yet to reach that stage'.[16] A final factor inducing caution among African leaders was the fact that the 1919 pass protests brought in a new social element – the urban unemployed, more volatile, more violent, and much less easy to organise than members of the working class. From 1920, for a few years, Congress's leadership was to be diverted into safer channels; into the Joint Council movement which provided a medium for consultation between black and white liberals, and the government advisory conferences which enabled a select group to advance grievances and discuss policy.

However, from 1922, two other organisations had arrived to complicate the African political scene. These were the Industrial and Commercial Workers' Union (ICU) and the Communist Party of South Africa. The origins of the ICU lay in the early post-war attempts by white socialists to organise black labour in Cape Town. A temporary shortage of unskilled labour and a tradition of multiracial (white and coloured) trade unionism in the Cape – predisposing the local labour movement to favour African trade unionism – both help to explain the early emergence of African labour organisation here. The ICU developed out of several attempts to organise dockworkers. It was founded in 1919 and immediately gained prestige by leading a successful strike in the docks. Its secretary was a school-teacher from Nyasaland, Clements Kadalie, a man of great charm and charisma. The Cape Town ICU's following was to spread and link up with other embryonic trade union groupings, first in the ports of the eastern Cape and then in Durban. In each case the movement owed its strength to powerful and flamboyant personalities, usually from a non-working class background, rather than any systematic organisation. A branch was established in Johannesburg in 1924 and from that year the ICU began to attract the attention of the Communist Party, now seeking to expand its African support (see pp. 7–8 below).

The ICU's transformation into a mass movement only began with its penetration of the countryside, first in rural Natal and then, most dramatically, in the eastern Transvaal. Here, despite the provisions of the 1913 Land Act, a relatively prosperous group of African labour tenants, sharecroppers and 'squatters' had survived outside the reserves on white land. From the 1920s these people were subjected to savage pressures as white farmers, responding to an increased demand for agricultural products, sought to convert quasi-feudal social relationships on the land to more recognisably capitalist relationships. Labour tenants had their land reduced and free labour obligations increased; sharecropper arrangements were transformed into rent-paying tenancies and squatters were being squeezed off the land altogether. Rural Africans responded in a general wave of unrest: refusals to work on the farmers' land, mutilation of animals, threats, assaults and other forms of insubordination. In their desperation they turned to the ICU, joining it in thousands, attracted by the millenarian promise of much of the ICU's rhetoric. But, as one of them said, it 'all ended up in speeches':[17] rural expectations of freedom and the restoration of land were to be disappointed. All the ICU had to offer were some rather shady land purchase schemes, legal manoeuvres, and attempts to improve conditions by negotiations with farmers. None of these could halt the advance of capitalist social relations or significantly soften their impact. Reaching a peak of 100 000 members in 1927 the ICU declined rapidly, crumbling through internal dissension and organisational paralysis.[18]

Ostensibly a workers' organisation, because of the character and ambitions of its petty-bourgeois leadership the ICU tended to function as a mass-based political party, its charismatic leaders voicing a broad range of popular grievances. Incapable of organising systematically on an industrial base it nevertheless attracted (and possibly diverted) massive support from Congress – an indication of considerable receptivity to political ideas among the urban and rural poor. In doing so it freed Congress's élitist leadership from the radicalising pressures emanating from below which had helped to condition its responses at the beginning of the decade. But the ICU also had a second, more positive effect on Congress. Its spokesmen infused into the courtly and often pompous discourse of African politicians a fierce anger and apocalyptic imagery. Here, for example, is James Thaele, later a Congress leader in the western Cape, writing in the ICU newspaper, *The Workers' Herald*, in 1923:

> We are fed up with the white man's camouflage, his hypocrisy, his policy of pinpricks in the land of our forefathers. I am appealing to the racial consciousness of the radical aboriginal to use all means to rouse the African race to wake from their long sleep of many a decade . . . when those in authority become so unreasonably notorious . . . disregard that authority, be blind and damn the consequences.[19]

Or Kadalie himself, three years later:

> We natives . . . have always given the game away . . . we are dealing with rascals, the Europeans are rascals. . . . There is no native problem, but a European problem of weakness, greed and robbery.[20]

Such sentiments were beginning to resonate among sections of the African National Congress (the title adopted by the SANNC in 1923) amid increasing disenchantment with negotiation and moderation in the face of an unprecedently repressive administration. By 1926 there was additional reason for bitterness. Two years earlier there had been a realignment in white politics. With the accession of the Labour/Nationalist regime under General Hertzog, an administration more sympathetic to the interests of white farmers and workers had come to power. It was less inclined towards co-optive strategies to blacks than its predecessor and more disposed to embracing the full political and economic implications of segregation. In 1926, two bills, one removing

Africans from the common roll vote in the Cape and the other expanding on the provisions of the 1913 Land Act, were tabled. Though they were not passed for another decade the implication for the African political leadership was clear: existing rights and privileges were thenceforward under constant threat. To underline the situation still further, in 1927 the Governor-General was empowered to legislate in African affairs by proclamation.

Before looking at how the ANC was behaving in the late 1920s we need to understand something of another radicalising influence, the Communist Party of South Africa (CPSA). The Communist Party had been founded in 1921 after a series of manoeuvres between various small left-wing groups on the Rand and in Cape Town.[21] When the Labour Party had split over the issue of whether to support the war effort, those who had contended that the war was an anti-working class imperialist struggle had broken away to form the International Socialist League. This eventually fused together with various other socialist, Marxist and Zionist organisations, many of them informed by the experiences of eastern European immigrants, into the Communist Party of South Africa, the outcome in part of the stimuli of the Russian Revolution and the subsequent formation of the Communist International. The CPSA was not a large body but it was well organised, its centralised structure being patterned on a Leninist model. A few of its members had been involved in earlier syndicalist attempts to organise black workers: though it did not apparently have any blacks in its original membership, it may well have had some informal following amongst black workers. The CPSA, however, was not a syndicalist organisation: it was a political party, prepared, because conditions were not yet ripe for revolution in South Africa, to work within and take advantage of existing political institutions. The adoption of this policy was to cause some internal disagreement, as well as, later on, criticism from other left-wing parties. Though it could, on occasion, be accused of opportunist expediency over the race issue, in general the CPSA adhered to the doctrine that working-class unity transcended racial divisions. White working-class consciousness as it developed would, the CPSA leadership assumed, ultimately eschew racialism. In the short term, therefore, communists were prepared to join forces with white labour on certain issues: in 1922, for example, communists were active in the Rand mineworkers' revolt despite the explicit racialism of the mineworkers' leaders. Similarly the CPSA supported the Nationalist/Labour alliance in the 1924 election, although this did to lead to reassessment: the racist overtones of the campaign led the CPSA to conclude – at its annual conference – that 'our main revolutionary task is among the natives'.[22] The initiative for this switch in policy came from Cape Town where the local branch had a substantial coloured membership, and where the ICU had originated.

The ICU, gathering strength in the mid-1920s, was the obvious target for Party workers. It had a massive working-class membership, and at that stage explicitly socialist goals. Communists joined the ICU and helped it by leaving the field open for ICU men to organise industrially. But by 1926 there were considerable tensions between the communists and the ICU, arising from both tactical and ideological differences. Firstly, the ICU was not functioning as a trade union organisation as the communists understood the concept. Its membership was scattered and diffuse and tended to be concentrated among farmworkers rather than the industrial proletariat. Communists within the ICU tried to reorganise the movement into industrial branches based on individual concerns, and this was sharply resented by ICU leaders. Secondly, the ICU's founders tended to view achievement in petty-bourgeois terms – status, wealth and individual power – and hence could with some justification be accused of using the organisation to enrich themselves. Kadalie viewed the struggle as primarily a political one and because of this was to seek institutional respectability for his movement – including international affiliations with reformist European labour organisations. Kadalie viewed social conflict in South Africa mainly in nationalist or colonial terms and did not share the communist vision of a class struggle complicated only by racist 'false consciousness'. These tensions eventually resulted in the expulsion of the communists and a sharp turn to the right by the ICU as it withered and decayed. Rejected by the ICU, communists began to establish their own industrial unions and placed fresh emphasis on African recruitment into the Party. By 1928 three members of the central committee were black, as were most of the CPSA's 1 750 members. Concurrent with the emphasis on African mobilisation was a reassessment of policy towards the African National Congress, hitherto treated as a purely reactionary movement.[23]

By 1927 many ANC leaders were disillusioned with the politics of diplomatic (and sometimes downright sycophantic) persuasion. Their susceptibility to more radical strategy was signified in an abortive scheme in 1926 for joint ICU/ANC mass demonstrations in protest against Hertzog's legislative proposals. In 1927, with the election of Josiah Gumede to the presidency, the ANC announced its intention to embark on a course of mass organisation involving the construction of branch memberships. The western Cape was already the scene of an energetic recruitment campaign among farmworkers by two communists working within Congress, Ndobe and Tonjeni. Here, in contrast to the Transvaal, wage labour as opposed to labour tenancy predominated on farms.[24] Significantly, the initiative within the CPSA to work with black organisations had sprung from the western Cape.

Josiah Gumede had been influenced in the early 1920s by the American negro doctrine of Garveyism – a separatist ideology based on race pride and black exclusiveness. But Gumede, by 1927 president of the Natal wing of the ANC, was receptive to other influences as well; he accepted an invitation to attend a communist-sponsored Conference of Oppressed Nationalities and later toured the USSR, returning to South Africa much impressed with what he had seen. At Brussels the Conference adopted a motion put forward by Gumede and his compatriot, James La Guma of the Cape Town branch of the CPSA, endorsing

> the right of self determination through the complete overthrow of capitalism and imperialist domination . . . the principle of Africa for the Africans.[25]

Under pressure from its African and coloured members as well as from the Communist International[26] (itself inspired by Stalin's reasoning on colonial problems), in 1928 the CPSA took an important step which laid the foundation for an alliance with African nationalist organisations. This was the adoption of a vaguely worded slogan defining the goal to which Party activists should work towards as 'an independent native republic as a stage towards a workers' and peasants' republic'. The formulation begged obvious questions which were never satisfactorily answered. The slogan was to be short-lived but one of its most important premises informed CPSA policy for a long time to come. This was the view that South Africa contained within itself a colonial situation and consequently socialism would be accomplished through two stages: first a nationalist democratic revolution, involving many issues over which it would be easy to cooperate with reformist African petty-bourgeois organisations, and only then a socialist revolution.

The 'native republic' slogan was produced at an opportune moment. First, it coincided with and complemented the impact of Garveyism on the ANC. Both Gumede and James Thaele, president of the western Cape branch of the ANC, were influenced by Marcus Garvey's doctrines. The millenarian accent of Garveyism would have reverberated strongly in rural parts of the Cape Province where there was considerable unrest among farmworkers and where the ANC had succeeded in building up country branches. Secondly, 1929 was a year in which coercive measures against Africans were intensified. A bitter election was fought that year on 'native policy' as the result of the Pact government's inability to gain the required two-thirds majority to alter the franchise arrangements. The election was accompanied by a vigorous tightening of pass laws. In response to this the Communist Party established a League of African Rights which was intended to agitate for freedom of speech, education, the vote and abolition of pass laws. Gumede supported the League on behalf of the ANC and was elected its president. But by late 1929 Gumede was almost totally isolated from his executive, and the ANC failed to support the League's proposed mass demonstrations against the pass laws.

In April 1930, after he had addressed the ANC annual conference on the need to mount a massive campaign on the basis of the native republic slogan, Josiah Gumede was voted out of office. In his place was elected Pixley ka Izaka Seme and with his ascendency the ANC shifted several degrees rightwards into almost total moribundancy. Meanwhile the Communist International, working on the assumption that 1930 marked a profound crisis for the capitalist world, called for the withdrawal of all communist parties from any association with reformist organisations. The League of African Rights collapsed. The CPSA, despite internal misgivings as to whether a revolutionary situation prevailed in South Africa, called for a general strike and launched itself on a confrontationist course which, heroic though it was, was to lead to the Party's decimation (aided by its internal purges) and the almost total destruction of its trade union organisation. The refusal of the ANC and ICU to support the pass-burning demonstrations organised by communists in Johannesburg in November 1930 created a legacy of ill-feeling between revolutionaries and nationalists. Within the western Cape where the ANC had been most radicalised (and closest to the communists) Congress split as dissidents, distressed by the right-wing swing by Thaele, set up their own, short-lived, Independent ANC.

The 1930s was a decade when both the ANC and the CPSA reached the nadir of their influence. The communists, from being the best-organised and most militant group active among black South Africans, were to lose much of their popular following. This was partly a consequence of the systematic policy of harassment pursued by the state, and particularly the Minister of Justice, Oswald Pirow, but the decline in the fortunes of the South African Communist Party was not simply the result of more energetic repression. From 1933, with the ascendency of Nazism in Germany, communist parties throughout the world, in conformity with the advice of the Communist International, formed so-called 'popular front' alliances with reformist anti-fascist groupings. In South Africa, confronted with the attempts by Afrikaner nationalist forces to capture the white labour movement, communists from the mid-1930s concentrated on combatting what they perceived to be fascist tendencies amongst white workers. An all-white 'People's Front' was established and tacit support was offered to the Labour Party. Symptomatic of their approach was a pamphlet addressed to white workers entitled *Communism and the Native Question.* Part of it read:

> If the Kaffir Boetie jibe doesn't get home, such people will follow up with the shameless assertion that it will end up by all the races getting mixed up and 'How would you like your sister to marry a native?'. This sort of talk shows a great want of confidence in South African women and is a cheap and unworthy insult to them. It overlooks the fact that neither race *wants* to mix with the other. Where racial intercourse does take place, it is largely due to the poverty and backwardness of the native woman which leaves them without self-respect.[27]

Party newspapers carried less African news, and according to the memories of some of its African members, increasingly they felt that with the SACP's strivings for a particular type of acceptability it was no longer *their* party.[28] Revival was only to come slowly with the transfer of the Party's headquarters to Cape Town in 1937 and its reintegration into the Cape radical tradition which had begun amongst African and coloured workers a decade earlier.[29]

Meanwhile an ever-shrinking Congress floundered its way through the decade. Under the leadership of Pixley ka Izaka Seme tensions between different leadership cliques increased and Congress's popular impact dwindled. Seme's approach and the reason for Congress's decline are apparent in this quotation from an article written by him in 1932:

> I wish to urge our educated young men and women not to lose contact with your own chiefs. You should make your chiefs and your tribal councils feel that education is a really good thing. It does not spoil people nor detribalise them. Most of the miseries which our people suffer in the towns and the country today is due to this one factor, no confidence between the educated classes and their own uneducated people. The former cannot open any business relations amongst the latter and get good support because to be able to establish a business anywhere you want confidence. The Indian trader succeeds because he makes friends with all classes and ever tries to win their confidence. You should try and do likewise. . . . Congress can make us learn how to produce our own wants as a nation. We can learn to grow cotton and wool and make our own leather boots and blankets in our factories.[30]

As well as reflecting the increasing difficulty the ANC was having in maintaining the allegiance of a chieftaincy ever more dependent for its position on the goodwill of the authorities, the economic message in the speech is also revealing. The general good is identified totally with the welfare of an aspirant African commercial class. Translated into practical terms, Seme's policies included the wooing of chiefs and the establishment of African Congress Clubs, which would function as savings organisations with the power to make loans and provide cheap wholesale goods for businessmen. To ensure their smooth operation ex-employees of the Native Affairs Department would handle Congress Club revenues.

Even the eventual passage of the Hertzog legislation in 1936, which removed Africans from the common roll, created for them a new set of segregated political institutions, including white 'Native Representatives' in Parliament and an elected advisory 'Native Representative Council', as well as entrenching the unequal distribution of land, did not provoke a dramatic response from African politicians. True, after a conference in Bloemfontein, a new organisation was established, the All-African Convention, with the original purpose of uniting oppostion to the legislation, but in the face of the unwillingness of establishment politicians to boycott the new institutions (a move which was urged by left-wingers from Cape Town) the All-African Convention (AAC) and its constituent organisations settled down into a familier routine: wordy protests through consultative machinery, delegations, vague calls for African unity, and national days of prayer. The AAC was dominated until the war by conservatives; its protestations were punctuated by affirmations of loyalty to South Africa and the Crown, and its policy documents, despite some attention to general socio-economic matters, were largely thought out within the tenets of Cape liberalism.[31]

In contrast to the political lethargy of the previous decade the 1940s was a period of ferment as political movements adjusted to the new pressures and opportunities created by the popular upheavals accompanying the massive wartime expansion of the African working class. The remainder of the chapter will focus mainly on Johannesburg, for here the developments within African urban communities assumed their most complex and dramatic form. We will start by looking at some of the socio-economic characteristics of South African urban society during these years.

The disruption of the international capitalist economy as a result of the Second World War created boom conditions for South African industry with the proliferation of more sophisticated forms of import substitution and the development of production geared to military demands. With the expansion of manufacturing (which in 1943 outstripped mining's contribution to the gross national product) and the diversion of a section of the white labour force into the army there was a rapid growth in the number of African factory workers, and for the first time African women began to be employed in manufacturing in large numbers. Between 1939 and 1952 the African urban population nearly doubled, the major proportion of this increase being the result of the movement of whole families from the countryside into the towns. The two most powerful impulses to this migration were the threat of starvation in the

11

reserves and deteriorating conditions on white farms. In the reserves overcrowding and sharp inequalities in stock ownership and landholdings had created a situation which for many was precarious even in years of good climatic conditions. For example, in 1943 a government commission found that in the Transkei nearly ten per cent of the households within the territory were landless, and in three typical districts nearly half the population had no cattle, and a similar proportion (not necessarily the same people) were without sheep or goats.[32]

The war years were, in any case, years of drought: in 1942, for example, the crop harvest in the Transkei was one-quarter of its normal size.[33] The situation had not improved significantly three years later when the District Surgeon in Pietermaritzburg claimed that 60 per cent of the African population were starving.[34] This was not attributable solely to the climate, for shortfalls in production of maize coincided with increased export commitments. As well as this, social differentiation within the reserves had led to a situation where in some areas wool production was substituted for cultivation.[35] On the farms the general trend towards proletarianisation of labour tenants and squatters continued, forcing large numbers off the land. High wartime food prices not only hastened the process of transition to a fully-blown rural capitalism but also led to a deterioration in the diet of farm labourers: between 1945 and 1946 farm rations were reduced by over two-thirds, and to make up the shortfall farmworkers had to buy maize from their employers at double the controlled price.[36]

The exodus from the countryside was at first facilitated by a brief suspension, between 1942 and 1943, of influx control in the major cities. This was one of several measures taken by the authorities in the early stages of the war so as to avoid confrontation and maintain African political quiescence. Other measures included school feeding schemes, pensions for certain categories of African employees and increased educational expenditure. All these tied in with manufacturing's requirement of a stable, urbanised, and relatively well educated industrial labour force.

Poverty amongst the urban African population, while not as atrocious as in the countryside, was nevertheless very widespread. Although wages were higher than in rural employment – and indeed rose in some sectors during the war – this was offset by unemployment and increases in the cost of staple foods and fuel. Mealie meal, for example, went up between 1939 and 1940 by 20 per cent and firewood by 50 per cent.[37] Unskilled workers rarely earned enough to cover the costs of essential food, shelter, fuel and clothing. As a result many people who depended on such wages simply did not survive: for example, in East London, six out of every ten African babies born were dead by the end of their first year.[38]

Such conditions were not always accepted passively. Where there was scope for leverage African communities were quick to attempt either to resist increased subsistence costs or to reduce the price of survival. The two most important of such struggles were the Alexandra bus boycotts of 1940 and 1945 and the Johannesburg squatters' movement of 1944 to 1947. Because our main interest is in the effects of these movements on political groups this is not the place to chronicle their development in any detail. Their history has already been written with sensitivity and compassion by two South African scholars,

A. W. Stadler and Baruch Hirson.[39] What follows is a bare summary of their evolution.

Alexandra was one of the few areas in which Africans enjoyed freehold property rights. It lay twelve miles to the north of Johannesburg, just outside the municipal boundary. It was lightly administered because of its freehold status and autonomy from Johannesburg and was consequently a catchment area for those people who had no official sanction to live in an urban area. It had other attractions for the least privileged: the absence of effective building controls meant that landlords could build shacks around their stands, making accommodation available for people who for economic and bureaucratic reasons could not find housing in municipal townships. Like the other freehold suburb of Johannesburg, Sophiatown, Alexandra's population had a relatively complex class structure, for access to property rights had made possible the development of African businesses. But from 1940 Alexandra appeared to be threatened with expropriation as white residents of neighbouring suburbs, who were opposed to its existence, managed to obtain an increasingly sympathetic hearing from the civic authorities. This background of insecurity was an important element in communal responses.

Transport was an obviously sensitive issue in Alexandra. There were no trains and its distance from the city centre made the existence of a cheap bus service vital to the continued existence of the township. African entrepreneurs had initially been able to exploit the demand for cheap transport but in the early 1940s the last of these, R. G. Baloyi, was squeezed out by better capitalised white-owned operations. The insecurity of African property owners and their continuing entrepreneurial aspirations in the transport field motivated them to play a leading role in the bus boycotts, though not always very successfully.

The first boycott occurred in 1940, nine months after the bus fare to town had been raised from 4d to 5d. The boycott only took place after the failure of negotiations between operators, the Council and a Transport Action Committee, which included C. S. Ramahanoe, an Alexandra resident and Transvaal secretary of the ANC, and Gaur Radebe, also of Alexandra and a member of Congress as well as the Communist Party. The boycott was brief, successful, and because it was scarcely reported in the press little is known of the form it took.

In 1942, after a second attempt to raise the fare to 5d, the buses were again boycotted, and the boycott was enforced through pickets and its conduct decided through a mass meeting in one of Alexandra's three public squares. On this occasion it was at first the fares which were boycotted rather than the buses, passengers simply refusing to pay the extra penny. The bus owners retaliated by moving the terminus to the edge of the township, hence shortening the route. Pickets were then set up which clashed with bus company employees and after negotiations between the company and a committee representing the ANC, Alexandra washerwomen and other special interests, the old fare was restored while an official investigation was held.

The investigation pronounced in favour of the bus companies and in August 1943 fares were raised once again to 5d. This time the boycott was longer and attracted much more external attention, lasting from 2–11 August. On this occasion the boycotters, 20 000 of them, walked to work across

Johannesburg's north-western suburbs. This involved getting up at three o'clock in the morning and arriving home after nine in the evening. To assist these people an emergency transport committee was formed, composed of members of the Communist Party, white left-wingers and liberals and various prominent Alexandra figures. Led by Senator Hyman Basner ('native representative' in the upper House for the Transvaal and a former CPSA member) the committee organised lifts. This was done with the cooperation of the police and traffic department and the Department of Native Affairs went so far as to appeal to employers to reinstate workers dismissed for lateness and absenteeism. In this boycott the ANC seems to have played an unimportant role in the day-to-day leadership of the boycott. In Alexandra, Congress tended to be identified with Baloyi who was rightly suspected of self-interested motives and neither he nor Xuma, the President-General, were at their best on a public platform. Negotiations faltered and were ended by government intervention after a dramatic procession of 10 000 Alexandra residents marched through town on 10 August. A commission of enquiry was set up and for the time being the 4d fare maintained.

Between 1943 and 1944 there seems to have been a significant shift in government policy: whereas in 1943 the state appears to have played a conciliatory and defusing role, in 1944 official attitudes were more combative. Hirson suggests this alteration was inspired by the self-confidence engendered from Allied war victories. Despite commission evidence which suggested that no urban African community on the Rand could afford increased transport costs, the government gave its assent in November 1944 to the 5d fare. This time the boycott lasted for seven weeks, despite considerable harassment by the state: lift-givers were intimidated by Transportation Board officials, pass offenders were arrested in large numbers and a proclamation banned meetings or processions of over twenty people. Attempts were made to extend the boycott to other parts of Johannesburg and an illegal meeting on 20 December threatened a communal strike if the issue was not resolved in its favour. The complexities of the various responses by the government, municipality and employers' organisations need not detain us here: eventually a subsidised coupon scheme was improvised in which people would buy tickets in advance for the old fare and the companies would claim the extra penny from the council. This was a temporary arrangement during which the bus companies were bought out by a Public Utility Corporation which, through economies of scale, would retain the old fares.

The conclusion of this final boycott found the leadership which had emerged in these struggles in disarray. In 1943 Basner, together with various African leaders disenchanted with the inability of Congress to function at a popular level, had formed an African Democratic Party. This fell apart during the 1944 boycott as a result largely of disagreements between its more radical African members (who included some Trotskyites) and the Senator as to the acceptability of the coupon scheme. As it appeared in December 1944, the scheme was a temporary and uncertain measure, Basner himself only favouring it because of his scepticism as to whether the boycott would hold after its introduction. The communists involved in the Workers' Transport Action Committee had fallen out with their colleagues after opposing the extension of the boycott to other centres, and after the entry of Russia into the war the Communist Party was in any case unwilling to undertake illegal forms of opposition as long as the war lasted. The ANC establishment was totally discredited in the eyes of the boycotters: its leaders had avoided involvement and Ramahanoe, one of the ANC leaders, was tainted with employment with one of the bus companies. During the boycott itself different approaches had emerged between the communists and the far left, the former arguing for the ending of the struggle as soon as a concession on fares had been made, the latter advocating its continuation until the state or the municipality itself took over responsibility for the provision of public transport to Alexandra.[40] We will return to these political tensions later. Apart from their influence on the politics of opposition the boycotts were also important in demonstrating the effectivness of a new tactic which was to be used again and again in the succeeding decade. They also served to promote a trend towards increasing state intervention in issues bearing on the subsistence of workers; the form this took in the case of Alexandra's transport was modest – the subsidisation (from a levy exerted on employers) of the monopolistic Public Utility Transport Corporation which still to this day carries a major proportion of the Rand's labour force to and from work. In the case of the squatters' movements described below state response was to be rather more far-reaching.

In 1944 there were four municipal housing schemes in Johannesburg: Western Native Township, adjacent to the freehold area of Sophiatown, four miles west of the city centre; Eastern Native Township; and, much further out, twelve miles to the south-west, Orlando and Pimville. Orlando was the prototype for today's Soweto housing estate and, spartan and bleak as its accommodation was, Orlando was nevertheless considered a 'model' township by the city fathers, though as much for the ease of administering it as the quality of its facilities. Pimville, on the other hand, was conceded to be a horrible place, consisting of 99 former water-tanks sliced lengthwise, each housing a family and a rather larger group of African-constructed shanties. It had been conceived originally as an emergency camp for refugees from an outbreak of plague in the inner city, and had remained as a result of the reluctance of the municipal authorities to provide alternative housing for its inhabitants. In total there were about 14 000 houses in these townships, most of them two-roomed. Under the impact of the wartime population increase these became steadily more overcrowded. An insignificant number of houses was built during the war: skilled labour shortages and the meanness of the ratepayer-controlled Council both contributed to this failure. Instead, regulations governing sub-tenancies were relaxed. Stadler estimates that by 1944 a two-roomed Orlando house normally housed eight people.[41]

The housing shortage and consequent overcrowding was only one of several factors underlying the sudden emergence of squatter communities on the outskirts of Johannesburg which ultimately were to number some 90 000 inhabitants. With unskilled workers earning about £5 a month and rent accounting for around a fifth of this, squatting could be a vital strategy for survival, and the most effective way of meeting the cost of subsistence with pauper-level wages. Squatting could also be the resort of the unemployed, especially those who had left behind them the sheer hopelessness of rural existence and arrived to form the most marginal and desperate portion of the urban population. But it seems that squatters were not characteristically unemployed, and indeed their importance as part of an industrial labour force helped to protect them against attempts by the municipality to have them removed. As Stadler argues, the central government displayed little enthusiasm in assisting local officialdom in its persecution of the squatters. The latter were housed at no cost to the state or industry. For the municipality, though, the squatters represented a direct threat and challenge to its authority.

The squatters' movement began in March 1944 with the exodus of several hundred families of sub-tenants from Orlando to open land near the township where they built themselves shelter from sacking, scraps of wood and corrugated iron. This first camp had a structure which characterised those which followed it over the course of the next three years. It had a leader, James Mpanza, who controlled the camp through a tight organisation which regulated entry into, and membership of, the squatter community; administered justice as well as its own authority through fines and beatings; exerted a levy on traders; and from the finance deriving from membership fees, fines and trading levies, provided limited facilities (especially water) and an income for Mpanza himself. This last function should not be exaggerated: squatter leaders were often accused by their opponents of gangster-style behaviour, but their subsequent careers demonstrate little evidence of great affluence. Power itself was perhaps an important attraction and motive for squatter leaders, but there was also the vision of community development most clearly voiced by Oriel Monongoaha of Pimville, who in 1947 demanded larger sites for rehoused squatters so they could keep livestock and vehicles, form transport cooperatives, finance 'bursaries for Native children and students, and eventually contribute to the financial development of the African people as a whole'.[42]

The contest between the squatters' movements and the local authorities is, like the bus boycotts, too complex to do justice to in this introductory chapter. It ended in the destruction of the Johannesburg communities and their absorption into the massive complex of housing estates around Orlando which was begun in the late 1940s. Mpanza himself is referred to today as 'the man who founded Soweto' and in this there is a measure of truth. The squatters, like the bus boycotters, were to help shape state policy in the direction of greater intervention and control over housing and the other basic requirements of the urban African workforce.[43]

The relationship between squatters and political groups was an uneasy one. As far as the ANC was concerned, although the President-General, A. B. Xuma, spoke in 1947 in the Alexandra squatter camp and the previous year the ANC's Youth League was reported to have assisted Mpanza's movement,[44] there is no evidence of any great interest in the squatters on the part of the Congress leadership. This is not altogether surprising given the personalities concerned. Mpanza, a member of the Orlando Advisory Board, and convicted once for murder, was much closer to the syncretic proletarian culture of the township than the urbane Congressmen. Converted to Christianity in prison he drew on his new faith to inspire his followers with his own magnificent self-confidence:

> The position of the chieftainship is given to me like Jesus. Many people thought I was arrested, and yet I was not. The same as with Jesus. Many

thought he was dead, and yet he was not.[45]

A good example of the gulf which existed between Mpanza and his followers on the one hand and the ANC leadership on the other was demonstrated in an Advisory Board debate concerning the topic of domestic beer brewing. P. Q. Vundla, of the ANC, arguing for the restriction of brewing, said:

> We hear much about Kaffir beer forming part of our 'native customs' but we do not want these 'native customs' because our township being part and parcel of the town we have to follow the white way of living.

Mpanza was forced to leave the meeting after 'daring those who opposed homebrewing to express their feelings at a public meeting . . . where they would certainly be stoned to death'. 'The African', he added, 'when he supplicates his gods, slaughters a goat or sheep, and brews his traditional beverage.'[46]

Until 1946, the communists also held back from involvement in the squatters' cause despite initial overtures to them by Mpanza. The Johannesburg district committee's annual report mentioned him as a 'figure hardly worth taking seriously', and by implication a 'cheap demagogue . . . urging the people to irresponsible actions'. The report nonetheless conceded that communist activity in the townships had been 'almost entirely propagandist' and that Mpanza 'gave the people what they demanded; something to do about the housing shortage'.[47] It was to take nearly two years for the Communist Party to reassess the squatters' movement. The impetus to do so seems to have come from two sources. Firstly, in late 1946, Party members in Alexandra helped to lead a squatters' movement.[48] Secondly, a rent strike in Moroka, the camp established by the Council to house and control squatters, gained the active support of Councillor Hilda Watts, the first communist elected to Johannesburg's City Council; and in 1947 the communists formed a squatters' coordinating committee which drew in some of the squatters' leaders. Under the secretaryship of Edwin Mofutsanyana, editor of the Communist Party newspaper, *Inkululeko*, and a veteran Party member, the committee in fact achieved little. Mofutsanyana himself had never demonstrated any interest in squatters before, despite living in Orlando, and moreover had opposed Mpanza in Advisory Board elections. But by 1947 the squatters' movement was on the wane. Probably the Communist Party would have found it difficult to work with the squatters in any case: communists disliked and distrusted spontaneous populist movements, while the squatters' leaders jealously guarded their spheres of authority. In 1945 and 1946 communists in Johannesburg had other preoccupations: these lay rather in the attempt to build an electoral pact with the Labour Party so as to exert a greater degree of influence over white municipal voters, and in a trades union movement that had grown in strength during the war.

Besides the popular subsistence movements – the squatters' and the bus boycotts – the other spur which was to prod the African political leadership in a more militant direction was provided by organised labour. With the expansion of secondary industry in the late 1930s and during the war, and the consequent increase in the numbers of Africans employed in manufacturing, there was a flurry of trade-union activity, pioneered by the Trotskyite Max Gordon, but soon involving communists and liberals as well. Increasingly Africans were performing skilled and semi-skilled functions in industry and this made them less easy to replace and in consequence less vulnerable to dismissal. At the same time the rising cost of living meant that even in relatively well paid sectors of employment the value of real wages was declining. Between September 1942 and February 1943 worker discontent erupted in a sudden rash of strikes on the Witwatersrand. Those employers affected included sweetmakers, the railways, dairies, sawmilling, the Johannesburg municipality, meat wholesalers, flour mills and the mining industry. Many of the workers involved were migrants living in compounds.[49] Strikes continued despite being proclaimed illegal in 1942, and in 1943 and 1944 sixty strikes took place. Frequently these strikes were independent of trade union initiatives; indeed, trade unions organised and led by communists tended to be restrained by the party's reluctance to disrupt production after the entry of the Soviet Union into the war. Nevertheless, African trade unions achieved substantial improvements for their members at a time when many employers were beginning to favour their activities as a preferable alternative to industrial anarchy, and they steadily increased their strength. At the end of 1942 the Minister of Labour, Walter Madeley, even went so far as discuss the possibility of their recognition in the near future. The relatively concilatory official attitude to African labour during the war was reflected in the rush of minimum wage determinations; by the end of the war the number of African workers covered by these had increased sixty-fold.

On the Rand the most important African unions were – from the end of 1941 – affiliated to the Council for Non-European Trade Unions (CNETU). CNETU's leadership was from its inception dominated by communists, though for most of the war its president was Gana Makabeni, who had been expelled from the Party in 1932. He was succeeded in 1945 by J. B. Marks, the chairman of the African Mineworkers' Union and a member both of the Communist Party and the ANC. CNETU was to develop into the most powerful African trade union grouping ever to have existed in South Africa (it remains so today) with, by 1945, a (probably exaggerated) affiliate strength of 158 000 members grouped in 119 unions, accounting for 40 per cent of African employees in commerce and manufacture. During the war years African labour was in a stronger bargaining position than it ever had been or was to be in the future. Yet for political reasons CNETU was unwilling to challenge either the state or employers on the crucial question of recognition during the war years, doing so only in 1946 with the mineworkers' strike when CNETU no longer occupied such a strategically advantageous position.[50]

The development of the African trade union movement was to be a significant radicalising influence on the ANC, especially in the eastern Cape (see Chapter 2). As far as the ANC leadership in Johannesburg was concerned the workers' struggle which was to have the greatest impact on its outlook was that of the African mineworkers.[51]

African mineworkers were recruited in the South African reserves as well as, in increasing numbers, in the adjacent colonial territories. They were one of the most difficult groups within the industrial labour force to organise. A contract labour system, a migrant workforce, and the fact that they were housed in tightly controlled compounds – all presented formidable obstacles to the creation of a durable trade union organisation. As a result of monopsonistic recruiting practices, mineworkers' wages were very low – in 1942 actually below what they were in 1890. The Chamber of Mines set wage levels at below the cost of reproduction of the mineworker and his family, justifying this with the increasingly untenable assertion that the worker and his dependents had – through the migrant labour system – recourse to agricultural production in the reserves. The fixed price of gold and the high capital outlay required to extract it served further to rationalise the low wage structure of the mining industry.

In the 1930s and 1940s the material position of mineworkers deteriorated. Mineworkers tended to be drawn from the landless portion of the reserve population and hence the section most affected by fluctuating food prices. As we have seen, the cost of food and other basic necessities was rising sharply. Even those miners who had access to some land were finding that the period between contracts during which they could afford to work on it was becoming shorter and shorter.

In 1941, on the initiative of two communists within the ANC leadership, Gaur Radebe and Edwin Mofutsanyana, a conference was held under Congress auspices to discuss the formation of a mineworkers' trade union. Amongst those present at the conference was James Majoro, a representative of the Native Mine Clerks' Association. The mine clerks, though not subject to the same restrictions and hardships as surface and underground workers, had by virtue of their employment within the mining industry been excluded from the cost of living allowance and this motivated them to affiliate to the new African Mineworkers' Union (AMU). As union officials were to be systematically excluded from the compounds the mine clerks – with their access to the workforce – were to play an important organisational role.

In early 1943, after sporadic strikes in individual mines and representations by the AMU, the government appointed a commission to investigate mineworkers' wages and conditions. But the commission's recommendations, which included modest wage increases for the lowest paid and 'some form of collective bargaining' system, did not go far towards meeting the main demands of the AMU – regular wage increases, union recognition and the abolition of the compound system. The Chamber of Mines granted a small wage increase below the level considered by the commission to be necessary to make up the shortfall between income and expenditure of each mineworker and his family. Meanwhile, despite the harassment of its officials and a prohibition of gatherings on mining land the AMU steadily grew in influence, claiming in 1944 25 000 members. In 1945, post-war food shortages led to a decline in the quality of mine rations; with the substitution of canned for fresh meat, food riots and protest broke out on many mines. At Crown Mines, on the border of Johannesburg, miners went on a hunger strike.

At its annual conference in April 1946 the AMU resolved to claim a minimum wage of ten shillings a day, family housing, paid leave and a range of other improvements. Its memorandum to this effect to the Chamber evoked no other response than a printed postcard stating that the resolution was 'receiving attention'. In May, in the wake of wildcat stoppages in support of the minimum wage demand, a meeting held on 19 April, attended by 2 000

19

mineworkers, voted in favour of a general strike if their demands were not met. Subsequently an organising committee was formed by union officials and the Johannesburg district committee of the Communist Party. In June CNETU pledged itself to give full support to any mineworkers' strike.

On the morning of 12 August between 60 000 and 70 000 miners refused to go on shift in at least twelve mines. On the following day the CNETU leadership called for a general strike in sympathy. The strike was to last a week, and the response of the state was ruthless. Those compounds affected were surrounded by police and the AMU offices were raided and its main leaders arrested. An attempt to stage a sit-down strike at the rockface was broken with great brutality, the miners being driven up to the surface and back into the compound. Groups of mineworkers marching from the East Rand compounds to the Chief Native Commissioner's office in Johannesburg were savagely repulsed by police. The strike was ferociously suppressed at a cost of 12 dead and 1 200 wounded. CNETU's attempts to mount a strike in sympathy were thwarted by a massive police presence in townships at stations and bus terminals.

The strike effectively destroyed the African Mineworkers' Union and seriously weakened CNETU. In 1947 22 African affiliates were to secede from the Council, citing as their reasons disenchantment with communist leadership and disillusion with the strike weapon.[52] It also signalled the end of any serious consideration by the African political leadership of any reformist proposals put forward by the government. In the course of the strike the Native Representative Council was adjourned at the insistence of its African members, some of whom had conferred with miners while changing trains in Germiston on their way to Pretoria. The adjournment was an important stage in the realignment of African politics which took place in the 1940s, and it is to this that we now turn.

The two most important developments in African politics during the 1940s were the emergence of the Congress Youth League and the consolidation of its influence on the ANC leadership and the strengthening of the relationship between Congress and the Communist Party.

In April 1944, after a series of meetings and discussions between young ANC members and the ANC leadership, a Youth League was formally constituted. Membership was to be open to all Africans (and those from other sections of the community 'who live like and with Africans') between the ages of twelve and forty. Youth League members over the age of seventeen were automatically members of the ANC. After asserting that 'no nation can free an oppressed group other than that group itself', the League's manifesto went on to make some pungent criticisms of the ANC. The ANC, it argued, had developed a habit of yielding to oppression and was thus unable to advance the cause of African freedom. It was weakly organised, represented only the most privileged members of the African community and hence was concerned mainly with the preservation of rights which were enjoyed only by an élite. Its thinking lacked 'national feeling' and its strategy was an overwhelmingly negative one of reaction. The Congress Youth League's purpose would be to infuse into the national liberation movement 'the spirit of African nationalism' and act as the 'brains trust' of the ANC. The manifesto went on to outline the CYL's 'Creed'. This involved a belief in 'the divine destiny of nations', a rejection of 'foreign leadership', an insistence that leadership should express 'popular aspirations and ideals', and a belief in the unity of all Africans from the Mediterranean to the Indian and Atlantic oceans: 'Africa', it said, 'must speak with one voice.'[53]

The guiding personality behind the Youth League's inception was a former school-teacher and articled clerk, Anton Muziwakhe Lembede. Lembede was born in 1914, the son of a Zulu farm-labourer. Educated at home by his mother, he succeeded in winning a bursary to Adams Teacher Training College near Durban. In the late 1930s he taught in the Orange Free State while taking BA and LL.B. degrees by correspondence through the University of South Africa (UNISA). In 1943, having given up his teaching post, he arrived in Johannesburg to work in the legal office of Pixley ka Izaka Seme. Lembede's formidable intellectual gifts were developed in a very different context from the environment in which the ANC establishment had been brought up. He was self-educated to a large degree and had never lived or worked abroad. His origins lay in an impoverished peasantry. The time he had spent in the Orange Free State had made him a fluent Afrikaans speaker, while his awareness of the growing strength of Afrikaner nationalism contributed to his own heightened sense of race-consciousness. This factor, together with the rise of European fascism, did much to influence Lembede's political outlook. He was a devout Roman Catholic, and in 1945 wrote an MA dissertation in philosophy for UNISA entitled 'the conception of God as expounded by, and as it emerges from the writings of philosophers from Descartes to the present day'.

Lembede and his co-founders of the Youth League were inspired by the popular responses to material deprivation in wartime Johannesburg which we have just been examining. Here, for the Youth Leaguers, was the potential source of mass support which the Congress movement had so shamefully neglected to exploit. But in order to link this rapidly growing urban proletariat to the ANC a crucial problem had to be overcome. With all the puritanism of a recent rural arrival in the corrupt urban world of Johannesburg, Lembede wrote in 1946:

> Moral degradation is assuming alarming dimensions . . . [and] manifests itself in such abnormal and pathological phenonema as a loss of self-confidence, inferiority complex, a feeling of frustration, the worship and idolisation of whiteness, foreign leaders and ideologies. All these are symptoms of a pathological state of mind.[54]

What was required to channel the latent energy of working-class Africans in the direction of Congress was an appeal that would overcome the psychological inhibitions produced by racial oppression. This appeal, Lembede believed, should consist of a racially assertive nationalism which would serve to foster sentiments which were part of the 'natural' psychological make-up of all Africans.

The Youth League would therefore place its emphasis on indigenous leadership and national self-determination. 'The leaders of the Africans must come out of their own loins' and 'Africa is a Black man's country'; political collaboration with other groups could take place only with Africans acting as 'an organised self-conscious unit'. In particular, the Youth Leaguers were wary of the left. Quite apart from the suspicion that communism simply served to cloak another variant of white paternalism, there was a great gulf between an analysis based on class and one which made ethnicity the crucial determinant: 'Africans are a conquered race – they do not suffer class oppression – they are oppressed as a group, as a nation.'

There was little philosophically original about the Youth League's 'Africanism', as it came to be known. It drew extensively on nineteenth-century Romanticism and Social Darwinism. Few of Lembede's colleagues were in any case very interested in his theories about racial destiny. Where Africanism had a more lasting impact was in the sphere of strategy, for its exponents, while they may not have been profound political theorists, seem to have been unusually imaginative in their reactions to the social eruptions around them. Alone among political groupings they attempted to involve themselves in Mpanza's movement; the ANC, by contrast, preferred to negotiate on behalf of the Orlando squatters with the City Council but with no popular mandate to do so, while the communists regarded the squatters as irresponsible.[55] In a revealing speech in 1949 a Youth Leaguer addressed his audience of Kroonstadt teachers as follows:

> A significant thing has happened recently. In the tram boycott of Western Native Township the lead has been taken by African youth who in their enthusiasm even use violence to make this a success. . . . These [sic] are manifestations of the new spirit – the spirit of nationalism. Only these youngsters haven't the correct orientation. The spirit is there and undeniable.[56]

It was this recognition of the political opportunity presented by these spontaneous popular outbursts that was the most important contribution made to the nationalist movement by the Africanists. From such struggles they distilled a strategy of mass action, centred on the use of the boycott weapon (which had been employed with such effect in the economic context of the bus disputes in Alexandra) but also involving strikes, civil disobedience and non-cooperation. Africanists were never to demonstrate any clear conception of exactly how and in what order these tactics should be employed to achieve their goal of 'national freedom'. Rather it was assumed that in the course of an almost mystic communion between leaders and the popular classes the path would become clear:

> Every Youth Leaguer must go down to the masses. Brush aside all liberals – both white and black. No compromise is our motto. We recognise only one authority – the people, and our leader can only be he who is with the people.[57]

To understand why the Africanist vision was to become so influential within African politics in the late 1940s we need to look at the overall political environment of the 1940s. Whatever hopes and aspirations may have been raised by early wartime hints and promises of reform made by the Smuts administration were to be disappointed later in the decade. Not that these hopes were entirely without foundation. The shifts in government policy towards certain classes within the African community were not simply the result of political expediency but reflected important social divisions within white society. Collective bargaining rights for African workers, social welfare provisions and educational improvements, a degree of material security, and legal recognition of the right of African town-dwellers to permanent residence, were all concessions which the increasingly powerful manufacturing interest viewed as being to its long-term benefit; all were under consideration by government commissions in the second half of the 1940s. On the other hand, there were powerful groups opposed to any improvement in the material conditions, rights and status of the urban African population: farmers suffering from a shortage of labour as the result of the exodus from the countryside to the cities; white workers fearful of the inroads that an organised black working class could make on their preserves of skills and protected employment (for the first time in South African history the proportional wage differentiation between black and white workers was narrowing); and nascent Afrikaner capitalists unable to afford the concessions being contemplated by established industry and commerce. It was these groups which threw their weight behind the Nationalist Party with its advocacy of increased political, social and racial segregation, greater coercion of black workers, and the retention, expansion and sophistication of the migrant labour system in the interests of a more rational allocation of labour between different sectors of employment.[58] In 1948, to the surprise of the incumbent administration, the Nationalists were voted into power. Were any further proof needed of the futility of the traditional lobbying tactics used by the African National Congress, the Nationalists were ready to supply it; unlike their predecessors, they did not have at that stage any reason whatever to meet the most sectional African aspirations. But by then even the most conservative African politicians had little faith in the capacity of any white administration for conceding more than token reforms. Notwithstanding the albeit very limited proposals of some United Party spokesmen in favour of some degree of integration, the brutal treatment of the mineworkers, the extension of urban influx controls to many centres in the Cape, the creation of segregated political institutions for coloureds and Indians and the demonstrable uselessness of the Native Representative Council had all served to undermine any residual faith in the tactics of persuasion through deputation, memoranda and negotiation via sympathetic intermediaries. The Africanist emphasis on confrontation accorded well with the political climate of the decade.

African political expectations were also heightened by the international political context. In common with nationalists in other parts of Africa and Asia, black South African politicians tended to interpret the Atlantic Charter's endorsement of national self-determination rather more literally than its authors in the Allied camp intended. In 1943 a committee of leading professionals, educationists, and ANC and Communist Party members produced a document called 'African claims in South Africa'. Calling in its preamble for the application of the Atlantic Charter to all parts of the British empire it went on to outline a bill of rights. This included provisions for the abolition of all political discrimination based on race and the extension to all adults of voting rights, freedom of residence and of movement, equal rights in the spheres of property and occupation, equal pay for equal work, free compulsory education, equal state assistance to African farmers and the universal extension of a variety of welfare services and social security measures. The proposals provide an interesting contrast to the economic self-help philosophy of Seme a decade earlier, and the importance attributed to the role of the state was itself a reflection of the slightly more enlightened way the state was responding to urban African needs in the early 1940s. 'African Claims' was summarily rejected by Smuts when it was presented to him in 1944. But as well as its importance in marking a stage towards the development of a coherent social alternative to the *status quo* by the nationalist movement, the document was symptomatic of an increased interest by educated Africans in the international environment. For, as never before, there was much to excite them. Quite apart from the stunning defeat of a European empire by an Asiatic power there was the sight of a rapidly growing anti-colonial movement in India and, from 1945, an international forum in the United Nations which would listen with some sympathy and interest to their representatives.

Economic factors also encouraged middle-class Africans to adopt a more politically aggressive outlook. Teachers and clerical workers occupied less strategically advantageous positions than semi-skilled industrial workers at a time of inflation, but the mid-1940s nevertheless witnessed an extraordinary degree of open disaffection by African teachers during the course of their angry but vain campaigning for improved conditions and wages (see Chapter 5); teachers, indeed, were to form a disproportionately large group within the early membership of the ANC Youth League. Even the relatively privileged position of someone like the ANC Treasurer-General, R. G. Baloyi was under threat. His original business was built on African transport, on linking Alexandra's commuters with the workplace and Johannesburg with its rural hinterland. By 1940 a combination of legislation designed to entrench the position of South African Railways and competition from recently arrived Afrikaner and Italian migrants to Johannesburg forced Baloyi and other African entrepreneurs out of the black transport business. In the 1940s, local white interests began to threaten the right to freehold in those citadels of African entrepreneurial interests, Sophiatown and Alexandra: petty-bourgeois Africans were confronted with fresh threats to their security.

Even before the birth of the Youth League there were indications within Congress of a more vigorous reaction to the new pressures and challenges created by a rapidly industrialising society. In 1940 the ANC elected A. B. Xuma as its President. Then aged 47 Xuma was a comparatively young man to accede to this position. Up until that time he had not been very active in politics, although he had helped to organise the first meeting of the All-African Convention of which he was a vice-president. His distinction lay rather in his impressive professional achievements. After a brief spell as a primary school teacher he had trained for fourteen years, mainly at American universities but also in Hungary and Britain, before starting a medical practice in Johannesburg in 1928. Xuma was an energetic and intellectually capable man, though in manner aloof and authoritarian. His major political achievement was to streamline the ANC's organisation. This was done through drawing up a new constitution in 1943, which scrapped ex-officio chiefly membership and abolished the 'House of Chiefs' envisaged in the constitution of 1912, gave full equality to women members, centralised authority by creating a working committee of five executive members living within fifty miles of the President, and attempted to create an effective branch structure by allowing the branches to retain a portion of subscriptions. Xuma himself paid the expenses of full-time organisers until Congress finances were on a sound footing, something which was achieved briefly in the late 1940s. An attempt was made – with some effect in Natal – to build up rural branches, and in the Transvaal urban branches began holding regular weekend open air meetings. By 1947 membership had reached a peak for the decade of 5 517, over half of which was in the Transvaal. In addition, through its mass meetings in locations – often attended by thousands of people – Congress had generated a much larger, less committed, informal following.[59]

Xuma's talents did not extend to the popular touch: he was no orator and preferred the atmosphere of the committee-room to that of the mass meeting. But it was an indication of his receptivity to new ideas that he was initially responsive towards the young men who brought to him the proposal to establish a Youth League. There is an interesting record of his reactions to the draft manifesto:

> . . . the deputation went on to say that the erratic policy of the ANC was shown by the fact there was no programme of action – no passive resistance or some such action. Dr Xuma replied that the Africans as a group were unorganised and undisciplined, and that a programme of action such as envisaged by the Youth League would be rash at this stage. The ANC lacked people who were concerned about the movement and who knew what they wanted. Action would merely lead to exposure. The masses of the people were unorganised and only committees existed in the ANC. . . . His own feeling was that some members of the Youth League should be on the executive of the ANC. . . . He felt that what was really wrong with the manifesto was the tone of the criticism and the expressions used. The committee should start off without antagonising anyone.[60]

The men of the Youth League were precisely the kind whom Xuma was attempting to bring into the organisation: creative, committed, well qualified young professionals. At the same time the exchange demonstrated what was to persist as the main issue of contention between Xuma and the League: the question of organisation. The Africanists were uninterested in organisational problems, and the League itself remained small and loosely structured; for them the key question rather was that of ideology. Xuma insisted that organisational preparation was a vital prerequisite before any form of mass compaigning, and this led him to oppose the Youth League's attempts in the late 1940s to persuade the ANC to boycott Advisory Board and Native Representative Council elections. Xuma's predeliction for organisation and his pragmatic approach to doctrinal issues are useful in understanding his willingness to form alliances with both the Communist Party (with which he was in considerable tactical agreement) and in 1947 (possibly with an eye on the international gallery) the Indian Congresses in their campaign of passive resistance against the Asiatic Land Tenure and Representation Act. Xuma's support for the latter never got beyond a joint statement on principles but in the case of the communists, in reaction to the sudden intensification of pass law prosecutions, he agreed in 1943 to chair a joint CPSA/ANC anti-pass committee. The anti-pass campaign, though expected to culminate in a general strike and pass burnings, was a premature gesture: neither the ANC nor the Communist Party could muster much enthusiasm for it and Xuma's participation was essentially rhetorical and rather half-hearted. The Africanists were hostile, disliking the degree of Communist and Indian participation in the leadership. Africanists, by 1947 well represented on the ANC national executive, combined with conservative Natal leaders in opposing effective cooperation in the Indian passive resistance campaign.

The Indian passive resistance of 1946 to 1948 (see Chapter 2), unsuccessful though it was in gaining the repeal of the offending legislation, was nevertheless important in impressing upon the ANC national executive in 1949 the need to adopt rather more forceful tactics, particularly in the light of the 1948 election. Since Lembede's death from an unknown illness in 1947 a document prepared by Africanists had been circulating at various levels of the Congress leadership. By 1949 this was in the hands of a drafting committee appointed by Dr Xuma and drawn from the left, the establishment, and the Africanist sections of the ANC's leadership. At the 1949 annual conference the ANC committed itself to implementing the final formulation of this document, the Programme of Action. The Programme was the most militant statement of principles adopted by the ANC to date. Congress, it said, should struggle for the rights of national freedom, political independence, and self-determination (these were not clearly defined) and the rejection of white leadership and all forms of segregation. The means employed to reach these ends should include the following: the creation of a national fund and a national press; the appointment of a council of action which would organise a boycott of all differential political institutions, plan a 'national stoppage of work in protest against the reactionary policy of the government', and as well as boycotts and strikes employ the weapons of civil disobedience and non-cooperation; the expansion of African economic power through African-owned businesses, reserve development and trades unions; the improvement of African education through the creation of scholarship funds, trade union educational programmes and a 'National Centre of Education'; and various cultural activities articulated through a 'National Academy of the Arts and Sciences'. Finally, Congress recognised 'that ultimately the people will be brought together by inspired leadership under the banner of African Nationalism'.[61]

The Programme was the product of an eclectic range of influences: the reference to political independence and self-determination being obviously Africanist-inspired; the strategic component derived from the experiences of the Indian Congress and the Communist Party as well as some of the popular struggles of the decade; and the self-help theme a throw-back to the economic nationalism of Congress in the 1930s. Simultaneously with its adoption the leadership changed hands; Dr Xuma, with his distaste for mass-based political activism, being replaced by the Free State physician, Dr James Moroka. As socially eminent as his medical colleague, Moroka had the additional advantage of being sympathetically inclined towards militant forms of action. He was, however, politically inexperienced – not actually being an ANC member at the time of his election – and although personally courageous lacked the sophistication to hold together the increasingly complex organisation the ANC was shortly to become.

Joining Dr Moroka on the new ANC national executive were some of the young men who were to predominate in African nationalist politics in the 1950s. Of the Youth Leaguers elected to leadership positions Nelson Mandela, Oliver Tambo and Walter Sisulu were to play the most prominent roles in the events of the subsequent years. All three had originally come from the Transkei. While Tambo and Sisulu were born into fairly modest peasant households Nelson Mandela's origins were patrician; his family belonged to the Tembu royal house. After high school and two years at Fort Hare university (he was expelled in the aftermath of a student protest) Mandela arrived in Johannesburg to study law, first by correspondence and then at the University of the Witwatersrand. Mandela was a tall, aristocratic-looking man with a remote but commanding personality. A foundation member of the Youth League, he had not been one of its main theorists despite his intellectual abilities. In the events which followed the ANC's adoption of the Programme of Action, Mandela would prove himself to be a pragmatic and astute strategist.

Oliver Tambo – like Mandela, a law student – had also been expelled from Fort Hare, in 1949 after a student strike. He then taught at St Peter's, a prestigious African school in Johannesburg, where he was an inspirational influence on some of the students who were to assume leading positions in the ANC in the late 1950s. Tambo helped to found the Youth League and became its treasurer, though like Mandela he was never one of its principal ideologues. Less charismatic than his future legal partner (he and Mandela were to open an ill-fated legal practice in 1952) he was rather an austere figure, then a puritanical Christian, characteristically silent and thoughtful.

Sisulu had a very different background from his two Youth League associates and friends. From a poor peasant household near Engcobo, before joining the ANC he had worked in a variety of labouring jobs in East London and Johannesburg, and had a brief spell on the gold mines as well. The original sources of his political inspiration were in Xhosa oral traditions as well as Wellington Buthelezi's millenarian movement which had had its main following near his village while he was a boy. In 1940 he had tried to organise a bakery strike and in 1946 had been involved in CNETU's efforts to instigate a general strike in support of the mineworkers. In appearance Sisulu was a dour-looking figure: short, stocky, often hidden in the folds of a wide-lapelled overcoat, bespectacled and with a habit noticed by journalists of biting his bottom lip in between making terse polemical statements. Behind this guarded exterior there was taking place a remarkable intellectual and emotional transformation, for Walter Sisulu, from being one of the most fervent exponents of racially exclusivist nationalism, was one of the first former Youth Leaguers to advocate alliance with political groups drawn from other sections of the population. Sisulu was elected as secretary-general of the ANC. Although the Youth League could with justice represent the 1949 conference as a triumph for its guiding political philosophy – with its Programme of Action adopted and six of its members on the national executive of the ANC – the ANC's leadership nevertheless remained eclectic in its composition and ideology. The communists were still represented and two of them, Moses Kotane and J. B. Marks, would remain influential throughout the 1950s. Both were about twenty years older than the Youth Leaguers, both had been politically active since the 1920s, had received training at the Lenin School in Moscow, and unlike some African communists they had a long history of commitment and loyalty to the ANC. Of the two J. B. Marks was the better educated – he had worked for some time as a teacher – but Kotane, self-taught and educated at a Communist Party night-school, was more at home with Marxian theory and more capable of independent thought. The two men were widely respected, even by Africanists, as political veterans, for their integrity and evident courage.

Finally, there was the traditional liberal African political leadership, represented after the 1949 executive elections in the dignified figure of Professor Z. K. Matthews. One of only two black professors in South Africa, Z. K. Matthews, the son of a Kimberley diamond miner and café-owner, epitomised the traditional African middle-class ideal of success. Gentle and apparently lethargic in manner, he was regarded by many of the African politicians as being firmly within the ranks of the old guard of conservative leaders. In fact Z. K. Matthews' aura of respectability and his natural conservatism were tempered by a personal modesty and sense of honour. Fastidiously courteous in all his dealings with the authorities, who until the advent of the Nationalists had frequently sought his advice and participation on official committees, he was nevertheless an uncompromising political leader. Together with his eldest son Joe, who joined the executive a few years later, he was to be one of the key intellectual influences on the ANC's evolution and in particular in the preservation, alongside an apparently confrontationist strategy, of a conciliatory and racially inclusive form of nationalist ideology.[62]

While populist orientation had been developing within Congress, the Communist Party had been undergoing a comparable change of direction. At the beginning of the war, after six years of popular front activity and committed to an anti-war stance in line with Soviet policy, its influence was at its nadir. Membership had sunk to 280, 150 of whom were in Johannesburg.[63] In the following years it achieved a remarkable recovery, particularly in the size of its African membership. The outstanding feature of its development during the decade was an increasing involvement with the affairs of Congress.

During the war itself the Party's influence was extended chiefly through the indirect means of building industrial trade unions among African and Indian workers, and, on the white political front, in municipal elections. The Party's prospects improved greatly after 1941 as a result of the entry of the Soviet Union into the war and its subsequent 'Defend South Africa Campaign', and for the first time it gained a certain institutional respectability. Its press was allowed extra newsprint and the circulation of two communist-controlled newspapers, *Guardian* and *Inkululeko*, soared to a weekly total in 1945 of 67 000.[64] This was at first mainly due to trade union work which remained the chief source of the Party's strength amongst blacks in Durban and the Cape, though in the Transvaal, particularly on the East Rand, the Party began to play quite a prominent role in township politics, taking up basic bread and butter issues (see Chapter 5). On the East Rand the communists managed to establish a foothold on most of the Advisory Boards, although in Johannesburg itself this did not occur since their preoccupation here was with white municipal elections. But this did result in their winning a seat on the Johannesburg City Council, and it encouraged the local branch to cherish the illusion that it could increase its white working-class following. The lack of any recent activism in local township politics was at the root of the failure of the communist's anti-pass campaign to generate any enduring support in its centre, Johannesburg.

As a result of the lack of interest the CPSA leadership showed in African political affairs in the 1930s and early 1940s, African members of the Communist Party had begun to work more energetically within the ranks of Congress. In certain instances there were tactical reasons for this: it was felt that Congress, because of its access to the traditional leaders in the reserves, would be useful in the organisation of mineworkers. In 1945 three leading African communists, Moses Kotane, J. B. Marks and Dan Thloome were on the ANC national executive. Disillusioned with white labour, these men were successful in influencing the Party to promote causes which would appeal to a wide range of African opinion, rather than just the working class: hence the pass laws and the franchise were at the centre of the Communist Party's national campaigns after 1945. On the whole communists enjoyed the support of the more conservatively inclined members of the ANC national executive: in 1945 and 1947 the Africanists were narrowly defeated in their bids to have Communist Party members expelled from the ANC. At the ANC's annual conference of 1947 communists and the establishment joined together in repudiating the Africanist policy of boycotting Advisory Board and Native Representative elections; both were agreed that these provided a useful platform which should not be yielded to political opponents.

In 1950, shortly before its enforced dissolution, the Communist Party's (still predominantly white) central committee discussed the problem of the Party's relationship with the nationalist movement in its annual report for the previous year. The report first of all argued that with the election of the Nationalist Party, South Africa was entering a bitter national conflict, in which, with an 'exclusive nationalist consciousness' being promoted by an intensified racial oppression, the objective reality of class divisions was being concealed. In these circumstances the Party should be careful to avoid dogmatic hostility to nationalism. The report went on to argue the case for working with and through the national movement:

> From the analysis here presented, the conclusion must be drawn that the national organisations can develop into powerful mass movements only to the extent that their contents and aims are determined by the interests of workers and peasants. The national organisations, to be effective, must be transformed into a revolutionary party of workers, peasants, intellectuals and petty bourgeoisie, linked together in a firm organisation, subject to a strict discipline, and guided by a definite programme of struggle against all forms of racial discrimination in alliance with class-conscious European workers and intellectuals. Such a party would be distinguished from the Communist Party in that its

29

objective is national liberation, that is the abolition of race discrimination, but it would cooperate closely with the Communist Party. In this party the class-conscious workers and peasants of the national group concerned would constitute the main leadership. It would be their task to develop an adequate organisational apparatus, to conduct mass struggles against race discrimination, to combat chauvinism and racialism in the national movement, to develop class consciousness in the people, and to forge unity in action between the oppressed people and between them and the European working class.[65]

With this formulation the communists had finally recognised that the path to a socialist revolution lay through a nationalist struggle, and from 1950 the South African revolutionary left was to devote its energy to influencing the course of the nationalist movement. As we shall see, this was to give rise to bitter conflicts within the ANC.

Notes

1 Gwendolyn Carter and Thomas Karis, *From Protest to Challenge*, Volume 1, Hoover, Stanford, 1971, p. 20.
2 *Ibid*, p. 44.
3 Author's interview with Mr William Letlalo, Soweto, 1979.
4 Carter and Karis, *From Protest to Challenge*, p. 118.
5 SANNC constitution, *ibid*, p. 78.
6 *Ibid*, p. 72.
7 *Ibid*.
8 *Ibid*, p. 78.
9 Peter Walshe, *The Rise of African Nationalism in South Africa*, Hurst, London, 1970, p. 38.
10 Author's interview with Mr William Letlalo.
11 Brian Willan, 'From tram shed to assembly hall' in University of London, Institute of Commonwealth Studies, *Collected Seminar Papers on the Societies of Southern Africa*, Volume 8, p. 8.
12 Philip Bonner, 'The Transvaal Native Congress, 1917–1920', in S. Marks and R. Rathbone (eds), *Industrialisation and Social Change in South Africa*, Longman, London, 1982, pp. 277–8.
13 Frederick Johnston, 'The IWA on the Rand' in Belinda Bozzoli (ed.), *Labour, Townships and Protest*, Ravan, Johannesburg, 1979.
14 See Bonner, 'The Transvaal Native Congress, 1917–1920', and also Philip Bonner, 'The 1920 black mineworkers' strike' in Bozzoli (ed.), *Labour, Townships and Protest*.
15 Carter and Karis, *From Protest to Challenge*, p. 124.
16 Bonner, 'The Transvaal Native Congress', p. 275.
17 Helen Bradford, 'The ICU and the Transvaal rural popular classes in the 1920s', University of the Witwatersrand History Workshop paper, 1981, p. 11.
18 Apart from Bradford's recent research the major treatment of the ICU is Peter Wickens, *The Industrial and Commercial Workers' Union of Africa*, Oxford University Press, Cape Town, 1978. I have also drawn upon Philip Bonner, 'The decline and fall of the ICU', in Eddie Webster (ed.), *Essays in Southern African Labour History*, Ravan, Johannesburg, 1978.
19 Carter and Karis, *From Protest and Challenge*, p. 215.

20 *Ibid*, pp. 300–1.
21 These are described in Sheridan Johns, 'The birth of the Communist Party of South Africa', *International Journal of African Historical Studies*, ix, 3 (1976).
22 Martin Legassick, 'Class and nationalism in South African protest', unpublished seminar paper, n.d., p. 1.
23 Information on the CPSA during this phase of its development is drawn mainly from Legassick, 'Class and nationalism', and Jack and Ray Simons, *Class and Colour in South Africa*, Penguin, Harmondsworth, 1969.
24 Michael Morris, 'The development of capitalism in South African agriculture', *Economy and Society*, v, 3 (1976), p. 293.
25 Legassick, 'Class and nationalism', p. 3.
26 The impetus for the adoption by the CPSA of the 'native republic' slogan is a subject of controversy. Edward Roux, in *Time Longer Than Rope*, Wesleyan University, Wisconsin, 1964, views it primarily as the consequence of external influence whereas the Simonses are prepared to accord more importance to pressures in its favour within the Party.
27 Communist Party of South Africa, Johannesburg District, *Communism and the Native Question*, Johannesburg, n. d. (*c.* 1935).
28 Simons, *Class and Colour*, p. 484.
29 Further detail can be found in Brian Bunting, *Moses Kotane: South African revolutionary*, Inkululeko Publications, London, 1975.
30 Carter and Karis, *From Protest to Challenge*, p. 310.
31 Opposition to the legislation is discussed in Richard Haines, 'The opposition to General Hertzog's Segregation Bills' in University of the Witwatersrand Development Studies Group, *Conference on the History of Opposition in South Africa*, Johannesburg, 1978.
32 Union of South Africa, *Report of the Witwatersrand Mine Natives' Wages Commission*, Pretoria, UG 21 1944, pp. 125–30.
33 Alfred Stadler, 'Birds in the cornfield: squatter movements in Johannesburg, 1944–1947', *Journal of Southern African Studies*, vi, 1 (October 1979), p. 111.
34 *Eastern Province Herald* (Port Elizabeth), 8 February 1945.
35 Alfred Stadler, 'Food crisis in the thirties: a sketch', University of the Witwatersrand History Workshop paper, 1981, p. 5.
36 Stadler, 'Birds in the cornfield', p. 111.
37 *Ibid*.
38 *Daily Dispatch* (East London), 2 May 1946.
39 See Stadler, 'Birds in the cornfield', and Baruch Hirson, 'Prices, homes and transport'. I am very grateful to Baruch Hirson for allowing me access to this unpublished paper which forms part of a larger study of African politics in the 1940s on which he is currently engaged.
40 I have drawn upon Alfred Stadler, 'A long way to walk', University of the Witwatersrand African Studies Institute seminar paper, 1979, and Hirson, 'Prices, homes and transport', for this discussion of the bus boycotts.
41 The analysis which follows is drawn mainly from Stadler's 'Birds in the cornfield'.
42 Stadler, 'Birds in the cornfield', p. 108.
43 *Ibid*.
44 South African Institute of Race Relations, Johannesburg, SAIRR papers, AD 1189, ANC Notebooks, ANC working committee minute book VII.
45 Stadler, 'Birds in the cornfield', p. 107.
46 *Bantu World* (Johannesburg), 3 September 1951.
47 Communist Party of South Africa, Johannesburg District, *Democracy in Action*, Johannesburg, 1945, p. 6.
48 University of the Witwatersrand, Rheinnalt Jones Papers, AD 843 B 3 1, Hilda Watts, 'The facts about Moroka Township', typed memo.

49 Mark Stein, 'The Witwatersrand strikes of December 1942', unpublished paper.
50 For discussion of CNETU's policy during the war see Philip Bonner, 'Black trade unions in South Africa since World War II', in Robert Price and Carl Rosberg (eds), *The Apartheid Regime*, University of California, Berkeley, 1980, pp. 179–80.
51 The following section is based on Dan O'Meara, 'The 1946 African Mineworkers' Strike', *Journal of Commonwealth and Comparative Politics*, xiii, 2 (July 1975).
52 *Sunday Express* (Johannesburg), 23 November 1947.
53 Unless otherwise indicated all CYL documents quoted are taken from Carter and Karis, *From Protest to Challenge*, Volume II, Hoover, Stanford, 1973.
54 Gail Gerhart, *Black Power in South Africa*, University of California, Berkeley, 1978, p. 58.
55 SAIRR papers, AD 1189, ANC notebooks, ANC working committee minute book 1.
56 SAIRR papers, AD 1189, ANC 111, File 4, speech by H. J. Hleti, 21 October 1949.
57 SAIRR papers, AD 1189, ANC 111, File 5, undated memo on provincial congress elections.
58 For elaboration of this argument see Martin Legassick, 'Legislation, ideology and economy in post-1948 South Africa', *Journal of Southern African Studies*, i, 1 (1974).
59 See Walshe, *The Rise of African Nationalism in South Africa*, Chapter 14.
60 SAIRR papers, AD 1189, unsorted box, notes of an interview with A. B. Xuma, 21 February 1944.
61 Carter and Karis, *From Protest to Challenge*, Vol. 2, pp. 338–9.
62 A good source of biographical information on African politicians is Gwendolyn Carter, Gail Gerhart, and Thomas Karis, *From Protest to Challenge*, Volume IV (Political Profiles), Hoover, Stanford, 1977. Here I have also used information from Anthony Sampson, *The Treason Cage*, Heinemann, London, 1958.
63 Alan Brooks, 'From class struggle to national liberation: the Communist Party of South Africa, 1940–1950, M.A. thesis, University of Sussex, p. 25.
64 Anon., 'Wartime history of the comrades', *Forum* (Johannesburg), 29 July 1944.
65 Union of South Africa, *Report of the Select Committee on the Suppression of Communism Act*, Cape Town, SC 10 1953, pp. 205–17.

CHAPTER 2

The creation of a mass movement: strikes and defiance, 1950–1952

During the 1940s under the stimuli of industrial action, communal protest and passive resistance and an increasingly repressive social and political climate, the African National Congress's leadership had reached the point of embracing a strategy based on mass action: the strikes, boycotts and civil disobedience entailed in the Programme of Action adopted in Bloemfontein in 1949. The form this programme would assume was indefinite: it was a statement of principle rather than a detailed strategem. But the months following the December conference allowed little time for careful planning. In 1950 the government began its first major offensive against organised African opposition. The Suppression of Communism Act was not directed solely at the Communist Party and left-wing multiracial trade union groupings; it sanctioned the persecution of any individual group or doctrine intended to bring about 'any political, industrial, social or economic change . . . by the promotion of disturbance or disorder, by unlawful acts' or 'encouragement of feelings of hostility between the European and non-European races of the Union'.[1]

The Communist Party's leaders were already affected by banning orders on J. B. Marks, Moses Kotane and Yusuf Dadoo. It was announced at a 'defend free speech convention' held in Johannesburg on 26 March and presided over by Dr Moroka that May Day would be marked by a stay-away from work in protest against the restrictions and low wages.

The May Day protest was not unanimously supported by the ANC despite Moroka's presence at the convention. A *Bantu World* columnist accurately summed up the feelings of many Youth Leaguers – including Mandela and Tambo – when he commented that the 'People's Holiday' was 'deliberately intended to divert people from the Bloemfontein Programme'.[2] It certainly looked as if the Africanists had been upstaged as there had been up to that point no evident attempt to implement the Programme's call for 'a national stoppage of work for one day as a mark of protest against the reactionary policy of the government'.[3] In fact the African National Congress in the Transvaal appeared to be sharply divided, the May Day protest being endorsed by communists who were also important Congress members (Bopape, Marks, Thloome) and opposed in Johannesburg as well as Evaton and the East Rand by Youth Leaguers.[4]

Despite disagreements between political leaders the stay-away call evoked a significant response. Within the working-class communities on the

Reef, experienced political and trade union organisers of the calibre of Marks, Bopape, and Thloome had at that stage probably greater local standing than the young intellectuals of the Congress Youth League. Nearly 2 000 police were put on duty in anticipation of the event and in the course of clashes between police and crowds in Alexandra, Sophiatown, Orlando and Benoni, eighteen people were killed. Police and newspaper reports describing the events tell us very little about their real character. We know something about some of the victims. Of the eleven people who died, five were under the age of twenty-one, three of them school-children, two were suffocated in a cinema which had been set alight, one man was looking for his child and another was returning from work. Most of the dead and wounded were under the age of thirty.[5] But the composition of the crowd and the motives of those who were out on the streets that day are difficult questions to answer. It is likely they varied in detail in each centre. In Sophiatown there was a well-established tradition of street violence spearheaded by gangsters. In Orlando, violence only developed later in the day when police were escorting workers home who had ignored the strike call. In Benoni, the police were on the offensive, breaking up a large political meeting with bayonets, then firing on the apparently infuriated crowd which threatened to encircle them. While the conservative *Bantu World* was inclined to view most of the violence as due to the action of 'groups of vicious youth',[6] support for the stay-away from the working-class population of Sophiatown and the East Rand townships suggests that street actions did not merely involve an anti-social minority. Loathing for the police was widespread – especially in the Western Areas, for long the haven of those living on the edge of legality. On the Rand, the period 1948–9 was marked by a sudden tightening of the pass and liquor laws (and a 25% increase in convictions under them)[7] which would have had an especial impact in the 'open' freehold locations such as Alexandra, Sophiatown and Benoni. It was not merely that controls on mobility had tightened; they were also implemented in an increasingly brutal fashion. From 1949 there evolved in Johannesburg a new blanket technique of police raiding, the effect of which 'appears to be, not to trace and trap known criminal gangs, but to conduct what resembles a punitive expendition against the entire location population'.[8]

These raids were to become especially frequent in the early months of 1950 after protracted and bloody battles between police and supporters of a municipal tram boycott in the Western Areas. The tension of the crowds on the Reef that May Day is best understood in the context of this sudden intensification of official harassment.

The May Day strike was succeeded by a series of discussions between nationalist and left-wing African leaders culminating in a decision by the ANC national executive to call for a national stay-at-home in protest against the shootings and the Unlawful Organisation Bill (subsequently the Suppression of Communism Act). The 'Day of Protest' would be on 26 June. In the intervening period, in anticipation of the Suppression of Communism Act, the Communist Party dissolved itself. But much of its membership remained politically active – in the case of its 1 500 African members many already had positions within the ANC hierarchy.[9] The preliminaries to 26 June included discussions with Indian Congress leaders who were to call out their own followers that day. A committee to co-ordinate the activities of both organisations was established with Walter Sisulu and Yusuf Cachalia as joint secretaries. The Transvaal Youth League issued a fiery statement supporting the protest and stirringly concluding 'Up you Mighty Race'.[10] Unlike the May protest, 26 June could be viewed as an unequivocally nationalist assertion: the day itself (apparently chosen at random) had no distracting working-class or internationalist connotations.

The second 1951 stay-at-home was considerably more decorous than the first. To avoid confrontations with the police, people were told to 'remain quietly at home and think seriously about the plight of their people'.[11] The most noticeable effects of the Day of Protest were in Durban and Port Elizabeth where even the hostile *Bantu World* admitted there was a 'most effective' stay-away by African workers. On the Rand the organisers at the time claimed – in the face of hostile press reports – important successes, though the ANC's national executive report at the end of the year conceded that response to the strike call in the Transvaal was very poor.[12] In Port Elizabeth, campaigning before the stay-away centred as much around the Native Urban Areas (Amendment) Bill as the impending restrictions on political organisation. The amended Urban Areas Bill appeared especially threatening in Port Elizabeth, by 1950 the only major urban centre exempt from the provision of influx control (see below p. 49).[13]

In Port Elizabeth, the Communist Party had a following within both the trade union movement and sections of the Congress leadership. As we shall see later, local developments in the preceding decade had provoked the most extraordinary transformation in a population which 'had earned the reputation for loyal behaviour in response to considerable municipal policy'.[14] On Monday 26 June much of the unskilled labour was withdrawn from industry; the harbour, commerce and services, which drew most of their labour from the African population, were the most seriously affected.[15]

In Durban, where political influence had been linked with labour organisation because of the provincial presidency of the aged ICU leader, Champion, a bitter personal conflict between Champion and his provincial secretary, Selby Msimang, had stimulated local Congress organisation. Champion was later to complain that Msimang built 'Congress branches in every hostel and street-corner in Durban with a view to organising factions hostile to me'.[16] Here, too, the Natal Indian Congress had developed into a radical mass movement as a result of the passive resistance movement and the wartime development of working-class consciousness within the Indian population. The Congresses were to claim a 60 per cent abstention by the workforce, affecting 70 factories. Municipal workers were worst affected by victimisation dismissals, and the Council, despite its dismissal of 115 African workers, warned that in future it would discriminate against Indian as opposed to African labour in its employment policy – apparently the absenteeism rate was especially high in the Indian workforce.[17]

The level of participation between different urban centres in these mass political demonstrations was beginning to fall into a pattern which would characterise organised black opposition in urban centres for the rest of the decade. We will be looking at the background to the outstanding feature of this pattern – that is the consistently strong response to Congress campaigns in the eastern Cape – as well as variations elsewhere, later in this chapter. But a brief digression is needed here to make a few points about the stay-at-home tactic which since 1950 has remained the most important political weapon in black protest politics. Support for the stay-at-home should be related to the realisation amongst black politicians of the potential strength of black workers, discussed in the last chapter. The Programme of Action had called for a protest strike and this was to characterise Congress's approach to the stay-away throughout the decade. General withdrawals were intended as demonstrations of strength; they were not in themselves direct attacks on the power of the state or employers. Only in isolated and localised instances would the stay-aways be called for an indefinite period and assume the characteristic of a classical general strike. The organisation of the stay-at-home took place mainly in the townships, through open air meetings and door-to-door canvassing. South African urban geography holds certain advantages for the organisation of such protests: black people are concentrated in crowded and isolated housing complexes. Because of their compact nature and few points of communication with the rest of the city, mobilising or immobilising their inhabitants is relatively easy. The township-based stay-at-home tactic had legal advantages as well: formal prohibitions on African industrial strikes were inadequate counter-measures to the stay-aways. Organisation at the workplace was considerably riskier, though it had advantages. When the local Congress leadership had strong links with trade unions (as in Port Elizabeth) the stay-at-home would have the most dramatic effect, worker solidarity being greater in the factory than at home.

The stay-at-home appeared a useful and appropriate means of protest. But it had disadvantages. As the events in the 1950s were to demonstrate, police action against a township as opposed to a factory-based strike was considerably simpler. Moreover, the stay-away left certain workers untouched: when there were no controlled compounds or hostels the effects of such strikes would be much more widespread. Here again Port Elizabeth was exceptional.[18]

In the two years between the 26 June strike and the first acts of civil disobedience in 1952 there was little organised political activity outside the western Cape. For the African National Congress, nevertheless, they represented a crucial phase. The adoption of the Programme of Action and the movement's involvement in political strikes did not signify a thorough-going transformation from an élitist to a popular movement. The period which followed the Day of Protest was characterised by conflicts concerning both strategic and ideological questions. The two main issues were the position of marxists within Congress and the question of collaboration with non-African organisations. Until there was a degree of unanimity within Congress's leadership over these, further implementation of the Programme of Action would have to wait. Of the five members of the 'Council of Action' appointed in early 1950, by the end of 1951, one had withdrawn from political activity and two had identified themselves with a dissenting ANC faction, the National Minded bloc.

The Simons's remark that with the dissolution of the Communist Party on 20 June 1950, and the absorption thereafter of its activists in the affairs of

Congress, 'the class struggle had merged with the struggle for liberation'.[19] This was precisely what Youth Leaguers had feared, since they believed that Africans were oppressed 'by virtue of their colour as a race'[20] rather than through their position as a class. Some Youth Leaguers were to join older conservatives within the Transvaal Congress to oppose the successful election of J. B. Marks as president of the provincial organisation in November 1950. However, the most bitter opposition to Marks came not from those who opposed 'imported' ideologies and 'obscure' influences but rather from people who looked back with nostalgia to an era when politics was more socially exclusive:

> Congress wants a leader with simple methods of teaching the masses how to live; a man who has himself proved a success in life as apparent from his economic, social and political well-being.[21]

The similarities between the conservative and Youth League opponents of Marks were superficial. Both stressed race pride in their popular appeal. But the former placed their main emphasis on the virtues of upward social mobility on the part of Africans[22] – a major concern being opposition to Indian trading activity within black residential areas. The latter saw an ethnically derived nationalism as the key to mass mobilisation. For a time the conservatives, banded together as the 'National Minded bloc', appeared a serious threat. In the first months of 1951, J. B. Marks and other Transvaal leaders devoted much energy to establishing their authority at public meetings in the Johannesburg and Reef locations.

The Youth League was going through an important transition. Collaboration with other national executive leaders modified the Africanist position of Mandela and Tambo, the older and less ideologically dogmatic Sisulu being a key influence upon them. Youth League spokesmen began to pay more attention to class-based analyses. Dilizantabe Mji, president of the Transvaal Congress Youth League from early 1951, was a good example, with his reference to:

> . . . foaming racialist slogans that have perverted the minds of their fellow white men . . . driving the white workers away from the ranks of the toiling masses . . . the ordinary white man must be forgiven . . . he is not an oppressor . . . the people never to be forgiven are those who build round the lives of simple people this facade of a black peril.[23]

Mji's position was not shared by everyone – in 1952, indeed, he was only re-elected after criticism of his 'ideological unreliability'.[24] In the early 1950s the League divided into two camps: one was to promote, in the words of Joe Matthews, 'a healthy, democratic, non-racialist, anti-colonial, anti-imperialist nationalism'.[25] The other was to adhere to Africanist orthodoxy. The former camp was closer to the decision-making levels of Congress. Its leaders tended to have greater professional status and hence economic independence than the latter, many of whom were teachers, and hence less politically active. For the time being, the Africanists were to content themselves with issuing ephemeral newsletters from their centres in Orlando and East London.

African communists were often ideologically rather eclectic and hence in 1950–2 a more sensitive issue than their presence in Congress's leadership was that of cooperation with the Indian Congress.

Anti-Indian sentiments were not confined to African businessmen. In 1948, the Newclare Youth League passed a resolution calling on the Minister of the Interior to tighten African/Indian residential segregation.[26] In Benoni, in July 1952, Indian shopkeepers were attacked and their stores looted after one of their number had fatally beaten up an African boy he suspected of stealing.[27] Conservative opponents would often accuse the ANC leadership of being under control of Indians. However, though cooperation between Indian and African organisations remained a contentious issue in some quarters, several factors made this considerably easier by the beginning of the decade than it had been before. First of all, like the ANC, the Indian Congresses in Natal and the Transvaal became more popularly oriented during the 1940s. This reflected the increase in the size of the Indian industrial working class and its corollary, the spread of Indian trade unionism; the development of a professional non-commercial middle class; the spreading influence within these groups of the South African Communist Party; and – especially in the Transvaal – the growing vulnerability of small retailers threatened by both legislation and Afrikaner nationalist trading boycotts.[28] In 1946, in protest against the new Asiatic Land Tenure Act, the Indian Congresses embarked on a two-year campaign of civil disobedience in which over 2 000 volunteers were arrested, usually for the illegal crossing of provincial borders or the occupation of selected sites in 'white' areas of Durban. By the late 1940s there seemed less to be gained than before from isolating Indian struggles from those of other blacks, while at the same time the new marxist leaders of the Indian Congress were eager to form links with other communal struggles for moral and ideological reasons. This was achieved at a symbolical level with the 'Joint Declaration of Cooperation' signed by A. B. Xuma, G. M. Naicker, and Yusuf Dadoo. This promised a combined struggle by Africans and Indians against all forms of discrimination, as well as the participation of a small band of African volunteers in Germiston in one of the final acts of civil disobedience.[29]

A firmer commitment to alliance with the Indian Congresses was stimulated by the Durban 'race riots', which, in highlighting the tense everyday relationships between Africans and Indians, helped to persuade leaders of both communities of the dangers of polarisation and the virtues of collaboration. The Defiance Campaign itself would demonstrate in tangible form the benefits of communal cooperation, for small traders apparently provided an important financial contribution,[30] and the influence of newly independent India at the United Nations helped to attract international attention to the campaign. Two additional factors served to bring the movements closer. In both the African and Indian Congresses marxists had become – by the late 1940s – influential at the level of leadership. In both, the influence of well-established (and hence competitive) groups of businessmen had lessened with the adoption of a mass-based strategy. In the case of the Natal and Transvaal Indian Congresses this was a consequence of the withdrawal in 1946 of the Indian High Commissioner in South Africa and hence the end of the favoured tactic of the wealthy, lobbying.[31] In the case of the ANC, the formation of the National Minded bloc in late 1950 was an important development. The bloc's influence was greatly exaggerated by the *Bantu World* – whose editor was Richard Selope Thema, the bloc's president – but its emergence was nevertheless significant for this reason.

The above discussion helps to elucidate what were rather dramatic developments given the racial isolationism of young African politicians in previous years. The joint co-ordinating committee which emerged during the 26 June stay-away provided a precedent for the Council of Action's recommendations – presented to the ANC national executive on the afternoon of a founding member's funeral – for a joint campaign with Indian and coloured organisations against pass laws and stock limitation. On the 28 June 1951, a five-man planning council was established consisting of Moroka, Sisulu, Marks, Dadood and Yusuf Cachalia. The council's purpose was to establish the appropriate strategy of mass resistance to six 'unjust laws'.

Events in the western Cape helped to strengthen the conviction of those who believed that conditions favoured a mass campaign, as well as contributing to the emergence of the Congress alliance. In the Cape, political disaffection among coloured people was becoming more militant and assertive in its expression.

The radicalisation of coloured politics began in the 1930s with the formation in Cape Town of the National Liberation League and later the Non-European United Front: both were founded in response to the threat of segregationist legislation, and after demonstrations and riots in District 6 this was postponed. The 1939 congress of the NEUF was attended by representatives of the Cape ANC and the Communist Party. Political organisation within the coloured community received a further impetus with Smuts's proposal in 1954 to establish a 'Coloured Affairs Council'. In response an Anti-CAD movement was formed. Anti-CAD's main purpose was to deny any legitimacy to segregationist political institutions, and this objective – together with the fact that much of its following was among teachers who were proscribed from activist politics – meant its major weapon was the electoral boycott. Initially, this created a distance between Anti-CAD and both the Communist Party and the ANC, both of which, through the 1940s, made use of whatever political platform was available. The Anti-CAD movement and the All-African Convention were both affiliated to the Non-European Unity Movement (NEUM). The NEUM was the major political force among coloured intellectuals, while the Communist Party succeeded in bringing coloured workers under its indirect influence through a few well-organised trade unions.

By the end of the decade the relatively privileged position of the coloured population in relation to Africans was being eroded. Between 1948 and 1951 prohibitions on sexual relationships and marriage between whites and coloureds, a humiliating system of racial classification under the Population Registration Act, apartheid on trains in the Cape peninsula, stricter residential segregation and the Separate Registration of Voters' Bill – all appeared as new threats to coloured security and status.

Resistance to these measures was at first unpromising. When train apartheid was announced on 13 August 1948, a large meeting was convened by the Communist Party in front of Cape Town's town hall. A train apartheid resistance committee was elected including communists, Unity Movement leaders, and members of the African People's Organisation – the oldest coloured political organisation. Tensions within the committee swiftly developed. The Unity movement and APO people were opposed to small-scale passive resistance.[32] The communists accused the rest that their insistence on wide-scale organisation as a precondition for resistance was merely an excuse for inactivity.[33] A call for 2 000 volunteers[34] to fill whites-only coaches attracted 300 who succeeded in delaying the departure of one Cape Town train for thirty minutes.[35] The committee broke up shortly afterwards, amid charges and countercharges of adventurism and cowardice.

However, by 1951 the focus of protest had shifted to something rather more important than first-class railway accommodation. In February, a conference was held in Cape Town attended by representatives of the African People's Organisation, the South African Indian Congress, the ANC, and local community groups and trade unions, to discuss the opposition to the removal of coloured voters from the common roll. Out of this meeting grew the Franchise Action Committee. FRAC, as it was known, was a curious alliance involving both left-wing trade unionists and some of the most accommodationist coloured politicians, including supporters of the state-sponsored Coloured Advisory Council. Although the alignment of such diverse figures as Sam Kahn, one of the leading figures in the Communist Party, and George Golding of the National Convention, attracted the derision of the Unity Movement, it was nevertheless quite effective in organising well-supported protests. Speeches at FRAC meetings give some idea of the tension and anxiety underlying these. As one speaker pointed out:

> If you lose your votes you will become like the African people. You will be placed in locations . . . you will be judged by Coloured Commissioners . . . if you lose your votes, you will lose everything you have.[36]

In April, a FRAC conference resolved in favour of a 'political strike' which was eventually called for 7 May. The strike had a considerable impact upon industry in Cape Town, although *Torch* claimed that in many cases employers and workers had prior agreements to work on a public holiday instead. It was supported by both coloured and African workers. At a conference in June 1951, 233 of the delegates were from FRAC factory groups.[37] Despite the amorphous nature of its leadership FRAC had become an effective force among working-class coloureds who were most affected by new protectionist policies in favour of white workers. Their volatility was expressed dramatically when a mainly coloured crowd, responding to the insurrectionary flavour of a Torch Commando demonstration, began to converge on the House of Assembly only to be violently repulsed by police.[38]

Though coloureds were responding to the threat of losing privileges which differentiated them socially from Africans, these events nevertheless served to strengthen the argument of those who advocated a multiracial campaign. The Joint Planning Council reported in November 1951 and recommended that an ultimatum be presented to the Government to repeal the 'unjust law ' by the end of February. If the ultimatum was not met a campaign was to begin on either 6 April (van Riebeeck's Day) or 26 June. The struggle would involve the courting of arrests by trained volunteer corps through contravening selected laws and regulations. In the first stage, it was envisaged that the campaign would be limited to the major urban centres, in the second the number of corps and centres would increase, and finally the struggle would 'assume a general mass character' in both town and the countryside. In towns, ANC volunteers would defy the pass laws and in the countryside people should be persuaded to resist stock limitation. In the case of SAIC members, provincial barriers, the Group Areas Act, apartheid regulations at railway stations, post offices and so forth would be the main targets. FRAC volunteers would als oppose the Group Areas Act and apartheid regulations.[39]

The report also considered the possibility of strike action but concluded that it should not be a major strategic component until possibly later in the campaign. The authors of the report were concerned to ensure that the campaign attracted as wide a range of participation as possible. Limiting it to various forms of industrial action would, they believed, deny the opportunity of involving, for example, the large number of people affected by the Separate Registration of gvoters Act who were not industrial workers. The importance accorded to rural action reflected the increasingly bitter struggle in the reserves against Gtvernment rehabilitation schemes. In particular, the Witzieshoek disturbances of 1950–51 had helped to draw the attention of African politicians to rural problems. The personal inclinations of the Council members undoubtedly helped to shape their recommendations. Moroka himself, a country doctor in Thaba Nchu, was much more aware of disaffection in the countryside than his predecessor, Xuma. Yusuf Cachalia was, of the five, the nearest to being a Gandhist and both he and Dadoo brought to the Council their own experiences in the 1946–48 passive resistance campaign. However, it was the former Africanist, Walter Sisulu, who was the first to elaborate a civil disobedience strategy.[40] And notwithstanding the misgivings of some of his colleagues, the campaign was not inconsistent with an Africanist strategy; mobilisation was to be along communal rather than class-determined lines and only in exceptional cases would 'mixed' volunteer units be formed.

The underlying motives of the plan's authors and of those who adopted it are difficult to determine. The apparent divisions in white politics (it was only in 1952 that the Nationalist Party consolidated its control over the electoral process) and the evidence of militantly expressed dissent within the black communities may have persuaded some that civil disobedience would provide a strong enough challenge to change government policy. Such considerations may have helped to influence the choice of civil disobedience which, while it challenged the moral authority of the law, did so in a way which minimised the risk of violence and did not seriously inconvenience the white population. It is unlikely that many subscribed to Gandhi's notion of Satyagraha in which the suffering of those punished for disobedience was supposed to activate the inherent goodness of the rulers. More conceivably, a large number of those who eventually participated in the campaign probably hoped that their actions would succeed in disorganising authority by filling the prisons and the courts to capacity. This was not how the leadership viewed the purpose of defiance, at least not at first. Naboth Mokgatle, a former member of the CPSA in Pretoria, records in his autobiography his dismay at the selective and cautious way in which the ANC set about recruiting volunteers. Stating that 'hundreds and thousands' of potential resisters were turned away by

Congress officials he goes on to recall

> . . . talking to a group of Congress Youth League men at Atteridgeville. They were holding their meeting next door to where I lived and it was very well attended. Nelson Mandela was National Volunteer-in-Chief, which meant that he had to go all over the country to see that committees were formed and that the people were defying everywhere. I was not a Youth Leaguer, but I asked for permission to come along and say a few words and it was kindly granted to me. I said to them in Mandela's presence that if they were serious and wanted to break the Apartheid machine, the right way to break it was to throw into its spokes, its wheels and all its parts everything they could – sand, rags, stones – to jam it. By that, I told them, I meant that hundreds and thousands of volunteers should flood police stations, courts and prisons. I told them, further, that their methods were not aiding the people, but Malan's Government. I said that their actions were like throwing things into a machine, then allowing the owner to dismantle it, clean it, sharpen it and put it together again before throwing in another thing. My advice was ignored.[41]

As things turned out, in those areas in which the campaign reached its peak, it was to come very close to functioning in the fashion envisaged by Mokgatle, but even so the organisers would continue to insist that the volunteer units remained both small and disciplined. The retrospective claim made by ANC leaders that the main aim of the campaign was to mobilise an effective mass following for the nationalist movement[42] was probably accurate given the campaign's essentially demonstrative flavour.[42]

The Joint Planning Council report was endorsed in December by the delegates at the ANC's annual conference, over half of whom, according to Joe Matthews, were people 'closely connected with the trade unions'.[43] A National Action Council composed of four ANC and three SAIC leaders was set up to direct campaigning. The only expression of dissent came from the Natal provincial organisation. This was now led by Chief Albert Lutuli, after a bitter struggle between the old incumbent, A. W. G. Champion, and the Youth League. For various reasons, Congress was in disarray in Natal and Lutuli and other delegates doubted the organisation had the capacity to mount a mass struggle in that province. A month later, indeed, the provincial secretary, Selby Msimang, publicly condemned the joint African/Indian leadership of the campaign as being especially inappropriate in the Natal context, in view of the communal tensions which existed.[44]

In January 1952 an ultimatum signed by Dr Moroka and Walter Sisulu, calling for the repeal of six 'unjust laws', was sent to the Prime Minister. The laws they had singled out were in themselves a telling reflection of the additional pressures black people had been subjected to since 1948. First there were the pass laws, a long-standing grievance, but recently enforced with new vigour. Stock limitation and the Bantu Authorities Act, fiercely resisted by Africans, were attempts by the state to restructure local economic and political relations in the reserves. The Group Areas Act extended residential and occupational segregation and threatened in particular those who owned property or operated a business in a 'white' area. Included in the six laws were two affecting political rights: the Voters' Representation Act and the

Suppression of Communism Act. To nobody's surprise the ultimatum was rejected in a letter from the Prime Minister's secretary.

On 31 May, encouraged by the success of huge rallies organised on 16 April in protest against the van Riebeeck tercentenary celebrations, the executives of the ANC, SAIC, and FRAC decided that the Defiance Campaign should begin on 26 June. The campaign was to be the most sustained and – in terms of numbers of participants – the most successful organised resistance the ANC was ever to initiate. Because much of the scholarly analysis of Congress campaigns has emphasised bureaucratic inadequacies as the key to understanding their shortcomings, it is worth looking at the state of Congress organisation at the inception of the campaign. Certainly, judged by narrow bureaucratic criteria the ANC was in no state to organise a major campaign. The report of its executive for 1951 drew attention to the financial crisis it faced and the difficulties caused by disputes over the leadership in Natal and the Transvaal. The organisation could afford only one full-time paid official, Walter Sisulu. Though membership was on the increase (7 000 on the eve of the campaign) it was concentrated in a small number of active branches: 25 in the Transvaal, 14 in the Cape, 17 in the Free State, and an unspecified number in Natal.[45] A plan to break the provincial organisation into less cumbersome and geographically more coherent units had only just begun to be implemented.[46] Clearly, if the campaign was to be successful it would have to rely on informal channels of communication and local initiative.

Despite these difficulties the campaign's programme was remarkably consistent with the JPC recommendations. It opened in the main urban centres on the Reef and Port Elizabeth on 26 June. In Boksburg, 50 people, led by the veteran passive resister, Nana Sita, walked through the gates of the African location without the appropriate permits and were arrested. That night 52 men, including Mandela and Cachalia, broke the curfew laws in central Johannesburg. In Port Elizabeth, 30 walked through the 'Europeans only' entrance of the New Brighton railway station. The next day, nine volunteers opened the campaign in the western Cape, standing at the white counter of Worcester post office. Worcester was a small town, but a logical starting point for resistance in the western Cape, since it was an important centre for the canning industry and hence the main focus of activity of one of the largest and most militant black trade union organisations, the Food and Canning Workers' Union and its African sister union. The opening moves set the pattern for the campaign: until the police actually tried to prevent acts of defiance they were warned well in advance so they could be present. Volunteer groups remained small and easily manageable. Their acts of defiance were watched by a much larger crowd of supporters, and were often preceded by meetings and street processions. The regulations disobeyed were very minor ones: use of white facilities at post offices, railway stations and on trains, breaching curfew regulations and pass laws, and entering African locations without a permit. Despite the increasingly heavy sentences handed out by magistrates (including flogging for young people), almost without exception volunteers opted to serve prison sentences which could last two or three months rather than pay the alternative fine.

A mood of religious fervour infused the resistance, especially in the eastern Cape. When the campaign opened it was accompanied by 'days of prayer', and volunteers pledged themselves at prayer meetings to a code of love, discipline and cleanliness. Manyanos* wore their uniforms and accompanied Congress speeches with solemn hymn singing, and even at the tense climax of the campaign in Port Elizabeth – where there were strong syndicalist undercurrents – people were enjoined on the first day of the strike to 'conduct a prayer and a fast in which each member of the family will have to be at home';[47] and thereafter they attended nightly church services. A few Congress spokesmen, especially in Johannesburg where the Youth League provided an important component in the local leadership, spoke in the strident idiom of Africanism: 'To you who are young and whose blood is hot, we say catch the bull by its horns, Afrika.'[48] But more typically the verbal imagery of the campaign involved ideas of sacrifice, martyrdom, the triumph of justice and truth. The speech that J. B. Marks made in anticipation of his arrest for breaking a banning order just before the campaign opened set the tone for much of what was to follow. Referring to the ANC as the real Noah's Ark he went on to announce: 'This is the hour now. I am being crucified and I feel the weight of the cross.'[49]

By the beginning of August the campaign had spread from its original centres to East London, Uitenhage, the West Rand, Vereeniging, Pretoria, Grahamstown, and Cape Town. Already it was apparent that the most dramatic levels of participation were in the towns of the eastern Cape. One early morning in August, for example, between 12.01 a.m. and 8.15 a.m., eleven groups broke railway apartheid regulations at New Brighton and the Main City stations, 245 volunteers being arrested.[50] There were other regional variations as well. The pattern on the Rand was for groups to travel out from a main Congress stronghold and break the law in an outlying township. Consequently the regulations that were broken most frequently in the Transvaal were the location permit requirements. In the eastern Cape, on the other hand, there was far more dependence upon local initiative: here, people were encouraged to defy in their home areas.

The campaign reached its peak in September, 2 500 resisters being arrested that month in 24 centres, amongst them both Bloemfontein and Durban. It received a fresh impetus at the beginning of October when India successfully moved that South Africa should be debated at the UN General Assembly. The leaders of the campaign, most of them now facing charges under the Suppression of Communism Act, called for an intensification of the campaign in response. By October it had drawn volunteers in every major town in the union and in addition had attracted some rural support: most dramatically in Peddie in the Ciskei, but also from 31 farmworkers in the eastern Transvaal who had been organised in a farmworkers' union by the ANC leader, Gert Sibande, since the late 1930s. In Port Elizabeth the campaign appeared to have reached the first stage projected by the Joint Planning Council. By mid-October nearly 2 000 had volunteered. They had on several occasions managed to fill to capacity the city's smart new jail, and police reinforcements had to be drafted in from other parts of the country.[51] The more generalised resistance envisaged in the projected third stage of the campaign appeared to be taking place in the Eastern Province: in Peddie

* Manyanos were members of church-based township women's welfare groups.

several hundred people were under arrest for breaking curfew regulations and there were reports of widespread resistance and lack of cooperation with cattle-dipping measures. In Port Elizabeth, from quite early on, strike action was combined with civil disobedience, despite the injunctions of a section of the ANC leadership. Volunteers returning to work after having served their prison sentences would be refused re-employment. Workers, encouraged by ANC activists, would then empty the factories. In three weeks six strikes involving 850 workers took place.[52]

But between 18 October and 9 November the campaign virtually ground to a halt, and there were less than 300 arrests thereafter. In its two main centres, where resistance seemed to be losing its momentum in any case, the movement was paralysed by events surrounding the outbreak of rioting – on 18 October in Port Elizabeth and on 9 November in East London. The riots will be discussed more fully later but they arose essentially out of the increasingly tense relationship between blacks and police which the campaign had generated. The Port Elizabeth riots were followed by bans and curfews which made political activity very difficult. In reaction to the measures taken by both the police and the city council, the leaders of the Port Elizabeth branch of Congress called for a workers' stay-at-home. Like the bus boycott which had followed the introduction of armed police on railway buses after the riots, this enjoyed almost total support from the African workforce and was backed by many coloured workers as well. Left-wing activists had wanted the strike to be indefinite, but they were overruled, and it was limited instead to a one-day demonstration. Its success appeared to have set the pattern for the future development of the campaign. By February 1953, rank and file feeling at both the Cape and Transvaal provincial conferences was clearly in favour of continued 'industrial action'. This was prompted by two recently enacted laws, the Public Safety Act (enabling the government to declare a state of emergency) and the Criminal Law Amendment Act which set the seal on any further civil disobedience efforts by imposing a three-year imprisonment sentence and/or flogging for any violation of the law 'by way of protest against the law'. The strike call, though accepted in principle by the Congress national executive, was never implemented. In 1953 bans on political leaders and organisational confusion – caused in part by the immense expansion of the movement as a result of the campaign – effectively immobilised any further resistance.

Out of this necessarily selective account of the campaign several questions arise which the rest of this chapter will attempt to answer.[53] These are: How does one account for the extraordinary response in the eastern Cape? What was the connection between the campaign and the riots? Why was participation in the campaign in Natal so limited (300 arrests and none outside Durban)? What were the achievements of the campaign? We will begin by considering the background to events in the eastern Cape.

The strength of Congress's following in the eastern Cape during the 1950s is generally attributed to a unique combination of a variety of factors. These include the ethnic homogeneity of the local population; the deep

Defiance Campaign resister arrests, 1952

East Cape

Port Elizabeth	2007 (DC)
East London	1322 (DC)
Uitenhage	600 (DC)
Peddie	669 (TL)
Grahamstown	372 (TL)
Fort Beaufort	157 (TL)
Queenstown	133 (DC)
Kirkwood	110 (DC)
Kingwilliamstown	98 (DC)
Port Alfred	297 (TL)
Adelaide	64 (DC)
Cradock	53 (DC)
Alice	37 (DC)
Jansenville	22 (TL)
Regional total:	5941

Transvaal

Johannesburg	521 (DC)
Germiston	245 (DC)
Boksburg	138 (TL)
Brakpan	127 (DC)
Pretoria	101 (TL)
Springs	74 (DC)
Vereeniging	82 (TL)
Krugersdorp	95 (TL)
Benoni	48 (TL)
Roodepoort	85 (TL)
Bethal	31 (TL)
Evaton	20 (TL)
Witbank	11 (TL)
Regional total:	1578

West Cape

Cape Town	157 (TL)
Stellenbosch	114 (TL)
Kimberley	88 (TL)
Worcester	76 (TL)
Mafeking	20 (TL)
Paarl	20 (TL)
Ceres	15 (TL)
Regional total:	490

Orange Free State

Bloemfontein	125 (TL)
Regional total:	125

Natal

Durban	192 (TL)
Regional total	192

Regional totals

East Cape	5941
Transvaal	1578
West Cape	490
Orange Free State	125
Natal	192
Total:	8326

Above figures taken either from David Carter's 'The Defiance Campaign' or from my own calculations based on press reports in *Advance*, *People's World*, *Clarion*, *Bantu World* and *Eastern Province Herald*. Two less detailed sets of figures were made available shortly after the end of the campaign:

ANC/SAIC (cited in Carter and Karis, *From Protest to Challenge*, Volume II):

East Cape	5719
Transvaal	1411
Orange Free State	258
Natal	246
West Cape	423
Total:	8057

South African Police (in *Annual Reports* for 1952 and 1953):

Total arrested and charged:	8429
Total convicted:	7986

historical roots of modern political culture; the more relaxed legal environment – in particular the absence in influx control in Port Elizabeth; the greater sense of deprivation as the eastern Cape was brought into conformity with the harsher segregationist policies of the north after 1948; the persistence of attitudes generated during a bloody phase of primary conflict; the strength of trade unionism and the existence of a large concentration of African industrial workers in Port Elizabeth; the stability of family life; the extent of conversion to Christianity; the lack of divisive communist influence in African politics.[54] However, this hypothesis needs testing in a more detailed examination of the local context if it is to provide a convincing explanation. With the exception of ethnic homogeneity most of these factors would have been operative on the Rand where a major proportion of the African population had several generations' acquaintance with 'modern' political activity, trade unionism and Christianity, and where important centres had only recently been subjected to the full rigours of influx control under the Urban Areas Act.[55] There is little evidence that ethnic or linguistic differences either within the African community or between Africans and Indians inhibited political response in the

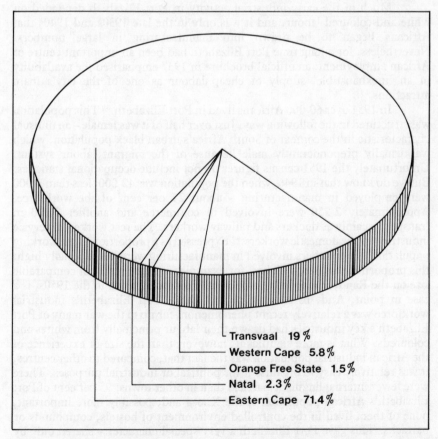

Transvaal 19%
Western Cape 5.8%
Orange Free State 1.5%
Natal 2.3%
Eastern Cape 71.4%

Fig. 1   Location of arrests by province during Defiance Campaign resistance

Transvaal. Only a detailed consideration of the eastern Cape political environment and local antecedents of the campaign can provide an understanding of its course in this area. Let us look, therefore, at its two major centres, Port Elizabeth and East London.

Port Elizabeth is one of South Africa's oldest industrial centres, the town's prosperity being initially based on its importance as a port as well as the local leather industry. In the 1920s it was the obvious site for South Africa's fledgeling motor industry, and both its port facilities and its central position between major population conurbations made it the logical choice. In 1923 work began on the Ford assembly line. The major vehicle manufacturers were followed by components industries as well as clothing and food processing factories. By the 1930s Port Elizabeth's population was increasing more rapidly than anywhere else in South Africa.[56] The Second World War halted the rate of industrial expansion but it also had the effect of stimulating the existing factories to diversify their output. The late 1940s, however, were a period of unprecedented industrial growth with the establishment of two tyre factories, a Ford and a Volkswagen plant, stainless steel, canning, metallurgical and electronics concerns, and many others.[57]

Much of the early industrial activity in Port Elizabeth depended on white and coloured labour, and it was only in the late 1930s and 1940s that Africans began to be drawn into manufacturing in large numbers. Nevertheless, for a long time Port Elizabeth had been an important centre of African employment: an official brochure in 1937 emphasised the availability of an 'inexhaustible' supply of cheap labour as one of the city's main attractions.[58]

In 1951 over 60 000 Africans lived in Port Elizabeth.[59] This population was structured in the following way. Just over half of it was female – an unusual characteristic in the context of South Africa's urban black population, which was usually preponderantly male because of the migrant labour system. Unfortunately the 1951 census figures do not include occupational statistics. But we do know that in 1946, when the population was 42 000, less than 3 000 were employed in manufacturing – about 21 per cent of the workforce. Approximately 2 250 were involved in commerce and another 2 000 in transport, mainly as dockers and railway workers. The rest worked in service industries and as domestic workers.[60] Expressed as a proportion of the working population, the numbers involved in manufacturing were not especially high: this proportion was much higher, for example, in many towns of comparable size on the Rand; Roodepoort, a politically quiescent town in the 1950s, is a case in point. And, in contrast to the Rand, Port Elizabeth's industrial workforce was a relatively recent phenomenon, for up to the war many of Port Elizabeth's key industries had drawn their labour principally from whites and coloureds. What is more significant, however, than the size or experience of the African industrial population was the fact that, compared to other centres, it was relatively easy to organise it for political or industrial purposes. There were fewer internal linguistic barriers than in other towns; 95 per cent of Port Elizabeth's African population spoke Xhosa and, possibly more important, none of them lived in the controlled environment of hostels, compounds or barracks. This gave Port Elizabeth a very special character – shared only by East London – for most workers in Port Elizabeth lived with their families in the various townships and locations. A final demographic feature was that this population was increasing rapidly: in the fifteen years between 1936 and 1951 it more than doubled, though it should be added that this was characteristic of many other urban black populations in South Africa at this time. A more unusual feature of this population expansion was the fact that because of industrial growth, unemployment does not seem to have been a major problem: as late as 1948 city councillors were complaining of difficulties in obtaining domestic servants because of the local aversion to this type of work.[61]

Because of its housing policies and its reluctance to impose restrictions on the flow of Africans from the surrounding countryside into the city, Port Elizabeth's local government had a relatively liberal reputation. Much of this was based on enlightened self-interest. For example, the town's administrators, looking forward to a spurt of industrial expansion, argued in 1946 that 'it was imperative for the demands of industry and contractors to have a floating reserve of native labour in the City'.[62] In the absence of powerful vested interests with competing industrial labour demands this was an important factor in the City Council's liberalism.

Port Elizabeth's black population originally lived in five inner-city locations, demolished at the beginning of the century on the insistence of the Plague Board. The inhabitants of these slums trekked over the municipal boundary to Korsten, which by the 1930s had become a huge, rack-rented, shanty village, arousing considerable official disapproval because of its overcrowding, consequent disease, a high crime rate and the effects of all these on surrounding suburbs. In the late 1930s work began, five miles from the city centre, on the huge municipal housing complex of New Brighton, funded by a state loan. The 9 000 African inhabitants of Korsten (where the poor of all races lived) began to be evicted and expropriated and rehoused in the new township.[63] By 1941 New Brighton had a population of 20 000 people living in tidy rows of bungalows. Korsten, however, still had an African population of at least 8 000, and people continued to pour into the town in search of work. Another 4 000 lived on employers' premises.[64] Building continued in New Brighton, and by the end of the war it accommodated 35 000.[65] In contrast to municipal townships elsewhere, New Brighton's population lived in relative freedom from official restrictions; there was no curfew, no pass regulation, no registration of employment and even domestic brewing was allowed.[66] Not surprisingly, because of these freedoms, the city had the lowest black crime statistics in the country.[67] Port Elizabeth's industrial employers, for their part, needed a relatively skilled workforce with a low rate of turnover, and this was just what the city fathers were very efficiently providing.

But during the late 1940s municipal policy began to change. In Port Elizabeth's hinterland, smaller towns nearer to the African reserves began to close themselves off from a rural population suffering from increased land shortages and a savage series of droughts. The number of desperate men and women seeking shelter and work in Port Elizabeth grew larger as opportunities elsewhere shrank. By 1948, Korsten's African population was bigger than it had been ever before, and many of its inhabitants had to rent miserable rooms constructed from packing cases in which motor-car parts had arrived. Such dwellings were being built at a rate of 60 a month,[68] with one 9' × 7' room housing as many as thirteen people.[69] The problem worsened as farmers began to evict squatters and workers' dependants from their land.[70] The City Council attempted to check this growth by sudden demolition orders but the effect was only to create more overcrowding; a more effective means of demolition were the terrible fires, weekly occurrences which could destroy hundreds of shelters at a time. In 1946, a local survey showed that Port Elizabeth – of six major urban centres – had the poorest African population;[71] and by 1949 it was reckoned that Port Elizabeth shared with East London the worst tuberculosis rate in the world.[72] Within the council chambers, traditionally liberal policies began to appear anachronistic. In 1949, 'foreign' (i.e. non-Cape Province) Africans were told to register with the municipality if they wanted to remain in Port Elizabeth.[73] At the end of 1950 controls of this kind were being seriously contemplated for the 'local' African population as well.[74] And in early 1952 a labour bureau was established by the City Council: work seekers were no longer allowed to remain in Port Elizabeth for an unlimited period.[75]

To summarise: in 1952 Port Elizabeth's black population, despite a tradition of paternalism on the part of the municipality, was almost universally poor and frequently ill-housed. Relatively few had benefited directly from the city's industrial boom, most being employed in the tertiary sector. A large proportion had recently escaped from the desperate poverty which characterised much of the rural hinterland of the eastern Cape (see p. 58 below). In comparison with Africans elsewhere they did have certain freedoms, and these were to be crucial in determining their response to local conditions. But in 1952 it was clear that existing freedoms would shortly be eroded.

Local concerns apart, in order to understand popular responses of the early 1950s, one also needs to keep in mind the general political climate of the 1940s. For this was a decade of dramatically shifting political expectations, reflected, perhaps a little exaggeratedly, in a series of trials involving officials of an 'African Legion'. The Legion was led by a self-styled 'Prince of Abyssinia'. He and his 'Knights of the Grand Cross' had toured the Port Elizabeth and East London locations at the beginning of the war, warning of a coming catastrophe and raising money to build an army which would – with the aid of the Japanese – overthrow the Europeans. People were encouraged to buy 'trademarks' of the firm 'Prince Yusuf' claimed to represent.[76]

Fortunately, charlatans and dreamers did not significantly detract from the more serious efforts to organise Port Elizabeth's Africans. With the wartime expansion of the African industrial workforce came the first serious efforts at trade unionism since the collapse of the ICU fifteen years before. The initial organisation was done by A. Z. Tshiwula, a protégé of the Friends of Africa, a British-based Fabian group, which took an interest in labour relations in South Africa. Tshiwula's approach was hardly militant: in 1945 W. G. Ballinger, one of the people associated with the group, had to chide him for signing a letter to the railway systems manager as 'your obedient servant'.[77] However, Tshiwula was responsible for establishing two years earlier the first union for Port Elizabeth's African railway workers.

In 1941, in a second liberal trade union initiative, the Institute of Race Relations sent a Trotskyite, Max Gordon, to Port Elizabeth. Unlike Tshiwula, Gordon had the support of the local Trades Council and was able, during his short visit, to organise seven unions among cement, soft drinks, food and canning, engineering, leather and distributive workers.[78] It was these unions which were to provide the backbone of industrial struggle in the 1940s. During the war they were taken over by officials who were members of the local branch of the Communist Party.[79] The communists were also successful in reducing the influence of Tshiwula among railway workers, and by 1944 he had to content himself with leading a white-collar staff association.[80] The following year Tshiwula's opponents were active amongst domestic workers.[81] In 1945 the nineteen Port Elizabeth affiliates of CNETU claimed a membership of 30 000.[82] This was obviously an inflated figure given the size of Port Elizabeth's workforce, but it was nevertheless evident that trade union membership amongst Port Elizabeth's African workers was unusually high.

The strength of trade union consciousness in Port Elizabeth was evident in the laundry workers' strike in April 1948 when 200 blacks walked out of city laundries after a demand for a 2/6d weekly pay increase had been refused. During the strike, which lasted a month, the six dry-cleaning and laundry establishments affected were picketed by large crowds, delivery vans were stoned and set alight, and blacklegs and police were fiercely attacked in pitched street battles. Thirteen strike leaders, some of them communists, were arrested under the Riotous Assemblies Act though charges were later dropped when the strike was legalised by the Department of Labour. Trades and Labour Council support was crucial to workers' resistance and all strikers received a weekly strike pay. Large mass meetings were arranged by the New Brighton Communist Group to publicise the strikers' demands and win communal support.[83]

A vital characteristic of organised popular resistance in Port Elizabeth was the interpenetration of the trade unions and political movements of those years.[84] Office-holders of both the Communist Party and – more untypically for the 1940s – the ANC, were trade unionists. Raymond Mhlaba, a laundry worker until his dismissal after the 1948 strike, was secretary of the local Communist Party branch and ANC chairman in Port Elizabeth from 1947 to 1953. A. P. Mati, organiser of railway and distributive workers was also a member of the Communist Party district committee and an ANC branch chairman in the 1940s. Caleb Mayekiso, president of the local textile workers' union, was to become an important ANC leader in the early 1950s. Gladstone Tshume, who led the 1946 dock workers' strike was another important ANC leader as well as the Communist Party candidate in the 1948 Advisory Board elections. Frances Baard was secretary of both the Food and Canning Workers' Union and the ANC Women's League. There is no need to go on: while Congress in other centres was led by a professional élite, in Port Elizabeth, because of the relative strength of trade unionism, working-class leaders dominated African politics. Nor was their position under serious challenge from Youth Leaguers. In the Cape, Youth League organisations began in late 1948 with the establishment of a branch at Fort Hare.[85] One year later a branch was formed in New Brighton, but in June 1950 its membership was still very small.[86] The Youth League tended to draw its membership from young professionals: university students, teachers, lawyers and articled clerks and doctors. Such a group was small enough in Johannesburg, in Port Elizabeth it was smaller still: excluding soldiers, the 200 or so members of Port Elizabeth's African 'professional' class listed in the 1946 census was mainly composed of teachers, policemen and priests. The city had one African doctor, did not have a university, and there were no black lawyers or legal workers. For a town of its size Port Elizabeth also had a very small number of African traders (half the number of East London, a smaller town). In this context the popular orientation of local political leadership was understandable.

Of the local Youth Leaguers only one was to play a really prominent role in eastern Cape politics. This was James Njongwe, one of the first medical graduates of the University of the Witwatersrand. He joined the Youth League in Johannesburg and served on its national executive before returning to the eastern Cape to open his practice in New Brighton in 1947. Dr Njongwe was already a politician of some stature and he immediately assumed a leading role in the local affairs of Congress. A gifted speaker and brilliant organiser, it is to him and Robert Matji, the branch secretary, that much of the credit is due for establishing the basis of a local mass organisation.

In Port Elizabeth popular political participation was an established tradition by 1952. In contrast to other centres local leaders had successfully bridged the gap which existed elsewhere between direct community action ('the politics of the poor') and more self-conscious organised forms of protest. They helped to set a particular local style: the crowded meetings, and massed street processions through the city centre which developed during the 1945–47 rent and food shortage protest; the preference for direct action as opposed to lobbying and negotiation. Partly this was a consequence of the climate of municipal politics as well: because the authorities had a liberal reputation there were fewer intermediaries between them and the crowds.

The militancy of local leadership in Port Elizabeth was demonstrated particularly in the 1949 bus boycott, the curtain-raiser for of the drama which was to develop over the following years; it lasted nearly four months, from 19 April to the first week in August. Transport between New Brighton and the city was controlled by South African Railways which operated both a train and a bus service. On 1 April, without any warning, the 3d fare was raised to 4d. In the month before the boycott, the New Brighton Advisory Board had been informed that it could expect a general $7\frac{1}{2}$ per cent increase in South African Railway fares, so the disproportion between this and the one-third rise in bus fares appeared extremely unjust. The fare rise – representing an extra four shillings a month for every commuter in the household – came at a time when the real value of household incomes was dropping, and school attendance in New Brighton was reported to have fallen sharply in 1949 because parents could not afford clothes or school fees for their children. As well as the fare rise, other long-standing grievances were voiced by the people who attended a mass meeting in the township on Sunday 17 April. The bus service was erratic and unreliable; passengers had sometimes to wait for two hours after work before boarding a bus to take them home, and unsheltered bus queues could stretch half a mile away from the bus terminus in the city. On top of this, bus drivers and conductors were arrogant and abusive, departing from the scheduled route when it pleased them to do so, driving off with only half their complement of passengers, and on occasions depositing them outside the police station where they would be subjected to humiliating searches. The buses themselves were less convenient than before: the older models had plenty of space for parcels but now these were being replaced with vehicles with no room for luggage.

This was especially annoying for the large number of female food vendors who travelled into town each day to sell their wares to workers during the lunch-hour.

The meeting resolved to mount a boycott of buses on Tuesday 19 April, the 18th being Easter Monday which gave plenty of time to publicise the boycott. The meeting also elected an action committee which consisted of 28 people. The committee was led by Raymond Mhlaba and its membership included a large contingent of left-wing Congressmen, as well as James Njongwe and W. M. Tsotsi, the president of the All-African Convention. On the 19th the SAR buses travelled to and from the township empty and 15 000 people used alternative means of transport to work. Many went on the trains but several thousand made use of the services provided by entrepreneurially-minded vehicle owners in the township. At first a free lift service was run by white sympathisers. Meanwhile the committee telegrammed A. B. Xuma and the parliamentary Native Representatives requesting them to make representations on its behalf. Mrs Ballinger did succeed in gaining an interview with the Minister of Transport who, claiming that SAR made a loss of £20 000 a year, implied that the Ministry would welcome a takeover of the route by private enterprise.

Thereafter the boycott committee canvassed the idea of an African initiative in this direction and many of the speeches of subsequent meetings contained a strong strain of economic nationalism. As it turned out nobody within New Brighton appeared to have the capital resources for such a venture, and negotiations with the rural Kingwilliamstown-based Organised Bantu Partnership Bus Service was unfruitful. On 8 May a mass meeting resolved to organise a train boycott calling on people to walk to work on the 16th, and requesting the Chamber of Commerce to refrain from victimising late-comers. This seemed to jolt the local authorities into responding, for in the week between the meeting and the proposed train boycott members of the action committee met Council officials and began discussing the possibility of the municipal tramway company taking over the route. Meanwhile the bus boycott continued, though by the beginning of June it required fairly energetic picketing to enforce it and many people were being picked up by the railway buses outside the borders of the township and hence away from the pickets. However, later that month the boycott received an extra fillip when the Cape ANC held its provincial congress in New Brighton and national leaders of the standing of A. B. Xuma and Z. K. Matthews spoke at a mass meeting in support of the boycott.[87]

At the end of the month the action committee announced that the boycott was suspended pending the outcome of negotiations between the committee and the Transport Commission, then holding its hearings in Port Elizabeth. The commission recommended a subsidy scheme in which the municipality and private employers should reimburse the transport operator, according to the number of their employees, to make good the loss that pegging fares at 3d would incur. Unfortunately, it is at this point that the press reportage ceases; presumably the boycott ended, despite a popular sentiment that employers should subsidise all buses, and not just one company, thereby allowing African operators to compete. The only other shred of information we have is a letter written to the left-wing pro-Congress newspaper, *Advance*, in

1954 by G. X. Tshume, describing the takeover of Port Elizabeth's African transport from the SAR by the Bay Transport Bus Service. For the first time there were African bus drivers and conductors, and this was seen as a tremendous victory, the news being greeted with shouts of 'Mayebuye' at joyful township meetings. Tshume, a member of the 1949 action committee, traced this achievement back to the 1949 struggle, 'which failed to bring immediate results'.[88] So it would appear that the people of New Brighton had a long wait before they could savour the taste of victory.[89]

The development of the Defiance Campaign in Port Elizabeth reflected this rich heritage of protest. The strategic formulations of the Joint Planning Council were reinterpreted in the light of local traditions. This was evident, for example, in the series of lightning strikes which developed after employers had refused to reinstate volunteers. At a New Brighton meeting in July, one G. Simpe told his audience they 'could force an election tomorrow if they stayed away from work for thirty days'. Dr Njongwe, however, opposed such moves, criticising those who wished to drag 'side issues . . . into the defiance of unjust laws campaign'.[90] Njongwe, who during the campaign presided over the Cape ANC in the absence of Professor Z. K. Matthews, also found himself at odds with the local brand of leadership over the question of the duration of the November stay-at-home. The strike was originally called in Njongwe's absence by the local leaders, and was intended to continue until 'God Almighty has changed the hearts of the City Councillors', who had just imposed a curfew and ban on meetings.[91] The strike call was enthusiastically accepted at a series of open-air meetings held in New Brighton, Korsten, Veeplats and Walmer on Sunday, 2 November. Njongwe, though, did succeed in reasserting his authority on his return. The stay-away lasted only a day, and Njongwe owed his success in this direction to the outcome of negotiations with the mayor who, in return for a token strike, promised to reduce the curfew to three months and to lift the ban on meetings after a month.[92] But the council's conciliation was only tactical; in January 1953 it decided the city would be proclaimed under the Urban Areas Act thus enabling the Native Commissioner to 'weed out the tsotsi, vagrant and "won't work" element'.[93]

Njongwe, however, was not insensitive to the particular dynamics of local politics. Advising the Durban Defiance Campaign leaders he recommended that:

> Resisters should also start defiance at their own places and not come to Durban to defy away from home . . . the spiritual aspect of the resistance movement must be exploited. Whenever resisters go into action they must first go to church for prayer and dedication.[94]

This strategy was followed in the eastern Cape where branches tended to act independently of any central direction, following rather a well-established pattern of popular political involvement. This contrasted with the more structured and centralised organisation attempted in the Transvaal.[95]

To recapitulate: the Defiance Campaign succeeded in arousing massive support in Port Elizabeth for the following reasons. A rapid expansion of its African population in the 1940s introduced socio-economic tensions which were beyond the capacity of a paternalistic local administration to alleviate.

Industrialists who were the powerful voice in the local economy favoured an urbanised workforce and a floating pool of labour. Great poverty, comparatively few restrictions and a sizeable African industrial workforce led to the development of a powerful African trade union movement which deliberately concerned itself with issues well outside the scope of conventional economistic trade unionism. By 1950 politics was in the hands of working-class leaders to a degree which clearly distinguished Port Elizabeth from any other centre. As more and more restrictions on African mobility were imposed elsewhere in the Cape, so – in the last years before the campaign – Port Elizabeth became more crowded and life more intolerable. In 1952, there appeared the new threat of municipal influx control. Drawing on a well-established local tradition of mass protest, the African community was able to link parochial concerns with more general political ideas: popular politics transcended the usual anxieties over subsistence which predominated in everyday life.

East London shared some of Port Elizabeth's characteristics, being a port with an industrial sector which had grown quickly during the war, recruiting African labour to replace whites involved in the war effort. In common with Port Elizabeth, there were no compounds or hostels. Demographically the African population displayed similarities: an even ratio between the sexes, linguistic homogeneity and so on. But in some respects the towns were very different. In East London attempts to enforce strict influx control dated from the early 1930s. The majority of workers in East London returned every weekend to the Ciskei to visit their families. The municipal authorities constructed no housing at all between 1926 and 1940, and when money became available after the city's proclamation under the Urban Areas Act, progress on the first sub-economic scheme of Duncan Village was so slow that in the main location four-fifths of the population lived in privately constructed wood and iron shacks.

Despite the balance between the sexes, East London's African population was largely one which oscillated between working in the town and visiting their families over weekends. Eighty-six per cent of the population was rural-born,[96] and surveys made in the early 1950s indicated that the majority of men between the ages of 30 and 50 spent several years of their adult lives as peasants before coming to East London.[97] Philip Mayer found in 1955 that just under half the male working population could be categorised as 'Red'; that is, having a preference for traditional clothing and ancestor beliefs as opposed to Christianity. In East London, then, a large proportion of the population was strongly influenced by an indigenous rural culture and more still maintained family links with the countryside. Christianity and schooling, not surprisingly, had a marked effect on political and social aspirations. Mayer's survey found a detached attitude to white South African culture prevalent among 'Red' workers: 'I like nothing about the white man being quite satisfied with what I am myself'. Among 'School' people the assertion of a common cultural identity with whites, combined with resentment at white social exclusiveness, was far more common.[98]

It was a population afflicted by dreadful poverty. The 40 000 inhabitants of the location on the east bank of the Rooikrans river lived mainly in corrugated iron tenement buildings, honeycombs of crudely constructed rooms, usually opening on a yard which itself could be dotted with low kennel-like structures, used as kitchens by day and as sleeping quarters by night for poorer families. Even these families were lucky in comparison with the alcoholic bush community, some hundreds of men and women who led a terrible existence, shivering under sacks each night in the surrounding scrubland. The location itself had an ugly social complexity arising out of differential access to property. At its social apex there was a small group of owners, many of them based in the countryside, and supported by rents paid by lodgers; sometimes the high rents they charged forced the lodgers to share his or her room with sub-tenants. Within each room this structure would be reflected in sleeping arrangements; the official lodger perhaps having a bed by the window, his first sub-tenant, probably an age-mate, making do with a blanket on the floor next to the bed, and the last and least privileged sub-tenant sleeping in the least comfortable corner. For such accommodation people paid on average nearly a pound a month – approximately ten per cent of their wages.[99]

There were indications that conditions were deteriorating sharply in the late 1940s. East London's population would have been sensitive to rural conditions to an extent paralleled only by Durban. Between 1945 and 1951 the Ciskei, East London's rural hinterland, was hit by a terrible series of droughts, destroying crops and pasture and killing large numbers of cattle – for many people their only source of economic security.[100] In 1949, for example a quarter of the existing cattle population was lost; four years earlier it had been double the size. For people living in the countryside, when the nearest water could involve a seven-mile walk, when they had lost their animals and crops – if they were not already among the growing number who had lost all access to land – even the misery of East London's locations offered a ray of hope. D.H. Reader, writing in the early 1950s, reported that 'relative to the size of the city, the Bantu offer themselves for work, probably in larger proportions than in any comparable centre in the Union'.[101] Resultant low wages, unemployment, the increasing poverty of rural dependents – all intensified the horror of location life. In 1945 six out of every ten African babies born in East London died in their first year; the comparable figure for whites was less than one in a hundred.[102] In 1953 there were still only thirty communal lavatories serving a population of some 40 000.[103] According to the official census an extra 10 000 people had been squeezed into the location between 1946 and 1951. But it seems that the 1951 census was apparently particularly inaccurate in the case of East London; an independent survey in 1955 concluded that the location housed over 55 000, 141 people to each acre.[104] Unlike Port Elizabeth, East London's African population was under constant harassment from irregularly administered, often savagely effective influx control measures.

In the absence of first-hand oral testimony one has to use one's imagination to recapture the feelings of rural people, forced out of the countryside by starvation and land shortage (or in the case of the squatters and labour tenants, by white farmers), confronted with the glaring discrepancy between urban white affluence and black poverty; and bringing with them a world view in which the only whites were representatives of a bitterly resented officialdom. It comes as no surprise to find that the most vigorous political group in the location was a branch of the Youth League which set itself apart from the national leadership as early as 1952 with its adherence to an Africanist political philosophy. Gerhart has argued that the intellectual evolution of Africanism was influenced by the peasant background of its original exponents. Certainly its emphasis on racial dichotomy, cultural self-sufficiency and a heroic past would have found a special resonance in the bitter antecedents of many of East London's proletarians. The East London Youth League was exceptional in the history of political groups in the town in that it brought both 'Red' and 'School' people together.[105] The Cape Youth League was unusual in that it developed first in a rural context, round Herschel (the home of A. P. Mda, a founder of the Youth League), thereafter spreading to the coastal towns. Many of its original nucleus at Fort Hare had initially been close to the AAC,[106] whose leadership looked to the peasantry for their political base. Accordingly young student Youth Leaguers in the Cape had begun by organising literacy classes for farm labourers and peasants.[107]

The Youth Leaguers would have had less influence if other political groupings had not been so weak in East London. In particular that organic link between trade unions and political activity which distinguished Port Elizabeth was missing in East London. From 1947 personality differences split Congress into two factions, Congress A and Congress B. Congress B's dominant figure, V. M. Kwinana, a secondary school-teacher, was – despite his collaboration with communists in the 1946 Advisory Board Elections[108] – rather a conservative figure. At the 1949 Cape ANC conference he led the opposition to the adoption of a boycott strategy, and Congress B was to be at best luke-warm in its attitude to the Defiance Campaign.[109] Relations between Kwinana and the Youth League activists, many of them recent graduates of nearby Fort Hare University College, were poor. In 1950 he complained that they were insubordinate and ignorant of procedure.[110]

Communists in East London had succeeded in building a substantial trade union movement, and in 1944 a hostile observer allowed that they had as many as ninety African members in the location.[111] Communist influence was based on the wartime industrialisation of the African workforce. A local trade unionist working in 1941 observed that 'Africans here are clamouring to be organised and we are being forced, by their insistence, to form more unions than we can take care of at present'.[112] African trade unionists were responsible for the rejuvenation of Advisory Board elections in the 1940s; hitherto they had been the concern of no more than a very small number of people. Black East Londoners were obviously receptive to trade union organisation; even allowing for some degree of exaggeration, CNETU's figure of ten unions and 15 000 workers in 1945 was impressive. So why did local communists not have the same degree of success as their comrades in Port Elizabeth in reorienting local politics? There seem to have been three reasons. Firstly, strictly enforced curfew laws made political activity in the township difficult, particularly for a party with a multiracial leadership. Secondly, the nature of the location and its population made it more difficult to build political support through protest over subsistence issues. Unlike Port Elizabeth, the main landlords were not the municipality, but absentee Africans; since the location was close to the city centre transport costs were not a serious problem; and the lodger status of many location inhabitants meant that many of them saw their homes as being in the countryside. Workplace organisation was possible and communist activity centred on the factory-gate meeting. Community mobilisation was hampered by the incoherency of location society. Thirdly, Congressites and communists had to compete with the residual influence of Clement Kadalie's Independent Industrial and Commercial Union which, because of the still charismatic local presence of its founder, retained a surprising degree of vitality.

During the war the ICU had enjoyed a revival that recaptured some of the élan it had lost in 1930. Then an 80 per cent effective nine-day general strike failed to gain widespread wage increases and Kadalie himself was accused of misappropriating funds.[113] However, by the 1940s, Kadalie's prestige had risen, especially amongst the well-to-do educated population who had always dominated the local leadership of the ICU. Aroused by the successes of the communists and his own deep antipathy to them, Kadalie tried to compete with them in organising railway and harbour workers,[114] and in 1947 200 workers at a textile mill came out on a wildcat strike to reinstate an ICU shop steward.[115] But most of the energies of Kadalie and his lieutenants were concentrated on location affairs – the securing of more lavatories, raising local subscriptions to build a community hall, and such like. His popularity remained high.

In 1950 the debilitated state of local Congress politics was demonstrated in the disputes that broke out between conservatives and left-wing leaders over the question of participation in the 26 June stay-away. Congress leaders eventually decided to ignore the strike call despite a well-attended outdoor meeting voting in favour of participation.[116]

Established political leaders in East London had then, by 1950, lost much of their authority. Kadalie was dying and the old Congress discredited. It was this political vacuum which explains the unusual importance of Youth Leaguers who played the really decisive role in shaping the Defiance Campaign in East London. Of the various local factors determining the high level of participation in the campaign in East London, though, the most important was a peculiar combination of rural and urban popular preoccupations and the ability of local politicians to respond to them.

The inter-relationship between town and countryside in East London helps us to understand the dramatic impact of the campaign in the Ciskei. Social discontent was especially widespread in the Ciskei where the effects of land shortage and landlessness took their most acute form.[117] Government rehabilitation measures had been the object of deep resentment and at times violent opposition. Members of the Ciskei Bunga were to complain in 1952 of 'younger men taking control of the districts', of an 'ugly spirit of hostility and antagonism' manifested in hut burning, assaults on government employees and the destruction of fences.[118] Resistance to cattle culling dated back to its initial implementation in 1939, Ciskei being the first area in the country where stock limitation measures were taken.[119]

Whilst rural dissatisfaction was widespread elsewhere in South Africa in 1952, it is clear that the Ciskei was an extreme case. It was only here that Congress managed to penetrate rural society and obviously the nature of the social relationship between East London and its hinterland is very important in explaining this. In the Transvaal the ANC was cautious in its approach to rural organisation, still reluctant to alienate the chiefs. In consequence it recruited on an individual basis and attempted to retain friendly links with traditional authorities. This contrasted with the considerably more combative attitude of the eastern Cape leaders:

> Your duty is now to go and spread the message of freedom to the people in the reserves. They know what oppression is, what it is to have their cattle killed. They know what has been done to their chiefs and they are ready. They have been ready for years waiting for you. Even your trade union movement in the towns becomes futile because of the scab labour they can get any time in the reserves. Organise the reserves and there will never be any scab labour.[120]

The riots of Port Elizabeth and East London can only be briefly discussed here. Each arose out of a specific incident involving the police. In Port Elizabeth, during the afternoon of 18 October a railway policeman attempted to arrest two men disembarking at New Brighton because he had been informed that they had stolen a tin of paint. The men resisted arrest and gained the sympathy of other passengers on the platform. In the course of the ensuing scuffle, the policeman fired his gun into the crowd, killing one man and wounding two others. Rumours of what was happening circulated swiftly; in a few minutes a large crowd gathered outside the police station and police reinforcements, arriving on the scene, were stoned. The police then fired on the crowd, killing several people. The crowd turned away from the station and entered the location. A white lorry driver who was unfortunate enough to be in its path was killed and his lorry destroyed. Thereafter, three other whites were killed in a series of attacks on white-owned property. In the course of suppressing the riot, the police killed seven Africans.

In East London the initial incident which sparked off subsequent events was more sinister. In reaction to events in Port Elizabeth all public meetings had been banned but local ANC officials managed to obtain permission to hold a Sunday prayer meeting. The police maintained that on their arrival at the meeting it was indistinguishable from a political gathering and that it refused to obey their orders to disperse. Its organisers disputed this, contending that the police actually arrived while a hymn was being sung. Before people had a chance to leave, the police charged the crowd with bayonets. What seems indisputable is that the police – who had acceded to the initial request for permission to hold a meeting – were extraordinarily well-prepared for a fight. They arrived heavily armed in three troop-carriers and subsequently their commanding officer admitted they were 'expecting trouble'.[121]

The meeting was thus broken up. A lot of shots were fired and those attending the meeting were driven at gunpoint into the location. In the course of their retreat, two whites, including a Dominican nun, were brutally killed. The police surrounded the location with a tight cordon and the sound of gunfire from the location was to trouble nearby white suburbs until midnight. At least eight people died as a result of police action. Municipal buildings, a dairy depot, the Roman Catholic mission school and church were set alight and gutted.

The evidence is too fragmentary to make possible a satisfactory assessment of the cause of these outbreaks. Obviously the local impact of the campaign was a factor in explaining the extraordinarily aggressive behaviour of the police and the heightened popular sense of injustice which lay at the heart of the original incidents. The murder of the unfortunate white bystanders was the tragic consequence of the crystallisation of fear, frustration and anger which the behaviour of the police and provoked. In such a situation normal social inhibitions and moral restraints would have had little force. On both occasions, too, young teenagers played a disproportionate role in the disturbances, and it later emerged from subsequent investigation that many of these came from the most disrupted and deprived social surroundings. With the worsening overcrowding and unemployment the size of such a group must have grown rapidly over the previous ten years, and in the despairing and hopeless circumstances in which they lived social restraints would have been of little significance. White lives and white property were symbolic targets, chosen spontaneously in a mood of collective irresponsibility generated by police violence. We know too little about the faces in the crowds to attribute to them a more rational set of motivations. That they represented the most socially alienated seems likely given the local reaction to events – in the case of East London, mass migration to the countryside and political stagnation, though both these were the outcome also of repression and fear of the authorities.

Turning from the eastern Cape a few brief points must suffice for an explanation of the limitations of the Defiance Campaign in Natal. In Natal Congress had traditionally enjoyed a strong following in the smaller rural centres. This was now being disrupted because of evictions of peasant communities established outside the 1936 land delimitation.[122] Leadership conflicts had weakened the African National Congress. Indians had already participated in one passive resistance campaign which had failed to obtain any concessions from the authorities. But more important than these factors was the spirit of caution with which African and Indian leaders had approached the campaign. In 1949 inter-communal riots in Durban had brought to the surface a whole complex of tensions arising out of the conflict-ridden relationship between Africans and Indians in the sphere of commerce, transport, housing and jobs, in which Indians were popularly perceived as exploiters or unfair competitors. They had resulted in 142 deaths, 50 of which were Indians and 87 were Africans.[123] Despite the willingness of some local Indian and Congress leaders to try and effect some degree of reconciliation between the communities through political collaboration, not even the most optimistic of these pretended that this would be popular. Consequently in Durban the Congresses were cautious and kept a tight rein on acts of defiance, eight of the total of thirteen groups of volunteers being arrested at Berea railway station in the central industrial district. Organisational unreadiness, predicted at the 1951 conference by the Natal ANC provincial president, Albert Lutuli, helped to inhibit the spread of the campaign to smaller centres. The Natal Indian

Congress was no better equipped. In 1952 it had only two active branches.[124]

The main achievement of the Defiance Campaign lay in gaining widespread popular support for the African National Congress. By the end of the campaign ANC leaders claimed a following of 100 000.[125] Although membership estimates were to fluctuate wildly in the coming years, the number of paid-up subscriptions on which such figures were based were hardly an accurate guide to the movement's degree of influence. In the inactive years following the campaign, paid-up membership dwindled to 29 000.[126]

More striking was the proliferation of Congress branches, especially in the Cape. On the eve of the campaign the total here stood at 14, but at the provincial conference in 1953 87 branches were reported to be remitting subscriptions to the provincial treasurer – many of them in the countryside.[127]

Congress had also succeeded in jettisoning some of its more conservative spokesmen; in the rather uncharitable words of Robert Matji, it had rid itself of 'pleading, cowardly and hamba-kahle (go slow) leaders'.[128] This is not to say that it had been transformed into 'the revolutionary party of workers, peasants, intellectuals and petty bourgeoisie' envisaged by the communists in 1950.[129] Passive resistance, though adopted as much for tactical as ideological reasons, was in itself hardly revolutionary, especially when clothed in the Gandhist rhetoric of sacrifice, martyrdom and individual morality. The conflict between Njongwe and the left-wing leadership in Port Elizabeth is illustrative of the limitations of mainstream Congress radicalism. In the negotiations with the City Council (in which an Institute of Race Relations representative played an important intermediary role)[130] a preference for compromise as opposed to confrontation was still evident. Nevertheless, the reorientation in leadership was very real; Lutuli's election as national president at the ANC's 1952 annual conference marked this change. Albert John Lutuli, teacher, Methodist lay preacher and chief of a small reserve in Natal was a man of a very different stamp from his urbane, wealthy, cosmopolitan and somewhat remote predecessors. A man of great dignity and courage, he was immediately at home in the world of popular politics, combining eloquence with personal warmth. His experiences as a local administrator gave him an insight into the parochial worries and concerns of ordinary people. His religious faith and training brought to his politics a principled belief in non-violence and a remarkable optimism about the capacity of whites to undergo a change of heart. For him, passive resistance, even on a mass scale, held no fears:

> It is not subversive since it does not seek to overthrow the form and machinery of the state but only urges for the inclusion of all sectors of the community in a partnership in the government of the country on the basis of equality.[131]

For those like Lutuli, who still hoped for the peaceful transformation of South Africa into a harmonious multiracial society, optimistic conclusions could be drawn from the campaign. Despite crippling restrictions placed on political activity (legislation followed by a series of banning orders), supported by the official parliamentary opposition, there were some encouraging demonstrations of support from within the white community. One of the final acts of defiance, in Germiston on 8 December, when a group of volunteers broke permit regulations, was especially important in this context. Their number included several whites, one of them the son of a wartime Governor-General, Patrick Duncan. Duncan's participation in the campaign seemed especially important, for unlike his fellow volunteers, he came neither from a radical nor even a liberal background. His social origins were the nearest to what could be termed aristocratic in a white South African context, his natural conservatism reinforced by education at Winchester and Oxford and his subsequent entry into the British colonial service in Basutoland.[132] Another of the Germiston defiers was Manilal Gandhi, son of the Mahatma, and initially reluctant to identify himself with an African passive resistance movement. Exponents of a common society could also be comforted by the absence of bickering during the campaign between Indian and African leaders as well as the first significant involvement of Indians in an African-led movement. Direct involvement apart, the campaign itself inspired a regrouping of the white left – both socialist and liberal – out of which developed the small Congress of Democrats, officially allied to the ANC, as well as the South African Liberal Party. In retrospect, the hopes inspired by such movements can be seen to have been based on false premises. At the time they appeared to have great symbolic importance and contributed significantly to the ideological formulation of African political life.

Notes

1 Ellen Hellmann and Henry Lever, *Conflict and Progress*, Macmillan, Johannesburg, 1979, p. 87.
2 *Bantu World* (Johannesburg), 8 April 1950.
3 Gwendolyn Carter and Thomas Karis, *From Protest to Challenge*, Volume II, Hoover, Stanford, 1973, p. 338.
4 *Bantu World*, 29 April 1950.
5 South African Institute of Race Relations (Johannesburg), SAIRR papers, AD 1189, unsorted box, list of 'May Day Victims'.
6 *Bantu World*, 6 May 1950.
7 Ruth First, 'Newclare – sign of revolt', *Freedom* (Cape Town), 1 March 1950, p. 2.
8 *The Guardian* (Cape Town), 12 February 1948.
9 The CPSA reformed in the early 1950s as the South African Communist Party. According to a recent article in the *African Communist* (London), most former CPSA members rejoined it. There is little evidence of any serious activity during the 1950s by the SACP nor of its members acting as a self-conscious and united caucus within the Congress movement at that time.
10 Carter and Karis, *From Protest to Challenge*, Volume II, p. 445.
11 Minutes of the annual conference of the Cape ANC, 24/25 June 1950, Carter and Karis microfilm (available from Co-operative Microform Project, Evanston, Illinois), Reel 8a 2 DA 17: 30/10.
12 Draft national executive report to ANC annual conference, December 1950, Carter and Karis microfilm, Reel 8a, 2 DA 14: 30/42.
13 *Eastern Province Herald* (Port Elizabeth), 29 May 1950.
14 *Ibid*, 19 January 1950.
15 *Ibid*, 27 June 1950.

16 *Bantu World*, 17 May 1952.
17 Robert Johnson, 'Indians and Apartheid in South Africa', Ph.D. thesis, University of Massachusetts, 1973, and *Eastern Province Herald*, 1 September 1950.
18 Many of the points made in the above discussion are drawn from Eddie Webster, 'Stay aways and the black working class since the Second World War', University of the Witwatersrand African Studies Institute seminar paper, April 1979; and Socialist League of Africa, 'Ten years of the stay-at-home', *International Socialism* (London), 5, 1961.
19 Jack and Ray Simons, *Class and Colour in South Africa*, Penguin, Harmondsworth, 1969, p. 608.
20 SAIRR papers, AD 1189, ANC 111, A. P. Mda to G. M. Pitje, 24 August 1948.
21 *Bantu World*, 21 October 1950.
22 *Ibid*, 3 November 1951.
23 *Ibid*, 11 October 1952.
24 *Ibid*, 29 March 1952.
25 *ANCYL Journal* (Johannesburg), 2, 1953.
26 University of the Witwatersrand, Xuma papers, ABX 480813, R. M. Nkopo to A. B. Xuma, 13 August 1948.
27 *Bantu World*, 12 July 1952.
28 Essop Pahad, 'The development of Indian political movements in South Africa', Ph.D. thesis, University of Sussex, 1972, pp. 234–43.
29 These do not appear to have been ANC members. See *Passive Resister* (Johannesburg), 21 October 1946.
30 David Carter, 'The Defiance Campaign', University of London, Institute of Commonwealth Studies, *Collected Seminar Papers on the Societies of Southern Africa*, Volume 2, 1971, p. 92.
31 Pahad, 'Indian political movements', p. 253.
32 *The Torch* (Cape Town), 27 February 1954.
33 *Forum* (Johannesburg), 11 November 1948.
34 *Rand Daily Mail* (Johannesburg), 9 September 1948.
35 *Forum*, 11 September 1948.
36 Brian Bunting quoted in Union of South Africa, *Report of the Select Committee on the Suppression of Communism Act*, SC 10 1953, p. 33.
37 *The Torch*, 12 June 1951.
38 Michael Fridjohn, 'The Torch Commando and the politics of white opposition', African Studies Institute, *Papers presented at the African Studies Seminar*, University of the Witwatersrand, 1977, pp. 188–9.
39 Carter and Karis, *From Protest to Challenge*, Volume II, pp. 458–65.
40 Mary Benson, *South Africa: the struggle for a birthright*, Penguin, Harmondsworth, 1969, p. 134.
41 Naboth Mokgatle, *The Autobiography of an Unknown South African*, C. Hurst & Co., London, 1971, p. 307.
42 See Albert Lutuli quoted in Carter and Karis, *From Protest to Challenge*, Volume II, p. 426, and Nelson Mandela, *The Struggle is My Life*, International Defence and Aid, London, 1978, p. 34.
43 Quoted in *Peoples' World* (Cape Town), 9 October 1952.
44 *Bantu World*, 5 January 1952.
45 National executive report to ANC annual congress, December 1951, Carter and Karis microfilm, Reel 2a, 2 DA 14: 30/43.
46 *Bantu World*, 27 October 1951 and 10 November 1951.
47 *Advance* (Cape Town), 6 November 1952.
48 Leo Kuper, *Passive Resistance in South Africa*, Jonathan Cape, London, 1956, p. 18.

49 *Bantu World*, 14 June 1952.
50 *Eastern Province Herald*, 20 August 1952.
51 Union of South Africa, *Annual Report of the Native Affairs Commission for 1952*, Pretoria, UG 48 1955, p. 37, and *Forward* (Johannesburg), 15 August 1952.
52 *Eastern Province Herald*, 13 August 1952.
53 The above summary of the campaign is based on accounts in the following newspapers: *Bantu World, Eastern Province Herald, Clarion* (Cape Town), and *Peoples' World*, as well as Carter and Karis, *From Protest to Challenge*, and Kuper, *Passive Resistance*.
54 See Julius Lewin, *Politics and Law in South Africa*, Merlin, London, 1963, p. 27; Carter, Defiance Campaign, pp. 76–7; Kuper, *Passive Resistance*, p. 123, Carter and Karis, *From Protest to Challenge*, Vol. II, p. 420, and Donovan Williams, 'African nationalism in South Africa', *Journal of African History*, xi, 3 (1970), p. 373.
55 For example, Benoni.
56 Port Elizabeth Publicity Association, *City of Industry and Commerce*, Port Elizabeth, 1937, p. 59.
57 R. Schauder, 'Industry revitalises commercial life', *Commercial Opinion* (Cape Town), March 1948, p. 352.
58 Port Elizabeth Publicity Association, *City of Industry and Commerce*, p. 56.
59 Union of South Africa, *Population Census*, 1951, Pretoria UG 61 1954.
60 Union of South Africa, *Population Census*, 1946, Pretoria, UG 41 1954.
61 *Eastern Province Herald*, 30 January 1948.
62 *Ibid*, 2 February 1946.
63 SAIRR papers, B boxes, AD 843, B 26 8, R. P. Hannan to R. Jones, 10 August 1937.
64 University of the Witwatersrand, Rheinallt Jones Papers, Ja, 2 6 (Labour/Port Elizabeth), Memo on economic, health, social conditions of natives in urban areas, 1941.
65 *Eastern Province Herald*, 6 February 1945.
66 *Ibid*.
67 *Ibid*, 6 February 1948.
68 *Ibid*, 7 July 1948.
69 *Ibid*, 9 April 1949.
70 *Ibid*, 3 March 1949 and 11 May 1949.
71 University of the Witwatersrand, Margaret Ballinger papers, File A, 410/B 2 5 1946, National Building Research Institute Survey.
72 *Eastern Province Herald*, 15 July 1949.
73 *Ibid*, 9 August 1949.
74 *Ibid*, 28 November 1950.
75 *Advance*, 16 April 1953.
76 *Daily Dispatch* (East London), 10 October 1946, and *Imvo Zabantusundu* (King Williamstown), 19 June 1943.
77 Margaret Ballinger papers, A 410, B 2 8 20, William Ballinger to A. Z. Tshiwula, 23 August 1945.
78 Rheinallt Jones papers, Ja, 2 6 (Labour/Port Elizabeth), Statement by Eastern Province Trades Council on the activities of Mr Max Gordon.
79 Baruch Hirson, 'African trades unions in the Transvaal', unpublished paper, p. 30.
80 Margaret Ballinger papers, A 410, B 2 8 20, A. Z. Tshiwula to William Ballinger, 14 August 1944.
81 Margaret Ballinger papers, A 410, B 2 8 20, Kwaza to Margaret Ballinger, 9 October 1945.
82 Rheinallt Jones papers, Ja, 2 11, Minute on African Trade Unions.

83 *Eastern Province Herald*, 24 April 1948–4 June 1948.
84 Desiree Soudein, 'The Food and Canning Workers' Union', B.A. dissertation, University of the Witwatersrand, 1981, p. 26.
85 SAIRR papers, AD 1189, ANC 111, A. P. Mda to G. Pitje, 24 August 1948.
86 *Inkundla ya Bantu* (Durban), 27 August 1949.
87 Minutes of the annual conference of Cape ANC 24/25 June 1950, Carter and Karis microfilm, Reel 2b, 2 DA 17: 30/10.
88 *Advance*, 19 August 1954.
89 This section is based on press reports in *Bantu World*, *Eastern Province Herald*, *Inkundla ya Bantu*, and *Guardian*.
90 *Eastern Province Herald*, 14 August 1952.
91 *Advance*, 6 November 1952.
92 *The Torch*, 11 Nobember 1952.
93 *Advance*, 22 January 1953.
94 Minutes of the executive committee of the Natal ANC, 2 November 1952, Carter and Karis microfilm, Reel 3b, 2 DA 19 1: 30/1.
95 Carter and Karis, *From Protest to Challenge*, Vol. 2, p. 80.
96 D. H. Reader, *The Black Man's Portion*, Oxford University Press, Cape Town, 1961, p. 47.
97 Philip and Iona Mayer, *Townsmen and Tribesmen*, Oxford University Press, Cape Town, 1974, pp. 68–9.
98 *Ibid*, pp. 62–5.
99 Reader, *Black Man's Portion*, p. 141.
100 Union of South Africa, Native Affairs Department, *Annual Reports*, 1944–1951.
101 Reader, *Black Man's Portion*.
102 *Daily Dispatch*, 2 May 1946.
103 *Advance*, 16 April 1953.
104 Reader, *Black Man's Portion*, p. 42.
105 Mayer, *Townsmen and Tribesmen*, p. 81.
106 *Inkundla ya Bantu*, 23 July 1949.
107 *Ibid*, 7 May 1949.
108 *Daily Dispatch*, 16 February 1946.
109 Reader, *Black Man's Portion*, pp. 25–6.
110 V. M. Kwinana to ANC (Cape) HQ, 31 July 1950, Carter and Karis microfilm, Reel 2b, 2 DA 16: 41/39.
111 Clements Kadalie papers, Clements Kadalie to Rev. Alex Kadalie, 9 November 1944.
112 Rheinallt Jones papers, Ja 2 1, Rose Behr to A. R. Saffrey, 22 October 1941. I am very grateful to Mrs Rose Schlacter (née Behr) for information on politics and trade unionism in East London.
113 Monica Hunter, *Reaction to Conquest*, Oxford University Press, Cape Town, 1936, pp. 69–70.
114 University of the Witwatersrand, Clements Kadalie papers, Clements Kadalie to Alexander Kadalie, 22 February 1943.
115 Margaret Ballinger papers, A 410, B 2 14 5, Clements Kadalie to Margaret Ballinger, 29 July 1947.
116 *Eastern Province Herald*, 27 June 1950.
117 See Union of South Africa, *Report of the Witwatersrand Mine Natives' Wages Commission*, UG 21 1944, pp. 146–9.
118 *Ciskeian General Council Proceedings*, 1952, pp. 47–70.
119 *Ibid*, 1945 special session, p. 2.
120 Dr J. Njongwe quoted in Kuper, *Passive Resistance*, p. 140.
121 Excerpt from trial record, Carter and Karis microfilm, Reel 3b, 2 DA 24: 96/7.
122 See minutes of 37th annual conference of the ANC, 15/19 December 1949, Carter

and Karis microfilm, Reel 8a, 2 DA 14: 30/47.

123 Eddie Webster, 'The 1949 Durban "Riots": A case study of race and class', unpublished seminar paper, University of Durban.

124 Johnson, 'Indians and Apartheid in South Africa', p. 85.

125 Carter and Karis, *From Protest to Challenge*, Vol. II, p. 427.

126 National executive report to the ANC annual conference, December 1953, Carter and Karis microfilm, Reel 8a, 2 DA 14: 30/47.

127 Cape ANC, circular letter to branches, 7 January 1954, Carter and Karis microfilm, Reel 2b, 2 DA 17: 40/13.

128 Carter and Karis, *From Protest to Challenge*, Vol. II, p. 426.

129 Report of the Central Committee of the CPSA, 18 January 1950, reproduced in Union of South Africa, *Report of the Select Committee on the Suppression of Communism Act*, Cape Town, SC 10 1953, p. 214.

130 South African Institute of Race Relations, *Report by the Director on Visits to Port Elizabeth, East London and Kimberley in connection with the Riots*, RR 9/53, 12 January 1953, para. II.

131 Albert Lutuli, 'The Road to Freedom is via The Cross', Karis and Carter, *From Protest to Challenge*, Vol. II, p. 488.

132 This episode of the campaign is described best in C. J. Driver, *Patrick Duncan: South African and Pan-African*, Heinemann, London, 1980, pp. 91–100.

CHAPTER 3

African political organisations, 1953–1960

This chapter will concentrate on the development of the African National Congress in the years succeeding the Defiance Campaign. The emphasis will be upon the organisation as a whole: there will be discussions of particular campaigns in local settings in the chapters which follow. Here our concern will be with the general process of transformation of African politics at the levels of ideology, strategy and organisation. Although the African National Congress was to remain the largest black political movement and the only one with a national following, it did not hold the monopoly of political protest. We will be examining, therefore, some of its rivals, and particularly, the offshoot Pan-Africanist Congress which was to decisively influence events at the end of the decade. Before looking at the organisations themselves it is useful to recapitulate the main features of the social, political and economic context within which they had to operate.

In 1953 the Nationalist Party consolidated its position in a second electoral victory. More confident of its long-term prospect of ascendancy it began to quicken the pace of social restructuring, implementing with greater alacrity the measures enacted in the previous parliament. Urban influx controls were now compulsory in all municipalities and the flow of labour was to be regulated and channelled through an extensive network of labour bureaux. Further measures aimed at the more effective control of the urban African population included fresh restrictions on the activities and rights of African trade unions, the resettlement of the African inhabitants of inner-city locations and freehold suburbs in remote and carefully planned and administered townships, and, from 1956, the attempt to halt the process of African urbanisation through subjecting women to all the mechanisms of influx control. Black social and political aspirations were checked through the imposition of an ethnically discriminatory educational curriculum, and blacks were excluded from inner-city commerce and property ownership far more rigorously than hitherto. Resistance to these measures was made additionally difficult by the Criminal Law Amendment Act, which imposed draconian penalties for civil disobedience. At the same time a slowing rate of economic growth was to increase the problem of unemployment and poverty amongst Africans as wages failed to keep up with rising prices. Within the urban African population property owners and small businessmen were threatened as they never had been before. This, together with attacks on the status and social mobility of African professional people, helped to push petty-bourgeois Africans into an increasingly defensive posture. Under a regime which – unlike its predecessor – was totally unconcerned over the extent to which it alienated middle-class blacks, such people were much more willing to participate in the creation and leadership of mass political movements than they had been a decade earlier. There were of course limits to their radicalism; they still had a material position to defend which could differentiate their political responses from those of working-class Africans. But given the fresh receptiveness of African political leaders to mass-based strategies, they became increasingly influenced by the concerns and the anxieties of the least privileged. As a result, in the 1950s, Congress was to develop – in a halting, uneven fashion, it is true – into a movement seeking a profound social transformation.

The years 1953 and 1954 were not marked by any major Congress campaigning. The Criminal Law Amendment Act made any repetition of the Defiance Campaign impractical: civil disobedience would only be encouraged again by ANC leaders in 1958 with the women's pass protests in Johannesburg, and even here there was disagreement over this within the leadership of the ANC. It was replaced for the time being by boycotts of one form or another, demonstrations, and non-cooperation, all technically within the confines of the law. Before the end of 1954 banning orders were served on many major Congress figures, and this helped further to immobilise the movement. Nevertheless, despite this lull in activity these years were important for Congress for they saw a confirmation of the trend towards collaboration with other groups, and in the process the elaboration of a programme which defined the ANC's ideological position more sharply than hitherto. At the same time the first attempts were made to build an organisational structure suited to the requirements of a mass movement operating in an increasingly hostile legal environment.

 With Chief Lutuli's election as president-general in December 1952 the rhetoric of 'self-determination' and 'national freedom' which distinguished the Programme of Action from previous ANC policy documents appeared less frequently. Lutuli himself saw the ideal future in terms of African 'participation' in government rather than absolute control of it and his nationalism was of a considerably gentler quality than that of the Africanists who had supported him originally.[1] He spoke of a 'progressive and liberal' nationalism with the goal of African 'partnership in the government on the basis of equality',[2] an 'all inclusive' position based on the acceptance of 'the fact of the multiracial nature of the country'.[3] Where Lutuli differed from his predecessors was not so much in his vision of a perfect society but rather over the means to attain it. He had neither Xuma's patrician distrust for mass action nor Moroka's apprehension about its repercussions. Mass demonstrations, suffering and sacrifice were all needed, in Lutuli's view, to induce a change of heart amongst whites. But unlike his fellow executive colleagues who were former Youth Leaguers, Lutuli still placed great faith in the moral impact of African struggle.

 To those leaders like Lutuli who drew encouragement from white political divisions and the existence within white society of a liberal minority, the isolated expressions of sympathy and support from whites during and after the Defiance Campaign seemed very important. In November 1952 a public meeting was held in Johannesburg under the auspices of the ANC and the SAIC. The few hundred people who assembled at Darragh Hall at the appointed date listened to Oliver Tambo and Yusuf Cachalia urge them to form an organisation which whites could join, and which would coordinate its activities with those of the Congresses. Also on the platform was Cecil Williams, chairman of the left-wing ex-servicemen's organisation, the Springbok Legion. Almost a year later this idea came to fruition with the founding of the South African Congress of Democrats (SACOD). SACOD was presided over by the trade-unionist and former Labour Party member, Piet Beyleveld, and though its small following came to include many communists it also succeeded in attracting people from other backgrounds. Small as it was to remain SACOD was to play an important role in the nationalist movement of the 1950s. Its members, many of them highly experienced in the fields of political and trades union organisation, with a mobility, level of affluence and education denied to most blacks, helped shape the overall development of the Congress movement. Individuals within SACOD controlled a newspaper and several journals which provided Congress with consistently sympathetic publicity on a scale it had never enjoyed before. Less positively, their presence on Congress platforms was to have the unintended effect of promoting dissension within the lower reaches of the movement.

In 1953 the ANC did not have a clearly articulated ideological position. The Programme of Action's emphasis was on means rather than ends, on strategies as opposed to social goals. The ideological content of the document was vague and ambivalent, lending itself to differing interpretations so that opposed factions within Congress could each legitimise their position by reference to it. In the wake of the Defiance Campaign ANC leaders were confronted with the problem of how to sustain the enthusiasm of their vast new following. The National Action Council (successor to the ANC/SAIC Joint Planning Council) reported a 'disquieting lull which has descended over the mass activities of Congress'. Future campaigning, it argued, should be based on strengthened organisational machinery and should arise from 'the concrete conditions under which people live'.[4] An ANC 'Programme of Economic Advancement' announced in mid-1953 displayed a new sensitivity to the preoccupations of the poor and insecure: it called for the end to the labour colour bar, the right to organise, the extension of social security, free trading rights and a minimum wage of £1 a day.[5] At the Cape provincial congress in August 1953 Professor Z. K. Matthews suggested the summoning of a 'national convention at which all groups might be represented to consider our national problems on all all-inclusive basis' to 'draw up a Freedom Charter for the Democratic South Africa of the future'.[6] The provincial congress's adoption of the idea was endorsed at the ANC's annual conference in September. In the light of the later controversy over the origin of the Freedom Charter, it is worth pointing out that the initial impulse to formulate a Freedom Charter came from within the African National Congress, from one of its less radical leaders, and that the proposal did not at first attract enthusiastic support from either the SAIC or the new Congress of Democrats.[7]

On 23 March 1954 the executives of the ANC, SAIC, SACOD and a new coloured organisation, the South African Coloured People's Organisation (later Coloured People's Congress), which had been formed in September the previous year, chiefly from the surviving members of the Franchise Action Council, met in Tongati near Durban to discuss plans for a national convention. At this meeting it was decided to establish a National Action Council for the Congress of the People. It would consist of eight delegates from each of the organisations sponsoring the Congress. A national organiser was appointed, T. E. Tshunungwe, one of the eastern Cape Youth Leaguers who had become prominent during the Defiance Campaign. It was envisaged that there would be, ideally, three phases to the creation of a Freedom Charter. First, provincial committees would have to be established on the model of the National Action Council. At the same time the recruitment of a huge army of 'Freedom Volunteers' was to begin, their task being to publicise the Congress and collect demands for the Charter. The provincial committees would then work to establish committees in every workplace, village and township. The final stage would involve the election of delegates from each locality who would then meet and assist in the drafting of the Charter. 'The Charter will emerge from countless discussions among the people themselves. It will truly be, in every sense of the word, the charter of ordinary men and women.'[8]

Many of the Charter's critics were to charge that these plans were not properly implemented once the campaign had begun. Certainly by August provincial committees had been formed in the Cape, Transvaal and Natal. In the case of the Transvaal committee, members included representatives of the Liberal Party and Arthur Blaxall, a well known Anglican priest, as well as people from the four Congresses. In Cape Town 27 of the 200 organisations invited to attend the meeting at the city hall sent delegates. They included six trade unions, the Federation of South African Women, the Cape Peace Council, a number of location vigilance organisations and the Liberal Party. However, the next stage, the formation of local committees, never really got off the ground and much of the process of collecting demands was carried out through Congress branches and visits by provincial organisers. But the campaign did succeed in evoking some degree of popular response: by May 1955 the Natal committee described itself as being flooded by suggestions for inclusion in the Charter,[9] and from the description of the content of some of them the feelings they expressed were spontaneous enough:

> Dr Athur Letele, for example, has said that messengers to tribal locations near Kimberley naturally asked leading questions, such as 'What is your idea of being free?' One reply was 'ten wives'. One of the non-African members of the NAC has stated that a committee of the council received 'thousands of little bits of paper, many of them with specific demands, for example, "The District Commissioner is not fair to us; we want his removal".'[10]

That there were organisational inadequacies in the preparations leading up to the Congress was admitted quite openly by the National Action Council and the pro-Congress newspaper, *New Age*. Bannings under the Suppression of Communism Act restricted an ever-growing number of the most experienced activists: for example, by November 1954 nearly the entire Natal Indian Congress executive elected at the end of the previous year had been banned.[11] At the same time the ANC was attempting to mobilise resistance to the

Western Areas removals and Bantu Education (see Chapters 4 and 5). But organisational shortcomings of the Congress of the People were not the main reason for the hostility towards it that was evident in some quarters. More important was the prominent role which members of the Congress of Democrats seemed to have in the arrangements leading up to the holding of the Congress of the People. This attracted criticism from outside the Congress movement from people who were initially willing to participate in the campaign; in particular from members of the small multiracial Liberal Party which had been launched after the 1953 election. From within the ranks of the ANC there was also concern over the role of their new allies. This arose partly out of tactical considerations: T. E. Tshunungwa, reporting after a visit to the western Cape, complained of the 'extreme . . . confusion' that was created when people discovered 'the COD men are taking a lead in the ANC meetings . . . a politically raw African who has been much oppressed, exploited and victimised by the European sees red whenever a white face appears'.[12] There was also the fear among the Africanists in the Youth League that white participants had the deliberate intention of diverting the ANC away from 'clear cut' African nationalism.[13] We will return to these anxieties shortly.

While the rather hurried process of electing delegates at public meetings in different centres was taking place, in April 1955, sub-committees of the National Action Council began sorting into various categories the multitude of demands and suggestions that had flowed in. Eventually, a small drafting committee produced the Charter, drawing on the material prepared by the sub-committees. The document that emerged had a rather distinctive poetic style, possibly the influence of Lionel Bernstein, one of the drafters,[14] and it was duly presented to the seven members of the ANC's national executive on the eve of the Congress of the People. Neither Chief Lutuli (immobilised by his ban) nor Professor Matthews, whose original idea it had been, saw it then.

The Congress itself was a dramatic affair. It lasted two days and was held in an open space near Kliptown, a coloured township near Johannesburg. It was attended by 3 000 delegates from all over the country, including 320 Indians, 230 coloureds and 112 whites. The various clauses of the Charter were introduced, there was an opportunity for impromptu speeches from delegates present, and the clauses were then read out and acclaimed by a show of hands. The proceedings were brought to an exciting close by the arrival of large detachment of policemen bearing sten guns in the afternoon of the second day. They took over the speakers' platform, confiscated all the documents they could find, announced that they had reason to believe that treason was being contemplated, and took the names and addresses of all the delegates before sending them home. Clearly the state was now confident that with the holding of the Congress the ANC and its allies had been given enough rope to hang themselves: hence the degree of toleration with which it had been treated up to that point.

Read out of its context the Charter itself appears a bland enough document. It consists of a list of basic rights and freedoms. Beginning by reaffirming the multiracial character of South African society ('South Africa belongs to all who live in it, black and white'), it went on to promise equal status for 'all national groups', to argue for the transfer of the mines, the banks and monopoly industry to the ownership of 'the people as a whole', to guarantee equal opportunities to all who wished to trade or manufacture, to advocate the redivision of land 'among those who work it', the ending of all restrictions on labour and labour organisations, unemployment benefits, a forty-hour week, a minimum wage, free compulsory education, and other welfare provisions with regard to health, housing, the aged and the disabled.[15]

What was the significance of all this? As far as its critics were concerned the Charter and the process which produced it were the results of manipulation and conspiracy. Peter Hjul, one of the Liberal Party members of the Cape Town local committee until his resignation from it at the beginning of 1955, contends that his function – along with other committee members – was merely to endorse prearranged decisions. To Liberals the dominant influence in the campaign was the Congress of Democrats, in their view no more than a front for the communists. They found especially offensive the attempts made by white Congressmen to align the nationalist movement with the Soviet bloc in the Cold War. The Liberal Party itself dissociated itself from the Congress of the People after a meeting of its executive on 26 January 1955.[16] The socialist implications of parts of the Charter appeared to them to vindicate their apprehensions. Africanists were at first less concerned about the content of the Charter though later their objections would centre on the sections concerning rights and guarantees for all national groups. It was rather the rôle allowed to representatives of the other Congresses in the leadership of the campaign that they found disturbing. In particular, the structure of the National Action Council with its equal representation of the four sponsoring organisations, despite their numerical disproportion, was in their view an ominous sign. They saw the council as a vehicle through which the ANC could be influenced and even controlled by non-Africans.

There was some substance to both sets of accusations. The Congress of Democrats, not surprisingly given the background of many of its activists, tended to identify itself rather more strongly with the Soviet bloc than did its partners in what had come to be known since March 1954 as the Congress alliance. *New Age*, for example, under the editorial control of SACOD members, devoted much of its space to descriptions of Soviet achievements, justifications of Russian foreign policy, and criticism of Soviet dissenters. Given their tiny following, SACOD personalities certainly did appear to exercise a disproportionately important function, playing a leading rôle at most public meetings and contributing significantly to the drafting of the Charter itself. This was predictable enough; many SACOD leaders were highly experienced politicians with considerable intellectual ability. Whatever their colour one would expect such people to play a dynamic rôle. Finally, it is also true that the formulation of the Charter involved only a limited amount of consultation: certainly popular demands were canvassed but the ultimate form the document assumed was decided by a small committee and there were no subsequent attempts to alter it in the light of wider discussion. The forum provided by the Congress of the People was scarcely suited to any kind of debate.

What such arguments do not take into account is the nature of the Charter itself. Despite the attempts that were made during the Congress to emphasise its revolutionary content ('There will be a committee of workers to run the gold mines . . . the workers will take over and run the factories'),[17] its authors seem to have taken care to respond to a broad range of interests. As Nelson Mandela commented one year later:

It is true that in demanding the nationalisation of the banks, the gold mines and the land the Charter strikes a fatal blow at the financial and gold-mining monopolies and farming interests. . . . But such a step is absolutely imperative and necessary because the realisation of the Charter is inconceivable . . . until the monopolies are first smashed up and the national wealth of the country turned over to the people. The breaking up . . . of these monopolies will open up fresh fields for the development of a non-European bourgeois class. For the first time in the history of this country the non-European bourgeoisie will have the opportunity to own in their own name and right mills and factories and trade and private enterprise will boom and flourish as never before. . . . The workers are the principal force upon which the democratic movement should rely but to repel the savage onslaught of the Nationalist Government and to develop the fight for democratic rights it is necessary that the other classes and groupings be joined. Non-European traders and businessmen are also potential allies. . . .[18]

In 1955, despite its increasing sensitivity to the preoccupations of the least privileged, and despite the increasing strength of its links with worker organisations, the ANC was not a movement oriented strongly towards the working class. As we shall see in following chapters, its leadership, particularly in local contexts, reflected a composite of interests, and at the national level could sometimes miscalculate the degree of receptiveness to its appeals on the part of black workers.

Of course it could easily be argued that the Charter had revolutionary implications – that it was a blueprint for a society that could not have been created without considerable structural changes which could not have been accomplished peacefully. But many Congress leaders believed that change would come without violence.[19] The presence as supporters and allies of a small number of whites on their platforms and at their meetings, people who appeared to have no traces of paternalism or reservation in their commitment, helped sustain this optimism. For men and women who had been schooled in liberal institutions and a Christian morality the generosity and courage with which white Congress supporters involved themselves in their movement outweighed in importance any 'ulterior motives'.[20] Not that this was simply an emotional issue: multiracial political activity brought to the nationalist movement material resources it otherwise would not have enjoyed, and was in itself an act of defiance in a society where inter-racial contact invoked official disapproval. In such circumstances it would have required considerable powers of self-denial on the part of SACOD members not to have assumed important functions in the Congress alliance.

As it turned out the Charter was not adopted immediately by the ANC. The executives of the four organisations met together at the beginning of August 1955 and agreed to recommend the adoption of the document by each respective Congress. A 'million signature' campaign was conceived to popularise the Charter and the 10 000 'Freedom Volunteers' apparently succeeded in collecting nearly 100 000 signatures to the Charter, half of them in the Transvaal.[21] The campaign was administered by a National Consultative Committee, a permanent successor to the National Action Council. Though the new committee was to have important functions the signature campaign was not one of them: it petered out towards the end of the year with few signs of any enthusiasm for it being shown outside the Transvaal. Many of the forms were confiscated in police raids. The ANC's annual conference in 1955 was shortened by a day because of objections to its being held at all by the municipal authorities in Bloemfontein. Many important leaders were unable to come because of their bans and branches had not received copies of the national executive report. Much time was taken up with a debate as to whether the conference should exclude a reporter from the *Bantu World* and there were acrimonious exchanges between the national executive and the Africanists. The latter now had the indirect support of Dr Xuma who had written an open letter to Congress accusing it of losing its identity and turning against the nation building programme of the 1940s. In the end there was no conclusive discussion of the Charter as the Transvaal delegates had to leave the conference early so as to catch their trains on Sunday evening.

Four months later a special conference was held with the purpose of discussing ways of opposing the introduction of women's passes. Despite noisy protests from a small group of Africanists from the local Orlando Youth League branch the Charter was accepted by the majority of the delegates. If any of them had any misgivings about the economic clauses (there was some unease among certain Natal delegates) they were reluctant to associate themselves with the Africanists' dogmatic advocacy of the Programme of Action and their hostility to 'foreign' allies and ideologies. It is likely that lack of interest was more widespread than any antipathy towards the Charter; as the national executive complained in its annual report of 1955:

> In the Congress of the People campaign, although the ANC was responsible for the creation of the Congress of the People, many of its leaders and many of its branches showed a complete lack of activity as if some of them regretted the birth of this great and noble idea.[22]

The endorsement of the Freedom Charter by the ANC reflected the changing character of the movement's leadership: in contrast to the previous decade it was younger, less affluent, and more likely to be drawn from a legal, trade union or non-professional background than the politicians of the 1940s who tended to be churchmen, doctors or substantial businessmen. But despite a more radical leadership the ANC was often slow and ineffective in its efforts to resist fresh infringements on existing freedoms and rights. As we shall see in later chapters, part of the problem arose from the social tensions which existed within local communities which could be reflected in the resistance movement itself. At times there were also strategic differences within the national executive – this was the case, for instance, during the efforts to mount a boycott of Bantu Education. The main difficulty, though, lay in the field of organisation.

In the course of the Defiance Campaign the ANC had become a mass movement with a membership of approximately 100 000 by the close of the campaign. Its estimated following fluctuated during the 1950s, paid-up membership dipping sharply during 1953 to about 30 000 but then reviving from about 1957, so that in the Transvaal it passed its 1952 peak in 1958; it then acquired thousands of new followers in Natal in 1959.[23] But official membership figures do not accurately reflect the full extent of the ANC's influence: subscriptions were only occasionally collected and not always reported accurately to the treasurer-general, and a large number of people clearly identified with Congress and participated in various campaigns without always holding a current membership card. In response to this expansion as well as to the prospect of legal constraints being placed on Congress activities a new organisational system was proposed in late 1953 by Nelson Mandela. Critical of the 'old methods of bringing about mass action through public mass meetings, press statements and leaflets',[24] and anticipating a time when the ANC would no longer be permitted to mobilise so openly, Mandela proposed that the branches – some of which had grown to a size of several thousand members during the course of the Defiance Campaign – should be divided into 'cells' based on a single street and headed by a cell steward. Seven street cells would make a 'zone' and the 'chief steward' of each zone would unite with four others in a 'ward'. One of their number would be a 'prime steward' and these prime stewards would form a branch secretariat so as to administer the ANC within a township.

As it turned out the 'M Plan' was only implemented in a few instances, mostly in the towns of the eastern Cape, which began to divide themselves up early in 1953, but also in Cato Manor in Durban. A national executive report later commented that in contrast to the eastern Cape very few branches in Natal or the Transvaal had been restructured,[25] and in December 1955 the national executive commented:

> The National liberation movement has not yet succeeded in the organisational field in moving out of the domain of mass meetings and this type of agitation. Mass gatherings and large public activities of Congress are important, but so is house to house work, the building of small local branches and the close contact with members and supporters and their continual education.[26]

It was a comment that held good for the decade as a whole. The reasons for this failure are not difficult to understand. The new system would have involved an immense amount of work, in many cases well beyond the capacity of spare-time volunteers. As a Natal leader pointed out: 'most people were so busy with their ordinary work that they could not find time for Congress duties'.[27] Long working hours, poor public transport, and residential areas far away from places of employment meant that there was little time in the evenings for political activity. Shortage of money was another obvious impediment: the eastern Cape was estimated by the national executive to need 35 full-time organisers to carry out the scheme. They received in 1953 £100 from Johannesburg to pay them.[28] Membership subscriptions were 2s 6d annually and even at this modest level were difficult to collect in a desperately poor community, for such a sum could make a significant inroad into a weekly household budget. The ANC had very few full-time workers, and it was still stressing the need for them in 1959.[29] The M Plan also could help to lessen the standing of local political personalities as part of its purpose was to reduce the size of administrative units. Many branches, therefore, remained cumbersome and difficult to administer because of their numbers, and communications both within the branches and between them and the national leadership remained poor. Throughout the decade there were references in national executive reports to letters not answered and policy decisions being ignored by branches. The movement had expanded swiftly and many of its activists were not people who wrote letters easily. A further factor that contributed to the weakness of communications was the fact that the strongest ANC centres were outside the Transvaal whereas the national executive was Transvaal-dominated and effective decision-making in any case was in the hands of a working committee of NEC members who lived within 50 miles of Johannesburg.

Harassment by the state added to organisational difficulties. By the end of 1955 42 ANC leaders had been banned, many of them being forced to give up office and membership in the ANC; some of these, like Walter Sisulu, still played an important role in directing the movement, but they could not do so overtly. Bans affected eleven of the 27 members of the national executive elected or co-opted in 1952. By then 40 SACOD members and 19 SAIC members were similarly restricted.[30] One year later 156 prominent figures in the Congress alliance were arrested and subsequently charged with treason. For the next five years the state vainly attempted to prove in court that a communist-inspired conspiracy to violently overthrow it had been prepared by the Congress alliance. The Treason Trial, as it was known, served as a drain on the energy and resources of the accused, many of whom suffered a total disruption of their livelihoods during its proceedings. It also removed from active political life some of the ablest and most experienced men and women in the Congress movement, leaving their places to be filled by people who were often less capable.

The consequences of these bureaucratic difficulties were, firstly, that effective campaigning often had to depend on local initiatives and therefore on the personal qualities of local leaders to a much greater extent than would have been the case had an efficient administrative machine existed. This was not always to Congress's detriment: both the education protest and the Alexandra bus boycott provide examples of occasions when cautious national leaders were pushed into a more militant posture by pressure from the rank and file. But it did mean that campaigns were localised and uneven in impact (hence the justification for looking at Congress activities 'from below'). It also meant that the movement was built on strong personal loyalties rather than bureaucratic control and for this reason the ideological conflicts which could strain the movement at the centre had a limited significance for the mass of its followers. The extent to which the ANC interested itself in questions of everyday life was in the ultimate analysis more important in sustaining its support than its attitudes towards whites, socialism, or the Cold War. Only if such issues could be shown to have an immediate relevance did they have much popular significance. Arguably, the way in which in certain contexts the Pan-Africanist

Congress was to draw upon ordinary people's experiences of contact with whites in articulating its ideas of racial exclusiveness was an example of this link being made successfully.

Nevertheless, ideological issues were important since they had a significant bearing on strategy and the manner in which the movement attempted to appeal to and to control its mass following. During the 1950s the ANC was not a revolutionary organisation and it did not have a carefully worked out long-term strategy. The Freedom Charter itself, although it sketched out a society which inevitably would have involved the nationalist movement in sharing, if not controlling, the power of the state, gave no indication of the means through which this was to be done. To have spelt these out would of course have been very unwise even if they had been worked out, but the Congress leadership nevertheless seemed very uncertain over the whole issue. As Oliver Tambo put it in 1955:

> We shall not have to wait long for the day when only one method will be left to the oppressed people in this country – precisely what that method will be is impossible to say, but it will certainly be the only method, and when that has been employed and followed up to its logical conclusion, there will be no more struggle, because the one or the other of the conflicting forces – democracy or fascism – will have been crushed.[31]

Of course some of the younger leaders – Mandela, for example, with his organisational reforms – were anticipating a period when Congress would be forced to operate as a clandestine movement. Joe Matthews, national president of the Youth League saw these reforms as a preparation for the broadening of the civil disobedience campaign of 1952 into 'a mass campaign and industrial action',[32] reflecting the syndicalist vision which appears to have inspired a section of the eastern Cape leadership. But this does not appear to have been representative of mainstream Congress thinking.

Through all the major campaigns of the 1950s a common underlying motive seems to have been the hope of influencing a section of the white population so as to weaken the hegemony of the ruling class. As late as 1959, for example, the Congress movement's anti-pass planning council argued:

> It is essential that the European public should be given a systematic and thorough education about the evils of the pass laws. It is evident that many are ignorant of these evils and not sufficient work has been done to educate them. Many sympathetic Europeans cannot imagine what the country would look like without the pass laws and in particular without influx control. The Planning Council recommends that a pamphlet should be written specifically for the European public and that certain leading personalities amongst the Europeans should be approached to raise and discuss the pass issue with various institutions and to lead deputations and to government and local authorities. We should regard this as a second front in out anti-pass struggle.[33]

Similarly, in 1958 the ANC attempted to sway the behaviour of the white electorate by planning a demonstrative stay-away from work to coincide with the general election. Hopes of a massive disaffection of whites from Nationalist policies did not only arise from the encouraging experiences of the multiracial political and social activities of the 1950s; both liberal and marxist orthodoxy held to the view that economic expansion and apartheid were essentially in contradiction with one another.[34] Politics were seen in terms of exerting enormous pressure on the system, rather than its systematic destruction. From 1953 onwards protest was preferred to disobedience. Whilst there were excellent tactical reasons for this, and Congress was organisationally too weak to withstand the sanctions of the state, the style of protest was nevertheless indicative of a desire to persuade through moral example. In 1958 the Women's League and the Federation of South African Women were instructed to call off the deliberate courting of arrest by women anti-pass demonstrators. Thereafter proposals for action by women on passes took the form of nationwide prayer meetings.[35]

Otherwise Congress strategy seems to have been to use every possible means to build up a large and disciplined following which would allow it to exercise the decisive weight in a crisis of political authority which was only vaguely conceptualised but which all were sure would shortly arrive. At the time it was difficult to resist the sense of exhilaration created by the victories of anti-colonial movements elsewhere in Africa. Another factor that contributed to the belief that sudden and dramatic change was imminent was the fresh international interest in South Africa – which in itself provided another good reason for trying to maintain moral pressure upon the government. With this end in view Congress leaders advocated a far greater degree of tactical flexibility than was suggested by the 1949 Programme of Action. The programme had insisted, for example, that all differential political institutions should be boycotted and for Africanists this became a cardinal principle. But by 1957 it was being argued that the boycott of such institutions as Advisory Boards merely deprived the ANC of a platform for communicating with people in an atmosphere where alternative methods of political representation were becoming increasingly restricted.[36] The ANC participated in Advisory Board elections on the Rand throughout the 1950s (though it boycotted them in Port Elizabeth) and in 1956 Leslie Massina, a national executive member and prominent trade unionist, stood for election in Dube.[37] During the mid-1950s the ANC controlled three Transvaal Advisory Boards, and this appeared to be a symptom of their popularity rather than isolation from ordinary people: in two cases, Natalspruit and Benoni, the local ANC branches were powerful and militant.[38]

The reasoning which underlay the ANC's position on electoral boycotts appears in retrospect sound enough: participation did not involve loss of following. (This was in contrast to the Coloured People's Organisation which made a huge miscalculation by putting up candidates for the coloured vote in the 1958 election. Apathy and a well developed boycott tradition among the potential electorate prevented the Congress candidates from attracting more than 900 votes.)[39] But in some instances the ANC was very inflexible in its tactics. In 1957 a stay-at-home call evoked a gratifying working-class response. The following year workers were called upon to make a similar response, despite the fact that the main issue had shifted from wages to the election. In 1959 the ANC succeeded in organising a highly successful consumer boycott of

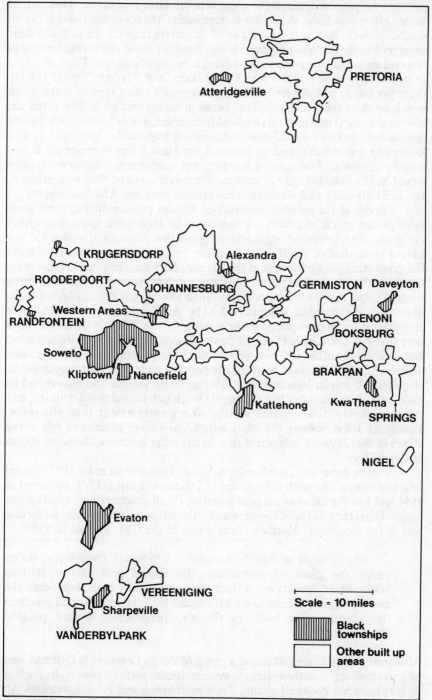

Fig. 2   African townships on the Witwatersrand, 1950–1960

potatoes in protest against the treatment of farm labourers. This led its leadership to conclude, somewhat mysteriously: 'the economic boycott can be used effectively against the pass laws'.[40] In certain respects the lack of a clear predetermined strategic programme was a virtue; it did encourage leaders to respond creatively to spontaneous upsurges of popular revolt. Their attempts to capitalise on rural protests were a good example of this (see Chapter 11). On the other hand, it could lead to an unimaginative reflex type of reaction, in which no clear relationship existed between means and ends. But given the historical context in which this leadership emerged, a unanimous and coherent approach to strategy would have been almost impossible. Ideologically this leadership was eclectic and in terms of the class forces represented it was socially complex. Attempts to hammer out a common long-term strategy would have succeeded only in splitting the movement and thus weakening it. Its social diversity and ideological eclecticism were the ANC's strengths.

Many of the existing accounts of African politics during these years have placed much emphasis on conflict over ideological questions within Congress. The foregoing argument suggests that ideological issues did not have a great deal of significance in many branches: the two areas of main Congress strength by the end of the decade, Port Elizabeth and Natal, were unaffected by internal disputes. This was not the case in the Transvaal or the western Cape, and the branches around Johannesburg, in particular, appear to have been divided and demoralised. The ANC itself suggested that this contributed to the unevenness in the response to the 1958 stay-at-home.[41] It is here that one could have expected most tension: the Johannesburg township and location branches did not seem to have been characterised by the same degree of interpenetration between the political and the labour movement as elsewhere. It was in Johannesburg that the Youth League had always had its main base. Johannesburg had the largest black population in the country, and it was probably differentiated socially to a greater extent than elsewhere. Finally, in Johannesburg the white left played a more prominent role in the affairs of the Congress movement than in any other centres with the exception of Cape Town.

As we have seen, the Congress Youth Leaguers were by 1952 divided into two camps, and with the election of Dilizantaba Mji as CYL president in 1951 and Joe Matthews as national secretary (both incidentally students at the 'open' University of the Witwatersrand), the left-wing non-Africanist faction was in the ascendant. Matthews later wrote in the CYL journal in 1953:

> . . . of a struggle within the League . . . to smash those forces which under the cloak of protecting 'the sacred principle of African Nationalism' have taken a right-wing reactionary path, hampered the mass struggles, sought to cut off contact with the masses, and maintain the League as a body in the air, periodically issuing political statements.[42]

Africanist dissent coalesced round a group of Youth Leaguers in Orlando, one of Johannesburg's south-western townships (today part of Soweto). Its leading figures included Potlake Leballo, Zeph Mothopeng and Peter Raboroko. All three were teachers who had lost their jobs during the Defiance Campaign (though Leballo's dismissal happened after a conviction for fraud). Leballo was born in 1924, in Modderpoort near Basutoland, enlisted during the war and by his own account led an army mutiny in North Africa, was later expelled from Lovedale teacher training college after a student strike, and eventually completed his training at the Evaton Wilberforce Institute. After his dismissal from his teaching post he settled in Orlando, working as an insurance salesman. Leballo was no intellectual but a colourful and effective orator, dogmatic and energetic. Mothopeng was a little older than Leballo, born in 1916 in the eastern Transvaal, better qualified professionally – he held a correspondence course B.A. – was a president of the Transvaal African Teacher's Association and for a short time on the CYL national executive. He lost his post at Orlando High School after campaigning against the Bantu Education proposals (see Chapter 5). Thereafter he held a variety of jobs before serving law articles in 1957. Peter Raboroko, a Free State farm labourer's son, a Youth League founder and Defiance Campaign volunteer, was the theorist of the movement, his impassioned advocacy of the revival of African culture and the need for a syncretic vernacular national language first appearing in the *Bantu World* in the early 1950s. All three men's backgrounds had features which seemed to distinguish the Africanist dissenters from the mainstream ANC leadership: a rural upbringing in the more harshly polarised racial climate of the Free State and the Transvaal (in contrast to the Transkei/Cape origins of many of the ANC leaders); relatively modest professional qualifications and career achievements; and at best superficial social contacts with whites.

The Orlando East Youth League and ANC branches together formed – AFTER Sophiatown – the largest concentration of ANC members in the Transvaal. It was not, however, one of the most militant groups. This may have been a reflection of the difficulties of mobilising people in a municipal location as opposed to a freehold community such as Alexandra or Sophiatown, as well as the social characteristics of much of Orlando's population.[43] The leadership of the ANC branch was involved – in 1953 – in a secret intrigue known as the *Bafabegiya* ('Those who die dancing')[44] under the aegis of Macdonald Maseko, chairman of the Orlando branch and a member of the ANC's national executive, which aimed to supplant the Transvaal leadership, sever any links with the Indian Congress and commit the movement to more confrontationist strategies.[45] Maseko and his co-conspirators were expelled from Congress in 1954. Meanwhile the Orlando East Youth League had also become increasingly rebellious under the chairmanship of Leballo. His speeches, criticising the ANC's linkages with non-African organisations and charging these Youth League officers who had accepted invitations to the 1953 World Youth Festival with being 'Eastern Functionaries', were enthusiastically reported in the *Bantu World*. The ANC, said Leballo, had repudiated the principles of the Programme of Action by participating in Advisory Board elections and succumbing to 'foreign ideologies'. In May 1953 Leballo was expelled by the League's Transvaal executive but subsequently reinstated by his branch. In November, Leballo and his confederates began to produce a cyclostyled journal, *The Africanist*.

Over the next few years the Africanists remained a small coterie, most influential in some of the Soweto branches but with support in Evaton and

Alexandra as well. In Alexandra the ANC branch was chaired for a while by Josias Madzunya, a hawker from Vendaland. He had little formal education but was a strident and persuasive demagogue beloved by the press and even regarded with some affection by the targets of his street corner polemics, the liberal and left-wing white Congress sympathisers. Madzunya was exceptional in operating within a very different social milieu from most of his fellow Africanists, and he was the only one with a popular personal following (see Chapters 5 and 7).

In 1957 a crisis of authority developed in the Transvaal provincial ANC, and the Africanists were swift to take advantage of it. Because of the spate of bannings as well as the involvement of much of the senior leadership in the Treason Trial, many provincial office-bearers were politically inexperienced and in some cases incompetent. Banned leaders who exercised behind-the-scenes authority sometimes appointed nominees to take their place, rather than going through the cumbersome process of having new office-bearers elected. In October 1957 the provincial executive insisted at its annual conference that it should be re-elected *en bloc* as a show of unity and defiance against the government. This and other administrative irregularities led to the formation by certain branch leaders of a 'petitioners' committee who drew up a list of complaints against provincial leaders, accusing them of rigging elections, financial malpractices and contempt for grass roots membership. Leading the petitioners was a Sophiatown politician, Stephen Seghali, who was thought to have Africanist sympathies.[46] He was reputed never to carry a pass, had served a prison term on a Bethal farm and often tinged his speeches with racist invective. The petitioners combined forces with the Africanists to demand a second provincial congress which – under pressure from the national executive – provincial leaders were forced to concede. It was held on 23 February 1958 and was an undignified affair; there was brawling between Africanists and supporters of the executive, and it ended inconclusively. Two days later the provincial executive were replaced with a temporary leadership chosen by the national leaders and of course including no Africanists. Bitter disputes continued through the year. In April, Africanists campaigned against Congress's stay-at-home. For this and a bizarre exploit in which Congress headquarters was raided and the ANC motor car removed, Madzunya and Leballo were deprived of their Congress membership. This did not deter them from establishing an 'Anti-Charterist Council' which, in anticipation of fresh elections at the November provincial conference, ran Madzunya as a candidate for Transvaal president with a manifesto penned by Peter Raboroko. At the conference itself, however, the Africanists were frustrated. Many of their delegates had their credentials rejected and on the second day they were prevented from entering the hall by Congress youths armed with sticks and iron bars. Sensibly the Africanists withdrew, announcing their intention to form their own organisation which would function as a 'custodian of ANC policy as formulated in 1912'.[47]

Although the Africanists' influence had been considerably exaggerated in the press this was nevertheless a more serious rupture in the nationalist movement than the disaffections which had occurred in the past. First, it took place when the movement in the provinces affected had already been weakened through organisational breakdown and campaign reversals. Second, unlike splinter movements like the National Minded bloc, it was led by young militants eager to see Congress embark upon a more adventurous course. The aggressive and vengeful mood they conveyed in their speeches was to have a particular attraction for the young and, as we shall see, in Cape Town it accorded well with the embittered feelings of Xhosa migrant workers. There had always been a potential constituency for a political leadership which played upon violent emotions and identified oppressors in racial terms. Impressionistic evidence suggests that this was beginning to include young and well educated middle-class Africans to a greater extent than before.[48] Hitherto ANC leaders, by virtue of their social background and moral beliefs, had not cared to exploit this. The Africanists were to show no such inhibitions.

The Africanist social landscape was painted with harsh and glaring colours. Their sensitive and sympathetic historian, Gail Gerhart, traces the Africanists' vision back to an essentially peasant outlook uncomplicated with the moral dilemmas posed by emotional involvement in a western urban industrial society:

'What can you do with the white men?' That's what they would tell you. 'The white man is all right; there is nothing that we can do.' They would also use some of the texts from the Bible, some of them, in order to show how God dictated things to be; there's nothing that can be done about them. But here you would have to use methods of persuasion. You draw examples from as many sources as you can, show the fight that went on in our country. . . . The question of land, for instance, touches the African to the core of his heart. Now if you draw from the fights of Moshesh in defence of the land, every Mosotho respects Moshesh very much. Once you talk of Moshesh . . . he is bound to listen. Or you talk of Hintsa, you talk of all the other heroes, Sekhukhuni and Tshaka and his warriors, that the land is the central point. Let us get back the land that was given us by our forefathers.[49]

Of course their appeals were self-consciously made in the knowledge that:

The masses do not hate an abstraction like 'oppression' or 'capitalism'. . . . They make these things concrete and hate the oppressor – in South Africa the White man.[50]

But this need not imply that the appeals were made cynically. As we have seen, the life histories of principals in the Africanist movement could reinforce a parochial and polarised outlook. They had two major disagreements with the Congress leadership as it was developing in the 1950s. The first was over the rôle allowed to whites in the Congress alliance. Africanists felt that white Congress sympathisers had mainly sectional interests; the proof of this, they said, was to be found in the Freedom Charter with its clauses guaranteeing the rights and status of all national groups. Their influence had succeeded in dissolving the ethnically assertive nationalism which Africanists believed to have been adopted by the ANC with the acceptance of the Programme of Action in 1949. In doing so the whites had deprived the ANC of the most effective ideological means of inspiring a mass following. 'Multiracialism', as they termed it, served to perpetuate the psychological subservience and dependency on whites upon which minority domination rested. The second major disagreement was over the question of spontaneity. The difference in the approaches of Congressmen and Africanists is evident in the following passages:

> . . . when a spontaneous movement takes place the duty of leadership is not just to follow spontaneously but to give it proper direction. (ANC National Executive, 1958)

> We must be the embodiment of our people's aspirations. And all we are required to do is show the light and the masses will find the way. (Robert Sobukwe, 1949)

From these two positions flowed most of the other elements in Africanist thinking: ethnic nationalism was a natural predisposition among the masses; all that was needed was an effective ideological articulation of popular consciousness by leadership for the masses to rise; organisational questions were of secondary importance; South Africa was a colonial society no different from any other African country, its basic internal contradiction a racial or communal one that could only be resolved through racial conflict; all attempts to win the sympathy or at least the neutrality of a section of the white population were futile and would detract from the effectiveness of any African political movement.

Four months after their secession the Africanists held the inaugural conference of the new organisation, the Pan-Africanist Congress, in Orlando. In a highly charged atmosphere, the conference was opened by the chairman of the Federation of Independent African Churches, the Reverend W. M. Dimba, who began his address by denouncing those 'hooligans of Europe who killed our God', and went on to salute 'a black man, Simon of Arabia who carried Jesus from the cross'.[51] The delegates then elected a president, rejecting, rather to the surprise of observers, Josias Madzunya (who had disgraced himself by calling for 'God's Apartheid', that is, Africa for the Africans and Europe for the Europeans), choosing instead Robert Sobukwe, a lecturer in African languages at the University of the Witwatersrand.

Sobukwe had been a prominent figure in the Fort Hare Youth League, rising to be the League's national secretary in 1949. In a graduation address he had distinguished himself in a bitter attack on the paternalism of the university authorities, equating 'broadmindedness and reasonableness' in Africans as 'treachery to Africa'. He lost his job at a rural Transvaal school as a result of his participation in the Defiance Campaign, though later he was reinstated. In 1954 he obtained his university post in Johannesburg. A self-effacing man with considerable intellectual gifts he remained in the political background, chairing an ANC branch at Mofolo in Soweto, and contributing anonymously to *The Africanist*. It was Sobukwe who was chiefly responsible for the refinement and degree of intellectual depth in the Africanist position which emerged at the PAC conference. Sobukwe did not subscribe to the crude racialism of Madzunya: in the columns of *The Africanist* he had called upon sympathetic whites to adjust their outlook in such a fashion that the slogan 'Africa for the Africans . . . could apply to them even though they are white'.[52]

But despite his comparative subtlety and thoughtfulness he shared with his colleagues their romantic belief in the political integrity of the masses.

Sobukwe's presidential address outlined the basic principle o the new movement. The PAC stood for government by the Africans for the Africans – 'everybody who owes his loyalty to Africa being regarded as African'. Whites, however, were for the present unable to owe their loyalty to Africa, even if they were intellectual converts to the cause of African freedom, 'because they benefit materially from the present set-up' and so 'cannot completely identify themselves with that cause'.[53] Pan-Africanists were opposed to 'multiracialism' in as much as it implied insuperable differences between various national groups and tried to safeguard minority interests. Sobukwe's view, rather, was that 'there is but one race, the human race'. Indian South Africans should reject the leadership of their merchant class and join forces with the 'indigenous majority'. He went on to stress his admiration for Kwame Nkrumah's and Tom Mboya's policy of non-alignment, rejected South Africa's 'exceptionalism', affirmed its common destiny with the rest of Africa and looked forward to the creation of a 'United States of Africa'. Similarly the PAC manifesto condemned the 'capture' of a portion of the black leadership by a section of the 'white ruling class' and called upon the movement 'to forge and consolidate the bonds of African nationhood on a Pan-African basis', as well as to:

> . . . implement effectively the fundamental principle that the domain or sovereignty over and the domination or ownership of the whole territory rests exclusively and inalienably in the indigenous people.

The manifesto also prescribed 'an Africanistic Socialistic democratic social order' and cited the Pan-Africanism of the All-African Peoples' Organisation's conference at Accra (which had excited great interest among Africanists when it was held in December 1958) as the nationalist creed to which the PAC subscribed.[54]

The founding conference optimistically set a target of 100 000 members by 1 July 1959.[55] In fact the PAC itself was to admit at the end of the year that less than a third of this target had been reached and even this was disputed by the ANC and members of the Liberal Party.[56] But the ANC had demonstrated during the Defiance Campaign how a movement could swell rapidly to many times its original size if it succeeded in catching the popular mood. Leballo was to claim that the PAC had 101 branches.[57] If each of these had consisted only of a few energetic activists this would have been sufficient to launch an effective mass campaign provided the PAC could inspire the crowd with its appeals.

The PAC did not build its bases in traditional ANC strongholds. It never had much impact in Natal. In the case of the Transvaal, while it did not extend it support in the Johannesburg area beyond the original Africanist groups in Alexandra and Orlando, it succeeded in acquiring a following in the Vereeniging district. For reasons which will be discussed in a later chapter, this was a region which had been neglected by the ANC. Similarly, in the Cape, the first PAC organisers were sent, not to the Eastern Province towns but to the Cape peninsula where the ANC was troubled by tensions which paralleled those which existed in the Transvaal. The ANC in the western Cape was traditionallly weak, Africans being a minority in the population in the area, and a large proportion of them contract workers from the Transkei, a group to which the local political leaders had never paid much attention. It was in this part of the country, for reasons which will become clear later in this book, that the PAC succeeded in establishing a strong following.

For the next eight months the PAC's strategy remained indefinite. Sobukwe himself announced in August a 'Status Campaign' which would take the same form as some of the ANC-inspired consumer boycotts in Port Elizabeth and exert pressure for more courteous treatment of Africans in shops. Its more fundamental purpose was to exorcise any traces of 'slave mentality' and encourage the assertion by people of their 'African Personality'.[58] Such modest intentions fell short of the expectations of rank and file members of the PAC, and under pressure from them, as well as being motivated by a desire to keep the initiative from the ANC, the PAC's national executive decided – at its first annual conference in December – upon a more dramatic course of action. The ANC at its annual conference had resolved to step up its anti-pass campaign and the PAC now followed suit.

Their plans were very different. The ANC proposed a series of demonstrations on days of symbolic importance, leafletting, and other educational activities, and the use of 'industrial action' led by SACTU factory committees. The Anti-Pass Planning Council also considered the possibility of civil disobedience, but concluded ambiguously:

> . . . a thorough study of the meaning of civil disobedience should be made, since there are so many interpretations of what it is. And before we can embark on any form, we should be specific as to what we contemplate doing.[59]

The PAC plans were specific: on an appointed day all African men should heed the call of their leaders, leave their passes at home and present themselves for arrest at their local police station. People should stay away from work and soon there would be a complete paralysis of the economy and the administration. All that was required was for heroic leaders to set the pace and the necessary conditions for a spontaneous popular uprising would be present.

In this chapter we have been concerned with examining the progress of African political movements which succeeded in acquiring mass support. There were, though, various other political movements active amongst the black population, the three most significant of which, in terms of resistance politics in the 1950s, were the All-African Convention and its affiliates; the Liberal Party; and the South African Communist Party.

The All-African Convention (AAC) had developed out of the opposition to the Hertzog land and franchise legislation of 1936 as a federal body to which different organisations could affiliate. By the end of the war it had become subject to the influence of a small group of African Marxists which had developed around Isaac Tabata in Queenstown. Tabata saw the main social forces for revolution in South Africa as existing in the countryside, and to this end he and his colleagues were active during the 1940s and 1950s in promoting the cause of peasant resistance to state land rehabilitation schemes in the Transkei. Their work mainly took the form of pamphleteering, holding public meetings, and, later, offering legal services to peasants who ended up in court. The AAC was influential amongst certain sections of the African teaching profession, notably in the case of members of the Cape African Teachers' Association, an AAC affiliate. But outside the Transkei it was not an activist organisation. Through affiliated groups, which included the (coloured) Non-European Unity Movement until 1959 and the Society of Young Africa, it functioned mainly at an intellectual level, producing vitriolic abuse of all those agencies which it perceived to be essentially collaborationist; these included the ANC, largely because of its participation in urban Advisory Board elections. The political tactic most favoured by the AAC and its constituents was that of boycott, and its impassioned advocacy of this often masked a considerable reluctance on the part of many of its members to become involved in any form of political activism. Nevertheless the AAC, through the Non-European Unity Movement, held considerable sway over the political behaviour of the black population in Cape Town, where it published a well-produced, if acerbic, newspaper, *The Torch*. In the Transvaal the Society of Young Africa enjoyed a certain vogue in the early 1950s amongst the young and usually well educated men and women who attended its discussion groups.

The Liberal Party, started in 1953 by a group of whites who up until then had placed their hopes in the more enlightened currents existing in the official opposition United Party, at first appealed to more conservative African political opinion. Though intended from its inception to be multiracial, it advocated a qualified franchise (only entirely dropped in 1959), and its appeal to Africans was rather limited. Its most important African member was Jordan Ngubane, a founder of the ANCYL who had left the ANC because of his belief that it was increasingly susceptible to communist manipulation. Notwithstanding Ngubane's hostility to Congress, good relationships existed between Liberal and ANC leaders in Natal, and in 1956 Liberal Party members participated in the opposition in Natal to the issue of passes to African women. Though it later developed in an increasingly radical and activist direction, the Liberal Party's chief importance was in helping to shape African political perceptions, firstly as a result of the friendships which existed between some of its principals and Congress politicians, and secondly as a source of hope and inspiration for the conciliatory brand of nationalism characteristic of the Lutuli era. It could also, on occasions, play an important intermediary rôle at moments of crisis arising out of conflict between African resistance movements and the state.[60]

The Communist Party of South Africa was disbanded, against the wishes of some of its members, shortly before the enactment of the Suppression of Communism legislation. It was re-formed as the South African Communist Party (the change in nomenclature indicative of a shift in its theoretical position with regard to African nationalism) in 1953. The SACP's membership seems to have included only the more active people in the CPSA and there is no evidence that during the 1950s it tried to recruit new members, preferring instead to involve itself in the campaigns of the Congress alliance. As we have seen, its members were especially prominent in the Congress of Democrats. Only in 1960 did the SACP begin to reconstitute itself as a separate and distinct political force (see Chapter 10).

In this chapter we have been principally concerned with the development of the nationalist movement at the level of its leadership. But to understand properly its evolution and slow transformation from an elitist to a popular movement, a knowledge of the local contexts within which it operated is essential. The following chapters will explore rather more intensively some of the ground we have just covered. The focus will be narrow and the picture at best partial, but the faces, at least, should stand out more clearly from the crowd.

Notes

1 Gwendolyn Carter, Gail Gerhart and Thomas Karis, *From Protest to Challenge*, Volume III, Hoover, Stanford, 1977, p. 14.
2 Gwendolyn Carter and Thomas Karis, *From Protest to Challenge*, Volume II, Hoover, Stanford, 1973, p. 425.
3 SAIRR papers, AD 1189, unsorted box, National Executive Report to the 1955 annual conference of the ANC, p. 3, South African Institute of Race Relations.
4 Report of the National Action Committee to the secretary-general of the ANC and the joint honorary secretaries of the SAIC, 5 December 1953, Carter and Karis microfilm (CAMP), Reel, 2b, 2 DA 14/4: 62.
5 *Advance* (Cape Town), 9 July 1953.
6 Carter, Gerhart, and Karis, *From Protest to Challenge*, Volume III, p. 12.
7 *Ibid*, p. 59.
8 *Advance*, 25 March 1954.
9 *New Age* (Cape Town), 19 May 1955.
10 Carter, Gerhart and Karis, *From Protest to Challenge*, Volume III, p. 58.
11 Robert Johnson, 'Indians and Apartheid in South Africa', Ph.D. thesis, University of Massachusetts, 1973, p. 91.
12 Carter, Gerhart and Karis, *From Protest to Challenge*, Volume III, p. 58.
13 SAIRR papers, AD 1189, ANC III, the Bureau of African Nationalism, Political Commentaries, No. 1.
14 Carter, Gerhart and Karis, *From Protest to Challenge*, Volume III, p. 93.
15 *Ibid*, pp. 205–8.
16 Janet Robertson, *Liberalism in South Africa, 1948–1963*, Oxford University Press, Oxford, 1971, p. 166. See also Jordan Ngubane, *An African Explains Apartheid*, Praeger, New York, 1963, p. 164.
17 Carter, Gerhart and Karis, *From Protest to Challenge*, Volume III, p. 195.
18 Nelson Mandela, 'In Our Lifetime', *Liberation* (Johannesburg), June 1956.
19 Nor were they alone in this. Michael Harmel, a leading theoretician of the Communist Party, was to argue as late as 1959 that economic pressures might induce revolutionary social changes without accompanying violence; see Michael Harmel, 'Revolutions are not abnormal', *Africa South* (Cape Town), January–March, 1959.
20 See Robertson, *Liberalism in South Africa*, p. 169.
21 Johnson, 'Indians and Apartheid in South Africa', p. 97.
22 SAIRR papers, AD 1189, unsorted box, National Executive Report to the 1955 annual conference of the ANC, p. 13.
23 For membership figures see: Cape ANC's circular letter to branches, 7 1 1954, Carter and Karis microfilm, Reel 2b, 2 DA 17: 40/13; Secretary's report to the

Cape ANC provincial conference, 15–16 August 1953, Carter and Karis microfilm, Reel 2b, 2 DA 17: 30/19; SAIRR papers, AD 1189, unsorted box, National Executive Report to the 1955 conference of the ANC; SAIRR papers, AD 1189, ANC 111, National Executive Report to the 46th ANC conference, 1958.

24 Report of the National Action Committee, Carter and Karis microfilm, Reel 2b, 2 DA 14/4: 62.

25 SAIRR papers, AD 1189, ANC 11, National Executive Report to the 42nd annual conference of the ANC, 16–19 December 1954.

26 SAIRR papers, AD 1189, unsorted box, National Executive Report to the 1955 annual conference of the ANC.

27 M. B. Yengwa quoted in Edward Feit, *African Opposition in South Africa*, Hoover, Stanford, 1967, p. 74.

28 Secretary's report to the Cape ANC provincial conference, 15–16 August 1953, Carter and Karis microfilm, Reel 2b, 2 DA 17: 30/19.

29 SAIRR papers, AD 1189, ANC 111, National Executive Committee report to the 47th annual conference of the ANC, 12–13 December 1959, p. 12.

30 SAIRR papers, AD 1189, unsorted box, National Executive Committee report to the 1955 annual conference of the ANC, annexure C.

31 Carter, Gerhart and Karis, *From Protest to Challenge*, Volume III, p. 39.

32 *Ibid*, p. 36.

33 SAIRR papers, AD 1189, ANC 111, Anti-Pass Planning Council Plan, 1959, p. 3.

34 See for example, H. J. Simons, 'An addendum', *Africa South*, October–December 1958. Also: 'It is no mere rhetoric to say that Apartheid is proving to be a Frankenstein. . . . Oppression in any guise cannot pay any country dividends' (Albert Lutuli in National Executive Report to the 47th annual conference of the ANC, 12–13 December 1959, SAIRR papers, AD 1189, ANC 111).

35 SAIRR papers, AD 1189, ANC 111, Anti-Pass Planning Council Plan, 1959, p. 2.

36 SAIRR papers, AD 1189, ANC 111, Memorandum dealing with the Programme of Action, 1957; see also Nelson Mandela, 'Our struggle has many tactics', *Liberation*, February 1958, pp. 14–17.

37 Carter, Gerhart and Karis, *From Protest to Challenge*, Volume IV, Hoover, Stanford, 1977, p. 77.

38 *The World* (Johannesburg), 8 December 1956.

39 Most of those who did vote refrained from supporting the SACPO candidate, Beyleveld. The triumphant candidate was a member of the United Party. The political conservatism of a large section of the coloured community was another factor which placed the Congress alliance at a disadvantage. See *The Torch* (Cape Town), 8 April 1958, for election report.

40 SAIRR papers, AD 1189, ANC 111, National Executive Committee annual report to the 47th annual conference of the ANC, 12–13 December 1959, p. 5.

41 SAIRR papers, AD 1189, ANC 111, National Executive Report to the 46th annual conference, 13–14 December 1958, p. 11.

42 *ANCYL Journal*, 2, 1953.

43 Orlando was established as a 'Model Native Township' by the Johannesburg municipality in 1932. Its distance from the city and consequent transport costs, and its high rents, would have limited the attraction of living there to those who could afford the relative comfort of its single and and semi-detached houses. A *Bantu World* correspondent (4 August 1951) chided those of his readers who lived there, along with the inhabitants of Dube (a section of the township where Africans could erect their own houses), for 'isolating themselves from the masses'.

44 The group began as a fundraising society during the Defiance Campaign with the purpose of raising money to support the families of imprisoned volunteers. To this end it would hold night-time dances to which admission fees were charged, hence its name: 'those who would die dancing'.

45 Information on the *Bafabegiya* drawn from reports in *Advance*, 22 October 1952; *Liberation*, 7 February 1954; *The Torch*, 2 March 1954.

46 This was according to a report on the petitioners in *Contact* (Cape Town), 3 March 1958. The report may be misleading though, or Seghali may have become disillusioned with the Africanists, for in *New Age* (14 January 1960) there is an article about a Steven Segale, who served a prison sentence for helping to organise the 1958 stay-at-home (which the Africanists opposed). He was quoted at his trial as saying in a speech: '. . . . be very careful of Africanists who are playing a double role. . . . They appear to be with the people when in truth they are with the Government.'

47 Peter Raboroko, 'The Africanist case', *Africa South*, April–June 1960.

48 Gerhart's interview with Z. B. Molete, quoted in Gail Gerhart, *Black Power in South Africa*, University of California Press, Berkeley, 1978, pp. 167–72.

49 Gerhart's interview with Z. B. Molete, quoted in Gerhart, *Black Power in South Africa*, p. 149.

50 *Golden City Post* (Johannesburg), 29 March 1959.

51 Peter Rodda, 'The Africanists cut loose', *Africa South*, July–September 1959, p. 23.

52 Sobukwe quoted by A. B. Ngcobo in *The New African* (London), November 1965.

53 Robert Sobukwe, 'The Africanist case', *Contact*, 30 May 1959.

54 Carter, Gerhart and Karis, *From Protest to Challenge*, Volume III, pp. 326–7.

55 *Contact*, 18 April 1959.

56 *Contact*, 8 August 1959 and 20 September 1959.

57 *Contact*, 8 August 1959.

58 Gerhart, *Black Power in South Africa*, p. 227, and Carter, Gerhart and Karis, *From Protest to Challenge*, Volume IV, p. 329.

59 SAIRR papers, AD 1189, unsorted box, Anti-Pass Planning Council Paln, p. 4.

60 For analysis of the development of the South African Liberal Party see: C. J. Driver, *Patrick Duncan: South African and Pan-African*, Heinemann, London, 1980, pp. 87–209; Janet Robertson, *Liberalism in South Africa*, pp. 106–231; Tom Lodge, 'Patrick Duncan and radical liberalism', Centre for African Studies, *Africa Seminar: Collected Papers*, Volume 1, University of Cape Town, 1978, pp. 108–125; Moira Levy, 'Opposition to apartheid in the fifties: the Liberal Party and the Congress of Democrats', B.A. Honours dissertation, University of the Witwatersrand, 1981.

CHAPTER 4

The destruction of Sophiatown

In this and the following four chapters we shall examine rather more carefully the ground surveyed in Chapter 3. Understanding popular political responses depends on a detailed knowledge of particular communities and social groups. It is beyond the scope of this book to provide an appreciation of the local background and underlying special interests in the case of every act of resistance in the period. Instead a selection has been made of the most important protest movements and constituencies. These include the opposition to urban residential removals (discussed in this chapter), the boycott of government schools in protest against 'Bantu Education', the 1950s bus boycotts, the attempts by African women to resist the introduction of women's passes, and, finally, the development of the labour movement. In the course of discussing this resistance particular local environments will be examined with the intention of providing an explanation of the regional variations in degree and form of black political activity in the early apartheid period. We have already looked at one of the storm centres of African protest, the eastern Cape; our understanding of resistance politics would be very incomplete without comparable insights into the political sociology of the Johannesburg and East Rand townships where the ANC, for most of the decade, had its most active following outside the eastern Cape. Congress enjoyed a tremendous revival of support in Natal in 1959 and the reasons for this revival will be discussed in the treatment of women's resistance in Chapter 6.

In 1955 the South African government began the demolition of a black freehold suburb in Johannesburg and the relocation of its inhabitants in a state-controlled township. Resistance to these moves was led by the ANC. It was short-lived and unsuccessful. Despite this the attempt to oppose the destruction of Sophiatown was historically significant. There are four reasons for this. First, the preservation of this suburb was an issue considered by African politicians to be of national importance. Their degree of success in mobilising opposition and the extent of coercion the government would need to employ would both have an effect on the development of 'an accumulated heritage of resistance'[1] conditioning popular political responses later in the decade.

Second, the resistance throws light on a currently influential hypothesis that in the immediate post-war years the ANC was transformed 'by its new class base' into a class-conscious movement of proletarian orientation.[2] This contrasts with an earlier analysis by Edward Feit. Here the ANC during this period is ascribed with a 'bourgeois' dynamic. Feit suggests the entry into politics of any member of the black petty-bourgeoisie was:

. . . perhaps less due to his own wish to participate in radical politics than to feelings that, being forced to the same level as the masses by external constraints, he must break the system to establish his supremacy over them.[3]

Not surprisingly, ANC supporters perceived their situation rather differently. 'The oppressed have no tradition of private ownership', asserted the pro-Congress newspaper, *New Age*, in 1955. With the black 'middle class' growing very slowly or even declining and the black proletariat undergoing rapid expansion we can expect to 'find the national movement [acquiring] a definite working class character'.[4]

Such claims are being revived as a new orthodoxy. Bernard Magubane argues that the various struggles of the 1950s 'convinced the people that they had common class interests'.[5] Within black South African society one cannot refer to the existence of social classes:

The few who escape from the ranks of unskilled labour cannot develop separate 'class consciousness' because they are forced to live with and among proletarians and share their disabilities.[6]

From within the ANC, Joe Slovo too, though acknowledging a degree of stratification within the black population, does not discern any major clash of interests. In South Africa there are merely 'black middle strata' of tightly limited social mobility whose fate is linked with that of worker and peasant.[7]

From this perspective it is argued that the struggles of the 1950s represented a manifestation of the general will. The inability of ANC efforts to achieve a reversal of government policies should not be viewed as failure. The ANC was a revolutionary movement and it is 'often only through the experience of these so-called failures that the masses begin to understand the need for conquering state power and thus for revolution'.[8]

This is not unreasonable if it is maintained that this was the objective effect rather than the subjective intention of ANC campaigns in this period. But something more than this is claimed: Slovo, Magubane and O'Meara refer to Congress as a working-class movement with a revolutionary strategy. The anti-removals campaign demonstrates this was not the case. Both the organisation and its context were socially complex.

Nevertheless, to understand the political leadership as having been inspired solely by selfish considerations seems harshly mechanistic. Though there may have been conflicts of interest within ghetto society in the 1950s these were not always consciously realised. Many petty-bourgeois Africans of the 1950s had intimate personal experience of the poverty and insecurity most people lived in. African townships, though socially heterodox in a number of ways, did not have the 'geography of class' that was and is a feature of white suburbia. Given these conditions it is artificial to define interests with rigid precision: they were bound to have an ambivalent quality. And given these conditions it was understandable that politically conscious men and women should have believed their feelings were a true reflection of popular concerns. Certainly, intellectuals and small entrepreneurs in the African community may have had petty-bourgeois aspirations, but there is also evidence in their literary culture, in their welfare activities and in their political commitment of a degree of social compassion and depth of anger that went well beyond their immediate class interests.

The third reason for looking at the Sophiatown removals is because they were representative of a much wider social process in which many old-established inner-city African communities were uprooted and reconstructed under the supervision of the authorities. In the course of these upheavals old relationships and social networks were disrupted and sometimes destroyed. The political quiescence of the 1960s was at least in part the result of the social disorientation which accompanied the transition from city location to state-administered township during the 1950s.

The final reason for the campaign's importance is because it helps testify to the social purpose of apartheid: the forces the government was endeavouring to protect and those it was most concerned to destroy. It has been convincingly argued that 1948 represented a turning point. A regime representative of established manufacturing and commercial interests timidly contemplating reform was replaced by a political order reflecting the concerns of a group who were served better by the intensification of existing labour-repressive measures: farmers, financiers, small industrialists, and white workers threatened by African acquisition of industrial skills.[9] But much of the recent analyses has concentrated on the changing balance of forces represented by the state, neglecting the active role Africans may have had in influencing this process.[10] The exact nature of the threat posed to established and ascendent interests by the African community is rarely detailed.

Questions such as 'Why did the government wish to destroy Sophiatown?' or 'Why did Africans resist its destruction?' are often taken for granted. Yet without understanding the social matrix of resistance it is difficult to provide adequate answers and it would be premature to form conclusions about the class content or revolutionary nature of African political responses of this period.

Sophiatown was one of several places in the Transvaal where Africans had succeeded in buying land before the prohibitive 1923 Urban Areas Act was passed. The Western Areas townships, Sophiatown and its neighbours, Martindale and Newclare, were not intended originally by the speculators who founded them for black occupation. The siting of a municipal refuse dump in their vicinity discouraged white inhabitation and the area became predominantly settled by Africans, some of whom invested their savings in stands. Their presence was opposed by neighbouring white ratepayers, as well as estate companies anxious about the impact of a high density poor community on property prices. Such opposition, strongly expressed at the municipal level, was unable to outweigh emergent industrial interests, reluctant to subsidise working-class housing and unwilling therefore to support any municipal attempts to assume responsibility for African housing. By 1928, the Western Areas had a population of 12 000.

Six years later this population had doubled. There were two causes. First, in 1933, with the exception of the Western Areas, Johannesburg was proclaimed under the Urban Areas Act: this meant residential areas were to be segregated and blacks living in predominantly 'white' areas were to be rehoused. The freehold suburbs absorbed a large proportion of those so displaced whom the municipality could not accommodate in its locations, Western Native Township and Orlando. Second, with the post-1933 growth in manufacturing, there was a fresh demand for black working-class housing, and in response to this tenants and landlords in Sophiatown began taking in sub-tenants and housing them in rows of back yard shanties. So, despite local opposition, the Western Areas grew as a densely packed lively African community, free from the normal administrative regulation of the African location. During the 1930s and the war, the central government chose to ignore the increasingly shrill municipal objections to the existence of these freehold suburbs. The Western Areas were providing social facilities for a swiftly growing industrial workforce that both the state and employers were unwilling to afford. There was also the consideration that the suburbs provided an outlet for black petty-bourgeois aspirations which, if totally denied, could be dangerous in a period of developing class consciousness amongst African workers.[11]

Before considering the fruition of these efforts to remove Africans from the Western Areas, let us look at the community that had developed by 1950. Sophiatown was situated four miles west of Johannesburg' centre on the slope of a rocky outcrop. Running along its southern border was the narrow strip of Martindale, separated from the municipality's Western Native Township by the Main Road. South-west of Western Native Township stretched Newclare. Trevor Huddleston has provided one of the best physical descriptions:

> Sophiatown is not, and never has been, a slum. There are no tenements: there is nothing really old: there are no dark cellars. Sometimes looking up at Sophiatown from Western Native Township, across the main road, I have felt I was looking at an Italian village somewhere in Umbria. For you do 'look up' at Sophiatown, and in the evening light, across the blue grey haze of smoke from braziers and chimneys against a saffron sky, you see close packed, red-roofed little houses. You see, on the farthest skyline, the tall and shapely blue-gum trees. . . . You see, moving up and down the hilly streets, people in groups: people with colourful clothes: people who, when you come up to them, are children playing, dancing and standing round the braziers. . . . In the evening, towards the early South African sunset, there is very little of the slum about Sophiatown.[12]

Nevertheless, living conditions were very unpleasant for many of the Western Area's inhabitants. By-laws forbade the construction of more than one building on each stand, but this regulation had never been enforced and most stands were crowded with rows of corrugated iron shacks, each room often housing an entire family. Up to forty people could share a couple of lavatories and a single tap. People would cook outside using fire buckets as stoves.[13] In contrast, the municipality's Western Native Township was less congested. Within its fence were rows of small brick houses, 2 000 of them each with two or three rooms, built just after the First World War. Here there dwelt approximately 13 000 people in an atmosphere of 'orderly respectability'.[14] Like most of the inhabitants of Sophiatown, those of the

Western Native Township were not provided with electricity or indoor water but there was a communal hall and a couple of playing fields as well as a clinic.[15] Certainly, measured by such criteria as living space, building regulations, provision of social facilities and so forth, the inhabitants of the Western Native Township were better off than their Sophiatown neighbours. But to adopt such a narrow perspective is to ignore the crucial characteristic of Sophiatown, Martindale and Newclare. The point was that the Western Areas were not locations, they were suburbs. Admittedly they had many features of the ghetto: poor inhabitants, external ownership of most businesses, little local investment, a high birth rate, indebtedness, and a socially heterodox population with members of different classes forced to live in close proximity with each other. But there were also two cinemas, twenty churches, seventeen schools, many shops, craftsmen, herbalists, shebeens and jazz clubs. Unlike locations, these townships were not fenced off, there was no superintendent, nobody had to ask permission to live there, and compared to the geometrically planned municipal location, these densely packed suburbs were very difficult to police.

Sophiatown had a particularly emotional significance: it was an African town in a way that few other places were:

> Sophiatown. That beloved Sophiatown. As students we used to refer to it proudly as 'the centre of the metropolis'. And who could dispute it? The most talented African men and women from all walks of life – in spite of the hardships they had to encounter – came from Sophiatown. The best musicians, scholars, educationists, singers, artists, doctors, lawyers, clergymen.[16]

Perhaps such sentiments were mainly indicative of petty-bourgeois aspirations. Perhaps the glamorisation of Sophiatown as the place of 'sophisticated gangsters, brave politicians and intellectuals'[17] satisfied only a small and relatively privileged group. But though the urban sophistication of the Western Areas was one of their most important attractions, it was not their only one. As we shall see, Sophiatown provided a chance of economic survival for various groups who would have been hard pressed to find it elsewhere.

The Western Areas had a richly heterodox population including nearly 54 000 Africans, 3 000 Coloureds, 1 500 Indians and 686 Chinese. It could be categorised in a number of ways. 82 per cent of the families were tenants, 14 per cent were sub-tenants, and 2 per cent were landlords.[18] In itself this tells us little: there were considerable disparities of wealth within the landlord group, for example. It is considerably more helpful to view the population as falling into three classes. At its apex there was a petty bourgeoisie consisting of professional people, teachers and ministers, clerical workers as well as traders, craftsmen and landlords (a minority of landlords depended on their property for their sole income: they tended to be extremely poor as a result). This group comprised in the case of each suburb roughly 11 to 14 per cent of heads of families.[19] This group was very amorphous: it could embrace on the one hand A. B. Xuma, the former president of the ANC and a wealthy medical practitioner, whilst on the other hand there were itinerant traders or craftsmen who earned less than industrial workers.[20] Three-quarters of the Indian population fell within this group; most of the shops and much of the landed property was Indian-owned. Though Indians formed a substantial proportion of the more prosperous section of the community it should be said that at least half of the 400 or so Indian families were living on incomes of less than £25 a month.[21]

It is difficult to generalise about property owners in the Western Areas. Just under half the stands were owned by 829 Africans, most of whom owned only one stand, but a tiny minority (nine in Sophiatown) owned between five and ten stands. There were 66 Indian standholders owning 113 stands (mainly occupied by shops) and the rest were owned by non-resident businessmen.[22] A majority of African owners were paying off bonds. These would frequently absorb the income from rents.[23] Indeed, only a minority could afford to occupy their whole house and some would live in a shack constructed alongside their tenants in the back yard.[24] Even if landlords were able to extract enough rent to pay off their bonds this was not the end of their difficulties: the municipality charged them for sewage, rubbish disposal, and water according to how many tenants they had.[25]

On average the family income of property-owning households was slightly higher than that of other families. But average figures are deceptive in that nearly a third of the property owners had a monthly income of less than £5 while only a fifth enjoyed an income of above £10, though within this group there was a small number deriving a monthly income of as much as £223 from their property.[26]

It would be misleading to classify all African standholders as petty bourgeois. Over half were in working-class occupations and most of these were receiving less than half their income from rents.[27] Given that many of these would have been making bond payments it is unlikely their economic position would have been much less precarious than the rest of the community. They would have differed only in that they would hope that ultimately their property would bring economic security and perhaps the eventual prospect of opening up their own business. To summarise: property owners formed about two per cent of the population. Within this group there were huge disparities of wealth. The majority were not much better off than their tenants and differed from them more in their social aspirations than objective situation. In general, landlords were heavily indebted, mainly to bondholders.

The working class were the largest group. Of all those in regular employment in 1951, 82 per cent were in working-class occupations, over half in domestic or unskilled capacities, the rest were semi-skilled factory operatives, service workers, lorry drivers and delivery men.[28] Average monthly wages ranged between £5 4s 4d for domestic workers to £16 5s 6d in the case of drivers. It is likely that three-quarters of this population had lived in Johannesburg for over ten years and one third had been born there.[29] The workers of Sophiatown, Newclare and Martindale seem to have been drawn from the most experienced and longest established layers of Johannesburg's working-class population. This was manifest in an intense degree of class-consciousness: Sophiatown was one of the few African townships where the Communist Party enjoyed a significant African following before its banning in 1950.

The final group, much the most difficult to discuss with any precision, were the lumpenproletariat. Approximately 10 to 15 per cent of the potential workforce was unemployed. Probably a fifth of all households would include at least one man without regular employment. A third had been jobless for at least six months.[30] An important group among the unemployed were former Basotho mineworkers. They were concentrated in Newclare where housing conditions were worst; here too illegal brewing and the incidence of anti-social crime were highest.[31] The Western Areas with their comparatively light influx controls would have attracted unemployed workers from the British protectorates. Members of this lumpenproletariat employed various survival strategies. Brewing was extremely important for single women with no means of support. It could be quite rewarding: one woman in 1951 claimed she was able to earn £40 a month from brewing.[32] It was forbidden by the authorities who derived a substantial income from their beer monopoly but this stricture was energetically resisted. In 1939 an almost total boycott of the Western Native Township beerhall was organised. Another lumpenproletariat response to material conditions was gangsterism. The Western Areas also provided opportunities for prostitution, gambling, casual craftwork and hawking, which, given the absence of municipal regulation and the geographical situation of the suburbs, were rather more yielding than elsewhere.

These social categories should be seen as fluid and blurred at the edges. Landlordism could embrace people drawn from both working-class and petty-bourgeois occupations. The lumpenproletariat would expand and contract with economic fluctuations. Complicating and cross-cutting class alignments were other perceived distinctions. For example, Indian and Chinese shopkeepers were usually the first to have their properties looted in the event of riots (though African traders might have fared equally badly had they been as obviously prosperous).[33] Certain Basotho inhabitants had organised themselves into gangs known as 'The Russians'. With their extortive protection rackets they earned for Basotho in general an undeserved reputation for anti-social violence.[34]

The Western Areas had a rich range of organisations and less formal associations to express all these interests. African landlords, from 1926, advanced their cause through the Non-European Ratepayers' Association. Property owners were prominent within the higher echelons of the local ANC branch: Simon Tyeku, chairman of Sophiatown ANC in 1955, was a landlord and coal merchant.[35] Other important local ANC leaders included J. D. Matlou, an insurance land agent, and, of course, A. B. Xuma. But it would be incorrect to view the ANC in this area as being totally dominated by businessmen and landlords. The post-war years had witnessed the infusion of men and women with backgrounds of trades union experience, community protest and revolutionary politics. In the Western Native Township, for example, P. Q. Vundla and H. Nkadimeng were politically influential, both members of the ANC and the local Advisory Board, Vundla in addition being the chairman of the Western Areas ANC region. Vundla had also been a full-time organiser for the African Mineworkers' Union, whereas Nkadimeng was in 1950 secretary of the Transvaal Municipal African Workers' Union and a member of the Communist Party. In Newclare, the ANC was led in the early fifties by J. B. Marks, one of the most important Communist politicians before 1950 and a founder of the African Mineworkers' Union. The ANC was well organised in Sophiatown with about 1 700 members grouped in cells along the lines of the M Plan.[36]

Besides the ANC, until 1950, the Communist Party enjoyed some influence in the area, chiefly through its night-schools, though it had also been involved in a short-lived Newclare Tenants' League and more recently, in 1949, a tram boycott. There were groups like the Coffee Carts' Association, formed to protect the interests of street vendors who were being squeezed out of business by café-owners.[37] And finally there were the gangs, huge and sometimes well-armed street armies with exotic names.

Association and organisation were symptoms of the cohesion and vitality of social life in Sophiatown. But for people who lived in the crowded conditions of the back yards the essential quality of life in the Western Areas, the one they miss most today, was neighbourliness. There was no privacy, families would play out their individual dramas on a densely inhabited stage, each with the advice, sympathy, interference and interest of everybody else. Certainly, the freehold townships were uncomfortable and often violent places to live in, but they were also characterised by mutual aid, interdependence and solidarity which would extend to the most ordinary (and therefore the most important) details of everyday life.[38]

Notwithstanding their virtues as far as their inhabitants were concerned, the Western Areas had for a long time been disliked by different groups within Johannesburg's white population: the history of attempts to destroy these suburbs dates back to 1932. André Proctor, in his history of pre-war Sophiatown, has argued how the sectional interests opposed to its existence, while vociferous in City Council debates, were unable to outweigh in importance the labour supply and reproduction requirements of ascendant manufacturing interests.[39] Despite City Council resolutions concerning the Western Areas in 1937, 1939 and 1944, the Minister of Native Affairs on each occasion excused himself and his department from taking action: the £4 000 000 estimated cost of providing alternative black accommodation was an expense the wartime administration would not contemplate, nor was it in the mood to gratuitously antagonise African politicians or an increasingly militant black workforce.

After 1948 different considerations prevailed. Now there was in power a government for whom a major preoccupation was the reallocation of labour between mining, manufacturing and agriculture. This involved tighter restrictions on the flow of workers and their families into the cities and increased state intervention in housing through levies on commerce and industry.[40] The corollary of this was that the government no longer accepted that places like Sophiatown were serving a useful function. Indeed their lack of effective controls and their congestion made them obviously attractive to those people intent on evading the more stringently applied pass laws. But these could not have been the only considerations influencing the government to take a fresh interest in removal schemes. Action against other African freehold areas was to be delayed for another decade. What particular characteristics of Sophiatown and its neighbours made their removal appear so important?

The point was, surely, that the Western Areas were perceived to be hotbeds of African resistance, in the words of the Native Affairs Commission, 'for many years a source of difficulty'.[41] Their recent history indicated reasons for the government's alarm. In late 1949, after the municipality had (against ministerial advice) announced an increase in tram fares from Sophiatown, a boycott of the service was organised. An Anti-Tram Fare Action Committee was established which planned a protest march into the city on the first day of the fare rise. Because of a massive police presence the march did not take place but the boycott was to be effective for over two months. It culminated in open battle between boycotters and police on the evening of 1 November after an incoming tram carrying one female passenger had been stoned. Then, three months later, fighting again broke out when on 29 January police attempted to arrest a man who was carrying a four-gallon tin of illegal liquor. On this occasion the crowd which immediately assembled compelled the police to abandon their prisoner and retreat. On returning with reinforcements they were confronted by 200 people who began stoning them and, according to the government report, firing guns. Newclare railway station was also stoned and the rioters barricaded Hamilton Street. A white man driving a jeep was stopped. After having surrendered his revolver and his cargo of vegetables, he was beaten up and told 'Jy stem most vir Malan en dus ook vir Apartheid' (You vote for Malan and therefore for Apartheid). Cars driven by Africans were also attacked. After two hours the police managed to clear the streets with tear gas.[42]

This produced only a short interruption in the unrest for on 14 February a similar outbreak took place in Newclare. This time the catalyst was the evening arrest of a pass offender. The man struggled to free himself, and attracted the attention of a crowd. The ensuing riot lasted until the following day. Again it featured road blocks and stoning of cars, though on this occasion African drivers were warned so they could turn off into side streets. Street lamps were stoned to make things more difficult for the police. On the second day several Asian-owned shops were set on fire. Roadblocks hampered the entry of fire engines and firemen's hoses were uncoupled.[43]

The fourth outbreak of popular violence in six months was the most serious. In March the ANC, the Communist Party and the Transvaal Indian Congress called for a general stay-away from work on May 1st. This was in protest against bannings imposed on J. B. Marks, Moses Kotane and Yusuf Dadoo. The strike was also to lend weight to a call for higher wages. Not surprisingly, given J. B. Marks' prominence locally, the call had a considerable impact in the Western Areas. Tension between policemen and strikers led to shooting. A total of thirteen people were killed. In Sophiatown, several hundred men armed with sticks massed in Good Street in the morning. The police managed to disperse this crowd which melted into the side streets only to regroup at street corners to stone the troop-carriers in which the police were patrolling. One of these vehicles stopped and the police leapt out firing their guns, killing one person and leaving another near to death. Events then followed in the now almost ritualised sequence: groups at each end of the stretch of Main Road running through Sophiatown stoning cars, attacks on police patrols, a lull towards the evening and then the destruction of street lamps accompanied by looting of local shops and cafés. And throughout one could hear the harsh clang of the metal columns of the street lamps as they were struck by iron bars to warn of the arrival of police.[44]

There is room here only for a superficial inquiry into the underlying causes of these disturbances. Each arose from an incident involving an issue which concerned everyday matters of tremendous importance. In the case of the first this was transport costs; in the second, liquor, for many people a major source of income; in the third, increasingly repressive pass laws; and finally, the May Day demonstrations were in part a response to low wages. Another common feature is that with the exception of the last, each riot was a spontaneous reaction to police provocation. Finally there was the discriminating nature of the rioters' behaviour: the attempt to warn African drivers so that they would not be stoned; the victimisation of Asian shopkeepers; the expressed political motivation of those who assaulted the white jeep driver in Hamilton Street; the systematic character of the rioters' actions. With these points in mind, there is a strong case for arguing that the riots were a spontaneous manifestation of the antagonism that existed between an impoverished but experienced working class and the agents of external authority and exploitation.[45]

But an understanding of these events would be incomplete without any reference to the activities of the gangs in the Western Areas. For the gangs, huge and sometimes fearsomely armed street armies, were the first to resist any unwelcome incursions into what they regarded as their legitimate territory.

In the historiography of black South African resistance the rôle of criminal gangs has been largely ignored. This is due to the traditional focus on institutionalised forms of opposition and also the ostensibly apolitical character of gangsterism. Recently, historians, concerned with the documentation of informal manifestations of class consciousness, have begun to pay attention to criminality. Charles van Onselen, in his study of the responses of Johannesburg domestic servants, describes the *Amalaita* gangs, which 'sought to give its members who laboured in alienated colonised isolation a sense of purpose and dignity'.[46] Don Pinnock, in his analysis of gangs in Cape Town's District Six,[47] also views gangsterism as an activity in which an especially rightless group could assert its identity. Crime was first and foremost a class response to oppression and gangs were regiments in a 'lumpenproletariat army at war against privilege'.

It is in a Fanonist adaptation of Hobsbawm's social bandit that these groups have been assigned a role. In its idealised form this would imply an outlaw group viewed as criminals by the state but perceived by their own society as champions, avengers and fighters for justice. This would have the corollary that such men would not prey on their own community.[48]

How well does this model fit the Sophiatown gangs? The question has a general importance because it was popularly recognised that Sophiatown was the centre of gangland activity and the incubator of more gangs than any other single township or location.[49] The period 1944–9 witnessed a 20 per cent increase in the incidence of violent crime in Johannesburg. Though there was no comparable dramatic increase in the rate of African unemployment it seems sensible to assume that unemployment was one of the underlying causes of this increase. In 1951 there were about 20 000 African teenagers in the city who were neither at school nor in regular employment. School-leavers found it especially difficult to find jobs because employers were unwilling apparently to employ educated blacks if the job's requirements did not include literacy.[50] African wages were no longer rising as fast as they had during the war and actually declined in real terms after 1948.[51] Such details provide a useful background for an understanding of why gangsterism was so prevalent in Sophiatown after the war.

Gangs often had different characteristics and habits. Of the Sophiatown adult gangs, the Gestapo, the Berliners and the Americans were the most famous. In addition there were the child gangs of which the best organised was the Vultures. The Gestapo grew out of a group of boxers who trained during the week and who would compete with each other over the weekend to see how many people each could knock out. They were led by a professional fighter and they do not seem to have attached much importance to crimes against property. Much of their energy was expended in defending their territory and women against the invasions of their rivals, the Berliners.[52]

The Berliners, in addition to defending their territory, were preoccupied with small-scale crime, in particular wage-packet robberies. The Berliners were comparatively well armed, reputedly with .303 rifles brought back by soldiers from the war.[53]

The Americans were formed a few years later. For a time they were led by a man known as 'Kort Boy', who after arriving from Benoni in the late 1930s had joined the army for the duration of the war. The Americans did not prey on the Sophiatown community[54] – of all the gangs they were the most interested in large-scale crime. They would steal from city shops but their favourite target was the railway delivery trailers. The Americans were flashy: they were smart dressers, they were reputed to go out with the prettiest girls, and some of them even drove round in large expensive imported cars.[55]

The Vultures, a huge child gang, was started in 1950 by Don Mattera, the offspring of a Tswana mother and an Italian/Griqua father. Don's father was a gambler but his grandfather was one of the wealthier men in Sophiatown – the owner of a substantial property and, until the mid-1940s, a bus company. The Vultures began, like many children's gangs, round a single 'strongman' figure who could offer protection against bullies, and it was based in Curtis Street where Mattera lived. It developed partly in conscious imitation of the adult gangs, but was also inspired by the cinema: its name, indeed, was derived from a film called 'Where no vultures fly'. Like their older colleagues, the Vultures profited from protection rackets, first based on rich school-children, later drawing upon the resources of Indian traders. Like the Berliners, the Vultures' main concern was with territoriality; like the Berliners they sometimes possessed firearms, but unlike them the Vultures did not feed upon the community indiscriminately.

These gangs were frequently very large, often had a quasi-military structure and in addition to their internecine conflict they were to be found in the vanguard of any communal confrontation with the police. Mattera recollects that the Berliners played a prominent rôle in the riots during the tram boycott. The commission of inquiry also attributed to the 'tsotsi organisations' a major responsibility for the attacks on the police in the disturbances of 1949 and 1950.[56]

How did gangsters perceive their own actions? Mattero says quite simply: 'It was like Robin Hood.' E. R. G. Keswa, a prison official, recalls: 'I often heard prisoners boast that they did not steal from fellow blacks . . . I overheard prisoners singling for ridicule a prisoner who was in prison for committing an offence against another black.'[57] The gangs were popularly characterised as marauders into the white city, as heroes; and it is clear that the glamour and ostentation of the gangster myth fulfilled an important function for both the participants and perhaps their immediate audience. As Mattera puts it: 'the boys could be somebody and society at that time did not help them to be somebody'.

Certainly some aspects of Sophiatown gangsterism conform to the Hobsbawn model. Though it would be an exaggeration to assert that the working-class community saw gangs as fighters for social justice, nevertheless it was popularly believed that gangs 'seldom harm ordinary folk'.[58] Most of their noninternecine violence was directed at universally disliked people: the more prosperous traders, the South African Police and the municipal 'Blackjacks'. Gangsterism could not right wrongs nor remedy injustice. But it could provide a sense of identity for the gangsters, and more vicariously, a heroic mythology for the community from which it sprung. Like social bandits, the gangsters were constrained by their individualism, their limited social vision, and their lack of an ideology. Occasionally political forces sought to employ them: Mattera remembers the time of the 1957 bus boycott when both the Berliners and the Vultures were being offered payment simultaneously by the bus company, PUTCO, and the ANC. The gangs profited both ways: they would take PUTCO's money and ride the buses in the evenings wearing woollen balaclavas, and be the first to turn up the next morning to add their weight to the boycotters' picket at the bus terminal. Nobody could control them; their path was dictated by their own preoccupations.

Nevertheless, for all their limitations, the gangsters must have been a source of considerable anxiety to the authorities. They presented an anarchic, violent and elusive current of resistance which lay beyond the capacity of the state to control, co-opt, or suppress. Their concentration in Sophiatown and neighbouring suburbs was no accident. Such places, with their proximity to the white metropolis, their relative freedom from administration, and their cluster of informal sector opportunities, offered the gangsters the best terrain for survival and prosperity. For this reason alone the destruction of the Western Areas would have served the state well.

The government opened its campaign for the removal of the Western Areas in 1950. On 17 February a meeting was held between Native Affairs Department representatives and the Chairman of the Council's Non-European Affairs Department. At this meeting the position of the Council was outlined. It was prepared to implement any removal scheme decided upon, but only if the government provided the necessary funds.[59]

In March 1951 the Minister of Native Affairs announced that 'Black Spots' in the Western Areas were going to be cleared. By April 1952 a slightly embarrassed City Council was claiming to African ratepayers that it had no responsibility for the scheme which was going to be financed by the government. This contradicted an earlier announcement that the council would assume responsibility for the removals. A joint City Council/government committee was established and this reported in 1952, blandly recommending the movement of all Africans from Sophiatown, Martindale and Newclare, to Meadowlands, an empty stretch of land next to Orlando, fifteen miles away from the centre of Johannesburg.[60] The council added a rider to its recommendations: those who desired it should be allowed to buy land in Meadowlands on a freehold basis.[61] However, the council was swift to absolve itself of any further responsibility for determining the course of events. In early 1953 it sold Meadowlands to the government, placing the latter in a position in which it had complete freedom to dictate the terms of any settlement.

Having accomplished this manoeuvre, the municipality could now afford the luxury of indulgence in moral condemnation. Indeed in terms of municipal politics this was increasingly expedient as the Institute of Race Relations, various churches and a hastily convened Western Areas Protest Committee under the chairmanship of Father Huddlestone were beginning to exert considerable moral pressure on the council. There was after all a glaring inconsistency between, on the one hand, rehousing the Western Areas' inhabitants, many of whom lived in perfectly good houses, whilst on the other, continuing to tolerate the dreadful conditions that the squatters in Moroka Emergency Camp had to endure.[62] And so, in late 1953, the Johannesburg City Council announced it would no longer cooperate with the government.[63] Unperturbed, the minister established a new local authority, the Western Areas Resettlement Board. Original ideas that Meadowlands would function as a site-and-service scheme were dropped: in late 1954 the first houses began to be constructed under the watchful eyes of a police detachment placed there to ensure they would not be occupied by the squatters of neighbouring Moroka. The state loaned the Board £850 000 and promised it a further one million pounds for the following financial year. Such munificence should have deceived no one. Rentals from Meadowlands would finance the interest on these loans, while the profits realised from the sale of former African property would pay them off.[64] With all these preparations completed, the removals could begin. In the middle of January 1955, the first 152 families received their notices to quit the premises they were inhabiting by 12 February.

Though the state's intentions had been clear from 1951, concerted moves to oppose the removals only really started in 1953. Before then, the ANC had been preoccupied with the Defiance Campaign and it was left to the property owners, who had in 1951 formed an Action Committee, to carry on a desultory and unrewarding correspondence with first the Minister of Native Affairs, and later the council.[65]

By 1953, less sedate forces were busy. In June, shortly after the minister had made it clear that expropriated Africans would not be granted freehold elsewhere, a public meeting was held at Sophiatown's Odin Cinema. It was called by the provincial executive of the ANC as well as the Transvaal Indian Congress. It was attended by 1 200 people who agreed to oppose the removals. The police contributed to the proceedings by turning up in force, armed to the teeth, and arresting one of the main speakers, the Defiance Campaign leader, Yusuf Cachalia, whom they later released, having been unable to conceive of even the thinnest pretext for holding him. The Congresses then arranged a series of meetings in all the main Reef townships, to publicise the removals and link them with other more general issues such as the pass laws and the Group Areas Act in the hope of generating wider opposition. The Indian community was not neglected. This was a time when Indian-owned businesses were being forced out of central city areas under the terms of the Group Areas Act. Of the Transvaal Indian population, nearly two-thirds depended on commerce for their livelihood and consequently the expropriation of the Western Areas' traders would have been of profound significance.[66] In Sophiatown itself, the local ANC organised weekly meetings from this time onwards. On 22 August, the Institute of Race Relations held a conference attended by representatives from 51 organisations. In its findings, the Institute argued that African opposition to the removals was widespread and that their implementation would 'further undermine confidence in the faith and goodwill of Europeans' as well as creating a united and determined spirit of opposition.[67] The conference argued in favour of a slum clearance; it had no wish to protect rack-renting landlords.

The first indication that opposition to the scheme was neither as widespread nor as unanimous as the ANC assumed was shown at the Advisory Board's congress in January 1954. Here the delegates were officially informed by the Secretary of Native Affairs of the Meadowlands scheme. It was only the presence of ANC members amongst the delegates that ensured the congress's decision to oppose the removals.[68]

The next significant development was the intervention of the ANC's national executive in April 1954 when it resolved to take over from the provincial leadership the direction of opposition to the removals. One motive in doing this may have been the factional disarray within the Transvaal organisation: Africanists were said to be influential in two important Johannesburg branches, Orlando and Newclare, and could be counted upon to subvert the implementation of any decisions taken by the provincial leaders (particularly if the Indian Congress was involved).[69] But this is unlikely to have been the most important consideration. Subsequent events revealed no deep divisions within the Youth League in the Western Areas, and the main local organiser, Robert Resha, while loyal to the national executive, was nevertheless capable of evoking much the same sort of popular response as the Africanists. Probably much more important was the leadership's professed reason at the time. As the joint ANC/Indian Congresses' National Action Council put it:

> . . . examining the issues before the country it came to the conclusion that the proposed Western Areas removal scheme was the most ruthless and brutal of them all.[70]

The Congresses sensed that the government saw the removals as crucial in the implementation of apartheid, and if they could demonstrate its wider implications, opposition to the removals would serve as a catalyst to mobilisation elsewhere. It was hoped that, even in the event of failure, the campaign against removals would politicise a great many people.[71] It was this point in their analysis that brought the Congress leadership closest to the idealised revolutionary strategy referred to at the beginning of this chapter. More immediate considerations were also important in influencing the way in which the ANC's leadership viewed the issue. Some of the most important political leaders lived in the Western Areas and were sensitive to local disquiet. In addition, one of the largest and certainly the best-organised ANC branch existed in Sophiatown.

On 27 June a 'Resist Apartheid' conference was held in Johannesburg. The day was declared one of 'Solidarity with the Western Areas'. Chief Lutuli called for the enrolment of 50 000 'Freedom Volunteers'. Members of the audience carried placards bearing such legends as 'What about shops?' and 'What about transport?' and 'I like it where I am'. The emphasis on subsistence issues was significant; the ANC appeared to be distancing itself from the property owners. Earlier in the year the owners had arranged a meeting attended by 1 000 people. At this meeting the slogan 'We are not moving, we are not selling' was adopted and afterwards a statement was issued which included the following appeal:

> . . . the tenants as well must join hands with property owners as the scheme denies them any hope of future land ownership, security and responsibility.[72]

On 27 July the Ratepayers' Association also convened its own meeting in Sophiatown.[73] Some property owners, by nature conservative, would have been uneasy about the transformation of their cause into a major nationalist campaign. The tension that existed between some of the older middle-class Africans and the ANC was to surface early in 1956 in an open letter written by Dr Xuma to *The World* in which he attacked Congress, charging it with increasingly losing its African identity to outside influences.[74]

However, in 1954–5 these rifts were not particularly noticeable in the Western Areas branches of the ANC. Here, as we have seen, businessmen and property owners still retained influence. On the other hand, there were other men who did not have comparable vested interests: these included P. Q. Vundla and Robert Resha. One should remember also that in the second half of 1954 the government moved onto the offensive by imposing bans on many of the more important national and provincial politicians. This had the twofold effect of emasculating the organisational ability of Congress while making the influence of local leadership considerably more decisive than it would have been otherwise.

Now the national leadership seemed to have had a different conception from that held by local ANC activists of the form resistance should take. For example, E. P. Moretsele, president of the ANC in the Transvaal, said shortly before the first removals: 'There can be no talk of defiance in this matter.'[75] Oliver Tambo, defending Congress's role during the removals, argued: 'The Congress is not in a position of a gladiator.'[76] As P. Q. Vundla pointed out: 'While Congress policy on the Removal Question was to protest, the people of Sophiatown shouted "We won't move".'[77] Other observers were to accuse the

ANC leadership of having no appetite for confrontation.[78]

However, this mood of hesitation had not permeated down to the level of local organisation. Here the ANC seemed more resolute. Speeches by both Vundla and Resha are indicative of this:

P. Q. Vundla:

> Those who refuse to move will be brought before magistrates. Congress will engage legal representation to defend them.[79]

Robert Resha:

> You will have to fight the African drivers of the lorries . . . I stand here to ask you to defend your homes to the bitterest ends, to the last ditch.[80]

Robert Resha was a key figure in the campaign. He had recruited 500 Freedom Volunteers. They were intended to mobilise and discipline the resistance; they were to train like soldiers, though on no account to behave violently.[81] Resha's background was interesting. During the war he had worked on the mines and on being dismissed for political agitation he had worked as a freelance journalist. He was imprisoned during the Defiance Campaign. He had lived most of his life in Sophiatown. Resha was widely regarded as one of the most militant ANC politicians and his reputation for toughness extended even to the gangsters of Sophiatown.[82] This reputation was sustained by the tone and content of his public statements:

> . . . uneducated people wherever they are in this country know very well the oppressor is the white man. If you could give the Pedi firearms and tell them to use them they will come to shoot the Europeans without being told. But you give a revolver to an educated African. . . . He will say 'Thank you, now I am safe from Tsotsis' because we are taught at school that a European is a superior and our fathers were thieves.[83]

Resha was one of the first Congress politicians to try and bring gangs into the political arena. Mattera remembers him recruiting Vultures as leaflet distributers. A passage in one of his speeches was clearly directed at the gangster community. He advocated that in the days before the removals youth were

> . . . to stop playing dice, abusing women and going to the bioscope, for the next twelve days. The police know they are helpless to stop crime here in Sophiatown. . . . You must show them that the removals is uppermost in your minds . . . boycott pleasure.[84]

Though it seemed that local Congress organisers were determined to confront authority, there were signs that they were not altogether happy about the configuration of interests they were attempting to defend. Certainly they could point to the material disadvantages of living in Meadowlands: the tighter controls and the insecurity of tenure;[85] the possibility that not all Western

Areas residents would be allowed to remain in Johannesburg;[86] the increased expenditure on rents and transport; the difficulties that people dependent on the informal sector would encounter.[87] But the local ANC branches, reflecting as they did a socially heterodox constituency, a composite of interests, could not afford to risk disunity by attacking the property owners or basing their stand only on tenants' concerns. J. J. Matlou, the branch organiser, appealed to tenants not to estrange themselves from landlords who were abusing their position by demanding key money and shutting off water to those who were behind with their rent payments. Congress would deal with such people when the struggle was over.[88] Resha was also very aware that some people viewed the prospect of occupying a house in Meadowlands with satisfaction. Certainly, there would no longer be exploitation by landlords, 'but these beautiful houses, do they belong to you?'; 'Even if you have a private tap and a private lavatory you cannot use it all day long.'[89] Again and again Congress spokesmen emphasised that now was not the time to bring up local conflicts of interest, that a united front was vital.[90] Congress insisted it was defending a right that had a universal significance:

> It doesn't matter how many Africans own land in Sophiatown. It doesn't matter if there is only one African landowner. The principle of the right of that one African is still at stake.[91]

Notwithstanding the complexity of the situation the ANC was vulnerable to the charge that it was defending privilege. When the Freedom Volunteers appeared in uniform on the streets for the first time during the evening of 7 February *The World* sourly reported that 'many of the volunteers were the sons and relatives of property owners'.

ANC plans seem to have included the following measures. On the 12th, a Saturday, everyone in the Western Areas should stay at home. People should not cooperate with any attempts to move them, though, as we have seen, there were different conceptions between national and branch levels as to what exactly non-cooperation involved. Both were agreed, however, that protest or resistance should be non-violent. In the case of the local activists this position was upheld despite considerable pressure. There was tension between local organisers and the young men who came into Sophiatown from other parts of the Reef demanding violent action against the authorities. Nor were all the violently disposed people from outside.[92] *Drum* reported that a section of Sophiatown's Youth League was flirting with the Berliners who were said to be trying to intimidate Congress into employing violence.[93] A high degree of local resolution would ensure that huge numbers of policemen would be needed to carry out the removals. Meanwhile Congress was to organise a stay-at-home throughout the Reef, beginning on the 14th, so as to make it as difficult as possible for the Government to concentrate its forces in the Western Areas.[94] But a full understanding of these plans was confined to the organisers: the strategy was to be publicised only on the day of the removals.[95]

The Congress scheme proved to be still-born. On 8 February a ban was placed on all public meetings in the Johannesburg area. The same day, the Resettlement Board announced that the removals would be advanced and would begin the next day, the 9th. Local organisers responded to this crisis by sending around Volunteers during the night to each threatened household and helping those who did not wish to be sent to Meadowlands to move their belongings into shelters on unaffected properties. Twenty-two families were helped in this fashion. Then there was silence broken only by the sound of eighty lorries and two thousand armed police moving into Sophiatown. There was no resistance of any sort. When the lorries departed with their human cargoes the demolition squads moved in. Only at 3 o'clock the following Monday morning was there to be a flicker of defiance when groups of youths ran along streets hitting the telegraph poles after a meeting of local Congress leaders decided to persist with their attempts to mount a general stay-away from work. But that morning the police were alert, arresting the pole-hitters and ensuring the buses left as usual with their full complement of passengers.[96] On 19 February the ANC tried to repeat their earlier manoeuvre when the second lot of families were removed. This time only one family was sheltered before forty Volunteers were arrested. The attempt to forestall the authorities was abandoned. By this stage the futility of these efforts was becoming obvious: of the families moved in the previous week by the ANC, fourteen had applied to the board for Meadowlands houses. A change in strategy was needed. Resha announced obliquely: 'We have our plans but we are not going to carry them out until a later stage when we think the time is opportune.'[97]

But this was the end of any attempts to organise mass resistance to the removals. *The World* of 26 March noted the first removals on the east side of Sophiatown. They were very quiet and unaffected residents took little notice. By July the minutes of a Sophiatown ANC Youth League meeting contained the admission that 'we have accepted the removals as routine' although they also stated that young people were 'dead scared' and were 'craving to have guns'.[98]

At this point the focus of resistance shifted from the tenants to the property owners. The Sophiatown Ratepayers' Association held a meeting to persuade all standholders to refuse to sell their properties to the Resettlement Board. By the end of March, 651 standholders in Sophiatown and Martindale had signed such an undertaking. From now on the struggle was confined to legalistic manoeuvres and its objectives were to become increasingly limited: by 1956 standholders were not challenging the principle of their deprivation of tenure but instead were trying to negotiate the fixed official values set on their property. Government strategy seems to have followed the lines of least resistance: first the tenants of non-African landlords were moved, then African traders who occupied stands owned by Indians and Chinese,[99] then in 1956 the tenants of African standholders, and finally, from 1957, the by then isolated African property owners.[100] Spreading the removals over a period of five years (the final resettlement of coloured inhabitants was complete only in 1960) also helped to dissipate any stronger currents of resistance.

Attempts to mobilise enthusiastic resistance to the Western Areas removals scheme failed. Congress organisers and their critics saw the failure in terms of a confusion of aims. As J. B. Marks pointed out, there were considerable flaws in the direction of the movement:

The people were given the impression that some last minute instruction would be issued. Those on whom resistance depended were in doubt as to what exactly they were expected to do.[101]

The assumption that there was sufficient unanimity concerning the removals has been challenged. For instance, *The World* reported Sophiatown sub-tenants as favouring the removals because of the higher standard of housing on offer at Meadowlands.[102] But the sub-tenants represented a small minority of the population. Sometimes they had to share single rooms with tenants and so it was not surprising that they would have been glad of the chance to obtain better accommodation. More serious are the charges that the organisers had lost touch with their popular constituency; that by and large there was little opposition to the move; that attitudes were determined largely by ownership or non-ownership of property; that the popular mood was apathetic rather than being vigorously opposed to the prospect of resettlement.[103]

Such contentions represent an oversimplification of a complex picture. The Western Areas offered a means of economic survival to a much larger group than just the landlords. Secondly, any analysis should recognise the fluidity and ambivalence of the social structure. A single household could embrace a landlord who nevertheless derived a major portion of his income from working in a factory, his wife, involved in brewing to supplement the family earnings,[104] their children, and finally perhaps, an unmarried lodger who would most likely be compelled to move into a hostel if he or she was not endorsed out of Johannesburg altogether. The observation that many of the Freedom Volunteers seemed to be the sons of property owners should not be taken too literally. For men and women who did not live with their families the removals represented a serious threat. All tenants were subject to a screening process before being sent to Meadowlands to ensure that only family units were housed there.[105] This helps to explain the desperation of young people as described in the Youth League minutes mentioned above, as well as the efforts by the Berliners to influence Congress in favour of violent confrontation. It was a fear that did inspire a discernable theme in speeches by Youth League spokesmen. Not everybody could go to Meadowlands, they insisted, there were homes there only for the servants (employees) of white people. For the others, the young unemployed and the illegally resident, labour camps were being constructed.[106]

The local ANC leaders showed an awareness of the latent social tensions within the community. Vundla's and Resha's constituency was not that of the privileged or the wealthy. These men were grass roots activists and they were in touch with some of the most alienated and underprivileged sections of the community.[107] ANC meetings were well attended and the months following the removals were to indicate no signs of declining local support. There is no convincing evidence to support the assertion that opposition to the removals was motivated mainly by elitist considerations. It seems fairer to argue that the ANC was caught in a web of social contradictions that reflected the situation of its petty-bourgeois national and local leadership. Elements in this group still had a material position to defend. Such people, because of their upbringing, their socialisation and their beliefs, were hardly going to relish the possibility of bloody confrontation with the state. Others were more prone to view society in starkly polarised terms; the implicit violence of Resha's speeches is indicative of this. Organisationally the ANC was too weak and under too much external pressure to risk internal disunity by bringing latent tensions out into the open. The Congress movement was changing, there can be no question of that, but its transition from an elitist to a popular movement was a complicated, gradual and often painful process.

But in the ultimate analysis, the decisive factor was the massive force the state was prepared to deploy to destroy Sophiatown. This was no slum clearance scheme. For years the Western Areas had been a strong centre of African resistance and its removal was too important a measure for the state to concede.

Notes

1 Joe Slovo, 'South Africa' in Basil Davidson, Joe Slovo and Anthony Wilkinson, *South Africa: the new politics of revolution*, Penguin, Harmondsworth, 1976, p. 167.
2 Dan O'Meara, 'The 1946 African Miners' Strike' in Philip Bonner (ed.), *Working Papers on South Africa*, University of the Witwatersrand, Johannesburg, 1977.
3 Edward Feit, 'Conflict and communication: an analysis of the "Western Areas" and "Bantu Education" campaigns', Ph.D. thesis, University of Michigan, 1965.
4 Treason Trial Record (original copy held by the South African Institute of Race Relations), p. 1169.
5 Bernard Magubane, *The Political Economy of Race and Class in South Africa*, Monthly Review Press, New York, 1979, p. 300.
6 Bernard Magubane, 'African opposition in South Africa', *The African Review*, (Dar es Salaam), ii, 3 (1972).
7 Slovo, 'South Africa', p. 126.
8 Slovo, 'South Africa', p. 167 and Magubane, *The Political Economy of Race and Class*, p. 304.
9 Stanley Trapido, 'South African in a comparative study of industrialisation', *Journal of Development Studies*, vii, 1970–1, p. 317.
10 See Belinda Bozzoli, 'A comment on capital and state in South Africa' in African Studies Institute, *Papers Presented at the African Studies Seminar During 1977*, University of the Witwatersrand, Johannesburg, n.d., p. 84.
11 I am indebted to André Proctor's 'Class struggle, segregation and the city: a history of Sophiatown, 1905–1940' in Belinda Bozzoli (ed.), *Labour, Townships and Protest*, Ravan, Johannesburg, 1979, for the points in the above two paragraphs.
12 Trevor Huddleston, *Naught for your Comfort*, Collins, London, 1956, pp. 121–2.
13 City of Johannesburg Non-European Affairs Department, *Report on a Sample Survey of the Native Population Residing in the Western Areas of Johannesburg*, 1951, mimeo, pp. 15–16. Henceforth referred to as *Sample Survey*.
14 City of Johannesburg Non-European Affairs Department, *Survey of the Western Areas of Johannesburg*, 1950, mimeo, p. 39. Henceforth referred to as *Survey*.
15 Conditions in Western Native Township are described by Marion Brindley in *Western Coloured Township: problem of an urban slum*, Ravan, Johannesburg, 1976.
16 Miriam Tlali, *Muriel at Metropolitan*, Ravan, Johannesburg, 1975, p. 70.
17 Essop Patel (ed.), *The World of Nat Nakasa*, Ravan, Johannesburg, 1975, p. 5.
18 *Survey*, 1950, p. 63. The survey was based on a questionnaire completed by nearly all heads of households in the freehold suburbs and Western Native Township.
19 *Ibid*, p. 50.
20 *Sample Survey*, 1951, p. 113.

21 *Survey*, 1950, p. 87 and p. 101.
22 *Sample Survey*, 1951, pp. 190–4.
23 *Ibid*, p. 166.
24 *Survey*, 1950, p. 63, and p. 194.
25 University of the Witwatersrand, Xuma Papers, ABX 520401, p. 8, Memorandum to the City Council on Western Areas Removal Scheme.
26 *Survey*, 1950, p. 68 and *Sample Survey*, 1951, p. 192.
27 *Survey*, 1950, p. 68.
28 *Sample Survey*, 1951, p. 110.
29 *Ibid*, p. 31.
30 *Ibid*, p. 125–32.
31 *Survey*, 1950, p. 17 and p. 27 and *Sample Survey*, 1951, pp. 183–4.
32 *Sample Survey*, 1951, p. 147
33 *Ibid*, p. 17, and Huddleston, *Naught for Your Comfort*, p. 102.
34 *Ibid*, pp. 102–6.
35 Gwendolyn Carter, Gail Gerhart and Thomas Karis, *From Protest to Challenge*, Volume IV, Hoover, Stanford, 1977, p. 163.
36 Feit, 'Conflict and communication', pp. 65–73.
37 Kathleen Vundla, *PQ: the story of P. Q. Vundla*, Moral Rearmament, Johannesburg, 1973, pp. 24–6.
38 All points made to be me in discussions with former Sophiatown residents in Johannesburg during November 1979.
39 Proctor, 'Class struggle, segregation and the city'.
40 See Richard de Villiers, 'The state, capital and labour allocation', *Africa Perspective* (Johannesburg), 12 (September 1979), pp. 29–30.
41 *Report of Native Affairs Commission*, 1 January 1948–31 December 1952, Pretoria, UG 36/1954.
42 For details of these riots see Union of South Africa, *Report of the Commission of Enquiry into Acts of Violence Committed by Natives at Krugersdorp, Newlands, Randfontein and Newclare*, Pretoria, UG 47/1950.
43 See *Rand Daily Mail* (Johannesburg), 14 February 1950 and *The Star* (Johannesburg), 14 February 1952.
44 *Rand Daily Mail*, 2 May 1950.
45 *Sample Survey* statistics suggest that most people living in Sophiatown were born in an urban area and lived on below-subsistence level incomes.
46 Charles van Onselen, *Studies in the Social and Economic History of the Witwatersrand*, Volume 2, *New Nineveh*, Longman, London, 1982, Chapter 1, 'The witches of Suburbia', pp. 1–41.
47 Don Pinnock, 'From Argie Boys to Skollie Gangsters: the lumpenproletariat challenge of the street corner armies of District Six', paper delivered at the University of Cape Town History Workshop Conference, 1979.
48 Eric Hobsbawm, *Bandits*, Penguin, Harmondsworth, 1969, Chapter 1.
49 'The Americans', *Drum* (Johannesburg), September 1954.
50 L. I. Venables, 'Report on crime in Johannesburg', in *Journal of Racial Affairs* (Stellenbosch), ii, 2 (January 1951), p. 5.
51 Rob Davies, *Capital, State and White Labour in South Africa*, Harvester Press, Brighton, 1979, p. 332.
52 Details of the Gestapo from 'The Americans' in *Drum*, September 1954.
53 *Ibid*, and author's interview with Don Mattera, Johannesburg, 28 October 1979.
54 Author's interview with Mattera. E. R. G. Keswa, 'Outlaw communities', unpublished dissertation, 1975, p. 44.
55 Author's interview with Mattera. *Drum*, September 1954.
56 Union of South Africa, *Report of the Commission of Enquiry into Acts of Violence . . .*, UG 47/1950, p. 10.

57 Keswa, 'Outlaw communities', p. 30.
58 Feature on the Torch gang, *Drum*, April 1955, p. 31.
59 University of the Witwatersrand, Xuma papers, ABX 520401, letter from Town Clerk to Dr A. B. Xuma, 1 April 1952.
60 SAIRR, *Annual Survey of Race Relations*, 1951–2, Johannesburg, 1952, p. 43.
61 SAIRR, *Annual Survey of Race Relations*, 1952–3, Johannesburg, 1953, p. 57.
62 An inconsistency which was pointed out *inter alia* by the ratepayers in a memo. to the Joint Committee; see Xuma papers, ABX 521008, p. 3.
63 Huddleston, *Naught for Your Comfort*, p. 189.
64 SAIRR, *Annual Survey of Race Relations*, 1954–5, Johannesburg, 1955, p. 95.
65 See Xuma papers, ABX 510531 and 510613.
66 Muriel Horrell, *Group Areas: the emerging significance*, SAIRR, Johannesburg, 1966, p. 93.
67 South African Institute of Race Relations memorandum, RR 131/1953.
68 University of the Witwatersrand, Hoernlé papers, Urban Affairs, AD 843 B4 2, handwritten report by W. B. Ngakane.
69 Feit, 'Conflict and communication', pp. 97–8.
70 *Ibid*, p. 97.
71 *Ibid*, p. 98.
72 Xuma papers, ABX 540321.
73 Xuma papers, ABX 540627.
74 *The World* (Johannesburg), 28 January 1956.
75 'What will happen in the Western Areas?', *Drum*, February 1955, p. 17.
76 'How yellow is Congress?', *Drum*, May 1955, p. 27.
77 'Masterpiece in bronze', *Drum*, January 1956, p. 59.
78 See University of York, Patrick Duncan papers, PD 5 45 15 and PD 5 45 39.
79 Freedom Square Congress meeting reported in *Bantu World*, 22 January 1955.
80 Robert Resha in Treason Trial Record, p. 7492. See also 'ANC decided on Mahatma Gandhi type resistance' in *Bantu World*, 5 February 1955.
81 Treason Trial Record, p. 1202 and p. 7498.
82 Author's interview with Don Mattera.
83 Treason Trial Record, p. 2479.
84 *Ibid*, p. 7489.
85 *Ibid*, p. 7472.
86 *Ibid*, p. 7500.
87 *Ibid*, p. 7492.
88 *Bantu World*, 12 February 1955.
89 Treason Trial Record, p. 7484 and p. 7500.
90 See, for example, 'Vundla at property owners' meeting' in *Bantu World*, 26 February 1955.
91 *Bantu World*, 'Vundla's call to Africans', 12 February 1955.
92 *Bantu World*, 19 February 1955.
93 *Drum*, June 1955.
94 Feit, 'Conflict and communication', pp. 126–32.
95 *Bantu World*, 22 January 1955.
96 Anthony Sampson, *Drum: adventure into the new Africa*, Heinemann, London, 1956, pp. 236–9.
97 *The World*, 22 February 1958.
98 Treason Trial Record, p. 1289.
99 *The World*, 3 December 1956.
100 *The World*, 27 July 1957.
101 *Fighting Talk* (Johannesburg), April 1955.
102 See *Bantu World*, 22 January 1955 and 19 February 1955.

103 Feit, 'Conflict and communication', see especially chapters 1, 2, and 9.
104 Author's interview with William Letlalo, Soweto, 10 December 1979.
105 *The World*, 27 July 1957.
106 Treason Trial Record, p. 7492.
107 Both men had trade union experience with some of the most underprivileged members of the workforce, the migrant mineworkers. Neither was wealthy, even in relative terms. Vundla, in his capacity as an Advisory Board member, used to keep 'open house' so that all those people in any kind of difficulty could visit him. Also, though in rather a different way from Resha, Vundla had certain contacts with the gangster world and in later years was to play an important arbitration role in their internecine disputes.

Chapter 5

The parents' school boycott: the eastern Cape and East Rand townships, 1955

In 1955 the South African government assumed control over black education. The Bantu Education Act transferred responsibility for the administration of black education from the provincial authorities to a government department. The content of the syllabus, the employment of teachers, the admission of pupils – all previously matters over which schools themselves had a degree of autonomy in decision-making – were now subject to central authority.

The Bantu Education Act was vigorously opposed in the South African press, various public forums and by some white and many black opposition politicians. The opposition was ineffective in altering government policy and in many areas did not succeed in arousing much popular participation. In this chapter we will be looking at those instances in which opposition to Bantu Education *did* transform itself into a popular movement. This was particularly the case in the East Rand townships as well as, to a lesser extent, the eastern Cape urban centres and black rural communities. In tracing the local antecedents and history of this movement it is hoped the chapter will provide an understanding of the broader traditions of popular resistance in these places, as well as an appreciation of why these were stronger in some centres than in others. So, first of all, this chapter is about local history, with an especial concern for documenting some of the popular movements of the East Rand, a region hitherto unexplored by most researchers. Secondly, the intention is to identify education and the popular desire to participate in it – and have some control over it – as one of a range of issues which in the post-war period in South Africa struck a particular resonance with poor people; to see it as an issue which together with such concerns as the cost of transport, the price of food, the availability of housing, and freedom of movement, lay at the heart of mass political responses in those years.

Before 1955 most African schooling was run by missionary societies. Schools could qualify for state financial aid if they registered with the provincial education department. Registration required conforming to syllabuses laid down by the department but the day-to-day administration of the school was in the hands of a school manager or superintendent, usually a white missionary. Schools which did not receive a government subsidy determined their own syllabuses and trained their own teachers. As well as mission schools, in the

Transvaal there were 600 community schools, which had been built from funds supplied by the local community and matching government grants. In such cases control was in the hands of a superintendent employed by the province and advised by an elected parents' school committee. School syllabuses varied between provinces but were all specially written for African primary school-children though secondary school pupils followed the same curriculum as their white peers.[1]

Though the system included some justly prestigious schools, it had serious shortcomings. Being atrociously paid, teaching was not an attractive profession and many teachers were under-qualified. Mission control could be heavy-handed and paternalistic and resentment of it (especially at rural boarding institutions) would often boil over in fierce and destructive riots.[2] There was a vast imbalance in the number of primary and secondary schools. Until 1945 the system was seriously under-financed as expenditure depended on the level of revenues from African taxation. Finally, wartime industrialisation and its corollary, urbanisation, had contributed to fresh pressure on the educational system. By 1953 African school enrolment had risen by 300 000, or 50 per cent, since the war. Classrooms were crowded, teachers overworked, and parents desperate to get their children into schools already filled beyond capacity. The need for some form of public intervention was beyond dispute. The ANC's 'African claims' in 1943 had called for free compulsory education to be provided by the state,[3] and by 1949 800 of the 2 000 mission schools in the Transvaal had been placed under direct departmental control in response to the feelings of African parents.[4] Black communities themselves were willing to make considerable sacrifices, raising the money for extra teachers' salaries, classroom buildings, and equipment, as well as establishing their own independent schools. 'Shanty' secondary schools existed in 1948 in Orlando, Western Native Township, Brakpan and Atteridgeville.[5] In Alexandra, an independent primary school, Haile Selassie School, founded in 1950, was to play a significant role in the 1955 boycott.[6]

The Nationalist government accepted the need for intervention, though its first concern was not so much with meeting African educational needs, but rather in attempting to control the social consequences of educational expansion. Consequently its concern was to restructure rather than reform the system. Increasing numbers of literate job-seekers with basic clerical skills were being thrown into an employment market increasingly reluctant to absorb them. Crude sociological considerations were foremost in the minds of the policy-makers. In the words of Verwoerd, Minister of Native Affairs:

> . . . good racial relations are spoilt when the correct education is not given. Above all, good racial relations cannot exist when the education is given under the control of people who create wrong expectations on the part of the Native himself, if such people believe in a policy of equality, if, let me say, for example, a communist gives this training to Natives.[7]

It is doubtful that many missionaries had quite such egalitarian beliefs as Verwoerd attributed to them and certainly none were communists, and the government was to considerably underestimate the difficulties of instilling an ideology of subordination. Official thinking on African education was tendentious, naive, and brutally simple. In 1949 the Eiselen Commission was set up to produce a blueprint for 'Education for Natives as a Separate Race'. Its report was published in 1951. Its 'guiding principles' included the reconstruction and adaption to modern requirements of 'Bantu culture', the centralisation of control, the harmony of schools and 'Bantu social institutions', increased use of African languages and personnel, increased community involvement in education through parents' committees, efficient use of funds, and an increased expenditure on mass education. Black social expectations were to be orientated to the reserves ('there is no place for him in the European community above the level of certain forms of labour').[8] Community participation in partly elected committees and boards would serve to legitimise the system as well as giving neo-traditional 'Bantu Authorities' tighter control. Central dictation of syllabuses would ensure the production of skills appropriate to a subordinate role in the economy:

> A beginning [at the end of Standard II] should be made with the teaching of at least one official language on a purely utilitarian basis, i.e. as a medium of oral expression of thought to be used in contacts with the European sector of the population. Manipulative skills should be developed and where possible an interest in the soil and in the observation of natural phenomena stimulated.[9]

Cost per pupil would be lowered and expansion facilitated by the use of shorter daily sessions, the employment of under-qualified female assistants, and the pegging of the state financial contribution (the balance to be drawn from African taxation). As much as possible, post-primary schools were to be sited 'away from an urban environment' in the reserves.

In 1953 the Bantu Education Act was passed transferring direct control of education from the provinces to the Native Affairs Department. All schools had to be registered, all state-aided schools had to be staffed by government-trained teachers, and all would have to use official syllabuses. From 1957 mission schools could continue only if they registered – they would receive no subsidy. Syllabuses for primary schools outlined in 1954, though in operation only from 1956, stressed obedience, communal loyalty, ethnic and national diversity, the acceptance of allocated social roles, piety, and identification with rural culture.[10]

Superficially, the new order had some features which may have appeared attractive to some African parents. Access to education was to become a little easier and school boards and communities provided an illusion of local accountability. But to parents whose children were already at school (as opposed to those whose children were not) Bantu Education promised obvious disadvantages. Amongst these was the insistence on primary schoolchildren learning the fundamentals of both official languages (making it less easy to acquire proficiency in the one, English, which was a minimum requirement for most white-collar employment). The shortening of primary school hours made life more difficult for working mothers, as did the closing down of nursery schools. School boards and committees were at best only partly elected – nominated members were likely to be unpopular (and in rural areas were compliant servants of local authorities). Fierce competition for elected places on such committees probably testified more to parental anxiety than approval of the system.[11] The rural and 'tribal' bias of proposed syllabuses would have been especially objectionable to parents in long-established urban communities. The linking of education with 'development' ensured its unpopularity with societies resisting government land 'rehabilitation' and 'stabilisation' schemes. Less apparent at the scheme's inception was that it was likely to impose increasing financial obligations on African communities. For example, a two-shilling monthly education levy was implemented on urban households,[12] while teacher:pupil ratios would increase,[13] per capita expenditure would decrease,[14] school meals services would be shut down and the abolition of caretakers' posts would make pupils responsible for school cleaning.[15] For an underprivileged society in which access to education provided the most common means of social mobility for one's children these were serious blows.

Popular involvement in educational issues considerably predated opposition to Bantu Education. In its most positive form, there had been a number of local African initiatives in starting schools entirely independent of external administration or finance. The shanty school movement of the Reef townships mentioned above is an example of this. Popular concern could take the form of resistance: for example in 1944 the Amalgamated Mission School in Brakpan was boycotted by the parents of some of its 900 African pupils. Mothers picketed the school's entrance and persuaded children to return home in protest against the dismissal by the Education Department of a politically active school-teacher (see below, p. 132).[16] This incident was not unique. In 1952 a parents' protest committee organised a boycott of Orlando High School after three teachers, who had publicly opposed the Eiselen recommendations, were sacked (see below, p. 120). The parents established a 'people's school' for boycotters. The protest committee was headed by the chairman of the local ANC branch, I. M. Maseko, and apparently gained wide local support. Less than a third of the pupils attended school in the two month long boycott. Parental indignation in this case was intensified by the venality of the local superintendent.[17] Political groups sometimes attempted to enhance their following through sharing popular educational concerns. The South African Communist Party's night school programme was a good example of this. Less well known was the ANC Youth League's establishment of a shanty school in Newclare to cater for children who had been refused admission at local schools through lack of accommodation[18] or the League's projected night school and literacy campaign in 1949.[19] There is evidence that in urban African communities at least, education was an issue evoking common interest and, at times, anxiety.

Not surprisingly, the earliest concerted resistance to Bantu Education proposals came from that group most directly affected and most sensitive to their implications – the teachers. Bantu Education, because of the 'Africanisation' of lower reaches of the inspectorate and the expansion of schools, did offer to teachers a slight improvement in promotion prospects. However, in many other respects the profession was to be degraded. Teachers would have to work a double session day with larger classes, employment qualifications would be lowered, salaries (it was made quite clear) would remain at their existing (and inadequate) levels, and teachers would be reduced to the level of state employees.[20] They would also be directly subordinated to the sometimes uneducated members of school boards which had the power to recommend their dismissal.[21] Verwoerd made little effort to conceal official hostility to the profession:

> The Bantu teachers must be integrated as an active agent in the process of the development of the Bantu community. He must learn not to feel above his community, with a consequent desire to become integrated into the life of the European community. He becomes frustrated and rebellious when this does take place, and he tries to make his community dissatisfied with such misdirected ambitions which are alien to his people.[22]

Teachers' opposition to Bantu Education came mainly from two sources: the Cape and Transvaal African Teachers' Associations (CATA and TATA).[23] Let us examine developments in the Cape first. Of all the different teachers' organisations CATA was the earliest to become politicised. In the Cape the Non-European Unity Movement, founded in 1943 and drawn principally from coloured teachers, took an interest in educational issues from its inception. The NEUM and a sister organisation, the Teachers' League of South Africa, were both affiliated to the All-African Convention (AAC), an organisation which had been transformed in the early 1940s by the departure from it of the ANC and the infusion into its leadership of a number of Marxist intellectuals. The AAC had originally been founded as a response to Hertzog's franchise and land legislation of 1936, and Marxists within its leadership differed from the more orthodox South African communists in their preoccupation with agrarian issues. The AAC consequently attempted to build a following among peasants in the Transkei and Ciskei (areas then rather neglected by other national organisations) through its immediate constituency, the teachers in the dense network of mission schools long established in the region. CATA affiliated to the AAC in 1948 and helped organise peasant resistance to the rehabilitation scheme.[24] The Transkeian teachers' faction of the AAC (W. M. Tsotsi, L. H. Sihlali, A. K. Manglu, M. Mbalo, Z. Mzimba, L. Mkentane, N. Honono et al.) later broke away from more theoretically purist Cape Town colleagues because they favoured redistribution of land on an individual private basis to the peasantry.[25]

The first serious instance of conflict between CATA and educational authorities came in 1950 when CATA, together with the AAC, attacked new provincial regulations aimed at easing overcrowding by imposing a quota system on schools, effectively excluding 30 000 pupils in the eastern Cape.[26] In 1952 CATA's annual conference condemned the Eiselen regulations, calling on its members to 'organise the people and explain to them the recommendations of the report', and the following year, in defiance of warnings from the authorities, 200 teachers met at Queenstown to discuss ways of resisting Bantu Education. This had been preceded by a well-attended public meeting in Langa, Cape Town, called jointly by CATA and the

Vigilance Association to protest against the proposed legislation.[27] CATA's attempts to mobilise public opinion were unusual for an African professional body. They were obviously influential, and the authorities' alarm at the teachers' agitation against land rehabilitation led to the closure of a school near East London in December 1953.[28] The following year, spurred by the introduction of double sessions in the Cape, CATA's annual conference called upon 'teachers and parents to do everything in their power to oppose the Herrenvolk schemes for their enslavement', although it was not very explicit as to what exactly should be done. The state responded to this opposition by withdrawing recognition from CATA and bestowing it on the newly established and supportive Cape African Teachers' Union (a similar process took place in the Transvaal); and having isolated the militants, ensuring their dismissal through the rural school boards[29] – largely composed of Bantu Authorities personnel and their supporters – as well as redundancies through especially strict application of higher teacher/pupil ratios.[30]

The militant stance of Cape teachers and the severity of departmental response should be understood in the context of the much wider struggle against land rehabilitation and the reorganisation of local government under Bantu Authorities, which took a particularly intense form in the Transkei and Ciskei.[31] Interestingly, teachers were not the only people to link Bantu Education with Bantu Authorities and rural 'development' programmes. In Cildara, in the Ciskei, the local Masizakite (acceptance) Assocation arranged a school competition to popularise Bantu Authorities and promote the substitution of academic with manual subjects.[32]

It should be noted that teachers in rural communities during the 1950s were potentially the natural leaders of opposition to authority. First of all they were educated men in societies which placed a high premium on education.[33] Secondly, they were men with no formal power, as well as being badly paid; there was little to set them apart from the rest of the community. Thirdly, the Bantu Authority and school board systems, which elevated traditionalist (and hence often illiterate) leaders to greater power, confronted teachers with a direct threat to their security and status. When teachers were politically motivated, they could be a very important element in rural opposition movements and it is no coincidence that the Bantu Education boycott movement (see below) had its most significant rural impact in the eastern Cape and adjoining reserves.

The Transvaal African Teachers' Association (TATA), in contrast to CATA, was a primarily urban-based organisation. African teachers on the Witwatersrand had been very sharply affected by wartime price rises – TATA's journal the *Good Shepherd*, complained in 1942 that Johannesburg domestic servants could earn more than a female teacher – and in 1944 teachers had demonstrated for higher salaries in the streets of Johannesburg.[34] Through its partially successful campaign over salaries, TATA became a dominant, and in some cases a politicising, force among Transvaal African teachers.

By the end of the decade some of TATA's leaders were tending to identify with the militant assertion taking place in African politics at the time. An editorial in the *Good Shepherd* in 1949, taking its cue from Z. K. Matthews, called for the formation of an 'African Association' 'for the purpose of keeping our heroes remembered'.[35] One year later TATA's Rand District Conference was addressed by G. M. Pitje of the ANC Youth League (ANCYL) who informed his audience that 'God placed Africans in Africa, Europeans in Europe, Asiatics in Asia'.[36] In 1954 Pitje was to become editor of the *Good Shepherd*. The ANCYL's Africanism, though, was only one of several influences affecting the political outlook of Transvaal teachers. Eskia Mphahlele attributes to the AAC considerably more appeal at the time. Young intellectuals and junior teachers in the Orlando branch of TATA also tried to persuade their branch to take some stand in respect of the May Day strike which the ANC and the Communist Party were organising in protest against the Suppression of Communism Act.[37]

However, unlike its sister organisation in the Cape, TATA never linked educational issues with broader concerns and it resisted calls by some of its members for a similar political affiliation to CATA's.[38] It was, though, forthright in its condemnation of Bantu Education, its journal summing up the purpose of the scheme quite succinctly:

> It [the government commission] wants to find out how it can give the African the training necessary to make him an efficient worker, without giving him any real education, for the simple reason that it would be dangerous if the oppressed sector of the population were sufficiently advanced to fight for their freedom.[39]

A group of Orlando teachers, who were elected to leading positions on the TATA executive in 1951, began to campaign quite effectively along the Reef, organising meetings of teachers and parents to explain and condemn the findings of the Eiselen Commission. Matters came to a head when the Transvaal Chief Inspector of Education was heckled at a prize-giving ceremony. The principal reported the teachers he suspected of organising the students to the department and they were later sacked. The success of the ensuing boycott (mentioned above) is testimony to their effectiveness in arousing parental concern at the threatened changes.[40] From 1952 TATA began organising anti-Bantu Education teachers' conferences in Johannesburg and the East Rand and attempted to set up or revitalise parent/teacher associations, so as to lend some popular weight to resistance to Bantu Education. However, progress was slow and by late 1954 these had been formed only in Johannesburg's South-West Townships, Lady Selborne and the East Rand.[41] At least one of the parent/teacher associations demonstrated the trend of local feeling when, in February 1954, 500 people at a Moroka-Jabavu PTA meeting called for a boycott of schools in the near future.[42]

Compared to Cape teachers, the opposition to the Bantu Education Act demonstrated by Transvaal teachers was less widespread. Relatively few Transvaal teachers suffered dismissal from their jobs as the consequence of criticism of the authorities. Unlike their Cape colleagues, Transvaal teachers were subjected from 1950 to a strict provincial prohibition on political activity. Nor did the ANC (unlike the Cape-based organisation) interest itself in the preoccupations of teachers in the early 1950s.[43] Nevertheless, in the links they did establish with parents through the associations in Johannesburg and the East Rand, their activity forms an important part of the backdrop to the communal boycott of schools that took place in those areas and to which we now turn.

The conception and preparation of the ANC's campaign to resist Bantu Education has been the subject of one monograph as well as detailed treatment in Karis and Carter's documentary collection.[44] The ANC's approach to the issue was characterised by uncertainty and disagreement between different sections of the leadership and between leaders and rank and file. The decision to oppose Bantu Education was taken shortly after the passage of the Act, when the ANC announced the launching of a 'Resist Apartheid Campaign' in May 1954, which included the Bantu Education Act amongst its six issues.[45] Concrete plans for resistance emerged only at the ANC's annual conference held at Durban in December 1954. Here the national executive recommended the withdrawal of children from schools for a week. At the same time, the executive noted in its report that 'progress on Bantu Education was very slow in all provinces'.[46] However, the conference itself overruled the executive, resolving in favour of an indefinite boycott, timed to begin on 1 April (the date of the administrative transfer of schools). It was decided that local organisation for the boycott should be in the hands of the Women's and Youth Leagues.

Preparations in the Transvaal began quite buoyantly with the Youth League organising a meeting in Sophiatown in early January, which called for 1 000 volunteer teachers to provide alternative educational facilities. At the same time the Transvaal Youth League established a number of local 'anti-Bantu Education committees'.[47] By February, though, the initial caution of national leaders was beginning to reassert itself. A national executive committee meeting held in Durban on 5 March at the instigation of Chief Lutuli and Z. K. Matthews, agreed to postpone the boycott to an unspecified later date. Those who favoured this course were influenced by reports of the intimidation of teachers by the authorities, the announcement that the new syllabus would not be implemented until 1956 and the fact that 1 April was in any case during the Easter recess. They also felt preparations to be inadequate.[48] Such apprehensions were not limited to the more conservative leaders. The left-wing pro-Congress journal *Fighting Talk* pointed out in March: 'to imagine that the ANC has yet the power to bring about such a boycott in a few months would be totally unreal'. Instead of beginning the school boycott in April, the national executive decided that the ANC should take on the more modest task of mounting a boycott of school boards and committee elections.

This decision prompted open dissension. A special conference held in Sophiatown the following week reaffirmed the December decision. The Transvaal Youth League enjoyed the support of the Johannesburg-based members of the national executive committee (including Oliver Tambo) and to prevent a serious breach from taking place yet another conference was arranged. This was held in Port Elizabeth on 9 and 10 April, the weekend before schools were due to open.[49]

The 700 delegates, drawn from all four organisations of the Congress alliance, as well as two delegates from the Liberal Party, eventually decided on a compromise. In principle, it was agreed government schools should be boycotted indefinitely. The date for the initiation of this boycott should be left to the national executive to decide. If any area had completed its preparations (including the provision of alternative facilities) before that date then, with the permission of the national executive, it could begin its local boycott. Meanwhile the ANC was to discourage participation in school committees and boards. The national executive would establish a national educational council which would make provision for a network of cultural clubs providing informal education.[50] The mood of a majority of the delegates was in favour of immediate action, and a proposal to limit the boycott for a trial period to the Port Elizabeth area was decisively rejected.[51]

The underlying tensions within Congress which are reflected in these hesitations and compromises are not a major theme of this chapter. In brief, they were caused by the isolation of some members of the leadership from more activist branches as a result of bureaucratic inefficiency; the presence on the national executive of men who belonged to an older and less militant generation of African politicians; provincial and ideological rivalries; class considerations; and well-founded apprehension concerning Congress's organisational vigour.[52] They have been discussed extensively elsewhere. In this chapter our concern rather is to examine the local response to the ANC's boycott appeal and the reasons for its peculiar strength in certain areas. First, we will consider the area in which the boycott movement was to have its greatest impact: the townships along the Reef.

Reports of fairly energetic Youth League campaigning on the issue of Bantu Education begin to occur several months before April 1954, particularly in the Western Areas (Sophiatown, Newclare, and Western Native Townships) which were threatened by the government's removal scheme.[53] Despite regular rallies and street corner meetings, local politicians appeared to be a little disappointed by the public response. One spokesman pointed out at a Sophiatown meeting on 2 January: 'It is a pity that I see very little youth here, as they are the people directly affected [by Bantu Education].'[54] One month later there seems to have been little improvement: P. Q. Vundla, regional chairman, complained: 'your organisation [the ANCYL] is very important indeed; but it should be much stronger in this area'.[55] However, lack of interest amongst many young people did not appear to dampen the confidence of the organisers in Western Native Township:

> From 1 April is the time we must sit down and work and have our own schools. We have got well educated people like Dr Matthews, Mr Robert Resha, Mr P. Q. Vundla and Dr Conco to draft the syllabuses for the children.[56]

Outside the Western Areas, the most active centre appeared to be Benoni, and here there were indications from early on that the movement would receive substantial popular support. For example, in February the *Bantu World* reported 'growing feeling in Benoni against the Bantu Education Act'. A teacher was threatened at a women's prayer meeting and people were contributing generously to the branch chairman's fund-raising appeal.[57]

Another encouraging sign was the apparent popular antipathy to the new school committees which were being established under the Act: in early March noisy parents' meetings considered these in Roodepoort, Moroka, Jabavu and Sophiatown.[58] In Alexandra, too, there seemed to be plenty of enthusiasm, though here the branch was divided between those who accepted the need for alliance with non-African political groupings and the Africanists. The latter were led by the soon-to-be-expelled branch chairman, the flamboyant, bearded figure of Josias Madzunya, who used to address his audience as 'fellow slaves of Africa'. On Bantu Education the Africanist leader proclaimed 'they want to teach them that white people originated in Africa'.[59] Among Madzunya's opponents on the branch executive was J. J. Hadebe, a former teacher who was to play an important role in the boycott movement later on (see below).

With all this activity it is not surprising that the ANC national executive's decision in early March to postpone the boycott aroused considerable local discontent. On 13 March speakers at a meeting in Orlando proposed that there should be two ANC branches at Orlando – one in opposition to that which obeyed leadership directives. The former squatters' leader, Schreiner Baduza (not a Congress member), said: 'If I was a member of the Youth League I would say the leaders of the ANC are sellouts, and otherwise I would say "let us do away with Congress".' Another speaker concluded: 'Congress here is nothing. I am sure that the ANC members will do nothing about Bantu Education.'[60] In the case of Orlando he may have had a point – the branch was riddled by factional disputes and tended to be dominated by Africanists totally at odds with provincial and national leaders.

Elsewhere on the Rand branches ignored the national executive's postponement decision. In Benoni the ANC resolved to boycott as had been decided, though it amended the date for the inception of the boycott to Tuesday 12 April, the first day of school after the Easter holidays.[61] The meeting was addressed by both Robert Resha, national leader of the Youth League, and its Transvaal president, H. G. Makgoethi. A week later a well-attended gathering in Lady Selborne pledged its support for the boycott.[62] By the end of the month the Transvaal Youth League and even some of the older leaders were in open rebellion against the national executive. A 'Save our Children' conference in Orlando came out in favour of the boycott and several prominent individuals, including P. Q. Vundla and Bob Ngwendu (Transvaal ANC executive member), promised to withdraw their own children from school.[63]

As we have seen, this rank and file feeling forced the national leaders to reconsider and the Port Elizabeth conference gave a qualified assent to those areas which favoured an immediate withdrawal of school-children, subject to national executive approval in the case of each local movement. By this stage, however, branches were acting independently of any higher authority. On Tuesday 12 April children were withdrawn or stayed away from schools in Benoni, Germiston (and Katlehong), Brakpan and Alexandra. In Benoni, Youth League volunteers and mothers visited the ten primary schools in the Old Location and ordered all the children home.[64] In Germiston, events were more dramatic with ANC Youth League volunteers marching through the location streets at 3.30 a.m., shouting slogans and calling on children not to go to school. All school-children remained at home until the Congress branch announced that it had opened an 'independent school', rounded up the children and took them there.[65] In Katlehong, the new Germiston township, five miles away, 22 women were arrested after police stopped them from taking children out of school. There the local effectiveness of the boycott was to be enhanced as the result of the location's superintendent advising people to keep their children from school the following morning.[66] In Alexandra, the ANC branch canvassed houses through the night of the 11th and half the township's school-children stayed at home. In the case of Alexandra the provincial ANC president, E. P. Moretsele, attributed the main responsibility for the boycott to parents rather than the ANC.[67] The ANC was apparently anxious to dissociate itself from some rough behaviour, blaming intimidation of school-children on 'tsotsis'.[68]

In the days which followed the boycott movement was to widen considerably. By Wednesday 3 000 Brakpan children were out of school – the highest figure for any single location. In Germiston, parents marched with children in a procession. All Benoni and Germiston schools were empty and in Katlehong Township only 70 out of the 1 000-odd pupils at a community school attended.[69] On Thursday the Minister of Native Affairs announced that any school-children still absent by 25 April would receive no further education. The same day a march by women and children in Benoni was broken up by police. By the following Monday the boycott movement had penetrated Johannesburg with six primary schools in Western Native Township and Newclare abandoned by their 3 500 pupils after visits from Youth League youths and women.[70] The marches and processions continued more or less daily in the effective locations and became increasingly violent in nature. By the end of the week two unsuccessful attempts at arson had been staged against school buildings in Benoni and near Katlehong. On Friday the total number of children out of school exceeded 10 000 and the boycott, still strong in the original centres, had spread to Moroka/Jabavu schools in Soweto and to Sophiatown, though here disaffected parents sent their children, with the apparent approval of the ANC, to the newly established unregistered church school run by Anglican missionaries. Over the weekend, though, threats by the authorities were having an effect: in Western Native Township 1 000 parents resolved to return their children before Verwoerd's deadline. P. Q. Vundla, the most prominent local ANC leader, supported their decision – an action which was to earn him a beating-up by youth leaders and, later, expulsion from the ANC.

Notwithstanding Verwoerd's ultimatum, as well as criticism from conservative African politicians and the *Bantu World*, the third week of the boycott began with nearly 7 000 school-children absent and hence banned from further schooling. The most resilient boycott centres were Johannesburg's Western Native Township and Brakpan, where loudspeaker vans successfully exhorted parents to keep their children at home, and where a teacher's house was set alight.[71] In Brakpan, 1 300 children were expelled and in the Western Areas 2 000 were reported to be still out of school by the beginning of June.[72] In several townships schools were closed down permanently and the 116 redundant teachers sacked.[73]

The national organisation's reaction to these events was somewhat sluggish. The Transvaal-based working committee congratulated the boycotters in a circular dated 23 April and called for an intensification of the boycott for the next week.[74] However, unanimity within the national executive was achieved only a month later, on 21 May, when an ambitious three-phase campaign was announced. The boycott could no longer depend on 'haphazard and spasmodic efforts whose origin is unknown'. Phase one would involve an educative campaign; phase two, withdrawal of children in areas of readiness where alternative facilities had been prepared; and finally, total non-cooperation with all activities directly or indirectly connected with Bantu Education.[75]

A serious effort was made to improve 'alternative education' facilities with the establishment of the African Educational Movement at a meeting in Johannesburg on 23 May, attended by representatives from churches, the ANC and Congress of Democrats. The AEM, however, only began operating from the end of June (see below),[76] and meanwhile local Congress organisers ran illegal 'independent schools' in some of the centres; two of them, accommodating 300 children, were broken up by police in Alexandra in June.[77] Notwithstanding the courage and commitment of local activists, Congress branches were scarcely equipped to provide facilities for thousands of small children. Organisers made brave promises about Congress running private schools[78] but some parents in other townships were beginning to consider other options. In some areas the position of anti-boycotters was strengthened by the failure of the ANC leadership to provide branches with any solid support. A Brakpan school committee member informed the press:

> When the boycott started we called on the ANC members to tell us what the position was. We asked them what alternative plans there were for the children. They said there were none and they had no instructions from Head Office about that yet. In the meantime nothing would be done.[79]

In most of the affected locations local parent organisations tried to establish schools independently of ANC/AEM initiatives. In the Western Areas, by August 1955, the Matlehomola Private School had 950 children, almost half the total number of children affected by the bans. ANC officials had sounded out the school's secretary on the possibility of their serving on the school's committee. They had been told that before they could stand for election 'they must confess to their followers that they have changed and that they support the present system'.[80] AEM records mention independent schools in Orlando and Sophiatown, apparently not antagonistic to the ANC.[81] In Brakpan a school was opened in September 1955 by the Brakpan Civic Protection Society, a group which grew out of the Brakpan school committee mentioned above. There was stiff opposition from the ANC. The school was attended by only 230 pupils in contrast to the local ANC Cultural Club which attracted about 800 boycotters[82] – and many parents would have been unable to afford high fees. In Germiston there is no evidence of hostility between the ANC branch and any parents. Perhaps this was because here the ANC had succeeded in establishing, despite police interference, a proper school. The 380 children were taught by trained teachers who were Congress members and possibly because of this the school decided to legalise its status by applying for registration. Registration was refused on the grounds of a technicality but it was suspected that the department regarded it as a 'protest school'. The school reopened as a cultural club – within the limits of the law so long as no formal education was provided.[83] Similarly, there are no indications of a rift in Alexandra but here it was the dissident Africanists who were involved in a community school: the Haile Selassie School, which had existed over the previous five years, increased its enrolment by nearly 1 000 children. The AEM organiser (probably Hadebe) mentioned in a report that there were difficulties between him and the school because of the involvement of one H. S. Madzunya (Josias?) who was 'reluctant to work with a committee which has on it Europeans, Coloureds and Indians'. The report also mentions a 'dissatisfied element' amongst Haile Selassie's pupils and friction between parents and the school. This would not have been very large; the local cultural club formed partly from dissenchanted Haile Selaisse children had only 200 members. But like the Germiston school, Haile Selaisse failed in its bid for registration.[84]

How genuinely popular was the boycott movement in its local centres? Were the Congress branches reflecting local feeling or trying to dictate parental response to Bantu Education? This is difficult to assess as the available evidence is thin and patchy. The press, uniformly hostile to the boycott from its inception, reported the progress of various deputations from the affected locations which pleaded with the department for the admission of the expelled children (this was eventually granted over a two-year period). But such groups need not have been very representative of the whole community. Apart from the reports concerning tsotsis in Alexandra and an allegation from an obviously partisan Brakpan school committee member there were few accusations of intimidation of parents. The tension which appears to have developed in certain areas between the ANC and boycotters' parents might not have existed at the inception of the boycott: it was probably a result of worries over the quality of alternative educational options offered by the ANC as well as the increasing isolation of the movement. It seems a little unlikely that branches on their own initiative, with no encouragement from higher authority, would have imposed an unpopular policy on their own local constituency. Most telling of all, there are no signs of any apparent decline in ANC support in the East Rand. For example, in Natalspruit and Benoni, in the 1956 elections, the ANC won control of the location Advisory Boards.[85] In Brakpan, the Civic Protection Society, the main local critic of the school boycott, showed its true colours when in March 1956 it opposed a well-supported bus boycott led by the ANC and the Vigilance Committee. Obviously the society's leaders were well insulated from the concerns of most of the inhabitants of the location.[86]

The other area in which the boycott had some impact was in the eastern Cape, like the East Rand an area in which in the urban locations and townships Congress had a strong following. Here again the boycott movement appeared to suffer from a lack of central direction; the Cape-based members of the national executive were in any case unenthusiastic, and in general the boycott was much weaker than in the East Rand. Reports of preparations are sparse: a meeting in Korsten (Port Elizabeth's oldest location) in March, attended by 3 000 parents, called for action on 1 April in conformity with the December ANC resolution[87] and no less than six electoral meetings were held in Grahamstown by the authorities, all of which failed to persuade parents to choose a school committee. Their unwillingness to do so was attributed to Congress influence.[88] In the event, despite local rank and file feeling in favour of the boycott, evident at the Port Elizabeth conference in April, all the children attended school on 12 April. The next reported activity was in May when Port Elizabeth's New Brighton branch called for a regional boycott of schools from the 23rd. East London's ANC denied any knowledge of this decision. Apparently there had been leadership difficulties which left the local branch in total disarray.[89] In any case, in East London some ANC members had accepted positions on the new school committees.[90]

The Port Elizabeth boycott only slowly gathered impetus from the 23rd. There was a significant police presence that day and many parents escorted their children to school. Parental fears were probably aroused by Verwoerd's threat of instant dismissal of any school-children who participated, which precluded even a symbolic limited withdrawal. Despite a house-to-house canvass the day before there were no pickets outside schools.[91]

Despite this unpromising start the movement slowly gathered strength, particularly in the small rural towns and villages around Port Elizabeth.[92] The *Evening Post* reported a fairly effective primary school boycott in Kirkwood, the centre of a closely settled citrus-farming area.[93] ANC influence in this area may have been linked to the local strength of the Food and Canning Workers Union.

In Port Elizabeth and Uitenhage a second attempt to mount a boycott was made in July despite considerable opposition from sections of the location community. Clashes between police and some parents on the one hand and pickets of young men on the other occurred in both centres on the 18th, but despite these difficulties at the end of the first week in August Congress claimed that 1 700 children were staying away from schools in Port Elizabeth.[94] Altogether the boycott in the eastern Cape was to involve, according to the AEM, over 2 500 children from Uitenhage, New Brighton, Korsten, Kirkwood, Missionvale, Kleinvee, Kleinschool and Walmer location.[95]

It was a surprisingly light response when one remembers that the eastern Cape was the region most affected by the Defiance Campaign and an area in which the ANC and the trade union movement were comparatively strong and links between the two well developed. Part of the explanation lies in the deep cleavages between grass roots membership and a very cautious leadership still much more schooled in the pre-1950 liberal tradition in African politics than that which prevailed in the Transvaal. T. E. Tshunungwa, the ANC's 'national organiser', wrote in a revealing letter to Oliver Tambo:

> Well my duty here [in the eastern Cape] is to toe the line in the best interests of the organisation and to strictly confine the disputes and the differences to the officials and the organisation only and that masses should never know it was a mistake to carry out the boycott.[96]

Joe Matthews of the Youth League, writing to Walter Sisulu later that year, accused the Cape leaders of 'passivity', complaining that he was 'really fed up with the whole leadership'.[97]

The most sustained local reactions to Bantu Education in this area were encountered in the reserves, already, as we noted, the scene of some agitation by affiliates of the All-African Convention. The AAC opposed the school boycott as 'adventurist' (after all, had it been effective, many of the members would be without jobs) and confined its campaigning to opposing school committees and boards. Opposition to these institutions and to nominations to them is reported to have taken place in Tsolo and Butterworth in the Transkei in early 1955 and in the Ciskei villages at intervals between 1955 and 1958. The committees and boards were linked with the issue of increased taxation; at Butterworth officials were asked:

> Where are the monies to come from which school committees are to handle? Seeing that this is a government affair, why are the people going to be taxed?[98]

In Glen Grey, it was reported that at 11 out of 24 villages represented at a meeting between headmen and magistrates in early 1955, school committees could not be established because of local opposition.[99]

Besides widespread passive opposition and suspicion, there were a few instances of more active revolt. The Police Commissioner's report for 1955 mentions arson of school buildings in Peddie[100] and in September 1955 fifty men entered a school in Mgwalane, Peddie, dismissed the children, locked the building and removed the keys.[101]

There were, therefore, indications of considerable anxiety and tension provoked by state intervention in eastern Cape schools which might have been more effectively exploited by determined political organisation. In rural areas more oppressive local government, rising taxation and increasingly generalised economic hardship were powerful and explosive factors. Had rural and urban movements been more closely articulated the challenge to authority might have been formidable. A revolutionary movement might have been able to exploit the situation successfully but neither Congress nor the Convention was this in the mid-1950s. By the end of the decade local Congress leaders themselves were participating in the new system, energetically contesting and winning school board elections despite official ANC disapproval. Boycotts often involve the renunciation of power: the boards and committees had real if limited powers. Christopher Gell, reporting from Port Elizabeth in 1955, mentions African members of school boards influencing appointments in direction of relatives and friends.[102] Men and women struggling to survive economically and to provide a better world for their children are not necessarily revolutionaries. The pressures arising from everyday life require inspired and powerful political leadership if they are to be disregarded.

What Congress did try and provide was some kind of alternative to Bantu Education and its efforts in this direction deserve consideration if only for their persistence. As we have seen, in the wake of the boycott some branches tried to establish 'independent schools'. By June, the African Education Movement, chaired by Trevor Huddleston and with energetic support from Johannesburg's Congress of Democrat activists, was beginning to assist these ventures. The formal aims of the AEM were threefold: the establishment of private schools; the assistance of cultural clubs for those boycotters whose parents could not afford private school fees; and a home education programme. In practice the cultural clubs became the AEM's main preoccupation. These, for legal reasons, were conducted on an informal basis. The children would be taught, through a programme of songs, stories and games, the rudiments of mathematics, geography, history and general knowledge. Club leaders, supported financially by the modest fees that were charged would be provided by the AEM with cyclostyled teaching material, encouragement, and a training programme.

Given the limitations of what could be achieved, the clubs were in some centres surprisingly well attended, Brakpan being the outstanding example: here, a year after the boycott began, the club still had over 700 members, and leaders paid up to £16 a month from local resources.[103] One of these was a fully qualified teacher, who had resigned his post to join the club, bringing his pupils with him.[104] Amongst the problems mentioned in a memorandum by the AEM's full-time organiser, J. J. Hadebe, were the poor qualifications of club leaders, only a minority of whom were trained teachers; shortage of leaders, insufficient money to pay them and a lack of facilities and equipment – clubs often being held in the open.[105] The material provided by the AEM was well prepared and imaginative, emphasising a tactful and sensitive approach to certain topics:

> The Freedom Charter – to be taught to the children as they understand it. Care to be taken not to offend parents, the Charter not to be imposed on the people. The importance is not the name but the ideas embodied in it. The Freedom Charter to be the basis for our education.[106]

The AEM's approach involved a reversal of normal South African educational conventions; considerable demands were placed on future club leaders: 'Trust the children – let them take responsibility for themselves'.[107]

Even in terms of formal criteria, the clubs could be successful. Some of their members wrote and passed Standard VI examinations, and in Benoni and Brakpan as late as 1956 were even winning recruits from government schools.[108] The AEM and the cultural clubs were a brave experiment, but their significance became increasingly symbolic as numbers dwindled and children were re-absorbed into government schools. Their interest lies in their being the first sustained effort by Congress members to attempt to flesh out in educational terms an alternative world view: something that had been called for often in political rhetoric but seldom attempted before.

Opposition to Bantu Education, though widespread, only developed into open political rebellion in a few areas. In fact most of the opposition movements of the 1950s were geographically isolated and sporadic: amongst a fearfully poor and politically rightless population a peculiar combination of factors had to be present before anger could be translated into active defiance. The remainder of the chapter will concentrate on isolating those factors which help to explain why this happened in the East Rand townships.

The driving force of South Africa's industrial revolution was located in the

East Rand townships. Gold mining operations began in the 1880s, and the presence in the Transvaal of large coal and iron deposits led to the establishment in Benoni of the first steel works in the Union. By the end of the First World War engineering was beginning to be the most important local industry and this trend was strengthened during the 1930s, with an influx of foreign firms, and in the 1940s when wartime import substitution policies gave rise to another spurt of industrialisation. By 1947 Benoni was the country's largest centre of heavy industry, and together with the neighbouring town of Boksburg it made up South Africa's most densely industrialised area. To the west, Germiston grew in importance, first as a mining centre, then as the main railway junction on the Reef and centre for lighter industries – 400 of which were established in the period 1917 to 1957.[109]

The relatively early establishment of secondary industry in this area had important social consequences. The towns became important employment centres for black workers and early centres of black urbanisation: with the exception of Nancefield (in what is today Soweto) Benoni's African location, with its 9 600 inhabitants, was by 1929 the biggest on the Rand.[110] Secondary industry required a relatively skilled and permanent workforce, and by the 1950s the men and women who lived in the locations of the East Rand were members of a long-established proletariat. Nevertheless, these were small towns and at a municipal level the major political force was not the industrialists and businessmen who predominated in the affairs of the nearby metropolis, Johannesburg, but white workers. Given their constituency, Labour and Nationalist town councils of the 1930s and the 1940s were reluctant to embark on ambitious programmes of public works, and conditions in the African locations on the East Rand were notoriously bad. In some, squalid living conditions were exacerbated by the uneven application of the provisions of the Urban Areas Act. Areas of municipal neglect tended to coincide with inefficient or negligible control. Benoni's location was to develop into a refuge for people driven out of other Reef towns by the enforcement of the Act.[111] These places were always the object of public indignation. As one wartime sanitation official pointed out in Benoni: 'the conditions under which the Natives are living are vile',[112] and as recently as 1981 a *Star* report had this to say of Germiston's old location:

> Fetid rivers of liquid filth run down the side of each dirt road, collecting in noxious pools of swirling scum. Peeling and rusting corrugated iron plastered walls form shelters for humiliated families.[113]

Nor was the disgust limited to external observers. In Benoni, for example, an African Housing and Rates Board existed from 1945 and squatter movements unilaterally occupied buildings and land kept empty by the council.[114]

The chances of escape from the poverty-stricken despair of the locations through individual enterprise and initiative were just that much more limited in the East Rand than in, for example, Johannesburg. The small towns did not supply the same degree of administrative or commercial white-collar employment: local lack of demand for well-educated blacks was reflected in the lack of any secondary schools in the area until the 1960s.[115] Despite the frequent employment of women in the food and textile industries, for which the East Rand was an important centre, household incomes were well below Johannesburg's.[116]

The 1950s were an important transitionary phase for these communities. For in this decade the African populations of Germiston, Benoni and Brakpan were to be subjected to the full thrust of Afrikaner and Nationalist social engineering. Vast geometrically planned and tightly administered 'model' townships were erected – in each case at a considerable distance from the city centre – and location inhabitants were gradually screened and sorted and resetttled according to the dictates of Verwoerdian dogma. Germiston, with its Katlehong township, and Benoni, with Daveytown, were, in 1949 and 1950, among the first municipalities in the Union to comply with the Group Areas Act. In terms of living space, housing standards and sanitation, the new townships may have represented an improvement on the old locations, but to some groups within the community they would have appeared threatening,[117] and the manner in which these changes were implemented evoked widespread resentment.[118] The removals tended to speed up a process of social differentiation within the local communities. The new townships, being isolated from city centres, provided improved business opportunities for African traders and their own administrations created a certain amount of clerical employment. This, together with their geographical characteristics, tended to make it less easy for political leaders to evoke a united communal response to a particular issue. The strength of political movements of the 1950s in the old locations of the East Rand was no accident. With the onset of the removals – a process which lasted more than a decade – the old locations became even more neglected and their inhabitants increasingly insecure about their future.[119]

The socio-economic history of the East Rand is, to a large extent, a story of African working-class communities characterised by the depth of their proletarian experience, a measure of poverty unusual even among urban black South African people, and – because of their relative smallness and the importance of industrial employment among their male and female members – a high degree of social solidarity. With these points in mind, it is easier to understand the political radicalism which took root in the East Rand locations during the 1940s and the 1950s. The strength of the 1955 boycott is better understood if it put in the context of political and trade union responses in the preceding years.

The most active and militant political force on the East Rand during the 1940s was the Communist Party of South Africa, which seems to have won considerable support with its involvement in small local disputes, usually arising out of day-to-day difficulties of economic survival. The issues could include municipal prohibition on female hawkers (Benoni, November 1943);[120] police violence against location inhabitants (Brakpan, December 1943);[121] intimidation of rent defaulters (Brakpan, March 1944);[122] location conditions and the behaviour of the location superintendent (Brakpan, August 1944);[123] dismissal of teachers (Boksburg and Brakpan, March to November 1944);[124] housing shortages (Benoni, June 1945 to September 1947);[125]

brewing (Springs, July 1945);[126] bus services (Brakpan, April 1946);[127] food shortages (Brakpan, May 1946);[128] extension of municipal passes to women (Brakpan, July 1946).[129]

Let us look more closely at Communist Party involvement in local issues in the town where there seems to have been most activity – Brakpan. Though by no means the worst of the East Rand townships in terms of overcrowding or living conditions,[130] the small location community (5 000 in 1939)[131] seems to have been in a state of constant ferment in the 1940s. Brakpan was exceptional on the East Rand in the 1940s in having a Nationalist town council and provisions for control of its African population seem to have been particularly rigorous. The City of Johannesburg's 1939 *Survey of Reef Locations* makes especial mention of recent increases in the size of the Brakpan municipal police force, erection of fencing and a clamp-down on illicit brewing.

During the 1940s, Brakpan's Native Affairs Department was headed by a Dr Language, whose other claim to fame was as the leading theoretician and 'native expert' of the Ossewa Brandwag. (The OB appears to have had quite a following on the East Rand, doubtless enhanced by the blowing-up of Benoni's post office in 1942 by some of its local enthusiasts).[132] Even by the standards of his calling, Language seems to have been a formidably intolerant and unpleasant man. He began his term of office by reorganising local influx control into the location, raising lodgers' fees, and harassing minor rent defaulters. Differences between the council and the location community came to a head when, on Language's initiative, the council secured the dismissal of an important local politician, David Bopape, from his teaching post at Brakpan's Amalgamated Mission School.[133]

Bopape was one of the most energetic and active of the grass roots Congress leaders of those years. Initially drawn into politics by his involvement in the TATA salary campaign of 1940–41, he became a founder-member of the Youth League, and was by 1943 a forceful and effective spokesman for the Brakpan African community. He does not appear to have shared the normal Youth League antipathy to communists, perhaps because, unlike many young Congress intellectuals, he was himself involved in bread-and-butter political issues, and by 1946 is thought to have actually joined the South African Communist Party, while retaining an important position in the Transvaal ANC.[134] Bopape's activities appeared to have gained him a large personal following, for his dismissal was to provoke a school boycott affecting 2 000 children and a one day stay-at-home of the location's 7 000 workers on 10 August 1944.[135] Bopape had apparently angered Language by campaigning for better living conditions in the location, and the issue of his dismissal was to fuse with a range of other grievances, including the housing shortage, inadequate and expensive transport, low pay for municipal workers, high municipal rents, no running water within the location, and Language's racism.[136]

The action of Brakpan's parents inspired a similar protest the following year in Boksburg after teachers' dismissals there. In this case parents organised themselves under the slogan 'African education run by Africans' and their case was taken up by TATA, which had already begun to establish parent/teacher associations in the East Rand. The existence of these may have something to do with the effectiveness of both these and later school boycotts.[137]

The communal support for Bopape did not succeed in gaining his reinstatement (despite initial promises by the Brakpan council) and discontent within the location continued to simmer. In May 1945 the council announced that it was going to use beer hall profits for general street cleaning, refusing at the same time to grant the Advisory Board extensions to its powers which would have given it some say in the expenditure of location revenue. Three months later a fresh permit system was introduced and a wave of arrests of illegal location residents took place. In all these local disputes, the Communist Party's local spokesman played a prominent part, and in their African language newspaper, *Inkululeko*, reported these extensively. In its sensitive approach to local issues and its down-playing of more remote and abstract political problems, it seems to have gained a real popularity. A former Youth leader and Brakpan resident remembers:

> The ANC missed out a great deal [in the 1940s] because it would not interest itself in the little things that bug the people . . . the popularity of the Communist Party in places like Brakpan was because they took up such things.[138]

The Advisory Board elections in December 1945 illustrated the effectiveness of the approach. Communist candidates stood and were elected in Springs, Brakpan, Benoni and Nigel. The newly elected Brakpan Board went on to win a significant victory by organising a bus boycott which successfully reversed a council decision to relocate the bus terminal to a longer distance from the location boundary.[139]

Brakpan's African community was administered unusually heavy-handedly. For example, the municipality was the first on the Reef to consider enforcing a registration system on African women.[140] The role of an exceptional individual like Bopape was obviously important in consolidating the local representation of communists. But the latter's performance here was not untypical of their activity on the East Rand as a whole; the Benoni squatters' movement was given energetic leadership by the local branch of the Communist Party which held mass meetings, encouraged occupation of empty premises and organised the biggest political demonstration in Benoni's history when in 1945 several hundred people marched through the city centre bearing placards saying 'We are homeless', 'We are starving', 'Slums cause crime', and 'We sleep in tents this winter'.[141]

The communists established a tradition of involvement in local socio-economic issues that was taken up by later nationalist politicians. Communists were also important in the work place struggles that took place on the East Rand during the 1940s. Their rôle in the 1946 African Mineworkers' strike is well known, though the effect on location residents of the brutal treatment of miners who marched out of their compounds into the East Rand towns has yet to be considered. Communists had a rôle in the organisation of the African Iron and Steelworkers' Union, one of the two strongest regional affiliates (along with the Food and Canning Workers' Union), the Council for Non-European Trade Unions, and later the South African Congress of Trade Unions.

The East Reef in the mid-1950s, then, was an area in which a tradition of radical politics had existed for a comparatively long time among its black communities, a tradition which was characterised by a sensitivity to parochial concerns, and the successful intervention in these by African nationalist and socialist politicians. With this background, it becomes easier to understand why the parents within these communities responded in the way they did to the call for a boycott of schools in 1955. The boycott should be seen as flowing out of a well-established momentum by poor people to retain some control over their lives.

Notes

1 Muriel Horrell, *African Education: some origins and development until 1953*, SAIRR, Johannesburg, 1963, pp. 35–41.
2 See Baruch Hirson, *Year of Fire, Year of Ash*, Zed Press, London, 1979, pp. 20–34, for examples.
3 Gwendolyn Carter and Thomas Karis, *From Protest to Challenge*, Volume II, Hoover, Stanford, p. 217.
4 Horrell, *African Education*, p. 37.
5 *The Good Shepherd* (Johannesburg), March 1948, p. 27.
6 *Drum* (Johannesburg), June 1955.
7 Quoted in E. Murphy, 'Bantu Education in South Africa', Ph.D. thesis, University of Connecticut, 1973, p. 118.
8 Brian Rose and Richard Tunmer, *Documents in South African Education*, Ad Donker, Johannesburg, 1975, p. 266.
9 *Ibid.*, p. 254.
10 Murphy, 'Bantu Education in South Africa', p. 199.
11 Mia Brandel-Syrier, *Reeftown Elite*, Routledge and Kegan Paul, London, 1971, p. 38.
12 South African Institute of Race Relations, Johannesburg, SAIRR Library, Box File 26A, Federal Council of African Teacher's Memorandum to Department of Native Affairs, April 1956. A new school built in Tyutyu near King William's Town cost the location's inhabitants £411 – two-thirds of the total; *The Torch* (Cape Town), 11 November 1958.
13 R. Hunt Davis Jr., *Bantu Education and the Education of Africans in South Africa*, Centre for International Studies, Ohio University, 1973, p. 46.
14 Murphy, 'Bantu Education in South Africa', p. 121.
15 Federal Council of African Teacher's Memorandum to Department of Native Affairs.
16 *Imvo Zabantsundu* (Kingwilliamstown), 12 August 1944.
17 Reports of this boycott appear in *The Torch*, 26 August 1952 and 4 November 1952, and *The Spark* (Johannesburg), 5 September 1952.
18 SAIRR papers, AD 1189, unsorted ANCYL papers, Report of proceedings at ANCYL meeting, Newclare, 5 December 1948.
19 SAIRR papers, AD 1189, unsorted ANCYL papers, Agenda, Bloemfontein Youth Conference.
20 Misconduct which could justify the dismissal of a teacher could include political activity and any public opposition to any state agency. Murphy, 'Bantu Education in South Africa', p. 165. In fact the Transvaal province had already made this a regulation in 1950. See *The Voice of Orlando* (South West Townships), May 1950.
21 Leo Kuper, *An African Bourgeoisie*, Yale University Press, New Haven, 1965, p. 184.

22 Rose and Tunmer, *Documents in South African Education*, p. 262.
23 Organised opposition from Natal teachers developed later: perhaps partly because of the absence of political organisations prepared to involve themselves in educational issues and also, possibly, because in Natal direct state control of school, in contrast to other provinces, was common before the passage of the Act. See Kuper, *An African Bourgeoisie*, pp. 187–90, and Horell, *African Education*, p. 36.
24 See, for example, 'Tsolo people will not suffer oppression', *The Torch*, 29 January 1952, p. 2.
25 The best history of the evolution of the AAC and associated bodies is a University of Cape Town B.A. Honours dissertation by R. Gentle from which many of these details are drawn. *The Torch* contains useful information, as does the breakaway faction's *Ikwezi Lomso*, Queenstown.
26 *The Torch*, 26 December 1950.
27 Leo Sihlali, 'Bantu Education and the African Teacher' in *Africa South* (Cape Town), i, 1 (October–December 1956); see also *The Torch*, 10 November 1953 and 22 December 1953.
28 Sihlali, 'Bantu Education'.
29 *The Torch*, 24 December 1957.
30 *Ibid*, 3 December 1957.
31 The history of resistance in these areas to various government land schemes should be linked with the especially overcrowded conditions characterising these areas as early as the 1940s. See *Report of the Witwatersrand Mine Natives' Wages Commission*, UG 21/1944, pp. 10–12.
32 *The Torch*, 4 November 1958.
33 Ciskeian school attendance figures, for example, were the best in the country. See *Ciskeian General Council Proceedings* (Kingwilliamstown), 1954, p. 18.
34 *The Good Shepherd*, March 1942 and November 1946.
35 *Ibid*, June 1949.
36 *The Voice of Orlando*, April 1950.
37 *Ibid*, May 1950.
38 *The Good Shepherd*, March–June 1950.
39 *Ibid*, January 1950.
40 Interview with Professor Es'kia Mphahlele, Johannesburg, 1980; see also *The Torch*, 5 August 1952 and 26 August 1952.
41 *The Torch*, 3 August 1954.
42 *Ibid*, 2 March 1954.
43 Professor Mphahlele remembers approaching ANC activists in 1952 and attempting to discuss Bantu Education with them but failing to elicit much interest. The ANC, at the time, had all its energy caught up in the organisation of the Defiance Campaign. There were relatively few teachers in the higher echelons of the ANC and those teachers which remained in Congress after 1952 tended to be Africanist-inclined (e.g. Zeph Mothopeng, A. P. Mda, Godfrey Pitje, Peter Raboroko, Robert Sobukwe, Potlake Leballo, and Tsepo Letlaka).
44 Edward Feit, *African Opposition in South Africa*, Hoover, Stanford, 1967, and Gwendolyn Carter, Gail Gerhart and Thomas Karis, *From Protest to Challenge*, Volume III, Hoover, Stanford, 1975.
45 Hirson, *Year of Fire, Year of Ash*, p. 47.
46 SAIRR papers, AD 1189, ANC 111, Annual Report of the National Executive Committee to 42nd annual ANC conference, 16–19 April 1954, p. 10. Brakpan must have been atypical: here energetic campaigning against Bantu Education began as early as June 1954, according to a report in *Advance* (Cape Town), 1 July 1954.
47 Feit, *African Opposition in South Africa*, p. 164.

48 See Carter, Gerhart and Karis, *From Protest to Challenge*, Vol. III, pp. 31–2.
49 *Ibid*, pp. 32–3.
50 Legal Advice submitted to the conference by the Liberal Party lawyer J. Gibson made it clear that the law could not tolerate any formal education outside that provided by the schools registered with the new department.
51 Information on this conference drawn from: Carter, Gerhart and Karis, *From Protest to Challenge*, p. 33; Federation of South African Women papers, C111 (4) (IV) 15 10 55, ts. memo. by Congress of Democrat delegation; University of the Witwatersrand, Margaret Ballinger papers, File B 2 14 1, ts. memo by Liberal Party delegation.
52 This has been exhaustively discussed in both Feit, *African Opposition in South Africa* and Carter, Gerhart and Karis, *From Protest to Challenge*, Vol. III.
53 The earliest Congress campaigning appears to have been in Brakpan; see note 46.
54 Treason Trial Record (original copy held by the South African Institute of Race Relations), p. 2265.
55 *Ibid*, p. 7485.
56 *Ibid*, p. 2266.
57 *Bantu World*, 26 February 1955.
58 *Ibid*, 12 March 1955.
59 Treason Trial Record, p. 2472.
60 *Ibid*, p. 2438.
61 *Ibid*, p. 2450.
62 *Bantu World*, 26 March 1955.
63 'The girl who will not go to school again', *Drum*, April 1955.
64 *Bantu World*, 16 April 1955 and *Cape Argus* (Cape Town), 13 April 1955.
65 *Bantu World*, 16 April 1955.
66 *The Torch*, 19 April 1955 and Treason Trial Record, p. 2413.
67 *The Star* (Johannesburg), 12 April 1955.
68 Treason Trial Record, p. 2413.
69 *Cape Argus*, 13 April 1955 and *The Torch*, 26 April 1955.
70 *The Star*, 18 April 1955.
71 *Rand Daily Mail*, 26 April 1955.
72 *Bantu World*, 11 June 1955 and 27 August 1955.
73 *The Star*, 4 May 1955 and *Pretoria News*, 29 April 1955.
74 Carter, Gerhart and Karis, *From Protest to Challenge*, Vol. III, p. 33.
75 Feit, *African Opposition in South Africa*, p. 183.
76 University of the Witwatersrand, Federation of South African Women papers, C111 (2), Cyclostyled letter on origins of the AEM.
77 *Bantu World*, 25 June 1955.
78 Germiston meeting reported in *Rand Daily Mail*, 2 May 1955.
79 *Bantu World*, 7 May 1955.
80 *Bantu World*, 10 September 1955.
81 SAIRR papers, AD 1189, ANC IV, pencilled memo. on the cultural clubs.
82 Trevor Huddleston, *Naught for your Comfort*, Collins, London, 1956, p. 174.
83 See *The Torch*, 5 July 1955 and 5 June 1956, and *AEM News* (Johannesburg), i, I (June 1956), p. 4.
84 See report in *Drum*, June 1955, SAIRR papers, AD 1189, ANC IV, pencilled memo on cultural clubs; *Bantu World*, 10 December 1955 and 17 December 1955.
85 *Bantu World*, 8 December 1956.
86 *Bantu World*, 25 June 1956.
87 *Eastern Province Herald* (Port Elizabeth), 15 March 1955.
88 *Ibid*, 7 April 1955.
89 *Daily Dispatch* (East London), 15 May 1955.
90 *The Torch*, 24 April 1955.

91 *Evening Post* (Port Elizabeth), 23 May 1955.
92 Helen Joseph (interviewed by the author in January 1981) recalls that local enthusiasm for the boycott was very evident in smaller centres when she visited the eastern Cape in June 1955.
93 *Evening Post*, 25 May 1955.
94 *Evening Post*, 19 July 1955 and *The Torch*, 26 July 1955.
95 *AEM News*, i, I (June 1956).
96 Quoted in Feit, *African Opposition in South Africa*, p. 184.
97 Carter, Gerhart and Karis, *From Protest to Challenge*, Vol. III, p. 34.
98 *The Torch*, 15 February 1955.
99 *The Torch*, 5 April 1955.
100 Union of South Africa, *Annual Report of the Commissioner of the South African Police*, 1955, Pretoria, UG 52/1956, p. 5.
101 *Cape Times* (Cape Town), 21 September 1955 and *New Age* (Cape Town), 10 November 1955.
102 *Africa X-Ray Report* (Johannesburg), October 1955, p. 12.
103 SAIRR papers, AD 1189, ANC IV, pencilled memo on cultural clubs.
104 *Counter-Attack* (Johannesburg), 2, 11 March 1956.
105 Pencilled memo on cultural clubs.
106 Federation of South African Women papers, C111, 3, handwritten note on political instruction.
107 Federation of South African Women papers, C111, 4 x 9 13 56.
108 *Counter-Attack*, 2 11 March 1956.
109 See Chapter 7 of D. Humphriss, *Benoni, Son of my Sorrow*, City of Benoni, Benoni, 1968 and City of Germiston, *Official Guide*, 1957.
110 Humphriss, *Benoni*, p. 99.
111 *Ibid*, p. 99.
112 *Ibid*, p. 97.
113 *The Star*, 26 January 1981.
114 Humphriss, *Benoni*, p. 113–6.
115 Muir and Tunmer, 'African desire for education in South Africa', *Comparative Education*, ix, 3 (October 1965).
116 *Ibid*.
117 See Chapter 4.
118 Ethnic grouping policies were universally disliked by urban Africans. Both Humphriss and Brandel-Syrier (*Reeftown Elite*, p. 8) mention resistance to the removals but more research is needed to uncover the details.
119 See, for example, 'Benoni hit by glaring class-room shortage', *Imvo Zabantsundu*, 2 December 1961.
120 *Inkululeko* (Johannesburg), 9 November 1943.
121 *Ibid*, 4 December 1943.
122 *Ibid*, 4 March 1944.
123 *Ibid*, 14 August 1944.
124 *Ibid*, 24 November 1944.
125 *Ibid*, 9 June 1945, September 1947; Humphriss, *Benoni*, p. 184.
126 *Inkululeko*, 28 July 1945.
127 *Ibid*, 4 April 1946.
128 *Ibid*, 15 May 1946.
129 *Ibid*, 1 July 1946.
130 That distinction belongs to Benoni. For a brief review of location housing statistics, see City of Johannesburg, Non-European and Native Affairs Department, *Survey of Reef Locations*, May 1939.
131 *Ibid*.
132 Humphriss, *Benoni*, p. 85.

133 *Inkululeko*, 4 March 1944 and 24 November 1944.
134 A brief biography appears in Carter, Gerhart and Karis, *From Protest to Challenge*, Volume IV, Hoover, Stanford, 1977, p. 10.
135 *Inkululeko*, 18 April 1944.
136 *Ibid*, 4 October 1944.
137 *Ibid*, 10 May 1945.
138 Author's interview with Dr Nthato Motlana, Soweto, January 1981.
139 *Inkululeko*, 4 April 1946.
140 *Ibid*, 1 July 1946.
141 Humphriss, *Benoni*, p. 184, and *Inkululeko*, 9 June 1945.

CHAPTER 6

Women's protest movements in the 1950s

Protest movements drawn from African women were especially prominent in the popular resistance of the 1950s. This chapter will concentrate mainly on the actions of urban women; only in the case of the Natal riots of 1959, where events taking place in Durban were intimately linked with unrest in the countryside, will rural women's oppostion be considered. The reaction of rural African women elsewhere to new controls on their movements and reinforced economic deprivation is discussed in Chapter 12.

The 1950s was a period of unprecedented activity by African women in political organisations as well as in more spontaneous forms of protest. On occasions such movements were exclusively female and could be characterised by an appetite for confrontation qualitively sharper than that usually displayed by those in which men predominated. In the course of their protests women would sometimes show an angry awareness of the way African men could be emasculated by their situation, a reaction to the frequent failure of men to perform their customary rôle as protector and defender of the household.[1] To understand why women were beginning to play such an important rôle in a hitherto male-dominated political environment one needs some insight into the changing position of African women, and especially working-class African women, in South Africa's political economy.

The development of an industrial economy in South Africa initially affected African men and African women in different ways. Men were required as labour whereas women under a migrant labour system were chiefly responsible for the maintenance of the household, taking over more and more of the duties traditionally carried out by men in their capacity as head of the household. Increasingly it was women who represented the most economically active permanent element in the population of the reserves. However, land shortage – which together with land rehabilitation measures (see Chapter 11) could deprive women of their customary role as cultivators – and the requirements of manufacturing industry, were both to induce growing numbers of women to leave the reserves for the town. Between 1921 and 1946 the proportion of women to men in the African urban population was to grow from 1:5 to 1:3.[2] During the 1940s there was a significant increase in the numbers of women employed in manufacturing. In 1951 they represented – at 7 000 – one per cent of the total manufacturing workforce;[3] but this was not the main reason for their importance to secondary industry. Rather, their growth in numbers signified the development of a stabilised urban population suited to the particular labour requirements of manufacturing. Most urban African women did not have industrial experience, working instead in the considerably more isolated environment of the home (domestic service), or in the informal sector. Hard as conditions in South African towns were, they offered opportunities for survival which for many simply did not exist in the countryside.

Up to the 1950s African women were exempt from many of the provisions of influx control. Women had only started to arrive in towns in large numbers the decade before and formed a very small minority of the total industrial workforce. Controls on their movement had only been attempted earlier in the Orange Free State, where at the turn of the century, unlike other parts of South Africa, domestic servants were female and where there were also acute labour shortages on the farms. Protests against passes culminated in passive resistance campaigns in Bloemfontein, Winburg and Jagersfontein in 1913 and the relaxation of the regulations thereafter.[4] The effectiveness of the Free State resistance may have served to delay any further consideration of women's influx control.

In 1948, with the advent of the Nationalist administration, there were fresh compulsions to control the mobility of African women. In contrast to their predecessors, the Nationalists believed that the labour requirements of secondary industry could be met through a more sophisticated and controlled system of migrancy rather than the creation of a stable urban proletariat.[5] The mass movement to the towns of the 1940s had led to an acute social crisis which for both municipal and central authorities was assuming an increasingly threatening political character (see Chapter 1). For the state, the relative degree of freedom from official regulation that African women enjoyed was by the 1950s a dangerous anachronism. In 1952 the Aboliton of Passes and Coordination of Documents Act made provision for women to carry reference books. However, it was denied at the time that the clause affecting women would in their case be enforced. In early 1950 extensive demonstrations in many of the main urban centres, as well as more muted protests from the Advisory Boards, had greeted proposed amendments to the Urban Areas Act to tighten up the process through which women sought permission from the local authorities to remain in a municipal area.[6] The offending clauses were dropped: at that stage the state was not ready for major confrontations.

The political responses of African women were probably affected by the above processes in several ways. The social dislocations resulting from colonialism and the migrant labour system helped to disrupt family life and undermine both women's rights and status in patriarchal rural societies. The insecurity of urban existence would have also contributed to a weakening of traditional patriarchal controls. Marital instability, a growing number of female breadwinners, an increase in spinsterdom and single parent families as well as domestic conflicts engendered by the humiliations and subservience of most men's work experience, all these could have influenced women to be more socially assertive. More tangibly, the economic difficulties confronting poor people during the 1940s, especially those directly connected with the upkeep of the household, had in certain instances a politicising effect. For example, in Cape Town, the queues of housewives which regularly congregated in front of the food vans which sold basic foodstuffs in short supply in the townships developed their own committees. These were first of all intended to maintain fair dealing within the queue, but soon linked up with each other and developed a centralised organisation which successfully protested outside parliament again the proposed withdrawal of the vans. The Cape Town Women's Food Committee, representing fifty-nine queues throughout the peninsula, had links both with the trade unions and the Communist Party. By 1948 its leaders had moved beyond subsistence issues and linked the question of food supply and availability with popular suffrage.[7] A similar organisation developed in Johannesburg and local Communist Party members led women in angry raids on Fordsburg shopkeepers suspected of hoarding.[8] African women had also become important as trade unionists since entering the clothing and textile industries in the 1930s. Small as their number was they were to play a vital role as political leaders in the 1950s. Lilian Ngoyi, Frances Baard and Bertha Mashaba, to name three of the most important figures in the Federation of South African Women, all drew their first organisational experience from trade union activity.

The majority of African women in towns, though, did not work in industry. This, together with their freedom from the pass laws, helps to explain their political militancy: for them, involvement with urban industrial society was neither as humiliating nor as brutal as that experienced by their menfolk[9] and this may have conditioned attitudes to authority. Confronted with the threat of pass laws they could compare their present degree of independence from official restriction with the position of men and perceive they had something worth defending.

Up until the late 1940s organised activity by African women tended either to focus around church-based voluntary associations, the exclusively female *Manyanos*, or, at the other social extreme, the organisations which worked for the upliftment and upward mobility of African women such as the Zenzele Clubs led by Mrs Xuma, or the National Council of African Women. With the exception of the Communist Party, African women were not greatly involved in political organisation. The communists drew African women into their ranks because many of the issues they took up – the cost of food, the right to brew beer, lodger permits – were of fundamental importance to women in their domestic capacities. Many of the informal popular movements which developed during the 1940s – the squatters' movement and the bus boycotts – also brought up the question of maintaining the integrity of the household and probably also served to politicise women. But African politicians were rather slow to recognise this potential new constituency; though it was mooted in 1943, the proper establishment of the ANC Women's League had to wait until the founding of a Sophiatown branch in 1948.[10]

By 1950 government policies were beginning to contain a specific threat to the position of African women. The Defiance Campaign of 1952 attracted thousands of female volunteers, and on occasions there were exclusively women's days when only women defied. Four months after the close of the campaign a group of women met in Port Elizabeth to discuss the launching of a national women's organisation. The meeting was attended by, amongst others, trade unionists, ANC Women's League members, and some of the women who were at the same time involved in the establishment of the Congress of Democrats (see Chapter 3). Following this meeting Ray Alexander of the Food and Canning Workers' Union, and Hilda Watts, a former Johannesburg City

Councillor (the only communist ever elected to such a position) worked energetically to organise 'a national meeting at which women of all races will come together to discuss women's disabilities, and to promote women's rights'.[11] With their Communist Party and trade union background, both women were well suited to the task of establishing a non-racial women's organisation. By virtue of not holding passes black women had been able to join registered trade unions and, as we have seen, the communists' concentration on subsistence matters in the 1940s had provided some basis for mobilisation of women across colour lines.[12]

On 17 April 1954, 150 delegates from different parts of the country met in Johannesburg to adopt a 'Women's Charter' and launch a new organisation, the Federation of South African Women (FSAW). As its title implied, the new movement was federal in character, functioning as a coordinating body to which different groups affiliated rather than constituting itself on the basis of individual membership. The Charter, while pledging women to an active rôle in the struggle for 'National Liberation', placed much of its emphasis on women's legal disabilities:

> The Law has lagged behind the development of society; it no longer corresponds to the actual social and economic position of women. The law has become an obstacle to the progress of the women, and therefore a brake on the whole of society. This intolerable condition would not be allowed to continue were it not for the refusal of a large section of our menfolk to concede to us women the rights and privileges which they demand for themselves.[13]

As things turned out national liberation was to take priority over specifically feminist demands. The main FSAW affiliates were various trade unions and the ANC Women's League as well as the Congress of Democrats, the Indian Congresses, and SACPO. Its first president and secretary were Ida Mtwana and Ray Alexander, to be succeeded in 1956 by Lilian Ngoyi, former garment worker and ANCWL president, and Helen Joseph, previously a social worker and a founding member of the Congress of Democrats. Both women had been drawn into the Congress movement as a result of the Defiance Campaign. It was to be a highly effective political partnership. It also had the effect of confirming the nature of the FSAW's position within the Congress alliance. Ray Alexander had been keen that the FSAW should be an organisation which one could join as an individual, and she also viewed the Federation's major function as being a women's rights movement. The ANC and the Transvaal section of the Women's League favoured a federal organisation, and the transferring of the national executive from the Cape to the Rand (as a result of Ray Alexander's banning) served to endorse this position.

The 150 delegates at the founding conference were mainly from towns, Johannesburg contributing the greatest number, many were trade unionists and most had had only a limited amount of formal education (there were no representatives of farm workers or women in the reserves.) For them the most pressing issue was the threat of passes and this was discussed extensively at the meeting.[14]

During the first months of the Federation's existence, the energies of its office-holders were channelled into Congress campaigns, which – especially in the case of the Bantu Education boycott – drew upon the resources of the Women's League and the Congress of Democrats. The first major FSAW initiative had to wait until the second half of 1955. After months of campaigning on the issue of passes the Transvaal branch of the Federation decided to mount a demonstration in Pretoria against unjust laws – a decision provoked also by a recent intensification of pass raids on the Rand resulting in a 25 per cent increase in convictions for pass offences.[15] The inspiration for the form of demonstration was drawn from the vigils outside the Union buildings held by the Black Sash, a white women's organisation at that time concerned with defending constitutional principles. Helen Joseph and Bertha Mashaba, Transvaal secretary of the Women's League, drew on Congress networks to mobilise 2000 women; despite various forms of legal harassment, they arrived in Pretoria on 27 October, and marched up to the Union buildings, each carrying their own copy of a petition compiled by a FSAW/Women's League joint committee. This form of individual protest was a neat solution to the legal problem posed by Pretoria City Council's ban upon the organisation of any meetings or processions by FSAW. FSAW leaders demonstrated a similar flexibility when confronted with the withdrawal by the authorities of the licences of the buses they had chartered: township groups were swiftly contacted by the indefatigable Mrs Joseph who told them that they should go by train. In one instance the local ANC branch helped with fares but for many this meant considerable financial sacrifice.

Shortly before this first demonstration the government announced its intention at last to issue women with reference books; with deceptive pedantry it argued that these were not the same thing as passes. A cautious strategy was adopted: mobile units would first circulate in the remoter parts of the country and in the smaller towns which were unaffected by African political organisation. The first such centre to be visited was Winburg, centre of the 1913 Free State anti-pass resistance. Here, in March 1956, nearly 1 500 women were induced to take out the new reference books. Women from Winburg requested assistance from the ANC, and Lilian Ngoyi visited the town to find that many of the local women were ready to act on the established local tradition and burn their passes. Despite ANC advice to the contrary, those passes which were collected overnight were burnt the next day outside the office of the location superintendent.[16] Refusing to accept passes was not illegal (they were not made compulsory for women until 1963 when they had all been issued), but burning them was. The Federation contributed money towards the women's defence costs.

For the next six months no more passes were issued by the mobile units,[17] but the Federation and the League were not idle over this period: from March 1956, in virtually all the major towns, women marched from the locations into city centres to hand in petitions and protests to Town Clerks, Native Commissioners, Magistrates and other local officials. These demonstrations were particularly frequent and lively on the East Rand where municipalities, taking advantage of amendments made to the Urban Areas Act in 1952, had begun to control the presence of African women within their boundaries by the issue of employment and residence permits.[18]

Certain groups were especially angered by recent control measures: in

June 1956, 360 African domestic workers in Johannesburg, threatened by new regulations prohibiting flat cleaners and servants from living in, marched to the Native Commissioner to protest against women's passes. They were led by Bertha Mashaba.[19] In general, the sentiments expressed in the various protests and petitions had three main themes: the passes would affect the ability of women to move about and sell their labour freely; women would be exposed to sexual abuse at the hands of licentious officials; pass arrests would have a dramatic effect on the welfare of their children and homes.[20] The following extract from a leaflet issued by the Port Elizabeth ANC is a good reflection of some of the worst fears felt by African women:

> It means that no husband can ever be sure any day that his wife is his wife; nor can he be sure that his child may not be taken away from him and sold to farmers under the pretext of failing to comply with the pass regulation . . . how can any decent home be built for the proper upbringing of the children. . . . A man has only to come into any home or stop a woman on the street and say he is a policeman or detective and the law of the country empowers him to take away that woman and to touch any part of her body as they can do with men under the pretext they are searching for a pass. Even in the days of slavery there was nothing like this. This is the basest method of humiliating people and destroying the honour of its womanhood.[21]

The reference to farm labour was significant. It was commonly believed (with some justification) that the introduction of passes was partly motivated by a labour shortage in the badly paid sectors of agriculture and domestic service. One of the most interesting petitions recorded was in Bethlehem, in the Free State:

> We the mothers have contributed enough to the uplifting of South Africa by producing strong sons and daughters, who go underground and sweat to bring to the earth's surface the wealth of our country. People who clean your houses and are the caretakers of your children. People who provide you with the necessary cheap labour. We are sorry for the Government. We are not at all convinced these documents are necessary. We wish to remind the Government that we want freedom not serfdom.[22]

The predominant preoccupation of the women appeared to be the effects of the new controls on their customary domain: their children, the household, family relationships. This seemed the main basis for their solidarity.

By August 1956, after thousands of women had been involved in these local protests, the stage was set for a massive repetition of the previous year's demonstration in Pretoria. After Helen Joseph and Bertha Mashaba had made a tour of the country, 20 000 women travelled to the capital from all four provinces. The seventy delegates from Port Elizabeth had chartered an entire railway coach at a cost to themselves of £700, many of them reputedly selling their furniture in order to come. The 20 000 petitions were delivered to an empty Prime Minister's office, and then, in the forecourt of the Union Building, the women stood in silence for thirty minutes before an astonished audience of clerks and typists. Before leaving they sang their triumphant anthem, 'Strydom you have tampered with the women, you have struck a rock', afterwards quietly filing away down the hill.

At the end of the year FSAW's main leaders were arrested and charged with treason alongside other Congress activists. At the same time the authorities began to use increasingly intimidatory tactics to enforce the use of passes. In the more isolated towns of the eastern Cape and Transvaal where these efforts were now concentrated, husbands whose women had refused passes would be threatened with dismissal from their jobs; women without reference book numbers could find it difficult to collect pensions or receive medical treatment; teachers were drafted in to inform their pupils of the necessity for their mothers to carry passes, and employers were told to register their female labour with labour bureaux.[23] Confrontations between women and the authorities became increasingly violent with women burning passes in several centres and police dispersing demonstrations outside Native Commissioners' offices with baton charges. In September the Criminal Law Amendment Act, which imposed severe penalties, began for the first time to be employed against female pass protesters.[24] This was in Lichtenburg where nearly a year before two women had died in a struggle between police and demonstrators against a mobile pass unit. In Standerton and Nelspruit men joined women in their protests. In Standerton, on the day of the arrival of the pass-issuing team, the entire location stayed away from work and buses and taxis were boycotted. This was after a huge prayer meeting had been held some days before in the neighbouring hills. Women picketing the entrance to the location defied police orders to disperse and then marched in groups of eight to the magistrate's office: the first to arrive were locked in a yard, and as hundreds more came they too demanded to be arrested. Eventually they were driven away with a baton charge and 914 were charged with holding an illegal procession. In Nelspruit, 95 per cent of the African workforce stayed at home one day in October in protest against the treatment by police of women pass protesters.[25] The most sustained and widespread resistance was in the Marico reserves of the eastern Transvaal where several people lost their lives in the bitter conflict over passes and the Bantu Authorities (see Chapter 11).

By the end of 1957 the battle in the countryside had largely been won by the state and the pass units began to move into the main urban centres. The recently passed General Laws Amendment Act provided fresh difficulties for effective opposition since African public meetings were now confined by law to townships. Instead of issuing passes indiscriminately the pass units concentrated on especially vulnerable groups. The Nursing Amendment Act made identity numbers compulsory for all nurses, and in October 1958 Johannesburg housewives were sent a notice telling them to send their female servants to the pass offices. A FSAW-inspired demonstration of nurses outside Baragwanath Hospital attracted much publicity in March and succeeded in embarrassing the state into dropping the identity number ruling. But domestic servants, in contrast to nurses, were a very insecure and isolated group. Members of FSAW and the Congress of Democrats leafletted those suburbs where the pass units were concentrating their efforts (which were principally inhabited by less affluent Afrikaans-speaking whites) to correct the misleading impression the official notice gave that women's passes were compulsory.

Meanwhile, Sophiatown and Alexandra branches of the Women's League organised large numbers of women to march or go by bus to the Johannesburg pass office in the centre of town to protest. In the last ten days of October nearly two thousand women deliberately courted arrest this way, for the marches and meetings, being outside the townships, were illegal. Of the 1 200 women crowded into the cells of the Johannesburg Fort, 170 were accompanied by their babies. Most of those arrested were charged under the Criminal Laws Amendment Act.

Organised as it was by local-level leaders, the scale of the protest surprised the FSAW and ANC executives. The Federation responded quickly by calling for the enlargement of the campaign and twenty thousand volunteers and argued that no fines or bail should be paid. However, its leadership was overruled by the ANC. Bail was to be paid and no more women were to invite arrest. Instead of confrontation the Federation should concentrate on organisation and educative campaigns against passes. While the FSAW and ANCWL leadership expressed regret at this decision they did not contest it and contented themselves with organising a legal protest on 27 November when 4 000 women outwitted the police by arriving at the city hall in twos and threes to hand in their signed petitions.[26]

It is possible to interpret in the ANC's restraining influence at this point the assertion of patriarchal attitudes emanating from a political leadership chiefly composed of men. Certainly there was some evidence both within and outside Congress that many men tended to remain passive bystanders in the women's struggle. An ANC directive complained of 'men who are even more affected by the pass laws [playing] the role of spectators . . . the tendency of regarding this as a women's struggle must be forthwith abandoned'.[27] The FSAW itself criticised 'men who are politically active and progressive in outlook [who] still follow the tradition that women should take no part in politics'.[28] In early 1959 a Federation report spoke of the 'impatience' with which 'the active entry of men into the campaign' was awaited.[29] However, there is no substantial evidence that suggests the ANC's intervention resulted from any disapproval of female political militancy. Certainly the ANC leadership was susceptible to pressure from rank and file men anxious for bail to be paid and their wives to be released. But this was not the only consideration. Penalties under the Criminal Law Amendment Act were very severe and the Congress movement hardly had the resources for the defence and support of the dependents of twenty thousand volunteers. There were tactical reasons for caution, particularly at a time when ANC leaders had also to deal with internal ideological dissension within their organisation.

November 1958 was the last instance of a major organised protest against women's passes. Though Helen Joseph wrote hopefully at the end of the year that there was 'a long way to go and much may yet happen',[30] there was little coordinated resistance thereafter. The ANC, in acknowledgement of the courage and effectiveness of the women, proclaimed 1959 to be 'Anti-Pass Year' and established a National Anti-Pass Planning Council. Removed from the small group of deeply committed women of the Federation, the anti-pass resistance suffered from bureaucratic inertia, and a detailed strategy was not formulated until the end of 1959 (see Chapter 3).

This was not the end of militant protest by women. In mid-1959 there developed, first of all in the sprawling Durban shanty area of Cato Manor, later throughout Natal, resistance of a rather different kind to the formal and disciplined movement led by the Federation. The initial catalyst to these upheavals was provided by a sudden intensification of illegal liquor raids in Cato Manor itself.

Durban had an unusually severe shortage of housing for its African population. Initial plans for the erection of municipal townships to cater for the enormous wartime population growth had foundered on objections by the Minister of Native Affairs, Dr Verwoerd, to the use of crown land, the Umlazi Mission Reserve, as an urban housing scheme. Only by the late 1950s had the conflict between state and municipality been resolved and work started on Kwa Mashu, fourteen miles away from Durban. Meanwhile the major part of Durban's African population lived in the 4 500 acres of Cato Manor, on land owned by Indians, but let out to African tenants who would then divide up their plots and let portions to hundreds of sub-tenants who had built themselves dwellings from whatever materials they could find. By 1959, 125 000 people lived here, Indians, Africans and even a few thousand whites. As might be imagined, their presence and the conditions under which they lived were a continual source of civic anxiety. The Council had managed to obtain permission from the Native Affairs Department to develop part of Cato Manor as a temporary 'emergency transit camp' in return for an undertaking that ultimately Cato Manor would be reserved for white occupation. Within the camp, shacks were thinned out and with funds from the Native Revenue Account (chiefly drawn from beerhall sales) lavatories and a few washing facilities were installed. But the municipality was parsimonious: little actual improvement in living conditions resulted and their interventions often made things more difficult; they harassed unlicensed traders, demolished overcrowded buildings, and paradoxically, contributed to the overcrowding by moving the occupants of other shanty areas into Cato Manor.

In 1958, with the first houses in Kwa Mashu completed, the process of removal and resettlement began. First of all the authorities felt it incumbent on themselves to discover who had the legal right (in terms of Section 10 of the Urban Areas Act) to live within Cato Manor, intending that those people who had no legal status would be returned to the countryside. Being virtually impossible to administer efficiently, Cato Manor was an obvious haven for those who could no longer endure the poverty and hopelessness of life in the rural areas. The threat of deportation affected thousands of women. Even the relatively fortunate ones who had working husbands had to prove their married status to officials who often demanded evidence of more than customary unions: as a result, there was a sudden rush of civil and church weddings that year in Cato Manor. But many women were single and unemployed; 1959 was a year of economic recession and Natal was especially badly affected. In the light of later events the enforced exodus of large numbers of embittered urban women to the reserves was very significant. The authorities required documentary proof of women's residential qualifications and in desperation hundreds took out the despised reference books. Those without documents would have their homes and sometimes their possessions within them flattened without warning by bulldozers. A deputation to the

Mayor in June 1958 elicited reassuring promises but produced no relaxation of the removals. Even those who were guaranteed a home in Kwa Mashu would not necessarily have been pleased by the impending move: Kwa Mashu was far from their jobs, more money would be needed for fares and rents, and the relative degree of freedom from official interference that could be enjoyed in Cato Manor would disappear.[31]

In June 1959 the City Council introduced a final provocation. Attempts to improve sanitation in Cato Manor so as to forestall a typhoid epidemic were frustrated by hidden caches of illegal alcohol. Municipal labourers were brought in Cato Manor to destroy all the stills they could find. This move affected not only the shebeen queens who sometimes actually distilled liquor but the much larger group of women who brewed traditional beer. People were allowed to brew a small amount of beer for domestic consumption provided they obtained a permit from the municipality. The restriction on home brewing enabled the Durban Corporation to draw a large revenue from its beer halls where all social drinking took place. The existence of these establishments was for most women itself a grievance. The beer hall usurped a traditional domestic function of women, it caused men to spend a portion of the household income on refreshment which could be supplied for social occasions by women at home at a much lower cost, and when the limits on home brewing were enforced women were thus denied a potential source of income. The new sanitation measures were indiscriminate, and they affected both distilling and brewing; the beer halls themselves formed a natural focus for people's anger. On 17 June the first beer hall in Booth Road was invaded by an army of furious women: its male customers were driven outside, beer vats were overturned and brewing machinery was destroyed. The following day a crowd of 2000 women was broken up by police, many of the women being hurt in the process. In the riots which followed municipal buildings and vehicles were destroyed in retaliation. Three people were shot dead while setting fire to a beer hall. For two weeks the African women of Durban expressed their outrage in demonstrations, invasions of beer halls, and clashes with the police. Those beer halls which were not burnt to the ground were picketed, and with ANC support a highly successful beer boycott was instituted. In some instances anger was effectively mixed with ribaldry and sexual assertion:

> These women were very powerful. Some came half-dressed with their breasts exposed, and when they got near this place the Blackjacks [municipal police] tried to block the women. But when they saw this, the women turned and pulled up their skirts. The police closed their eyes and the women passed by and went in!
>
> . . . women took off their panties, filled them with beer and said, 'Look, this is what happens', as they squeezed them out.[32]

Though by the end of June unrest in Cato Manor had subsided this signified only a temporary reprieve for the authorities. For the events of Cato Manor were to have effects that rippled outwards into the surrounding countryside. Natal had a rather unusual social geography. Though the smallest of the four provinces (less than ten per cent of Union's area) it contained within its borders a fifth of South Africa's inhabitants. Its densely inhabited reserves were situated within a few miles of the major towns, and between the African townships and the reserves, rather as in the case of East London, there was a constantly oscillating traffic. Cato Manor itself, with its freedom from official controls, was the main locus of contact between rural and urban people, and over weekends its population doubled under the impact of visitors from the countryside.

The indignation of urban women was infectious, and it found fertile ground in rural worries and distress.[33] Because of the removal of large numbers of economically active men through the migrant labour system, those who were left to confront the everyday difficulties of material existence were more often than not female. Women in rural Natal in the late 1950s were faced with particular problems. First there was an increasing pressure on available land as the result of elimination of 'black spots' (especially numerous in Natal) as well as the 'repatriation' of illegal Durban residents. Secondly, stock controls were being vigorously enforced once again (see Chapter 11). After widespread resistance to government attempts to assess and then limit the number of reserve cattle the assessment process was then linked with dipping, a measure to control disease. Dipping was additionally unpopular because it was believed to make cattle more susceptible to illness, and an outbreak of stock deaths did in fact coincide with a dipping offensive. To add insult to injury, local women were obliged to fill and maintain the dipping tanks: a tiring, and in the eyes of the majority, an utterly irrational duty. The betterment schemes had additional penalties for women. They were no longer guaranteed their own fields under the new and alien system of land allocation which was imposed, and forestry schemes, too, involved novel and unwelcome obligations. In addition, an increased tax on wives in 1959, together with more stringent influx control measures introduced as a result of urban unemployment, contributed to a mounting crescendo of rural dissatisfaction. Symptomatic of the excitement and tension in rural Natal was the large influx of rural people to attend the annual Freedom Day meeting of the ANC held in Curries Fountain, Durban, on 27 July 1959.

The first eruption of rural rebellion was at Harding on 21 July. That day a meeting was to have been held at which the agricultural officer would present proposals for closer settlement and soil conservation. The meeting was postponed following reports that a band of armed men were on their way to break it up. Thirty women were later arrested when they were caught pushing over a hut belonging to the Department of Bantu Administration and setting fire to a drum of oil. The women were convicted on 11 August. In the court case there emerged four main factors in this discontent: closer settlement (which in imposing a village structure on people distanced them from their fields), increases in taxation, influx control, and the collaboration of the local headmen with the authorities. After the women's imprisonment a group of men marched to the jail and demanded the release of their wives. This was refused and so in reprisal they started to light fires in the surrounding sugar plantations. Later they attempted to block the railway lines to Port Shepstone where it was rumoured that the women would be transferred.

The Harding incident was the only one which involved large numbers of men. More typical was the incident in Umzinto, where, on 29 July, 500 women marched on the magistrate's court, demanding the abolition of reference books, influx controls, and calling for a minimum wage of £1 a day. In the weeks that followed there were similar occurrences in Idutywa, Weshula, St Faith's, Port Shepstone, Hibberdene, Camperdown, Ipoxo, Umtwalume, Mehlomyami, Umsinsini, Isopofu, Hlogkozi, Edendale, Donnybrook and the Mdhal reserve. Dipping tanks were smashed, cane fields burnt down, police were stoned, women marched on police stations and magistrates' courts, armed with sticks and calling for the end of afforestation schemes, labour obligations, influx control and women's passes. In the course of these protests roughly 20 000 women were actively involved and nearly 1 000 were arrested. Nearly three-quarters of the dipping tanks were destroyed. The movement reached its climax in mid-August when a meeting at St Faith's could attract 1 000 women and then subsided, as the demoralising effects of heavy fines and long prison sentences began to take their toll. The last chapter of the revolt was in Ipoxo in October where local ANC leaders organised a deputation of 500 women who marched into the town and demanded a reply from the Native Commissioner to the list of grievances they had submitted to him in August. They were told to return home and channel such requests through their husbands and headmen. Instead of returning home the women went down on their knees in prayer, saying they would not go until they had seen a Native 'Women's Commissioner'; 366 of them .were arrested and sentenced to four months' imprisonment with the option of a £35 fine.

The events at Ipoxo were the only ones which were instigated by the ANC. On the whole the ANC played only an auxiliary rôle in the unrest; its leadership expressed sympathy with the women over their grievances, but warned against physical violence or the destruction of property. Nevertheless, through the politicising effects of the disturbances and the despatch of supportive messages and counsels of caution Congress succeeded in attracting tremendous rural support. On 6 September a Congress-inspired 'Natal People's Conference' was held in Durban. Fifty rural locations were represented by delegates.

The protests of African women during the 1950s were an important contribution to the history of post-war African resistance. Industrialisation, urbanisation, the restructuring of rural social relations, and a fresh intervention by the state into the lives of African women all helped to create a vast new political constituency. No understanding of the radicalisation of black politics in those years would be complete without a knowledge of the emergence and behaviour of this constituency. It provided the base for one of the most militant and disciplined political movements of the decade. It was also one of the most successful: of all the apartheid measures, the incorporation of women into the influx control system was the most fiercely contested, and with the exception of land rehabilitation in the reserves, the most difficult to implement.

This was not a feminist movement. Women were not seeking an extension of rights or an alteration in their domestic relationships and responsibilities. It is possible to detect in their sexual solidarity and occasional scorn for their more acquiescent menfolk the needs of a feminist consciousness. But in the forefront of their minds was a more immediate motivation: new controls threatened their rights and status in both urban and rural society and in doing so could subvert the basis of their traditional domestic role. The most powerful sentiment was matriachal, captured most vividly in the magnificent phrase of Lilian Ngoyi's: 'My womb is shaken when they speak of Bantu Education.'[34] Men were viewed as weak and passive, enmeshed in an emasculating system: significantly, one of the themes of the anti-pass protests was that the women's passes involved a usurpation by officialdom of African men's domestic authority.[35] In many respects it was a highly conservative rebellion, though no less justifiable for that. Therein lay its strength and moral passion.

Notes

1 For example: 'When Josie Palmer [a leading member of the CPSA in the 1940s] was asked why women were so much more politically active than men, she promptly replied, "Because men are cowards! They are afraid of losing their jobs". The implication, of course, is that women did not have jobs worth losing.' From Julia Wells, 'The day the town stood still: women's resistance in Potchefstroom, 1912–1930', University of the Witwatersrand History Workshop paper, 1981, p. 42.
2 Cynthia Kros, *Urban African Women's Organisations and Protest on the Rand*, Africa Perspective Dissertation no. 3, Johannesburg, 1980, p. 20.
3 Janet Schapiro, 'The political and economic organisation of women in South Africa: the notion of sisterhood', *Africa Perspective*, 15, 1980, p. 12.
4 Julia Wells, 'Women's resistance to passes in Bloemfontein during the inter-war period', *Africa Perspective*, 15 1980, pp. 22–3.
5 See Martin Legassick, 'Legislation, ideology and economy in post-1948 South Africa', *Journal of Southern African Studies*, i, 1 (October 1974), pp. 15–24.
6 Draft National Executive report to ANC annual conference, 1950, Carter and Karis microfilm (CAMP), Reel 8a, 2 DA 14: 30/42; Moses Kotane to Z. K. Matthews, 2 March 1950, Carter and Karis microfilm, 2 DA 16: 41/32.
7 Cheryl Walker, '"We Fight for Food": women and the food crisis of the 1940s', *Work in Progress* (University of the Witwatersrand), 3 (January 1978).
8 See report in *Eastern Province Herald* (Port Elizabeth), 27 May 1946, 'Rand Shops Raided, Alleged Black Market in Food, Communist Action', and Naomi Mitchison, *A Life for Africa: the story of Bram Fischer*, Merlin Press, London, 1973, p. 55.
9 Kros, *Urban African Women's Organisations*, p. 14.
10 *Ibid*, Chapter 4.
11 Cheryl Walker, 'The Federation of South African Women', Development Studies Group, *Conference on the History of Opposition in South Africa*, Johannesburg, January 1978.
12 Walker, in '"We Fight for Food"', claims that the Food Committees contained the seeds of a national women's movement.
13 Reprinted in *Africa Perspective*, 15, pp. 70–2.
14 Richard de Villiers, 'Resistance to the extension of passes to African women, 1954–1960', University of the Witwatersrand African Studies Institute seminar paper, 24 September 1979, p. 7.

15 Calculated from Union of South Africa, *Annual Report of the Commissioner for the South African Police*, 1954, UG 54/55; 1955, UG 52/56; 1956, UG 41/58.
16 Recollections of Lilian Ngoyi read out at Durban meeting, 22 March 1980; compiled by Julia Wells.
17 Helen Joseph, 'Women and passes', *Africa South* (Cape Town), January 1958, pp. 26–31.
18 *New Age* (Cape Town), 10 May 1956.
19 *Ibid*, 14th June 1956.
20 Joseph, 'Women and passes', p. 26.
21 'The pass must be resisted', leaflet issued by the ANC in Port Elizabeth, 1956, Carter and Karis microfilm, Reel 2b, 2 DA 17: 84.
22 *New Age*, 21 June 1956. 'Freedom, not Serfdom' was a traditional Congress rallying slogan.
23 *New Age*, 20 September 1956, 15 November 1956, 10 October 1957, 9 May 1957.
24 *New Age*, 12 September 1957.
25 *New Age*, 31 October 1957, 18 July 1957, 25 July 1957.
26 Helen Joseph, 'Women and passes (II)', *Africa South*, April 1959.
27 Statement by the ANC National Executive on Women's Pass Demonstrations, 1958, Carter and Karis microfilm, Reel 3b, 2 DA 22: 33/2.
28 Walker, 'The Federation of South African Women', p. 200.
29 *Ibid*, p. 199.
30 Joseph, 'Women and passes', p. 28.
31 A good analysis of the tension in Cato Manor is R. R. Butcher, 'Poverty and insecurity: the case of Cato Manor', *The Forum* (Johannesburg), September 1959, pp. 9–10.
32 Ken Luckhardt and Brenda Wall, *Organize . . . or Starve: the history of the South African Congress of Trade Unions*, Lawrence and Wishart, London, 1980, p. 304.
33 The following section draws upon Joanne Yawich, 'Natal 1959: the women's riots', *Africa Perspective*, 5 (1977), pp. 1–16.
34 Quoted in *Bantu World* (Johannesburg), 8 October 1955.
35 See the passage quoted above from 'The pass must be resisted'.

CHAPTER 7

'We are being punished because we are poor': the bus boycotts of Evaton and Alexandra, 1955–1957

The two major subsistence protests of the 1950s, the Alexandra and Evaton bus boycotts, with their almost theatrical quality of plot and characterisation, help to illuminate many of the important problems confronting black South African resistance movements. In particular they are useful in discussing the processes of political mobilisation in the context of a period when, despite promising objective conditions, mass response to African political organisation was uneven and often disappointing.

Most discussions of African opposition in the 1950s tend to bring to the surface, not always intentionally, the tensions between leaders and followers, between political organisation and its potential constituency, between formal institutionalised resistance and informal 'spontaneous' protest. There are three principal approaches. The first we have met before, the one adopted by many of those who participated in the political struggles. With the wisdom of hindsight history is interpreted as the careful unfolding of a continuous grand strategy which has the purpose of raising the level of mass political consciousness to fresh heights, hastening the arrival of all the necessary conditions for revolution. The party has a vanguard rôle: it plans campaigns which in terms of their proclaimed objectives are doomed to failure, but which in their very frustration will succeed in lifting the scales from the eyes of those who hitherto believed the existing system was capable of significant reform. Each campaign elicits a cumulatively more savage response from the state. This deepends the masses' hatred of authority and reinforces their determination to confront it whatever the penalty or cost.[1] The first approach, therefore, conceives of a politically inert mass which initially must be activated by a catalyst – in this case the African National Congress and its allies.

The second approach, sometimes adopted by those who for one reason or another are critical of the African National Congress, is to contend that in actual fact the ANC functioned during the 1950s in precisely the opposite way. The people, the masses, did not need to be cajoled and prodded into resistance, they had no illusions about the iniquity of the system. Rather, it is argued, the leadership actually perpetuated certain illusions and curbed popular militancy. Guided by its own class interests, which were those of an aspirant petty bourgeoisie, it sought to restrain the course of protest and guide it into channels in which it would serve the interests of this class as opposed to those of the masses. So that when there was an outburst of protest, political organisations would institutionalise it, bureaucratise it, and blunt the keenness of popular anger. For such critics the history of the 1950s is the history of lost opportunities, of chances squandered.[2]

A third approach, favoured by the sociologists Fatima Meer and Leo Kuper,[3] falls somewhere between the other two. For while recognising the existence of spontaneous mass-murmerings which can suddenly erupt into violence, they imply that there is something qualitively different about the nature of protest involved in, say, a beer hall riot, compared to that of an orchestrated campaign against, for example, Bantu Education. In spontaneous movements the agencies of oppression are ignored while the wrath of the crowd breaks on a specific or associated grievance. It is the grievance, not the system of which it is but a symptom, which makes the direct emotional impact and dominates the perception of the crowd. This contrasts with the behaviour of a political movement which deliberately concentrates its energies on attacking a symptom – for example, pass laws – but articulates this attack in a general strategy directed against the system itself. The behaviour of the mass can be likened to that of a psychotic: the mass cannot see beyond the immediate provocative trifle to the root of its passion. The trifle restored or the grievance alleviated will reduce the passion, which though considerably more violent and excitable than the disciplined application of political energy, is never very sustained. Nevertheless, the incident that provokes this essentially apolitical disturbance, though it arises from a particular grievance, is embedded in a matrix of grievances. Ideally the rôle of the political organisation is an ambivalent one. On the one hand it tries to control and direct the energies of spontaneous protest – often attempting to divert it away from activity which is perceived to be unprofitable and wasteful – and thus in a sense it seeks to curb the implicit violence of mass disaffection. On the other hand, organisations try to 'sympathetically interpret' popular emotion – to locate the immediate grievance in the matrix of grievances. They try to employ the raw energy of communal protest in a politically constructive manner. They try to ensure that short-term victories are gained and seen as victories, as signs of weakness in authority, and hence stages along a road of confrontations involving progressively more vital and important issues. In this sense, compromises to gain short-term victories, while they are open to the accusation of reformism and of blurring the focus and dissipating the emotion of spontaneous protest, are tactically vital in any long-term strategy of revolutionary implications. As Martin Legassick has pointed out:

> . . . the means by which any revolutionary party mobilises its social base are reformist, whether one talks about a 'mass line', 'immediate demands', or a minimum program. The problem is whether 'reformist' demands can win and retain popular support and whether their internal logic leads to questioning of the system as a whole, and a stronger power base for challenging that system.[4]

The bus boycotts provide promising material for the testing of these assumptions concerning the interplay between the behaviour of the organisation and of the crowd. In examining these two movements, the bus boycotts of Alexandra and Evaton, the following questions will be implicit in the analysis.

What was the rôle of the political organisations in these movements? Did they perform the vanguard function suggested by Joe Slovo in the first of the three approaches cited above? Did they help to raise the level of consciousness of a politically inert population? Or did they attempt to bureaucratise mass assertions and divert them along channels dictated by the class interests of their petty-bourgeois leadership? Or was the process the dialectical one suggested by Meer and Kuper: the behaviour of the crowd conditioning and being conditioned, in an increasingly potent fashion, by the activity of the political organisations?

Was there a distinct pattern to the development of these protests which can lead us to suppose that they could have formed part of what Martin Legassick calls 'institutionalising' popular power? In other words, could they have been linked to a strategy which would have involved short-term objectives, acceptable to the authorities in the sense that they could have been compelled to accept them? Such a strategy would have consisted of a gradual process of consolidating popular power at a local level through subsistence issue struggles. These, while they would not have directly threatened the state's authority, would nevertheless have stimulated an expansion of the popular classes' awareness of their potential power. Such a development would have been a vital precondition for the mounting of any serious challenge to the political and economic system as a whole.

We will begin with the Alexandra boycott because, though it occurred later than the Evaton protest, Alexandra had already provided the archetype, and the movement which developed in 1957 was self-consciously modelled on what had happened before.

The Alexandra bus boycott was the response of an African community to a penny rise in the single bus fare between the township and the centre of Johannesburg, nine miles away. Now the failure of the African National Congress to evoke a consistently massive response during the 1950s is explained by Fatima Meer, who suggests: 'revolution is not a popular cause . . . [the] security of a familiar system, even if limiting, is invariably preferred to the risks of change'.[5] It has also been asserted that rising black expectations were being matched by the pace of economic growth; that urban Africans had too much to lose if administrative tranquillity and economic productivity were interrupted or disturbed.[6] The bus boycotts help to demonstrate that the economic climate of the 1950s did precious little to provide for the needs of a large proportion of the members of the urban black community. The African family budget rested on a knife edge: in 1956 the average income was £91 a year.[7] A penny increase in bus fares amounted to another 1·4 per cent of income being devoted to the cost of going to work – regardless of the transport needs of the wage-earner's family. When one also considers that well over 80 per cent of Johannesburg's black families had incomes below the level needed for 'minimum essential expenditure',[8] it does not take very great perception to see that attempts to explain failure in political mobilisation as a result of satisfaction of African economic aspirations are pretty far-fetched.

The other point to consider is that the rise in bus fares brought up a number of issues arising out of transport problems. Transport was a major issue in urban African communities. Bus boycotts were a very common form of protest in the 1950s[9] and the Alexandra boycotters attracted an enormous amount of support and interest throughout South Africa. As well as the townships directly affected by the fare rises, there were well-supported sympathy boycotts among communities which had not recently suffered from fare increases; these included Moroka, Port Elizabeth and East London. In part these bore testimony to the African National Congress's organisational strength – but they were also a reflection of the accumulated frustrations that developed out of the problems of transport in towns. It was not simply the cost of transport that was an issue in bus boycotts. In 1943 the complaints of Alexandra commuters had included such matters as routing, overcrowding, departures from schedule, danger, unsheltered terminals, and rude staff.[10] Fourteen years later there had not been much improvement. Buses were still crowded, they were badly ventilated and insufficient in number. African residential areas were often far away from the workplace and in addition to the journey time there were also the periods spent waiting in long bus queues, often without shelter. In 1953 it was estimated that Alexandrans spent three and a half hours a day commuting.[11] There was little consultation over timetabling and when the buses reached townships they would often stop at a single terminal: people would sometimes have to walk a considerable distance to their homes from the bus stop. And on top of all this the buses were certainly not cheap: transport was quite often the second major item in the family budget. It is not difficult to understand the way transport issues seemed to touch on an exposed nerve in the black community.

To understand the boycott we must know something of the history and character of Alexandra township. The first thing that is significant is that Alexandra was a freehold area: as in Sophiatown, Martindale and Newclare, Africans could own land.[12] There seems to be a correlation between well-supported bus boycotts and the existence of freehold property rights; there had been major boycotts in Sophiatown, Lady Selborne and Evaton – all areas in which Africans owned property – as well as in Alexandra. Such places were often very densely populated, which helped to create in them a strong feeling of communal solidarity.[13] Alexandra's population was growing rapidly in the 1950s; in 1943 it was estimated at 50 000, and less than ten years later it was thought to have 80 000 inhabitants.[14] The pace of this growth was in part a response to the recent industrial development in the neighbouring areas of Wynberg and Bergvlei. Alexandra was a township which had evolved organically over forty years rather than, as was the case with the South West Townships, being suddenly and artificially constructed by external agencies. The political liveliness of the community must have owed something to the fact that it was extremely difficult to police; despite pleas from standholders there was no police station in the township,[15] and in the 1950s police entered it only with the greatest reluctance.[16] It is also possible that the character of Alexandra's class base would have contributed to its reputation for militancy. As an old township it would have included in its population some of the most skilled and experienced members of the working class as well as an established petty bourgeoisie. Both groups were on the defensive in the 1950s.[17] And Alexandra had a tradition of bus boycotts. The first took place in 1940 and succeeded in forcing bus companies to reduce fares by a penny to 4d. The operators attempted to put the fares up three times in the next five years and on each occasion a boycott prevented them from doing so. The longest of these boycotts lasted for six weeks from 15 November 1944. As well as the boycotts there had been an important squatters' movement led by Schreiner Baduza in 1946-7. In Alexandra, in short, there was a well-developed history of collective action by the community.

Alexandra was administered by the Alexandra Health Committee. The township lay outside the municipal area and consequently the committee had very few sanctions or resources to make its authority effective. Its six officers could do little to control building (one of the designated functions of the committee) and Alexandra was therefore very crowded. Standholders were often heavily in debt: in the 1940s 85 per cent of the property was bonded.[18] Money-lenders charged high interest and standholders in some instances built up to fifteen lean-to rooms to their stands,[19] letting each room to a family for rents that could be as high at £4 per month.[20] There was the most appalling poverty: an ANC representative claimed that most wage-earners earned on average £2 10s 0d a week[21] (the SAIRR figure for an average Johannesburg black family income was £15 18s 11d a month[22]). Alexandra's poverty was reflected in the infant mortality figures: 23 per cent of the children born there died within a year, mainly of malnutrition.[23] There was an unusually high degree of youth unemployment: influx control regulations prevented people who were born in Alexandra from seeking work in Johannesburg.[24] This, combined with the absence of policing in Alexandra which caused it to be a catchment area for people seeking to avoid the clutches of authority, helps to explain the flourishing gang activity in the township. With all these factors it is small wonder that the people of Alexandra reacted so vigorously to a penny rise in bus fares.

Some understanding of the position of the bus company is also helpful. The Public Utility Transport Company (PUTCO) was formed in 1945, taking over licences and stock from several smaller companies which had serviced locations in the Pretoria and Johannesburg area. Some of PUTCO's difficulties can be traced to this takeover, which was on excessively advantageous terms for the companies which were being bought out. But to compound this PUTCO faced the problem of rising costs. By local standards, PUTCO paid high wages and these had risen by 50 per cent since 1945; the cost of buses and spare parts had doubled since this date as well.[25] But fares on certain routes, which were in any case sub-economic, had remained static since the 1930s. In 1954 PUTCO had applied for permission to increase its fares but this was refused by the cabinet. Then, in 1955, the National Transport Commission (NTC) agreed that PUTCO could raise its weekend fares: the new fares were implemented, despite the efforts of the Alexandra branch of the ANC and other groups to oppose them.[26] But this did little to solve PUTCO's problems. By the end of 1956 the 440 shareholders were in a dissatisfied mood; they had only begun to receive a dividend in 1952, and at six per cent it was hardly a generous one.[27] In fact PUTCO was only able to pay a dividend because the government was subsidising unprofitable routes with an annual grant of £207 475.[28] The government was reluctant to increase the subsidy and so the NTC granted an apprehensive PUTCO a fare increase to take effect on all save Soweto routes from 7 January 1957.

The Alexandra bus boycott lasted three months. The tenacity of PUTCO's efforts to maintain the new fares was partly motivated by its desperate financial position. But there was another factor. PUTCO was no ordinary company: as well as providing the subsidy the government appointed two of PUTCO's five directorships and approved the chairman of the board.[29] The quasi-public nature of the company could well have contributed to the inflexibility of its negotiating position.

In response to PUTCO's announcement on the fare rise a meeting was called on 2 January 1957 by the Alexandra Vigilance Committee, a group of community leaders which, amongst its other functions, elected two standholder representatives to the Health Committee. Twenty-four people came to the meeting, representing seven different groups – the Standholders' and Tenants' Association, the African National Congress, the ANC National-Minded Bloc, the ANC (Madzunya) Group, the Movement for Democracy of Content, the Tenants' Association and the Workers' League.

The Standholders' Association represented about a thousand people who owned stands or who rented or sub-let them from external property owners. S. Mahlangu and J. S. Mathebula of the Association became chairman and secretary of the Alexandra Peoples' Transport Committee (APTC), which was formed from those who attended the meeting. The fact that property owners were to play a leading rôle in the boycott was to be very significant, but it is not easy to explain. There does not seem to have been any intention, as there had been in earlier boycotts, on the part of local entrepreneurs to establish an alternative bus company, though there was a proposal that African businessmen from Durban should be approached.[30] It is possible that landlords would have been keen to resist rises in the cost of living which may have affected people's ability to pay rents. According to one of the more radical APTC members the majority of the standholders favoured a legal contest in the courts with PUTCO rather than direct action.[31] They were overruled by the rest of the committee.

The ANC had the largest representation on the APTC: three men and three Women's League members. The ANC had had a tumultous history in Alexandra recently because of disputes between Africanists and supporters of the Freedom Charter. The current leadership was inexperienced and fairly young. The branch chairman, Alfred Nzo, had only recently been elected to office. He was employed by the Health Committee as an inspector.[32] The other leading ANC spokesman was Thomas Nkobi, a laboratory assistant. Up until the mid-1950s the local ANC had been led by businessmen such as Phineas Nene and R. G. Baloyi. That they no longer predominated reflected the increasingly radical character of the movement at this time. It was important that the boycott coincided with the opening hearings of the Treason Trial: the Congress leadership was unable to pay very close attention to the affairs of the branches and for a time the local ANC was left to take its own initiatives. The presence of women on the committee was also significant. The ANC had submitted a memorandum of transport grievances in 1943 to show how the inadequacies of the system specially affected women: examples included the plight of washerwomen (servicing the northern suburbs), who had to deliver their bundles of washing using the overcrowded buses, as well as the situation of any woman at a crowded bus stop where the strongest will always win the struggle for space on the buses.[33] Women were to be prominent in the initial picketing of bus stops.

The ANC (Madzunya) group was a faction which had developed out of the disputes between Africanists and Charterists which were affecting most ANC branches on the Rand. The Madzunyites were Africanists: after being expelled from the ANC they formed an African nationalist nucleus in Alexandra. The Alexandran Africanists were considerably less middle-class in character than those elsewhere.[34] They were led by Josias Madzunya who had been ANC branch chairman until his expulsion in 1955. He was born in Vendaland and arrived in Johannesburg in 1931 to work as a domestic servant. As a casual labourer he attended a Communist Party night school and later took a correspondence course in public speaking. He currently earned his living selling cardboard boxes on a Johannesburg street corner where he would deliver lengthy political harangues. He was an energetic activist, played quite an important part in the Bantu Education Boycott – Alexandra being one of the few townships to respond – and he was very outspoken:

> These whites are just bluffing you by saying that they are friendly to you. They will never be friendly. . . . Europeans are like lice. They are parasites, busy sucking on blood by means of work for unequal pay.[35]

Madzunya was a member of the APTC as was one of his colleagues, M. Motsele, a former ANC branch secretary expelled with Madzunya.

The ANC National Minded bloc were a conservative splinter grouping which emerged in 1952 in opposition to cooperation with the SAIC and what they alleged to be communist influence on the nationalist movement. It was a small group with a heavy preponderance of relatively wealthy businessmen. Those of its members who lived in Alexandra included R. G. Baloyi, a former ANC treasurer and bus boycott leader of the 1940s and, more important in the context of the 1957 boycott, Dan Gumede. Gumede was the only member of the APTC who provided a personal link with the boycotts of the previous decade. In 1942 he was ANC branch secretary[36] and in the following year he belonged to both the Alexandra Transport Action Committee and the Anti-Expropriation Committee.[37]

The Movement for Democracy of Content (MDC) seems to have been composed of people who had broken with the Unity Movement and its youth wing, the Society of Young Africa, both of them components of the All-African Convention. A leading figure in the movement was the poet (and distant relation of the Minister of Justice), Vincent Swart. Swart had been a member of the African Democratic Party during the war and was peripherally involved in the 1943 and 1944 boycotts. He was later a member of the Trotskyite Workers' International League (which, for a short time, included Madzunya amongst its adherents). In the late 1940s, Swart visited the United States. The Movement for Democracy of Content, which he helped to start, was inspired by an American grouping of the same name, which published a journal called

Contemporary Issues. MDC had been established in Alexandra for a couple of years, and like the Convention, was often sharply critical of the ANC. The MDC was a small coterie of intellectuals. Their thinking was inspired principally by insights drawn from mass theory and led them to a strong faith in popular spontaneity. Of the political groups they were the least concerned to inject externally derived ideas and themes into the boycott movement. The reasons for such restraint were explained by Dan Mokonyane, a University of Witwatersrand law student and the assistant secretary of the APTC. He wrote in his memoir of the boycott:

> Spontaneity does not mean aimless retort or a passive reflection to conditions, because spontaneous acts appear at various levels of political consciousness. But the masses as masses are governed by different rules from those governing individuals. The movement of the masses is elemental and centres exclusively round the next possible step. . . . In general the reaction of the masses is against intolerable pressure which they bear either passively or actively. But when they enter into such activity, their action is not only decisive but can, and often does, take the movement further than its most alert and developed theoreticians dared to imagine.[38].

Finally there were the Workers' (local craftsmen's) and Tenants' Leagues. These were the least well-documented groups. The Workers' League was led and represented on the APTC by George Hlongwe. An Alexandra Workers' Union was involved in bus fare negotiations in 1942,[39] and in 1955 Hlongwe – as leader of the Workers' League Transport Action Committee – was proposing a boycott in response to the weekend fare rises.[40]

There was a diverse collection of sectional, and in some cases conflicting, interests represented on the APTC. Broadly these fell into three groups: the property owners and businessmen, now largely alienated from the local ANC; the political parties each with a competing popular appeal; and groups which confined themselves to the immediate worries of the poor.[41]

The APTC organised a meeting on Sunday 6 January which was attended by 2 000 people. The meeting voted to boycott the buses until the fares were restored to their old level. The next day the buses ran virtually empty; 15 000 people walked the nine miles from Alexandra to Johannesburg. Simultaneously boycotts began in Sophiatown and the Pretoria townships, also affected by the PUTCO increases (see below). Altogether 60 000 people stopped using the green PUTCO buses. Many of them had the alternative of a train service but the people of Alexandra had no such choice; for the next three months they walked to and from work, eighteen miles a day. Several factors were important in sustaining the boycotters' enthusiasm. First, the boycott committee held frequent open air mass meetings in one or other of the squares in Alexandra. Here speeches were made by representatives of the different factions and groups, but most important of all, people were informed of the progress of negotiations with the company, the municipality and employers' organisations, and given a chance to express their opinions. Decision-making was done at the mass meeting; a show of hands would determine the acceptance or rejection of proposed solutions. This direct democracy was crucial in the maintenance of boycotters' morale. It is significant that there was little evidence of any kind of intimidation; even the *tsotsis* contented themselves with the levying of 1s 6d 'boycott tax'.[42]

The second point is that there was considerable sympathy for the boycotters among the white community. This was important for two reasons. First, efforts were made to provide boycotters with lifts during the early stages of the boycott. Secondly, it was not long before various white groups began to search for a compromise: unlike industrial struggles or overtly political campaigns the bus boycott seems to have had a much greater potential for exploiting conflicting interests within the white community. It is worth looking at these groups quite closely. Perhaps the one that had the most influence on the course of events was the Johannesburg branch of the Liberal Party. They were to perform a crucial intermediary function between the employers' organisations and the boycott committees. A white group which had much closer contacts with the ANC was the Congress of Democrats, but they lacked the relationship with employers enjoyed by Liberals and in any case many of their leading members were caught up in the Treason Trial proceedings. Quite apart from their humanitarian feelings, the Liberals were anxious to increase their influence and membership among the black community; the boycott offered an excellent opportunity. The Liberals quickly formed a boycott sub-committee and set about organising a relay of lifts (though lift-giving was by no means restricted to Liberals or COD members). Members of the committee also began sounding out contacts in the City Council and the Chamber of Commerce. After 22 January a series of meetings was held between the Liberal sub-committee and the APTC. Out of these an important moderating principle was established: the boycotters demands would not go 'beyond the preservation of pre-boycott fares'.[43] This contrasted both with the Evaton boycott (see below) and previous Alexandra boycotts.

We will return to the Liberals later. Also very important were the employers' organisations, for it was their attitude that was likely to decide the final outcome of the boycott. First, the Johannesburg Chamber of Commerce. The Chamber had played an important rôle in the 1944–5 boycott negotiations and on 23 February it offered to fund a transport allowance which would be paid to employees. Contrasting with the relatively conciliatory position towards the boycotters taken by the Johannesburg Chamber of Commerce was the attitude of the Transvaal Chamber of Industries. This became clear in the statement issued by the Chamber's President, Lulofs, on 11 January. In it he complained of a sharp increase in the rate of absenteeism (commercial employers were emphatic that absenteeism had not increased) and a lowered productivity because of physical exhaustion of the workforce. He also said that industry was reluctant to subsidise to any further extent the Native Services Levy – a fund contributed to by industry and commerce which financed various services and housing projects. Lulofs pointed out that many employers were exempted from this contribution (e.g. municipalities, who paid atrociously).[44] Two weeks later, the Chamber called on boycotters to 'accept their situation'. Plans for long-term solutions were being formed, it loftily informed them. Absenteeism, it said, would result in wholesale dismissals.[45] At this stage, the Chamber of Industries had been influenced by the transport minister's denunciation of the boycott as being politically inspired. At the beginning of February the Chamber said it was not prepared to raise wages to end the boycott (a solution advocated with some force by PUTCO which was one of the best employers in Johannesburg).[46] Even more striking was industry's refusal to support the Chamber of Commerce's transport allowance scheme. This was after one of the major industrial bodies, the Steel and Engineering Industries' Federation of South Africa, had decided that the boycott was 'too dangerous to touch'.[47]

The contrasting attitudes of the two employers' organisations need some explanation. First, it may have been that many of Alexandra's industrial workers were employed nearby (in Bergvlei and Wynberg) and consequently the boycott would not have made a great deal of difference to them or their employers. Second, the Chamber of Industry was a Transvaal body whereas the Chamber of Commerce represented Johannesburg firms only: in the case of the latter the Alexandra boycotters – as a proportion of their total workforce – may have been more important. Third, industry may have been penetrated to a much greater extent by Afrikaner capital than was the case with Johannesburg commercial firms, and hence been more receptive to government injunctions to have nothing to do with the boycotters. Finally, commercial firms would have had an immediate interest in the economic welfare of blacks as consumers. This concern would have been shared only by some industrialists.[48]

But as well as taking account of the positions of various organisations one should not neglect the general sympathy the boycott evoked from Johannesburg's white community – at least until the first terms were rejected. The boycott received a reasonably favourable press, and the lifts also provided a great deal of encouragement. The boycott's impact is not difficult to understand: visually it was dramatic – the steady procession of men and women marching to and from Alexandra every day shouting 'Azikwelwa' (we will not ride) and 'Ha Bongoela' (we don't drink any more) and 'Gein Ukudla' (keep food for a rainy day)[49] and 'Asinimali' (we have no money). And as they walked they sang the boycott song which was soon banned by the South African Broadcasting Corporation. To get to work the boycotters had to cross nine miles of white residential areas along a busy main road. For a while the black people of Alexandra had become visible to the affluent northern suburbs of Johannesburg.

However, behind the determination and unity of the people who were walking to work divisions were beginning to emerge amongst the groups represented on the APTC. These were the result of moves by the employers and PUTCO itself. As we have seen, the first move came from the Johannesburg Chamber of Commerce (JCC) when they persuaded their members to pay an extra shilling a week transport allowance. This was refused by the APTC; after all, many employers were not members of the JCC – how would domestic servants and municipal labourers persuade their employers to give them an extra shilling? Nevertheless the APTC, in collaboration with members of the Liberal Party, drafted a set of proposals for the JCC to consider. PUTCO meanwhile had produced an ultimatum on 18 February: if the boycott was not called off by 1 March the buses would be permanently withdrawn. At this point the government stepped in. Minister Schoeman had already said that the boycott was a political challenge to the state – a boycotters' victory would be an ANC victory. He now announced that in the event of PUTCO withdrawing their buses, no one would be allowed to take over their routes: Alexandra would never have a bus service again.[50]

This provoked the first erosion in APTC solidarity. A mass meeting was held on 20 February; it voted for the boycott to continue. Five days later a secret meeting was held between six members of the APTC and PUTCO executives. The six were drawn from the property owners on the committee, and were led by Mr Mahlangu. Though they were beginning to make conciliatory noises a mass meeting of 5 000 people simultaneously voted again for a continuation. By the beginning of March the divisions were clear: the Vigilance and Standholders' associations and the ANC National Minded bloc were trying to reach towards some form of compromise, whereas the other groups were opposed to any concessions being made to PUTCO.[51] These latter groups seemed to be reflecting the feelings of the overwhelming majority of Alexandra residents who had been walking to work for nearly two months. The Standholders' position was understandable: if there was to be no bus service for Alexandra in the future they would be ruined, for Alexandra would lose much of its attraction and they would lose their tenants.

On 28 February the Chamber of Commerce, in response to APTC proposals, produced a fresh offer. Employers were to put up a fund of £25 000: this would finance a scheme in which people could claim a penny back on a cancelled ticket at the end of their journey. This was put to the APTC at a meeting attended also by the Bishop of Johannesburg, Ambrose Reeves (who was working closely with the Liberals and who had a friendly relationship with Transvaal ANC leaders), A. B. Xuma and Liberal Party representatives. At this meeting ten members of the APTC voted in favour of the proposals – including the ANC representatives. Madzunya, Motsele and Mokonyane voted against them.[52] On 1 March PUTCO delayed withdrawing its buses so that mass meetings could consider the JCC plan that evening. They were due for a disappointment: in Alexandra the public meetings rejected the proposals and the Africanist Motsele burnt a copy of them in front of the crowd.[53] Significantly, women were said to have organised the main Alexandra meeting which rejected the proposals.[54]

By this stage the divisions between the groups represented on the APTC were public knowledge. The ANC National Minded bloc were openly opposing the boycott[55] while the Standholders were discreetly wavering. On 3 March they had a meeting where they anxiously discussed the economic implications of the withdrawal of the bus service.[56] The Africanists and Mokonyane, as we have seen, were totally opposed to any compromise. The position of the ANC leaders was less clear cut. In the negotiations of the 28th the ANC representatives voted in favour of the refund scheme. Here it is possible that the presence of Reeves and Xuma had a persuasive effect. Both were in favour of the proposals[57] and the Bishop was closely in touch with the ANC's national leadership gathered in Johannesburg for the Treason hearings.[58] It was known that he enjoyed their confidence and therefore he was in a position to exert considerable pressure on the Alexandra ANC leaders, some of whom were new to the movement. But it is also likely that there was confusion over the choice of strategy among Congress alliance leaders. For the day the terms were rejected at the mass meetings a leaflet was circulated in the township advising people to reject the JCC offer. The leaflet was issued by the Congress of Democrats and was evocatively entitled 'What is to be done?'.[59] An article in *Africa South*, a journal generally sympathetic to Congress, gives us an indication of the way the left within the nationalist movement perceived the boycott. The boycott, it asserted, did not merely involve an economic issue, a rise in the cost of public transport. The boycott had aroused massive retaliatory measures by the state. The participants were claiming the right to protest against all the major and minor iniquities of apartheid. To separate the economic background of this particular conflict from the more general political issues was to make distinctions which were meaningless in the eyes of most Africans.[60]

Revolutionaries within the Congress movement were well aware of the boycott's political significance: theirs was rather a sin of omission. At no time was there any evidence that senior left-wing Congressites actually provided any suggestions to the local leaders as to how to develop whatever potential the boycott had for more general political action.[61] That other groups were able to influence the APTC to limit their demands to the fare alone is an indication of the weakness of the left at this time. In the later stages of the boycott there were signs that it could develop into a more open challenge requiring a higher level of political commitment but these owed little to the influence of outsiders.

Political considerations aside there were sound material reasons for rejecting the JCC terms. First, the scheme was inconvenient: it involved queueing twice rather than once on every journey, thus adding to commuting time. Second, there was no assurance that there could be a permanent settlement: the £25 000 would be exhausted in three months. Mokonyane viewed the scheme as a lure to draw people back on to the buses without any formal commitments being made. Third, Pretoria had been left out of the scheme.[62] When these terms were rejected PUTCO withdrew its buses. Bishop Reeves and the Liberals did not despair: they continued to negotiate with the City Council and the JCC and also obtained the ANC's agreement that it would attempt to persuade boycott committees to accept improved proposals. All these efforts were fairly secret: both Reeves and the Liberals felt that PUTCO and the APTC would be made more amenable if they were kept in the dark for a while.[63]

The state preferred a more heavy-handed approach. The police played a major rôle. They patrolled Louis Botha Avenue in force and stopped as many cars as they could which seemed to be carrying boycotters, subjecting them to checks on minor traffic regulations. Five hundred people (mainly illegal taxi operators) were detained after breaching such rules. Not content with this petty harassment, the police raided Alexandra twice in February: altogether 14 000 people were held under some pretext, tax defaulting and illegal residence being the two most common offences.[64] The government was also making more long-term threats. An official publication stated:

It was found that of all the townships where boycott attempts were made, the only really successful boycotts occurred in uncontrolled townships where no formal authority is exercised over the Bantu inhabitants in terms of the normal legislation applying to Bantu townships. It is also these uncontrolled areas which generally show the highest crime rates and other disturbances.[65]

It was time, announced the Minister of Native Affairs, to bring Alexandra 'under very strict control'. The proper population of the township should have been around 30 000 and steps would be taken to reduce it to that number.[66] The government obviously viewed the boycott as a major threat. It devoted two numbers of its *Digest* to analyses of the boycott, replete with sensational revelations concerning 'underground red workers', 'red termites', and 'ANC Youth League Stormtroopers'.

Such hysteria should be seen in the context of the state's attempt to implicate the Congress leadership on a treason charge: its external propaganda should not therefore be taken altogether at its face value. Nevertheless, it is likely that the authorities were genuinely alarmed by the boycott. Efforts to exploit its political implications were not limited to state agencies. By March ANC spokesmen were claiming that 'the boycott was no longer an economic struggle but was becoming a political one'.[67] By this time there were signs of a move to convert the boycott into a form of general strike. At a mass meeting on 27 February Mokonyane told the people:

> When we are tired we shall rest. . . . They are punishing us because we are poor . . . save food and prepare for the offensive.[68]

By the first week in March Nzo was actually using the phrase 'stay-at-home', a term linked to the South African Congress of Trades Unions' '£1 a day' campaign which was just beginning. Nzo told his audience on 6 March that when they were tired they should stay at home and wait until commercial and industrial firms came to pick them up for work.[69] This resolution then became rather less ambivalent, and the following week the APTC produced an ultimatum: the City Council should provide transport for the boycotters; if this was not done by Monday the 18th the workers would stay at home.[70] To an extent this may have reflected the onset of fatigue, but there is a strong case for arguing that the ANC was thinking in such terms from the start of the boycott. Amongst the Treason Trial evidence were some notes for a speech by Tennyson Makiwane. Makiwane, a defendant in the trial from 1956 to 1958, had previously lived for two years in Alexandra after his expulsion from Fort Hare for ANC Youth League activities. The notes were for a speech made in February 1956. The speech is about the Evaton boycott but it seems to have been intended for an Alexandra audience. In it, Makiwane suggests that consumer grievances should be linked with those of transport workers, that a common union should be formed to represent passengers and workers and that the political organisation should link up people's struggle for transport in a location into a general struggle of all people in townships.[71] Makiwane used to use his lunch breaks in the Treason Trial to consult with APTC leaders.[72]

In broad outline this did approximate to the strategy the ANC was pursuing in the February/March period. In Alexandra itself it would have been difficult for passengers to make common cause with PUTCO staff: their interests were diametrically opposed; PUTCO employees were better paid than most Alexandra workers and were faced by the threat of losing their jobs.

However, in Bloemfontein, where the local ANC tried ineffectively to organise a 'sympathy boycott', issues discussed included the upgrading of black staff into jobs reserved for whites. The sympathy boycotts affected East London, Randfontein, Port Elizabeth, Germiston, Moroka-Jabavu and Edenvale. These were in addition to the boycotts which arose from the PUTCO fare increase (Pretoria, Sophiatown and Western Native Townships). In each centre, Peoples' Transport Committees were formed and despite the frequent opposition of Advisory Boards they could be, as in the case of the Eastern Province centres, 90 per cent effective. Though the ANC was accused of using the boycotts 'solely for a political purpose . . . not economic',[73] these sympathy protests were linked to local issues: in Bloemfontein, for example, as well as the question of black staff the municipality were also accused of using profits derived from black bus services to subsidise white facilities. For the main boycott centres (Alexandra, Pretoria and Sophiatown) a co-ordinating committee was established: this was chaired by Alfred Nzo of the Alexandra ANC.[74] In Alexandra the ANC underwent a massive expansion in membership, from 600 to 6 000, making it one of the largest branches in the country. The degree of politicisation of the boycott was perhaps indicated at the Alexandra meeting where Nzo first mentioned a stay-at-home. The Africanists were also present. Mr Motsele spoke of Ghanaian independence and of Nkrumah. There were cries of 'Afrika!' and 'This is our mother country. We will die first!'[75]

However, there was no stay-at-home on 18 March. Instead, negotiations began, with the ANC playing an intermediary rôle between the Peoples' Transport Committees (PTCs) and representatives of PUTCO, the Chamber of Commerce, the municipality and the Liberal Party. The fresh proposals were based on a coupon system: at the beginning of the week people would buy a book of coupons with the effect that the 5d tickets would cost 4d; the Chamber of Commerce would then make up the difference to PUTCO. By the time the JCC funds were exhausted it was hoped that the JCC and the municipality would have succeeded in obtaining a rise in the Native Services Levy. The ANC undertook to persuade the PTC to accept the proposals on conditions that the deal would include Pretoria. The Bishop and Liberals agreed to look for sources to fund coupons in Pretoria. There was also a general undertaking that employers' organisations would encourage a rise in wages. In response to this latter point the ANC, when it presented the settlement terms to the community, included the demand of a £1 daily wage.[76]

The events of the final week of the boycott were complex, and they resulted essentially from a threefold split between the APTC leaders. It seems clear that the local ANC were under considerable pressure from the national leadership, who seem to have been open to influence from Reeves and Liberal Party spokesmen.[77] Meanwhile the property owners had made a completely independent secret approach to PUTCO guaranteeing an acceptance of the coupon system regardless of whether it was implemented in Pretoria. Obviously they were seriously worried by Verwoerd's declared intention to reduce the township population, and they were not prepared to risk any possibility of a continuation of the boycott in the hope that if a settlement was reached the attention of the authorities would be diverted elsewhere. PUTCO agreed to reintroduce the buses if enough people turned up to ride them on

Monday morning. Mokonyane, for reasons that will be explored below, remained opposed to a settlement whilst the Africanists were undecided. On Sunday 31 March public meetings were held in all boycott centres. These voted for an acceptance of the terms, provided (a) that they were approved by Alexandra residents, and (b) that Pretoria was included.

On the 31st three meetings were held simultaneously in Alexandra – two of them organised by pro-settlement factions (who had published a circular the day before advocating a return to the buses), and one by the rest of the APTC. The latter meeting was by far the best attended. Despite the intentions of the ANC it rejected the proposals. It was felt that: (a) because the tickets for which people were meant to exchange the coupons had 5d printed on them they were intended to accustom people to paying 5d when the JCC money ran out, and (b) that PUTCO should pay compensation for police action, arrests and deaths (in Pretoria) that had occurred during the boycott.[78]

By now there was total confusion. Liberals met APTC leaders on Sunday evening and criticised them for failing to unanimously support the settlement, whereupon some promised to urge the people to reverse the decision. On Monday PUTCO buses were reintroduced and in the absence of any clear directions, and indeed with conflicting advice in the form of pamphlets from the ANC (declaring a victory and telling people they could ride the buses) and from the non-ANC members of the APTC (see below), people once again started using the buses. In Alexandra the boycott was over.

It continued, though, in the other Johannesburg locations and townships for another fortnight. In Moroka-Jabavu, where people had to walk seven miles to a railway station, and which had not been affected by bus fare increases, the boycotters went on walking for another two weeks. Both here and in the Western Areas, where Africanists were said to have a commanding position on the People's Transport Committee, large public meetings resolved to carry on the boycott until Pretoria was included in the settlement. Only after the Co-ordinating Committee made a public commitment to negotiate for the inclusion of Pretoria in any final agreement did the boycott end in these centres. Meanwhile, in Alexandra, conflict between the APTC leaders helped to diminish popular morale. As well as its opponents within the township, the local ANC branch had to contend with criticism from an unexpected source. An analysis in the 4 April issue of *New Age* by Michael Harmel commented on the 'marked failure of . . . Congress to give positive leadership to the people of Alexandra. The local Congress branch did not play a positive part either before or at the crucial meeting on Sunday.'

It is difficult to evaluate the ANC's decision to accept the terms and end the boycott. As well as looking at the pros and cons of continuation it is necessary to come to some assessment of the ANC's strategy throughout the boycott. The case against settlement included the following points.

First, the offer was a temporary one: there was no guarantee that the government would heed the Chamber of Commerce or the Johannesburg City Council. Significantly, the *Afrikaanse Sakekamer* had refused all along to support the JCC. An APTC leaflet distributed on 7 April made the point well:

When the £25 000 runs out from the Chamber of Commerce – what then? We cannot sell our fourteen weeks' struggle for a twelve week settlement. The government has promised to step in when the boycott is smashed and the Chamber is bankrupt to bring about their permanent settlement. Why drive the Chamber to bankruptcy, why drive the people to distraction? An authority which behaves in this way is highly suspect. We refuse to settle our economic affairs on the basis of PROMISES – from the enemy. Since when must we have confidence in a white government who are the source of our ruin?

The ANC and the Standholders, by accepting the offer had sold out, 'they [had] tried to sell out many times'.[79] The JCC was 'prepared to spend £25 000 now in killing the boycott in order to guarantee hundreds of thousands profit in the future'.[80] At the time the argument had some force to it. A permanent settlement was by no means a certainty. The Minister of Transport did agree in May to raise the Native Services Levy – but only if both the main employers' organisations agreed. For two months the employers were divided on the issue, the Chamber of Commerce favouring the scheme, the Chamber of Industry being 'adamant' in its opposition.[81] Industrial employers only extended their backing grudgingly and slowly.

The second point, which may well have tipped the balance in favour of settlement, was that the situation in the townships was hardly stable either. As an APTC leaflet of 14 April pointed out:

> Wherever we look there is confusion. Some people proclaim a victory, others say . . . the boycott must go on. Some people ride. Others carry on walking.[82]

Liberals, by the beginning of May, were seriously worried that the boycott might be restarted. The APTC leaders (including the local ANC men) had been left out of the negotiations with the Minister and the employers: 'They feel isolated, hurt, slighted and do not know what to tell their people . . . [the] first lesson of the boycott, consultation, has already been forgotten by the Europeans.'[83] Had the boycott in fact exhausted its potential? Would the people of Alexandra have gone on walking? The main meeting in Alexandra did reject the scheme: it was attended by 5 000 people and it was held on Sunday (so the APTC could not be accused of holding a meeting when most of the normal bus users were still at work or on the way home). Against this one must bear in mind that people were getting very tired: the theme of exhaustion is very common in the later boycott speeches. With the removal of the buses in March one of the objective tests of the boycott's effectiveness was gone: there was nothing to boycott. However, a unified leadership might have exploited the situation more deftly: a recurrent theme of APTC leaflets after 1 April was that 'if we, the people, having united on this issue, won a victory, we would feel our strength and continue to fight for much more than 1d'.[84] So it was possible to argue that acceptance of the deal dissipated the strength and unity built up over three months. We will return to this in a moment.

The third point favouring continuation was that the coupon scheme was applicable to the Johannesburg routes only; it was not going to apply to Pretoria where there were separate employers' organisations who were completely opposed to raising the contribution to the Native Services Levy.[85]

The Pretoria boycott continued into 1958 without enjoying any support from elsewhere. The development of the Pretoria boycott requires some explanation. First, even compared with Alexandra, people in Pretoria locations were poor. Early in the boycott a special report was produced by the manager of the Non-European Affairs Department. It revealed that 70 per cent of Pretoria's black population earned less than £9 0s 0d a month. The last wage award had been in 1942. To give some idea of the impact of the 1d fare rise the budget of a family in Vlakfontein is illuminating. Municipal rents were £2 7s 3d. Monthly transport costs were £2 4s 3d. This left less than £5 for everything else.[86] The leadership and impetus of the Pretoria boycott came from Lady Selborne, like Alexandra a freehold township. Here, even the relatively conservative Advisory Board was in favour of the boycott.[87] Women played an especially important rôle in the Pretoria boycott. It was reported in a case at Mooiplaas location in January that: 'The menfolk want to use the buses but the women insist on the boycott continuing and are apparently prepared to use force to prevent the use of the buses.'[88]

Because of the domestic division of labour women could be expected to be more sensitive to issues of subsistence than men. There seem to have been fewer political rivals to the ANC's position than was the case in Alexandra. However, the ANC was fairly weak and inexperienced, and the branch had only been reformed in 1955 after a period of inactivity.[89] This was possibly one reason why, after the Alexandra settlement, the Pretoria boycotters never succeeded in mobilising the ANC nationally in the way that Alexandra had. Alexandra's branch, over the years, had contributed many people who now had important functions within the organisation. This was not the case with Pretoria – and this may have had the effect of making them more autonomous of, but less influential with, the national leadership. But the poverty of the people and autonomy of the ANC are not the only factors that explain the extraordinary resilience of the 10 000 boycotters of Pretoria. Unlike the people of Alexandra, most of them had the alternative of a train service: indeed, in December 1958 Lady Selborne PTC requested that PUTCO services should be permanently withdrawn. The trains were cheaper and the station was nearer the centre of the location than was the bus terminus.[90] Hence the boycott caused rather less hardship than elsewhere. Nevertheless, this did not prevent moments of considerable bitterness: during the boycott buses were burnt, as was an office of the Peri-Urban Areas Board, and a man was killed and several were wounded when the police broke up meetings during the early stages of the boycott. The only concessions offered to the Pretoria Committees were:

    (a) the inclusion, because of its geographical position, of Vlakfontein in the Johannesburg settlement, and

    (b) the shortening of some bus routes for the old fare price.

Consequently there was considerable bitterness among Pretoria boycotters when they found that they had been deserted by Alexandra: after all, they had been united under a single co-ordinating committee. It is not surprising that when the Pan-Africanist Congress was formed, some of the main defections from the ANC were in the Pretoria townships.

But a strong case could be made for accepting the JCC proposals as they stood. Though the remnants of the APTC did contend that settlement involved a retreat from a strategically advantageous position of strength and unity, it might be said that settlement was the best option if maximum unity was to be preserved. Certainly, the situation was volatile after 1 April, but the reintroduction of the bus service and the coupon system were substantial temptations for those who were tired. A continuation would probably have provoked deeper divisions in the community than settlement: Mokonyane's meetings thereafter, in which he called on Alexandra to come out in support of Pretoria, had a certain moral force but little impact.

There was much less morale-boosting sympathy from the white community: this declined notably after the rejection of the JCC refund scheme. Fewer lifts were being offered and press coverage was increasingly impatient, not to say hostile. As argued previously, the feeling that the boycott was having an impact on the white community helped to encourage a realisation that victory was possible.

Then, the JCC offer at the end of March might have been the last chance of even a partial victory: if the offer had been rejected it might never have been repeated. PUTCO had lost nearly £90 000 as a result of the boycott:[91] if it had continued, PUTCO's losses could have been so severe that no increase in the Native Services Levy that employers would have been willing to contemplate would have made good these losses. As we have seen, the Alexandra leaders were far more susceptible to pressure from above than were the Africanists or Mokonyane. Pressure from above came from people who could gauge more sensitively the mood of civic and business leaders.

The final and seemingly clinching argument in favour of the ANC's decision was that the nationalist movement was able, to use Mokonyane's words, 'to pick the fruit' of the struggle of Alexandra. This happened more or less fortuitously. On 26 June, 80 per cent of Johannesburg's African workforce stayed at home in response to a Congress call for a demonstrative action on its Freedom Day anniversary. The decision to call for a strike emerged from the lower echelons of the ANC; the national leadership envisaged the occasion as a day of prayer, sporting and cultural activities, religious services and torchlight processions in the evening, and this was the form the 26 June demonstration took in the other main towns. In Johannesburg, though, there appeared to be a compelling popular tendency towards a withdrawal of labour as a result of the bus boycott. It was most obviously apparent in the Western Areas where, in the wake of the boycott, a large proportion of the population had been involved in protests against a system of permits recently introduced to stem the flow of men and women who were still trying to enter and reside in the doomed freehold township. Under the leadership of an Anti-Permit Committee, a series of protests were arranged, culminating in a huge march of over 30 000 people to the City Hall in what virtually amounted, as the *New Age* observed, to a 'general strike'. The permits were withdrawn shortly thereafter. According to Mokonyane, the march was opposed by senior ANC men and it may have been significant that the Sophiatown ANC at that time included Africanists in its leadership.[92]

Out of the dilemma of whether to jettison Pretoria in order to conserve their Alexandra base, or to take a principled position and perhaps erode their strength in Alexandra and retain support in what was never a strong ANC area, the ANC chose the tactically correct option. But in general strategic terms they were open to criticism. First, there were moments of inconsistency in the conduct of ANC leaders during the boycott which suggest that they lacked a clear vision of how the boycott could be developed. The acceptance of the second JCC offer, the call for a stay-away in March only to be followed by a hasty withdrawal to the negotiating table, the early assurance by the national leadership that they would persuade local leaders to accept the coupon system: these do not suggest a long-term strategy nor do they indicate a very high valuation being placed on the process of popular decision-making that was such an important feature of the boycott. And this leads one to the second major flaw in the ANC's approach: they did not attempt in any real sense to 'institutionalise' the popular power, the popular political participation, that had developed out of the boycott. True, they drew on its energy for the 26th June demonstration, but this ritualistic effort did little to perpetuate or channel constructively the forces of the boycott. Here an interesting comparison can be made with the 1944–5 boycott in which communists urged people to go on walking despite the fare settlement until the transport system was socialised.[93] Of more obvious relevance to the 1957 situation was the Evaton settlement which placed considerable power in the hands of the Peoples' Transport Committee (see below). But in Alexandra, as we have seen, the APTC was influenced to limit its concerns to the fare rise. Nevertheless, the democratic forms of the boycott could have been adapted to produce permanent and far-reaching structures with enterprising political leadership: an unofficial, democratised township administration might have been a possibility. Then there were issues which arose out of internal class differentiations: landlords had shown themselves as a distinct interest group during the boycott; surely a move to create some form of rent control mechanism would have been widely acceptable? Although in general the ANC made a valuable contribution to the blossoming of the boycott movement it can be contended that having picked it they then threw away the fruit.

The following analysis of the Evaton boycott will begin with a bare chronology. Out of this will arise several questions and in answering them some comparisons will be drawn with the Alexandra protest. The treatment will close with an evaluation of the Evaton settlement. We will then be in a position to resolve some of the issues raised at the beginning of this chapter.

The first post-war bus boycott in Evaton, a township situated twelve miles from the Vereeniging/Vanderbijlpark industrial complex and 30 miles from Johannesburg, took place in January 1950. The bus company had decided to collect passengers on the Evaton–Vereeniging route from the edges of the township as tarmac roads did not extend within its boundaries.[94] In August 1954 there was a one-day token boycott in protest against the inefficiency of the service between Evaton and Johannesburg provided by the Evaton Passenger Company (EPC). The director of the EPC, a Mr V. d'Agnese, suggested that a liaison committee of influential Evaton inhabitants should be formed, and on 24 August 1954 the Evaton Peoples' Transport Council (EPTC) was elected at a public meeting.[95] That same month the EPC applied for a fare increase and despite protests from the EPTC it was granted by the Road Transportation Board. In October 1954 a boycott took place in Kliptown, another community served by the EPC. The boycott was successful: after four weeks, during which 6 000 people walked daily to Nancefield railway station, a sixpenny weekly fare rise was withdrawn and improvements in the service were promised by d'Agnese.[96] Towards the end of this boycott a joint meeting was held between the Kliptown Bus Committee and the EPTC to discuss d'Agnese's application for a fare increase on the Evaton–Johannesburg route.[97] The two communities decided to co-ordinate their activities. Early in 1955 an EPC bus broke down one night on a level crossing. Ten people were killed by an oncoming train.

In July 1955 the EPTC issued a bulletin calling for a public meeting on 24 July. At this meeting the 2 500 users of the Evaton–Johannesburg service resolved to boycott the EPC until the monthly and weekly fares were reduced to their old levels, that is, from £2 15s 0d to £2 5s 0d and from 18s to 15s, respectively.[98] The following morning people began walking to Nancefield railway station at 4.00 a.m. Buses carrying passengers were stopped by pickets and people were told to get off. The boycott also affected nearby Annandale. Much of the picketing was done by groups of women.[99] The following day a woman threw herself in the path of a moving bus to halt its progress.[100] For the next seven weeks buses were picketed and stoned and there were occasional clashes between police, boycotters and an anti-boycott group which was beginning to coalesce round Ralekeke Rantube, the leader of Evaton's Basotho community. This tension came to a head on 7 September when two attempts – one of them successful – were made to burn out buses which had entered the location. The EPC then withdrew its buses altogether until 24 October. One incident that occurred during this interval deserves mention: on 25 September a car fixed with a loudspeaker toured the location. The men inside announced their intention to establish an African-owned bus service for Evaton.[101] The wreck of the car was discovered the next day in Evaton.

On 24 October the EPC resumed its service. The buses were greeted by large angry crowds, stones and roadblocks. That afternoon a procession of about one thousand people marched through Evaton. Fighting broke out between pro-boycotters and Ralekeke Rantube's followers, the 'Russians'. Two boycotters were killed and Rantube's house was damaged. The conflict was deepened in October when the EPC took to employing Ralekeke and several other Basothos to protect the buses and attack picket lines.[102] In December five boycott supporters were murdered including Khabutlane, a Basotho sub-chief.[103]

At some point during early 1956 the EPTC applied for four National Transport Board certificates and announced its intention of establishing a bus service for the community. Meanwhile the boycott went on with sporadic outbreaks of tension. EPC employees were taking the brunt of the boycotters' anger and on 6 May a bus conductor, Johnson Choke, was badly beaten up and died from his injuries shortly afterwards. In the days preceding his funeral, as well as on the day of the funeral itself, 11 May, Basotho groups boarded buses on their way to Evaton, and rode into the location in them, emerging at the terminus to assault the picketers. Sustained fighting between armed groups of boycotters and 'Russians' took place between 24 and 29 June. Nine people were killed altogether, several houses were destroyed, thousands of people sought refuge on the ground surrounding the local police station (Evaton's population was estimated to have fallen by 40 per cent – 20 000 – during these troubles).[104] A hundred policemen armed with sten guns were needed to control the situation. The police prevailed upon the EPTC leader Molefi and Rantube to go through the motions of a public peacemaking and shortly afterwards the violence simmered down. At this point the bus company announced that the old fares would be reintroduced.[105] It would seem that at this stage the EPTC leaders were in favour of a settlement but the public feeling against the EPC was too bitter for a return to the status quo to be sufficient. A meeting was held which rejected the settlement and collected £23 13s 7½d towards boycott funds.[106] An EPTC meeting was held on 10 July. At this meeting it was resolved to negotiate on the basis of the following demands (in addition to the maintenance of pre-boycott fares): Sunday workers should be able to use their normal weekly or monthly season tickets; a concessionary student rate should be introduced; the bus depot and booking office should be located within the township; a penalty clause should be included within the settlement making the EPC liable to a payment if it took action without consulting the EPTC.[107] On 11 August the EPC and the EPTC met to negotiate and managed to come to an agreement. Some of the above terms were incorporated into the settlement which was made public on 19 August. As well as agreeing that the pre-boycott fares should remain operative, the EPC gave an undertaking that £500 would be paid to the EPTC if the fare was increased or if it sold interests without consultation. In addition the EPC would run its buses on the basis of a timetable drawn up by the EPTC, 50 per cent of the inspectors were to be black, and shelters would be constructed at the Evaton and Johannesburg terminals.[108] At this point the EPTC managed to satisfy rank and file boycotters that they had won a substantial victory and shortly thereafter the EPC buses began to carry their full complement of passengers to Johannesburg. The boycott had ended but at a cost of fifteen deaths, the polarisation of the Evaton community and £52 000 in lost fares to the company.[109]

Several questions seem immediately relevant. Firstly, why did the boycott (which only affected the immediate interests of 2 500 bus users and their dependants) create such a deep rift in the community? More particularly, why did Rantube and his followers oppose the boycott? Secondly, what rôle did any political organisations play in the events; were there any attempts to develop the boycott into a more deliberate, self-conscious political movement? Thirdly, how do we interpret the settlement: why did the EPC make such important concessions and what were their implications? First of all, though, it is useful to have some knowledge of the type of community Evaton was.

Evaton's origins are similar to those of Alexandra. The area originally belonged to a land speculation company which began selling off allotments to Africans in 1905. Its formal status as a released freehold African area was confirmed by the 1936 Land Act. At first the location mainly accommodated farm labourers but with the development of manufacturing industry the population trebled in ten years: from 10 000 in 1936 to 30 000 in 1946.[110] Thereafter, it continued to expand, but at a more modest rate: in 1955 Evaton was believed to have 50 000 inhabitants. It was divided by a stream into two areas: the location proper and Evaton Small Farms. Despite its name, the Small Farms area was considerably more congested than Evaton location. This was because allotments there were sold during the 1930s to meet the expansion of demand: they were smaller, and relatively more expensive (a high initial price being, as we have seen in the case of Alexandra, an impetus for rack-renting).[111] Evaton had an even lighter degree of administration than Alexandra. A health committee, which was the most rudimentary form of local government, did not exist: no whites from the surrounding area could be found who were willing to serve on such a body.[112] Instead there was a Native Commissioner and, to assist him in his duties, 22 policemen. The lack of an administrative body comparable even to Alexandra's meant that there was very little in the way of services. A more positive side of this neglect, as far as the people of Evaton were concerned, was that they did not pay rates[113] and they were free from many influx control restrictions.[114] However, during the 1940s local ANC leaders had been pressing for self-government in the form of a local authority which would include six elected Africans and three nominated members. Nothing was done about this, largely because of the unwillingness of the Department of Native Affairs to finance the facilities which would be needed as a consequence of bringing the location into administrative conformity with owner townships.[115] This undercurrent of discontent with the way the community was governed is an important factor to bear in mind.

Because of its unusual status and freedom from external controls, Evaton was most attractive for people who might have found it difficult to live legally in any other location, as well as those who had more complicated reasons for avoiding the authorities. Because of the absence of rates and the possibility of growing or foraging foodstuffs[116] it was relatively cheaper to live there. Consequently Evaton had a fairly large unemployed group. A major proportion of these people were Basotho migrants who had worked out their contracts on the mines. The mining industry enjoyed an 'unprecedented' flow of labour during the 1950s. One mining journal went so far as to comment that the situation had reached 'the point of embarrassment' when there was no longer any employment for experienced and skilled miners who would, of course, normally qualify for higher rates of pay. This might help to explain the concentration of ex-miners in Evaton.[117] Some of these people were involved in criminal protection rackets harassing the hundred or so traders who operated within or around Evaton.[118] There were approximately 2 000 Basotho altogether in Evaton.[119] From their number the Native Commissioner chose a 'chief' to 'stop people doing bad'.[120] The Basotho lived mainly in the Small Farms area: here conditions were most crowded and uncomfortable and rooms were cheaper.[121] But as well as its attractions for a lumpenproletariat, the Evaton population also included a significant petty-bourgeoise group, represented by the Evaton Property Owners' and Residents' Association. Traders must have done well in Evaton as they were well insulated from Johannesburg competition. A symptom of their prosperity was the formation in 1956 of the first African turf club in South Africa: it held six race meetings before it was forbidden the use of the ground which it had improvised as a race course.[122]

Evaton's population was prevented under Section 10 of the Native (Urban Areas) Consolidation Act of 1945 from finding work in the Veereeniging/Vanderbijlpark area – the major employment centre nearest to Evaton.[123] So instead 2 500 people commuted sixty miles a day to and from Johannesburg. The rest of the population who were not pedlars, craftsmen, criminals or in shopkeeping would have had to pick up what work they could in the surrounding white-occupied areas: as farm labourers, domestic servants, service workers and so forth. The post-war restriction of employment opportunities for Evaton's inhabitants helps to explain the slackening in its rates of population expansion.

To sum up, Evaton was a community which, like Alexandra, had developed organically, which was negligibly administered with little in the way of coercive sanctions of authority. In 1956 it had fairly longstanding grievances: the uncertainty of its municipal status was coupled with insecurity for property owners who could not obtain deeds of transfer,[124] an insecurity which may have filtered downwards and been reinforced by the presence of organised criminal groups and the threat of unemployment. It seems likely that the 2 500 Johannesburg commuters represented a relatively privileged group: Johannesburg wages were higher than elsewhere on the Rand and they were earning enough to make the expenditure of £2 5s 0d a month (and considerably greater expenditure on train fares during the bus boycott) worthwhile.

Transport facilities were considerably worse than those provided by PUTCO to Johannesburg's townships. The Evaton Passenger Service was a small, privately owned concern which operated seventeen buses on the Evaton–Johannesburg route. The company, because it serviced a community which lay outside the borders of a major municipal area, did not benefit from any subsidy or Native Services Levy. The company had taken over from Dickenson's Bus Services which had been unable to make a profit on the route.[125] It was owned by a group of Johannesburg businessmen known by the boycotters as 'the Italians'. Fares had risen by 25 per cent since 1945 but the service had not improved. The buses were old, they let in the rain, and frequently broke down, sometimes at night, which meant that people would have to sleep out of doors until the morning. They were often late, always overcrowded, there were no shelters at the terminals, and the staff, in particular those who managed the bus queues, treated passengers badly.[126] Then there was the appalling incident of the train crash when an EPC bus had broken down on a railway line. Nevertheless, despite these shortcomings, the bus was preferable to the train: the bus journey was half as long (one hour), took you all the way to the location, and was one third less expensive.

As we have seen, the EPC directors were conscious of these faults and, hoping to allay some of the discontent, suggested that a consultative body should be constituted to advise them on transport problems. The composition of the Transport Council was interesting: unlike the corresponding organisation in Alexandra, leading members of the Property Owners' Association were not represented on the committee. The EPTC had a core of nine members: they included two shopkeepers, four factory workers, one law student, one manufacturer's representative and one articled clerk.[127] Its chairman and secretary were both ANC members and adherents of the Africanist line. In 1955, the chairman, Vus'umzi Make was 24. He had joined the ANC Youth League at school, had lived in Evaton all his life and was studying law. Joe Molefi, EPTC secretary, was a year older than Make. He was born in the Orange Free State but moved to Evaton at the age of nine. He went to secondary school at St Peters, Johannesburg, where he was taught by Oliver

Tambo, one of the original Africanist founders of the Youth League. On leaving St Peters (where he had joined the ANC) he studied medicine at the University of the Witwatersrand. At that time he lived in Alexandra, where in 1952, having given up medicine, he helped to organise Defiance Campaign volunteers. After serving as branch secretary in Alexandra he moved to Evaton in 1953 to organise the ANC there, and under his influence it became strongly Africanist. Meanwhile he worked as a company representative.[128] Also members of the EPTC were two Transvaal Indian Congress activists, Suleiman Nathie and Mohammed Ismal (sometimes spelt Asmal), both of them shopkeepers. All the EPTC members were fairly young men in their twenties or early thirties. It is significant that the EPTC had a relatively experienced political leadership but one that was at odds with the ANC establishment: indeed it was later claimed in court that 'the ANC had nothing to do with the boycott and took very little part in it' (though by this stage the ANC leadership may have been anxious not to be implemented in a murder trial).[129] Apart from the shopkeepers the EPTC was reasonably representative of the sort of people who might be expected to use the bus to Johannesburg.

However, the one group it did not represent were the Basotho residents, and it is to them that we now turn. Nobody has ever provided a very satisfactory explanation of just why the Basothos should have opposed the boycott. Their violence is attributed to the anti-social nature of the 'Russians' whose behaviour conformed to a widely-held stereotype of the Basotho being an especially violent people.[130] The 'Russians' originated in Newclare which did have a substantial Basotho colony. They organised a protection racket which became notorious and which led to fighting in 1952.[131] It should not need to be said that the 'Russians' were not the only gangsters in Johannesburg, neither were all Basothos gangsters, nor were all gangsters Basothos. However, partly as a result of the conduct of the blanketed 'Russians' of Newclare the popular press tended to identify all Basotho migrant workers as 'Russians'. This sort of stereotyping was sometimes deliberately exploited, as in the case of the Dube Hostel riots of 1957 when gangsters would disguise themselves as Basothos and assault and rob Zulu workers and then present themselves as Zulus robbing the Basothos. This was considerably facilitated by ethnic grouping in separate buildings.[132] In the same way, it is quite likely that the Basotho community in Evaton was being similarly stereotyped at the onset of the boycott by the activities of a small group, and were then forced into a defensive solidarity after being attacked indiscriminately. Indeed, one of Ralekeke's rivals, Khabutlane, made a point of emphasising that not all Basothos opposed the boycott.[133] Basotho gangsterism can be explained without recourse to generalisations about ethnic characteristics: Basutoland, a desperately poor country, exported half its economically active male population to South Africa; those who for one reason or another were no longer engaged under contract would probably do their best to remain in South African urban centres, since chances of adequate subsistence, let alone a cash wage in Basutoland, were very limited.[134] Consequently, unemployed Basotho migrants could be expected to form a fairly important element within the informal sector: without skills, family, or capital resources they would have to resort to the less legitimate fringes of that sector. And in one important sense they had a considerable advantage over other participants in this field: being non-Union citizens there were fewer restrictions on their movements. It is interesting that the leaders of two major groups of 'Russians', Hlalele of Newclare, and Ralekeke of Evaton, knew each other from the time they had worked together on the mines.[135] Aside from these general considerations there were factors specific to Evaton which help to explain the lines along which tension developed.

The Native Commissioner appointed a chief for the Basotho migrant community. He had an ill-defined status but considerable informal power. Ralekeke was placed in this position in 1952. The previous year he had come out of prison after serving a two-year sentence for killing a previous incumbent, Palama. From 1952 he worked for a tailor in Evaton.[136] The Basothos lived in the Small Farms area of Evaton – the poorer district. In some of Ralekeke's speeches there was an underlying theme of antagonism towards 'educated people', of resentment that he, Ralekeke, a recognised leader in the Evaton community, had been slighted because he had not been consulted by the boycott planners (who, as we have seen in the composition of the EPTC, were often well-educated men in better paid jobs than the majority of the population).[137] It is possible that the inclusion of shopkeepers on the EPTC may also have contributed to the antagonism of an underprivileged group towards the boycott. Apart from the Basothos' feelings about the boycott, the way in which they were perceived by the rest of the community was of great importance. Whatever the conduct of the majority of Basotho residents, the man in a position of authority over them was somebody with two convictions for violent assault and a known involvement in gangster activities. There was also a more generalised resentment: the Native Affairs Commission, reporting in 1947, mentions complaints in Evaton that whereas Basotho citizens were free to seek employment in Vereeniging, people who had been born in Evaton were prevented from doing so by the Native (Urban Areas) Consolidation Act.[138] Given such tensions and the prevalence of certain stereotyped perceptions (which were at least indirectly stimulated by official policies) the rift that came to light in the boycott becomes easier to understand. At a fairly early stage – the records are unclear as to exactly when, but at least by October – the EPC started drawing upon the services of a strong-arm squad to break pickets, paying them between £2 and £3 a week.[139] Naturally it found them amongst the most isolated and alienated sector of the community. Apart from the dozen or so of his followers employed like himself by the EPC, Ralekeke was able to involve larger numbers of Basothos in the struggle against the boycotters: they need not all have been 'Russians', for those that opposed him were summarily dealt with; fear could have been an important factor. Ralekeke was able to reinforce his position by calling upon other 'Russian' groups elsewhere on the Rand.[140]

It should not be thought that the 'Russians' were the only people who opposed the boycott: the EPC only served a minority of the community and most of Evaton's inhabitants would not have been materially affected by the increase. For example, a prominent independent African church leader, Bishop Sims, was outspoken in his opposition[141] and was later killed. But the involvement of the gangsters on the side of the bus company would probably have created considerable sympathy for the boycotters' cause among those who were not immediately affected by the fare rise.

Given the length of the boycott, the involvement of local political leaders, and the passions it seems to have aroused, it is a little surprising that the ANC should have done so little to help the boycotters (there were no sympathy boycotts) and that it did not really attempt to make any political capital from it. It is true that the national chairman of the Youth League, Robert Resha, did visit Evaton; in his speech he declared that unless the people of Evaton had their own transport system there would never be any peace, but this was an exceptional instance of interest by a member of the national executive. It is possible that the ANC was wary of the Africanist element involved, and for this reason the Evaton branch may have been considered with disfavour; and it is also likely that the violence involved may have caused the ANC leadership to be cautious. The EPTC received some encouragement from Africanist groups elsewhere.[142] However, in their leaflets and bulletins[143] one does not find any attempt to situate the boycott in any wider context than the struggle between bus company and passengers – this despite the fact that the police and courts were believed to be acting in collusion with the bus company and the 'Russians'. However, despite the absence of a self-consciously 'political' character to the boycott it did have one aspect which could have developed political implications. Unlike the case of Alexandra in 1957, there can be detected in the conduct of the boycott a recurrent theme of economic self-help. The EPTC had shown itself from the start to be extremely effective in fund-raising: by the fifth week several of its leaders were on bail after having been arrested for picketing, and the bail money collected amounted to £250. It was perhaps this and Resha's suggestion that prompted the EPTC to apply for four certificates from the Road Transportation Board so it could run buses on the EPS routes. It contested the EPC's efforts to renew its licence, though no significant sum was collected towards the project. The interesting thing is that these plans did not involve the wealthier businessmen of the Property Owners' Association; they had entered into quite separate negotiations to establish a private bus company.[144] The EPTC project may have been motivated by the idea of establishing a service which would be properly responsive to consumer needs, a service over which bus users would have some control. The project does not seem to have sprung from a desire for economic aggrandisement among members of the EPTC. As we have seen, fares were not the only issue involved in the dispute. If a community bus service had been established it could have been the first step towards the organisation of other aspects of township life outside the framework of state authority. Given the administrative vacuum described above this was not an altogether unlikely possibility. It seems that the EPTC had received some encouragement from Indian businessmen that finance for such a venture would be made available – and it may be that the presence of Indians in the EPTC was helpful with regard to this.[145]

The final feature of the boycott which should be considered is the nature of the settlement, the totality (in contrast to Alexandra) of the boycotters' victory. The extraordinary thing was that the EPTC was asking for considerably greater concessions: it was actually demanding a degree of control over the operation of the bus service. The company offered several compromise solutions which included reversion to old fares; despite the substantial economic sacrifice involved in boycotting the service, the EPTC, under popular pressure, then held out until the company offered the terms outlined above. The following six features of the struggle had a bearing on the boycotters' victory.

(1) The boycotters were able to hold out for a very long period, the existence of alternative transport facilities being crucial in this. The bus company was a small one and had few other routes. Unlike PUTCO, the EPC was totally independent; there were no constraints on the sort of agreement it might reach with the boycotters.

(2) The bus company came to be identified with gangsters who were willing (and encouraged) to use violence against the boycotters. Feelings were bitter against the bus company, so much so that a mere reversion to the pre-boycott status quo was not acceptable. It is clear from the EPTC minutes that this was a case of a leadership falling in with the mood of the crowd rather than attempting to spur it to greater intransigence.

(3) There was complete unity among the leadership. This is one of the most important contrasts to Alexandra. Several factors explain this unity. First, there was comparatively little external interest in the boycott: no white liberal organisations tried to play a mediating role, although at one point the Institute of Race Relations was in fact approached. The boycott occurred in a township located at some distance from a major urban centre, was visually undramatic – to begin with at least – and did not involve the vast numbers of Alexandra. It did not affect employers and was not so obviously visible to humanitarians. So we do not find that the local ANC was being put under any pressure from the national executive, and there was in any case considerable tension in their relations. Secondly, there was no standholder element within the EPTC committee, and there were therefore no major clashes of economic interest, which might otherwise have occurred after the fighting in June 1956. Thirdly, there seem to have been no political rivalries either – somewhat surprising in view of the fact that one of the main complaints of Orlando Africanists was the closeness of the ANC's relationship with the South African Indian Congress.

(4) Like the 'Russians', the EPTC was capable of exercising fierce sanctions against those who challenged its policies: EPC staff were murdered; civic guard units were mobilised; people who spoke against the boycott were attacked; picketing was energetic and effective, and it was generally made impossible to run a normal bus service. Though ostensibly peaceful in intention – there were occasions when EPTC leaders actually protected EPC executives and police from angry picketers – from the beginning opposition was expressed in a violent idiom. Buses were burnt and constantly stoned. Here the particularly appalling service the EPC provided and the atrocious incident of the train/bus crash were obviously important in stimulating initial antagonism.

(5) Then there was the attitude of the government. In contrast to its reaction in Alexandra, in the case of Evaton the state does not appear to have interpreted events as constituting a challenge to its authority. As we have seen, governmental authority was only very sketchily represented at Evaton, but it nevertheless could have made the boycott far more difficult: interfering with the train timetable would have been an obvious strategy,[146] as well as subjecting Evaton train commuters to police checks. The fact that the boycott

was largely ignored by the national ANC, and that politically it was low-key (the economic self-help aspect was seldom expressed in nationalist terms), was obviously significant in determining the government's response. The internecine nature of the violence might have also contributed to its unwillingness to interfere: the violence did not represent a threat to the authorities, it was not primarily directed against them, and indeed appeared to reinforce the tenets of state ideology. The leaders of the Evaton boycott actually requested the government to endorse out the 'Russians', but ironically this was refused.[147]

(6) Finally, the possibility that the community might have been able to raise the resources to finance their own bus company could have had some bearing on the EPC's willingness to capitulate.

Yet the victory of the Evaton boycotters was a Pyrrhic affair. The events of June 1956, which received some attention in the foreign press,[148] highlighted and drew attention to the lack of administrative machinery in the township. Evaton was proclaimed in African township under the full gamut of municipal regulations. A governing council was constituted with nine elected advisory members and nine nominees under the chairmanship of the Native Commissioner. Influx control was introduced.[149] The response of both the 'Russians' and the EPTC was indicative of the political limitations of the movement: there was no protest against the new controls and instead they showed their willingness to cooperate by putting themselves up for election with other community leaders.[150] The first to suffer under the new dispensation were some of the EPTC leaders and Ralekeke Rantube; they were 'endorsed out'. The Evaton boycotters had failed to transcend the original limited objective of their action: their immediate enemy, the bus company, had been defeated, but authority and the system it rested upon had not been questioned.

It is possible now to provide some answers to the questions raised at the beginning of this chapter. In terms of the rôle of political organisations in these movements, there seems to be a good case for contending – on the basis of their activity in Alexandra and their comparative inactivity in Evaton – that they can perform a useful function. In the case of Alexandra, the ANC, with a system of intelligence vastly superior to that of the more localised groupings, was able to make strategic and tactical decisions that ensured a victory over the fare issue. By co-ordinating struggles elsewhere with those of Alexandra and Pretoria the ANC was to add substantially to the boycott's impact. But the ANC could also be criticised for moving from a specific to a generalised struggle too quickly, without any consideration of how the political energies released by the boycott could be most effectively used. The logic of the boycott process seemed to lead to the 'stay-at-home':

> When we are tired we shall rest. . . . They are punishing us because we are poor . . . save food and prepare for the offensive.[151]

But a poor community cannot sustain a stay-at-home long enough to make a serious impact on the economy. Even if it had accumulated the resources for a prolonged withdrawal of labour, the police would show far less hesitation in entering a township and driving people back to work than they would in interfering with a struggle situated within the workplace itself. A stay-at-home can be an effective demonstration; only in very exceptional circumstances can it be anything more.

Evaton represented a sin of omission for the ANC. Though their neglect of the boycotters gave the ANC a free hand in their negotiations with the bus company, nevertheless it is possible that the bitterness of the internecine conflict was at least in part a function of the absence of a perceived powerful external enemy. No attempt was made to channel resistance towards political ends: the struggle was reformist in the true sense of the word; to use Legassick's words, 'its internal logic did not lead to a questioning of the system as a whole'. Perhaps communal divisions were too profound for this to have happened: Evaton's obvious attraction as a catchment area for the Basotho lumpenproletariat made overall solidarity very difficult. There were opportunities which were lost, not least the numerous trials of picketers and EPTC members culminating in a murder trial in December in which the EPTC was charged; no support came from the national movement. The rôle a political organisation could have played at Evaton – providing a 'sympathetic interpretation' of the violence of the boycott – would have been valuable but problematic. Was there a distinct pattern to boycott behaviour which could have led to the 'institutionalising' of popular power? It is possible that the boycott form of protest had potential which could have been developed. First, a widespread participation was easier to achieve because it involved (in the case of a walking boycott) no immediate sacrifice in economic terms (except for those accustomed to earning overtime payments). It was not illegal – indeed it was one of the few forms of protest left to Africans that did not involve breaking the law. It must be conceded that certain conditions favoured the development of a boycott – the relative degree of freedom, the comparative ease of political and social organisation, and the strong sense of communal identity that existed in the freehold townships.

The boycott process was itself immediately suggestive: large-scale meetings and instant democracy, emphasising the dialectical relationship between leaders and crowd, and in the case of Alexandra, the processions of walkers, the very tangible feeling of being involved in protest: unlike other boycotts (electoral, rent, education) this demanded a degree of activism. The possibility of martyrs, court cases, mass oratory, the slogans, the songs – each boycott had a symbolism and imagery of its own but drew on a developed tradition: the Evaton boycotters reminded their followers of the people's struggle in Alexandra in 1944, the Alexandra boycotters were spurred by the Evaton victory of the previous year, and Molefi and Make, indeed, used to visit the APTC to advise them on the organisation of the boycott.[152] Furthermore, bus boycotts were often successful: the crowd's immediate target – the bus company – was at their mercy for without their patronage it could not function. Initially the agencies of the state could do little more than play a secondary harassing role, enough to focus people's attention towards authority but not enough to cow them into submission. The mode of protest and its immediate objectives made it difficult to systematically crush by arresting a few ring-leaders. The boycott did not depend on formal structure or key personalities; it acquired its own momentum and only ground to a halt through exhaustion, the point at which an organisation's intelligence system was most crucial if it was going to tap the power of the boycott. Yet, to the extent that the boycott would condition people, accustom them to direct communal action, unite them in action, and exploit differences of interest within the dominant community to gain immediate victories, then popular power was on the way to being institutionalised. These processes were apparent in Alexandra in 1957.

It is possible, therefore, that the boycotts can help to show us an important shortcoming in the campaigning of the Congress alliance during the 1950s. The two movements we have just been examining both demonstrate the possibility of obtaining through struggle immediate material improvements, and of drawing political capital from these. Too frequently the possibilities that such struggles presented were disregarded. For Christians in the ANC the road to freedom was via the cross, salvation through martyrdom:

> . . . we appeal to you to become the apostles to do this noble and holy job of delivering the people of Africa into the kingdom of heaven on earth.[153]

For social revolutionaries within the Congress alliance nothing succeeded like failure: the oppressive character of the state had to be revealed, time and time again. From this perspective, the heroes were the vanquished, not the victorious. The ultimate victory would only be realised through a succession of defeats.

Notes

1 Basil Davidson, Joe Slovo and Anthony Wilkinson, *Southern Africa: the new politics of revolution*, Penguin, Harmondsworth, 1976, p. 170.
2 Socialist League of Africa, 'Ten years of the stay-at-home', *International Socialist* (London), 5 (Summer 1961), pp. 7–9; Edward Feit, *African Opposition in South Africa*, Hoover, Stanford, 1967, pp. 29–31.
3 Leo Kuper, *An African Bourgeoisie*, Yale University Press, New Haven, 1965; Fatima Meer, 'African nationalism: some inhibiting factors', in Heribert Adams (ed.), *South Africa: sociological perspectives*, Arnold, London, 1971.
4 Martin Legassick, 'Class and nationalism in South African protest', unpublished seminar paper, n.d., p. 17.
5 Meer, 'African nationalism, p. 150.
6 Feit, *African Opposition*, p. 130.
7 This is calculated on the basis of figures provided in *African Poverty* (South African Institute of Race Relations, Johannesburg, 1957), p. 30. Alexandra incomes were, on average, lower than those in other townships, and many expenses (e.g. rent) were substantially higher. Ruth First, 'The bus boycott', *Africa South* (Cape Town), July, 1957, p. 58, argues that the real value of African wages was in decline. The deficit between income and minimum essential expenditure for subsistence, health and decency had increased from £4 17s 10d to £7 11s 5d in 1954.
8 SAIRR, *Annual Survey of Race Relations, 1956–1957*, Johannesburg, 1957, pp. 166–170.
9 At least 23 bus boycotts were reported in the two main Johannesburg newspapers, *The Star* and the *Rand Daily Mail*, between 1948 and 1961.

10 University of the Witwatersrand, Xuma papers, ABX 430711e; Union of South Africa, *Report of the Commission Appointed to Inquire into the Operation of Bus Services for Non-Europeans on the Witwatersrand*, Pretoria, UG 1/1944.

11 *Rand Daily Mail*, 1 October 1953.

12 Alexandra Township was laid out in 1905 and was originally destined for white occupation. Its distance from Johannesburg made it unattractive to potential purchasers and in 1912 (one year before the passage of the Natives' Land Act) the land speculation company obtained official permission to sell stands to Africans and coloured people. Its status as an African freehold township was recognised by the Native Trust and Land Act and though there were efforts in 1943 by the Johannesburg City Council to abolish the township (which was situated outside the municipal boundaries), wartime economies prevented their success. Alexandra still exists today, though a large proportion of its inhabitants arer now housed in migrant workers' hostels. See 'Challenge to democracy: Rand's problem township', *Libertas* (Johannesburg), August 1942.

13 Modikwe Dikobe, who lived in Alexandra in the 1940s before moving to Soweto, has pointed out to me the considerable difficulties of political organisation in a township where everybody lives in separate detached houses as opposed to the crowded terraces and lean-to rooms of Alexandra.

14 'Alexandra Township – 1952', *Fighting Talk* (Johannesburg), September 1952.

15 SAIRR papers, B Files, AD 843 (B 30) d.

16 Ben Turok, 'South Africa: the search for a strategy', *Socialist Register* (London), 1973, p. 355.

17 I am grateful to Charles van Onselen for this suggestion.

18 The problems of landlords are discussed in a booklet published by the Alexandra Health Committee, *The Future of Alexandra Township*, Alexandra, 1943, and in 'Challenge to democracy', p. 12.

19 *The Star*, 22 March 1957.

20 *Natal Witness* (Pietermaritzburg), 22 February 1957; *The Star*, 22 March 1957.

21 *The Star*, 18 January 1957.

22 *The Star*, 5 February 1957.

23 *The Star*, 7 February 1957; *Fighting Talk*, September 1952, cites a 1951 figure for 40 per cent.

24 Trevor Huddleston, *Naught for your Comfort*, Collins, London, 1956, pp. 26–8.

25 *The Star*, 8 January 1957.

26 Union of South Africa, *National Transport Commission Report for 1954–1957*, UG 26/1958, p. 11.

27 *Rand Daily Mail*, 22 December 1956.

28 First, 'The bus boycott', p. 58.

29 *Ibid*.

30 *The World* (Johannesburg), 9 March 1957. Also, a D. G. Mtshaulana of the Bantu Bus Service spoke of applying to take over PUTCO routes but he seems to have had no Alexandra connections.

31 Dan Mokonyane, *Lessons of Azikhelwa*, Nakong ya Rena, London, 1979, p. 35.

32 Gwendolyn Carter, Gail Gerhart and Thomas Karis, *From Protest to Challenge*, Volume IV, Hoover, Stanford, 1977, p. 123.

33 Xuma papers, ABX 430711b.

34 The main Africanist centre was the ANC Youth League branch at Orlando: here the leading Africanists were well educated men, some with university degrees, and employed as journalists, teachers, articled clerks, etc.

35 Treason Trial Record (original copy held at the South African Institute of Race Relations), p. 2482.

36 South African Institute of Race Relations, Johannesburg SAIRR papers, B Files, AD 843 (B 74) c.

37 SAIRR papers, B Files, AD 843 (B 74) c; Xuma papers, 430913d.
38 Mokonyane, *Lessons of Azikhewelwa*, pp. 76–77. I am grateful to Baruch Hirson for information on the Movement for Democracy of Content.
39 SAIRR papers, B Files, AD 843 (B 74) b.
40 *Rand Daily Mail*, 19 November 1955.
41 I would place the Workers' League, the Tenants' League, the Democracy of Content in this category. Mokonyane, unlike some of the other political spokesmen, insisted that the boycott had no wider political ramifications. Over this there was some tension between him and the Society of Young Africa: see *The World*, 2 March 1957.
42 *The Star*, 25 January 1957 and 29 January 1957.
43 'History of the Bus Boycott' (describes Liberal Party involvement – henceforth: Liberal Party memo), unsigned typescript held in South African Association of Newspapers' Library, Transport Files, p. 3.
44 *The Star*, 11 January 1957.
45 *Rand Daily Mail*, 24 January 1957.
46 *Rand Daily Mail*, 2 February 1957.
47 Liberal Party memo, p. 5. See also *Digest of South African Affairs*, 15 March 1957, p. 3.
48 I am indebted to Belinda Bozzoli for this suggestion.
49 An article in *The Listener* (London), 25 April 1957, quotes a different version of this slogan: 'Store food and prepare for the offensive'.
50 *The Star*, 28 February 1957. The government even went to the length of introducing legislation to this effect.
51 *Rand Daily Mail*, 27 Februarty 1957.
52 Liberal Party memo, p. 5.
53 *Rand Daily Mail*, 2 March 1957.
54 Liberal Party memo, p. 6.
55 *Rand Daily Mail*, 27 February 1957.
56 *The Star*, 3 March 1957.
57 Liberal Party memo, p. 5.
58 Anthony Sampson, *The Treason Cage*, Heinemann, London, 1958, p. 212.
59 *Rand Daily Mail*, 2 March 1957.
60 First, 'The bus boycott', p. 63.
61 Mokonyane, *Lessons of Azikhwelwa*, p. 39, asserts that the ANC 'took instructions from Treason Trial big-shots'.
62 *Rand Daily Mail*, 10 July 1957. Pretoria employers were totally opposed to an increase in the levy.
63 Liberal Party memo, p. 6.
64 *Digest of South African Affairs*, 1 April 1957, p. 12.
65 *Ibid*, p. 5.
66 *The Star*, 21 March 1957.
67 *Rand Daily Mail*, 11 March 1957.
68 *Rand Daily Mail*, 28 February 1957. In his book Mokonyane claims that the Movement for Democracy of Content began calling for a stay-at-home in the first week of the boycott. See: Mokonyane, *Lessons of Azikwelwa*, p. 42.
69 *Rand Daily Mail*, 7 March 1957.
70 *Digest of South African Affairs*, 1 April 1957, p. 10.
71 Carter and Karis microfilm (CAMP), Reel 21b, 2 YE1 96/3.
72 Carter, Gerhart and Karis, *From Protest to Challenge*, Vol IV, p. 69.
73 *Pretoria News*, 12 February 1957.
74 The formation of the Co-ordinating Committee enabled the ANC to take a leading rôle in negotiations, for its position was under less challenge in the other boycott centres than in Alexandra. Nzo chaired this Committee throughout the boycott,

though Mokonyane claims that the APTC members withdrew their support from him after he had received several reprimands from them for taking initiatives on the Co-ordinating Committee in the negotiations without consulting the APTC; see Mokonyane, *Lessons of Azikwelwa*, p. 40.

75 *Rand Daily Mail*, 7 March 1957.
76 Liberal Party memo, p. 7.
77 Sampson, *The Treason Cage*, p. 213.
78 Liberal Party memo, p. 9.
79 Gwendolyn Carter, Gail Gerhart and Thomas Karis, *From Protest to Challenge*, Volume III, Hoover, Stanford, 1977, p. 394.
80 Carter and Karis microfilm, Reel 21b, 1 YE1.
81 University of the Witwatersrand, Margaret Ballinger papers, A 410/B2 Native Affairs (b), Jimmy Dey to Walter Ballinger, 7 May 1957.
82 Carter and Karis microfilm, Reel 21b, 2 YE1.
83 Margaret Ballinger papers, A410/B2 Native Affairs, Jimmy Dey to Walter Ballinger, 7 May 1957.
84 Carter and Karis microfilm, Reel 21b, 2 YE1.
85 *Rand Daily Mail*, 10 July 1957.
86 Margaret Ballinger papers, A 410/B2 Native Affairs (b).
87 *The World*, 26 January 1957.
88 Margaret Ballinger papers, A410/B2 Native Affairs (b), Jimmy Dey to Walter Ballinger, 7 May 1957.
89 *Bantu World*, 8 October 1955.
90 *Rand Daily Mail*, 3 December 1958.
91 Union of South Africa, *National Transport Commission Report for 1954–1957*, UG 26/1958, p. 11.
92 *The World*, 6 April 1957; 4 May 1957; *New Age*, 4 July 1957; 27 June 1957; 13 June 1957; 23 May 1957; 16 May 1957.
93 Edward Roux, 'The Alexandra bus strike', *Trek* (Johannesburg), 21 September 1945, p. 12.
94 *Rand Daily Mail*, 31 January 1950.
95 Memo of Crown evidence, Part 2, Section B, paragraph 2, Carter and Karis microfilm, Reel 21b, 2 YE1 95.
96 *Rand Daily Mail*, 2 November 1954.
97 *The Star*, 2 November 1954.
98 *The World*, 30 June 1956.
99 Memo of Crown evidence, Part I Section B, paragraphs 5195, 5916, 5942, Carter and Karis microfilm, Reel 21b, 2 YE1 95.
100 *Ibid*, paragraph 5969.
101 *Ibid*, paragraph 5973.
102 *Ibid*, paragraph 5975.
103 *Ibid*, paragraph 5947.
104 *Ibid*, paragraph 5960.
105 *Ibid*, paragraph 5937.
106 Minutes of EPTC executive meeting, Carter and Karis microfilm, Reel 21b, 2 YE1 32/2.
107 *Ibid*.
108 SAIRR, *Annual Survey of Race Relations, 1955–1956*, Johannesburg 1956, p. 100.
109 Fare loss computed on basis of EPC losing three-quarters of its passengers a month, as was admitted by the bus company; *The World*, 25 February 1956.
110 Union of South Africa, *Report of the Native Affairs Commission, 1946–1947*, Pretoria, UG 15/1949, p. 30.
111 *Ibid*, p. 30.
112 *Ibid*, p. 35.

113 Ezekiel Mphahlele, 'The Evaton riots', *Africa South*, January 1957, p. 56.
114 See Verwoerd's speech as reported in *Rand Daily Mail*, 7 August 1956.
115 Union of South Africa, *Report of Native Affairs Commission, 1946–1947*, p. 35.
116 An article in *The World*, 7 April 1956, as well as Mphahlele's 'The boycott that became a war' in *Drum* (Johannesburg), July 1956, makes the point that Evaton children seemed comparatively well fed and healthy, attributing this to the possibility of access to wild fruit and agricultural produce.
117 R. Rodseth, 'Flow of native labour to South African mines', *Optima* (Johannesburg), 1959, pp. 102–4.
118 Union of South Africa, *Report of Native Affairs Commission, 1946–1947*, p. 37.
119 *Rand Daily Mail*, 28 June 1956.
120 Memo of Crown evidence, Part I, Section B, paragraph 13, Carter and Karis microfilm, Reel 21b, 2 YE1 95.
121 Union of South Africa, *Report of Native Affairs Commission, 1946–1947*, p. 34.
122 *The World*, 28 April 1956.
123 Union of South Africa, *Report of Native Affairs Commission, 1946–1947*, p. 38. Mphahlele, 'The Evaton Riots', p. 60, confirms that this was still the case in 1956.
124 'The Evaton riots', p. 57.
125 Union of South Africa, *Report of the Commission Appointed to Inquire into the Operation of Bus Services . . .*, UG 31/1944, p. 29.
126 *The World*, 28 April 1956. See also undated letter of complaint from J. M. Nhlapo to EPS, Nhlapo papers (University of the Witwatersrand), A 1006 A.
127 Profile based on EPTC minutes, Carter and Karis microfilm, Reel 21b, 2 YE1 32/2, and a report in *The World*, 20 October 1956.
128 Biographical details from Carter and Karis microfilm, Reel 12a, 2 XM 117, and Reel 11a, 2 XM 19.
129 Carter and Karis microfilm, Reel 21b, 2 YE1 95, paragraph 5.
130 See, for example, 'Extracts from the Report of the Interdepartmental Committee of Inquiry into Riots on the Mines in the Republic of South Africa', *South African Labour Bulletin*, iv, 5 (September 1978), p. 51.
131 Huddleston, *Naught for Your Comfort*, pp. 101–2.
132 D. C. Theme, 'Inside Dube Hostel', *Drum*, November 1957.
133 *Bantu World*, 1 October 1955.
134 Francis Wilson, *Migrant Labour in South Africa*, South African Council of Churches, Johannesburg, 1972, p. 110.
135 Carter and Karis microfilm, Reel 21b, 2 YE1 95, paragraph 6145.
136 *Ibid*, paragraph 6111.
137 *The World*, 25 August 1956.
138 Union of South Africa, *Native Affairs Commission . . .*, UG15/1949, p. 38.
139 Memo of Crown evidence, Part I, Section b, paragraph 11, and Part 2, Section b, paragraph 8, Carter and Karis microfilm, Reel 21b, 2 YE1 95; *Sunday Express* (Johannesburg), 29 July 1956.
140 *Ibid*; *Sunday Times* (Johannesburg), 5 August 1956.
141 Mphahlele, 'The boycott that became a war', *Drum*, July 1956, p. 22.
142 See article on boycott in *The Africanist* (Orlando), December 1956, p. 16. Josias Madzunya visited the Evaton boycotters.
143 Carter and Karis Microfilm, Reel 21b, 2 YE1 84/2; 2 YE1 84/3.
144 *The World*, 21 7 1956.
145 *Rand Daily Mail*, 28 6 1956.
146 As they did in Lady Selborne the following year; see *The Star*, 30 January 1957.
147 *The World*, 4 August 1956.
148 See, for example, *Time*, 9 July 1956.
149 Carter and Karis microfilm, Memo of Crown evidence, Part 1, Section b, paragraph 5982; *Rand Daily Mail*, 7 August 1956.

150 *The World*, 8 September 1956.
151 *Rand Daily Mail*, 28 February 1957.
152 Carter and Karis microfilm, 2 XM 117: 96/2.
153 Meer, 'African nationalism', p. 144.

CHAPTER 8

Labour and politics, 1955–1965

A corollary to the increasingly radical character of nationalist politics during the 1950s was the politicisation of African trade unionism, especially after the emergence, as a member of the Congress alliance, of a new trade union coordinating body, the South African Congress of Trades Unions (SACTU). This chapter's concern is with the political trade unionism of the 1950s and early 1960s. An examination of its historical development will be followed by a discussion of the controversy which this history has given rise to. First, though, an understanding of the political and economic environment within which trades unions had to operate is needed.

Government labour policies became increasingly repressive in the course of the 1950s. African trade unions never actually became illegal but instead legislation was enacted which made it increasingly difficult for them to function effectively. This legislation reflected the coalition of interests the Nationalist administration represented. Its predecessor had presented in 1947 an Industrial Conciliation (Natives) Bill which, with the support of employers' organisations drawn from secondary industry, had provided for a degree of recognition for African trade unions. This trend was continued by the Nationalist-appointed Industrial Relations Commission which, again taking the side of manufacturing, argued the case for control of African trade unionism through a process of certification and registration. At the same time African unions would be debarred from any political affiliation or activity as well as joining any trade union confederation.[1] Industrialists believed that left outside any industrial relations framework African trades unions were vulnerable to 'irresponsible' political leadership. Conciliation machinery to which unions had access would help to bureaucratise their leadership and deflect them from involvement in strikes. In making their recommendations employers obviously had little faith in the repressive capacity of the state: legal prohibition during the 1940s had failed to prevent considerable industrial unrest.

Powerful groups were opposed to recognition. Farmers believed that any enhancement of black industrial bargaining power would accelerate the drift away from the very badly paid agricultural employment sector. White workers had in the 1940s seen for the first time the wage differential between white and black industrial labour narrow. Confronted with an increasingly skilled and militant black workforce, white workers were preoccupied with the legal protection of their preserves of skilled employment. A cooptive strategy towards black labour implicitly threatened these. Moreover, by 1951 when the Commission reported, the enthusiasm of secondary industry for withholding union recognition had substantially abated: the decline of the Council of Non-European Trades Unions (CNETU) group following the suppression of the 1946 mineworkers' strike (from a claimed 158 000 membership in 1945 to 17 296 in 1950)[2], and the effects from 1950 on trade union organisers of the Suppression of Communism Act, both served to reduce in the eyes of employers the dimensions of the problem that African trade unionism had represented. In 1953 the government began unfolding its programme for the control of African labour with the Native Labour (Settlement of Disputes) Act. It set the tone for what was to follow. As well as reaffirming the wartime strike prohibition it established separate conciliation machinery for Africans, a highly bureaucratic and cumbersome procedure in which workers would be represented by works committees functioning under the guidance of white 'Bantu Labour Officers', and from which union representatives were to be excluded. Successive amendments deprived African trade unionists in 1957 of the right to sit on wage determination boards and to collect dues (1959) through stop orders.

A further legislative measure was aimed directly at weakening the unity of the trade union movement itself. In 1956 the Industrial Conciliation Amendment Act ended any future recognition of unions with a white and coloured or Indian membership and required existing 'mixed' unions to either split into 'uniracial' unions or form separate racial branches, each with a white-controlled executive. African men, of course, had never been permitted to belong to a registered union.* The Act also empowered the Minister to declare strikes illegal in essential industries as well as giving legal force to white 'job reservation' practices. In 1959 the food industry was so defined in a move to curb the activities of the registered coloured Food and Canning workers' Union, a powerful SACTU affiliate.

As well as laws specifically aimed at trade unions, African worker organisation was increasingly hampered by more general legislation. The extension of influx control and the establishment of labour bureaux in 1952–53 further curbed worker mobility and made the consequences of dismissal considerably more serious. Such measures enabled the state to reduce the political threat represented by large numbers of unemployed workers when concentrated in the urban centres.

Legislation apart, economic conditions in the 1950s were less favourable for the development of African trades unions than in the previous decade. Economic growth slackened and unemployment increased, and in many cases this helped to weaken the bargaining position of black trade unions. The value of real wages declined: between 1948 and 1957 a 25 per cent average wage increase in four representative industries was outstripped by a conservatively estimated 44 per cent increase in the cost of living.[3] All these points should be borne in mind when the achievements of political trade unionism are evaluated later in this chapter.

The repressive political climate led to a realignment in the trade union movement. The largest of the trade union organisations, the South African Trades and Labour Council (SAT&LC), had, through the banning of

---

*Note: African women, who until 1956 did not carry passes, could be defined as employees in terms of the 1924 Industrial Conciliation Act and hence belong to registered unions. Many African men did join registered unions illegally.

left-wing trade unionists on its executive under the Suppression of Communism Act, become increasingly paternal in its approach to African trade unions. When the provisions of the Industrial Conciliation Bill were made public in 1954 the SAT&LC was deeply divided, for its affiliates included Indian, coloured and African as well as white trade unions. The Council had recently suffered defections from white craft-based unions hostile to the organisation of African workers. In October 1954 the SAT&LC decided on a compromise which it hoped would keep the loyalty of its white artisan membership while still retaining for it some influence on the development of African unionism. A reformed coordinating centre, the South African Trade Union Council (later TUCSA) would exclude African trade unions from direct affiliation and instead created for them a liaison committee. Members of this committee should eschew politics and in return for their cooperation the corresponding white registered trade unions in the same industry would negotiate on their behalf. It was a strategy known as 'parallelism'.[4] Nineteen unions voted against this arrangement, the most important of them being the Food and Canning Workers' Union and the Textile Workers' Industrial Union and their respective African branches. * These four unions, together with ten others, then established – between October 1954 and March 1955 – a Trade Union Co-ordinating Committee which met with CNETU representatives (whose following had dwindled to 22 unions and 10 000 members) to organise an inaugural conference for the South African Congress of Trade Unions at the beginning of March 1955. SACTU was to emerge finally with 19 affiliates representing 20 000 workers. Accounting for the bulk of its strength were three registered unions and their African branches: the Food and Canning Workers' Union, the Textile Workers' Industrial Union and the National Union of Laundry, Cleaning and Dyeing Workers. What these had in common was the fact that they represented semi-skilled workers in labour-intensive industries, a factor which distinguished them from most of those unions which remained affiliated to TUCSA. The laundry workers included about 400 whites who throughout the 1950s were the only white workers SACTU represented. Their small number notwithstanding, they were of considerable symbolic importance to SACTU's organisers, reaffirming its non-racialism.

From its inception SACTU recognised that it would have a role in political as well as economic struggles. To obtain a real transformation in the position of black workers would inevitably involve conflict with the state. To stay within the boundries set by TUCSA for black unions meant acceptance of job reservation, exclusion from legalised collective bargaining, racially based wage differentials as well as the rapidly tightening restrictions on African urbanisation and geographical mobility. The inclusion of the word 'Congress' in SACTU's title was a deliberate identification with the nationalist movement. Less than three months after its formation SACTU delegates attended the Congress of the People; later that year it formally became a member of the Congress alliance with representation on its National Co-ordinating Committee. Here SACTU was drawing on an already well

*Note: In 1946, after threats of de-registration from the Department of Labour, separate African unions were formed. These differed from parallel groups in that joint meetings were held by both the registered and unregistered leadership and both could exercise democratic checks on the registered union's leadership.

established tradition of union political involvement. As we have seen, CNETU itself, at moments of crisis, had joined with the Communist Party and sections of the ANC in calling demonstrative general stay-aways aimed primarily at the state rather than individual employers. In certain areas, Port Elizabeth in particular, trade unions had provided a stepping stone to politics for many Congress leaders and liaison between political and worker organisations was close. Individual unions like the FCWU, from the time of their inception, looked beyond the immediate conflict at the workplace:

> On looking through your agenda I find that it differs from that of many other unions. You do not only attend to the elementary duties of a trade unions, but your agenda and the Secretary's report covers a wide field and covers that, that is of interest to the workers as a whole. That is right – the trade union must take an active interest in all that affects the people.[5]

Nevertheless despite its political connection SACTU was first and foremost a trade union organisation and it is to its more conventional function of organisation and intervention in industrial disputes that we now turn.

Organisation was mainly in the hands of local committees established from 1955 in most of the main industrial centres. Their effectiveness depended on the local strength of the branches of SACTU's 'core' of registered affiliates, for these provided most of the money needed to pay organiser's salaries and other running expenses. According to its official history, the Laundry Workers' and the Food and Canners' carried SACTU financially.[6] The first of these committees was set up in Johannesburg, but despite the initial concentration of SACTU affiliation on the Rand, organisers had least success in creating new and stable unions and recruiting new members: overall SACTU affiliation on the Witwatersrand remained static at 15 000 between 1956 and 1961, but declined proportionately from a half to a third of SACTU's following. The Rand local committee was seriously depleted by Treason Trial arrests and one of its main bases, the ATWIU branch at the Amato textile mill in Benoni, was virtually destroyed in the wake of dismissals following a strike in 1958. Nevertheless despite such difficulties 17 unions were founded or revived on the Rand and in Pretoria, many of them resulting from SACTU initiatives in strikes or wage disputes involving unorganised workers. Many were short lived but in the process over 5 000 African workers were introduced to trade unionism.

In the eastern and western Cape the picture was somewhat brighter. In Port Elizabeth, for example, six new unions were formed in 1956 in the sweet, milling, stevedoring, biscuit, cement and leather industries. Here the nationalist movement had been dominated by trade unionists for over a decade (see Chapter 2) and was unusually well organised, thereby enabling it to support SACTU campaigns effectively. The local committee in Cape Town could draw on the resources of the Food and Canning Workers' Union which had its largest branches in the western Cape; here also a good working relationship with Congress assisted in the creation of several new unions amongst the largely migrant African working class. Durban's local committee was led by the textile workers Billy Nair and Stephen Dhlamini, both of them

Treason Trialists. Despite this, Durban and Natal generally was to be the scene of SACTU's most outstanding organisational success. Generated by the upsurge in popular militancy arising from the Cato Manor riots of June 1959 and encouraged by the enthusiasm for trade unionism of Chief Lutuli, 13 500 Natal workers joined SACTU affiliates that year and new local committees were formed in Pinetown, Ladysmith and Pietermaritzburg.

Until 1958 the energies of SACTU organisers were concentrated on traditional spheres of African unionism: light manufacturing, food processing and services. The most important industries in the country in terms both of employment and economic significance – agriculture, mining, transport and metal – were relatively unorganised. Agricultural workers were scattered and isolated and in the other three sectors, much of the labour was migrant and housed in the highly controlled environment of compounds and hostels. Recognising the limits of their resources, SACTU's leaders proposed that organisational work should be limited initially to transport and metal. In the case of the former there was already a base to build upon: railway and harbour workers' unions existed in Durban, Port Elizabeth, Cape Town and Johannesburg. Here, under heavy pressure from a hostile administration, the most courageous local organisers could do was to conduct a holding operation: that the South African Railway and Harbour Workers' Union could still in 1960 claim nearly 5 000 members was itself an achievement. With half the African labour force employed on a 'casual' 24-hour basis and under the vigilant eyes of the railway police, union organisers were limited to taking up individual instances of injustice and attempting to reduce the level of victimisation of their members. Dockworkers, being privately employed, were slightly less vulnerable than railways employees but their position also deteriorated. This was especially evident in the case of those in Durban, from whom had emerged during the war years a resourceful and militant leadership, well placed to take advantage of Durban's massive industrial expansion.[7] Because of the sharply fluctuating labour requirements of the port, dockworkers were employed on a daily basis so that at busy periods employers had to compete for their services. While lacking the security of a regular income they enjoyed a degree of independence. In the course of a series of bitterly contested struggles supported by the SACTU local committee the dockers were by 1959 brought under a centralised labour supply company which eliminated competition between employers and confined the workers within a single compound. When this innovation was greeted with renewed wage demands and a refusal to work overtime the employers and the state used their ultimate sanction. The entire labour force was deported and speedily replaced with new workers from the Zulu reserves.

Attempting to defend the interests of transport workers quickly and inevitably brought trade unionists into confrontation with the state. Though the struggles were often heroic, they were seldom successful. SACTU's record in the metal industry was more positive. In Cape Town, Port Elizabeth and the East Rand from 1956 new unions were founded for metal workers. The Transvaal union developed eight branches and was still flourishing in 1963 when it recruited 927 new members. In its first year, five strikes were supported on the Rand, two of which resulted in pay increases. In 1960 employers responded to worker militancy by granting a 6d per hour increase on the general wage. By the early 1960s SACTU organisers were active among the tightly controlled workers of the state-owned iron and steel monopoly, ISCOR.

The African Mineworkers' Union had collapsed in the years following the 1946 strike and mineworkers thereafter were successfully isolated from trade union organisations. Intermittent leafletting campaigns and clandestine contacts with African mineworkers enabled SACTU to claim nearly 100 paid-up trade unionists on the mines in 1961, but the committee established to organise mineworkers had to content itself with producing propaganda and memoranda. At the same time a serious effort was made to organise farmworkers, drawing on the expertise of Gert Sibande who had led farmworkers in the eastern Transvaal since the 1930s. The Farm, Plantation and Allied Workers' Union built up a following in early 1962 of over a thousand but its function was primarily legalistic, resorting to the courts to defend farmworkers against evictions and brutal treatment.

SACTU's total affiliation grew from 20 000 in 1956 to 55 000 in 1962. Many of the new unions were hasty constructions, often the results of interventions by SACTU in industrial disputes. SACTU's achievement is easy to criticise in terms of its bureaucratic shortcomings and is difficult to measure. One can point to individual instances where wage increases or improved conditions were won; this was especially the case with the old-established registered affiliates and their African branches, but there were more where disputes ended in dismissals, arrests and destruction of existing organisations. Although, as we shall see, SACTU could be credited with some of the responsibility for a general rise in wages towards the end of the decade, its record should be evaluated in the much wider context of African working-class struggle at that time. For despite the new legal weapons at its disposal, the state was to experience great difficulty in enforcing industrial discipline on black workers: strikes actually increased in the second half of the decade, 569 occurring between 1955 and 1961, the majority involving African workers. The official system of conciliation machinery was widely rejected. Only ten works committees were successfully established in this period.

But whether or not SACTU was effective in terms of a narrow conventional perspective of trade unionism is scarcely the point. For SACTU's original purpose was to link economic struggles with political assertions of working class consciousness.

SACTU's first two years of activity were concentrated in the building of industrial unions. Although its officers could involve themselves in township-based campaigns such as the struggle to protect Soweto tenants conducted by the Witwatersrand local committee, nevertheless their main concern was situated at the workplace. The period 1955–57 was, for employers, the most turbulent time of industrial unrest since the mid-1940s.

A switch to a more broadly based strategy was stimulated by the massive protest movement that developed around the issue of bus fare increases in Alexandra in the first months of 1957. Three hundred trade union delegates attended a 'National Workers' Conference' convened by SACTU at which it was resolved to mobilise a national campaign for a £1 a day minimum wage. The campaign was to have three functions: first, and most obviously, to arrest the steady deterioration in the value of working-class incomes; second, to sustain the political militancy that was being generated out of the bus boycott; and finally, to assist in the process of mass enrolment in trade unions.[8] It was felt that recruitment of workers should not wait until there was an appropriate industrial union in existence; rather, workers should be brought in as SACTU members first and then placed in a suitable union as soon as one had been created. £1-a-day committees were to be formed in the main towns and these were to organise rallies and publicity campaigns. In fact the mass enrolment only began properly two years later, but the 1957 conference nevertheless represented an important departure from the strategy of industrial unionism which had been adhered to by the African labour movement since the 1930s. It is worth stressing at this point that the impetus for the minimum wage campaign came from the trade unions. Don Mateman, a former Textile Union branch secretary and a SACTU official in Johannesburg, remembers:

> We had to convince the people in the ANC about it. . . . These people were not trade unionists. . . . So our first job was to convince all the people round us about the wisdom of the £1 a day campaign and it was a job at the time. . . . The idea came from the union.[9]

Inevitably, with its adoption by SACTU's allies in the Congress alliance there was a qualitative shift in the nature of the campaign. This was at first only slightly evident. In June 1957 the campaign opened dramatically with a revival of the stay-at-home tactic. The Congress alliance's national consultative committee called for a 'Day of Protest, Prayer and Demonstration', and it was only in Johannesburg and Port Elizabeth that workers were called out on strike. It was these two centres which had been most deeply affected by the bus boycotts four months before. Other centres simply held evening prayer meetings and processions. On the Rand, according to Mateman, organisational work was concentrated on the factories: leaflets were distributed outside gates and shop stewards were contacted. The printed publicity placed the main emphasis on the call for a minimum wage, though workers were told that the strike was also in protest against passes and permits. On 26 June, the anniversary of the second 1950 stay-away and the opening of the Defiance Campaign, a large number of workers stayed at home in Port Elizabeth and Johannesburg. In Johannesburg the strike was said to have been 70–80 per cent effective. This was despite threats of dismissal from jobs and subsequent banishments to the rural areas (actually implemented by the Johannesburg City Council which was having to contend with a new SACTU affiliate, the African Building Workers' Industrial Union). The success of the 1957 demonstration was not limited to the impressive turn-out. Together with the high level of industrial strikes that year and the bus boycott it helped to provoke a flurry of wage determinations after government recommendations which led to a rise in real wages after 1958.[10]

Out of these events was generated a revived faith among political leaders in the potency of working-class forms of struggle. At the 1957 ANC annual conference Lutuli, in his presidential address, called for a revaluation of 'our idea of indifference to a White general election. Such periods properly used can be most fruitful politically. It provides a favourable climate for the political education of our people'.[11] Lutuli went on to call for a repetition of what he conceived the previous year's protest to be: a day of mass gatherings, prayer and dedication. Meanwhile SACTU's annual conference discussed the possibility of a general strike for a minimum wage.[12]

The final decision on the 1958 stay-away was made at a second National Workers' Conference held in Newclare, Johannesburg, on 16 March. The conference, which was attended by 1 673 delegates and 3 000 observers and which had been preceded by regional conferences, resolved in favour of a 'week of national stay-at-home' (later it was decided that three days would be more practical). A speech by Lutuli just before the conference contained a warning which hinted at some uneasiness within ANC circles:

> Because of the name of the Conference, some people in our Congress are treating it as though it were a trade union affair primarily concerning the active trade unionists and confined to delegates elected from factories.

Congress represented a broader range of interests than just those of workers, Lutuli claimed, and work in the factories should not be at the expense of organisation in the townships 'where we are strong'.[13] The two main slogans to emerge from this conference were '£1 a day' and 'the Nats must go', reflecting the two impulses underlying the strike proposal. But despite the prominence given to the wage issue by the Workers' Conference, in the weeks which followed it, to quote SACTU's official history, 'the strike call had become less and less a SACTU-oriented campaign and more and more one focusing on the white elections'.[14] Compared to the 1957 stay-away, on the Rand there was much less trade union involvement in the preparations, most of the organisation taking place in the townships rather than outside the factories.[15] The ANC ruled against picketing. The state, in contrast to the previous year, took no chances: in the days before the election there was an intensification of pass raids in townships, police leave was cancelled, prison labour placed on standby and meetings of over ten Africans prohibited. Employers also took considerable precautions, denouncing the illegal strike and making the customary threats.

On 14 April, the first day of the elections, large contingents of armed police entered the townships at 2 o'clock in the morning. This was probably not necessary; on the Rand only about ten per cent of the workforce stayed away from work, though in Sophiatown, where Congress was exceptionally well organised, there was almost total abstention. Port Elizabeth and Durban were the other two centres affected and here the absenteeism rates were 50 and 30 per cent respectively. To the disappointment of trade unionists in these towns the Rand-based ANC national working committee called the strike off on the evening of the 14th. SACTU's leaders were not consulted over this decision nor was it accepted unanimously in ANC branches. Sophiatown's workers were to hold out for three days as had been the original intention.

Several explanations were offered at the time for the disappointing response to the 1958 strike call. The ANC's national executive, in its annual report, attributed most of the blame to its own organisational deficiencies. The strike had been opposed by Africanists, and many branch leaders had not understood the ANC's position on the stay-away, believing it to be a 'mere SACTU affair'.[16] Certainly preparations in most areas, with the exceptions of Port Elizabeth and Sophiatown, were at best haphazard. But though Congress's leadership was fairly self-critical, the nearest it came to evaluating the 1958 stay-away strategically was when Duma Nokwe, an executive member, admitted that a three-day strike call was probably asking too much from wage earners.[17] The problem was mainly defined in terms of organisation and communication. Lutuli's verdict was not untypical. The previous year he had called for greater sacrifice but 'The African people as a whole did not measure up to that call'.[18] It was left to the veteran trade unionist, Dan Tloome, in an article written for *Liberation*, to criticise the basis on which the attempt to mobilise people had been made: 'the slogan led a considerable section of the people to believe that the Congresses were in favour of the United Party coming to power'. The elections were obviously a much less effective rallying issue than wages as far as most African were concerned.[19]

Another important lesson drawn from these events was the importance of trade union organisation in making these political demonstrations successful. The efficient articulation between political and worker organisations in Port Elizabeth underlay the strong impact of the strike call there. Both the ANC and SACTU were to place renewed emphasis on worker organisation, Lutuli calling on political leaders 'to organise workers into trade union movements' and SACTU building a new network of factory committees drawn from the most experienced and politically conscious trade unionists. These were intended to play a vital role in the ANC anti-pass campaign. In addition, from 1959 General Workers' Unions were set up to broaden the basis of SACTU recruitment. Much of the organisation of General Workers' Unions was done in the townships in house-to-house visits by SACTU teams. Increasingly SACTU's activities were assuming a populist dimension; as Luckhardt and Wall put it in the case of the Port Elizabeth GWU: 'More than just a trade union to protect working class interests, it became an institution of and for the people.'[20]

The final protest in which SACTU played a principal role was in May 1961 when once again a three-day stay-at-home was called for, this time to coincide with the proclamation of the South African Republic. By this stage the overall political context had altered dramatically. The African National Congress had been prohibited, and some sections of its leadership as well as the clandestine South African Communist Party were beginning to favour the adoption of a violent strategy of sabotage with the long-term aim of mounting a guerrilla insurgency. A 'National Action Council' had emerged from two conferences which had tried to unite African political leadership, and its spokesmen had called for a national convention to decide South Africa's political future. The strike call for the 29–31 May 1961 was made six weeks before, on 14 April. SACTU, as the largest surviving legal component of the Congress alliance, was crucial in mobilising support for this demonstration. Despite elaborate and extensive countermeasures by the state, which included nightly searches through the townships by the police, 10 000 arrests without charges, a twelve-day detention law, road blocks and an unprecedented display of armed might with tanks, armoured cars and helicopters, the 1961 stay-away evoked a far greater response than any of the previous decade. This was all the more remarkable given the collapse of political organisation within the townships during the emergency. Nelson Mandela, secretary of the National Action Council, in reaction to press reports, called off the strike on the second day as 'it was not the success I had hoped for'. But afterwards it became evident that there had been considerable disruption of industry and commerce in Johannesburg, Cape Town, Durban and Port Elizabeth with many smaller centres affected as well. As the NAC report concluded: 'wherever workers were organised into trade unions there was a favourable response to the strike call'.[21] As in 1957, most of the organisation for the strike was done in factories, although special township strike committees were formed in Soweto, the East Rand townships, Sharpeville (where untypically the local PAC men supported the stay-away) and Alexandra. These committees sent leafletting teams from house to house and put pickets on bus and railway stations.[22]

In the light of this relative degree of success the decision thereafter to locate the main thrust of Congress activity in the sabotage campaign appears surprising.[23] It was obviously not one which involved much consultation. In the years which followed, while SACTU struggled to maintain and strengthen its organisation, many of its most competent and energetic personalities were drawn into the guerrilla movement, Umkonto we Sizwe. Edward Feit's charge, based as it is on the evidence of state witnesses, that SACTU was the recruitment funnel for Umkonto and that it ceased to perform any serious trade union functions, is an exaggeration.[24] What is more likely is that many SACTU activists, who were inevitably committed Congress members, would have found it emotionally difficult to resist the logic of armed struggle. The state itself promoted the identification of normal trade union activity with the clandestine ANC campaign. The 1962 Sabotage Act was drafted in terms sweeping enough to define strikes as acts of sabotage. Between 1960 and 1966 160 SACTU officials were arrested and many were convicted on sabotage charges. By the middle of the decade the movement had been paralysed.

This has been the barest synopsis of an exciting phase in South Africa's labour history. There is a well-developed literature on African trade unions in the early apartheid period, including two detailed studies of SACTU itself.[25] Within this literature there is extensive disagreement over the achievement of the black labour movement of that time and how one should evaluate them.

The most hostile review of SACTU's history is by the American political scientist, Edward Feit. Most of his criticisms stem from what he assumes to be the original conception of SACTU's purpose: that is a 'transmission belt' serving to drive workers in the direction of a political goal determined by an external agency. SACTU's subordination to the national liberation struggle, he argues, caused a constant and unproductive diversion of the militancy generated by shop floor struggle into futile political campaigns. Political failures rebounded back on the trade union organisation, thereby contributing to a decline in the enthusiasm of its following. At times basic organisational work was neglected in favour of political campaigning. To widen the Congress alliance's mass base ill-organised and understaffed unions were constructed which inevitably were corrupt and ineffectual. As the distance between SACTU and orthodox trade unionism widened, its propaganda became more self-delusory and its affiliation statistics increasingly unreliable. Potential opportunities for winning solid material gains for workers were lost by gratuitous antagonism of employers who initially were prepared to offer concessions. Through its final involvement with Umkonto we Sizwe it managed to extinguish itself.

Some of these accusations are quite easy to refute. For example, to argue that SACTU affiliates squandered the possibility of extracting concessions from an initially sympathetic management by a too hasty adoption of the strike weapon, is, firstly, to make unwarrantedly generalised presumptions about managerial attitudes of the time;[26] and, secondly, to forget that the wage determinations of the late 1950s were in response to a mounting wave of strikes. Moreover, SACTU's political linkages could bring it extra stature in the view of some employers. From 1954 onwards, beginning with the United Tobacco Company in Durban, Congress-organised consumer boycotts were used as a highly effective form of pressure in support of striking workers. In 1959 an ANC-inspired boycott of 'Nationalist products' forced the largest canning firm in South Africa, Langeberg Ko-operasie Besperk, into direct negotiations with the FCWU. The same year a boycott of potatoes organised jointly by the ANC and SACTU led to some very limited improvements in the official requirements for the treatment of farmworkers as well as a sharp fall in potato prices.

The view that SACTU mainly provided a vehicle for harnessing workers to a political movement is less simple to dismiss. The conspiratorial implication is of dubious validity; few of SACTU's officials were communists, and many activists, especially at the level of local committees, had received their organisational training within the trade union rather than the political movement.[27] It seems more sensible to conceive the relationship between trade union centre and nationalist party as a dialectical one. Certainly at times the nationalist leadership, particularly with its concern with demonstrative politics, could be rather insensitive to trade unionist preoccupations. The evidence of the stay-at-homes tends to suggest, though, that political strikes were not necessarily unpopular with unionised workers and that SACTU's organisational efforts after 1958 were rather successful, if judged in terms of the original intention to raise the level of workers' class and political consciousness.

But it is true that SACTU was never an equal partner in the Congress alliance, notwithstanding the contention of its official historians,[28] and the campaigns in which it was involved were led by a political leadership which itself had little experience of trade unionism. Feit's suggestion, however, that this was a leadership dominated by a revolutionary clique has little substance. Its typical response to moments of crisis was to call for days of prayer rather than to attempt to exploit those crises.[29] It must be admitted, though, that with the adoption of a guerrilla strategy in 1961, the Congresses chose to jettison a powerful weapon in the trade union organisation.

Political trade unionism was not the only option open to African workers. Unregistered unions could gain limited economic benefits by subordinating themselves to registered unions through TUCSA's liaison committee. Five important African trade unions did this. They later formed a short-lived PAC-aligned federation, the Federation of Free Trade Unions of South Africa, funded by TUCSA and the ICFTU. But for many trade unionists, particularly those schooled in the radical tradition of left-wing industrial unionism of the 1940s, this was unacceptable. It involved toleration of the racial division of labour as well as a tendency to view management-labour relations as ideally conciliatory. In any case TUCSA was extremely inconsistent in its attitudes to African trade unionism and it can be argued with some justification that the development of a more sympathetic posture by TUCSA's hierarchy to the aspirations of black workers which did develop in the late 1950s did so only as a result of ASACTU rivalry.

Finally, the criticisms of SACTU's organisational defects and populist tendencies should be judged in the context of a period of tremendous disaffection among African workers. The proliferation of haphazardly created unions at the turn of the decade was SACTU's response to an increasingly insecure and hopeless existence for black workers.[30] Perhaps it was better that there should have been weak unions than no unions at all.

Notes

1 Larry Welcher, 'The relationship between state and African trades unions in South Africa, 1948–1953', *South African Labour Bulletin*, iv, 5 (September 1978), pp. 25–35.

2 *Ibid*, p. 37. The 1945 figure was probably an overestimation. See Chapter 2.

3 Ken Luckhardt and Brenda Wall, *Organize or Starve . . . the history of the South African Congress of Trade Unions*, Lawrence and Wishart, London, 1980, pp. 156–7.

4 For an exposition of its benefits, see Linda Ensor, 'TUCSA's relationship with African trade unions, 1954–1962', *South African Labour Bulletin*, iii, 4 (1976).

5 Quoted in Desirée Soudien, 'The organisation of the Food and Canning Workers during the South African Congress of Trade Union years', B.A. Honours dissertation, University of the Witwatersrand, 1981, p. 21.

6 Luckhardt and Wall, *Organize or Starve*, p. 216. Much of the following information on SACTU organisation is derived from this source.

7 See David Hemson, 'Dockworkers, labour circulation and class struggles in Durban', University of London, Institute of Commonwealth Studies, *Collected Seminar Papers on the Societies of Southern Africa*, Volume 7, 1976.

8 *Organize or Starve*, pp. 159–161.

9 Don Mateman interviewed by Eddie Webster, March 1980. I am grateful to Eddie Webster for allowing me access to the transcript of this interview.

10 I have leant heavily on two analyses of the stay-aways: Eddie Webster, 'Stay-aways and the black working class since the Second World War', University of the Witwatersrand, African Studies Institute seminar paper, April 1979; Rob Lambert, 'Black resistance in South Africa, 1950–1961: an assessment of the political strike campaigns', University of London, Institute of Commonwealth Studies seminar paper, January 1979.

11 South African Institute of Race Relations, Johannesburg, SAIRR papers, AD 1189, ANC 11 File 3, annual report of the national executive committee to the 45th annual conference of the ANC, 1957.

12 Webster, 'Stay Aways and the black working class', p. 5.

13 *New Age* (Cape Town), 13 February 1958.

14 *Organize or Starve*, p. 354.
15 Don Mateman interviewed by Eddie Webster.
16 SAIRR papers, AD 1189, ANC 11, File 3, annual report of the national executive committee to the 46th annual conference of the ANC, 1958.
17 SAIRR papers, AD 1189 unsorted box, 'Stay away from work demonstration – report of the field officer', SAIRR unpublished manuscript.
18 Webster, 'Stay-aways and the black working class', p. 8.
19 Dan Tloome, 'Lessons of the Stay-Away', *Liberation* (Johannesburg), 32 (August 1958). A similar conclusion is reached in Socialist League of Africa (Baruch Hirson), 'South Africa: ten years of the stay-at-home', *International Socialism* (London), 5 (Summer 1961).
20 *Organize or Starve*, p. 212.
21 SAIRR papers, AD 1189, ANC unsorted box, 'Report from Organisers', typescript.
22 *Ibid*. See also Nelson Mandela, *A Review of the Stay-at-Home Demonstration*, National Action Council, Johannesburg, 1961.
23 According to Lambert ('Black resistance in South Africa, 1950–1961'), there were plans for a 'second phase' in the campaign for a national convention, involving mass non-cooperation based on strengthened industrial organisation. These were not implemented.
24 Edward Feit, *Workers without Weapons*, Archon Books, Hamden, 1975, pp. 170–2.
25 *Organize or Starve* and Feit, *Workers without Weapons*.
26 For an expansion of this point, see Rob Lambert, 'Political unionism in South Africa', *South African Labour Bulletin*, vi, 2 & 3 (September 1980), pp. 101–2.
27 Philip Bonner in 'Black trade unions in South Africa', in Robert Price and Carl Rosberg (eds), *The Apartheid Regime*, David Philip, Cape Town, 1980, argues that two ideological currents combined to influence SACTU strategy. One was the notion of a two-stage revolution as adopted by the SACP in 1950. Here a working-class revolution would be preceded by a national democratic revolution so that in consequence trade unions should subordinate their struggle to national democratic ends. The second idea was the Leninist view of the limitations of trade union consciousness, which even in the context of a national democratic revolution might induce unions to be economistic and reformist. Certainly SACTU's leaders were openly critical of economism but the evidence that African trade unionists generally subscribed to a two-stage theory of revolution is not substantial. Because of the Suppression of Communism Act's listing known former members of the SACP, the SACP could influence the trade union movement only indirectly.
28 *Organize or Starve*, p. 442.
29 See Lambert, 'Black resistance in South Africa', p. 6, and also Chapter 9 of this book.
30 For an amplification of this argument, see Bonner, 'Black trade unions in South Africa', pp. 182–3.

The Sharpeville crisis

In December 1959 both the African National Congress and the Pan-Africanist Congress announced their plans for a campaign against the pass laws. The ANC's proposals consisted mainly of massive protests: 31 March, the anniversary of the 1919 pass burnings, Africa Day, 15 April, Union Day, 31 May, and 26 June were all to be the occasions for nation-wide demonstrations against the passes. In cities the ANC believed it should combine with other sympathetic organisations in leading deputations to government and local authorities. Research would be conducted into the mechanics and effects of influx control and the findings publicised in pamphlets so as to arouse 'the indignation of all sections of our people', including whites. Many of the latter 'are ignorant of these evils [of the pass laws] and not sufficient work has been done to educate them'. As well as the white population who were to form a 'second front' in the campaign, special attention was to be devoted to mobilising women (nation-wide prayer meetings on 9 August) and workers. Industrial action 'should . . . be considered as a form of struggle in this campaign'.[1]

With the exception of the last provision these plans were far from radical. They were especially disappointing when viewed in the context of the explosive situation in urban and rural communities in Natal during that year. While the Anti-Pass Planning Council was considering prayer meetings and street processions Natal activists were talking in terms of a province-wide general strike to halt the Cato Manor removals. Many of the ANC leaders (including Chief Lutuli) had a principled abhorrence for the violence of the Natal protests. Though there was much talk of using economic and industrial power 'to defeat the government',[2] it was never explained quite how this was to be achieved without violence. Part of the problem stemmed from the absence of any serious analysis of the society which Congress leaders were confronted with. The assumptions contained within Lutuli's Presidential Address of December 1959 were typical:

> It is no mere rhetoric to say that apartheid is proving to be a Frankenstein . . . oppression in any guise cannot pay any country dividends. . . . Industry and Commerce are beginning to squeal. . . . We are not without strength. White South Africa is vulnerable.[3]

This type of thinking was not limited to liberal Congress spokesmen. In response to a pessimistic prognosis of the likelihood of revolutionary change in South Africa in the journal *Africa South*, a leading theoretician of the South African Communist Party had this to say:

Industrialisation is incompatible with . . . group or class monopoly of political (and ultimately of economic) power. . . . Nowhere outside the Union does a privileged minority claim to govern by divine right. This type of despotism [is] a freak, an anachronism which cannot have much longer to survive.[4]

Given this belief in the fundamental irrationality of apartheid it is not altogether surprising that Congress's leaders were persuaded of the potential educative protest campaigns could have in swaying a section of the white public. Allied to this conviction was the feeling, especially among older ANC leaders, that political activity, if it was to be effective, should have a moral dimension. As Chief Lutuli had put it in 1957, the road to freedom was 'sanctified with the blood of martyrs – in other words, no cross, no crown'.[5]

Obviously not everyone within the ANC leadership held to these tenets as seriously as Lutuli, but because of the social contradictions within the movement and its lack of ideological coherence, a show of unity was felt to be more important than any sustained debate over strategic problems. In the absence of any rigorous analysis long-term planning was next to impossible. Campaigning was increasingly in the course of the decade a matter more of protest than resistance.

But while the Pan-Africanists' conception of their pass campaign was more in tune with mass disaffection in certain areas, its intellectual foundations were equally shaky. Ideology (in the crude sense of a defined programme and accompanying set of slogans) was seen as a weapon, a crucial ingredient which up to that point had been absent from the spontaneous upsurges of popular rebellion of recent years. All that was required was the correct message expressed in terminology with which ordinary people could identify, and popular rage would cohere into revolutionary uprising. The PAC leadership was convinced that Africanism made articulate a deeply rooted ethno-nationalist popular consciousness. A political appeal founded on such sentiment would immediately attract massive support. Heroic and self-sacrificing leadership would inspire a similar degree of courage and selflessness by the masses. The fundamental problem of mounting an effective campaign was in the style and content of leadership offered to the African population. Few of the Pan-Africanist leaders had played an activist role in ANC campaigning and it is not surprising that they paid so little attention to the question of organisation. The community struggles which provided them with such convincing evidence of the possibilities of mass spontaneity had been conducted around immediate, tangible material issues. They ignored the difficulty of linking the resolution of these issues with a more far-reaching political struggle, a difficulty which had defeated Congress on numerous occasions. As we shall see, the response to the PAC campaign in the western Cape appeared to vindicate their thinking. This response, however, was conditioned by the particular situation of a section of the Cape Town African community. By defining South African oppression in terms of race and psychology the Pan-Africanists assumed a uniformity of African political behaviour which was naively idealist. Their narrow introspection led them, like the ANC, to grossly underestimate and simplify the power and coercive capacity of the state. The PAC's campaign for resisting the pass laws reflected their assumptions about South African society. On an appointed day PAC followers would leave their passes at home and follow their leaders to police stations and present themselves for arrest. This action would inspire massive participation and as prisons filled up and industry and commerce were paralysed by a general strike of national proportions (and indefinite length), irresistable pressures would build up forcing the government to abolish passes. This victory would be succeeded by a 'never-ending stream of campaigns' culminating in a struggle for political 'independence' to be concluded by 1963. The pass campaign itself would be conducted in a strictly peaceful fashion so as to offer no unnecessary provocation of violent police reaction. PAC leaders privately conceded that in the future violence would probably be unavoidable; their insistence on its avoidance in the pass campaign was tactical.[6]

Just over three months was to elapse between the adoption of a campaign strategy at the PAC conference and its launching on 21 March. This haste can be attributed partly to the disregard many Pan-Africanists had for organisational matters. But there were other factors which may have contributed to the PAC's impatience. First, since the movement's inception, the pass laws had been a central preoccupation in speeches made at township meetings, and indeed the characteristics of future PAC action were made quite clear well before December 1959. For example:

> People are being assaulted daily for passes which have been introduced by the Europeans, but come to the PAC to get a medicine to cure you and show you that a European is an enemy. I will pass a resolution in December 1959. What you should do away with is criminality. Don't kill your own people. We are going to throw the pass away because we are prisoners. (Joshua Mashaba, 20 September 1959)[7]

and:

> I will lead you, I will be in front. . . . The thing is [for] the mothers to put food away, put money away, we will call you. We may not come back from where we will be going to. Passes, permits, that is their waterpipe . . . close that waterpipe, we want to fight those acts one for all. (Robert Sobukwe, 1 November 1959)[8]

As the first excerpt indicates, the idea of a pass campaign came from below, from the ordinary members of the PAC, for whom Sobukwe's 'Status Boycott', mooted originally in August 1959 and launched formally in February 1960, had little appeal. Jordan Ngubane, a prominent African critic of the ANC and a member of the Liberal Party on good terms with the PAC leadership, has suggested that the PAC decision to embark swiftly on a confrontationist course was externally prompted. According to Ngubane's account, shortly after the PAC conference, while the PAC executive was divided over the timing of the proposed campaign, letters were sent through a foreign contact of Ngubane's to various African governments to ask for assistance. The Ghanaian authorities replied encouragingly, urging the necessity for a showdown with apartheid, and promising financial and diplomatic support.[9] Ngubane suggests that this served to weaken the position of the more cautious leaders like Sobukwe, who were concerned the campaign should not be mounted precipitately. A final motive for urgency was the desire to preempt the ANC whose first mass demonstration was to take place on 31 March.

Outside the Cape peninsula and the Vereeniging district of the southern Transvaal, where, for reasons which will be discussed below, the PAC had begun to constitute itself as a mass organisation, there was little evidence of systematic attempts to mobilise grass roots support for the movement. Open air meetings were held fairly frequently in Alexandra, the home of the one PAC leader who had a significant popular following, Josias Madzunya. Madzunya and the other main PAC figures absented themselves from the Rand on two occasions: once in early January to attend the annual conference of the Basuto Congress Party (support from Basuto politicians was going to be useful later on),[10] and for two weeks the following month when Sobukwe, Leballo and Madzunya toured Durban, Port Elizabeth and Cape Town. Except in Cape Town, attendance at the various meetings called on their behalf was disappointing.[11] In Durban, especially, they might have expected a more excited reception. Just over a week before their arrival, in the Ezinkawini area of Cato Manor, which was in the process of being screened and resettled, nine policemen were attacked and killed while on a liquor raid. The incident which provided the initial provocation was when a policeman stepped on a woman's toe while searching a shebeen, but underlying the conflict were all the unresolved tensions arising out of poverty, fear of resettlement and official harassment which had lain behind the previous year's unrest in Cato Manor. In Natal, however, the ANC was too strongly entrenched for the PAC to make any significant impression. Here the ANC was sensitive to the popular frustration and anger reflected in the Cato Manor riots: on 18 February, a 4 500-strong meeting called by Congress at Durban City Hall made plans for a general strike and a bus and beer hall boycott in protest against the removals to Kwa Mashu.[12]

Undeterred by the uneven impact of the movement, on 4 March Robert Sobukwe sent out final instructions for the conduct of the campaign to PAC branch and regional executives. Two weeks later Sobukwe wrote to the Commissioner of Police, General Rademeyer, warning him of the launching of the campaign on 21 March and assuring him of its non-violent intentions. In particular, he stressed that crowds should be given adequate time when called upon to disperse by the police. Two days later, simultaneously with the Cape leadership, Sobukwe held a press conference and outlined the PAC's intentions as well as exhorting his followers to refrain from any violent or emotional behaviour. The next day, Saturday 19th, at a meeting presided over by the African Clothing Workers' leader, Lucy Mvubelo, the FOFATUSA chairman, Jacob Nyaose, promised the support of FOFATUSA affiliates who would go on strike for the duration of the campaign.

Meanwhile, at a less public level other preparations were completed. As the response to the campaign would indicate, except in the case of Cape Town and Vereeniging the PAC had made little effort to create strong, committed branches in different centres. Instead, successive layers of leadership were prepared, each of which would take over the functions of the one above it as each echelon of the organisation was arrested. This was consistent with overall PAC strategy which hinged on the quality of leadership rather than organised mobilisation. A final precaution was taken on Sunday 20th, when two members of the national executive, Nana Mahomo and Peter 'Molotsi crossed the Bechuanaland border to raise external support for the campaign. Within the PAC, on the eve of the campaign there was dissatisfaction in certain quarters with the lack of organisational preparedness. At a meeting in Alexandra on the Sunday, Josias Madzunya publicly dissociated himself from the Orlando leadership and told his audience to ignore the PAC:

> Sobukwe and his gang can do what they like, but they have themselves failed to organise Orlando West, because they say they are intellectuals, and they only drink tea in their houses.[13]

Madzunya's defection ensured that whatever popular following the movement had generated in Johannesburg would be divided in its subsequent responses.

The following day the campaign opened in a dignified and quiet fashion in Soweto. Robert Sobukwe, having been up from 2 a.m. putting his papers into order and making last minute arrangements for the welfare of his family, left his house in Mofolo at six, and began his four-mile walk to Orlando police station. At various stages along the route, Phefeni, Dube and Orlando West, small groups of men joined him. Altogether nearly 170 PAC men were arrested under the provisions of pass laws in Johannesburg, some with Sobukwe in Orlando East, others in Moroka, George Goch, Jeppe and the Western Areas. In Pretoria, events were similarly undramatic: six men presented themselves for arrest at Hercules police station only to have their names taken and to be sent away. PAC activity in Pretoria seems mainly to have centred round Lady Selborne High School.[14] A handful of PAC volunteers were arrested in Durban and East London.[15] Only in the African townships round Vereeniging and in Langa and Nyanga near Cape Town did the PAC's call to action seem to have attracted a popular response. The events in the Cape will be examined shortly. First we will look at impact of the Pan-Africanists in the Vereeniging district, starting with the structural factors which helped to shape the African community's response to their campaign.

The industrial centre of Vereeniging, fifty miles south of Johannesburg, had grown up round the Union Steel Corporation, a steel works based on wartime surplus scrap-iron founded in 1912, conveniently near the Vaal River coal deposits. The town's industrial importance was confirmed in 1941 when the state-controlled Iron and Steel Corporation (ISCOR) established its second plant ten miles from Vereeniging, at a new township named after the ISCOR chairman, Vanderbijlpark. Round these two steel works there developed a wide range of steel-based industries which expanded rapidly during the Second World War as Vereeniging became the centre of South African munition production. By the end of the war Vereeniging's population included 12 000 whites and 30 000 blacks, a threefold expansion over the past decade. Originally Vereeniging's African population was concentrated in the Top Location, founded in 1912 on what was then the municipal boundry. On stands rented from the council African landlords built houses and lean-to shacks which they rented out. As the location's population expanded living conditions became increasingly unhealthy: in two months in 1946, out of a population of 15 000 nearly 150 had died of pneumonia, 85 of gastro-enteritis, and a further 24 from tuberculosis.[16] In 1937 socio-economic tensions sparked off by liquor raids had exploded into a violent riot in which two police were killed. Following the recommendations of the subsequent government commission of inquiry, but motivated also by the potential value of the Top Location land as well as a typhus epidemic, the council began to negotiate for the purchase of a new site from the Vereeniging Estate Company. The first houses of the new township were built in 1942 on a site two miles from Vereeniging, named after the Mayor, John Sharpe. At roughly the same time the two townships of Bophelong and Boipatong were constructed to house the ISCOR African labour force at Vanderbijlpark.[17]

By the standards of the time these were model townships, their neat rows of boxy dwellings being supplied with street lighting and running water, sanitation, and in some cases bathrooms. Sharpeville was tightly and effectively administered, with its own police station and a superintendent as well as other facilities provided by the munipality: a brewery, clinic and weekly film shows. By official criteria the new location was a glowing success: compared to the Top Location the incidence of disease was minimal and in the first quarter of 1946 only thirty-eight crimes were reported to the Sharpeville police, compared to 500 in the Top Location.[18]

The resettlement of the population of Top Location was a gradual process taking place over a period of fiteen years as houses became available in Sharpeville. There are no reports of resistance to the removals: compensation to the landlords was paid at a rate determined by the Advisory Board and the Council and they did not make any protest.[19] It would have been unlikely that they would have aroused much sympathy: in 1951 the mean rent for a lean-to shack in the Top Location was 15s on a stand which on average was shared by 21 people.[20] The Council was renting its new houses at 27s 6d and because the removals were so gradual, if people could not afford the higher rent they could always stay on in the Top Location for the time being.

Not all of Vereeniging's African population lived in Top Location or Sharpeville. Many of the major employers housed a large section of their workforce on their premises in single male hostels. In the Vereeniging District (which included Vanderbijlpark), in 1960 nearly 50 000 people lived in municipal townships and another 11 000 in employers' compounds.[21]

Despite its size, proximity to Johannesburg and industrial importance, Vereeniging had never been an important centre of political activity among Africans. Throughout the 1950s municipal officials would proudly assert again and again that the 'peace-loving and law-abiding' character of the black population and the absence in its townships of the 'riots and boycotts instigated by the Bantu' which had marred the recent history of so many other urban centres.[22] And indeed the available records support their testimony. In 1950 pamphlets did circulate in the Top Location and Sharpeville itself calling on people to support the May day strike, and a meeting was held in the Top Location, but with a subsequent ban on gatherings and threats of dismissal by employers, 1 May passed uneventfully enough.[23] Two years later, the only local reactions to the Defiance Campaign reported were a well-attended meeting held in Sharpeville in July by the Society of Young Africa (a Unity movement affiliate) at which its spokesmen attacked the ANC; and a second SOYA meeting held two months later after which SOYA claimed that its support in Sharpeville was 'very large'.[24] Further evidence of SOYA activity appeared in 1953 when the superintendent informed the Advisory Board of a secret meeting at which plans for a boycott of the coronation festivities were discussed. The shocked members of the Board advised the ejection from the township of these mischievious agitators who in any case, they believed, were almost certainly outsiders.[25] Whether this advice was followed is not known but the coronation was celebrated with picnics and souvenir mugs distributed to schoolchildren without protest or interruption.

For the next six years there were no further reports of 'agitation'. The degree of local political quiescence was evident in the lack of any resistance to the issue of women's passes; indeed, 'so many presented themselves for registration that the number had to be controlled daily'.[26] This obviously requires some explanation. The apparent local political apathy was particularly surprising, bearing in mind the liveliness of nearby Evaton during its two-year bus boycott. Yet in Sharpeville it seems that the ANC had failed to establish a token presence.[27] One reason for this may have been the controlled environment in which so many workers existed which made the organisation of trade unions very difficult, thus depriving the ANC of a normal source of energetic activists. Of the total African employment in manufacturing in Vereeniging, nearly 15 000 out of 16 798 worked in industries which relied chiefly on migrant labour recruited from the nearby Free State reserves and housed in inaccessible compounds.[28] Other inhibiting factors may have been the relative newness of the township communities and the strict official supervision under which they lived. The local authorities were unusually hostile to manifestations of African political life: even contestants for positions on the compliant Advisory Board were prohibited from canvassing votes at public meetings.[29]

By the end of the 1950s, for a variety of reasons, unemployment, influx control, poverty and police activity were having a peculiarly forceful impact on the Vereeniging African population, contributing to its receptiveness to militant political leadership. Sharpeville's population comprised nearly 21 000 children, nearly 7 000 adult women and 8 600 men.[30] It was therefore a predominantly youthful population. In the late 1950s youth unemployment was an increasing problem. The main local industries, with their requirements for cheap heavy manual labour, preferred to recruit from the reserves[31] and industrial wage-levels and conditions did not appeal to township school-leavers.[32] To exacerbate this, in 1959 there were not enough high school places in Vereeniging to accommodate Junior Certificate holders.[33] According to The World, 'scores of youths roamed the streets' and in Bophelong 7 000 residents had gathered to warn the authorities of the dangerous situation created by the pass laws which prevented their children from seeking work on the Rand and helped to turn them 'into jailbirds and criminals'.[34]

This was not the only reason, however, why influx control was likely to have aroused an unusually intense degree of antipathy in Vereeniging in 1960. In September 1959 the resettlement of the inhabitants of Top Location was finally completed. Whereas over the previous decade they had been moved out at a rate of a few families a month, towards the end of the process the pace quickened so that during August the final removals affected 3 000 people. In the last few months of the removals the official statistics indicate that not all the people moved out of Top Location were being accommodated in Sharpeville: the discrepancy in the declining population of the one and the rising population of the other amounted to 213 in December 1958, 75 in February 1959, 61 in March, 182 in April, 436 in May, 48 in June, 642 in July and 3 060 in August.[35] The Council's Director of Non-European Affairs explained the disparity by referring to the large number of families in Top Location who were unable to pay the higher rentals of Sharpeville and so could not live there. These people, accordingly, had been endorsed out to the reserves.[36] So what had happened was that in under a year 5 000 people, all of whom would have had close links with the recently settled element of the Sharpeville population, had been driven out of the area.

For those who remained there were other difficulties. Many of the new tenants in Sharpeville were hard put to pay their rent, particularly as the new houses were the most expensive in the location at £2 15s a month. If people were in arrears they were without warning locked out of their homes and refused certain services: in one case a family was not permitted to bury a corpse in the township graveyard.[37] In January 1960 the Town Clerk reported that in Sharpeville there were 2 310 rent defaulters – accounting for over a third of the households. An angry protest meeting took place at the beginning of March outside the township offices, at which, according to the newspapers, women stoned the superintendent.[38] The authorities denied the stoning and went on to allege that there was nothing spontaneous about the protest; they claimed that people had been intimidated into attending after receiving threatening leaflets issued by both the ANC and the PAC.[39] In addition to high rents Sharpeville residents were affected by the presence of a vigorous local police force: liquor raids were a daily occurrence and statistics indicate a rise in the level of influx control arrests and prosecutions in the first part of 1960. Unemployment figures were also increasing.[40]

All these conditions provided fertile ground for the first PAC activists who reportedly arrived from Johannesburg in mid-1959 to establish branches in Sharpeville, Bophelong and Boipatong. They need not have been particularly well informed about local grievances, for the Vereeniging area was an obvious place for them to choose. No opposition to their work would be forthcoming from the ANC, and in Evaton, twelve miles away, Africanists had played a prominent rôle in the affairs of the community for some years. The visitors from Johannesburg had their entry permits withdrawn after a couple of days by the superintendent for 'talking politics' but this did not inhibit the progress of the new organisation.[41] Its local recruits worked with caution and discretion, avoiding public meetings, and working instead through door-to-door canvassing, with small groups gathering indoors at night to discuss future strategy.[42] They were thus able to escape unwelcome official attention, although complaints began to be received by the authorities in September of PAC incitement against members of the Advisory Board.[43] The Board was an easy target on which to focus popular discontent; judging from its minutes its members either ignored or were unaware of the recent tensions and difficulties which have been described above. By the end of 1959 the PAC in Sharpeville had approximately 150 followers.[44] If its local leadership was typical it was an organisation of quite young, comparatively well-educated, working-class men and women. Members subsequently interviewed by a commission of enquiry were all in their twenties and included an unskilled labourer, a seamstress, a dry cleaning worker, a delivery man and a chauffeur. Most were junior certificate holders.[45]

In contrast to the Reef, PAC preparations on the eve of the pass campaign were systematic and extensive in the Vereeniging district. On Thursday 17 March a crudely reproduced typed leaflet was in circulation in the townships telling people to stay away from work the following Monday. On Sunday afternoon PAC activists approached bus drivers and warned them:

> We beg you, our people, tomorrow we must be as one. We are not going to fight the Europeans. We just want to alter this pass law because it is hard on us . . . if you run away you might get hurt. . . . We will lay our hands on the one that does not. . . .[46]

One bus driver testified to the commission of enquiry that he and some of his colleagues were taken away from their homes in the middle of the night and not released until after sunrise.[47] The evident attention PAC activists in Sharpeville paid to disrupting public transport may have been inspired by the experiences of the Evaton bus boycott. Telephone wires linking Sharpeville with Vereeniging were cut during the night of the 20th. Police patrolling the township on Sunday evening on several occasions interrupted large gatherings of young men.

Early on Monday morning the first passengers began forming queues at Sharpeville's Seeiso Street bus terminal, near the new police station. PAC pickets appeared and told them they should not go to work, but in any case no buses arrived. PAC groups were also posted on the road to Vereeniging to stop pedestrians and cyclists. By 10 o'clock a large crowd had formed in the open space in the centre of the township. Similarly, in Bophelong and Boipatong a large group of people gathered in both locations and then joined forces to march, 4 000 strong, in a procession to Vanderbijlpark police station. At Evaton 20 000 people assembled outside the police station.

The degree of success the PAC branches had had in mobilising the populations of these townships can of course be attributed partly to their success in halting public transport and picketing. But this could not have been the only explanation. Even where it was strong, the PAC was not a large organisation and did not have the capacity to coerce support. Police evidence of intimidation does not accord with the eyewitness accounts of the character of the crowds which had formed: these were expectant and cheerful rather than browbeaten and resentful. In any case the Vanderbijlpark commuters did not depend on public transport as the locations were within easy walking distance of the town. For pedestrians a few scattered pickets would not have presented unsurmountable obstacles to getting to work. Response to the PAC's campaign in these townships was surely a reflection of local conditions and in particular the local effects of influx control. This had had a particularly disruptive and aggravating impact on the lives of sections of Vereeniging's African population.

The size of the crowds took local police officers by surprise. Their subsequent reactions were to be conditioned by the relative novelty for them of handling large political demonstrations (more experienced reinforcements arrived later in the day) and an acute (if mistaken) consciousness of their vulnerability. Their behaviour may have been influenced by the memory of the recent attack on policemen in Cato Manor (the commission report accepted police testimony to this effect). In the cases of the crowds at Vanderbijlpark and Evaton, these were dispersed by 10 o'clock after a baton charge in the former and low-flying Sabre jets in the latter. In Vanderbijlpark one man was killed when police fired on a group of men whom they alleged were stoning them. At Sharpeville the aircraft failed to intimidate people. The police had already declined to arrest those PAC supporters who had presented themselves at the head of the crowd. According to the police, the PAC officials refused their order to disperse, the branch secretary, Nyakane Tsolo, saying 'We will not call them off until Sobukwe has spoken'.[48] Many members of the crowd believed that an important announcement concerning passes was going to be made and this contributed to their determination to remain where they were. Police reinforcements arrived through the course of the morning, some of them in Saracen armoured cars. At 1.15 p.m., with nearly 300 police facing a crowd of 5 000, a scuffle broke out at the gate which breached the wire fence round the police station. A police officer, accidently or deliberately, was pushed over. The attention of the front rows was focused on the gate and they surged forward, pushed by people behind them who wanted to see what was happening. At this stage, according to police witnesses, stones were thrown at them. The more inexperienced constables began firing their guns spontaneously. The majority of those killed or wounded were shot in the back. Altogether 69 people died, including eight women and ten children. 180 people were wounded.[49]

In the days which followed the shootings, while the population of Sharpeville mourned, Vereeniging was held in the grip of a general strike by the workers from the townships. The steel and metal industries managed to maintain production with their compound labour force, but the smaller industrial and all the commercial employers were affected. Domestic servants stayed at home (ironically they had been forbidden to live on their employer's premises the year before). Only after the mass funeral had taken place on Wednesday 30 March did the people of Sharpeville trickle back to their jobs.[50]

With the Sharpeville shootings the police had effectively broken the back of the PAC campaign in the Transvaal. In the Cape peninsula, however, a similar sequence of events marked only the opening act of a drama which was to reach its climax the day the African people of Vereeniging buried their dead.

The events of March 1960 came closest to representing a crisis for the South African state in its political capital, Cape Town. To understand the way this crisis developed and the fashion in which it was resolved an understanding of local political relationships, and in particular of the two political groups most directly involved in the events, the PAC and the Liberal Party, is essential.

Most members of the small and at that stage predominantly white Liberal Party were repelled by what they took to be the inherent racism of the PAC's rhetoric. Only a minority among them believed that the PAC's position was closer than that of the ANC to Liberal ideology. In particular there was the group which by 1958 had taken over the leadership of the Cape division of the

Liberal Party, and which though radical, was also anti-communist. The Liberal Party itself had been founded in 1953. Its founders had expressed a faith in the traditional institutions of Cape liberalism and they announced their intention to employ democratic and constitutional means, stating at the same time that they were opposed to all forms of autocracy, including communism. At first the Liberals advocated a qualified franchise and though they dropped this policy in 1954 they continued until 1959 to insist on the desirability of progressive stages of enfranchisement. Though they were well to the left of established parliamentary opposition, to black and white Congressmen the Liberal Party appeared to be gradualist, moderate and patronising. Increasingly, however, the Liberal Party came to be composed of people who rejected constitutional strategies; the most important figure in this respect was Patrick Duncan.

Since his participation in the Defiance Campaign (for which he served part of a three-month prison sentence) Patrick Duncan had steered an idiosyncratic political course. Disappointed in his efforts to join the ANC in 1953, and unable to accept the left-wing stance of the Congress of Democrats, he finally joined the Liberal Party, serving as its national organiser in 1956–7. In 1958 he sold up his farm on the Lesotho–Free State border and moved to Cape Town to edit *Contact*, a fortnightly newspaper. *Contact*, like its owner-editor, was to be a constant source of controversy. It embarassed the Liberal leadership as much by its criticism of Chief Lutuli's alleged susceptibility to communist influence as for its enthusiastic championing of African political aspirations. From the perspective of the revolutionary left Duncan appeared at best as misguided. But eccentric and undisciplined as Duncan's behaviour may have seemed to his contemporaries it was nevertheless motivated by deeply held moral and political principles. From the early 1950s he had been a Gandhist and it was his belief in the efficacy of passive resistance and the morality of Gandhi's *Satyagraha* which was to influence his response to the PAC. For when the PAC called for 'absolute non-violence' in the execution of its campaign, Duncan recognised in this the spirit of the Mahatma.[51]

Though *Contact* was not a Liberal Party newspaper those who worked on it were Liberal Party members. They shared with Duncan his anti-communism, a dislike of gradualism and a desire to make the Liberal Party a considerable force in black politics. They were not all as inclined as Duncan to criticise the ANC openly, but they were far less willing than Liberals elsewhere to work with COD, with whom they were competing for influence. Several of Duncan's associates felt, before he did, that the Pan-Africanists' misgivings about the Congress alliance were the same as their own and that the PAC's emergence was a promising development. They felt that the PAC could be persuaded to be less ambiguously non-racial. It was this group based around *Contact* which had managed to supplant the old Cape leadership of the party which had been hostile to mass action and in favour of franchise qualifications.

The PAC, in its public statements, was as critical of the Liberals as it was of white Congressmen, for it held that both groups, whether they meant it or not, could only dilute the force of the struggle. The PAC leaders pointed to the disparity between the living conditions of the black man and the most committed and radical white political activist and concluded that 'no white man can identify himself with the struggle of the black people in this country'.[52] The PAC president, Robert Sobukwe, warned his followers in May 1959 about their 'so-called friends' who were out to confuse them; in particular he mentioned Bishop Ambrose Reeves, Trevor Huddleston and Patrick Duncan.[53] Despite this, the PAC was prepared to accept help from white groups – provided it was given unconditionally. Peter Hjul, Liberal divisional chairman in Cape Town, remembers that the PAC had made an approach to the Liberal Party national executive in February 1960 to ask for money to support dependents of those who were going to take part in the PAC campaign.[54] Hjul also thinks that Sobukwe told Kgosana, the secretary of the Cape PAC, that only two organisations would provide disinterested help: the Liberal Party and the Black Sash, a movement of white women who concerned themselves with black civil rights and social welfare. Certainly PAC leaders had been willing to discuss their policies with Liberals in Johannesburg in the months leading up to the campaign.[55] The fact was the PAC was short of money, and while it was publicly hostile to and privately wary of the Liberals, at least the latter, unlike the COD, had no formal connection with the ANC.

The relative success the PAC had in attracting support in the Cape peninsula should be understood in the context of the especially aggravating situation of the local African population. Africans were traditionally a minority in Cape Town, the 75 000 estimated by the 1960 census representing 10 per cent of a total population which also included 411 000 coloured people.[56]

Notwithstanding its small size, the peninsula's population was the object of much official harassment. In 1955 the Minister of Native Affairs announced the curtailment of African migration to the peninsula. Ideally, it was argued, there should be no Africans in the western Cape. Coloured workers would be employed in their place. From 1957 the Urban Areas Act Amendment tightened influx control. As a result, between 1955 and 1962 the official number of registered male African workers fell by nearly 20 per cent.[57] The process of 'endorsing out' quickened towards the end of the decade. Between January 1959 and March 1962 18 931 men and 7 280 women were transported to the already overpopulated reserves.[58] Increasingly the African community was composed of male migrant labourers and anything that might strengthen the tendency towards a settled, balanced African urban community was discouraged officially. In 1960, therefore, the African population in Cape Town was suffering from recently imposed government measures which were more severe in their effect than elsewhere.

Most Cape Town Africans lived in two townships, eight and twelve miles from the centre of the city. Langa, established in 1927, had 25 000 inhabitants. Just over a quarter of this population lived in the small houses provided for families by the municipality. The vast majority of people who lived in Langa were male and inhabited single workers' blocks known as 'flats' because they were divided up into double rooms or in barrack-like hostels with large dormitories, little privacy, bleak surroundings and communal cooking and washing facilities. Of the population living in Langa, 66 per cent lived in the barracks and 5 per cent in the flats, a total of 18 276 men.[59] Just over a quarter of Langa's inhabitants were 'townspeople'; that is, people who had been born in Cape Town or some other town. The rest were migrant workers, mainly from the Ciskei and the Transkei, and it was they who occupied the barracks and flats. Generally the most recently arrived migrants lived in dormitories with workers from their own region. The more ambitious men who wanted to settle permanently in town attempted to share rooms in the flats.[60]

Although Langa was thought to be a serene African community compared to those around Johannesburg, conditions were deteriorating during the 1950s. From 1954 the government had refused to sanction the building of any more family accommodation in Langa.[61] Government policy was that eventually all families should be 'repatriated' to the reserves. At the same time there was an influx of 'bachelor' migrant workers who were being rehoused in the 'zones' (hostels and flats) as locations were concentrated and eliminated. 'Endorsing out' and its concomitant, influx control, required progressive restrictions on movement and employment opportunities for migrant workers. Migrant workers who had previously remained aloof from townspeople's preoccupations began to concern themselves more with political issues. Moreover, rural opposition to land rehabilitation and Bantu Authorities also affected the reactions of workers from the reserves.[62]

Nyanga was created in 1956 as an emergency camp for flood victims and evicted 'squatters'. Families forcibly resettled from Langa provided significant social links between the two townships. These were important as during the crisis the two communities tended to act together. In contrast to Langa, Nyanga mainly housed families but in accommodation which ranged between the minority of local authority-built houses rented at £4 15s a month to shacks constructed on plots for which occupants paid £1 a month ground rent.[63] People forced to resettle had received no assistance in building their new homes. Many had to do without sanitation and running water.[64] In 1959, with the arrival of 1 200 families from Windermere and other camps resentment flared into open anger. Former squatters attacked policemen on a liquor raid and shortly thereafter 200 women protested against the raids, rents and poor conditions to the Bantu Affairs Commissioner.[65] His reply to them was as brusque as his treatment of a more decorous delegation from the Advisory Board. If people disliked living in Nyanga they could go to the reserves; nothing was going to be done to encourage Africans to remain in Cape Town.[66]

Migrant workers had on the whole been neglected by established political parties. Migrants were commonly criticised for their apathy about working conditions and their lack of political motivation. By 1960 it is probable that social conditions were such that the migrant workforce was far more politically receptive than was thought. Quite apart from the pass system on which the increasingly repressive apparatus of influx control rested, there was also the simple fact that 50 per cent of the black population was living on incomes barely adequate for subsistence and certainly not enough to cope with rent or price rises.[67]

There is not enough evidence to indicate exactly how much support for the PAC came from the settled section of the population and how much from the migrants. Both groups found thmselves in deteriorating situations in 1960. The PAC's style was heroically and traditionally orientated. This might have had a considerable attraction for Xhosa workers from the culturally conservative Transkei and Ciskei. As we shall see, the PAC did manage to establish a following in the 'bachelor' hostels and flats. It could be argued that even if the degree of PAC organisation was fairly slight it was nevertheless valuable in obtaining a mass response to the PAC's call to do away with passes. In 1960 the grievances of both urbanised and rurally orientated Cape Africans were especially acute, and it can be argued that migrant workers were beginning to share the political concerns of the black townsfolk. The disturbed and unbalanced nature of Langa society, and the government's deliberate sabotage of any social stability in Nyanga, had created a mood which was volatile, angry and desperate.

The ANC had never been a powerful force in the western Cape. In the 1950s the movement was bedevilled by squabbles between those who favoured the Congress alliance and those who felt, with the Youth Leaguers of Orlando, that multiracialism weakened African control of their political destiny. The stronger branches were outside the metropolis, in the agricultural centres of the Boland where the SACTU-affiliated Food and Canning Workers' Union had its greatest support. In Cape Town itself there had been only token participation in the major ANC campaigns of the decade. Not surprisingly, bearing in mind Cape Town's demographic features, multiracialism was an important dimension of Congress activity, and in 1958 three ANC branches broke away as Africanists.[68] Apparently inspired by the proceedings of the Basutoland Congress Party conference at which some of them met prominent Transvaal Africanists,[69] the secessionists constituted themselves formally as PAC members from May 1959.[70] Beginning in Nyanga, under the leadership of Christopher Mlohoti, a labourer from the single quarters in Langa, branches were started in Langa Flats, Langa Township, Nyanga West, Nyanga East and in the remaining squatters' encampments at Windermere and Crawford.[71] It was in the bachelor zones of Langa that Philip Kgosana, a young university student, began to meet Pan-Africanists.

Philip Kgosana was a political novice. The son of a Transvaal village priest, he had managed to get an Institute of Race Relations scholarship to pay his university fees. He lived in great poverty in one of the Langa flats. He wrote to Patrick Duncan for help and was given £2 and a *Contact* sales commission. But it was his friendship with an Africanist which provided a measure of security: 'When I needed money I just told him like a child and he gave it to me'.[72] Drawn into the PAC, he failed his first year exams and decided to abandon his studies.

Much of the organisation of the PAC in the Cape peninsula was the work of Nana Mahomo, also a University of Cape Town student, but as well a politician of some experience. He had helped lead the 1957 bus boycott in Johannesburg's Western Native Township[73] and was a member of the PAC's national executive. He left Cape Town on the eve of the pass campaign to raise support abroad for the PAC. Mahomo and Kgosana were untypical in their backgrounds; most of the Cape Town PAC leaders would have been more comfortable in the company of Madzunya than with the Orlando intellectuals. While only seven of the 31 men put on trial for incitement after the campaign came from the migrant workers' quarters, none worked in a white-collar job.[74]

Twenty-nine of them were described in court as 'labourers', though in most cases they were men with some education and work-skill.

Philip Kgosana was not the only Pan-Africanist in Cape Town to have had some contact with Duncan or his friends. Nana Mahomo had lodged with Joe Nkatlo, a leading member of the Liberal Party (and a former Africanist within the ANC). Nkatlo was close to Duncan. Mlohoti had been to the Liberal Party office early on to put the PAC's case and so impressed one of them, Randolph Vigne, that Vigne sent a motion in favour of supporting the PAC to the Liberal Party's national executive in February 1960. The Cape Town Liberals, especially those associated with *Contact*, were seen by local PAC men as sympathetic.

By December 1959, the PAC had established a few branches and recruited 1 000 men in the area,[75] but they did not appear to have had an enormous impact on the African population. Initial enthusiasm appears to have waned. Kgosana found, after returning from the first PAC national conference in Orlando, that the regional executive had adjourned until 20 January, this despite the fact that the leadership had announced their programme of 'positive action'. On 24 January the regional executive was dismissed and a more energetic group including Kgosana and Mlohoti took over.[76] By late February, after a visit from Sobukwe and Leballo, they were capable of drawing 300 people to a meeting in Nyanga.[77] Leballo had been in particularly good form as he addressed a crowd in Kensington on the impending campaign.

> Everybody felt the electricity as Potlake Leballo, National Secretary, climbed on to the platform and waved his pipe in the air. His powerful voice rang out in Sesotho *'Ke Potlake was ho Leballo u gu thweng oa bona lefatshe es glno le thopilwe ka badischabo'*. (This is Potlake of the Leballos, of whom it is said 'hold your shield lightly, your father's land has been looted by foreigners'.)[78]

On 18 March, simultaneously with Sobukwe, Kgosana announced that the pass campaign would begin on Monday. Like Sobukwe he was emphatic that the campaign should eschew violence: 'We are not leading corpses to a new Africa,' he said and went on to warn that if

> violence breaks out we will be taken up with it and give vent to our pent-up emotions and feeling by throwing a stone at a saracen or burning a particular building; we are small revolutionaries engaged in revolutionary warfare. But after a few days, when we have buried our dead and made moving graveside speeches and our emotions have settled again, the police will round up a few people and the rest will go back to the passes, having forgotten what our goal had been initially.[79]

There is some evidence that in the weeks before the campaign PAC workers had attempted to organise African resistance in the Cape. The diary of one of the organisers, Ralph Mbatsha, had entries which included a mention of a visit to Worcester on 13 March.[80] The entry was perhaps significant; Worcester was an important centre for the Food and Canning Workers' Union, which was composed of both African and coloured workers, and was one of the few places where coloured workers were to join Africans in striking during the following weeks.[81] PAC men were able to enter the Cape Town docks on 19 March and with the tacit consent of the watchmen distribute their leaflets and persuade dockers to stay away from work.[82] A 'Task Force' of young volunteers had been formed.

On the eve of the campaign, Sunday 20 March, large meetings were held in Langa and Nyanga – both addressed by Kgosana, who claimed afterwards that he had spoken to 5 000 'sons and daughters of the soil':

> At the end of the meetings, the massive crowd poured their hearts out when I led them in singing '*Unzima Lomthwalo Ufuna Madoda*'. (The burden is heavy, it needs men).[83]

On Monday men began to assemble in the rain outside the bachelor zones at Langa New Flats early in the morning. By the time of Kgosana's arrival at 6.00 am, 6 000 men had gathered to listen to his instructions to march to Langa police station and surrender themselves for deliberately leaving their passes at home. Then Mlami Makwetu, a docker and a branch secretary, repeated the earlier insistence that there should be no violence. When the police arrived, they warned Kgosana that a march on the police station would be interpreted as an attack. Kgosana agreed to disperse the meeting, but also informed the police that no one would be going to work that day. In dispersing the crowd Kgosana allegedly told people to reconvene at 6 pm when there would be 'word from the national office'. The police station was subsequently picketed by PAC 'Task Force' men who kept demonstrators at a safe distance from it.[84]

Similarly, at Nyanga PAC supporters congregated on the rugby field. Women stood around bus stops mocking those who went to work. At 7.30 am the first batch of volunteers started for Philippi police station. A Liberal Party member who lived in Nyanga, Collingwood August, wrote in his diary:

> I am surprised at the large number of peasant-type demonstrators. Normally they take little interest in politics. They are the migrant labour and they are the section of Africans hardest hit by the pass laws. But it is still surprising and a revelation that at last a political call that appeals to them has been raised.[85]

The police station at Langa was reinforced: by the evening there were to be over 60 police armed with sten guns, riot sticks, revolvers and Saracen armoured cars.[86] At one o'clock the PAC leaders heard over the radio that over 40 demonstrators had been killed outside Sharpeville police station.[87]

Kgosana then travelled to Cape Town to visit men who had already been arrested at Philippi. In town he called at the *Contact* office where an excited Patrick Duncan told him: 'You have poked the bees but you must be careful. Anything can happen tonight'.[88] According to Duncan, Kgosana 'understood the dangers of the situation and the ever present possibility of violence erupting'.[89]

The exhilaration of the *Contact* Liberals was understandable. Their enthusiasm for the PAC arose from a complex set of ingredients. They mistook the PAC's tactical injunction on violence for a principle. Pan-Africanists' hostility to communism suited them too, particularly as they chose to ignore (or were unaware of) the lack of any doctrinal objections to communism in the speeches of PAC spokesmen (who mainly concentrated on the 'foreign-ness' of communism and its exponents in South Africa). There was emotional reason for identification with the PAC cause among younger Liberals. Like young black intellectuals (with whom there was more contact than had ever taken place before) whites of radical sympathies were infected by the end of the 1950s with a sense of crisis and of imminent change. As Lewis Nkosi has commented:

> It was a time of infinite hope and possibility; it seemed not extravagant in the least to predict that the Nationalist government would collapse . . . it was a time of thrust, never of withdrawal.[90]

The circumstances which stimulated this mood included the experience of a decade of mass political campaigning, the apparent inability of the state to suppress African opposition, the swelling chorus of international criticism of South Africa and the euphoria produced by decolonisation. It led some Liberals to take up rather illiberal positions: an admiration for mass militancy, for toughness and for confrontation. Duncan's adherents had little time for the pressure-group tactics favoured by many of their Liberal Party colleagues. They sought involvement in a popular struggle and saw in the sudden mushrooming success of the PAC the vehicle for this.

While Kgosana was in Cape Town 6 000 people gathered in the New Flats area in anticipation of the evening meeting. The police, who had toured the location in loudspeaker vans during the afternoon broadcasting a ban on public meetings, arrived in force with Saracens and sten guns at 5.45 pm. After giving an inaudible command to disperse two baton charges were made on the crowd. This only had the effect of transforming a peaceful gathering into a furious one. Some people began stoning the police and a large number surged forward. The commanding officer ordered his men to fire. Two people were killed and the rest fled. That night rioting broke out in Langa: police reinforcements were attacked; municipal offices were burnt to the ground, African policemen's houses were looted, telephone wires cut and roads blocked to prevent the entry of fire-engines. The mutilated body of a coloured man who had driven two white journalists into Langa was found the next day.[91]

The strike gathered momentum throughout the week. On Tuesday at 8 am the hostels in Langa were raided and policemen burst into rooms and beat up anyone they found in them.[92] Kgosana spent the morning in hiding but visited Duncan in the afternoon.[93] The PAC put up road blocks in Nyanga and the bus crews stayed at home.[94] On Wednesday Duncan held a bizarre dinner party to which he invited Kgosana, Thomas Ngwenya of the ANC, Randolph Vigne and Anton Rupert, the tobacco magnate.[95] Duncan's diary is cryptic: 'a useful and friendly meeting', but Randolph Vigne remembers Rupert, a committed government supporter, being heavily patronising, drawing comparisons between immature African political development and unripe fruit and telling Kgosana that these days were likely to be the great moments of his life and he had therefore better get on and enjoy them.[96] Duncan had

217

believed that Rupert, whom he saw as a figure with some influence, was open to persuasion to act on the PAC's behalf. Kgosana himself was to declare that the aim of the campaign had been to put pressure on industrialists who could appeal to the government to lift the pass laws so that the workforce would return to work.[97] But the meeting was inconclusive: by all accounts neither Kgosana nor Rupert made much impression on each other.

On Thursday, 24 March, Kgosana spent much of the day in Cape Town, both in the *Contact* offices and those of *New Age*,[98] despite his own warning to his followers not to heed what *New Age*, in particular, said about the campaign.[99] Duncan warned Kgosana that if he had anything further to do with the Congress of Democrats he would have to cease counting on Liberal support (the day before, Duncan had agreed to arrange for the Liberals to obtain food supplies for strikebound Langa).[100] Kgosana did not tell Duncan that he had already negotiated through Brian Bunting for the COD to deliver a truckload of food.[101] At the time, he ostensibly accepted Duncan's contention that to approach COD people was to contravene Sobukwe's orders.

That evening Wilson Manetsi, a PAC regional executive member, left Langa, and presented himself with 100 volunteers at Cape Town police station for arrest.[102] By now the Cape peninusla was the only area in which the PAC campaign was continuing. While workers were beginning to trickle back to their jobs in Vereeniging, in Cape Town the stay-away was increasing its impact; the next morning 50 per cent of the African labour force was on strike.

The PAC leaders, Makwetu, Kgosana, Nxelwa and Ndlovu, led a demonstration outside Cape Town's Caledon Square police headquarters. Estimates of its size varied between 2 000 and 5 000. Here there are different versions of what subsequently happened. Duncan's diary states that at 9 30 am a telephone call came from Philip Kgosana who was on the Grand Parade in the middle of Cape Town, which warned him that the people of Langa were on their way to hand themselves over to the police:'They have seen yesterday the police had room to arrest 101 men and they want to join them. Come quickly.'[103] At the time of Kgosana's telephone call only a small group had arrived, but soon the street was dotted with groups of men and when Kgosana approached the police station from the Grand Parade they gathered in a crowd in front of it. Kgosana's different accounts have it that the crowd had come merely to demand the release of those already mentioned (which contradicts what he told reporters at the time) and he does not mention phoning Duncan.[104] But Hjul, like Duncan, remembers that Kgosana *asked* Duncan to join him outside the police station.

Duncan arrived to find a 'good-humoured and relaxed crowd'; he noticed many dockers and saw approvingly that 'Task Force' runners were preventing the demonstrators from blocking the pavements or disturbing the traffic.[105] Ndlovu and Kgosana had already been arrested and taken inside the police station. Duncan then persuaded the police chief, Colonel I. B. S. Terblanche, who was facing the crowd, to negotiate with those PAC leaders still at liberty. This he agreed to do and at 11.40 am five PAC men, Terblanche and Duncan went into the building, where Makwetu told Terblanche that the people outside were ready to surrender themselves for being without passes. Terblanche replied that he had no intention of arresting anybody who was breaking pass laws at that moment and then went on to promise that for the next month no one would have to show his pass in the Cape Town area. The PAC leaders then demanded the release of Kgosana and Ndlovu and with Duncan's help they managed to persuade Terblanche to release them without bail. Kgosana and Ndlovu were released and at 12.10 pm went out in front of the crowd and were told by Makwetu that they should return home. The crowd shouted down the speaker but marched off chanting, singing, and carrying Kgosana shoulder high.[106]

Thtmevening Terblanche's local *ad hoc* suspension of the pass laws was dramatically extended to cover the whole country by General Rademeyer of the police and J. M. Erasmus, Minister of Justice. It was the first time that a Nationalist government had conceded to an African political initiative and the action reflected the uncertainty of the government's handling of the crisis.

Kgosana said later that he was furious Duncan had taken it upon himself to negotiate for the PAC.[107] There is no contemporary evidence for this and subsequent events suggest no break in their friendship at this point. After all, the PAC had won a considerable victory; they had succeeded in compelling the police to negotiate and offer concessions and Duncan's part in persuading both sides to talk to each other was crucial in this. Duncan helped to create the relationship which was emerging between the PAC leaders and the police, but it was also the result of Kgosana's own concern that tension should be avoided when dealing with the authorities. In the short term this relationship was to strengthen the PAC's hold on the townships. Hjul claims that Duncan's object was to enhance the importance of the PAC – to establish a *de facto* recognition of the PAC's control of the locations and to restrain the police from interfering in them. Judging by the increasing success of the strike in the days that followed it is probable that police harassment did lessen. An indication of the degree of PAC control is given in Collingwood August's diary:

> I put in a brief appearance at the *Contact* office, I must leave soon. The permission given to me by the task force, the youths of the PAC who have complete control of the townships, is due to expire.

In Langa this was probably consolidated by the closeness of the PAC to the Langa Vigilance Committee; the two organisations together arranged the funeral of police victims and money was collected by PAC men on behalf of both groups.[108] Duncan's diary says that by 26 March 'PAC committees were completely in charge of Nyanga and partly in charge in Langa'.

PAC influence was further strengthened over the weekend when they assumed control of the distribution of food supplies. Duncan, with the aim of prolonging the strike and with it PAC ascendancy in the townships, had energetically canvassed businessmen for funds as well as persuading wholesalers to replenish trading stores. Relief supplies were taken in by lorries driven by Black Sash women escorted by Kgosana and his task force. Duncan's support, though, was not altogether uncritical:

> The Nyanga East Committee came into the offices of *Contact*. . . . They asked us to introduce them to the police. . . . Before the committee went off to see Terblanche I told them I had sensed, on the Wednesday, that the police were very worried about the road blocks that had been built in

Nyanga. I said it was difficult to see the point of them, that the police could only regard them as a provocation and as a challenge to their authority and that it might be wise to pull them down. They claimed that they had been put up by the tsotsis but that they would do what they could.[109]

Contemporary sources suggest that by the beginning of the second week the strike involved 95 per cent of the African labour force.[110] The strike was given extra impetus by Lutuli's call for a one-day stay-at-home to mourn the dead of Langa and Sharpeville. The Johannesburg *Star* reported that coloured people were blacklegging in Cape Town but at Worcester, where the coloured and African workers were integrated into a single union, coloured workers joined the strike. On the day of the strike legislation was introduced to ban the PAC and ANC.

Nyanga PAC had been rendered leaderless earlier in the campaign by the arrest of its chairman, Mlohoti. The committee sent a message to Duncan asking him to discover from Terblanche what had happened to Mlohoti. We do not have Terblanche's reply; Duncan does not mention what happened when he raised this matter. We do know that Duncan used this opportunity to assure Terblanche that the Liberals were behind the police so long as they kept the peace 'by reasonable and humane methods'.[111]

Terblanche must have been suitably impressed because he helped Duncan and Kgosana persuade an electrical goods supplier to lend a public address system to the Langa PAC committee. Terblanche also agreed that no uniformed police would be at the funeral for which the electrical equipment was needed.[112] The 50 000 people who attended Monday's funeral in Langa included many ANC men who joined in the singing of '*Aphi no majoin?*' (Where is the soldier?).[113] The *Cape Times* recorded that apart from sporadic stoning of cars on Vanguard Drive, the major highway out of Cape Town, the occasion was peaceful. People arrived from all parts ot the western Cape to be greeted with shouts of 'Afrika' and the clenched fist PAC salute. A small group of whites were seen to give the salute too. PAC speakers told the crowd that the strike should continue, repeated their earlier warnings against violence and declared that in spite of recent events the Africans had no hatred for any other racial group.[114]

Up until Monday, the three PAC committees in Nyanga East, Nyanga West and Langa were unable to co-ordinate their efforts. The *Contact* group succeeded in creating liaison between them.[115] Food deliveries to the townships organised by Duncan and other Liberals provided some relief for the strikers, although it is difficult to estimate their impact. *Contact* claimed that the Liberals raised £1 500 worth of food.[116] The South African Coloured People's Organisation sent food donated by Indians into Langa,[117] and the COD provided a lorryload. As political gestures they were important: it must have enhanced the PAC's influence to be food distributors, but the food could not have gone very far in meeting the needs of 60 000 workers and their dependents.

On Wednesday over 1 500 people were arrested all over the country and the government declared a state of emergency. Most of the detainees were members of the ANC or allied organisations though their numbers included a few Liberals as well. No Liberals were arrested in Cape Town;[118] apparently the Minister of Justice had requested Duncan's arrest, but Colonel Terblanche had advised against it. Without Liberals providing him with a link with the townships he could not guarantee law and order.[119] Hjul thinks that Terblanche had a special regard for Patrick Duncan because Duncan's father, the Governor General, had been responsible for his early promotion. This may have been true but it was not enough to prevent Terblanche's men from repeating their attempts to break the strike. Police had broken into houses in Langa on 28 March and they had shot at those attempting to escape.[120] Early on Wednesday the police raided Langa with immense brutality.

It was this last action which provided the immediate provocation for the march of the 30 000. It came after ten days of political crisis, after a strike which had brought Cape industry to a standstill, after mass demonstrations had wrung concessions from authority, and after black people in Cape Town had had a chance to feel their power in a way that had never happened before. The march is thought to have been spontaneous. That is, it seems there was no elaborate organisation for it, it had not been planned in advance and it could not really be said to have been led. The impression one gets is that the march was as much the result of the growing groundswell of political confidence among Cape Town Africans, as a reaction to the police cruelty that morning. The Langa committee did claim at the time that such a march had been planned – but for Thursday rather than Wednesday.[121] Perhaps this explains the 'stewards' marshalling 'the crowd with wonderful control', observed by the *New Age* correspondent.[122] Another indication of preparatory work was that the marchers were not only from Langa; a contingent from Nyanga also began the long journey into Cape Town – though somewhat later in the day.[123] According to eye witnesses the mood of the crowd was peaceful, 'almost joyful',[124] and they marched in total silence.[125]

Whatever plans had been made beforehand, the PAC leaders were taken aback when it began. Kgosana admits that when he first heard the men were marching he was in bed and he had to be given a lift by an American reporter to get to the head of the procession. He caught up with the marchers as they came to the Athlone Pinelands railway line, asked them why they were marching and was told it was to protest to the police in Caledon Square about the attacks of the morning. Kgosana then suggested that the objective should not be Caledon Square but the Houses of Parliament where they could find the Minister of Justice.[126] This was agreed upon but in the event the march upon Parliament was called off. Afterwards there were those who argued that had the marchers stuck to their decision the day would have ended differently. But had Parliament been besieged would the government's resolve to continue have been broken? This is very doubtful, and in any event the mood of the crowd was hardly likely to provoke a confrontation. Kgosana, after all, continues to insist on the limited objective of the march and the campaign in general:

> I think we did our best to demonstrate our opposition to white domination and oppression. We were shot at, we never fired back we never killed a soul.[127]

The march ended, therefore, at Caledon Square. Thousands of people joined the procession at Mowbray railway station and the procession then took the De Waal Drive route into the city. The choice of route is significant: Kgosana was anxious not to disrupt traffic.[128] Again this makes nonsense of the claim that the situation had a revolutionary potential. One witness remembers that the line of marchers good-humouredly made way for cars containing whites. At an early stage of the march a Liberal Party member had tried to persuade Kgosana not to take the procession to Parliament – the police reaction, she insisted, would be too ruthless.[129] Kgosana refused to reassure her, saying the matter was out of his hands. But when he was confronted by Detective Head Constable Sauerman at the Rowland/Buitenkant streets intersection he agreed after some discussion to alter the destination of the marchers.[130]

The next decision was the most controversial. Kgosana had another meeting with Terblanche when he reached the police station and again he agreed to send the marchers home – this time in return for a promise of an appointment with the Minister of Justice, at Caledon Square at 5.00 pm that day. Janet Robertson states that Liberals persuaded Kgosana to disperse his men and praises them for doing so.[131] Writers less sympathetic to Liberals see this as a betrayal, suggesting that they persuaded Kgosana to negotiate and turn back the men, and were thus instrumental in the surrendering of Kgosana's power.[132] But the overwhelming weight of evidence suggests that no Liberals, and especially not Patrick Duncan, were involved on this occasion. Kgosana cannot remember Duncan or any other Liberal being present during the negotiations.[133] Duncan's diary does not mention any involvement – and as he publicly praised Kgosana's actions that day, it is unlikely that he would have failed to record any part he had played in directly influencing them.[134] Collingwood August remembers Liberals meeting in 'secret conclave' in their office building but he does not mention any contact between them and Kgosana.[135] Hjul insists that Duncan was not at Caledon Square. There was a similarity in the pattern of events on 25 March and 30 March, and indeed on the latter occasion, when the decision to turn back became known amongst those at the back of the crowd the rumour began to circulate that Kgosana had been swayed by Duncan and Terblanche.[136]

Liberals advised PAC men that Kgosana should not keep his appointment.[137] But Kgosana turned up at Caledon Square and was arrested. He never did see J. M. Erasmus. Finally, after ten days of indecision, the government reacted. Cordons were thrown around Langa. Not enough police or military units were locally available and sailors and soldiers were flown in.[138] The cordon could only be extended to Nyanga three days later[139] but from the moment Langa was sealed off, black Cape Town had lost the struggle.

Despite these events both Hjul and Duncan believed that their faith in Terblanche had been justified and that Terblanche had been overruled by the Union police chief, General Rademeyer and the government.[140] But Terblanche said later that he was so afraid that the blacks would try and release their leaders that he himself asked the army to put cordons around Langa.[141] It could be argued that although the *Contact* group wanted the PAC strong, and that some of their actions helped towards strengthening it (the food deliveries, Duncan's part in persuading Terblanche to suspend pass laws), their advice lost the strong negotiating position which the Cape Town PAC had temporarily won. Whatever the marchers might have achieved by staying in Cape Town that day, one thing is certain: they lost everything by going home. Liberals had, by contributing to the creation of an 'understanding' between the PAC leaders and the police chief, strengthened the impression that the police were to be trusted, and that Terblanche would act in good faith. All along they had sought to eliminate tension, to remove any possibility of violence. Duncan was even prepared to defend the forces of law and order:

> Today a State of Emergency was declared. In my view the Government was compelled to do this, and I defended their moderation (up to date) in dealing with the Cape Town situation.[142]

Moreover the *Contact* group had contributed to Kgosana's isolation from his followers. They had seen him as the key man, as the young messiah. Kgosana did have a hold on his followers, but, when he should have been with them, sharing their feelings, assessing their strength, working out a strategy of resistance, sensing the extent of their will to resist, he was elsewhere being interviewed and advised by well-intentioned whites. One has a feeling that throughout the crisis there was a four-cornered relationship: the police chiefs, the *Contact* Liberals, the Kgosana group and finally the people of Langa and Nyanga. It was these last who had least say in the decisions.

Resistance continued for over a week. By 2 April both townships were cordoned off by navy, army and police units. Before Nyanga was totally surrounded 1 000 men were prevented from marching on Cape Town.[143] As tension showed no signs of ebbing the government mobilised the reserves.[144] On Tuesday 4 April the police moved, determined to break the strike. Liberals had been forbidden to bring in any more food the day before. Men were beaten without restraint on the streets of Langa. On 7 April the suspension of pass laws was revoked and the situation in Langa was 'normal' enough for the cordon to be lifted. However, the men surrounding Nyanga needed reinforcing. By now PAC leaders who were unarrested and many of the Liberals who had been involved were lying low.[145] It took the police four days of continuous brutality to break the strike. They used sticks, batons, crow bars, guns and Saracen armoured cars to comb the townships and force the men back to work. On Wednesday 6 April PAC men in Nyanga told foreign journalists that the strike would go on until Sobukwe gave the word. The next day the police took the location by storm, arresting 1 500 people and detaining 250.[146] By the following Monday the strike was virtually over. For nearly three weeks the people of the Cape Town locations had presented the biggest challenge that had faced the South African government since the Defiance Campaign in 1952.

As resistance gathered impetus in Cape Town and reached its apogee on 30 March, elsewhere in the country an upsurge of protest began to assume national dimensions. On Thursday 24 March Chief Lutuli, responding to a suggestion by a *Drum* journalist,[147] called for Monday 28 March to be observed as a Day of Mourning with a worker stay-at-home. At the same time the ANC executive, anticipating the suppression of the Congresses, decided to send an ANC representative abroad. Oliver Tambo was chosen and was driven from Cape Town to Bechuanaland by Ronald Segal, the editor of *Africa South*. Tambo was on a brief visit to Cape Town at the time to help coordinate local ANC responses to the PAC campaign. On Sunday Chief Lutuli, then in Pretoria giving evidence in the Treason Trial and staying with the branch chairman of the Liberal Party, burnt his pass.

The next day response to the ANC strike call was almost total amongst Africans in many large towns. The stay-away was 90 per cent effective in Johannesburg and similarly successful in Port Elizabeth and Durban. In Port Elizabeth the local PAC men circulated a leaflet telling people to ignore the ANC protest; this conflicted with a message, apparently smuggled out of prison from Sobukwe and publicised by the acting leader of the PAC in Johannesburg, William Jolobe, which advocated a week long strike.[148] On the Rand participation in the protest was facilitated by employers who allowed their workers to do double shifts on Saturday to make up for the wages they would lose on Monday.[149]

Despite the ANC's insistence on the peaceful conduct of the stay-away, in the late afternoon of the 28th violence broke out in many parts of Soweto as tsotsi gangs attacked homecoming workers who had ignored the strike call. Large groups of teenagers gathered outside the railway stations and manned road blocks to stone alighting passengers. Municipal buildings were set alight and the Rediffusion radio system's wiring ripped out. As the tsotsis' attacks continued into the night the railway service was suspended, the remaining commuters spending an uncomfortable night on the platforms of Johannesburg railway station.[150] Meanwhile, small groups of ANC supporters stood in streets and backyards and lit small fires in which they burnt their passes. Similar demonstrations were organised by the ANC during the next few days in other centres.

The final eruption took place in Durban. On 31 March and 1 April huge processions attempted to march from Cato Manor by various routes through Durban's suburbs to the centre of the city. On both occasions the marchers were intercepted by police and driven back to the accompaniment of shooting by white civilian onlookers. One group of 1 000 people succeeded in getting through the police cordon and marched through Durban's shopping area to end up outside the central gaol demanding the release of ANC men detained on 30 March. Unrest continued in Durban over the next week or so as ANC activists tried to mount a ten-day stay-at-home which was fiercely contested by the authorities. Interestingly, the main support for the strike came from the migrant hostel dwellers rather than the inhabitants of the municipal townships.[151]

The Sharpeville crisis has been viewed as a historical moment when, to quote R. W. Johnson, extraordinary chances were missed:

> All over rural South Africa small and even medium-sized towns were suddenly denuded of their police, who were rushed to the urban centres. In almost no case did local Africans attempt to exploit the vacuum thus

created in the countryside.[152]

Leaving aside for the moment the question of neglected opportunities, could the occasion when the authorities were confronted with the greatest potential threat, a defiant African crowd capable of occupying the central institutions of the state, have been exploited by African politicians to better effect? There were obvious flaws in the leadership provided by the PAC. Its strategic vagueness hardly prepared its followers for the inevitable confrontations with the police provoked by the campaign. Insistence on tactical non-violence ducked the issue of how to respond to the use or threat of violence by the authorities. There was also the organisational inexperience of many key men within the movement: in the case of Philip Kgosana this contributed to his dependence on the Liberals and in consequence the degree of influence Patrick Duncan had on his behaviour on both occasions at Caledon Square. The lack of involvement in activist politics during the 1950s of the Soweto leaders may have helped to reduce the potential impact the campaign had in Johannesburg. The failure to picket public transport terminals effectively in the Johannesburg townships on 21 March was especially neglectful. The impromptu action of teenage gangs one week later is an indication of one constituency which the PAC omitted to identify and harness.

Possibly, had Kgosana refused to disperse his followers at Caledon square, more significant and long lasting concessions could have been negotiated. With better organisation the PAC might have succeeded in mobilising a larger following on the Rand. But it is unlikely that more would have been achieved. Unarmed demonstrations, however large, were a poor match for aggressive and well-armed police. The main thrust of the PAC campaign developed within the townships: here revolt was easiest to control and suppress. Many urban Africans still thought in terms of protest rather than resistance – the double shifts worked on Saturday 26 March were a telling instance of this – so revolt was in any case, outside Cape Town and Cato Manor at least, unlikely. Johnson's suggestion that while the state was concentrating its resources on securing control over the main urban centres, African nationalists should have unleashed rebellion in the smaller towns and the countryside overestimates the real extent to which the power of the administration was challenged. As one contemporary analysis pointed out during the Sharpeville crisis, 18 000 people were arrested in the countryside for normal legal infringements.[153] It also ignores the way the nationalist movement had developed during the 1950s: this derived much of its strength from concentrations of industrial workers and both ideologically and structurally was scarcely a revolutionary force.

The significance of the Sharpeville crisis was not that it was an occasion when revolutionary political and social conditions were present and consequently squandered. Instead it represented a turning point in the history of African nationalism, when protest finally hardened into resistance, and when African politicians were forced to begin thinking in terms of a revolutionary strategy. But this shift in their perception of their role was derived not so much from an accurate reappraisal of the strength and indivisibility of white South Africa as it successfully contained the challenge presented by African political movements, but rather from an illusion of its vulnerability. They were not alone in believing in the possibility of imminent political change. In the wake of the Sharpeville shootings there was a massive withdrawal of investors' confidence, giving rise to a short-term business slump; and a cabinet minister called for reforms in government policies affecting Africans.[154] The sense of crisis generated by the Sharpeville shootings and their aftermath appeared to be a vindication of a programme of armed insurgency.

Notes

1 South African Institute of Race Relations, Johannesburg, SAIRR papers, AD 1189, ANC unsorted box, Anti-Pass Planning Council Plan.
2 SAIRR papers, AD 1189, Box 11, File 3, Presidential address in the annual report of the National Executive Council of the ANC, 1959.
3 *Ibid.*
4 Michael Harmel, 'Revolutions are not abnormal', *Africa South*, January–March 1959.
5 Albert Lutuli, 'What June 26th means to African people', *New Age*, 27 June 1957.
6 Gail Gerhart, *Black Power in South Africa*, University of California, Berkeley, 1978, p. 220; CAMP microfilm collection, *Regina vs. Sobukwe and 22 others*, 1960, trial transcript, p. 510.
7 *Regina vs. Sobukwe and 22 others*, police evidence.
8 *Ibid.*
9 Jordan Ngubane, *I Shall not be Silenced*, unpublished autobiographical manuscript.
10 *The World* (Johannesburg), 9 January 1960.
11 Gerhart, *Black Power in South Africa*, p. 234.
12 *Rand Daily Mail* (Johannesburg), 25 July 1960 and 19 February 1960.
13 *Regina vs Sobukwe and 22 others*, trial transcript, p. 44.
14 Hannah Stanton, *Go Well, Stay Well*, Hodder and Stoughton, London, 1961, p. 178.
15 *Cape Times* (Cape Town), 16 May 1960.
16 F. H. C. Dixon, *The Story of Sharpeville*, Vereeniging Town Engineer's Department, n.d., mimeo.
17 See R. L. Leigh, *Vereeniging: South Africa, 1892–1967*, Courier-Gazette Publishers, Johannesburg, 1968; Vanderbijlpark Publicity Association, *Vanderbijlpark, 21 Years of Progress*, Felstar Publications, Johannesburg, 1964.
18 Dixon, *Story of Sharpeville*.
19 *Ibid.*
20 Vereeniging Town Council, Town Engineer's Department, *Memorandum on Housing and other facilities for Non-Europeans at Vereeniging*, 1951, mimeo.
21 Republic of South Africa, *Population Census, 6 September 1960*, Volume 2, number 11, Report on the Vereeniging–Vanderbijlpark Area, Bureau of Statistics, 1964.
22 Town Clerk's Office, Vereeniging, Non-European Affairs, 130/5/4, Volume 4, Sharpeville Advisory Board minutes, 28 October 1953, 24 November 1955, 26 May 1958.
23 Town Clerk's Office, Vereeniging, Old Location Advisory Board minutes, 24 April 1950.
24 *The Torch* (Cape Town), 8 July 1952 and 9 September 1952. The only events of the Defiance Campaign which touched Vereeniging were four attempts by Rand-based volunteer batches to enter Sharpeville location without a permit. There were no reports of any local participants.

25 Sharpeville Advisory Board minutes, 18 May 1953.
26 *Vereeniging and Vanderbijlpark News*, 10 October 1958.
27 Text of an interview with Joe Matthews, 1963, Carter and Karis microfilm, Reel 9a, 2 XM 61.
28 Republic of South Africa, *Population Census*, 6 September 1960, ii, 11.
29 Vereeniging Town Council, Non-European Affairs Committee, minute book, November 1959–July 1960, Report of the Town Clerk to special meeting, 22 September 1960.
30 Union of South Africa, *Summary of the Commission of Enquiry into the Events which occurred in the Districts of Vereeniging and Vanderbijlpark*, mimeo, 1960, p. 2.
31 *Vereeniging and Vanderbijlpark News*, 24 April 1959.
32 *Ibid*, 10 October 1958.
33 *Ibid*, 13 February 1959.
34 *The World*, 26 March 1960.
35 Statistics from the Town Clerk's reports to the Non-European Affairs Committee, minute book, November 1958–October 1959.
36 Minutes of the Non-European Affairs Committee, 12 January 1959.
37 *New Age*, 24 March 1960.
38 *New Age*, 24 March 1960, and *The Star* (Johannesburg), 8 March 1960.
39 Minutes of the Non-European Affairs Committee, 14 March 1960.
40 Town Clerk's reports to the Non-European Affairs Committee, minute book, November 1959–July 1960.
41 Transcript of the Commission of Enquiry into the events which occurred in the districts of Vereeniging and Vanderbijlpark, 21 March 1960 (copy held at the University of York Library), p. 429.
42 *Ibid*, pp. 425 and 2688.
43 *Ibid*, p. 430.
44 *Ibid*, p. 2469.
45 *Ibid*, pp. 2049–2503.
46 *Ibid*, p. 1933.
47 *Ibid*, p. 1916.
48 *Ibid*, p. 1255.
49 The Commission of Enquiry's findings were never properly published though a summary of its main conclusions was produced. The Commissioner accepted the veracity of police testimony on the hostile and aggressive behaviour of the crowd, despite the weight of evidence to the contrary submitted by other witnesses. Bishop Ambrose Reeves's *Shooting at Sharpeville*, Victor Gollancz, London, 1960, based on Commission evidence and cross examination, is an impressive refutation of police testimony.
50 *Vereeniging and Vanderbijlpark News*, 25 March 1960 and *Rand Daily Mail*, 29 March 1960.
51 Duncan's personality is discussed best in C. J. Driver, *Patrick Duncan: South African and Pan-African*, Heinemann, London, 1980.
52 Robert Sobukwe, 'The Africanist case', *Contact* (Cape Town), 30 May 1959, p. 3.
53 *The World*, 25 September 1959; *Die Burger* (Cape Town), 2 May 1959.
54 Author's interview with Peter Hjul, London, 1976.
55 Author's interview with Marion Friedman, London, 1976.
56 Sheila van der Horst, *African Workers in Cape Town*, Oxford University Press, Cape Town, 1964, p. 33.
57 *Ibid*, p. 10.
58 *House of Assembly Debates*, 30 March 1962.
59 Monica Wilson and Archie Mafeje, *Langa: a study in social groups*, Oxford University Press, Cape Town, 1963, p. 16.
60 *Ibid*, p. 25.

61 L. B. Lee Warden, 'The crime of Langa', *Africa South*, April–June 1957, p. 51.
62 Wilson and Mafeje, *Langa*, p. 18.
63 *Contact*, 20 September 1962, p. 12.
64 Phyllis Ntantala, 'African tragedy', *Africa South*, April–June 1957, p. 61.
65 *Cape Times*, 29 August 1959 and 12 September 1959.
66 *Contact*, 20 September 1962, p. 12.
67 Wilson and Mafeje, *Langa*, p. 3.
68 Mary Benson, *Struggle for a Birthright*, Penguin, Harmondsworth, 1966, p. 206.
69 Institute of Commonwealth Studies, University of London, Albie Sachs papers, File 31, p. A108, Regina *vs.* Synod Madlebe and 31 others, Case no. 313/1960.
70 *Ibid*, p. A25.
71 Philip Kgosana's letter to the author, November 1975.
72 Philip Kgosana, 'The story of my exciting life', *Drum* (Johannesburg), February 1961.
73 *The World*, 19 January 1957.
74 Author's interview with Randolph Vigne, London, 1975. It was Vigne and Joe Nkatlo who were chiefly responsible for creating good relations with the PAC in Cape Town well before the campaign. Joe Nkatlo's letter to the author, 20 July 1976.
75 *Cape Argus* (Cape Town), 11 May 1960.
76 Philip Kgosana, '30 000 obeyed me as one man', *Drum*, March 1961.
77 *Ibid*.
78 *Ibid*.
79 Union of South Africa, Report of the Commission of Enquiry into events at Langa Location, 21 March 1960, typescript, 14 July 1960 (henceforth Langa Commission Report).
80 *Cape Times*, 12 May 1960.
81 Muriel Horrell, *Days of Crisis in South Africa*, SAIRR, Johannesburg, 1960, p. 17.
82 Patrick Duncan papers, DU 8 71 6, Collingwood August's diary, entry for 19 March 1960.
83 Kgosana, '30 000 obeyed me as one man', *Drum*, March 1961.
84 Langa Commission Report; *Cape Times*, 5 May 1960 and 13 May 1960; *Contact*, 2 April 1960 and 16 April 1960.
85 Collingwood August's diary, entry for 21 March 1960.
86 *Cape Times*, 22 March 1960.
87 Kgosana, '30 000 obeyed me as one man'.
88 *Ibid*.
89 Patrick Duncan papers, DU 8 71 5, Patrick Duncan's diary.
90 Lewis Nkosi, *Home and Exile*, Longmans, London, 1965, p. 23.
91 Langa Commission report, p. 112.
92 *Cape Argus*, 20 May 1960.
93 Kgosana, '30 000 obeyed me as one man'.
94 Patrick Duncan's diary.
95 Collingwood August's diary, entry for 22 March 1960.
96 Author's interview with Randolph Vigne.
97 *Natal Mercury* (Durban), 12 May 1960.
98 Patrick Duncan's diary, entry for 24 March 1960.
99 *Contact*, 16 April 1960.
100 Patrick Duncan's diary, entry for 23 March 1960.
101 Author's interview with Brian Bunting, London 1975.
102 *Regina vs. Synod Madlebe and 31 others*, p. A 550.
103 Patrick Duncan's diary, 25 March 1960.
104 Kgosana in *Drum*, March 1961; Associated Negro Press (Chicago) bulletin, 19 July 1963; Philip Kgosana's letter to the author, November 1975.

105 *Contact*, 16 April 1960, p. 3.
106 *Ibid*, p. 8; *Regina vs. Synod Madlebe and 31 others*, pp A 480–481.
107 Associated Negro Press bulletin, 19 July 1963; Kgosana's letter to the author.
108 *Cape Times*, 12 May 1960.
109 Patrick Duncan's diary, entry for 26 March 1960.
110 *The Star*, 28 March 1963.
111 Patrick Duncan's diary, entry for 28 March 1960.
112 Collingwood August's and Patrick Duncan's diaries, entries for 28 March 1960.
113 Kgosana in *Drum*, March 1961.
114 *Cape Times*, 29 March 1960.
115 Patrick Duncan's diary, entry for 28 March 1960.
116 *Contact*, 16 April 1960, p. 8.
117 *Cape Times*, 29 March 1960.
118 Collingwood August' and Patrick Duncan's diaries, entries for 30 March 1960.
119 Patrick Duncan's diary, entry for 30 March 1960. Entry records a conversation with a journalist.
120 *Cape Argus*, 20 May 1960.
121 Patrick Duncan's diary, entry for 30 March 1960.
122 *New Age*, 8 September 1960.
123 Patrick Duncan's diary, entry for 30 March 1960.
124 *Contact*, 16 April 1960, p. 6; author's interviews with eyewitnesses, Cape Town and London, 1975–6.
125 Author's interview with participant, Cape Town, 1976.
126 Kgosana in *Drum*, March 1961.
127 Kgosana's letter to the author, 1975.
128 Kgosana in *Drum*, March 1961.
129 Author's interview with former member of the Liberal Party, Cape Town, 1976.
130 Kgosana in *Drum*, March 1961.
131 Janet Robertson, *Liberalism in South Africa*, Oxford University Press, Oxford, 1971, p. 216.
132 R. W. Johnson, *How Long Will South Africa Survive?*, Macmillan, Johannesburg, 1977, p. 19; Martin Legassick, 'Liberalism and social control in South Africa', unpublished seminar paper; Non-European Unity Movement, *The Pan-Africanist Congress Venture in Retrospect*, Cape Town, 1960; National Union of South African Students, *Dissension in the Ranks: white opposition in South Africa*, Cape Town, 1981, p. 11.
133 Philip Kgosana's letter to the author, November, 1975.
134 Patrick Duncan, 'Fortune favours the brave', *Contact*, 2 April 1960, p. 6.
135 Collingwood August's diary, entry for 30 March 1960.
136 Author's interview with participant, Cape Town, 1976.
137 Author's interview with Peter Hjul, London, 1976.
138 Anon, 'The nineteen days', *Africa South*, July 1960, p. 16.
139 Collingwood August's diary, entry for 2 April 1960.
140 Author's interview with Peter Hjul, London, 1976.
141 I. P. S. Terblanche, 'Die wonderwerk van 30 Maart 1960', *Die Huisgenoot*, 14 April 1961.
142 Patrick Duncan's diary, 30 March 1960.
143 Horrell, *Days of Crisis in South Africa*, p. 16.
144 Union of South Africa, Government Gazette, 2 April 1960.
145 Collingwood August's diary, 7 April 1960.
146 Anon, 'The nineteen days', *Africa South*, July 1960, p. 18.
147 Tom Hopkinson, *In the Fiery Continent*, Victor Gollancz, London, 1962, pp. 263–4.

148 Norman Phillips, *The Tragedy of Apartheid*, David McKay, New York, 1960, p. 63.
149 *Rand Daily Mail*, 28 March 1960.
150 Phillips, *The Tragedy of Apartheid*, pp. 31–7; *Rand Daily Mail*, 29 March 1960.
151 Horrell, *Days of Crisis in South Africa*.
152 R. W. Johnson, *How long will South Africa survive?*, p. 19.
153 Socialist League of Africa, 'South Africa: ten years of the stay-at-home', *International Socialism*, 5 (Summer 1961), p. 12.
154 Bernard Sachs, *The Road to Sharpeville*, Dial Press, Johannesburg, 1962, p. 49.

CHAPTER 10

Guerrillas and insurrectionists, 1961–1965

After the Sharpeville crisis and a confused period during which African politicians adjusted to new conditions of illegality the two nationalist organisations both produced insurgent offshoots. These were both dedicated to a revolutionary transformation of society and were both prepared to employ violent measures to attain this, but there the similarity between them ended. The ANC's military wing, Umkonto we Sizwe, and the PAC-orientated Poqo movement reflected in their divergent strategies the fundamental ideological and strategic differences which existed between their parent organisations before their banning. Umkonto we Sizwe was to advocate the implementation of a carefully controlled campaign of violence which in its initial stages would attempt to avoid bloodshed. Poqo's insurrectionary programme developed from the same vision of a spontaneous popular uprising which had informed the PAC's conception of their pass campaign. This chapter will outline the history of these two movements and the issues which their activities have given rise to.

Reorganisation of the ANC began seriously with the lifting of the state of emergency in August 1960 and the release of political leaders detained on 30 March. Before then ANC activity was limited to a hard core of activists who on two occasions, in April and in June, distributed leaflets in Johannesburg and Durban calling for stay-away strikes. In February 1961 an ANC newsheet announced that considerable progress had been made in reactivating branches in the Transvaal and the eastern Cape, though many branches had still not even started to restructure their membership along the lines of the M plan.[1] Even in Port Elizabeth, where before 1960 a measure of success had been claimed in implementing the plan, local leaders who had formed a caretaker committee opposed the reduction of surviving branches to cells and zones until they were visited by Nelson Mandela in April 1961.[2] Instead of building a cellular structure, branch committees continued to function under the guise of ostensibly apolitical cultural and social organisations.[3]

While rank and file members slowly adapted to new conditions the ANC's leadership played a dominant role in organising the final act of mass civil disobedience. In December 1961, prompted by a suggestion from the Inter-denominational African Ministers' Federation, a meeting of African political notables was held in Orlando. Both the PAC and the ANC were represented as well as leading African members of the Liberal and Progressive parties. At the insistence of PAC spokesmen whites and coloureds were excluded. The meeting passed several resolutions in favour of political unity, non-violent pressures against apartheid, non-racial democracy, and the calling of an 'All-in Conference representative of African people' to agitate for a national constitutional convention. A continuation committee under the chairmanship of Jordan Ngubane, a former Youth Leaguer and a member of the Liberal Party, was elected.

The work of this continuation committee was soon overshadowed by conflict between the Liberals and the PAC on the one hand and the ANC on the other. Ngubane claimed that the ANC, with financial assistance from the South African Communist Party (SACP) worked to control the committee and the All-in Conference. Without consulting other committee members ANC people drafted publicity for the conference to ensure its pro-Congress character. Though Ngubane's accusations were probably somewhat exaggerated it is likely that neither the PAC or the ANC had a particularly sincere concern for unity, at least not if this required making concessions to the other side. By mid-March the PAC men and Ngubane had resigned from the continuation committee and the All-in Conference held in Pietermaritzburg on 25 and 26 March was, despite the attendance of delegates from 140 organisations, a characteristically Congress affair. Among the 1 400 participants were whites, coloureds and Indians from the allied organisations. Traditional
NC rhetoric, songs and slogans predominated. The highlight of the event was the appearance of a recently unbanned Nelson Mandela who made his first public speech since 1952. In his address Mandela announced that the first phase of the campaign for a national convention would take the form of a three-day strike, the last day of which would coincide with South Africa's proclamation of a republic on 31 May. Preparations for the strike would include an ultimatum to the Government to call a convention. If this was ignored a campaign of 'mass non-cooperation' would follow. A 'National Action Council' would supervise these arrangements. Mandela was chosen as secretary of the Council but its other members were not identified so as to protect them from prosecution for incitement. Mandela himself disappeared after the Pietermaritzburg conference.

The scale of African response to the strike and the controversy surrounding it have already been dealt with in Chapter 8. Briefly, given the weakness of the political organisation, previous failures to persuade workers to stay at home, and the extent of the state's countermeasures, there was a surprisingly widespread degree of participation in the strike. Much of this could be attributed to support for the protest from SACTU and its affiliates. But despite its extensive impact the NAC's campaign was misconceived. Its tactics belonged to the previous decade when open campaigning was still possible; the preparations for it did nothing to further the transformation of Congress to a powerful clandestine movement. Though it demonstrated the potential for political mobilisation of SACTU's organisational network[4] it is difficult to see how this network could have been effectively employed in the second phase of the campaign. This, according to the National Action Council, would have consisted of attacks on rural Bantu Authorities, rent and tax boycotts, and withdrawal from participation in School Committees and

Advisory Boards.[5] The campaign for a national convention showed just how intellectually unprepared the leadership of the Congress alliance was in 1961 to embark on a revolutionary struggle.

With their failure to evoke anything from the state other than more repression and greater solidarity among the state's beneficiaries, ANC leaders began to consider violent tactics. Because the strike had not succeeded in obtaining political concessions many Congressmen assumed that the range of non-violent tactics had been exhausted. As there had only rarely been internal criticism of the way these tactics had been used and the purposes for which they had been deployed this was not altogether surprising. Methods such as strikes, civil disobedience and boycotts, which might have been applied to win short-term material gains, had increasingly been employed to underscore moral assertions. Resistance politics (which characterised some of the efforts of the early 1950s) had set into the politics of protest. As it was by 1961 demonstrably obvious that protest had little persuasive power it was assumed that the means which had been used to make these protests were equally futile. Those who like Chief Lutuli continued to publicly assert the validity of non-violent forms of political activity[6] did so on grounds of principle, not expediency. There was no internal debate on the adoption of violence within the upper echelons of the Congress alliance and therefore people who did have tactical as opposed to moral reservations were not consulted.[7]

Apart from the failure of the stay-at-home, another consideration influenced those advocating armed struggle. In some centres, especially in the Cape, it was evident that there was a powerful popular sentiment which favoured political violence.[8] Why this feeling should have been more widespread in Cape urban centres than those elsewhere will be discussed later in this chapter in the section dealing with Poqo. Such happenings as the murder of the Port Elizabeth District Police Commandant after he had interrupted ANC volunteers distributing leaflets thoroughly alarmed members of the Congress executive.[9] As Nelson Mandela put it later:

> Unless responsible leadership was given to canalize and control the feelings of our people, there would be outbreaks of terrorism which would produce an intensity of bitterness and hostility between the various races of this country . . . .[10]

Accordingly, in June 1961 a meeting of the ANC national executive considered a proposal from Mandela on the use of violent tactics, and assented to the extent that while Congress itself would not change its official non-violent standpoint those of its members who involved themselves in the campaign suggested by Mandela would not be restrained. The implication of this was that a separate organisation would have to be established. Mandela's testimony at his trial suggested that the founding of this organisation was the work of ANC men alone.[11] Umkonto we Sizwe (The Spear of the Nation), unlike the ANC opened its ranks to whites, Indians and coloured people, and through the agency of these, as well as some of its founding members, the South African Communist Party made an important contribution to its development.

During the emergency, the South African Communist Party issued its first public statement since its foundation in 1953 with a leaflet calling on communists to work within the Congress alliance for the first stage of a two-stage revolution.[12] The theoretical justification for doing this was formally elaborated in a document entitled 'The road to South African freedom' adopted as policy by the party's fifth underground conference in October 1962. The programme characterised the South African situation as being that of a 'special form of colonialism' in which:

> On one level, that of 'White South Africa', there are all the features of an advanced capitalist state in its final stage of imperialism. . . . But on another level, that of 'Non-White South Africa', there are all the features of a colony. The indigenous population is subjected to extreme national oppression, poverty and exploitation. . . . [13]

In such circumstances the national democratic programme of the traditional liberation movements had a progressive function which the workers' party should support.[14] With the banning of the main liberation movement and the subsequent disruption of the Congress alliance (COD was banned in September 1962), for the first time since the 1940s the Communist Party as a corporate body began to collaborate with the ANC. As with the ANC it remained institutionally separate from Umkonto, and had its own distinct sphere of activities.[14] And as with the ANC there was some disagreement within its leadership over the appropriateness of a violent strategy. For example, the Durban activist, Rowley Arenstein believed 'there was no obvious necessity' for violence.[15] Significantly, Durban communists, perhaps because of their relative degree of intimacy with the Mpondoland peasant revolt, tended to take a Maoist line in the Sino-Soviet dispute.[16] Other communists were also impressed by the events in Mpondoland without understanding the limitations of the movement and the situation which gave rise to it. Deducing from the localised rebellion in Mpondoland a generalised popular susceptibility for revolutionary violence, at its December 1960 conference, six months before the inception of Umkonto, the Communist Party resolved itself in favour of a campaign of economic sabotage to precede a guerrilla war.[17]

Umkonto we Sizwe geared its activity to a similar programme. Several considerations influenced the movement, in its first stages of development, to restrict itself to sabotage of economic installations and targets of symbolic political significance. First there was the hope expressed in an Umkonto leaflet distributed simultaneously with the first bomb attacks, that

> our first actions will awaken everyone to a realisation of the disastrous situation to which the nationalist policy is leading. We hope we will bring the Government and its supporters to their senses before it is too late, so that the Government and its policies can be changed before matters reach the desperate stage of civil war.[18]

The statement probably reflected real beliefs and fears. ANC leaders, still committed to the ideal of a common society, wished to avoid the racial polarisation which might develop with open warfare. SACP theorists were concerned that the revolution should have as much support as possible outside the African community and that in the eventuality of violent confrontation the divisions of conflict should not altogether coincide with those of colour. Sabotage did not irrevocably commit the movement to bloodshed. Great faith was still placed at this stage by African politicians on the power and pressure of international opinion in inducing change in South Africa; the weakness of the United Nations had yet to be demonstrated and the ANC's call for an international economic boycott of South African trade appeared to be taken seriously in certain quarters.[19] Economic sabotage would not risk jeopardising international support to the same degree that guerrilla warfare might. If suitable targets were destroyed capital would continue to flow out of the country and white confidence in the government would be shaken.[20] Despite such optimism, preparations for guerrilla activity began in 1961 with the despatch of men overseas, initially to China, for military training.[21] Nelson Mandela himself left the country in January 1961 to travel to various African and western European capitals to negotiate military and diplomatic support. In the course of his six-month journey he spent some time in an Algerian guerrilla training camp.

During the months which preceded the opening of the sabotage campaign the basic organisational framework was constructed. The leadership group, which included white SACP members with military experience (in one case derived from the Jewish Irgun movement in post-war Palestine), constituted itself as a 'national high command'. This was based in Johannesburg where, with the aid of funds derived from the SACP, a suburban property, Lilliesleaf Farm in Rivonia, northern Johannesburg, was bought as an operational headquarters. Then, independently of the regional and local ANC leadership, the national high command members began contacting carefully selected individuals to form regional commands. If the case of Natal was typical the regional commands were drawn mainly, not from prominent ANC office-holders but rather from full-time SACTU functionaries.[22] Such people had a degree of mobility and independence not enjoyed by most Africans and were generally more experienced in coping with organisational problems than in the case of many ANC men. The regions would establish lower echelons, the basic organisational unit ideally being a four-man cell. Whilst the high command would determine overall policy the regional commands were responsible for selecting the type of targets to be attacked in their areas and for approving specific targets chosen by the cells. In fact the organisational structure was never as tidy as this and local units often acted independently of the commands. This was especially so in the case of attacks which endangered human life. As well as laying down the organisational basis members of the regional commands were instructed in the use and manufacture of explosives and encouraged to stockpile bombs.

On 15 and 16 December (the Durban group acted prematurely ahead of the others) the first Umkonto bombings took place in Durban, Johannesburg and Port Elizabeth. The attempt to blow up the Bantu Administration Department's office in Durban failed, but the next day, the Day of the Covenant, a Fordsburg post office, the Resettlement Board headquarters in Meadowlands, and the Bantu Affairs Commissioner's offices in Johannesburg were damaged. Similar offices and an electrical transformer were attacked in Port Elizabeth. These were the first in a series of over 200 attacks which took place over the next eighteen months in all the major centres and many of the smaller towns. These will not be chronicled in detail here. Edward Feit's analysis of Umkonto[23] provides a convincing picture of the courage, enthusiasm and frequent amateurism with which the attacks were executed. Here there is room only for a few brief comments on the campaign. First, the bombings had a very uneven impact, varying between different centres and the nature of the target chosen. Of the actions listed in the indictment during the subsequent trial of the national high command leaders,[24] 72 were of a minor character (setting fire to letter boxes, severing electric cables, etc.), 95 were incendiary bomb attacks, mainly on public buildings, and a further seven were more ambitious still, involving dynamite and attempts to destroy railway signals systems, important electrical instllations and so forth. As might be expected, Port Elizabeth was the centre most affected by the campaign: here there were 58 attacks though of these 31 were fairly trivial (indicative perhaps of a greater degree of rank and file initiative). Cape Town followed with 35 attacks, and next in importance was Johannesburg (where most of the 31 targets were hit by incendiary bombs); and then Durban with 29 sabotage attempts, again mainly of the fire-bomb variety. Another 25 were distributed between East London (6), the Vereeniging district (5), Uitenhage (5), Pretoria (3), Paarl (3), Benoni (2), and one each in ten other places. The apparent non-involvement of many of the East Rand branches is surprising when one remembers the local strength both of the ANC and SACTU affiliates. Regional variations in the campaign do not altogether support Feit's contention[25] that SACTU's functions after 1961 were completely subordinated to its role as a recruitment funnel to Umkonto: if this had been the case one might expect rather more Umkonto activity in the East Rand industrial towns and rather less in Johannesburg.

The second point is that while the majority of these efforts adhered to the national high command's intention to avoid bloodshed, a substantial number did not. Twenty-three actions, eighteen involving the railways (including two petrol bombs thrown into railway carriages) and five beerhall bombs risked lives, and in addition there were 23 attacks on policemen, their informers or people regarded as collaborators.[26] Most of these took place in Port Elizabeth or Durban and indicated considerable indiscipline as well as enthusiasm for violence among Umkonto members in both places. Bruno Mtolo, a member of the Durban regional command who later turned state evidence, demonstrates in his autobiography that recruitment presented no difficulties if it was for people who would immediately undertake sabotage.[27]

Though the extent and scale of Umkonto activity in its main centres was impressive, considering the small numbers involved and the resources they had at their disposal, the sabotage campaign nevertheless did not go very far towards fulfilling its aims. Its impact on the white population was limited by the scanty press coverage and the usually superficial damage that resulted from the bombings, as well as being overshadowed by the considerably more frightening activities of Poqo.

Influencing white political reactions, though, was not Umkonto's sole purpose. Its leaders also anticipated a protracted guerrilla war, when a much wider degree of popular participation in the struggle than provided for by the sabotage campaign would be necessary. In this context the strength of the underground ANC and the nature of its relationship with Umkonto were very important issues. In Natal, where in 1960 the ANC had been especially strong, there was apparently some tension between ANC leaders and Umkonto's regional command.[28] The former appeared to dislike the autonomy of the saboteurs and attempted in vain to control their work. Much of the difficulty derived from the absence of any consultation by the ANC's national executive of lower leadership echelons when Umkonto was established. To remedy the consequent confusion and uncertainty the ANC held a national conference in Lobatsi, Bechuanaland, in October 1962. Here the prospect of a guerrilla war was openly discussed as well as the existence of a 'specialised military wing'. It was also emphasised that the ANC should continue to devote itself to 'mass political action' for 'political agitation is the only way of creating the atmosphere in which military action can most effectively operate'. 1963 was another anti-pass year in which campaigning proved to be especially energetic in the western Cape, the area most severely affected by influx control.[29]

Despite these professed intentions there is little evidence to suggest that the underground work of the ANC occupied much of the attention or energy of the Congress/SACP leadership. Little was done to coordinate the activity of Umkonto cells and ANC branches so that the latter could play a significant support rôle. Instead the ANC confined itself mainly to traditional forms of protest; for example, a leaflet issued in 1963 called for the observation of 26 June with a boycott of Afrikaner-owned newspapers, the non-use of electricity, and the lighting of bonfires.[30] One instance in which the ANC and Umkonto did appear to articulate their activity was, ironically, one of the occasions when a terrorist tactic was employed in contravention of official policy. In Durban the ANC's efforts to revive the anti-pass campaign by beginning with a boycott of beer halls[31] resulted in Umkonto's bomb attacks on the halls.[32]

Recruiting men for military training in sympathetic African countries as well as in China and the Soviet Union was the other important sphere of Umkonto's work. Approximately 300 recruits were sent across South Africa's borders though some of them were captured and repatriated by the British colonial authorities in what was then Northern Rhodesia. This tended to dampen the enthusiasm for recruitment and it was alleged that people were sometimes misled as to what exactly they were being sent abroad for.[33]

Whether or not the Umkonto campaign of 1961 to 1964 could have led to a popular insurgency was never put to the test as the authorities, taking advantage of the imperfections of Umkonto's security precautions, infiltrated the movement with spies. The police were also assisted by legislation which enabled them to detain people for long periods in isolated confinement without charging them. For the first time torture began to be used fairly frequently as a means of extracting information from political prisoners.[34] As the result of infiltration and betrayals most of the national high command were identified and captured. Nelson Mandela was arrested shortly after his return to South Africa on 5 August 1962 and many of his colleagues were taken a year later in a raid in Lilliesleaf Farm. Shortly before the Rivonia arrests a police agent had succeeded in joining the SACP and this was to lead to the destruction of its internal organisation by the end of 1965.[35]

Amongst the evidence gathered by the police at Rivonia were two hundred copies of a document entitled 'Operation Mayebuye'. The contents of the document provide a good insight into the strategic thinking of some Umkonto leaders, though it must be said that Operation Mayebuye had not, at the time of the raid, been adopted by the high command as policy.[36] The strategic proposals were prefaced by an analysis of the extent to which objective conditions favoured the promotion of guerrilla insurgency. It concluded that the strength and sophistication of the South African state was compensated for by the extent of of popular support Umkonto could expect to receive, and also the prospect of the diplomatic and economic isolation of the South African government. Umkonto would be aided by 'massive assistance' from African and socialist countries – 'in no other territory where guerrilla operations have been undertaken has the international situation been such a vital factor operating against the enemy'.[37] The guerrilla struggle would be launched by the infiltration of four well-trained groups of thirty men into four different areas: the hinterland of Port Elizabeth, and the Swazi, north-west Transvaal and north-west Cape border regions. Simultaneously with the preparations of these groups the internal group would recruit 7 000 auxiliaries and collect equipment and materials. While the insurgents began attacking carefully selected targets of vital strategic importance to the state, the internal organisations would step up the rate of sabotage and agitation and create as many opportunities as possible for ordinary people to participate in the struggle.

Discussion of Umkonto's sabotage campaign has converged on three issues: whether the switch to a violent strategy was the correct decision for African politicians; whether the appropriate form of violence was chosen; and the extent to which Umkonto was controlled by the South African Communist Party.

Critics of violence fall into two categories: those who argue that given the weakness of the movement and the power of the government a violent course was suicidal; and those who suggest that for sociological reasons violence was inappropriate. Both Johnson and Lambert suggest that a more sensible alternative might have been, in Johnson's words, 'to lie low and attempt to maintain some presence', perhaps through concentrating on industrial organisation.[38] The difficulty here was that such a policy would have probably split the underground movement and discredited the leadership in the eyes of the most energetic and competent activists. Mandela's assertion that one of Umkonto's functions was to *control* the level of violence should be taken seriously. Nevertheless it is difficult not to conclude that the planning and preparations undertaken for a guerrilla insurgency were, to say the least, premature.

It has also been suggested that political violence would have alienated rather than attracted popular support to the ANC and its allies. 'Africans', claims Fatima Meer, 'are singularly unaggressive'.[39] Edward Feit argues that in South Africa:

Stability . . . [is] attained not only by repression but also by the maintenance of order and by economic improvement, some of which, at least, spills over to the black people . . . to succeed the African insurgents would have to maintain an increasing rate of disorder, beyond a level which the government could control.

and

Most 'little' people are not much concerned with 'big' issues. . . . The people like the jungle are neutral. They will side with whoever can best protect them. Protection means order. Disorder makes life difficult. Order is, therefore, the crucial issue.[40]

This is not the place to discuss the validity of these statements in any detail. What this book has attempted to demonstrate in preceding chapters is that popular inclinations to revolt have to be understood in the context of often very localised and specific conditions. These make the formation of useful generalisations very difficult. The assumption, however, that the authorities were providing for most Africans stability, protection and a significant measure of economic improvement is questionable. As will be evident later in this chapter, it was precisely the denial of these things that underlay the formation of an insurrectionary movement of a considerably more massive and popular character than Umkonto we Sizwe. On the whole it seems more tenable to argue that political, as opposed to socio-economic, factors did not favour the insurgents. Umkonto cadres had not fully anticipated the coercive capacity of the state – as one former saboteur has put it: 'Having talked of fascism for a decade and more, the movements were nevertheless caught by surprise when the police behaved like fascists'.[41] The international pressure which played such an important part in their calculations proved to be a chimera.

Defending the choice of sabotage, one of Umkonto's major strategists, Joe Slovo, has argued that as a tactic it fulfilled three important functions. Its quality of restraint would place, in the eyes of the South African population and the outside world, the moral responsibility 'for the slide to civil war' on the regime, not the liberation movement. It provided a useful screening process 'for establishing which activists . . . could make the transition to the new tactics'. Finally, sabotage had a propaganda purpose 'to create an atmosphere in which other militants would be encouraged to join'. Slovo concedes that important mistakes were made, notably to do with inadequacies in security and organisational structure as well as the neglect of 'mass work'. Ben Turok, also of Umkonto, has been more bluntly critical: 'the sabotage campaign failed on the main count – it did not raise the level of action of the masses themselves'. The method did not create opportunities for people to join in and express their support.[42]

Slovo's justifications do appear somewhat weak. The first of the three functions he refers to was unnecessary and the second and third were at best imperfectly performed by Umkonto. Whereas it is rather doubtful that an insurgent movement under South African conditions could afford to be anything other than elitist, it is quite true that outside the membership of the SACP[43] no systematic provision was made for popular mobilisation in a support role.

The third controversy surrounds the question of direction and control. Edward Feit suggests that because of the domination of the national high command's membership by communists, and because of the lack of unanimity among ANC leaders over the question of violence, the SACP effectively controlled Umkonto. In his analysis, Umkonto, the ANC and all other Congress-affiliated organisations are reduced to the status of fronts. Policy consequently was subject to communist social analysis and rested upon the premises upon which it was based.

It is certainly true that with the formation of Umkonto, SACP theoreticians could influence policy decisions affecting the ANC more directly than before. But control of a movement would depend on a disciplined and cohesive organisation and this existed neither in Umkonto nor in the ANC. Moreover, Nelson Mandela, the most popular and influential figure associated with Umkonto, was perfectly conscious of the ultimate divergence in the aims of communists and social-democratic nationalists like himself.[44] The fact was, Umkonto's strategic preoccupations flowed as much from the liberal heritage of petit-bourgeois African nationalism as from the class-related concerns of South African Marxists. In the short-term both had plenty of common ground. In the absence of immediate conflict, accusations of control and domination are rather difficult to prove.

Umkonto was not the only sabotage group during this period. Shortly before Umkonto's campaign started a much smaller group began operations in Cape Town and Johannesburg. This was the National Committee of Liberation which in early 1964 restyled itself as the African Resistance Movement. NCL-ARM activity was distinguished by the technical expertise of its methods (it relied mainly on dynamite and electrical timing mechanisms) and the ambitious nature of its targets. In Cape Town these included a railway signalling system, a radio mast, a reservoir dam and powerline pylons. To avoid loss of life, sabotage required careful research, simultaneous explosions (the signal system was blown up in four separate places) and strict timing.[45]

The NCL-ARM group appeared in subsequent trials to be mainly white though in Johannesburg its members included a few Africans. It numbered about fifty people altogether, concentrated in Johannesburg (where the NCL was first formed) and Cape Town but with a handful in Port Elizabeth and Durban as well.[46] The origins of the group were complex. During the emergency a left opposition to the SACP had appeared. Leaflets critical of SACP/ANC strategy and advocating the formation of an independent working class party were distributed in the name of the Socialist League in Johannesburg and the Workers' Democratic Party in Cape Town. In the case of the Socialist League it was claimed that its members were 'nearly all inside the Congress Alliance'.[47] Of the main personalities who were later convicted for NCL-ARM activities at least one, Baruch Hirson, was a member of the League. The other main impetus for the formation of the NCL-ARM came from young members of the Liberal Party mainly, though not entirely, involved in radical student politics at the Universities of Cape Town and the Witwatersrand. The Cape Town group also included Randolph Vigne who had pro-PAC inclinations. The PAC influence in Cape Town may have been significant in affecting the reactions of the Cape group; by 1964 they had begun to argue the futility of an urban-based campaign of sabotage favouring instead the construction of linkages with the rural population.[48] This view was based on a considerably more realistic assessment of the likelihood of a successful revolution in the near future than that of Umkonto. But despite its relative sophistication the NCL-ARM was destroyed in much the same way as Umkonto, through security lapses and the inability of a few of its members to resist police questioning. With most of its activists captured, one of the few still at liberty, John Harris, violated the principles of his organisation by placing a bomb in the concourse of Johannesburg station. The bomb exploded hurting fifteen people, one of whom later died. John Harris was subsequently hanged, the only white saboteur ever to be executed in South Africa.

A parallel movement to Umkonto was inspired by the PAC, though in the case of the latter's adherents their activities were considerably more violent and involved rather greater numbers than was the case with the sabotage campaign. In mid-1964 the Minister of Justice confirmed that 202 Poqo members had been convicted of murder, 12 of attempted murder, 395 of sabotage, 126 of illegal departure from the country and 820 of other offences related to membership of an underground organisation.[49] Poqo was the first African political movement in South Africa to adopt a strategy that explicitly involved killing people and it was probably the largest active clandestine organisation of the 1960s.

The word 'poqo' is a Xhosa expression meaning 'alone' or 'pure'. The term was used first in the context of a separatist organisation when the Ethiopian Church of South Africa was established. Its members described themselves as *Ndingum Topiya Poqo* (belonging to the Church of Ethiopia). The word was used sometimes in the western Cape in 1960 by PAC spokesmen to desribe the character of their organisation in contrast to the multiracial dimension of the Congress alliance. Leaflets opposing the May 1961 stay-at-home in Port Elizabeth bore the legend: 'May demos a fraud, Poqo, Poqo, Poqo'.[50] The authorities and the press tended to employ the term to describe all PAC-connected conspiracies though only PAC supporters in the Cape identified themselves as Poqo members at first. Here, for the sake of simplicity, the state's usage of the term will be followed, though, as will become clear, the two main concentrations of PAC/Poqo affinity had quite distinct social characteristics. The remainder of this chapter will examine the movement, first by looking at the fashion in which it developed organisationally in the Cape and the Transvaal, and then at its various spheres of activity.

The western Cape, and in particular the Cape peninsula, had been one of the areas of strongest support for the PAC. This could be related to the particularly fierce effects of influx control in the Cape peninsula, the 'repatriation' of women and children to the Transkei, the refusal of the authorities to construct adequate housing, and sharply deteriorating living conditions. In addition to the reason for popular disaffection mentioned in the previous chapter, in the early 1960s the imposition of Bantu Authorities and land rehabilitation measures of the Transkei (see Chapter 11) also influenced the political responses of Africans in the Cape peninsula and its hinterland. The Pan-Africanist Congress's rhetorical militancy, the incorporation into its ideology of themes drawn from traditions of primary resistance, and the immediacy of its strategic objectives made it especially attractive to the increasingly large migrant worker population of Cape Town. The Pan-Africanists found an important section, if not the majority of their following in the 'bachelor zones' of Langa.[51] However, of the 31 PAC leaders who were subsequently put on trial in Cape Town after the 1960 pass campaign, only seven men were from the migrant workers' hostels in Langa and Nyanga. Unfortunately the trial documentation only contains full details of the backgrounds of a few of the leaders: they included a herbalist, a dry cleaning examiner, a domestic servant, a university student, a tailor and a farmworker and their ages ranged from 22 to 55 (the majority of the accused were over 30). At least seven were former members of the ANC and one had once blonged to the Communist Party.[52] The evidence suggests a not altogether surprising social pattern: a political movement with a large following amongst migrant workers, but with positions of responsibility held by men with at least some education, work skills and political experience.

Dring the 1960 pass campaign as well as before and after it, there was considerable contact between the local Pan-Africanist leaders and members of the multiracial Liberal Party. This was despite frequent attacks on white radicals who had been associated with the Congress movement.[53] Local Liberals were seeking a mass base and though wary of the racialist undrtones of Pan-Africanist ideology, they sympathised with and were attracted by the PAC's hostility to left-wing influences within the Congress movement. Cape Town PAC leaders, whatever their private feelings about the Liberals, were glad to accept offers of assistance that appeared to be without strings, and allowed certain Liberals to play an important intermediary role between them and the authorities during the 1960 troubles in Cape Town. Whereas this relationship had certain advantages at the time, it did have the effect of isolating the leaders from the rank and file membership, as well as the large informal following the campaign generated.[54]

In the months following the crisis of March–April 1960, this gulf between leaders and followers widened and took on a factional form. Some of the main leaders jumped bail and left the country towards the end of 1960. This considerably weakened the degree of influence of those who remained. Accounts by two Cape Town journalists tell of a struggle in the Cape Town locations between 'moderates and extremists'.[55] The 'extremists' identified the 'moderates' a those PAC men who had flirted with the Liberal Party. They were 'Katangese, the treacherous ones who are playing the same role as Moishe Tshombe in the Congo'.[56] These accounts are substantiated by some of the trial evidence. In a trial of a group of workers employed in an old age home, two of the accused in their statements to the police (possibly made after they had been tortured) mntioned a dispute within the PAC in Cape Town. One group was led by two Nyanga leaders, both former members of the regional executive of the legal PAC, Christopher Mlokoti and Abel Matross.[57] Mlokoti and Matross were the PAC men who made the initial contact with the Liberal Party in late 1959.[58] The other faction was allegedly led by Mlami Makwetu and Wellington Tshongayi.[59] Makwetu had been branch secretary at Langa New Flats in 1960 and was a docker.[60] Tshongayi also belonged to the PAC in 1960 and was secretary of the Crawford branch. He was imprisoned after the pass campaign.[61] What the evidence suggests is a struggle for dominance of the underground movement in early 1961 between upper and lower echelon leadership with the latter, by virtue of their stronger links with migrant hostel dwellers, gaining the upper hand.

Ttis split in the underground movement (which was accompanied by fighting between the different groups)[62] was followed by a period of extensive recruitment and organisation by the dominant faction. It seems that it was at this point that the 'cell system' was established.[63] Within Langa, and elsewhere in Cape Town, recruitment and organisation was often done by forming groups composed of men who had come from a particular rural region. Although this flowed naturally from a situation where migrant workers would often choose to live with friends or relatives from their homeplace, there was an element of self-consciousness in the way it was done. For example, in Langa there was a special 'Lady Frere' group drawn from men who lived in Zones 19, 20, 23 and 24 of the Langa single men's quarters.[64] This would have obvious advantages when Poqo began to extend its influence into the Transkei.[65] It also meant that Poqo cell members would not only live in close proximity with each other, but were also likely to be employed together.[66] Theoretically each cell was composed of ten men; in fact, they were often larger and in any case individual cells would combine for larger meetings, often involving over a hundred people. Similarly, large groups would sometimes accompany recruiters on their rounds.[67] Each cell would have a leader.

Langa seems to have been regarded by other Poqo groups as the local headquarters of the movement: certainly it was recruiting teams from Langa who played the most active role in spreading the influence of the movement. There were recorded instances of Langa activists establishing cells or branches in different parts of Cape Town. Men living in employers' compounds seem to have been a favourite target for recruiting operations: a Poqo group at the Cape Town Jewish Old Age Home also included workers from a nearby hotel. Another trial, which collapsed through lack of evidence, involved staff from the Brooklands Chest Hospital.[68] Poqo activists fanned out from Cape Town to the smaller urban centres and the farms surrounding them, either starting new cells or reactivating PAC branches. Considerable effort seems to have been devoted to building cells among farmworkers: according to state witness evidence in a trial involving a member of Tshongayi's cell, there was an unsuccessful meeting to recruit people on a farm near Somerset West in February 1961.[69] More successful in this context apparently was the establishment of a Poqo cell on a farm at Stellenbosch in October 1961 after a visit by three Poqo men from Cape Town.[70]

Poqo's message was stated in simple, direct terms. In December 1961 a leaflet in Xhosa was picked up in Nyanga. It read:

> We are starting again Africans . . . we die once. Africa will be free on January 1st. The white people shall suffer, the black people will rule. Freedom comes after bloodshed. Poqo has started. It needs a real man. The Youth has weapons so you need not be afraid. The PAC says this.[71]

Sometimes the message was more specific: farmworkers were told that Poqo intended to take the land away from whites and give it to Africans.[72] Men in Wellington were told that one day they must throw away their passes and take over the houses of the whites. All who did not join Poqo would be killed along 'with the white bosses'. Men in Paarl were told there was no need for whites; the factories and the industries would carry on as usual for was it not the black people who worked in them?[73] Chiefs should be killed for it was they who were responsible for the 'endorsement out' of Africans from the western Cape.[74] Sometimes Poqo members giving evidence would repeat some of the old PAC slogans – 'from Cape to Cairo, from Morocco to Madagascar',[75] – but often witnesses would claim that they knew nothing of the ANC or PAC.[76] This may have been prompted by caution on their part, but what is noticeable is that many of the distinctive attributes of PAC speeches given at a popular level had disappeared: there were no references to Pan-Africanism, communism or socialism and no careful clarifications of the movement's attitude with regard to the position of racial minorities. Ideological statements had been boiled down to a set of slogans: 'We must stand alone in our land';[77] 'Freedom – to stand alone and not be suppressed by whites';[78] 'amaAfrica Poqo'; 'Izwe Lethu' (our land). Poqo's lack of a 'political theory', the brutal simplicity of its catchphrases, the absence of any social programme save for the destruction of the present order and its replacement with its opposite in which white would be black, and black would be white, all this has helped to diminish its importance in the historiography of South African resistance movements. But because the slogans were simple does not mean that they were banal: they evoked a profound response from men who had been forced off the land, whose families were being subjected to all forms of official harassment as well as economic deprivation, who perceived every relationship with authority in terms of conflict: whether at the workplace, in the compound, or in the reserve. These were men who had no place to turn to. Hence the all-embracing nature of the movement's preoccupations, its social exclusiveness, and its urgency. The undertone of millenarianism, the concept of the sudden dawning of a more just era, the moral implications of the word 'poqo' (pure) – these are not surprising. For here was a group of men who were simultaneously conscious both of the destruction that was being wreaked upon their old social world, and the hopelessness of the terms being offered to them by the new order.

The strategy of a general uprising developed logically from this vision. The 21 farmworkers of Stellenbosch put on trial in June 1962 were found guilty on a number of charges which included making preparations to attack a farm manager and his family, to burn the farm buildings and then to march to the town, firing buildings on the way. For weapons the men sharpened old car springs into pangas.[79] The initiative for this strategy was probably a local one: most of the national PAC leadership was in prison in 1961 and early 1962 and had only fully regrouped in Maseru in August 1962.[80] But by late 1962, judging from the evidence of men involved in the Poqo attack at Paarl, Poqo members were conscious of a plan for a nationally co-ordinated insurrection, the directives for which would come from above.[81] In March 1963, Potlake Leballo, the PAC's acting president, told a journalist that he was in touch with leaders in the western Cape and other regional leaders.[82] Despite this co-ordination of the movement with the surviving political hierarchy of the Pan-Africanist Congress, there is a strong case for asserting that the insurrectionary impetus came initially from below and, as I have argued, can be directly related to the social situation of Poqo's local leaders and their followers.

PAC's clandestine organistaion in the Transvaal was more tightly structured and more hierarchical than in the Cape. It was also considerably less effective. Initially, with most of the Transvaal leadership in prison, there was little evidence of PAC activity. With the end of the emergency in August 1960 some important PAC men who had been detained along with Congress alliance people were released. In particular, two Evaton leaders, both on the national executive, who because of the dispersal of the Evaton crowd on 21 March had not been arrested for incitement, were once again at liberty. One of them, Z. B. Molete, was delegated the task of presiding over the underground organisation while the other office-bearers were in prison and he, together with Joe Molefi, began reviving branches. At this time it seems likely that the leadership of the Transvaal organisation did not have any clear strategic plans: their participation in the Orlando conference and the continuation committee established in its wake is an indication of this. Their withdrawal from the committee was prompted apparently by a message from their imprisoned colleagues brought to them by Matthew Nkoana, a national executive member who was released early as a result of his fine being paid.[83] Nkoana took over the leadership of the internal organisation in early 1961 when both Molete and Molefi left the country to avoid imprisonment. The latter joined the growing nucleus of PAC exiles concentrated in Maseru. Nkoana himself worked within the country for about seven months before avoiding arrest by crossing the Bechuanaland border in early 1962. By late 1962, with many of the PAC principals out of prison, the headquarters of the movement was firmly established in Maseru, Potlake Leballo arriving there in August 1962 to take over the direction of the movement.

As might have been expected, the PAC's strongest areas of support remained where they had been before the pass campaign: in the Vereeniging district and in Pretoria. In Vereeniging the main thrust of activity came from Evaton (the Sharpeville branch leadership was involved in a massive trial and many of its activists left the country). Under the chairmanship of David Sibeko, a young journalist who joined the PAC in Orlando during the emergency, recruitment and the revival of branches in Sharpeville, Vanderbijlpark, Sasolberg and Carltonville was successful enough to warrant forming a separate regional executive for the Vaal river industrial area.[84] In Pretoria, PAC activity continued to be centred on the high schools students, a group which had apparently been neglected by the ANC.[85] Hofmeyr Bantu High School at Atteridgeville, Kilnerton High, and Hebron African Teachers' Training School each had a PAC group.[86] The PAC probably had several hundred adherents in Pretoria: the Atteridgeville branch had five cells of which the largest numbered 100 members.[87] The Vlakfontein location branch was said by the Atteridgeville men to be even larger.[88]

As well as the Pretoria and Vereeniging areas the PAC continued to be active on the Witwatersrand where it managed to extend its following to Benoni and Krugersdorp.[89] Altogether, the PAC claimed, seventeen regional executives existed, each being intended to preside over branches divided up into ten-man cells, each cell insulated from the other with only the cell leader having any contact with other cells and upper echelons of authority.[90] In practice the system was rather untidier and evidence of PAC activity in 1961–3 outside the areas referred to above existed only in the case of the eastern Cape centres of Port Elizabeth, East London, Grahamstown and King Williamstown.[91]

Sociologically, the clandestine Transvaal PAC was strikingly different from the Cape Poqo. A group of eight PAC men from the Benoni township of Daveyton, led by a 23-year old clerical worker, included a caterer and a laboratory assistant.[92] As we have seen, teacher training and high school students were part of the PAC's Transvaal constituency. The PAC did not appear to have attempted to construct a following among migrant workers: its Transvaal members were typically young, totally urbanised, comparatively well educated and often drawn from a middle-class background.

As a result of its organisational and social character the Transvaal PAC was comparatively easy for the authorities to penetrate. In contrast to its organisation in the Cape, where the organisational pattern grew out of pre-existing and esoteric social networks in the Transvaal it was bureaucratically, and thus predictably, structured. Its lack of the social cohesion comparable to the Poqo groups in the Cape facilitated the infiltration of outsiders. A letter intercepted by the police from the Witwatersrand branch chairman to Maseru reflects this. The writer complains of the interception of crudely coded messages, the presence of police informers, members who were 'emotional and not very revolutionary in their behaviour or the lack of it', mistrust of branch leaders and different factions accusing each other of treachery, laziness and carelessness.[93] Unlike the Poqo groups in the western Cape, the Transvaal PAC cells did not protect themselves against informers by killing them.

PAC/Poqo violence during 1962–3 fell into four categories. First, there were defensive murders of suspected informers and policemen in Langa and Paarl. Then there were killings which appear to have had a terrorist function: their victims were white and seem to have been chosen indiscriminately. Thirdly, assassination attempts were mounted on the lives of Transkeian chiefs and their supporters. These should be understood in the context of more generalised rural resistance to land rehabilitation and Bantu Authorities and are examined in Chapter 11. Finally, the PAC/Poqo undertook preparations for a general uprising which came to fruition only in Paarl, prematurely, and in East London and King William's Town. The first three categories of violence were confined to the western Cape branches, and only the last – the preparations for a general uprising – was co-ordinated and directed by the Maseru-based exile leadership.

As has been suggested above, the PAC's insurrectionism grew partly from the millenarian impulses in the Cape Poqo cells. At the same time the vision of a spontaneous mass cataclysm being triggered off by a few exemplary acts of heroism lay at the heart of the PAC's strategy before Sharpeville. Stimulated perhaps by reports from the Cape – Nkoana visited Port Elizabeth shortly before his departure from the country and 'came back feeling that the PAC was going to be unable to control those chaps'[94] – the Maseru-based leaders began preparations for an armed revolt. Potlake Leballo's impatience may have been increased by an interview he had with Kwame Nkrumah on his way back from a visit to the United Nations headquarters in November 1962. The uprising was to take place on 8 April the following year, thereby fulfilling the earlier PAC prophecy of 'independence' by 1963.

PAC/Poqo branches and cells in the Cape and the Transvaal were informed of the plan by the fourth quarter of 1962. In contrast to the Cape, in the Transvaal branches there appears to have been some hesitation and scepticism. Cell leaders from Pretoria who had travelled to Maseru for instructions were reprimanded by Leballo:

> He said we in the Transvaal here, were not well enough organised yet and that the people in the Cape provinces . . . were already becoming impatient and that is the reason they have started the killing.[95]

In February, circulars from the PAC leadership to branches around Johannesburg indicated that some branches and cells were asking for the uprising to be postponed until a later date.

Leballo's conception of the uprising was simple and dramatic. Each branch should immediately begin a programme of mass recruitment (a target figure of 1 000 members per branch was proposed) and then on the chosen day there would be simultaneous attacks on strategic points such as police stations or power installations, to be accompanied by the mass slaughter of whites. This was to be completely indiscriminate; in Leballo's speeches the whites were referred to as 'the forces of darkness'.[96]

Preparations were to include the manufacture of petrol bombs and the collection of food and clothing. Branches were also instructed to form cells if they had not done so already. Leballo told emissaries from Pretoria that on the appointed day they should kill for four hours and then stop:

> Those Europeans that remained will, if they are willing to join them in their parliament that they are going to establish, they would be allowed to stay.[97]

In the event the police were able to forestall all this by arresting over 3 000 Poqo suspects. Branches had been infiltrated, couriers entering the republic from Maseru were intercepted, and Leballo could not resist informing a startled press conference of his plans two weeks before the revolt was due.[98] In the wake of Leballo's indiscretion a police raid on the PAC offices in Maseru resulted in the seizure of lists of 10 000 names. The PAC later claimed that these were handed over to the South African authorities. With the exception of Kingwilliamstown and East London, where, respectively, the charge office was petrol bombed and a police patrol was attacked, 8 April passed without incident. Most of the conspirators in other centres were under arrest or too demoralised to contemplate any action.

In the small Boland town of Paarl, however, a sequence of events which very closely resembled Leballo's conception of an uprising had already taken place. At 2.30, early in the morning of Thursday, 22 November 1962, 250 men carrying axes, pangas and various self-made weapons left the Mbekweni location and marched on Paarl. On the outskirts of the city the marchers formed two groups, one destined for the prison where the intention was to release prisoners, the other to make an attack on the police station. But even before the marchers reached Paarl's boundaries, the police had already been warned of their approach by a bus driver. Police patrols were sent out and one of these encountered the marchers in Paarl's Main Street. Having lost the advantage of surprise, the marchers in Main Street began to throw stones at cars, shop windows and any police vans which they came across on their way to the police station. The police at the station were armed with sten guns and rifles in anticipation of the attack. At ten minutes past four between 75 and 100 men advanced on the station throwing stones. When the attackers came within 25 yards of the station they were fired upon and two of them were immediately killed. The marchers then broke up into smaller groups and several were arrested or shot during their retreat. Some of the men who had taken part in the assault on Paarl police station met up in Loop Street with the group that was marching on the prison. These men regrouped and embarked on an attack on the inhabitants of Loop Street. Three houses and two people in the street were attacked: a seventeen year old girl and a young man were killed and four other people were wounded. According to police evidence, five insurgents were killed and fourteen were wounded. By five o'clock, the Paarl uprising was over; police reinforcements had arrived from Cape Town and the men from Mbekweni were in full retreat.

Because the Paarl insurrection was the one instance in which PAC/Poqo preparations developed, albeit prematurely, into a full-scale uprising, it is worth looking at the local circumstances which gave rise to this outbreak in some detail.

Paarl had had a turbulent recent history. In mid-1959 there were demonstrations against the issue of women's passes. These were followed in November by riots in protest against the banning of Elizabeth Mafeking, a local trade unionist and women's leader. One month later municipal police were attacked on several occasions in Mbekweni while on searches for illegal visitors to the location and an unsuccessful attempt was made to burn down the location administration offices. In March 1960 Paarl was affected by the pass campaign; many people destroyed their passes and a school in Mbekweni was set alight.

Paarl was a small town and its African population very small. The evident intensity of the opposition to the authorities is at first sight surprising. These recurrent confrontations need to be understood in the light of recent changes in the town's social structure. Paarl lies in the heart of the Boland region, a rich agricultural area dominated by fruit and vine cultivation. From the end of the Second World War it experienced a swift industrial expansion both in its traditional industrial sector based on agriculture and more recent manufacturing. Providing the labour requirements for this industry was a population of 17 000 whites, 30 000 coloureds, and 5 000 Africans. Paarl's African population had actually shrunk in the course of the 1950s as well as undergoing internal changes in its composition. Whereas in 1950 about 2 000 African families lived in or around Paarl, by 1962 there were only 400 families, the rest of the African population being composed of 2 000 migrant workers.[99]

Paarl's African population had originally been a 'squatter' population, many of its members being, in 1950, recent refugees from evictions from farms and other urban centres. Paaral was one of the last towns in the western Cape to be proclaimed under the Urban Areas Act and was therefore an obvious refuge for those displaced by influx controls elsewhere. Before Paarl's proclamation in 1950 its African population lived in four squatter camps. In 1950 the municipality assumed responsibility for housing and controlling this 'squatter' population. In the course of the subsequent decade Africans were reaccommodated in two municipal locations, four miles from town, Mbekweni and Langabuya. The squatter camps were redesignated as industrial land.

Mbekweni consisted of four blocks of single workers' barracks, each barracks divided into rooms for six men. In addition there were houses for thirty families. Langabuya was conceived of as a temporary emergency settlement for the inhabitants of the demolished squatter camps. The municipality provided refuse collection and small plots at a ground rent of R1.00 a month. It was sited on top of a ridge exposed to the wind. In 1962, 1 200 people lived a squalid, miserable existence there with whatever belongings and shelter they had been able to salvage from the former camps.[100] Two thousand men lived in Mbekweni.

The municipality's resettlement policies had been much resented. The new accommodation had no obvious advantages over the old. Because of the ground rent and new transport costs it brought fresh financial burdens to people who, because of the seasonal nature of much of the local employment, did not have consistent incomes throughout the year. There was widespread rent defaulting and frequent arrests of racalcitrant tenants.

As well as the economic hardships it caused, resettlement also involved the denial to many of urban residence: from 1955 women whose husbands had not lived in Paarl for fifteen years were 'endorsed out' and sent to the Transkei.[101] Their menfolk were sent to live in Mbekweni. Langabuya had quite a large population of women living there illegally. To add to the anguish and insecurity created by this policy, in 1962 the government called for a rapid replacement in the western Cape of black unskilled labour with coloured workers.[102]

The venal fashion with which Paarl's influx control measures were administered further accentuated the tension and uncertainty which they gave rise to. The local Director of Bantu Administration, one J. H. le Roux, together with his senior clerk, Wilson Ngcukana, manipulated the system for their private profit, selling passes, setting pass offenders to work on le Roux's farm, enforcing substantial fines for trivial infringements of regulations and so forth. In 1960 le Roux was tried for corruption but was acquitted after rumours of bribery and intimidation of witnesses.[103]

Up to 1960 African political activity in Paarl had been divided between the affairs of the Advisory Board, which mainly reflected the interests of the tiny upper social stratum of municipal employees and skilled workers, and the ANC. The ANC had a strong branch in Paarl which developed a considerable following during the demolition of the squatters' camps. Much of its strength and energy was drawn from the SACTU-affiliated African Food and Canning Workers' Union which interested itself as much in community as in purely workplace-oriented issues. The FCWU had about 400 members, half of whom were Mbekweni hostel dwellers.[104] Outside the traditional industries in Paarl (fruit processing, canning and wine) the African workforce was unorganised. In the new manufacturing factories many of the workers were fairly recent arrivals from the Transkei. It is likely, therefore, that the influence of the ANC amongst a large proportion of the Mbekweni population was at best superficial. It was among these people that the Poqo cells were first active.

A branch of the PAC had existed in Paarl before the organisation was banned.[105] The earliest record of revived activity by PAC members in Paarl is provided by documentation from a trial of three men convicted for recruiting on behalf of an illegal organisation.[106] All three were originally from Cofimvaba, in their twenties, and lived in migrant workers' hostels. Two worked in the Bakke plastics factory and one at Rembrandt Tobacco. Their recruiting activities, which took place between February and October 1961, were concentrated in Mbekweni. Recruiting was a simple procedure: men would be approached, told of Poqo, 'an organisation which stood alone', and asked to pay an initial subscription of 25 cents. State witnesses at Poqo trials tended to emphasise a coercive aspect to recruiting: they would claim that they were given little option but to join, for if they did not, they were informed, they would be killed, or at the very least would have to leave the location.

Such people, though, would naturally be anxious to dissociate themselves from the organisation. One Poqo member (who did not seem to be aware of the legal implications of turning state evidence) said he joined because:

I saw that a lot of people were supporting the Poqo organisation at Mbekweni location. That's why I joined, because a lot of people I know also joined.[107]

Social pressure there may have been, but this does not amount to coercion.

New members were told that the subscriptions (as well as the 25 cents, members paid an additional ten cents a month)[108] would be used by leaders in Langa 'to buy guns' or for burials and the dependents of the dead and arrested.[109] Each new member was organised into a cell of ten people,[110] the members of which would sometimes live in the same rooms. Once a week the members of the cell would meet in their cell leader's room.[111] Less frequently there would be much larger meetings involving members of several Mbekweni cells.[112] According to age, the Poqo members would also be placed either in a 'task force' (if they were under 25) or a 'general force'.[113] The younger group would be in the vanguard of any attack as well as being responsible for performing any defensive operations. Members of both forces would attend parades together in a plantation near the location. Sometimes outsiders, believed to be from Langa, would join the proceedings. Here the recruits would drill like soldiers in preparation for the great day when they would fight for the return of their land.[114]

Other preparations included the fashioning of crude weapons and, for those who could afford it, the scarification of their foreheads as a measure believed to ensure their invulnerability against the police. This was carried out by one of the main leaders and he would be paid ten rands for the operation.[115]

There are no firm indications as to the number of people who belonged to Poqo in Mbekweni or Paarl as a whole. At the final meeting before the attack, and in the march on the town, witnesses suggest that were about three hundred participants. This was the figure the authorities believed at the time to have represented the local strength of Poqo. From the backgrounds of some of the defendants and state witnesses in one of the trials that took place after the uprising the following generalisations can be made. These were fairly young men who had come to work and live in Paarl since the mid 1950s. They were mainly employed in the new manufacturing industries, in services or at the cigarette factory. They lived in one or other of the migrant workers' blocks at Mbekweni (with no noticeable concentration in any one block). Despite testimony from witnesses to the Snyman Commission that the leaders were 'educated men'[116] this feature does not emerge from the records of the trial.[117] From these rather sparse details a few tentative points can be made. Poqo's local leaders were drawn from the men who formed the most recently arrived section of Paarl's population. The absence of any employees from the traditional industrial activities in Paarl confirms that the FCWU had succeeded in influencing the political loyalties and the ideological outlook of its membership. Though the Poqo men in the trial would not have experienced all the hardships that have just been described (the removals from the squatters' camps and their economic consequences) they did come from the group which felt the severity of the system most intensely. They were unable to have their wives and children living nearby save illegally; they themselves were the most stringently subjected to influx control restrictions; and they had the most intimate knowledge of deteriorating conditions in the reserves. It is also reasonable to assume that the general insecurity of the community and the violent tradition of social protest in Paarl would have contributed to their motivation.

Before the uprising there had been at least eight instances of violence in Paarl which were eventually attributed to Poqo. On the night of 21 January 1962, eleven men took part in the murder of an employee of the municipal administration, Klaus Hosea. Hosea was believed by local Poqo leaders to have been an informer. He was seen writing down the numbers of lorries which had transported Poqo members from Paarl to a meeting in Simonstown. Four of the men functioned as look-outs and seven took part in the killing of Hosea. The murder took place between Mbekweni and Langabuya.[118] Nearly three months later, on 14 April, the police were told of a plan to burn down the houses of municipal employees and kill the inhabitants. Early on the morning of the 15th, a strong police patrol was sent to Mbekweni. In the middle of the location they came across a crowd of about 120 men who were singing. On being intercepted the men attacked the police, wounding three constables and their commanding officer. According to reports at the time, guns as well as sticks and stones were used in the attack.[119] The police reacted by raiding the location in strength on the night of 6 May. The raid involved 162 constables led by eight officers. By now the police were aware of the extent of Poqo's influence, but in spite of arresting a few suspects were able to do little to check the movement: they were unable to persuade anyone to come forward to incriminate those they had arrested.[120] From this time police raids became increasingly frequent in Mbekweni.

Two more suspected informers were killed by Poqo in the following months and in both cases their ending was terribly brutal. Then in the middle of June Poqo members dragged four women out of various rooms in the hostels and took them to the nearby plantation. Three of the women were hacked to death, one managed to survive her wounds and the attempt to set her body alight. The day after, a pamphlet written in Xhosa was found pasted to one of the kitchen block walls. It read:

> Here is something important to all of you. Girls must never be present again in our single quarters, even the individual they may be visiting will not be innocent of such charge. Never again must any preacher be heard making a noise in our single quarters by preaching. One who wishes to do so must go and do it in town.
>
> Those who are going around here with pamphlets of Watchtower it must be their last week-end, going about approaching people with this nonsense.
>
> People collecting washing for local laundries must cease to be seen collecting money in the single quarters. We will take our washing to the laundry ourselves.
>
> Christians will be allowed only this Sunday, June 24th, after which and until December 1963, never will any existing church which is calculated to oppress be allowed. There will only be one national church. All the above things will be abolished from next week until December 1963.
>
> You are being told. These are the last warnings of this nature. Therefore please tell or inform each other. The time itself tells you. It shines to each and every one, but you teach or preach falsehood to us so that the nation must remain oppressed forever'.[121]

Then on 22 September a white shopkeeper was killed in his shop in Wellington. According to police evidence he was attacked by a Poqo group from Paarl 'to show [the movement's] determination to kill whites'. The group used firearms and emptied the cash drawer.[122] Finally on 28 October a witness, who was helping the police in their investigations of the shopkeeper's murder, was killed in a similarly brutal fashion to previous victims.

By the end of October the police had arrested 25 men whom they believed to have been involved both in the murders and in Poqo.[123] Concern over the apparent extent of the movement's power had also affected the Bantu Advisory Board and the location's administrators. There was a history of antipathy between the members of the Advisory Board and the inhabitants of the single hostels. Several of them owed their position on the Board to the influence of le Roux's headman, Wilson Ngcukana. Board members had acquiesced in the system of pass selling and had supported measures taken against people who were behind in their rent payments.[124] In 1960, the Advisory Board had sent a deputation to the Mayor of Paarl to complain about the single men's behaviour.[125] This was during the period of le Roux's suspension, when control of the location was for a period loosened. At the weekends large numbers of women and children came into the hostels and lively parties were held. The Board members asked for the appointment of block supervisors, and requested the erection of a fence to prevent unauthorised entry to the location. In May 1962 a deputation, composed of 'leading members of the Bantu Community' alarmed by the recruiting and the drilling activities going on quite openly in the location, complained to the police district commandant of 'unlawful meetings' and 'unlawful visitors'. The commandant took up their complaints with the location administration. The administration's officials seemed to have been rather piqued that the deputation did not channel their complaints through them and Ngcukana went so far as to compromise deputation members by publicly warning them that Poqo was looking for the people who had betrayed them to the police.[126] At the beginning of November the Board asked the administration for permission to send a second deputation to the police, but despite the urgency of the request, no more was heard of the matter.[127] Obviously the municipal officials were anxious to maintain their power within the location and did not want to rely on external assistance.

However, by this time the municipal authorities were ready to act. Ngcukana had for some months been engaged in a series of brutal interrogations of various suspected Poqo members. At least one of the Poqo witnesses at the Snyman Commission had been in touch with the municipal police since the middle of the year.[128] Ngcukana had also been building up his own client group in the location: there was talk of a group of Mpondo who had been brought into the location recently; other members of this group included very young and recently arrived migrant workers who had just bought their passes.[129] On Sunday 18 November, at a meeting held at Wilson Ngcukana's house during the morning, the decision was taken to isolate the Poqo members by driving them out of their hostels and forcing them to occupy rooms in Block D of the location. The removals took place straight away. Men from Block A (who apparently composed the major force of Ngcukana's following),[130] dragged men out of their rooms, beat them up, threw their belongings out after them, and then herded them into Block D. The municipal police played a leading part in this operation and apparently used the occasion to pay off a number of old scores.[131] These removals did not occur all at once but carried on until they were completed on Tuesday.[132] The municipal police then set to work on the new inmates of D Block, and by Wednesday had succeeded in discovering three men allegedly involved in the murders which had taken place during the preceding months. These men were handed over to the South African Police.[133] With this blow, the stage was set for the Paarl uprising.

At 9 o'clock on the evening of 21 May the Poqo leaders called a meeting in D Block. By now they were thoroughly alarmed and were convinced of the need for a decisive counter attack on the authorities. The meeting was told that they should prepare for an attack on Paarl police station and the prison later that night with the immediate purpose of freeing the Poqo men arrested earlier. Another object of the attack would be to obtain weapons and ammunition for the movement. Despite Synman's assertion that the ultimate aim was to launch an attack on the white people of Paarl that night, the evidence is rather confusing with regard to what was supposed to happen when Poqo was in control of the police station and prison. But it was stressed by the speakers that that night was not the great night when all Poqo groups were to launch a general insurrection throughout the country. However, it was planned to co-ordinate the assault with the Poqo cells at Langa whom, it was hoped, would launch a diversionary attack on the police and prevent Cape Town from sending reinformcements to Paarl.[134] Three men immediately left Mbekweni in a taxi to contact the Langa people for this purpose. While they were away, the meeting broke up and people returned to their rooms to collect their weapons and get some sleep. The last routine police patrol occurred during this lull and the police saw nothing to arouse their suspicions that anything unusual was going on.[135]

In Langa, there seems to have been some reluctance to fall in with the plans of the Paarl group. The Langa Poqo leaders first of all suggested that the Paarl men should merely kill Ngcukana, but this suggestion was rejected by the visitors. Ngcukana slept out of the location and was not easily accessible, and in any case was working hand in glove with the police. By now things had reached a stage where the killing of a senior clerk would not in itself provide an adequate solution. But, said the Langa men, there were not adequate numbers of Poqo members at Paarl to launch a successful attack on the police station. Then Damane, the leader of the Paarl deputation, said 'If we are dead, then we are dead',[136] and the force of this argument seems to have convinced the men in Langa, for their visitors left them with the assurance that the Cape Town police would have plenty to occupy themselves with in Langa that night.[137] On their return, the Poqo members were marshalled for another short meeting and then at 2.30 a.m., on the morning of 22 November, the march on Paarl began.

The events of the march were described earlier in this chapter. Just two points about them will be made here. First, the sudden transformation of the march from a disciplined attack on the police station and gaol into a general attack on any whites in the path of the marchers requires comment. The fact that Poqo members actually went into houses in Loop Street to kill their occupants suggests that this was not merely a panic-stricken defensive reaction but rather involved an extension of the objects of the attack as it was originally conceived in the minds of the participants. Poqo members had for months discussed and planned for a general uprising. An insurrectionist strategy, as suggested earlier, arose quite spontaneously in a situation where men were caught in a web of pressures and tensions, in which neither the present nor the future held out any source of hope. At the point when the marchers turned upon the inhabitants of Loop Street, the attack which had been primarily a defensive operation, turned into an insurrection, and followed the lines of a preconceived model.

The second point worth making here is that, in the short term, the march on Paarl very nearly succeeded in attaining its immediate objectives. If it had not been for the observation of the marchers by a bus driver on his way to the location and the failure of the marchers to stop him from alerting the police, it is quite likely that the 39 policemen in the Paarl district[138] (many of whom were off duty) would not have been able to cope with the attack. It took over three-quarters of an hour for reinforcements from Cape Town to arrive.[139] The Paarl uprising still represents the occasion which came closest to the apocalyptic ideal of Poqo and many other movements before them: a black insurrection carried into the heart of the white cities of South Africa.

In contrast to the pervasiveness of the Poqo movement in the western Cape, in the Transvaal the PAC failed to gain the support of a comparably broad social stratum. In the Cape the movement had grown out of a complex social crisis affecting the most underprivileged section of the African population. In the Transvaal the PAC's following was more socially heterodox, materially more secure and without the inherent world view of the Cape migrants. Consequently the PAC cells in the Transvaal were more susceptible to control, direction and inspiration from above, less unified and in some cases less enthusiastic in adopting a violent course of action. Here tragedy gave way to melodrama. Notwithstanding the courage of some of the participants, in the context of the tiny Transvaal conspiracies for a general uprising there was an especial air of unreality and fantasy. Just one example, that of the PAC cells in Atteridgeville, Pretoria, will have to suffice.

Like the Mbekweni men, the Atteridgeville insurrectionists were young, between 16 and 34 years old, and half of the men eventually convicted were under the age of 20.[140] On the whole they were well educated (several were still at secondary school) and the group included two school teachers. In contrast to Cape Town, where Poqo affiliation ran into thousands,[141] the Pretoria PAC cells did not have more than a few hundred members. There were five small cells in Atteridgeville. Between the different township branches there existed considerable friction which also affected the Pretoria regional committee.[142] The fact that such a large proportion of the Atteridgeville membership were schoolchildren does not imply a local population that was very receptive to PAC influence. Nevertheless, despite the weakness of the movement, fairly determined efforts were made to prepare for the uprising. Men from the Pretoria branches received their instructions from Leballo in Maseru on 1 March. One of the Atteridgeville men at the meeting was a police agent who had joined two months previously.[143] After that meeting, hasty efforts were made to divide up the branches into cells and the Atteridgeville people retrieved unexploded shells from a nearby firing range. Schoolchildren were told to warn their parents to store 180 lbs of mealie meal and to buy strong khaki cloth. A detailed plan of attack was formulated in which groups of men would march simultaneously on Pretoria from four quarters on the appointed day. Two attempts were made on the lives of African special branch policemen, though both were somewhat half-hearted. Most of the conspirators were arrested towards the end of March.

PAC/Poqo groups continued to be active within the country until the close of the 1960s. Apart from the cells which developed among convicts in Leeuwkop prison[144] and other jails,[145] most of the cells uncovered by the police were in the smaller towns of the Cape. For example, 26 men were put on trial in 1968 for planning to attack the police station, a power station and a post office in Victoria West. These were to be the first acts in a local insurrection.[146] The following year twelve men, led by a Methodist minister, were found guilty of belonging to a Poqo group in Graaff-Reinet.[147] But despite the activities of these residual clusters of PAC followers the back of the movement had been broken with the mass arrests of April–June 1963.

Notes

1 *Congress Voice*, February 1961.
2 Edward Feit, *Urban Revolt in South Africa*, Northwestern University Press, 1971, p. 119.
3 See, for example, Bruno Mtolo, *Umkonto we Sizwe: the road to the left*, Durban, Drakensberg Press, 1966, p. 23.

4 Rob Lambert, 'Black resistance in South Africa, 1950–1961: an assessment of the political strike campaigns', University of London, Institute of Commonwealth Studies, seminar paper, 25 February 1978, p. 8.

5 National Action Council, *A Review of the Stay-at-Home Demonstration*, 1961, p. 12.

6 *Africa Digest*, February 1962.

7 See Lambert, 'Black resistance in South Africa', p. 7, and Gerard Ludi, *Operation Q-018*, Cape Town, Nasionale Boekhandel, 1969, p. 30.

8 One East London member of Umkonto, for example, records in an interview that in 1969 a police informer was killed, possibly by ANC activists. See Dennis and Ginger Mercer, *From Shantytown to Forest*, Richmond, LSM Press, 1974, p. 51.

9 Feit, *Urban Revolt in South Africa*, p. 148.

10 Mandela's statement at the Rivonia Trial, reproduced in Gwendolyn Carter, Gail Gerhart and Thomas Karis, *From Protest to Challenge*, Volume III, Stanford, Hoover, 1977, p. 772.

11 *Ibid.*

12 *Ibid.*, p. 351.

13 Alex La Guma, *Apartheid*, London, Lawrence and Wishart, 1972, pp. 222–6.

14 For examples of activities undertaken by a cell penetrated by a police agent, mainly consisting of solidarity work amongst young people and students at the University of the Witwatersrand, see Ludi, *Operation Q-018*, pp. 174–186.

15 Lambert, 'Black resistance in South Africa', p. 7.

16 Ludi, *Operation Q-018*, p. 197 and Mtolo, *Umkonto we Sizwe*, p. 24.

17 Lambert, 'Black resistance in South Africa', p. 6.

18 Karis, Carter and Gerhart, *From Protest to Challenge*, Volume III, p. 717.

19 *Ibid*, p. 358.

20 *Ibid*, p. 778.

21 One of the first ANC men to be sent abroad for training was Joe Gqabi who returned to South Africa in 1963 after completing an eighteen-month course at Nanking. He was later arrested in Livingstone, Northern Rhodesia, while leading a batch of recruits to Tanzania. Gqabi died in 1981 while serving as ANC representative in Zimbabwe. His assassination was attributed by the Zimbabwean administration to South African agents.

22 Mtolo, *Umkonto we Sizwe*, p. 15.

23 Feit, *Urban Revolt in South Africa*.

24 Altogether the indictment listed 193 actions but some of these were clearly not the work of Umkonto. The Minister of Justice said in the Senate that, up to 10 March 1964, there had been 203 serious cases of sabotage. Muriel Horrell, *Action, Reaction and Counteraction*, Johannesburg, SAIRR, 1971, p. 59.

25 Edward Feit, *Workers without Weapons*, Archon Books, Hamden, 1975.

26 Gary Longden, 'Umkonto we Sizwe and the reasons for its failure', University of York, B. Phil. dissertation, September 1976, pp. 24–5.

27 Mtolo, *Umkonto we sizwe*.

28 *Ibid*, pp. 23–7.

29 'The people accept the challenge of the Nationalists', ANC national executive report issued after the Lobatsi Conference, 1963.

30 '26th June is the Freedom Day', ANC leaflet, 1963.

31 Feit, *Urban Revolt in South Africa*, p. 116.

32 Mtolo, *Umkonto we Sizwe*, p. 56.

33 Arrested recruits would claim that they thought they were being sent abroad on scholarships. Given the circumstances of such statements their truthfulness is open to question. Mtolo's account suggests that recruitment for military training (as opposed to simply joining Umkonto and taking part in its activities) became increasingly difficult.

34 See Ellen Hellman and Henry Lever, *Conflict and Progress*, Johannesburg, Macmillan, 1979, p. 90.
35 See Gerard Ludi and Blaar Grobbelaar, *The Amazing Mr Fischer*, Cape Town, Nasionale Boekhandel, 1966.
36 Carter, Gerhart and Karis, *From Protest to Challenge*, Volume III, p. 676.
37 *Ibid*, p. 761.
38 R. W. Johnson, *How Long Will South Africa Survive?*, Johannesburg, Macmillan, 1978, p.23.
39 Fatima Meer, 'African nationalism – some inhibiting factors' in Heribert Adam, *South Africa: sociological perspectives*, Arnold, London, 1971, p. 145.
40 Feit, *Urban Revolt in South Africa*, p. 75.
41 Ben Turok, *Strategic Problems in South Africa's Liberation Struggle*, Richmond, LSM Press, 1974, p. 45.
42 Joe Slovo, 'South Africa – no middle road' in Basil Davidson, Anthony Wilkinson and Joe Slovo, *Southern Africa: the new politics of revolution*, Harmondsworth, Pelican, 1976, pp. 180–196, and Turok, *Strategic Problems*, p. 45.
43 Ludi, the police agent who joined the SACP in 1963, claims that SACP cells were racially segregated so that each cell could undertake propaganda work and the organisation of front activity in their own respective communities. Dubious as some of his assertions are, a convincing impression emerges that the SACP, unlike the ANC, did work systematically on political projects of a non-military character during this period. ANC activity seems to have been much more spasmodic and less carefully programmed.
44 Mandela discussed the relationship between nationalists like himself and communists in his Rivonia trial statement as well as outlining his own political ideals. See Karis, Carter and Gerhart, *From Protest to Challenge*, Volume III, p. 78. For an earlier statement of Mandela's attitude to communists, see C. J. Driver, *Patrick Duncan*, London, Heinemann, 1980, p. 194–5.
45 The most extensive description of NCL-ARM's development is Miles Brokensha and Robert Knowles, *The Fourth of July Raids*, Cape Town, Simondium Publishers, 1965. It concentrates on the Cape Town wing of the movement and is often inaccurate in points of detail.
46 Hugh Lewin, *Bandiet*, London, Barrie and Jenkins, 1974.
47 Socialist League of Africa, 'South Africa: ten years of the stay-at-home', *International Socialist*, no. 5, summer 1961, p. 14.
48 Albie Sachs Papers, Institute of Commonwealth Studies, University of London, AS/76 C6, ARM documentation from trial in Cape Town, October 1964.
49 Horrell, *Action, Reaction and Counteraction*, p. 83.
50 Govan Mbeki, 'An unholy alliance' in *New Age*, 3 August 1961.
51 See Chapter 9.
52 Albie Sachs papers, AS 31/11, Regina *vs.* Madlebe and 31 others, June–December 1960, list of names and addresses of accused.
53 AS 31/6. 4, Regina *vs.* Madlebe and 31 others, transcripts of PAC meetings.
54 See chapter 9.
55 Report of evidence submitted to Synman Commission by Frank Barton, Cape Town editor of *Drum* magazine in *Cape Argus*, 12 March 1963.
56 Howard Lawrence, 'Poqo – we go it alone' in *Fighting Talk*, Vol. 17, no. 2, February 1963, pp. 4–6.
57 As 69/8, State *vs.* Mandla and 31 others, June 1963 statements by accused nos. 21 and 23 and AS 31/11, Regina *vs.* Madlebe.
58 Author's interview with Randolph Vigne, London 1975.
59 AS 69/8, State *vs.* Mandla and 31 others, statements by accused nos. 14 and 23.
60 *Contact*, 16 April 1960.
61 AS 69/7, State *vs.* Mandla and 31 others, defence lawyer's notebooks.

62 *Contact*, 29 November 1962.
63 *Drum's* report of February 1963 mentions an 'inaugural meeting' in August 1961 by 750 *Poqo* activists in a hall between Paarl and Wellington, very near Mbekweni. I have come across no other reports to confirm this and it is not mentioned in the Snyman Commission report.
64 'Sobukwe was Poqo leader', report in *Cape Times*, 4 March 1963, on Queenstown trial of men involved in unsuccessful assassination attempt on Chief Matanzima.
65 See Chapter 11.
66 As in the case of those accused in State *vs*. Mandla and 31 others, AS 69.
67 AS 35/5, State *vs*. Matikila and 3 others, March 1962, defence lawyer's notebooks.
68 AS 70, State *vs*. Budaza and 3 others, August 1963.
69 AS 83/14, State *vs*. Xintolo, n.d. defence lawyer's notes on evidence.
70 See report in *Drum* (February 1963) and Lawrence, 'Poqo – we go it alone', as well as *Cape Times* reports of the trial, 28 June 1962 and 5 July 1962.
71 Quoted in *Rand Daily Mail*, 23 March 1963.
72 *Cape Times*, 28 June 1962.
73 Transcript of proceedings of the Snyman Commission, CAMP microfilm (henceforth: Snyman proceedings), p. 348.
74 Report on trial of men involved in Matanzima assassination attempt, *Cape Times*, 4 March 1963.
75 Snyman proceedings, p. 329.
76 *Cape Times*, 28 June 1962 and Snyman proceedings, p. 38.
77 *Ibid*, p. 271.
78 *Ibid*, p. 297.
79 *Cape Times*, 5 July 1962 and 28 June 1962.
80 *Cape Times*, 15 August 1962.
81 Snyman proceedings, p. 283.
82 Draft of article on interview with Leballo in Maseru dated 24 March 1963 on microfilm of South African political documentation held at School of African and Oriental Studies, University of London.
83 Author's interview with Matthew Nkoana, London, 1975.
84 Author's interview with David Sibeko, London, 1976.
85 Author's interview with Tommy Mohajane, York, 1975.
86 *Cape Argus*, 24 June 1963, 3 July 1963, and 12 July 1963.
87 State *vs*. Masemula and 15 others, June 1963. Transcript filmed by Co-operative Africana Microfilm project (CAMP MF 568), held at the University of York, p. 180 and p. 272.
88 *Ibid*, p. 287.
89 *Cape Argus*, 21 June 1963 for report of Benoni activity, and for West Rand PAC support see letter from Witwatersrand regional chairman to Maseru PAC headquarters, 30 March 1963.
90 Author's interview with David Sibeko.
91 Author's interview with Matthew Nkoana; Mary Benson, *South Africa: struggle for a birthright*, Harmondsworth, Penguin, 1966, p. 274; various press reports.
92 *Cape Argus*, 21 June 1963.
93 Letter from Witwatersrand regional chairman to Maseru, 30 March 1963.
94 Author's interview with Matthew Nkoana.
95 State *vs*. Masemula and 15 others, transcript, p. 232.
96 *Ibid*.
97 *Ibid*.
98 *Contact*, 5 April 1963.
99 Report on evidence submitted to Snyman Commission, *Rand Daily Mail*, 18 February 1962; Snyman proceedings, p. 600.

100 Snyman proceedings, p. 626 and p. 649. A portrait of the location is provided in Frank Barton, 'Condemned to nowhere' in *Drum*, July 1963.
101 Barton, 'Condemned to nowhere'.
102 *Cape Times*, 29 August 1962.
103 Snyman proceedings, p. 620.
104 *Ibid*, p. 513.
105 Albie Sachs Papers, AS 35/5, State *vs*. Matikila and 3 others, defence lawyer's notebook, notes on evidence of Lieut. S. Sauerman.
106 State *vs*. Matikila and 3 others.
107 South African Institute of Race Relations, Johannesburg, SAIRR 1/63, p. 110, State *vs*. Makatezi and 20 others.
108 Snyman proceedings, p. 251.
109 Snyman proceedings, p. 253; *The Star*, 23 March 1963; *Rand Daily Mail*, 23 March 1963.
110 Snyman proceedings, p. 350.
111 *Ibid*, pp. 251 and 344.
112 SAIRR 1/63, pp. 77–9, State *vs*. Makatezi and 20 others.
113 *Ibid*, p. 344.
114 Snyman proceedings, p. 255.
115 SAIRR 1/63, p. 54, State *vs*. Makatezi and 20 others, and Snyman proceedings, p. 247.
116 'Marked man tells of Poqo initiations', *Cape Times*, 8 February 1963.
117 State *vs*. Makatezi and 20 others.
118 *Drum*, February 1963; Snyman proceedings, pp. 237 and 335; *Cape Argus*, 22 February 1968.
119 Snyman proceedings, p. 258; *Cape Times*, 16 April 1962; *Rand Daily Mail*, 13 March 1963.
120 Snyman proceedings, p. 245; *Rand Daily Mail*, 13 March 1963.
121 'Court told of 13 grievances at Paarl', *Rand Daily Mail*, 24 January 1963.
122 Snyman proceedings, p. 242.
123 *Ibid*, pp. 244–5.
124 *Rand Daily Mail*, 28 January 1963.
125 *Ibid*, 25 January 1963.
126 *Report of the Commission appointed to inquire into the Events on the 20th to the 22nd November, 1962, at Paarl*, Pretoria, RP 51/1963 (henceforth *Snyman Commission*), paragraphs 213–7.
127 *Cape Argus*, 19 February 1963.
128 Snyman proceedings, p. 342.
129 *Ibid*, pp. 644–5.
130 *Ibid*, p. 321.
131 *Ibid*, p. 227.
132 State *vs*. Malatezi and 20 others, p. 131.
133 *Snyman Commission*, paragraph 264.
134 State *vs*. Makatezi and 20 others, p. 147.
135 *Snyman Commission*, paragraph 276.
136 State *vs*. Makatezi and 20 others, p. 147.
137 *Ibid*. They were to be disappointed. In Langa there was to be no uprising that night.
138 *Snyman Commission*, paragraph 316.
139 *Ibid*, paragraph 311.
140 *Cape Times*, 3 July 1963.
141 *Snyman Commission*, paragraph 98.
142 State *vs*. Masemula and 15 others, June 1963, p. 272.

143 *Ibid*, p. 164.
144 *Cape Argus*, 7 August 1965.
145 *Ibid*, 16 December 1965 and 25 June 1966.
146 *Cape Argus*, 18 October 1968 and 19 November 1968.
147 *The Star*, 5 July 1969 and 2 August 1969.

CHAPTER 11

Resistance in the countryside

For over two decades, between 1940 and the mid-1960s, there was a succession of bitter localised conflicts between peasants and authority in the African reserves of South Africa. During the 1940s, 1950s and 1960s, the state played an increasingly interventionist role in the countryside. The reserves were needed for new economic and political functions, and a series of attempts was made to restructure them accordingly. Established social relationships were disrupted, in the process traditional authority was to be robbed of what legitimacy it retained, and the area of conflict between people and government expanded rapidly. Popular reactions to the reshaping of rural societies were widespread and rather bloodier than those occurring within cities. This was partly because the manner in which they were dealt with could be considerably more brutal than in an urban context, but also because the conditions of rural existence were even harsher than those that prevailed in the townships.

We will begin by discussing the new pressures rural people were subjected to as well as the reasons for them. Then, rather than providing a comprehensive survey of rural resistance movements (well beyond the scope of a single chapter) four case studies of rural rebellion will be described: Witzieshoek, 1950; Zeerust, 1957 to 1959; Mpondoland, 1960; and Tembuland, 1962 to 1963. There were significant differences between them, and over the years there was a development in both the content of these rebellions and the form they took. By drawing out such comparisons the underlying unity of these isolated and localised disturbances as well as their wider importance will become clearer.

Government policy in African-occupied portions of the countryside should be understood within the broad context of the South African political economy. The boundaries of reserves (later 'Bantustans' and 'homelands', today 'black states') were fixed by two pieces of legislation, the 1913 Natives' Land Act and the 1936 Native Trust and Land Bill. The Land Act set aside the rapidly diminishing areas under African communal tenure for exclusively African occupation, and prohibited African land purchase outside their borders. It also set out, with limited success, to restrict the growth of African squatting on white-owned farmland. The 1936 legislation amplified the anti-squatting provisions of the 1913 Act, actually making squatting illegal (a provision which was not enforced until a decade later) and establishing a Native Trust to buy up land in 'released areas' to be occupied and farmed by Africans under stringent supervision by Trust officials.

Much has been written about the changing purposes these reserves served in the development of South Africa's industrial economy, and what follows is a very brief condensation.[1] The original function of the reserves was to subsidise the costs of mine labour. In other words, mine owners could pay migrant black mineworkers' wages which were set below the minimum subsistence needs for themselves and their dependants. The balance would be made up by agricultural production carried out by the miner's family and himself between contracts. Moreover, the retention of linkages with a rural economy obviated the need for employers to pay pensions or to carry any other social welfare costs. However, this system had as its premise a rising level of production in the reserves. The tight limits set on African land occupation, the expansion of population within these limits and the removal of the healthiest and strongest members of the population for increasingly long periods as tax obligations and other cash needs grew greater was inimical to rising production. By the 1920s agricultural output (both stock and crops) per head was falling and though economic historians disagree as to exactly when the 'collapse' of reserve agriculture took place, by the 1930s the inability of some of the reserves to provide sufficient food for their inhabitants was arousing official concern. A confidential report on conditions in the Transkei and Ciskei commissioned by the Chamber of Mines concluded that 'semi-starvation is a very insecure basis with which to build a permanent labour supply'.[2] Within these reserves access to land and stock had become concentrated (so that growing numbers of people were landless or stockless or both). Moreover, cash agriculture was carried out at the expense of food production: wool production for the market, which mainly benefited headmen and chiefs, was, in the words of the Chamber of Mines report, 'driving cattle off the land' (as well as substantially contributing to its deterioration).[3]

Proclamation 31 of 1939, which outlined a programme of livestock limitation and land conservation measures, the 'betterment' scheme, was – together with the Native Trust regulations – outlined in the 1936 Act, the first attempt by the state to deal systematically with this situation. Wartime manpower shortages delayed the proper implementation of any such measures. But mining found other sources of cheap mining labour: by 1946 only 41 per cent of mining labour came from within South Africa's borders. Meanwhile the labour requirements of an expanding manufacturing industry came not from the reserves but from white-owned farms, where labour tenancy arrangements were becoming increasingly disadvantageous to the tenants.

The industrialisation of the 1940s presented South Africa's rulers with two sets of problems. First, there were the social and political tensions resulting from rapid urbanisation and proletarianisation. Second, there was the imbalance of labour supply between different sectors of the economy: farmers were unable to offer wages to compete with manufacturing and by the close of the decade were experiencing an acute shortage of labour. The reserves were affected by the resolution of both sets of problems. They no longer had any direct economic function but instead performed a crucial role in the process of controlling African labour. Responding to the needs of commercial agriculture, the post-1948 Nationalist government sought to redeploy labour in its favour by centralising and streamlining controls on the movement of labour. The 1952 Native Laws Amendment Act made Section 10 of the Urban Areas Act automatically applicable to every municipality and divided the country into prescribed (urban) and non-prescribed (rural) areas, movement between them being subjected to strict official sanctions. Labour bureaux, which began to be established in the countryside in 1949, dictated the channels along which labour could flow. Control of labour mobility was to be facilitated by a new system of pass documents incorporating photographs and fingerprints. In recognition of the increasingly important role they had in the industrial workforce, this system was extended to women under the so-called 'Abolition of Passes and Co-ordination of Documents Act' of 1952. To encourage a more efficient use of labour by farmers and to stimulate mechanised agriculture, anti-squatting legislation was enacted in 1954 which *inter alia* relieved the state of the legal requirement to find new land for displaced squatters. Squatters in peri-urban areas (that is those who lived just outside towns so they could take up urban employment but evade municipal influx controls) were prohibited in 1951. The overall effect of these measures was to massively enlarge the reserve population as various groups were excluded from the urban economy and forced back into the reserves. They were joined by displaced labour tenants, squatters and the inhabitants of 'black spots'.[4]

To meet these new burdens there was to be a substantial reorganisation of life in the reserves. Conceding that they could no longer provide a significant proportion of the subsistence needs of many of their inhabitants, it was proposed to regroup people in non-agricultural villages which would function as labour dormitories for decentralised industry. In the case of the Ciskei, this was mooted as early as 1945 with respect to displaced squatters. For the rest of the population, access to and the use of grazing and cultivated land would be subjected to an increased range of controls and supposedly self-imposed voluntary measures, such as stock limitation. This would serve to check the now alarming ecological crisis apparent in all the reserves. To enforce and supervise 'rehabilitation' in the face of continued resistance to it, and to provide a cheap repressive administration for a potentially rebellious population, local government was reshaped in an authoritarian fashion under the 1953 Bantu Authorities Act. As this policy was developed in the 1950s, wealth and power became concentrated at the local level around compliant chiefs and their acolytes. Their political aspirations, together with those of the small group of government employees (teachers, clerical workers, agricultural demonstrators and so forth) would be met through the construction of quasi-independent administrations of each reserve or group of reserves. By the end of the period the main function of the reserves would be in the displacement of sociopolitical tensions from the towns to the countryside where they could be more ruthlessly controlled and constituted less of a threat. To put it more brutally, the problems of the weak, the unemployed and the starving would be relocated to where they mattered only to those who were personally affected by them.

Let us look at the effects these changes had on rural life. They can be divided into three groups: those arising from attempts to regenerate production; the effects of political restructuring; and the results of new controls on mobility. The scheme for 'reclamation' of the reserves had two main features: limitation of stock to what was conceived to be the land's carrying capacity, and the redivision of the land into residential, cultivation and grazing areas. Kraals would no longer be scattered but grouped together 'in convenient small villages'.[5] Those people without access to land would live in rural townships. Land would be reserved for forestry schemes and access to these for firewood would be restricted. The betterment scheme was at its inception meant to be voluntary, its adoption depending on acceptance by meetings convened by chiefs or headmen in each rural location. In many cases such meetings could not have been very representative, as one of the Ciskeian General Councillors admitted in 1947:

> In some places the people have accepted the betterment proclamation but if you ask them personally you will find they know nothing of the whole affair.[6]

Or as another observed in 1951: 'in my location, when the scheme was accepted it was accepted by educated men, who went behind our backs'.[7] In general, support for the scheme came from the 'land-owning types of natives . . . the man who makes his living from the land and works it from January to December'.[8] Such people were relatively privileged in the context of some districts of the Ciskei where 30% of the population could be landless.[9]

In 1949 rehabilitation regulations were proclaimed placing great powers in the hands of agricultural officers who could 'excise areas needing special care' and allocate land for different purposes. However, despite their efforts, in 1954 the Native Affairs Department had tacitly to admit defeat when it switched over to a less complicated and more extensive conservation system which it called 'stabilisation', which had as its objective the prevention of further deterioration rather than 'reclamation'. But by this stage the department was looking forward to when conservation measures would be 'linked up with the traditional tribal system of government . . . constituted under the Bantu Authorities Act', a system which would not depend on popular sanction.[10]

Land reclamation was extremely unpopular. Native Affairs Department officials regularly complained of 'suspicion' and opposition from 'recalcitrant tribal communities' to their proposals. But hostility to the scheme came often from those whom one might have expected to be least conservative: as one Ciskeian District Commissioner plaintively put it in 1952, 'the younger men are taking control in the districts'.[11] Quite apart from emotional or ideological objections to rehabilitation, it was regarded with very real fear by people who depended on a very narrow margin for physical survival. Stock culling was aimed initially at the removal of weaker animals and reductions could take place with no regard of size of herd.[12] The average cattle holding in the Ciskei was 3.5 beasts a family (though this figure concealed wide disparities).[13] A minimum of three cattle was needed to ensure a regular milk supply for household consumption.[14] Those with such a number were relatively fortunate. In seven Transkeian districts, as early as 1941 44 per cent of the homesteads were found to own no cattle at all.[15] For such people access to cultivable land was crucial. But this was becoming more difficult. The new demarcation of fallow areas removed from some people a vital source of food:

> This season, a number of residents, including helpless widows, were made to pay heavy fines ranging from £2 to £3 for cultivating, under stress of want, lands they used to cultivate. This was particularly unfair because the people have just been encouraged by the magistrates to try

and cultivate every piece of available land in view of the scarcity of food throughout the country. What was worse than that, these plots were confiscated. After they were destroyed by weeds, the Assistant Commissioner felt he had humiliated his victims sufficiently, and was now in a good humour to let them repossess their plots. The chiefs are disregarded . . .[16]

Landless households were sometimes deprived of access to grazing: this was the case in Victoria East in 1951[17] and more generally common pastureland in practice shrunk as officials fenced off forbidden grazing camps. Prohibitions on tree-felling for people who could not afford to buy fuel were especially arduous in the colder reserves and in any case contravened a customary right of free access to firewood.[18] Villagisation policies, especially among people who did not live in villages (such as the Cape Nguni), aroused resentment. They offended custom and in any case lengthened the walk to the fields. Material considerations aside there were other objections to the scheme. First of all, cattle represented wealth, savings and security – in the words of one of the Witzieshoek spokesmen:

Cattle are his bank and he says money is useless to him, for it does not give birth, as cows do, every year; it cannot confirm a marriage, it cannot serve at ceremonies. From cattle he gets meat and hides to make blankets, but he would rather his beast died on its own than slaughter it. . . . He dreams of no other wealth. Even if his beasts are miserable and thin, they are as valuable as fat ones.[19]

Secondly, the interference by Native Affairs Department officials into matters which previously were the concern of chiefs of headmen – land allocation or the regulation of the agricultural cycle – reduced the popular standing of chiefs and headmen and could conflict with the principle that each household had sufficient land for its needs. Meyer, writing of 'red' communites in the Transkei, suggests that the loss by lineage elders of their function in advising headmen in land allocation undermined 'red' ideology and social solidarity as elders lost their main sphere of authority.[20] Women also suffered from the new system of land allocation, losing their customary right to a field of their own as land was usually only alloted to men as heads of households.[21]

The other main objection to the betterment scheme and its successors was that they did nothing to solve what many people felt to be the most pressing problems. As one of the Ciskei Councillors pointed out in the Council's rejection of the Reclamation Scheme in 1945:

most of the land is given to the few and the smallest piece is given to the many and the result is that they are grouped together with their stock, which brings about soil erosion. . . . If we reduce the stocks we deprive the people of food and milk.[22]

Acceptance of reclamation, betterment, rehabilitation or stabilisation implied acceptance of the way land had been apportioned in the first place. And the injustice of that division was being compounded every day as more and more people were being forced back into the reserves: the squatters, the inhabitants of black spots, the urban unemployed; between 1955 and 1969 the average population density in the reserves rose from 60 to 110.[23]

Closely related to economic reorganisation was the redefinition of political institutions under the Bantu Authorities Act. The architects of the new system took as their model the British colonial 'Native Authority'. Local government would be based on tribal institutions in which chiefs and headmen would have greatly enhanced executive powers. The size and composition of each tribal authority would be decided by the Department for Native Affairs. The system, in the case of the Ciskei and Transkei, replaced a partly elected District Council system, and more generally removed the consensual element in the relationship between chiefs and their communities, making chiefs answerable to the Department rather than their subjects. The scope and sanctions of the chiefs' judicial powers were considerably extended. In brief, chiefs were made responsible for the local maintenance of law and order and the implementation of government-inspired measures – including of course the rehabilitation scheme. As far as traditional leaders were concerned, the attractions of the new order were uncertain. It enhanced their local powers but detracted from their legitimacy as they became responsible for implementing unpopular laws. Many would have shared the sentiments of Abram Moiloa of the Bafurutse:

> It seems to us that they just want us chiefs to sign a document which says destroy me, baas. Let them destroy us without our signatures.[24]

For others, though, collaboration with the Department brought with it increased wealth and ascendancy over less compliant rivals. The system encouraged a trend towards despotism: those who profited most were often those whose traditional status was at best doubtful. In the self-conscious oratory of Bantu Affairs Department officials chiefs were incited to:

> Be your own police in your own interest, find out those men who respect authority and tribal institutions and band them together as the chief's and headmen's *impi* which will turn out when called to help keep your tribes and locations clean and well behaved. . . . Use moderate violence . . . just like a good chief should do.[25]

But quite apart from the burdens imposed by abuse of new powers, the system was to bring with it less arbitrary obligations.

The Bantu Authorities system included an attempt to cheapen (for the government) the cost of administration by extending the rural tax base.[26] In the Transkei, direct taxation almost doubled between 1955 and 1959,[27] and throughout the whole country convictions of Africans for tax defaulting leapt from 48 000 in 1950 to 179 000 in 1960.[28]

The final element in rural discontent was provided by the tightening of influx/efflux controls and the population resettlements of the 1950s and 1960s. The extension of pass laws appeared to rural women as a direct threat to the security and integrity of the household. Such anxieties would have been particularly felt in communities where, because of the prolonged absence of

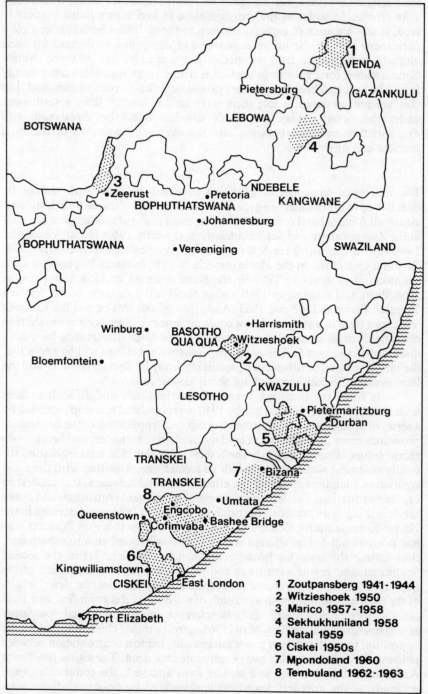

Fig. 3   Rural resistance in South Africa, 1940–1965

1 Zoutpansberg 1941-1944
2 Witzieshoek 1950
3 Marico 1957-1958
4 Sekhukhuniland 1958
5 Natal 1959
6 Ciskei 1950s
7 Mpondoland 1960
8 Tembuland 1962-1963

male migrant workers, the energetic and active members of the community were female. In so far as the reorganisation of agriculture limited access to land, it was a source of especial concern to those denied by influx control a permanent base in the urban economy and compelled to depend for their ultimate security on land or stock. For example, in 1951 the Native Commissioner for Tamacha in the Ciskei claimed that opposition came mainly from 'the industrial native . . . they do not beneficially occupy that land, but they are not prepared to lose their stake in that land'.[29] With resettlement under the Group Areas Act whole districts could be threatened with expropriation and incorporation into the ever growing ranks of the rural landless and unemployed.

The individual instances of rebellion to which we now turn should be understood in the context of a generalised background of unrest which affected almost all African rural communities. The main peaks of this disaffection were in the Zoutpansberg and Sekhukuniland in the early 1940s (today Venda and Lebowa), in the tiny Free State reserve of Witzieshoek in the early 1950s (Basotho Qua Qua), in the Marico reserve in 1958 (western Bophutatswana), Sekhukuniland again in 1958–9, the Natal reserves in 1958 and 1959, in Mpondoland, Transkei, in 1960 and in the Tembu districts of the western Transkei between 1962 and 1963. Also, throughout this period the Ciskeian territories were in a state of almost constant ferment. This book is too short to describe them all in detail. Some aspects of the Natal disturbance have been discussed in Chapter 8. The northern Transvaal rebellions will be neglected: the early ones are the subject of a pioneering study by Baruch Hirson[30] and the later events in Sekhukuniland are thinly documented.

In brief, the northern Transvaal reserves, hilly and difficult to farm under the best of conditions, but by 1940 overpopulated and impoverished by a series of droughts, were subjected to a rigorous application of the betterment provisions from 1939. Ploughed land was limited to taxpayers and because of a recent influx of new tribes into the reserve after the 1936 land legislation the family allotment was reduced to half its former size. Together with the rapid creation of a landless class and the effects of natural disasters, this created an explosive situation. Tactless enforcement of betterment regulations and heavy tax defaulting fines provided the catalysts to what in 1943 was described in the Native Representative Council as 'a state of armed warfare'.[31] Peasants who had overploughed their allotted areas were literally bombed into submission, thus setting the style for future repression.[32] The elements in the second Sekhukuniland revolt were more complex, involving the deposition of the Bapedi paramount who refused to accept Bantu Authorities, the deterioration of the local education system as a result of the Bantu Education Act, new local taxes, stock restrictions, and interference with traditional polygamy arrangements. An attempt in May 1956 to arrest a minor chief, who had led the opposition to the election of a new paramount, led to a confrontation between police and a crowd in which two people were shot dead. Thereafter pro-Bantu Authority chiefs, teachers and traders were attacked, the spiral of violence widening as the area was sealed off and invaded by police reinforcements headed by a special mobile column.[33]

The events in Witzieshoek were the first of these rural disturbances to attract the attention of an official commission of enquiry, and this, together with the fact that the participants had their own historian in the novelist, Atwell Mopeli Paulus, makes them unusually well documented.[34]

The Witzieshoek reserve, on the northern border between Lesotho and the Orange Free State, was originally granted by President Brand to a Basuto tribe headed by a brother of Moshesh, Paulus Mopeli, in a peace treaty after the war of 1866. Mopeli's tribe was joined in 1873 by the Batloaka under Chief Koos Mota. That the original boundaries of Witzieshoek were fixed by treaty and not by conquest was not without significance. Leaders of the rebellion would later claim that the treaty's existence invalidated those sections of the Land Act (1936) dealing with rehabilitation. Witzieshoek was administered by its paramount and an 'Additional Native Commissioner' who was chairman of a Reserve Board of four elected and two official African members. The Board was responsible for the upkeep of roads, bridges, sanitation, schools, local taxation and, until 1939, agricultural improvement.

In 1937, the grazing control measures of the Land Act were implemented in Witzieshoek with the fencing of six grazing camps. Residents in the enclosed areas were told to move and in the case of a sub-chief and his son, Howell and Paulus Mopeli, were prosecuted when they refused to do so. In 1939, at a public meeting after a meeting of the Board, the Betterment Areas Proclamation was accepted in Witzieshoek. In 1940 the reserve's 'carrying capacity' was set at 12 500 'cattle units' (one cow or five small stock) and the following year just under 1 000 cattle were culled. The only resistance came from the regent of the Batloaka who was fined for refusing to bring her stock to the cull. These developments were accompanied by the revival of a Vigilance Association which had existed since 1914. The Association was based in Johannesburg amongst migrants from Witzieshoek, who felt that as a result of the work of the betterment officials their own interests within the reserve (especially with regard to land allocation) were threatened. The Witzieshoek Vigilance Association was advised by the trade unionist, William Ballinger.

A second count was made in 1946 and it was proposed to cull nearly 1 300 cattle. This time hostility to the cull was more widespread. Four cattle owners, including Paulus Mopeli, ignored the culling order and were convicted in a local court. However, the judgement was set aside on appeal. Following this demonstration of the doubtful legal basis of the betterment proclamation many other people refused to sell off their culled cattle. These dissidents began to cohere into a movement under the leadership of Paulus Mopeli, known as the Lingangele. The Lingangele leaders began to assume a heroic status amongst many members of the community. It was popularly felt that the stock culling had involved a deception by the officials, that rather than being for the purposes of improvement of the reserves' stock by eliminating the weakest, the main intention was to reduce overall numbers. This, it was charged, was not what the tribe had accepted in 1939. In 1947, alarmed by the rising tide of dissatisfaction, the paramount, Charles Mopeli, with the support of the Native Commissioner, requested a commission of enquiry. However, this was refused by the Secretary for Native Affairs.

The chief then sent three delegates of the tribe, Paulus Howell Mopeli, Atwell Mopeli and Albert Mopeli, to interview the Native Senator, Hyman

Basner, in Cape Town. Basner promised to speak to the Minister of Native Affairs on their behalf, but according to the commission, told them that protest unaccompanied by action would be futile. He allegedly advised them to destroy the grazing camp fences. Atwell Mopeli's account does not mention Basner as giving this advice, though the commission's report asserts that against the wishes of the chief, Atwell himself relayed Basner's advice to the tribal *pitso* which was convened on the return of the Cape Town delegation.

At this meeting a split occurred between the delegates (who had been popularly elected) and those who, with the chief, were against any form of defiance of the administration. However, those who placed their hopes in some form of official intervention were to be disappointed. At the beginning of 1948 the Chief Native Commissioner informed tribal representatives that no official enquiry would be held. The following year, amid mounting dissatisfaction, a third cull was announced – with the carrying capacity of the reserves initially lowered to 10 000 units. Meanwhile, active resistance to betterment had begun with the firing of three plantations and the destruction of two miles of a seven-strand barbed wire fence. Stock found grazing in the now unfenced areas were impounded, only to be removed by a detachment of horsemen accompanied by large numbers of women.

In January 1950 the Under-Secretary of Native Affairs addressed a meeting of chiefs. He told them that 'cattle would be reduced in spite of the feelings of natives; that huts would have to be removed from mountain slopes; that there should be cooperation on the part of the natives; that the government could make laws whereby the whole community could be punished'.[35] Despite these threats the cull of 1950 was a total failure: the few people who actually brought their stock to the cattle crush had them driven off by Basotho horsemen. The authorities were further thwarted when ten convictions for refusals to allow cullings were set aside on appeal.

On 13 February 300 horsemen, armed with sticks and knobkerries, rode up to the court house. At their head was one Nehemiah Motleheng, who handed to the Native Commissioner a letter signed by himself as 'Tribal Secretary'. The letter warned the Native Commissioner that if bloodshed was to be avoided, grazing rangers should keep away from people's stock and that stock would not be submitted for branding. Motleheng and his escort subsequently seized the chief's stock which had been assembled at the auction sale pens. In reaction the chief wrote to the Commissioner requesting the removal from the reserve of Paulus Howell Mopeli and laying the main blame for events on the conspiratorial activities of the Witzieshoek Vigilance Association.

Opposition continued on an increasingly impressive scale. In March, another posse of armed horsemen delivered 1 000 stock cards and 700 land certificates (issued as part of the betterment controls) to the Native Commissioner, giving him also a fortnight's ultimatum 'to collect everything belonging to the Trust because if we have to assist we'll do so without exercising much care'. They were as good as their word: thereafter officials were threatened and driven out of certain areas, plantations and fences were destroyed and several veld fires started. In October it was announced a commission of enquiry would finally be held.

When the commission began its sittings, the Lingangele leaders at first refused to testify, only consenting to do so after intensive persuasion from Basner and Ballinger. On the day fixed for their testimony, the Lingangele representatives arrived accompanied by 1 300 tribesmen, according to the commission members, armed in some cases with sickles, axes, assegais and knobkerries. Paulus Howell Mopeli then demanded an open sitting so that all could hear the proceedings. This being refused, the four Lingangele witnesses withdrew and only after a considerable delay were then sworn in, too late to give evidence that day. The enquiry was then adjourned to the 27th, seventeen days later. The Lingangele agreed to meet again publicly just before the commission opened, on the 27th, at Namoka, the home of Paulus Mopeli.

On the 22nd all public meetings were forbidden by proclamation. However, this prohibition had little effect. According to defence witnesses at the ensuing trial, few were aware of any ban on meetings, and 800 people converged on Paulus's kraal on the morning of the 27th. According to Atwell Mopeli, 'people wanted to protect their spokesmen by accompanying them to court',[36] but Hyman Basner managed to persuade them that the safety of the four witnesses was guaranteed and left with the witnesses at midday. However, the fears of the *khotla* seemed confirmed when shortly after their departure, 39 mounted and armed police arrived, looking for the witnesses. On being told that they had already departed, the commanding officer told the assembly it was illegal. The crowd ignored this, and according to Atwell Mopeli, continued singing the hymn they had started before the arrival of the police, 'I have a shepherd'. Other sympathetic witnesses conceded that the police were met with shouts of abuse.[37] Shooting began when the ten minutes given by the police expired (though the exact circumstances of the initial shots were unclear). The tribesmen retaliated to the first shot with sticks and stones and in a battle lasting nearly half an hour fourteen tribesmen were killed and several more wounded. Police casualties were two dead and sixteen wounded.

The sequel to the skirmishes included mass arrests and searches in the mountains along the Basotho border and a huge trial which further depleted the material resources of the Witzieshoek community.

The Witzieshoek reserve is one of the most inhospitable in South Africa. In 1950 it consisted of 50 000 acres, most of it mountainside, only 4 000 of which was cultivable. Rivers dissecting the sharp valleys and running down to the Elands River leached away the soil, depositing it by the river banks in a marshy sponge difficult to plough. Winters could be bitterly cold – today the area is being developed as an alpine sports resort.

The original population had swollen dramatically in the 1920s and 1930s as the Free State was the one area where the anti-squatting provisions of the 1913 Land Act were enforced. Between 1918 and 1951 the population almost trebled, growing from 4 700 to 14 000.[38] Two-thirds of the menfolk had to migrate to feed their families[39] and this led to a third of the arable land being left uncultivated: migrants would naturally be anxious to retain their claim to a plot even if they were not present to work on it. Given the pressures on the land and the infusion of new settlers with no connections with the original tribal community, it is not surprising that there existed large numbers of people with access to no cultivated land at all. Within the land holding majority there was great inequality in the size of land allocation. In 1916 household portions varied between one and fifty morgens, those nearest to the sub-chiefs and chiefs, who controlled land allocation, benefiting most.[40] In these circumstances stock holding was a vital condition of most people's subsistence. The land was ill-suited for cultivation and in any case there was too little land of arable quality to produce a significant portion of many people's food requirements. Cattle was for migrants the crucial means of retaining a stake in reserve society and they would invest in stock purchases, farming their cattle out with relatives and friends.[41]

The implementation of Proclamation 31 in 1939 upset a balance of survival which for many people was at best delicate. The allocation of arable land was taken out of the hands of the chieftainship and was now decided by officials on whom the community could exert no pressure whatsoever. Plots were reduced to a norm of two or three morgens which may have corrected some previous inequities (there is no evidence available to prove this) but in some cases (widows, for example) the allocation was limited to one morgen. As we have seen, those who cultivated beyond the new boundaries were severely punished. Atwell Mopeli Paulus contends that people who had no stock lost all access to arable soil as well[42] and reports a widespread sentiment that too much ground was taken up with terraces and contours. In the process of allotment, 322 local taxpayers, that is, nearly a fifth of the total, were given no land.[43] Arable land varied in quality, ranging between fertile valley soils and rocky highland. According to Edwin Mofutsanyana, writing in *Inkululeko* in 1945, the best land went to the most powerful.[44] As well as the people who lived permanently within the reserve, the survey threatened the status and material security of migrant workers living outside it for much of their lives.

The cattle culls, affecting on each occasion about ten per cent of the stock within the reserves, were uneven in their effects; Atwell Mopeli Paulus reported that the 'rich suffer little, those with a hundred lost three as did those with five or ten'.[45] His claim was supported by a local white trader who testified to the 1951 trial that 'the culling of stock was carried out haphazardly and many of the poorer natives were prejudiced by it'.[46] Some people lost oxen in the culls, and owning no draft animals, were unable to plough their allotments.[47] The prohibition on tree felling also caused hardships and much resentment: the trees had been planted by the tribespeople and free access to firewood was a traditional right. A strong sense of injustice also shaped popular protest. There was a feeling that the tribe had been deceived; there was resentment that culling regulations had not been applied to traders (who grazed large herds in Witzieshoek), that the customary rights and privileges had been interfered with, that the scheme had accentuated material inequalities.

At the heart of this feeling was the knowledge that local political institutions had lost their meaning. As Atwell Mopeli Paulus put it: 'The chief is a chief when he can give land to his people to plough and food for them to eat. A man's home is where he can fill his stomach.'[48] The chief was no longer a chief, he could no longer do these things, he was now 'a servant of the Assistant Native Commissioner' and 'the people are never consulted'.[49] And one important aspect of the rebellion of the Lingangele – 'those who stand firm' – was the attempt to reinstate traditional rights and obligations. The rebellion was led by the chief's uncle, who himself had contested Charles's claim to the paramountcy. The chief as an individual may have been reproachable for his weakness but the institution was not rejected. In conserving the paramount's herd the Lingangele was also trying to maintain the integrity of the local polity. Their insistence on open debate, on consultation between representatives and followers, on the public accountability of the leaders, was a repudiation of the new closed bureaucratic mechanisms which had recently descended on Witzieshoek. At one level the rebellion was a reaction to a widely perceived series of injustices, and did not seek a fundamental alteration in society. The initial quest for a commission of enquiry was for a solution within the existing political framework, and the ultimate rejection of the commission by the Lingangele was more on account of its potentially biased personnel than the principle it represented. The inability of local officialdom to employ the full sanction of the law in curbing resistance to betterment (because of the regulations' doubtful legal basis) was an important ingredient in determining popular attitudes to authority.

At another level, of course, the rebellion was a desperate final act of resistance to proletarianisation. Mopeli Paulus reports a common feeling that the culls 'would bring poverty to the reserve and make it indeed a reservoir of labour for the farms and the gold mines'.[50] But to attempt to define it further would be to stretch the available evidence beyond its limits: we know too little of the participants and their motives. Along which lines, for example, the community split between supporters and opponents of Charles Mopeli is not known, save that it was not along the obvious ones of socioeconomic cleavage or ethnicity. Women played an unusually active role for what was still a very patriarchal society and there were many old men among the 79 in the following trial. Both features were understandable in the context of a community where active young men were for a large part absent for most of the year. The commission made much of the rebellion's external linkages, attributing an especially conspiratorial role to the Johannesburg-based Witzieshoek Vigilance Association; but while it is evident that its members advised and may have influenced Lingangele leaders, the form the revolt took indicates that it developed originally from within the community, drawing on traditional forms of organisation and concepts of political behaviour. At the trial, both the Lingangele and the 'loyalist' supporters of the chief placed rather more faith in the activity of Lingaka (medicine men) than they did in their respective legal councils.[51]

At the time of the revolt the peasants of Witzieshoek received scant attention from political parties. Edwin Mofutsanyana, a leading African member of the Communist Party of South Africa in 1945, wrote of the people of the reserve as 'terribly backward'.[52] Dr. Xuma of the ANC ignored an appeal in 1948 for information with regard to the formation of a branch by Atwell Mopeli Paulus.[53] Lingangele leaders did meet communists in Johannesburg a week before the shooting, but what advice, if any, they received is not known. Only in retrospect would the rebellion assume a significance for African politicians, helping to prompt the Congress leadership to pay fresh attention to the problems of the countryside when defining the scope of the Defiance Campaign.

The Bafarutshe reserve, situated along the Botswana border west of Zeerust, appeared to contemporary observers in the 1950s as relatively idyllic:

> It is a land of many streams. The children are fat and well cared for, crops flourish, the oranges in season are golden, and the whole area is lush with growth.[54]

The edge of the Transvaal maize belt, which mostly coincides with the borders of the Tswana reserves, included within its limits Dinokana, the village of the senior chief, Abram Moiloa, in the southern portion of the Luhurutshe. But in fact the Bafarutshe reserve was one of the most poorly endowed, despite its scenic beauty. Its apparent lack of obvious socio-economic distress was attributable more to its relatively easy access to the labour market of the Witwatersrand than any abundance in natural resources. Half its population worked outside the reserve, either on surrounding white farms or on the Rand. Significantly, the reserves of the western Transvaal had the highest proportion of female migrants – twelve per cent as opposed to a national average of three per cent.[55] Luhurutshe was thus able to escape the effects of overcrowding, having one of the lowest population densities of any South African reserve. Until the 1950s the reserve appears to have been comparatively neglected by the Native Affairs Department. Rehabilitation measures came late and seemed to have aroused little opposition, perhaps because in an area relatively thinly populated by people or stock, their effects were less drastic than elsewhere.

The extension of influx control measures to women would have represented an especially acute threat to an area with such a dependence on external sources of employment for both its male and female population. But this does not really explain why opposition to women's passes was so strong among the Bafarutshe. One reason may have been that people had up to then been relatively unaffected by the restructuring of reserve life which had begun in other places. But the proper explanation of the revolt only fully emerges from the course of the events themselves.[56]

In March 1957 a 'mobile pass unit' arrived in the small town of Zeerust and, despite talk of a boycott, most of the women in the location, led by the wives of government employees, lined up and handed over their three and sixpences in return for their reference books. The arrival of the unit had been anticipated with much discussion, both in the location and in the nearby reserve, popular alarm being aroused by the Lichtenburg incident. Here, four men were killed after stoning police who had baton-charged a deputation of women on their way to the Native Commissioner to ask him to explain the purpose of passes.

On 28 March Chief Abram Moiloa was summoned to the office of the Native Commissioner in Zeerust and told he must order women to attend a *kgotla* in Dinokana on 1 April so they could take out reference books. Now the relationship between Moiloa and Richter, the Native Commissioner, was far from cordial. Moiloa was not the most conscientious of administrators and indeed his slackness in attending to traditional duties had led to complaints being submitted by the elders of his council to Richter's predecessor in 1952. Moiloa had received an admonishment and the matter was for the time forgotten. Richter had, however, started a fresh investigation into Moiloa's conduct in 1956, dredging up the old complaints and discovering fresh grounds for disapproval. The underlying reasons for tension between the senior chief and the Commissioner were Moiloa's reluctance to sign the Bantu Authorities Act, and his lack of enthusiasm in persuading the inhabitants of two 'black spots', Braklaagte and Leeuwfontein, to give up their farms and move into the reserve proper. Moiloa, sensitive as he was to public feeling, was similarly disinclined to promote the cause of women's influx control. On 30 March he informed his villagers of the impending arrival of the unit but dissociated himself from the issue of passes, saying: 'The matter rests between you and the white authorities.'

Two days later the unit arrived and, mindful of the chief's reluctance to be involved, established itself outside the white-owned trading store, where 76 women, mainly school teachers and the dependents of Native Affairs Department officials, took out passes. The vast majority of the women of Dinokana, 4 000 altogether, kept well away from the unit. On 5 April a public meeting was called of the whole of the adult population to listen to an announcement of the regional Chief Native Commissioner. In front of a shocked crowd, Moiloa was stripped of his office and told to leave the area within fourteen days. It was later denied that there was any connection between the deposition of Moiloa and the women's refusal to take out passes, the department claiming it had been authorised three months earlier. Coincidental or not, the deposition, which was without local precedent, was fused in peoples' minds with the issue of women's passes and served to extend and harden the basis of popular opposition. Deposition of a chief by an external authority was a matter of serious concern to all the community's menfolk who, on the question of women's passes, were only indirectly affected.

The news of the deposition spread swiftly to the Witwatersrand among the concentrations of Bafarutshe migrants in Johannesburg's Western Areas and in Pretoria's Lady Selborne. As in the case of the people of Witzieshoek, Bafarutshe migrants maintained links with each other and with their homeplace through a voluntary association, the Bafarutshe Association. They lived concentrated in certain neighbourhoods, and were noted for their isolation and apparent lack of interest in urban political activity. The coherence of the urban migrant community was demonstrated by the swiftness of their response to Moiloa's deposition. On Sunday, 8 April a meeting was held in Johannesburg and it was decided to hire buses and find out what was happening at home. That weekend a delegation of Bafarutshe women from the Witwatersrand pre-empted the men by journeying to Dinokana. They brought with them news of a new tactic, the boycott, many of them having just lived through the exciting events of the Rand bus boycott. In Dinokana there were two obvious targets: the trader who had allowed his premises to be used by the pass unit, and the school, whose female staff had taken out passes. The store's daily turnover of £50 shrank to nothing and over 1 000 of the 1 200 local school children were withdrawn from school by their parents. Retribution was swift: the school was closed down and its teachers transferred by the Native Affairs Department, whose local representative allowed himself a biblical sanction, referring to the sins of the fathers being visited on the heads of the children.

The following Sunday, 150 men arrived from the Reef in two buses and after a meeting in the village decided to put on trial the men who had in 1952 unwittingly laid the basis of Moiloa's deposition by voicing complaints against him. The trial was brutal: the old men were beaten and sentenced to death. Fortunately for them, the police arrived with the Native Commissioner. The police departed with the elders, but in the face of a large and hostile crowd made no arrests. Thereafter there began a series of acts of communal revenge (interestingly, Hooper refers to them as acts of 'cleansing', of communal purification) in which the houses of people perceived as traitors were burnt down. The school principal and his wife were the first victims of this treatment.

In the meantime the revolt spread to the smaller village of Gopane, fifteen miles from Dinokana. Here it took a slightly different course. The local chief, Albert Gopane, was popular with the village. Moiloa's deposition convinced him that passes should not be resisted, and as a result of his gentle persuasion on 10 April one-third of the village's women were ready to accept passes. As with Dinokana, the Gopane migrants had organised a deputation to the village, and on their arrival these men were angered by the chief's actions. They, the heads of the households, had not been consulted. What right had the chief to encourage their wives to take such an important step without their sanction? Sensibly, Albert Gopane fled from that village that Easter weekend, and in his absence the men collected the reference books from those women who had them and burnt them publicly.

This is not the place to trace further developments in detail. Charles Hooper, the Anglican priest in Zeerust, who was falsely attributed with the major responsibility for the revolt by the authorities, has written a moving account, *Brief Authority*. In it he chronicles the various acts of official retribution. These first took the form of trivial harassment: the refusal of permits to doctors to enter the reserve; the insistence by the local tax office that taxes could be paid only by reference book holders; the cessation of pension distribution in villages where women had refused books; the discontinuation of the bus service to Zeerust; the closure of the post office. These served only to stiffen resistance as it spread through the villages in the reserves. A special police unit, which had been formed in Pretoria, the Police Mobile Column, began a series of raids on Luhurutshe, visiting the intransigent villages, beating up known resisters and people who refused to show them the way to their homes, making many night arrests and creating a climate of terror throughout the area. From April, a series of trials (most of which ended in acquittals, because for women to refuse a pass was not an illegal act) served to drain the community of its savings. Where the column was most active, near Dinokana and Braklaagte and Leeuwfontein, fields near the roadside were left untended, a development which anticipated a complete breakdown of the agricultural cycle as repression later spread to other parts of the reserve.

In June and July there was a lull in the activities of the police. But in August, after the appearance in Gopane of a Tswana-speaking stranger who encouraged the women 'to clear away rubbish' by burning it in the fire he lit, the remaining pass holders in the village destroyed their books. Subsequently, the Police Mobile Column came and compiled a list of about twelve women to present themselves for arrest a few days later. When the police vehicle arrived that day, over 200 women had assembled, all claiming that they had burnt their passes. Eventually, after much argument, two railway buses were commissioned to collect them and take them to Zeerust, where eventually they were told not to listen to Congress agitators. A common conviction amongst the police concerned was that the troubles were externally instigated by the ANC. The women were then told to go home and await their trial. The women replied that they had listened to no agitators from Johannesburg and that they themselves formed a 'Congress village'. Furthermore, they wanted nothing to do with their chief and wished him to depart from their village along with the police and other accomplices. And they refused to go home unless transport was provided. On the day of the trial similar tactics prevailed, this time over 400 women presenting themselves to the exasperated police officer and eventually forming a procession behind him singing their new songs composed during the troubles with the refain:

> Behold us joyful
> The women of Africa
> In the presence of our baas
> The great one
> Who conquers Lefurutshe
> With his knobkerrie
> And his asegei
> And his gun.

When they were tired of walking they sat down and demanded to rest for the night. The police returned to Zeerust without their unwanted charges and the case collapsed.

Farce was succeeded by tragedy. A commission of enquiry was set up in Zeerust in November which served mainly as a platform for local officialdom to denounce ANC agitation. Bafarutshe witnesses accompanied by thousands of fellow tribesmen were on two occasions prevented by police baton charges and low-flying Harvard aircraft from reaching Zeerust. Pass-burning spread to Witkleigat and Motswedi – this time the women concerned were swiftly arrested and sentenced to six months' prison for damaging government property. That month the police acquired local reinforcements: chiefs who had supported the issue of passes were encouraged to conscript bodyguards. The bodyguards instituted a reign of terror in each village. Husbands of women pass offenders were dragged before 'tribal' courts and subjected to heavy fines in stock and cash. In the case of Witleigat, where bodyguards had been in the habit of screening alighting passengers at the bus stop for 'ANC types', in December they were attacked by returning migrants from Johannesburg. After dealing with the bodyguards, the crowd marched to the kgotla and demanded the presence of the chief. He had fled, leaving his wife to be beaten up by the infuriated villagers who also destroyed his home and his new Chrysler motor car. One of the bodyguards was killed. In the aftermath of 70 arrests by the Mobile Column, another 36 houses belonging to supporters of the chief were gutted by fire.

January found the reserve in a state of virtual civil war, as a wave of arson attacks took place on those who had cooperated with the authorities (who included members of the Zionist church in Leeuwfontein), as chiefs and bodyguards fought back and as the police went from household to household in a search for evidence of ANC affiliation and weapons. A ban on meetings was imposed on the reserve in November and entry into it was prohibited in February 1958. Behind this legal screen the police lost all restraint and in one incident involving the arrest of one of the few genuine Bafarutshe ANC members in Gopane, killed four people. Two thousand people fled over the borders to settle in miserable encampments in Bechuanaland. The Zeerust revolt was over.

Its almost logical sequel took place on 7 August 1959 when, with elaborate ceremony, a Bantu Authority was established in Luhurutshe, presided over by Chief Lucas Mangope, whose family at Montswedi had distinguished themselves by the alacrity with which they had cooperated with the authorities. On this occasion, Chief Lucas (who was destined for much higher office) delighted his critics by imploring the Minister of Bantu Administration to 'lead us and we shall try to crawl'.[57]

How does one account for the extent and intensity of the Bafarutshe women's resistance? The region's reliance on the Reef labour market provides a tempting explanation. But in the accounts we have, the fear of being cut off from sources of employment does not figure prominently in the women's perception of their situation. Their prime concern was for the effects of the pass on the integrity of the household:

> When the men are fined, when the men are sent to jail, we can still care for the children. But what of their babies, when the women must carry these passports to prison. Who will care for the crops when we are arrested for pass offences?[58]

Their husbands too, as we have seen in the case of Gopane, viewed the issue in terms of external interference with their family domain. But such sentiments were not unique to the Marico district. What was unusual was the entanglement of passes with the question of the rights and prerogatives of the chieftancy. Such matters had an especial force in a district where, because the incidence of landlessness was low and serious socio-economic inequalities were absent,[59] traditional political relationships had been conserved to a possibly greater degree than elsewhere. The fact that the western Transvaal reserves were previously relatively unaffected by land rehabilitation measures and the conflicts and repression arising out of them, also helps to explain the initial determination not to accept passes. Amongst the neighbouring Barolong, in Genesa, Vryburg, Chief Setlhoapile declared himself opposed to passes and commanded the women in his village to refuse the reference books.[60]

How the community divided during the conflict is another problem. Hooper's account makes it clear that many of the minority of active government supporters were physically intimidated. But this could have not been the only consideration. There were small groups of government employees who were unwilling to risk their relatively privileged status and local livelihood. Then certain families actually gained significantly from the disturbances: it brought to the Mangopes both political office through government patronage and material wealth. Montswedi villagers could be fined as much as £5 or an animal in the chief's courts for burning their passes or refusing to join Mangope's bodyguard.[61]

The rebellion began as an act of conservation. By its close it had qualitatively changed. The deposition and subsequent behaviour of Moiloa's fellow chiefs served to undermine established loyalties. The women themselves began to demonstrate a consciousness of their importance within the village community and a sense of collective unity:

> Jail is a good school. When we went in we knew nothing. Now we are able to talk all day to our people from Johannesburg and to the women of other villages. We got organised in jail. We agree about those books; we know what they are for and we agree to refuse them.[62]

Even their singing had become more assertive and aggressive, reflecting a perception of their independence and strength compared to the helplessness before authority of men: 'Basadi bachola di-pas' ('The women carry passes and now they are just like men'). New patterns of identification emerged. Four young women in Witkleigat were subjected to 'tribal justice' for allegedly forming a branch of the ANC Women's League.[63] The charge may have been fabricated but it was nonetheless true that the constant accusations of Congress affiliation actually promoted identification and sympathy for Congress among the Bafarutshe. Ironically, the ANC leadership in Johannesburg were slow to react to and largely ignorant of events in Luhurutshe. An ANC branch had existed in Zeerust location since 1947[64] but it appears to have been inactive during the rebellion and Congress officials sent down from Johannesburg were unaware of the existence of any local ANC members.[65] External contributions to the struggle were important in determining its course: the experience of urban protest brought home by migrants influenced the form of resistance, as with the school and store boycott. The trial of elders in Dinokana was on the initiative of the migrants and was itself seen by the remainder of the village as a violation of custom. Migrant Bafarutshe, despite their association with each other on the Reef, would inevitably be freer of traditional ideological notions of propriety and they were thus an important catalyst in the popular reassessment of old loyalties.

The most dramatic instances of rural unrest took place in the Transkei. In the case of the Mpondo inhabiting the Bizana, Flagstaff and Lusikisiki districts in the north-east of the reserve, revolt took a uniquely structured and organised form and it is this feature which presents the main problem of any analysis. In brief, the Mpondo revolt lasted over a period of nine months, when resistance to rehabilitation and Bantu Authorities coalesced in 1960 under a hierarchical organisation.[66] This developed originally from local meetings held by each cluster of kraals to discuss difficulties, but soon became formalised as representatives from each group began to meet regularly at a hill near the village of Bizana. These meetings were public and came to be dominated by a small leadership group which appeared to have been selected more by ability than any ascribed status. The organisation, known as *Intaba* (the mountain), came to dominate the affairs of an area of about 4 000 square kilometres embracing a population of 180 000. By May, Intaba was in the process of establishing itself as an alternative political authority to the prevalent order, assuming, for instance, the functions of chiefs' courts in settling land allocation matters and other disputes, but in particular exerting great pressure on chiefs and headmen in the area to denounce and reject Bantu Authorities. Those who refused to listen to its bidding were punished: emissaries would be sent with the message 'the horsemen are coming' and warned to vacate their kraals, which in the event were burnt to the ground. If the recalcitrant chief remained he would be killed, though care was exercised not to physically harm any of his dependants. Seventeen chiefs, headmen or their bodyguards died through Intaba-inspired activity and a further five victims were suspected police informers. As a result there was a complete breakdown of the Bantu Authority system, many chiefs taking refuge in special camps in Bizana and Umzimkulu set up for the purpose.

The initial heavy-handed reaction by the authorities served only to intensify the revolt. A meeting at the foot of Ngquza Hill in Flagstaff called to discuss punitive action against the Eastern Mpondo paramount Botha Sigcau,[67] and attended by 400 tribesmen, was attacked by a specially assembled force of police. Eleven Mpondo men were killed, most shot in the back. In the following week 29 kraals belonging to government supporters were destroyed. An alarmed Bantu Affairs Commissioner at Bizana called for a mass meeting at Ndlovu Hill to discuss arrangements for the return of the chiefs who had fled, to appoint men to act in their place, and to request the meeting to nominate representatives to act as census enumerators. The first two points were refused discussion by the meeting – no one was prepared to assume chiefly office – and the third flatly rejected.

Meanwhile large numbers of Mpondo were being arrested and charged with murder, and high bail charges were beginning to drain the financial resources of Intaba, which initally drew on a membership levy exerted on all who attended the meetings. The leaders began to look for fresh sources of support, putting pressure on both African and European traders in the area to provide money, as well as lorries for transport to meetings and grain to support the dependants of those on trial. African traders, operating on small profit margins and living within the Mpondo communities, were very susceptible to pressure and took out £5 'licences', but in the case of white traders, boycotts of their stores had to be organised to induce cooperation. These were remarkably successful – a simultaneous boycott of three stores in one instance testifying to the discipline the organisation was able to impose on the community at a time of year when locally grown grain supplies would have been exhausted. Whether the Mpondo succeeded in gaining much financial assistance from white traders is not documented, but in November a traders' delegation to the Bizana magistrate apparently pleaded for a more conciliatory approach to the Mpondo.

In July the authorities established a commission of enquiry which had the probably intended effect of defusing tensions temporarily while grievances were submitted by tribespeople. From the time of its sitting aggressive actions against chiefs eased, though the mountain movement consolidated its influence by channelling popular militancy into a tax strike and a mass refusal to cooperate with the census enumerators. During this period a memorandum was prepared and dispatched with Mpondo representative, Enoch Mbhele, a Bizana tinsmith, to the United Nations.[68] This action and the testimony of witnesses to the commission showed a remarkable awareness of the wider context of their struggle, objections being made to Bantu Education, the lack of African political representation in parliament, restrictions on movement as the result of the pass laws, as well as more local wrongs. On 11 October, the Commissioner's conclusions were made public to a meeting of 15 000 Mpondos at Bizana airfield. It was conceded that certain minor grievances should be rectified, though within the existing political framework. All other complaints concerning taxation, influx control, and political representation were unfounded. Neither rehabilitation measures nor Bantu Authorities would cease to be operative.

The findings of the commission, together with the withdrawal of bail and the subsequent detentions in the following months, set the stage for the climax of the revolt. On 1 November 3 000 Mpondos accompanied their leaders into Bizana to witness their arrest, and then entrances into the villages were picketed and a trading boycott instituted with the purpose of persuading traders to make representations on behalf of the Mpondos to the authorities. From the 5th, unsuccessful attempts were also made to extend the boycott to labour recruiting agencies. The boycott was to continue until 5 January 1961, but in the meantime the three districts affected by the revolt were subjected to a massive police operation under the cover of a state of emergency proclamation. Nearly 5 000 people were arrested, interned in screening centres, and in some cases treated with great brutality. During this period all semblance of normal life disappeared. Cultivation ground to a halt and families were impoverished as they were forced to sell livestock so as to pay tax defaulting fines. On 5 January the boycott of Bizana was lifted and by the end of February resistance had collapsed to the extent that hundreds of tribesmen in Lusikisiki had taken part in humiliating public apologies to the paramount chief, Botha Sigcau.

The grievances underlying the revolt were not dissimilar to those which existed elsewhere: objections to land rehabilitation, heavier taxation as the region – like other reserve areas – began to contribute more to its administration, and an increasingly authoritarian local government. As elsewhere, rehabilitation had laid a heavy burden on the poorest members of the community. For example, the prohibition on keeping goats (disliked by conservationists because of their destructive feeding habits) removed access to the cheapest form of livestock.[69] Livestock taxation also trebled from the beginning of the rehabilitation scheme. An interesting point made by the UN memoranda concerned the switch to 'stabilisation'. The scope of the work of agricultural officers had been sharply restricted:

> Paid by our poll tax they are now remaining not to help us but to harm us. All that they do is to show us how to make barricades to prevent soil erosion. They no longer teach us improved methods of agriculture.[70]

Like other Nguni peoples, the Mpondo, not generally living in villages, had a particular objection to the concentration of settlement which could often distance them from their fields. But these complaints were not unique to Pondoland. While they formed an important part of the backdrop of the revolt, and informed the participants' subjective perceptions of the situation, they do little to explain the unusually structured and coherent form of the Mpondo revolt. However, when one turns to the local problems arising from the imposition of Bantu Authorities a possible explanation begins to emerge.

In the case of the eastern Mpondo districts, the paramount chieftancy was an unusually powerful institution, Mpondoland being the last area to be annexed by the Cape authorities, and the chief retained greater powers than traditional authorities elsewhere in the Transkei. This situation was reflected in the formation of the Tribal (Bantu) Authorities. Whereas normally taxpayers elected a quarter of the new councillors, the rest being chosen by the Native Commissioner and headmen (this was subject, of course, to pressure from the local chief, but was also susceptible to some influence from their community) in the case of Pondoland the paramount chose 75 per cent of the councillors, the balance being nominated by the Native Commissioner.[71] In such circumstances the personality of the paramount was very important. Botha Sigcau, having acceded to the paramountcy in 1938 as the less legitimate candidate in a succession dispute, owed his position to government patronage. Under his influence, especially after 1958 when he accepted Bantu Authorities despite the vociferous disapproval of his subjects, local government became especially corrupt. The Act, as we know, tended to remove communal sanctions on the behaviour of local authorities, and in eastern Pondoland there were unusually widespread reports of venality in such matters as land allocation, justice, and access to higher authority. Local chiefs additionally enriched themselves by imposing entirely novel charges, on, for example, the cutting of thatching grass or firewood.

In contrast to the rebellions discussed earlier, the traditional political structure was completely discredited and consequently dissatisfaction was unlikely to cohere around any representative of the old order. This was also in part a function of time: in the case of Witzieshoek and Zeerust people were responding to crises of fairly recent origin. By 1960 in the Transkei, on the other hand, disaffection had been simmering for well over a decade and had often previously been expressed in violent terms. A final point to remember about chiefs in Pondoland is that the unusual degree of power they retained within the pre-apartheid political framework allowed them to be the main beneficiaries of any increases in surplus agricultural production (Mpondoland was still exporting grain in the late 1920s).[72] In contrast to the rural societies of the Transvaal and the Orange Free State, internal class differentiation was probably wider. In 1968, nearly 20 per cent of Bizana district households had no land at all, another 75 per cent had less than 10 acres, and a small minority representing 0.25 per cent of the population – perhaps 800 people in all – were members of homesteads with more than 36 acres.[73] Confronted with the almost total incorporation of traditional leaders into an illegitimate social and political order, the Mpondo were compelled to create new leadership structures.

While the agitational and conspiratorial theories resorted to at the time by government spokesmen to explain the Mpondo revolt had no factual basis, it is possible that modern political groups may have provided some suggestive models. On the whole the influence of African political parties in the countryside was, by the 1950s, negligible, but the Transkei and the Ciskei had been less neglected than other reserves. In the handwritten minutes of the 1946 ANC annual conference, there is a reference to 'strong [Congress] activity in eastern Pondoland',[74] and the Cape provincial executive of 1958 claimed to be organising Transkei and Ciskei branches,[75] though there is no subsequent evidence of their activity. In Mount Ayliff in the neighbouring Zesibe District, a clandestine organisation, the Kongo, was formed in 1947 with the object of replacing a chief who had complied with rehabilitation. Two of its delegates appeared at an All-African Convention conference the following year.[76] Mbeki, then secretary of the Transkei Organised Bodies, was later to claim that 'Kongo' was a local rendering of 'Congress'.[77]

During the revolt itself the Mpondo leadership did have contacts with Congress members, though these did not begin until June. The Mountain leadership's appeal to the Mpondo Association in Durban introduced them to the Congress movement through the Association's chairman, Leonard Mdingi, an important local ANC member. Until his restriction order in October, the Durban attorney, Rowley Arenstein, a Congress of Democrat activist, provided valuable legal assistance and helped to raise money. Anderson Ganyile, a young Youth Leader expelled from Fort Hare, acted as a secretary to the Mountain committee when he returned home to Bizana. Such contacts were likely to shape perceptions of Intaba leaders. Mbeki claims that a Mpondo meeting 'adopted' the Freedom Charter.[78]

But one should not exaggerate these external influences. Much of the strength of the Mpondo revolt stemmed from precisely the lack of local familiarity with bureaucratic forms of political mobilisation. The reluctance to appoint delegates or spokesmen to advance their grievances (commission witnesses refused to identify themselves, Native Commissioners were summoned to public meetings) made it almost impossible for the authorities to defuse the situation through negotiation or co-option. Instead, the Mpondo worked through pressure and carefully orchestrated demonstrations of power, isolating their opponents and forcing potential allies to define their loyalties. The final strength of the movement was that it was drawn principally from youngish men of working age. 1959 and 1960 were years of a slump in the sugar industry and there was consequently considerable unemployment on the Natal sugar fields, which drew most of their workforce from the district affected by the revolt; as a result, in 1960 an unusually high proportion of the normally absent migrant workers had had to remain within the reserve.[79]

In terms of the extent of communal mobilisation and discipline the Mpondo rebellion was perhaps the most impressive of these rural risings. Its self-control extended to the deployment of violence which was discriminate and limited. In contrast, for our final case study of rural unrest, we now turn to a movement which included an unusual quality of insurrectionism.

The Tembu inhabit the Elliotdale, Mqanduli, Umtata and Engcobo districts of the Transkei, and a related subgroup, the Emigrant Tembu, live in the Cala and St. Marks districts, as well as enjoining Glen Grey, until 1964 administered as part of the Ciskei. The districts form a band of territory running for 250 miles across the southern portion of the Transkei. It is mainly highland, between 4 000 and 5 000 feet, with difficult communications and a landscape of badly eroded grass-covered hummocky hills. In contrast to Mpondoland, most of the working male population went westwards in labour contracts, mainly to the farms, services and industries of the western Cape, many of them living in the hostels of Langa described in Chapter 9.

Politics in Tembuland, as in other parts of the Transkei up to 1955, had revolved around the General Council, half the members of which were indirectly elected. The General Council, or Bunga, tended to be a rather compliant institution, its members, for example, supporting the rehabilitation programme from its inception, in contrast to those of the Ciskeian council. The majority were chiefs and headmen.

Nevertheless, despite its limitations, the abolition of the Bunga and its replacement by Bantu Authorities was unpopular and it was opposed in the various public meetings held to announce the introduction of the latter. The Bantu Authorities were also greeted with disfavour by many chiefs, especially in those areas which had been most resistant to rehabilitation measures. Of these, Tembuland was especially recalcitrant, being in 1961 almost untouched by any rehabilitation work. In May 1961, 1 000 Tembu chiefs condemned the scheme at a meeting summoned by the paramount, Chief Sabata Dalindyebo. In Emigrant Tembuland, however, which was under the authority of Chief Kaiser Matanzima, Chairman of the Transkei Territorial Assembly (the highest echelon Bantu Authority), the scheme was 'accepted' by most locations by 1960. However, the district magistrate was to admit that despite '100 per cent' endorsement of the scheme, shortly afterwards illegal meetings were held and anti-rehabilitation groups formed.[80] By 1960, rehabilitation proposals included the concentration of holdings into 'economic units', which taken to its logical conclusion would have made a further 113 000 Transkeian families landless.[81] In Matanzima's district, the scheme began to be implemented in 1962: it was intended that 2 400 consolidated farming units would be produced, and people began to be removed from their land to make room for a showpiece irrigation scheme.[82] It is worth remembering that this area, being the main source of migrant labour for the western Cape, would have been the most seriously affected by this region's coloured labour preference policies and by the expulsions from the peninsula which began in the late 1950s. Families forced off their holdings and into an ever greater degree of dependence on migrant earnings were confronted with increasing difficulties in finding employment opportunities outside the reserve.

Some of the dissatisfaction aroused by rehabilitation and Bantu Authorities in the 1950s had been channelled into political organisations. The African National Congress had little local influence. In 1954 it was still looking to the soon-to-be retired Bunga councillors for support.[83] But many local associations had affiliated to the All-African Convention (see Chapter 4). As a Cape parliamentary constituency Tembuland had traditionally the highest African vote, a testimony to the degree of impact of mission institutions. Electoral politics were for the most part an elitist affair but they may have contributed to the development of a wider political consciousness. In 1952, the Transkei Organised Bodies, which in the 1940s was responsible for the electoral boycotts of Native Representative elections, claimed the allegiance of fifteen different organisations – farmers' associations and vigilante groups, which had sent 200 delegates to its Mount Frere conference.[84]

In the 1960s resistance to rehabilitation and political restructuring in Tembu-inhabited areas assumed an increasingly violent form. As well as the grievances which underlay rural discontent everywhere, several factors distinguished the situation in Tembuland. Interference in land tenure and allocation arrangements had contributed to a feeling of insecurity among those Emigrant Tembu small-holders who were actually affected by consolidation, and would have seemed especially threatening to Tembu elsewhere. The effects of landlessness, an acute problem for at least two decades, were accentuated with the western Cape resettlements and the tightening web of influx control. Another important influence must have been the experience of Tembu migrants who mainly worked in the western Cape. The Cape peninsula had been the scene of the most dramatic upheavals in the crisis of March 1960. As we have seen (Chapter 9) migrant workers played a leading role in these. The PAC, which provided some political direction during the crisis, was especially influential in the workers' hostels. From the suppressed PAC developed the violent insurrectionary movement, Poqo. The movement, growing in the locations around Cape Town and smaller towns of the western Cape, drew its mass support from migrant workers (see Chapter 10). There may have been other influences affecting the political consciousness of western Cape migrant workers (Congress-affiliated trade unions were quite active in the western Cape) but it is likely that in the years following Sharpeville the Poqo movement was the most important.

The Tembu disturbances were sporadic and disjointed. Much of the unrest occurred under the draconian provisions of Proclamation 400, which imposed a state of emergency regulation on the Transkei in response to the Mpondo disturbances. In 1956, following the establishment of Bantu Authorities in Emigrant Tembuland, people in Cala and Glen Grey tried on several occasions to prevent the installation of pro-government chiefs.[85] In Tembuland proper, opposition to Bantu Authorities was influenced by the rivalry between the Paramount Chief, Sabata, and Matanzima, the regional chief of the Emigrant Tembu. Matanzima had gained government patronage as a result of his support for Bantu Authorities and he was busy expanding his area of jurisdiction. In 1958 the Ciskeian district of Glen Grey was placed under his control. His ascendancy was feared by Sabata and this helped to colour his attitudes to Bantu Authorities. Four of his advisers who had presented a memorandum to the Bantu Administration Department in Pretoria on 'The difficulties and tension arising from the imposition of Bantu Authorities' were deported at the behest of the Minister.[86]

The Tembu had successfully held up the progress of rehabilitation in their area but in the late 1950s there were renewed efforts by officials to limit stock and fence-off pasture and cultivated land. The region under Matanzima's control was especially affected, for here officials were supported by chiefs and headmen. Communities which attempted to hold out against the establishment of the Authorities were severely punished, a particularly notorious (but not atypical) incident taking place at Rwantsana near Lady Frere. Following the murder of an unpopular headman (preceded by the killing of three of his sheep), police, reinforced by men from Qamata, Matanzima's location, arrived and started rounding up the Rwantsana menfolk. Fighting broke out between the Qamata and Rwantsana people, which was quelled only when police fired their sten guns into the mêlée. Scores of men were then arrested and 35 subsequently charged.[87] In other locations in Lady Frere, Matanzima's impis were allowed considerable licence by the police. In Bolotwa, for example, over 100 huts were burnt by the chief's supporters with no official retribution. In 1960 one chief and eleven other people, regarded as government accomplices, were killed in Tembuland; though there was a decline in the number of killings the following year the killings obviously helped to influence the 1 000 or so chiefs who publicly declared their opposition to rehabilitation and Bantu Authorities at Sabata's kraal in Bumbane in two meetings held in May 1061 and 1962.[88]

In late 1962 there were three attempts on Matanzima's life. One will be described in detail below. All were Poqo-inspired. The first attack was on 14 October and was preceded by reports of Poqo 'preaching race hate' to the peasantry in Emigrant Tembuland.[89] Poqo activity was not limited to Emigrant Tembuland. Court trials provided evidence of Poqo influence in the Engcobo district as well as the Mpondo areas around Ngqeleni where 48 men were imprisoned for Poqo activities.[90] In Engcobo a 35-member Poqo cell was led by a chief and a school teacher.[91] At Bashee Bridge a white family was killed when their caravan was attacked by men who, according to the police, came from Mqanduli, Cofimvaba, Kentani and Bityi.[92] This was an unusually brutal incident: when headmen were attacked their families were usually left unharmed.

In 1963 the Engcobo and Umtata districts were said to be the most violent in the Transkei. Large numbers of people were arrested and accused of Poqo membership (the extent of Poqo affiliation is likely to have been considerably exaggerated). Mobile police units were brought in to suppress disturbances.[93] Illegal and violent opposition to the Authorities coincided with elections. In Tembuland hostility to Matanzima was reflected at the polls in an almost total defeat for his candidates. The year 1963 appears to have been the peak of the peasant unrest in Tembuland. By 1964, Chief Matanzima had enhanced powers through his control of the Transkeian government (as a result of support of nominated members of the territorial assembly). Chiefs who had stood out against Bantu Authorities were being intimidated or induced to support them. A drought which lasted until 1969, forcing another 35 000 Transkeians onto the labour market and killing a fifth of the territory's cattle, served to further demoralise popular resistance. One immediate provocation had in any case been removed: the semi-autonomous Matanzima administration made no attempt to implement any stock limitation measures thereafter.[94]

Before forming any conclusions about the unrest a closer look at two of the incidents will provide a clearer understanding of what was happening in the Tembu districts.

On 12 December 1962 a group of between twenty and thirty Poqo members travelled by train from Cape Town to the Transkei, with the intention of assembling with other groups near Qamata and launching a co-ordinated attack on Christmas Day on Matanzima's palace. According to the trial evidence, similar groups had already left.[95] Most of the twenty men later put on trial had been Poqo members since early 1961, but although there had been several meetings in the previous months the immediate preparations for the attack were only discussed at a meeting in Langa township on 10 December. At this and subsequent meetings members were told to contribute £6 for the railway ticket, and to collect weapons. The attack was supposed to incorporate the freeing of prisoners in Qamata jail who had been captured in earlier attempts on Matamzima's life. On the night before their departure a herbalist doctored the men by making incisions on their foreheads and rubbing in herbs.[96] Their weapons, which included a revolver carried by the cell's leader, were also treated.

Thus prepared, the men entrained the following morning. Most of them had not had the chance to give their employers an excuse for leaving their jobs and so, as well as forfeiting their pay packets, they had come away without getting their pass books signed. Their train arrived at Queenstown at 7.00 pm on the 13th. Here it was obvious that the police had been warned because they ordered everybody off the train and made them line up on the platform, where they began searching the passengers for weapons. On their discovery of a panga, the Poqo men made a concerted attack on the police, killing one of them and wounding several others. After a few minutes of fighting, police reinforcements arrived and the Poqo men retreated and tried to escape to a nearby hillside. Most were captured within the next day or two. Another group who had journeyed from Cape Town a few days earlier had succeeded in reaching Ntlonze mountain, near Cofimvaba, the rallying-point for the attackers,[97] but by now large impis and police units were searching the hills and the attack was not made.

The conspirators were all migrant workers; most of them did unskilled work in the construction industry or in various factories. They were mainly Emigrant Tembu and their home villages or districts included Glen Grey, Alice, Cala, St Marks, Qamata and Tsomo. Their wives and families were mentioned in the evidence as living in those places. It is clear that they regarded the Transkei as their home, and the evidence describing the various Poqo meetings in Langa indicates that they shared the same anxieties and preoccupations as the rural Tembu population. One was arrested with a letter from his mother in his pocket which contained a reference to his land being taken away,[98] and this was a predominating theme at meetings in Langa:

> The first thing he [Matanzima] did was to introduce fencing and now he is moving huts and kraals to some other place. It appears that he has sold the plots where the kraals were to the Europeans because there are huts there.* Now he is assaulting us . . .[99] Chief Matanzima has sold our land; we are going to kill him.[100]

The fencing and the other activities of the Native (Rehabilitation) Trust in St. Marks began to be discussed at Langa Poqo meetings in July 1962.

That the Poqo men were closely in touch with local realities is borne out by the second incident, which again arose out of conditions in the St. Marks district. As we have seen, discontent with land rehabilitation had led to the formation of secret village committees. In the middle of February 1963 the authorities tried to suppress these groups. In Qitsi the local headman was provided with some police from Qamata, and with these and other men he raided the kraals of leading critics of the land measures. Their houses were

---

*Note: the Europeans were experts who were there to construct a dam as part of the Qamata irrigation scheme (see page 284).

destroyed and some of their stock was taken.[101] However, the anti-trust men had already left Qitsi and found shelter in a kraal in Qulugu, Engcobo district, eight miles away across the hills. Quite apart from the headman's action, there was considerable anger in Qitsi because Matanzima had sent a large impi, which included fifty policemen, to search the area (possibly for Poqo men) and the location had had to provide food for them. There had also been removals. Though the headman was known to be rather reluctant to organise the fencing, he had had to do so: he had thus become 'the man who informs the people about the regulations'.[102] The bitterness of the feeling against him can be judged from the fact that among the men who killed him were two nephews and a man known to be 'a very great friend' of the headman.[103]

These men decided to kill the headman when they were at Qulugu. Rather inexplicably, they sent him a threatening letter which resulted in his being given a bodyguard and a revolver. The group at Qulugu were first treated by a herbalist who made incisions on their arms, foreheads and cheekbones. Then, on the night of the 26th, they marched to Qitsi, overpowered the bodyguards, dragged the headman out of his kraal and killed him. His family were allowed to leave the hut, which was then burnt down. There had been no attempt at secrecy (the bodyguards were allowed to get away) and shortly afterwards the conspirators were arrested.

There is a consistency in the details of these and other incidents during the Tembu unrest. Both conspiracies involved men who were, or had been, migrant workers (the Qitsi men were, with one exception, over thirty, and some of them had spent long periods in Cape Town). In both events there was a certain amount of traditional ritual used in the preparations. In both, the politically inspired Poqo men and the apolitical Qitsi group, the men felt threatened by the land rehabilitation scheme.

The involvement of Poqo in Tembu unrest is an indication of how local discontent could become consciously political. Poqo was not a movement that was brought into the Transkei by outsiders: its chief following was among migrant workers. It could be adapted to local traditions, beliefs and institutions. One man said at his trial that he had joined Poqo and 'its sort of church, Qamata' in 1961: Qamata is mentioned by Philip Mayer as a high god or ruler of the spirits that was commonly a feature of Red (traditionalist) Xhosa religious belief.[104] Nationalist politics had not previously gained much of a following among Red Xhosa migrants. A report that Poqo was linked to the Makuluspan,[105] and the existence of a Poqo group which was led by an Engcobo chief, are further indications of the considerable degree of support it may have had in Tembuland and the surrounding districts.

The Tembu disturbances lacked the coherence, unity and dramatic quality of the Pondo revolt. Unlike the Pondo, they evolved no clear strategy nor did they formulate a series of demands that went beyond the immediate causes of their hardships. Although one should not overestimate the part played in the events by Poqo, this weakness was very much its own: it was an insurrectionary movement which saw politics in the apocalyptic terms of a general uprising. Contrast this with the Mpondo store boycott which discriminated between those traders reckoned to be sympathetic and those who openly sided with the government.

One point should be made about the migrant workers. These men were not at that time a proletariat: they were not completely 'free' of access to the means of production. They still felt that land rehabilitation measures were a threat to their livelihood. Though the men who set out from Cape Town to attack Matanzima would probably have been destined to spend most of their working lives in the Langa hostels, nevertheless they were going to kill Matanzima because he was taking away their land. It has been suggested that the different experience of oppression for the worker, on the one hand, and his family in the reserve, on the other, introduces 'a structural division in the heart of the proletariat'. The worker would focus his opposition on the relations of production in the towns, while rural people would attack chiefs and headmen.[106] But in the 1960s this was not the case; migrants, at that time were not so detached from rural consciousness. Today things might be different: when people are forced off the land completely so that their entire subsistence depends on migrant wages, and when the migrant worker does not have the remotest prospect of ceasing to work in the towns and returning to his cattle and land, then perhaps he has become a member of an urban proletariat. In the early 1960s his situation was a transitional one.

It is in this context that his political reactions should be examined. At a time when the stay-away from work was the chief weapon of the nationalist movement, migrant workers hitherto had been considered apathetic politically, and the scale of their response to the Pan-Africanist Congress anti-pass campaign in 1960 surprised witnesses in Cape Town. Here they were responding to the frustrations of urban conditions: low wages, influx control, separation from their families and police raids. They could also be concerned about agricultural conditions: drought, rain, cattle sickness and the state of the fields.[107] This divided response could have been capitalised on by a well-organised political movement. Poqo was not that: it was an expression of a general desperation felt both in the reserves and in the locations, not a sophisticated organisation.

Traditional authorities also found themselves in an ambivalent position. The popularity of certain chiefs in Tembuland, the participation of one of their number in Poqo, even the Qitsi headman's lack of enthusiasm for implementing rehabilitation, is further evidence that the transformation from consensus gatherer to government functionary was not always undertaken willingly. Their change in function deprived them of legitimacy: their actions were an offence against tradition and custom. In this context the use of ritual and traditional beliefs by the Poqo movement and Qitsi villagers was significant.

But old loyalties, in contrast to Mpondoland, were not yet completely subverted. This, with the conspiritorial and apocalyptic features of the Poqo movement itself, mitigated against the emergence of a more structured and disciplined revolt.

Although the incidents described in this chapter were chosen because of their especially dramatic quality, they were not untypical of the experience of

Africans living in the countryside between 1940 and 1965. Rural revolt was extraordinarily widespread in South Africa, affecting vast numbers of people throughout the country. But with notable exceptions it was largely a parochial affair. Black rural communities are peculiarly isolated by vast distances, by the reserve system, and systematic barriers controlling the flow of people and ideas between town and countryside. Also, these were still peasant revolts: though the economic foundations of a peasant mode of existence had long been subverted, the contribution to peoples' subsistence represented by homestead output was still important enough to determine their subjective responses. As we have seen, the shape each revolt took was influenced by the degree in each case of social differentiation and ideological disintegration brought about in each rural community by the demands of a wider economic and political system. But these are variations of degree not kind. The reserve revolts of this period were all the result of a single historical process emanating from the centre. To an extent they helped to shape this process as well as frustrating its intended course. At times they were even, in terms of immediate aims, victorious. But the resilience of rural reaction depended on the survival of at least a residual peasant mode of production. By the mid-1960s, under the impact of the state rural resettlement policies (average rural population doubled between 1955 and 1969),[108] even a caricature of this had disappeared in many parts of the countryside.

Only intermittently was there contact between the rebellion in the countryside and the political movements of the towns. In this context, the Ciskei was exceptional, the result of the proximity of East London and the social characteristics of its population. Here, as we saw in Chapter 2, the ANC established an organised following. Subscription records indicate the existence in 1953 of ten branches in Pedi districts alone with over 1 000 paid-up members.[109] But on the whole the ANC's influence in the countryside was limited. At the end of the 1940s its leaders still worked to retain the loyalty of the chiefs rather than seeking to attract a more popular rural following. ANC leaders of the 1950s were conscious of the extent of popular unrest and from 1955 there are references to an organisation called Sebata Kgomo (a traditional Sesotho call to arms) which, under the leadership of the Bapedi farmworkers' organiser, Elijah Mampuru, apparently built up Transvaal rural support for Congress.[110] Nevertheless, by 1959 the ANC's Transvaal rural membership was reported to be in decline[111] following the sealing-off of Sekhukuniland (where the ANC had succeeded in establishing a branch in 1947[112]) and Marico reserve by the police. In rural Natal (where ANC influence had once been unusually widespread) local Congress leaders were swift to perceive the opportunities for channelling rural unrest into organisational activity,[113] only being prevented from effectively doing so by the prohibition of the movement in March 1960. But despite the evidence of a degree of sensitivity to rural tensions, Congress during the 1950s could do little to exploit them. Its organisational vulnerability apart, its social and ideological orientation during the 1950s helped to distance it from rural culture.[114]

Notes

1 See especially Michael Morris, 'State intervention and agricultural labour supply post-1948', in David Hendrie, Alide Kooy, and Francis Wilson (eds), *Farm Labour in South Africa*, David Philip, Cape Town, 1977; Michael Morris, 'The development of capitalism in South Africa: class struggle in the countryside', *Economy and Society*, v, 3 (August 1976); Harold Wolpe, 'Capitalism and cheap labour power in South Africa', *Economy and Society*, i, 4 (November 1973); Martin Legassick, 'Capital accumulation and violence', in *Economy and Society*, iii, 1 (1974); Martin Legassick, 'Legislation, ideology, and economy in post-1948 South Africa', *Journal of Southern African Studies*, i, 1 (1974); Mike Humphriss, 'The changing role of the reserves', *Africa Perspective*, 6 (August 1977); Charles Simkins, 'Agricultural production in the African reserves of South Africa, 1918–1969', University of the Witwatersrand African Studies Institute seminar paper, 24 March 1980; Alfred Stadler, 'Food crisis in the thirties: a sketch', University of the Witwatersrand History Workshop paper, 1981.

2 Francis Fox and Douglas Back, 'Preliminary survey of the agricultural and nutritional problems of the Ciskei and the Transkei', typescript, 1937, University of the Witwatersrand, microfiche A920.

3 Fox and Back quoted in Stadler, 'Food crisis in the thirties', p. 4.

4 'Black Spots' were areas in which Africans enjoyed freehold rights to land lying outside the boundaries of the reserves.

5 W. M. M. Eiselen, 'The development of native reserves', mimeo, n.d.

6 *Ciskeian General Council Proceedings*, Kingwilliamstown, 1947, p. 31.

7 *Ibid*, 1951, p. 32.

8 *Ibid*.

9 *Daily Dispatch* (East London), 4 January 1946.

10 Union of South Africa, *Native Affairs Department Annual Report*, 1950–1951, Pretoria, UG 30/1953, p. 6.

11 *Ciskeian General Council Proceedings*, 1952, p. 47.

12 South African Institute of Race Relations, Johannesburg, SAIRR papers, B Boxes, AD 843, B 10 5, letter from the Director of Agriculture, the Transkei, to the Librarian, SAIRR, 13 June 1941; Atwell Mopeli Paulus, 'The world and the cattle', unpublished manuscript, University of the Witwatersrand, Mopeli Paulus papers, A 974.

13 Union of South Africa, *Report of the Witwatersrand Mine Natives' Wages Commission*, Pretoria, UG 21/1944, p. 147.

14 William Beinart, 'The livestock levy in the Transkei', University of Cape Town, Centre for African Studies, *Africa Seminar: Collected Papers*, Volume 1, 1978, p. 128.

15 Union of South Africa, *Report of the Witwatersrand Mine Natives' Wages Commission*, p. 129.

16 University of the Witwatersrand, Margaret Ballinger papers, A 410/B 2 14 0, File 1, Memorandum drawn up by the Witzieshoek Vigilance Association, 1943, p. 3.

17 *Ciskeian General Council Proceedings*, 1951, p. 36.

18 Mopeli Paulus, 'The world and the cattle', p. 112.

19 *Ibid*, p. 107.

20 Philip Mayer (ed.), *Black Villagers in an Industrial Society*, Oxford University Press, Cape Town, 1980, p. 58.

21 Joanne Yawich, *Black Women in South Africa*, Africa Perspective dissertation no. 2, Johannesburg, June 1980, p. 12.

22 *Ciskeian General Council Proceedings*, 1945 special session, p. 17.

23 Simkins, 'Agricultural production in the African reserves of South Africa', p. 19.

24 Charles Hooper, *Brief Authority*, Collins, London, 1960, p. 105.
25 Govan Mbeki, *The Peasants' Revolt*, Penguin, Harmondsworth, 1963, p. 58.
26 *Ciskeian General Council Proceedings*, 1951, p. 23.
27 John Copelyn, 'The Mpondo Revolt', University of the Witwatersrand African Studies Institute seminar paper, 1975, p. 13.
28 Union of South Africa, *Annual Reports of the Commissioner of the South African Police*, 1950–1960.
29 *Ciskeian General Council Proceedings*, 1951, p. 32.
30 Baruch Hirson, 'Rural revolt in South Africa', University of London, Institute of Commonwealth Studies seminar paper, 1976.
31 Union of South Africa, *Verbatim Record of the Natives' Representative Council*, Pretoria, 3 November 1943, p. 79.
32 See Hirson, 'Rural revolt in South Africa', and Richard Haines, 'Resistance and acquiescence in the Zoutpansberg', University of the Witwatersrand History Workshop paper, 1981.
33 See 'State of war in an African reserve', *Contact* (Cape Town), 31 May 1958; James Fairburn, 'The Sekhukhuneland terror', *Africa South*, (Cape Town), October–December 1958.
34 The following chronology is drawn from Sean Moroney, 'The 1950 Witzieshoek rebellion', *Africa Perspective*, 3 (February 1976); Union of South Africa, *Report of the Commission of Enquiry into the Disturbances in the Witzieshoek Native Reserve*, Cape Times Limited, Parow, UG 26/1951; Mopeli Paulus, 'The world and their cattle'; Hirson, 'Rural revolt in South Africa'.
35 *Report of the Commission of Enquiry*, p. 7.
36 Mopeli Paulus, 'The world and their cattle', p. 127.
37 Moroney, 'The 1950 Witzieshoek rebellion', p. 127.
38 *Ibid*, p. 4.
39 *Report of the Commission of Enquiry*, p. 17.
40 Moroney, 'The 1950 Witzieshoek rebellion', p. 4.
41 *Report of the Commission of Enquiry*, p. 18.
42 Mopeli Paulus, 'The world and their cattle', p. 111.
43 *Report of the Commission of Enquiry*, p. 18.
44 Cited in Hirson, 'Rural revolt in South Africa', p. 9.
45 Mopeli Paulus, 'The world and their cattle', p. 111.
46 Moroney, 'The 1950 Witzieshoek rebellion', p. 7.
47 Mopeli Paulus, 'The world and their cattle', p. 116.
48 *Ibid*, p. 114.
49 Memorandum drawn up by the Witzieshoek Vigilance Association, 1943, pp. 4–5.
50 Mopeli Paulus, 'The world and their cattle', p. 109.
51 *Ibid*, p. 166.
52 Hirson, 'Rural revolt in South Africa', p. 10.
53 University of the Witwatersrand, Xuma papers, ABX 480331, A. S. Mopeli Paulus to A. B. Xuma, 31 March 1948.
54 'Zeerust: the full story', *Fighting Talk* (Johannesburg), February, 1958.
55 Joanne Yawich, 'The Zeerust Revolt', unpublished paper, p. 23.
56 The following narrative is drawn primarily from Charles Hooper, *Brief Authority*.
57 *Cape Times* (Cape Town), 8 August 1959.
58 See Hooper, *Brief Authority*, p. 133.
59 The official ethnological survey of the Bahurutshe ba ga Moilwa notes that 'the majority of the tribe is not poor compared with other tribes', reports 'sufficient grazing round Dinokana' and does not mention land shortage. The area was apparently well-watered and there was a successful irrigation scheme. Each family was allocated between four and ten acres. See P. L. Breutz, *The Tribes of the Marico*

District, Department of Native Affairs, Ethnological Publications No. 30, The Government Printer, Pretoria, 1953, pp. 139–62.

60 *New Age* (Cape Town), 24 April 1958.

61 *Ibid*, 13 February 1958.

62 Hooper, *Brief Authority*, p. 219.

63 *New Age*, 9 January 1958.

64 *The Guardian* (Cape Town), 26 June 1947.

65 Hooper, *Brief Authority*, p. 277. See also James Fairburn, 'Zeerust: a profile of resistance', *Africa South*, December 1958, p. 38.

66 The most thorough study of the events in Pondoland is John Copelyn, 'The Mpondo Revolt', B.A. Honours dissertation, University of the Witwatersrand, 1974. Much of what follows is based on this work and the seminar paper derived from it. The other standard source is Govan Mbeki, *The Peasants' Revolt*.

67 The incident is described in Rhona Churchill, *White Man's God*, Hodder and Stoughton, London, 1962, p. 64.

68 The memorandum was reprinted as 'Pondoland goes to the United Nations', *Fighting Talk*, October 1960, pp. 3–4.

69 *Ibid*, p. 4.

70 *Ibid*.

71 Copelyn, 'The Mpondo Revolt', seminar paper, p. 17.

72 See William Beinart, 'Peasant production, underdevelopment and stratification: Pondoland, c. 1880–1930', University of Cape Town, Centre for African Studies, seminar paper, pp. 18–20.

73 Johann Maree, 'The underutilisation of labour in the Ciskei and Transkei', University of the Witwatersrand African Studies Institute seminar paper, 4 June 1973, p. 35.

74 SAIRR papers, Ad 1189, National Executive Committee of the African National Congress minute book VII, 1946.

75 SAIRR papers, AD 1189, ANC 111, National Executive Report to the 46th annual conference of the African National Congress, 1958.

76 I. B. Tabata, *The Awakening of a People*, Spokesman Press, Nottingham, 1974, p. 60.

77 Mbeki, *The Peasants' Revolt*, p. 120.

78 *Ibid*, p. 129.

79 Colin Bundy and William Beinart, 'State intervention and rural resistance: the Transkei, 1900–1965', Martin Klein (ed.), *Peasants in Africa*, Sage Publications, Beverley Hills, 1980, p. 309.

80 University of York, South African Trials, Box 1, File 1, State *vs.* Nomapelisa Meji and 22 others, Butterworth, 21 August 1963.

81 Mbeki, *Peasants Revolt*, p. 76; Duncan Innes and Dan O'Meara, 'Class formation and ideology in the Transkei region', *Review of African Political Economy*, September–December 1976, p. 74.

82 Barbara Rodgers, *The Bantu Homelands*, International Defence and Aid, London, 1973, p. 28.

83 SAIRR papers, AD 1189, ANC 11, Annual Report of the National Executive Committee to the 42nd annual conference of the ANC, 1954, p. 9.

84 *The Torch* (Cape Town), 2 October 1952.

85 Patrick Lawrence, *The Transkei*, Ravan, Johannesburg, 1976, p. 36.

86 *Contact*, 18 October 1958.

87 SAIRR papers, AD 1196, 1, 8, 'A brief factual report on happenings in the Transkei', typescript.

88 See *Contact*, 9 March 1961 and 18 May 1961; Lawrence, *The Transkei*, p. 64.

89 *Contact*, 1 November 1962.

90 *Cape Times*, 17 September 1963.
91 *Cape Argus*, 28 August 1963.
92 South African Institute of Race Relations, *Survey of Race Relations 1962–1963*, SAIRR, Johannesburg, 1963, p. 19.
93 *Cape Argus*, 10 August 1963.
94 William Beinart, 'The livestock levy', University of Cape Town, Centre for African Studies, *African Seminar: Collected Papers*, p. 137.
95 University of York, South African Trials, Box 1, File 3, State *vs.* Ngconcolo and 19 others, CC 9/1963, p. 579.
96 *Ibid*, p. 581.
97 *Cape Times*, 9 November 1967.
98 State *vs.* Ngconcolo and 19 others, p. 611.
99 *Ibid*, p. 579.
100 *Ibid*, p. 581.
101 State *vs.* Nomapolesi Meji and 22 others, p. 20.
102 *Ibid*, p. 68.
103 *Ibid*, p. 27.
104 Philip and Iona Mayer, *Townsmen and Tribesmen*, Oxford University Press, Cape Town, 1974, p. 157.
105 See *Snyman Commission*. This official report contains the first published version of this claim. It was later taken up by the PAC leadership but no corroborative evidence has ever been produced.
106 Innes and O'Meara, 'Class formation and ideology in the Transkei region', p. 82.
107 Monica Wilson and Archie Mafeje, *Langa*, Oxford University Press, Cape Town, 1963, p. 18.
108 Simkins, 'Agricultural production in the African reserves of South Africa', p. 19.
109 Carter and Karis microfilm, Reel 2b, 2 DA 17: 40/13.
110 Ken Luckhardt and Brenda Wall, '*Organize or Starve . . . the history of the South African Congress of Trade Unions*, Lawrence and Wishart, London, 1980, p. 202; SAIRR papers, AD 1189, ANC 11, File 6, press statement, 1961, SAIRR papers, AD 1189, unsorted box, National Executive Committee to the 43rd annual conference of the African National Congress, 1955.
111 SAIRR papers, AD 1189, ANC 11, File 3, National Executive Report to the 47th annual conference of the African National Congress, 1959, p. 16.
112 *The Guardian*, 23 October 1947.
113 National Executive Report to the 47th annual conference of the African National Congress, 1959, p. 8.
114 For an elaboration of this point see John Blacking, 'The growth of the Africanist idea in South Africa', *Queens University Papers in Social Anthropology*, Volume 3, Belfast, 1978, pp. 122–132.

CHAPTER 12

Revolutionary exile politics, 1960–1975

The environment of exile politics presented South African political leaders with a fresh set of problems and difficulties. These can be grouped in three categories: those arising from the need to maintain sanctuaries in foreign states and sources of external assistance; those related to efforts directed at the re-establishment of internal activity and support; and finally, the problem of holding the exile movement together. Before examining how South African exiles coped with these difficulties a few general points about each category can be made.

Under exile conditions one of the major functions of political leadership is diplomatic; at certain points in their history the support of foreign powers and international organisations was more crucial to the survival of South African political movements than the existence of active membership within the country. External help could involve certain obligations: taking sides in international great power hostilities, or even in the internal political conflicts of the host state, were two of the more obvious of these. The requirements of diplomatic work and the habits created by it could serve to socially isolate leaders from rank and file. Liberation movement leaders were often encouraged by their hosts to behave in the manner of heads of states and members of government and this could help to fuel escapist illusions held by the leaders concerning the strength and importance of the movements they represented. Foreign assistance could also be in the form of large financial donations providing a source of affluence well beyond the scope of the finances of the movements in the earlier phase of legal domestic activity. So first of all, even in the context of a friendly and sympathetic exile environment, there were threats to the long-term effectiveness of the political movements.

As far as the problem of reactivating an internal organisation was concerned, the exile movements were confronted with formidable barriers. In the 1960s and early 1970s South Africa was protected by a *cordon sanitaire* of colonial territories themselves engaged in extensive counter-insurgent operations. Lesotho, Botswana and Swaziland, though all independent states by the end of 1968, were nevertheless too economically reliant on South Africa ~~provide secure~~ bases for exile South African organisations (though the PAC ~~guerrilla~~ rilla operations in Lesotho until 1965). Within South ~~succeeded~~ ed in destroying the ANC's network by the ~~usands~~ of suspected members in the eastern ~~Africa~~ Africa does not provide the terrain or ~~establishment~~ tablishment of successful guerrilla ~~Mozambique~~ ue or Angola. There, nationalist parties could initially base their struggles in superficially administered and economically fairly self-sufficient remote rural communities. In South Africa a repressive system of controls on popular mobility and political expression extends to the reserves where, for the most part, people live on the edge of starvation, dependent on migrant earnings. There is no group comparable to the 'middle peasantry' which comparative analyses of rural revolutions have found to be vital to the successful guerrilla movement.[2] In the towns, influx control and an extensive system of police informers served to inhibit political activity, as did the fear and demoralisation engendered by new security legislation and police powers. All these conditions helped to isolate exiled political leaders from the changing reality of life within the country, making it all the more difficult to devise realistic strategies.

Finally, each movement was vulnerable to behavioural tendencies arising from the circumstances of exile. In the absence of creative and rewarding mobilisation activity, political energy could focus itself around hairsplitting doctrinal disputes. Removed from the arena of real conflict, internal dissent and opposition to factions and personalities within the movement could serve as a substitute for externally-oriented aggression. Tensions between individual personalities could assume a reinforced significance and could be rationalised by both sides in ideological terms. The frustrations and material hardships of exile life (only a favoured few could live like diplomats) this could promote escapist delusions, mutiny, and apathy amongst rank and file. The crucial need to engage in propaganda activity (and compete with other movements in making extravagant claims) so as to retain foreign support, could contribute to the intellectual sterility of exile politics. Large sums of money and an unaccustomed degree of power over rank and file members (usually the host state took the leaders' part in internal dissent) could present obvious temptations to men and women with experience of neither.

Despite the frustrations and apparent triviality of much exile political activity, the experience of exile and the fashion in which South African political movements survived it was an important phase of the history of South African resistance. It was a rite of passage which could corrode the internal integrity of the nationalist and revolutionary organisations. Their ability to affect the course of black resistance in South Africa in the dramatically altered conditions of the late 1970s was more a result of the extent to which they had succeeded in overcoming the inherent difficulties of the exile environment, than their relative degree of influence within the country at the point when internal circumstances began to change in their favour.

The history of the exiled political movements is thinly documented and additionally difficult to research from within South Africa, because of the unavailability of their publications. The organisations th‑‑ ‑‑‑ ‑ tandably, do not describe their activities publi‑‑‑ ‑ official sources are by nature secretive and f‑ the press reportage is sensational in c‑ disputes within the movements have ‑ South Africa it is filtered through when more of the internal docum ‑

when the necessity for secrecy has disappeared will it be possible to write a comprehensive history of South African exile politics. What follows therefore is a tentative and inevitably incomplete account.

Up to the present the development of the external wing of the ANC has had four major phases. First, the establishment of a foreign mission in 1960, which from 1960 until 1963 devoted chiefly itself to fundraising and diplomatic efforts as well as establishing a military training programme. The second phase began with the arrest of most of the internal leadership at Rivonia in mid-1963 and the assumption by the external mission of responsibility for military decisions. With the Rivonia raid political leadership of Congress shifted from within the country to outside it. The period 1963 to 1969 was distinguished by efforts to infiltrate South Africa via Zimbabwe, the ANC forming an alliance with the Zimbabwe African People's Union and conducting joint operations against the Rhodesian army (and South African policemen) in the Wankie area. Dissatisfaction in the Umkonto we Sizwe training camps in Tanzania, arising partly from the Zimbabwean campaigns, helped to bring about the first major ANC conference since the Lobatsi meeting in 1962, and as a result of it important organisational reforms were introduced.

The third phase, 1970 to 1976, began with the collapse of the ANC/ZAPU joint operation as internal dissent debilitated the Zimbabwean movement, and ended with the accession to power of Frelimo and the Movimento Popular de Libertaçao de Angola (MPLA). This, together with the exodus of thousands of young people in the months following the Soweto uprising, created favourable conditions for the resumption of sabotage activity in South Africa. The third phase was characterised by attempts to infiltrate organisers through normal immigration channels as well as by considerable disunity within the ANC leadership. The fourth phase, the sabotage campaign in which the ANC reconstituted itself as a major force in South African black politics, will be discussed in the next chapter.

In anticipation of the prohibition of the ANC, its national executive despatched Oliver Tambo, deputy president-general, across the border of Bechuanaland and subsequently to London. He was a good choice, a skilful negotiator and strong personality who, like Mandela, had managed to avoid being strongly identified with the revolutionary left or the Africanist radical right within Congress. In June 1960, Tambo, together with Tennyson Makiwane who had left South Africa the previous year to help launch the international economic boycott of South Africa, and Yusuf Dadoo of the SAIC, joined with two PAC spokesmen, Nana Mahomo and Peter 'Molotsi in establishing a South African United Front (SAUF). The SAUF had a brief life of only eighteen months and was active mainly in Accra, Cairo, Dar es Salaam and London, soliciting support from European social democrats (in Britain both the ANC and important figures in the British Labour Party were involved in the establishment of the Anti-Apartheid Movement) and newly independent African states. The Front, the formation of which owed much to pressure from African leaders, broke up in early 1962 as the result of internal PAC leaders' hostility to cooperation with the ANC. By then the Umkonto sabotage campaign had begun and external Congress representatives, independently of the Front, had succeeded in obtaining Chinese military training facilities for Umkonto recruits. Meanwhile the PAC men concentrated on trying to win

Western support and forging an alliance with the Uniao das Populações de Angola (UPA).

The first training facilities on African soil were established in the wake of the inaugural conference of the Pan-African Freedom Movement for East, Central and Southern Africa (PAFMECSA) in February 1962. PAFMECSA had developed from the attempts in the 1950s by East African politicians to co-ordinate their anti-colonial struggles on a regional basis. Mandela's appearance made a most favourable impact; despite the reservations some African governments had about the multiracial character of the Congress alliance, large sums of money were promised by Nigeria, Ethiopia, Morocco and Liberia and Algeria's Front de Liberation Nationale (FLN) opened its training camps to South Africans. Mandela himself took a short course in guerrilla warfare in Algeria before returning to South Africa. One result of Mandela's Pan-African activity was an increased emphasis by the ANC leadership on the movement's African 'authenticity': Mandela was to appear at his trial in Xhosa traditional costume. At about the same time as Mandela's tour abroad, Arthur Goldreich, of the South African Communist Party (SACP) and Umkonto, visited Eastern Europe to arrange military assistance from the Soviet bloc. In the two following decades Soviet assistance was to be rather more valuable than Pan-African support. The third important diplomatic initiative of the ANC in 1962 would also have a long-term significance: in the middle of the year talks were held between ANC spokesmen and Marcelino dos Santos, secretary of the Conferencia das Organizações Nacionalistas das Colonias Portuguesas (CONCP). CONCP was an alliance of three Portuguese African groups, Frelimo, MPLA, and the Guinean PAIGC. Each was distinguished from their rivals by their multiracial membership and Marxist orientation. The ANC's agreement with CONCP to 'pursue their cooperation' and 'tighten their links'[3] assumed a fresh meaning in the context of the Frelimo and MPLA victories in 1974 and 1975.

In early 1963, perhaps in anticipation of the increased responsibilities the exile leadership would have in the context of a full blown guerrilla insurgency, Tambo and Makiwane were joined by Moses Kotane, general secretary of the SACP, and Duma Nokwe (rumoured also to be a communist), secretary-general of the ANC. From mid-1963 most important Congress alliance leaders were either outside South Africa or in prison, and in the two following years the internal organisation was destroyed. Kotane, appropriately enough considering the origin of most of the exile movement's funding, became the external ANC's treasurer.

In 1963, with the establishment of the Organisation of African Unity (OAU), the functions of PAFMECSA were taken over by the OAU's African Liberation Committee, presided over by the Tanzanian foreign minister, Oscar Kambona. Dar es Salaam became one of the main focuses of exile activity and the Tanzanian government the most important African supporter of the South African organisations. In the next few years the ANC established four guerrilla training camps there, at Kongwa, Mbeya, Bagamoyo and Morogoro with its headquarters at the last named.[4] Between 1964 and 1967 there was no evidence of any success in infiltrating trainees back into South Africa, but given the numbers in the camps (reportedly 2000 in 1970),[5] functioning ANC branches and Umkonto cells must have continued the work of recruiting men for military training and despatching them across the Botswana border. The first occasion on which the trained guerrillas were deployed in a military campaign was in 1967 with ZAPU units in Rhodesia.

The decision to embark on the Rhodesian campaigns was apparently taken without consulting the ANC's allies in the SACP. The SACP was to admit later that its central executive committee 'was totally unaware of the Zimbabwe events of 1967 until they hit the world's press'.[6] The incursions into Rhodesia had, for the ANC, two ostensible purposes. One group of Umkonto men was to march through Rhodesia with the help of ZAPU guides, keeping to the game parks on its western border, and hoping to reach South Africa without contacting Rhodesian security forces. Meanwhile another detachment of Umkonto guerrillas would assist ZAPU in establishing a base in Rhodesia.[7] Accordingly, in early 1967 Umkonto recruits were transferred from their Tanzanian camps to ZAPU's Joshua Nkomo camp outside Lusaka. The numbers involved were small; Norman Duka, one of the participants in the South African-bound detachment, claims there were 33 ANC men in his group.[8] On 8 August the ANC/ZAPU guerrillas crossed the Zambezi into Rhodesia. From Duka's account it seems that despite the sophistication of their equipment and their military competence the guerrillas were poorly prepared for their journey. The time it would take them to cross Rhodesia was badly underestimated, they ran out of food early, and lost their way through using inaccurate maps. Both Duka's group and the one in which ZAPU men predominated were spotted by game scouts. Fighting between ANC/ZAPU units and the Rhodesian army began on 14 August and continued into September. Both sides were to claim overwhelming victories in the various confrontations which took place over the three weeks of campaigning, neither sides' claims being independently verified. By mid-September the ANC/ZAPU forces were either killed or captured by the Rhodesians, or interned and later convicted for illegal entry by the Botswana authorities.

Encouraged possibly by the reception of the first group (the ZAPU-dominated detachment had considerable success in its initial attempts to mobilise villagers),[9] a second incursion into Rhodesia began at the end of December 1967. This time a much larger group under ANC command managed to survive undetected for nearly three months, the first contact with Rhodesian security forces occurring on 18 March 1968. Here the object of the ANC/ZAPU group, according to the Rhodesians, was to prepare rural people to participate in a ZAPU-led uprising. Fierce fighting took place intermittently between March and June, and the Rhodesians claimed to have killed 55 insurgents and captured many more. This did not discourage a third incursion in July in which a Rhodesian army camp was attacked. The Umkonto guerrillas were admitted by Rhodesians to be resourceful and determined, and those fighting in 1968 had the additional incentive of confronting South African policemen who had been sent to Rhodesia during the first campaign.[10]

Although the strategic purpose of the Rhodesian incursions was probably taken quite seriously by the ANC leadership in Morogoro (doctrines of rural-based guerrilla warfare were at the time very influential) there may have been subsidiary motives. The campaigns may have been intended to remedy the sagging morale created by inactivity and boredom in the camps as well as boosting the ANC's position with the OAU African Liberation Committee. This latter consideration could not have been very important though: in 1967–8, of a promised $80 000 only $3 940 was given by the OAU members through the Liberation Committee to the ANC.[11] The ANC had long since ceased to have much faith in Pan-African support. As far as improving internal morale was concerned the campaigns did not seem to have raised the spirits of rank and file members. In 1968 a batch of Umkonto defectors from camps in Tanzania sought asylum in Kenya, alleging that there was widespread dissatisfaction within the camps. They accused their commanders of extravagant living and ethnic favouritism. The first Rhodesian expedition, they said, was a suicide mission to eliminate dissenters. In political discussions no challenge to a pro-Soviet position was allowed.[12] Some guerrillas who had managed to return to Tanzania from prison in Botswana complained: 'There was no longer any direction, there was general confusion and an unwillingness to discuss the issues of the revolution'.[13]

In convening a 'Third Consultative Conference' (the first was in Pietermaritzburg and the second in Lobatsi) in Morogoro the ANC's leadership conceded that there were reasonable grounds for discontent within Umkonto. The conference lasted seven days and was attended by seventy delegates from the ANC and allied organisations. Most of the delegates were Umkonto men and only eleven were not African.[14] Discussion seems to have centred mainly around the role and structure of the external mission's leadership. It was criticised for isolating itself from the rank and file and devoting too much time to 'international solidarity work'. In addition, several executive members were attacked for personal misconduct and abuse of their positions.[15] Many of the criticisms were recognised by the leadership to have some justification; at the beginning of the proceedings Oliver Tambo announced that the executive had resigned en bloc and would be reconstituted in the light of conference decisions.[16] 'Unhealthy tendencies' were admitted to have existed within the highest echelons of the external mission and generally it was recognised that the body was 'not organisationally geared to undertake the urgent task of undertaking people's war'.[17] At the same time it was conceded that the ANC's internal organisation had been shattered and that no effective communication links existed with whatever remnants remained. In response to this groundswell of dissatisfaction several reforms were made: it was agreed that an internal commission would be established to listen to complaints and grievances and an oath and code of behaviour would be formulated. At the same time the day-to-day direction of Umkonto and overall supervision of military matters would be the responsibility of a revolutionary council, itself subordinate only to the national executive. The executive itself would be reduced from 23 to nine members.

The Morogoro conference did not limit itself to organisational reforms. Two important policy changes were introduced. The first concerned the position of whites, Indians and coloureds who had worked with the external mission. Many, though not all, of these were SACP members. Officially the South African Indian Congress (SAIC), Coloured People's Congress (CPC) (formerly SACPO), and the South African Congress of Democrats (SACOD) did not have external organisations. In the case of the SAIC this was because its provincial affiliates were still technically legal in South Africa and with the other two the numbers involved were very small (especially after the defection of several CPC men to the PAC in 1966). For white communists there was little to be gained by maintaining SACOD as a separate external organisation. Although unofficially these people had a close relationship with the external ANC leadership – a practice was made of including them in diplomatic delegations – nevertheless many of them wanted the relationship to be put on a more formal footing. Many, after all, had been involved in Umkonto and were not satisfied with the position of being merely favoured associates. With respect to Umkonto, after some internal disagreement, in 1965 the SACP – at the insistence of Kotane – decided to refrain from building its own cadre group among the military trainess. At roughly the same time as this decision, according to later ANC dissident sources, a discussion was held in London at the Slovos' house. Present were several SACP members and four ANC leaders: Oliver Tambo, Robert Resha, Raymond Kunene and Alfred Kgogong. The discussion centred on the question of whether non-Africans should be allowed to join the ANC, Resha and Kgogong being opposed to this. After the meeting, however, Resha was given the task of co-ordinating the efforts of the ANC's allies. The question was raised again the following year at a joint consultative meeting. The ANC and the SACP were divided over the issue; the same year a suggestion by Joe Matthews, a respected member of both groups, that a 'Council of War' should be formed which would include whites, Indians and coloured was rejected.[18]

At Morogoro it was decided that non-Africans could join the external ANC 'on the basis of individual equality' though they could not belong to the national executive. Yusuf Dadoo, Joe Slovo and Reginald September (formerly of the CPC) also became members of the revolutionary council. How popular this decision was is not known, but it could not have been made if it had encountered significant opposition from the delegates, most of whom were Umkonto men. Nevertheless it should be pointed out that a major change in ANC policy was made at a conference attended by not more than eighty people.

The second innovation was the adoption of a 'Revolutionary Programme' which essentially consisted of an elaboration of the different clauses of the Freedom Charter. Its phrasing was fairly cautious; on the whole it did not attempt to draw out the more radical implications of the Charter but rather provided a detailed commentary which served to correct some of the ambiguities in the original document. So, for example, in the section entitled 'The people shall govern' it was made quite clear that no political institutions would exist for the articulation of the interests of racial minorities. The question of land reform was tackled in rather greater detail than allowed for by the Charter's clauses: land formerly held by large capitalist concerns would be redistributed to individual peasants and a ceiling would be fixed on the extent of individual land holdings. Despite the claim that the programme represented an 'elaboration of [the Charter's] revolutionary message' its specifications still remained compatible with the preservation of a form of welfare state capitalism in South Africa.[19] This point is worth emphasising in the light of accusations that the external ANC was (and is) subordinated to the control of the SACP.[20] In contrast to the development of many exile African political organisations the ANC's ideological position remained noticeably conservative (and realistic).[21]

Its essentially nationalist character remained unchanged. As was pointed out at Morogoro:

> In the last resort it is only the success of the national democratic revolution which – by destroying the existing social and economic relationships – will bring with it a correction of the historical injustices perpetrated against the indigenous majority and thus lay the basis for a new and deeper internationalist appraoch. Until then, the national sense of grievance is the most potent revolutionary force which must be harnessed. To blunt it in the interest of abstract concepts of internationalism, is, in the long run, doing neither a service to revolution nor to internationalism.[22]

The Morogoro reforms of 1969 did not put an end to the ANC's internal troubles. In 1970 the new decade began inauspiciously with the collapse of ZAPU as an effective fighting force as a result of feuding which led to the emergence of a third Zimbabwean guerrilla group, Frolizi. The same year the final ANC expedition into Rhodesia ended prematurely with the ambush of Flag Boshielo and two others while they were crossing the Zambezi river from Zambia.[23] Boshielo, incidentally, had led the first Defiance Campaign volunteer unit in Johannesburg on 26 June 1952. Between 1970 and 1975 the known instances of attempts by the ANC at infiltration took the form of efforts to enter South Africa at official border points using forged identification documents. In 1971 one of the veterans of the first Rhodesian campaign, James April, after receiving some training in London from the revolutionary council's strategist Joe Slovo and the former explosives expert of the first Umkonto campaign, Jack Hodgeson, was arrested in Durban. The following year an Australian, Alexander Moumbaris and an Irishman, Sean Hosey, were arrested and accused of being ANC couriers involved in a scheme to land Russian-trained guerrillas on the Transkeian coast and begin organising local peasants into a military force. In 1975 Breyten Breytenbach, a famous Afrikaaner poet, returned from exile in Paris disguised as a priest, and on behalf of Okhela, a faction within the 'white' ANC, toured the country to make contact with potential sympathisers. Okhela, apparently, was an anti-communist faction within the ANC, with a mainly white membership clustered in Paris and Amsterdam. These cases naturally attracted much publicity but less obtrusively these were indications that ANC activists had succeeded in re-establishing a rudimentary organisational network in the country. For example, in August 1971 pamphlet bombs were exploded simultaneously in public transport terminals in Johannesburg, Cape Town, Durban and Port Elizabeth[24] and *Amandla-Matha*, an ANC newsletter, began to circulate inside the country the following year.

In the background of this activity there were continuing (and in some cases probably much exaggerated) reports of internal dissension. In April 1971 South African newspapers carried reports of a conflict between Oliver Tambo on the one hand and Duma Nokwe and Reginald September on the other.[25] In June a commission of enquiry, headed by Alfred Nzo, secretary-general, attempted to investigate the causes of tensions in the ANC's leadership. Amongst other things the commission reported that some NEC and revolutionary council members were not kept fully informed of certain decisions, raising the question 'of where exactly does power lie in the ANC?'.[26] The same year a national executive meeting held in Zambia, concerned at the continuing malaise in the organisation, established a committee to investigate ways of reinvigorating the movement. ANC dissidents later alleged that this committee was dissolved at the insistence of the SACP.[27]

Dissidents chose the occasion of Robert Resha's funeral in London to mount a public attack on the role of communists within the ANC leadership. Resha had opposed the extension of a form of ANC membership to non-Africans in 1969 and dissidents chose to make him a martyr to their cause. Finally, in October 1975, eight members of the ANC were expelled from the organisation. They were led by Tennyson Makiwane and met in London on 27 December to announce their intention of reconstituting the ANC as an authentic nationalist organisation. Like the Africanists of two decades earlier their main source of dissatisfaction was over the role of the SACP:

> The SACP white leadership who oppose the political philosophy embodied in the concept of African nationalism and who oppose the African image of the ANC reflect their social and class roots as petit-bourgeois white – roots firmly fixed in the historically-conditioned modes of thought that characterise white superior attitudes towards blacks in South Africa.[28]

The Communist Party produced an acidly contemptous pamphlet. Of the eight dissenters most had a history of factionalism (two had actually once been SACP members); their numbers included two former members of the African Resistance Movement and two former state witnesses in South African trials of former guerrillas.[29]

How much importance should be attributed to such conflicts? Did they reflect serious and widely entrenched divisions within the exile movement? It is not an easy question to answer. Certainly, despite reports of internal feuding affecting the discipline and morale of Umkonto cadres in the Tanzanian camps in 1975,[30] the expulsion/defection of the 'ANC African Nationalists' did not appear to generate more broadly based disaffection. The eight dissidents were drawn from leadership echelons rather than from rank and file. Unlike similar disputes in, for example, the Angolan or Guinean revolutionary movements, this one did not have the effect of dividing the political leadership from the military.[31] Yet because of the stature of some of the eight, the conflict did indicate the lack of unanimity over basic policy questions which continues to characterise the ANC's leadership, and which might therefore be a cause for more important and debilitating divisions in the future. The dissenters included two Treason Trialists (Jonas Matlou and Tennyson Makiwane) as well as Pascal Ngakane, Chief Lutuli's son-in-law and an important figure in the underground ANC in Natal during the early 1960s.[32] Interestingly enough, Tennyson Makiwane and several of the other dissenters were in the 1950s identified with the left wing of Congress. Makiwane later returned to South Africa and worked for the Transkei government. He was assassinated in 1980, apparently by ANC agents.[33]

In the mutual recriminations which followed the split it appeared that the question of white involvement in the ANC was the one key issue of disagreement. The split did not seem to involve questions of strategy or considerations of a more obviously ideological dimension: for example, at no point in their lengthy attack on the influence of the SACP on the ANC is there any mention, critical or otherwise, of the Freedom Charter. The only doctrinal issue raised in the document is the question of the class determination of white labour, on which the SACP is accused of taking a position which in fact it long ago abandoned.[34]

In the mid-1970s the exile movements were confronted with two fresh challenges. The first was provided by the decolonisation of the Portuguese colonies, which removed for the ANC one of the principal barriers to mounting an effective insurgency in South Africa – the protection afforded to South Africa by friendly colonial administrations to the north. The second came from the exodus of vast numbers of politically motivated young people as well as the changed internal circumstances in South Africa. This testified to the relative integrity, unity and strength of the exile movement, especially when compared to its rivals. Before turning to the fortunes of the exile Pan-Africanists the main factors which contributed to the ANC's survival should be discussed briefly.

Despite the criticism it evoked the ANC's link with the SACP was of great value in this period. It was ensured of a continual source of funds, equipment, training and diplomatic support – resources of a scale and quality its rivals could not hope to match. Soviet bloc-derived aid had, in the experience of African liberation movements, been proven to be more helpful than that obtained from any other source. Despite lavish promises the OAU donors have been fickle allies who, in any case, could themselves ill-afford their generosity. Chinese support for African movements has been meagre and unreliable; foreign policy reversals since the cultural revolution have made China an especially unpredictable source of support. Soviet aid, given the stability and continuity of the Soviet regime, has on the whole been more consistent and less subject to sudden changes of attitude than Chinese, American or African assistance. Moreover, its price, in the short term at least, has been a modest one. It costs African liberation movements little to align themselves loyally in favour of Soviet foreign policy. The alienation of the Chinese in 1964, when the ANC supported the USSR in the Sino-Soviet dispute, did the movement no significant harm. The ANC's endorsement of the Russian invasion of Czechoslovakia in 1968 was rather more offensive to its Western sympathisers,[35] but by this stage it was clear that enthusiastic and committed Western backing for the cause of African liberation was a chimera. The only Western governments regularly prepared to give financial grants to African guerrillas have been the Scandinavians and the Dutch, and here the money has been given for non-military purposes. The only Western military support has been from the CIA to right-wing African movements and its effects have been disastrous for the recipients.[36]

Apart from the material advantages of the aid it received, the fact that the ANC has had such a powerful external ally has meant that it has been able to steer clear of dependent relationships in African countries which have hosted it. Consequently it has avoided the dangers of local political entanglements. This has been in sharp contrast to the record of the PAC. The ANC has been able to afford to be selective and usually fairly principled in its choice of partners, alliances, and donors. It has been less susceptible than the PAC to OAU/ALC interference; significantly in 1971 and 1974 it was the PAC, under OAU pressure, and not the ANC, which announced itself willing to form a South African united front.[37] Finally, Soviet support does not appear to have had a marked influence on the ANC's strategy which has on the whole been pragmatic and flexible. Its consistent avoidance of terrorism (indiscriminate violence against civilians) can be attributed to its traditional aversion towards violence as much as the principled dislike of terrorist strategies of the SACP.[38] This again is in marked contrast to the PAC whose strategic policies, since 1965, have been dogmatically Maoist in character.[39]

Internally, as was evident at the Morogoro conference, the organisation has had its share of the difficulties which stem from the inactivity and sterility of exile conditions. Nevertheless, certain characteristics of the external movement have helped to prevent these from provoking serious fissions. Tightly centralised and apparently honest control of funds at the highest echelon helped to discourage one obvious source of corruption and low morale. There have been few reports of material hardships in the camps, possibly because of the relatively generous flow of resources to the ANC. In its pre-revolutionary period the ANC leadership had plenty of experience of containing disagreements over ideology and policy; this, together with the absence of sharp changes in ideological orientation help to explain why there has been only one major leadership split between 1963 and 1976. Within the SACP, too, there was evidence – in the early 1970s – of a degree of internal debate (on the subject of Black Consciousness) without this causing expulsions or defections.[40] The ANC and SACP leaders are on the whole well educated, politically sophisticated, and in some cases, affluent, and they have been less vulnerable to some of the temptations and delusions of the often pretentious world of exile politics.

There is too little evidence on which to base any firm conclusions about the state of the movement at rank and file level. Organisational inadequacies aside, the dissatisfaction of the late 1960s should be understood in the context of a situation in which men, drawn principally from an urban background in what is in African terms a rich society, had to come to terms with the conditions of existence in one of Africa's poorest rural communities. In addition it should be remembered that many Umkonto volunteers were not professional revolutionaries until their despatch abroad: the necessary discipline of life in a military training camp would have been strange, and to some, unwelcome. Significantly, in the post-1976 years, with the resumption of Umkonto's insurgent activities, reports of low morale in the camps have been less frequent.[41]

The Pan-Africanists in exile have had a turbulent history. By 1976, of their original fourteen-man executive committee, at least eight were in exile. Of these six, Nana Mahomo, Peter Raboroko, Peter 'Molotsi, Jacob Nyaose, Z. B. Molete and Abednego Ngcobo, had been expelled from the organisation as a result of conflicts between them and the acting president, Potlake Leballo. In addition, at least two other men who had joined the leadership after the PAC's ban, Matthew Nkoana and Tsepo Letlaka, were subsequently dismissed, Letlaka eventually becoming a member of the Transkeian government. Apart from leadership conflicts there have also been frequent internal rebellions resulting from the dissatisfaction of men in the guerrilla training camps. On several occasions these rebellions have taken the form of assassination attempts, the most recent being in 1979 when Leballo's successor, David Sibeko, was shot dead in Dar es Salaam. In its external relationships the PAC has had a disturbed history, incurring the wrath of the Organisation of African Unity in 1967 and 1968, and the Zambian government in 1968 and 1973; entering ill-starred alliances with the Frente Naçional de Libertaçao de Angola (FNLA) in 1963 and the Comité Revoluçionario de Moçambique (Coremo) in 1968; and attracting the dubious benefits of support from China and the Central Intelligence Agency. Its efforts to infiltrate its cadres back to South Africa were, in the pre-1976 period, even less fortunate than those of the ANC. For the Pan-Africanists, exile has been a traumatic and demoralising experience and through it the movement has been all but destroyed.

The following discussion of the PAC's history between 1960 and 1976 will have two dimensions. First, developments at the level of leadership will be examined, that is, alterations and reformulations of policy, strategy, and ideology, disputes and conflicts, and the shifting and sometimes uneasy relationships that existed between the PAC and various foreign powers. Secondly, the situation of the movement's followers will be described; here the focus will be on conditions in the camps, rank-and-file reactions to leadership, and the attempts to return insurgents to South Africa.

Until late 1962 there was very little organised activity by PAC members in exile. Refugees from South Africa had clustered in Maseru and in various centres in Swaziland and Bechuanaland. In Europe and in different African capitals Nana Mahomo and Peter 'Molotsi, independently of any direction from their colleagues, attempted to counter the influence of the ANC and obtain promises of financial, diplomatic and military support. Only in August 1962, with the arrival of Potlake Leballo, was a formal exile leadership constituted. In a letter from Robert Sobukwe dated 25 August, Leballo was designated as acting president of the PAC, and national executive members – together with the chairmen of the regional leaderships – were told to form a presidential council. The council was to have 'absolute power to rule, govern, direct and administer the PAC during the time the movement (was) banned and (during) the revolution'.[42] Maseru was, from 1962 to 1964, the headquarters of the organisation, though in the course of the following few months PAC representatives opened offices in London, Accra, Cairo, Francistown, Dar es Salaam and Leopoldville (Kinshasha). Later the PAC also sent men to Algiers and Lagos. Despite the theoretical consideration that all these centres should be subject to the Maseru headquarter's authority, they tended to function independently and occasionally in rivalry with Maseru.

The period August 1962 to August 1964 represented a fairly distinct phase of the PAC's exile history, characterised by strategic ventures which would have been inconceivable in the case of an external leadership more remotely situated from South Africa. During the Maseru period the PAC's leadership remained ideologically and strategically fairly consistent to the movement's origin: statements by its representatives featured references to a vaguely conceived 'African personality', advocacy of an African socialism derived from a 'continuity from older tribal democracies to present-day forms', and xenophobia.[43] Its insurrectionary preoccupations flowed from the same presumptions about mass behaviour as did the 1960 anti-pass campaign: the principal shackles inhibiting popular resistance were psychological; 'show the light and the masses will find the way'.[44] The one innovation in its policies was the admission of a white man, Patrick Duncan, to membership. Patrick Duncan joined the PAC in April 1963, having left South Africa the year before in defiance of his banning order. At this stage the PAC still hoped for support from the non-communist powers and in this context Patrick Duncan, with his reputation and social connections abroad, could obviously perform a valuable role.[45]

Initially the Maseru leadership did not anticipate a lengthy exile. The original plan was for a massive uprising in which, on an appointed day, PAC cells all over South Africa would mount attacks on police stations and other strategic targets to spark off a generalised insurrection. Preparations for this scheme began in late 1962 but were robbed of their crucial element of surprise on 27 March when Potlake Leballo staged a boisterous press conference in Maseru. Here he announced that the PAC's 155 000 members were impatiently awaiting his order to deliver the 'blow' which would end white South Africa.[46] On 1 April the Basutoland police visited the PAC office and questioned those whom they found there (Leballo had gone into hiding) and confiscated a quantity of documents including membership lists. Shortly afterwards the South African police began arresting several thousand suspected PAC men, using, it was alleged, the documents supplied to them by the British colonial authorities. For several months the PAC headquarters in Maseru were closed down only to re-open when Leballo resurfaced from his hiding in September 1963. Thereafter the PAC in Basutoland contented themselves with providing rudimentary instruction in guerrilla warfare.[47]

In the next year or so the major PAC initiatives took place in the fields of diplomacy and training. In June 1963 Nana Mahomo and Patrick Duncan (who had left Maseru for London in April) began a two-month tour of the United States, visiting trade unionists, United Nations officials, churchmen, senators, tate Department officials and businessmen. Apart from fund-raising their main purpose was to persuade influential Americans in favour of an arms and oil embargo of South Africa. Patrick Duncan succeeded in talking to Robert Kennedy who listened sympathetically to a plan for a Basutoland-based South African insurgency.[48] Mahomo concentrated on the American labour movement and was rewarded with a $5 000 donation from the AFL/CIO.[49] Mahomo's contacts with AFL/CIO officials provided the basis for rumours that the Pan-Africanists were being helped by the Central Intelligence Agency;[50] if this was the case then the CIA was being unusually miserly, for even by the standards of the time $5 000 was not an extravagant donation.

Nana Mahomo was responsible also for negotiating an agreement with the FNLA (another recipient of AFL/CIO generosity) through which PAC members would receive military training at the FNLA's Kinkuzu camp, near Leopoldville in the Congo. The incongruously named 'Operation Taperecorder' began in November 1963 with the arrival at Kinkuzu of a group of fourteen men from Dar es Salaam led by Nga Mamba Machema, a former

PAC organiser in Langa. It was hoped that the South Africans, together with recruits from the South West African People's Organisation and Mozambican nationalists would acquire practical experience from training and fighting alongside FNLA men against the Portuguese. In January the small PAC nucleus at Kinkuzu was augmented with a 'plane-load of completely untrained men from Francistown. By February the PAC force numbered about fifty men. Their strength, however, was rapidly dissipated. At the root of the trouble were the uncomfortable material conditions at Kinkuzu and the FNLA's ramshackle logistical system. In a letter written in April from one of the trainees to Abednego Ngcobo, then visiting Leopoldville, it was claimed that in the camp there was neither adequate food nor proper training facilities, that many of the trainees were afflicted with fever and that eleven had already deserted.[51] The Angolan troops were hardly an inspiring example: by this stage the FNLA had few activists inside Angola, and the men in Kinkuzu stagnated – no attempt even was made to get them to grow their own food despite the abundance of fertile land around the camp. The PAC men would in any case have been hardly inclined to do so; most of the recruits were from Johannesburg with no knowledge of farming, and the local crops and diet had little appeal. Their behaviour rapidly deteriorated: those who did not desert resorted to factional conflicts. Mutinous sentiments apparently assumed an ethnic/regional dimension; the officers (the Dar es Salaam group) tended to be Xhosa-speakers from the Cape and the lower ranks (the Francistown group) mainly from Johannesburg.[52] The nature of the leadership of the PAC was also partly responsible for the failure of the Kinkuzu project. Whereas Mahomo was reported to be in charge of the Kinkuzu office in December 1963,[53] by January the next year he was back in London. The fact that no high-ranking PAC official was sent with the trainess to share their experiences was significant and typical: very few members of the presidential council ever underwent any form of training. Not surprisingly the Kinkuzu group felt they had been deceived and neglected. By May 1964 the remaining Kinkuzu trainees had been flown back to Dar es Salaam. Notwithstanding their experience, the PAC's links with the FNLA continued,[54] and in April 1971 a PAC group under the command of one Mashombe was said to be operating with FNLA forces independent of any control from PAC headquarters in Dar es Salaam.[55]

The PAC's negligence concerning its recruits in the Congo can be attributed partly to the first of a series of leadership disputes which were to plague the organisation. This one concerned the behaviour of the two external representatives who were appointed in March 1960, Mahomo and 'Molotsi. In January 1964 the Dar es Salaam office was riven by feuds which largely centred on the question of who should control the PAC's finances. 'Molotsi had represented the PAC in Dar es Salaam since 1960 and was responsible for initial negotiations with the OAU/ALC. Abednego Ngcobo, the PAC's treasurer, had no access to ALC or other African-derived funding which was banked into an account to which 'Molotsi was sole signatory. The problem had wider dimensions than simply a personal squabble between Ngcobo and 'Molotsi: there was considerable discontent among PAC men in Dar es Salaam. Some were destitute and several had recently been sent back to Bechuanaland by the Tanganyikan authorities. 'Molotsi's assistant, Gaur Radebe, was in prison, suspected of complicity in a military coup against Nyerere. The Maseru headquarters, alarmed by the reports of corruption and low morale (many PAC men were defecting to the ANC), authorised Patrick Duncan to find out exactly what was happening. Duncan's efforts, together with those of Ngcobo and Jacob Nyaose, to establish which funds had been received and how they were being used, ended up with the intervention of the Tanganyikan government, which froze 'Molotsi's bank account and withdrew his travel documents. 'Molotsi himself was suspended from office and control over funds was restored to Ngcobo.[56]

This incident led to the estrangement of Mahomo from other PAC leaders. As in the case of 'Molotsi, Mahomo was responsible for negotiating much of the PAC's initial financial support and he too was unwilling to relinquish control of funds to the Maseru office. Mahomo was suspended in August 1964 charged with 'misappropriation of funds' and 'attempts to create personal loyalties' and 'sources of personal operation'.[57] In neither case was there any evidence of venality: Mahomo and 'Molotsi may have been simply motivated to maintain their own independent sphere of operation by the increasingly obvious reckless incompetence of Potlake Leballo and his colleagues. The AFL/CIO, incidentally, continued to provide funding for Mahomo's projects.

The PAC's problems were hardly resolved by the suspensions of Mahomo and 'Molotsi. Later in 1963 there were signs of a mounting wave of resentment and criticism of leadership in Francistown, Dar es Salaam and Maseru itself. In Francistown a rift had developed between one group of PAC refugees and another mainly as a result of the reluctance of some to undergo military training. They had left South Africa, they said, on the understanding that they would receive educational scholarships.[58] At the same time the local PAC representative in Francistown, Matthew Nkoana, with the support of 24 of the recruits, drew up a memorandum calling for a conference so that the command structure could be improved. This was rejected by Leballo in Maseru who claimed it represented a conspiracy aimed at his personal overthrow.[59] Leballo had good reason to feel personally threatened from within his organisation: in early 1964 PAC rebels blew up his house in Maseru; fortuitously, he was away at the time and escaped injury.[60] This took place shortly after Leballo had expelled nine of the Maseru-based group so as to forestall a local rebellion against his authority. Unrest spread to the PAC forces in Dar es Salaam with the arrival of the men from Francistown who had refused to accept military training at Kinkuzu. In August 1964 Potlake Leballo finally left Maseru to re-establish the headquarters of the exile movement in its centre of patronage, Tanganyika. Here the mutinous recruits were informed that no scholarships were available and all would have to go on military training courses. They were subsequently despatched to Ghana where it appeared that the PAC had eclipsed the ANC in obtaining Nkrumah's favour.[61] Shortly before Leballo's arrival in Dar es Salaam, Abednego Ngcobo, Peter Raboroko and Ahmed Ebrahim (the PAC's first Indian member) began a tour of China.[62]

The PAC's effort to obtain Chinese support was not the result of an ideological reorientation of its leadership. Significantly, two of the three men who took part in the initial negotiations were later expelled for 'right-wing deviationism'. And while they were in China their colleagues continued to cultivate the friendship of American millionaires and U.S. State Department officials.[63] The fact was that the organisation was desperately short of money: of an estimated requirement of £148 000 the PAC received from the OAU and other sources less than £30 000.[64] The expedient character of the PAC's new pro-Chinese sentiment was confirmed by a rebuke from Nyaose in Dar es Salaam to Leballo in Maseru: 'Wherefore your articles attacking communism when in fact you [should] be attacking the diabolical activities of Joe Matthews and other fellow travellers . . . [you are] prejudicing our support at certain quarters'.[65] Notwithstanding such sophistry, the Chinese 'alliance' was to have a profound effect on the organisation.

The following four years were exceptionally divisive ones for the PAC's leadership. Any analysis of the conflicts which arose in this period is complicated by a tendency by the protagonists to characterise any disagreement in polarised ideological terms. Of course, conflicts within the movement did have an ideological dimension – not all its members found the transition to a Maoist rhetoric easy or acceptable – but tension really centred around the question of who controlled the movement and its resources rather than opposed principles held by contending factions. Ideology at times appeared to be more a matter of etiquette than a system of beliefs and values held by leaders and followers. By 1965, after the expulsion of the PAC's remaining activists from Maseru (where amongst other things, they had attempted to organise the sabotage of the Cape to Johannesburg 'Blue Train'), most of the organisation's energies were devoted to internecine conflict. There is not the space here to document this in detail and a brief summary of the main events must suffice.

Most of 1965 and the first half of 1966 were relatively tranquil. Through the agency of Patrick Duncan, who had a rare attribute for a South African liberation movement representative – he spoke fluent French – the Pan-Africanists managed to obtain Algerian training facilities. Up to then the Algerians had tended to favour the ANC. Their training was considerably superior to that offered by the Angolans or Ghanaians, and for a time rank and file discontent appeared to subside. (Duncan was soon relieved of his Algerian post; his political sympathies and social background were increasingly inappropriate to the mannerisms and conventions the PAC leadership was now trying to emulate.) Meanwhile his colleagues diverted themselves with squabbles over the control and expenditure of Egyptian and Chinese funding.[66] At a more creative level, the PAC adopted a new name for South Africa and broadened its potential appeal by admitting to its ranks former members of the Coloured People's Congress. The new name was 'Azania', a name favoured by early cartographers for part of eastern Africa and derived originally from an Arabic expression. Some PAC men were apparently uncertain of its progeny and Evelyn Waugh, who, in his satirical novel *Black Mischief*, had called his mythical African country Azania, received a courteous letter of enquiry.[67] But whatever the inspiration for the name, the underlying motive for its adoption was a serious and important one – the desire to create an alternative cultural identity for black South Africans. Unfortunately for the PAC, this effort never really developed beyond the stage of symbolic gesture.

The defection of the CPC men to the PAC's ranks was a reflection of the tensions which existed between SACP members and other exiles within the

Congress movement in London. The PAC offered to non-communist CPC men what the ANC did not: full membership and responsibility in an African nationalist organisation, and the PAC had always held in its policy statements that coloured people were African. In fact the ex-CPC activists did not remain in the movement for long; by November 1967 they, together with other London-based PAC men, had constituted themselves as a nucleus of 'real revolutionaries' within the movement, and were highly critical of most of the rest of the leadership.[68] By 1969 most had been ejected from the PAC after Potlake Leballo had become aware of their efforts to challenge his authority.

Most of the movement's internal tensions were kept below the surface until mid-1966. But in August that year, at an anti-apartheid conference in Brasilia, the two PAC representatives ostracised themselves from the rest of the presidential council by reading statements which called for some form of international intervention in South Africa. According to his critics Leballo had approved of these first[69] but they nevertheless conflicted in principle with the more self-sufficient strategy of an initially rural-based 'protracted peoples' war' now advocated by PAC ideologues in the training camps.[70] The two PAC men concerned lent weight to the accusations of CIA manipulation directed against them by subsequently embarking on a visit of the United States.[71] A meeting held under the auspices of the OAU/ALC did not improve matters, Raboroko arguing for a properly representative 'national convention' which would include 'right-wing deviationists' and accusing Leballo of betraying the internal organisation in April 1963.[72] In July 1967 Ngcobo and Raboroko attempted to assume control of the Dar es Salaam office, and the ensuing scuffle was followed by the temporary closure of the office by the OAU/ALC. The two dissenters then held a press conference and called for an amnesty for all expelled and suspended members of the PAC. They were subsequently expelled for being 'on the pay roll of US imperialism' and of conducting a slanderous campaign against Leballo's leadership 'with two small voices of evil cherubim'.[73] Ngcobo, as former PAC treasurer, was for good measure accused of embezzling US and European-derived funds. Ironically, shortly after these expulsions the demand for a reconciliatory meeting was partially acceded to. In a bid to isolate these latest critics, the PAC announced the annulment of all previous suspensions and expulsions and the summoning of a leadership conference in Tanzania in September 1967.

The Moshi conference presents an interesting contrast to the ANC's efforts at internal reform at Morogoro two years later. Unlike the ANC, there was no attempt to make the conference proceedings representative of rank-and-file sentiment: the guerrilla units were represented by one member of the presidential council, T. M. Ntantala. In consequence it was not altogether surprising that despite the tone of 'rigorous but healthy self-criticism' which the PAC claimed predominated at Moshi, the conference mainly served to endorse the actions and behaviour of the PAC leadership. The expulsions of Ngcobo and Raboroko were confirmed and an anti-corruption committee chaired by Potlake Leballo was instituted to investigate allegations of misbehaviour by other senior PAC members. On the premise that 'the masses are ready for a long revolutionary war' the presidential council was replaced by a 'revolutionary command' under the authority of Potlake Leballo which established its headquarters in Lusaka in December 1967 in the hope that Zambia would provide a base for infiltration into hostile territory. It was admitted that hitherto the PAC had devoted a disproportionate effort to 'aimless international diplomacy' and that henceforth the main emphasis of its work would be on re-establishing its link with the internal struggle.[74]

The transfer of the headquarters to Zambia and the promise of greater activism in the future reflected the increasing impatience with which the PAC was being regarded by African statemen. Later in 1967 an OAU meeting in Kinshasha called upon the PAC to justify its continued existence and in February the following year at a council of ministers' meeting in Addis Ababa the movement was presented with an ultimatum: if the PAC did not mount any infiltration efforts by June all OAU aid would cease. To avert this catastrophe twelve men were selected from the group which had established a training camp at Senkobo near Lusaka. In April 1968 they were transported to the Mozambican border in Zambian government Land Rovers. Just before they crossed the border their weapons, which had previously been confiscated by the Zambian authorities, were restored to them. The intention was that the PAC men would cross Mozambique with the guidance of Coremo guerrillas and enter South Africa. In return Coremo would receive their help in sabotaging the Beira oil pipeline to Rhodesia and would receive weapons (without OAU recognition Coremo received very little external assistance). The PAC/Coremo group survived in Mozambique for nearly two months but were finally intercepted at Villa Piri at the beginning of June. Most of the PAC men were captured or killed. The Portuguese subsequently handed their prisoners over to the South African police. Two managed to evade capture and return to Zambia.[75]

The failure of the Mozambique expedition increased rank-and-file disenchantment with the revolutionary command. With the return of the two survivors of the expedition rumours that the guerrillas had been betrayed by the Zambian government and the Lusaka-based leadership began to circulate in the Senkobo base. At this stage, hoping to capitalise on lower echelon disaffection, Leballo's opponents, led by Tsepo Letlaka, first held a meeting in Dar es Salaam and announced the expulsion from the PAC of Leballo and his supporters and then travelled to Zambia. Letlaka, accompanied by Ngcobo, Molete, Nyaose and Raboroko visted the Senkobo camp with the hope of obtaining the guerrillas' support. Instead they were arrested and locked up. At this point the Zambian government intervened, raiding and closing down the PAC office in Lusaka, rounding up all the PAC members on Zambian territory regardless of their loyalties, and returned them to Tanzania. The Zambians then imposed a ban on any PAC activity, claiming that the Pan-Africanists had been involved in an attempt to overthrow the Kaunda administration. In Tanzania the dissidents were housed in a separate camp and most of them eventually made their way to Kenya. The OAU/ALC resolved to deny the PAC any further assistance until it put its internal affairs into order.[76]

What was the significance of all this? The dominant group within the PAC normally characterised such conflicts in grandiose historical terms, the Leballo faction being identified with 'the revolution' or 'the masses' and its enemies with 'imperialism' and 'counter-revolution' and so forth. The dissenters would attribute the organisation's troubles not to external interference but instead to the individual shortcomings of leading personalities within the movement. Both points of view had some justification. Some of Leballo's opponents did appear to have CIA connections. At the same time Leballo's behaviour could be vain, autocratic, self-centred and ill-considered. But neither external subversion nor personal deficiencies provide a satisfactory explanation of the PAC's weaknesses. The PAC was especially susceptible to corruption as a result of manipulation and personal failings, and the reasons for this can be traced back to the movement's essential character.

Three features of the PAC's development made it particularly vulnerable. First, its original ideological cohesion was based on the antipathy of its founders to external influences on the African National Congress. In particular they were hostile to the framework of multiracial alliances, within which the ANC conducted its affairs in the 1950s. For most Africanists this was the predominant consideration. 'African nationalism' on the whole remained a fairly abstract conception; the Africanists had only the vaguest conception of what their social ideal should be. In other words, their main basis for unity was essentially negative. In exile the issue of multiracialism was parochial and increasingly irrelevant. The PAC's previous hostility to 'foreign ideologies' made it especially ill-equipped intellectually to respond to the fresh challenges of a foreign environment. Casting around for new sources of support and inspiration, its leaders oscillated wildly between different international political camps. In place of any analysis and discussion there was substituted a sterile and externally derived dogmatism – for example, in a policy document of 1972, one finds the PAC advocating a rurally based popular insurgency aimed first of all at abolishing 'feudal relations in the countryside'.[77] In such circumstances the movement quickly shed its intellectual integrity.

The second source of weakness was the traditional indifference of most PAC men to the problems of effective organisation. In South Africa their dependence on notions of mass spontaneity and the concept of a charismatic leadership meant that they did not devote much energy to the task of transforming their movement into a carefully structured mass organisation. In exile this neglect led to bureaucratic chaos, and in the absence of well-defined democratic decision-making procedures, an increasing degree of authoritarianism. In such circumstances personal rivalries could have an especially debilitating effect.

Finally, in sociological terms the PAC's leaders often came from less privileged backgrounds than their compatriots in the ANC. They were thus more susceptible to the temptations, pretensions, and delusions of exile politics. The melodrama, hysteria, and grandiloquence inherent in their behaviour was probably a reflection of anxiety about status as well as an attempt to compensate for the insecurity and obscurity of existence in an alien environment. In this context it should be remembered that in many places the PAC did not have the institutional respectability of its rival.

A second meeting at Moshi of those who remained loyal to Potlake Leballo (whose numbers were rapidly diminishing – there were a spate of desertions in late 1968)[78] confirmed the expulsion of the five conspirators and once again reaffirmed the 'revolutionary leadership' of Leballo. Somehow the PAC managed to restore its position with the OAU/ALC, being granted recognition once again in early 1969. Because of continued Zambian intransigence there were to be no further infiltration attempts for several years. While the PAC guerrillas were confined in the Zimbabwe African National Union's training camp and did nothing (there were no weapons for them to train with),[79] Leballo busied himself with political intrigue in Dar es Salaam. In 1969 a group of leading Tanganyika African National Union politicians, whose business interests had led them to oppose Nyerere's Arusha declaration, plotted the overthrow of the government. Without access to the military they planned instead to draw upon the resources of the liberation movements encamped in Tanzania and for this purpose tried to recruit the PAC's Azanian Peoples' Liberation Army (APLA) (as it was known from 1968). The former ALC chairman, Oscar Kambona, then in exile, promised that in return for their cooperation, in the event of a successful coup, the PAC would receive lavish funding and facilities. Leballo, according to the prosecution in the later trial, informed the Tanzanian authorities and was encouraged to maintain contact with the conspirators so as to elicit more information. In 1970 the PAC acting president was the key prosecution witness in a lengthy treason trial.[80] From then onwards, Leballo could depend on the Tanzanian government's support in suppressing any resistance to his authority. The first sign of its approval was the inclusion of APLA men in a training programme being run from late 1970 by Chinese instructors at Chunya.[81]

Any chance that the APLA guerrillas would be able to use their newly learnt skills appeared to recede still further in early 1971, when the Basuto Congress Party (the probable victors of Lesotho's 1970 election), dropped their connection with the PAC in the aftermath of a coup d'etat by the incumbent administration. A rump group of the BCP was then offered a place in the post-coup administration if it ended any links between the BCP and South African liberation movements. Confronted with an increasingly hostile administration, the few remaining PAC members in Lesotho travelled north to Dar es Salaam.

From 1971 to 1975 the PAC made various attempts to negotiate a route back to South Africa for its guerrillas. From 1971 to 1973 the Zambians relented, allowing PAC men into the country for brief periods so they could then arrange their passage through Botswana. In November 1972 talks began with SWAPO representatives in the hope that SWAPO could be persuaded to guide APLA units through the Caprivi Strip into Botswana. The SWAPO people were unenthusiastic and eventually the PAC turned to the Uniao Naçional para Independençia Total de Angola (UNITA) for a similar arrangement. After the arrest of a PAC member for assault, the PAC was again exluded from Zambia.

By late 1973 the APLA guerrillas had been in the Chunya camp for four years, their boredom and sense of isolation relieved only by occasional training sessions, drill exercises, and political education classes. Their mood was becoming increasingly rebellious and appeared to affect some of Leballo's colleagues.[82] Once again the situation was saved by external circumstances. A renewed spate of diplomatic activity had resulted in the development of fresh sources of patronage. In November 1974 PAC lobbyists succeeded in obtaining the expulsion of South Africa from the United Nations General Assembly[83] and in July 1975 the OAU Kampala meeting adopted as official policy a long document prepared by the PAC arguing the case for the illegality of South Africa's international status.[84] Subsequently, both Uganda and Libya offered facilities. Libyan training helped to defuse some of the tension which had developed at Chunya, and 100 APLA men were flown to Libya.[85]

Frelimo's accession to power in June 1975 opened up fresh opportunities for infiltration. The PAC had had a poor relationship with the new rulers of Mozambique but Frelimo were nevertheless prepared to tolerate the passage of Pan-Africanists through their country to Swaziland. It was here that the PAC mounted its first sustained insurgent effort since 1963.

Between September 1975 and May 1976 a small group of guerrillas from Chunya ran a programme of military and political instruction for dissident members of the Mgomezulu tribe. The Mgomezulu straddle the South African–Swazi border and from 1970 had been politically divided by a chieftancy succession dispute, which had developed into intermittent fighting between factions supporting the two opposed claimants. Ntunja, the chief who had been appointed on the death of Mbikiza, was deposed by the South African and Kwa Zulu authorities in early 1974 and in his place Khatwayo, the rival claimant, was installed. Khatwayo's chieftancy began with fighting between his supporters and those of Ntunja. With the help of the South African police, Ntunja's faction was driven off their lands, and fled into Swaziland with their chief. Here they came into contact with PAC representatives who saw in the dissident Mgomezulu faction the potential social base for a rural guerrilla movement. The Mgomezulu were receptive to any offers of help, whatever motives underlay them. With only three old ·303 rifles and a shotgun between them they were anxious to acquire weapons and expertise in using them. They were aware that Pan-Africanists were concerned with a rather wider conflict than their disputed chieftaincy but their own political motivation remained locally orientated.

In October 1975 three men from Chunya who had travelled from Dar es Salaam by aeroplane and bus to Swaziland began training about thirty Mgomezulus. They started with basic lessons on firearms, naming the parts of the ·303 rifles and showing them how to aim and sight the weapon. They were unable to begin target practice as the consequent explosions would have attracted the Swazi police. The training sessions were conducted at Mkalampere, a disputed area on the South African–Swazi border. After a month the PAC men were able to obtain a couple of air rifles which they could allow their new recruits to fire. Training was suspended for six weeks over December 1975 and January 1976 because of the presence in the area of South African soldiers, but was resumed with their departure. Meanwhile PAC officials made several fruitless attempts to persuade President Machel of Mozambique to allow the transit of arms and reinforcements through Mozambique. Machel refused: it was known that a small group of PAC men were with UNITA in Southern Angola, and quite apart from UNITA's hostility to Frelimo's ally the MPLA, UNITA also appeared to have formed an alliance with the South African army. The OAU/ALC was reluctant to give the PAC any weaponry unless it could obtain the agreement of the Zambian and Mozambique authorities to ferry military equipment through their territories. Unable to supply the new followers with weapons, the PAC headquarters instead sent them some approved literature: speeches by Potlake Leballo and Mao's writings on guerrilla warfare. The instructors were told to investigate suitable routes and hiding places but to do nothing until the arrival of arms and further instructions. In April the Swazi police arrested some of the Mgomezulus, whom they had discovered in possession of home-made weapons. Then in early May South African police arrested the three PAC instructors at Mkalampere. With these arrests the PAC lost interest in the affairs of the supporters of Ntunja.[86]

The eve of the Soweto uprising found the PAC weak and once again divided. In Libya the guerrillas had revolted against the stringent code of behaviour imposed by their Islamic instructors and had had to be transferred to Uganda. Money promised by China had failed to arrive (after the defeat of its clients in Angola the Chinese lost interest in Southern Africa) and the OAU was being uncooperative. The most telling factor against the PAC was the system of alliances it had contracted: in the light of the Frelimo and MPLA victories the PAC's former connections with UNITA, the FNLA, and Coremo were extremely unhelpful. This, together with its failure to implement seriously any internal organisational reforms and the continuing rift between leadership and rank and file, was to inhibit its efforts to exploit the changed circumstances of the late 1970s.

This discussion of the PAC would be incomplete without some reference to the situation of the men in the training camps who represented the bulk of the exile movement. In examining their plight the tragic dimension of the PAC's history abroad becomes clearer. For many of them had spent well over a decade in various rural army bases in different African countries. The case of Isaac Mhlekwa, one of the men who worked with the Mgomezulu people, was fairly typical. Mhlekwa had joined the PAC in 1959 while working as a petrol pump attendant in Cape Town. Returning to his family in the Transkei in 1960 to get married he did not participate in the PAC's pass campaign in Cape Town. From 1960 to 1964 he was not politically active but in early 1964 he was visited at his hostel in Langa by the man who had recruited him in 1960. He was told to leave the country and report to the PAC in Francistown for military training. From February to August he stayed with other PAC recruits in Francistown waiting for transport northwards. In August a lorry came from Lusaka to fetch them. After two months of hanging around Lusaka he and his fellow recruits were sent to the Ngulana refugee camp in Tanzania. Then in late 1964 the PAC men at Ngulana were flown to Ghana for their initial military education. The Ghanian training was poor: the men were given conventional military drill by Ghanaian army officers and were badly clothed and fed. At the end of January 1965, after a revolt in the camp at Kumasi, the PAC men were transferred to Algeria. Here the training programme was considerably more sophisticated and the men's material needs more adequately provided for. After going on an officer's training course, Mhlekwa fell ill with tuberculosis and spent five months in hospital in Algiers. On his release from hospital in September 1965 he rejoined his comrades who were now at Mbeya in Tanzania. For ten months their military training lapsed as the PAC had no weapons for them. Instead the recruits occupied themselves with reading texts by Marx, Mao and Lenin and keeping fit with physical exercise. In October 1966 Mhlekwa was transferred to another camp, Ruanda, and was instructed in the use of weapons. Five months later he attended a further training session at Morogoro and was then – in June 1967 – sent to the

Zambian base camp. Mhlekwa spent over a year in Zambia, mainly working in the Lusaka PAC office and being treated for tuberculosis. He was deported in August 1968 with the other PAC members and spent the subsequent years either in Chunya camp or receiving treatment for TB at Mbeya. Most of the people who had been trained with him remained in Chunya.

Underlying the frequent desertions, minor revolts over food and conditions, and the more occasional full-scale mutinies which characterised the history of the camps, was the boredom and obvious futility of the daily existence of the training camp inmates. Because of their refugee status it was difficult for them to take up any form of local employment. There were no attempts to make the camps self-sufficient for their food supplies. What passed for political education comprised uncritical repetition of Maoist catch-phrases: if their public documents can form the basis of an accurate judgement, the PAC's strategic discussions were conducted within a realm of total fantasy.

The trivial and frustrating nature of much of the exile political activity of South Africans between 1960 and 1976 makes it tempting to belittle the significance of the exile phase of black South African resistance. Yet a knowledge of the development of South African political movements during this phase is essential to any understanding of post-1976 black South African politics. The relative ability of the exile movements to respond creatively to dramatically altered internal conditions was to be crucial in shaping the behaviour of a new political generation.

Notes

1   Sheridan Johns, 'Obstacles to guerrilla warfare: a South African case study', *Journal of Modern African Studies*, xi, 2 (1973), p. 274.
2   See Eric Wolf, *Peasant Wars of the Twentieth Century*, Faber, London, pp. 291–3.
3   John Marcum, *The Angolan Revolution*, Volume 2, MIT Press, Cambridge, Massachusetts, 1978, p. 225.
4   Richard Gibson, *African Liberation Movements*, Oxford University Press, Oxford, 1971, p. 66.
5   Kenneth Grundy, *Guerrilla Struggle in Africa*, Grossmann, New York, 1971, p. 195.
6   SACP, Central Committee Report on Organisation, March 1970, quoted in *Ikwezi*, London, ii, 1, March 1976, p. 34.
7   Dennis and Ginger Mercer, *From Shanty Town to Forest: the story of Norman Duka*, Liberation Support Movement, Richmond, Canada, 1974, p. 72 and p. 92.
8   *Ibid*, p. 71.
9   *Ibid*, pp. 92–4.
10 The campaigns are described from the point of view of the Rhodesians and South Africans in Michael Morris, *Southern African Terrorism*, Howard Timmins, Cape Town, 1971, pp. 40–55.
11 Johns, 'Obstacles to guerrilla warfare', p. 278.
12 *Intelligence Digest*, Cheltenham, 368, July 1969, pp. 17–18, cited in Johns, 'Obstacles to guerrilla warfare'.
13 Unsigned 'Reply to the Central Committee of the South African Communist

Party', unpublished statement issued in London by expelled ANC dissidents in February 1976, p. 35.

14 Central Committee of the South African Communist Party, *The Enemy Hidden under the Same Colour*, Inkululeko Publications, London, 1976, p. 15.

15 *Ibid*, p. 14.

16 *Ibid*, p. 15.

17 *Mayebuye*, Dar es Salaam, 10 May 1969, quoted in Johns, 'Obstacles to guerrilla warfare'.

18 The debate surrounding the admission of 'non-Africans' into the ANC can be followed in the two documents cited above, 'Reply to the Central Committee of the South African Communist Party' and *The Enemy Hidden Under the Same Colour*', as well as in *Ikwezi*, London, i, 1, November 1975, and ii, 1, March 1976.

19 The analysis was published in Alex La Guma (ed.), *Apartheid*, Seven Seas Books, Berlin, 1972, pp. 229–44.

20 This is a charge made frequently by ANC dissidents and the PAC and on a more academic level it is a favourite theme of the American scholar, Edward Feit. See also Richard Gibson, *African Liberation Movements*.

21 For purposes of comparison the programmes of the Angolan MPLA and Mozambique's Frelimo would be illuminating.

22 African National Congress, 'Strategy and tactics of the South African Revolution', reprinted in La Guma (ed.), *Apartheid*, p. 198.

23 *Ikwezi*, ii, 1, March 1976, p. 29.

24 Muriell Horrell, *Annual Survey of Race Relations*, South African Institute of Race Relations, Johannesburg, 1971, pp. 00

25 *Sunday Times*, Johannesburg, 11 April 1971.

26 'Reply to the Central Committee of the Communist Party of South Africa', p. 44.

27 *Ibid*.

28 *Ibid*, p. 35.

29 South African Communist Party, *The Enemy Hidden Under the Same Colour*, p. 5.

30 *Sunday Times* (Johannesburg), 27 July 1975.

31 See Marcum, *The Angolan Revolution*, pp. 197–206 and pp. 249–51, and *People's Power*, London.

32 See CAMP microfilm no. Mf-568, State *vs*. Pascal Ngakane, trial transcript, Pietermaritzburg, 1964, RC 139/64.

33 *Rand Daily Mail* (Johannesburg), 8 July 1980.

34 See 'Reply to the Central Committee of the South African Communist Party', pp. 10–14, and Michael Harmel, 'The Communist Party of South Africa', La Guma (ed.), *Apartheid*, p. 225.

35 John Marcum, 'The exile condition and revolutionary effectiveness: Southern African liberation movements', in Christian Potholm and Richard Dale (eds), *Southern Africa in Perspective*, Free Press, New York, 1979, p. 383. This sensitive essay is essential reading for anyone with an interest in exile politics and Marcum's analysis has been the main source of inspiration for this chapter.

36 See John Stockwell, *In Search for Enemies*, André Deutch, London, 1978.

37 Roland Stanbridge, 'Contemporary African political organisations and movements', in Robert Price and Carl Rosberg (ed.), *The Apartheid Regime*, David Philip, Cape Town, 1980, p. 82.

38 For detailed discussion of violent strategies see Joe Slovo, 'South Africa: no middle road', in Basil Davidson, Joe Slovo and Anthony Wilkinson, *Southern Africa: the new politics of revolution*, Penguin, Harmondsworth, 1976, and African National Congress, 'Strategy and tactics of the South African Revolution', in La Guma (ed.), *Apartheid*

39 See for example, Pan-Africanist Congress, *Principles of a United Front in People's War*, London, 1972.

40 See for example, Ben Turok, *Strategic Problems of South Africa's Liberation Struggle*, Liberation Support Movement, Richmond, Canada, 1974.

41 The only such report in the South African English language press since 1976 has been 'The ANC recruit who came home', *Drum*, September 1980, pp. 54–5. Gladstone Lunamfu, recruited in Gugulethu, Cape Town, in mid-1975 was despatched to a transit camp in Gaborone, Botswana. There he spent three months before becoming disenchanted with conditions and the behaviour of the camp's senior officers. He stole money from the camp office and deserted. After various adventures which included being kidnapped and beaten up by a group of SASO refugees, he was repatriated by the Botswana authorities. His testimony seems an unreliable basis on which to base any general conclusions about life in ANC training camps.

42 'Background to official appointments and policy statement', memorandum signed by Potlake Leballo and John Pokela, Maseru, 20 June 1964.

43 Joe Molefi, 'Approach to African Socialism', *New African*, London, i, 12, December 1962, and Elias Ntloedibe, 'Race and nationhood', *New African*, i, 9, September 1962.

44 See Chapter 3.

45 The circumstances surrounding Duncan's recruitment are discussed in C. J. Driver, *Patrick Duncan: South African and Pan-African*, Heinemann, London 1980, pp. 221–4.

46 *Contact*, Cape Town, 5 April 1963, p. 6.

47 See trial reports in *Contact*, April 1965, July 1966, and October 1966.

48 C. J. Driver, *Patrick Duncan*, p. 229.

49 Details of this donation are provided in a letter from the PAC headquarters to the PAC treasurer, A. B. Ngcobo, dated 3 March 1964. See also Matthew Nkoana, *Crisis in the Revolution*, Mafube Publications, London, 1968, Chapter 3.

50 The AFL/CIO's external programme was believed to serve as a conduit for CIA funding. The PAC leadership implied that Mahomo was working with CIA agents in 'Official statement of expulsion and repudiation of the call for United Nations intervention', PAC headquarters, Lusaka, 1967, p. 6.

51 Letter from recruit at Kinkuzu base to A. B. Ngcobo in Leopoldville, dated April 1964.

52 John Marcum, *The Angolan Revolution*, Volume 2, p.

53 *Africa Confidential*, London, December 1963.

54 See report on Potlake Leballo's visit to Kinshasha in supplement to *Le Progres*, Kinshasha, 2 April 1967. Cited in Marcum, 'The exile condition and revolutionary effectiveness', Potholm and Dale (ed.), *Southern Africa in Perspective*, p. 384.

55 *Africa Confidential*, London, April 1971.

56 Driver, *Patrick Duncan*, pp. 235–6.

57 'Instrument of suspension from office', Potlake Leballo to Nana Mahomo, Maseru, 10 August 1964.

58 State *vs.* Stanley Thabo Pule and two others, Supreme Court Natal Division, Case No. ec 133/77, trial records.

59 Open letter from Matthew Nkoana to Potlake Leballo, London, 2 December 1966, p. 6.

60 See report entitled 'Exiles in terrorist activities' in *South Africa: Information and Analysis*, Congress for Cultural Freedom, Paris, no. 25, June 1964.

61 The PAC's espousal of Nkrumah's Pan-Africanism helped in their relationship with the Ghanaian authorities. In March, Jacob Nyaose was claiming that Nkrumah was displeased with the local ANC representatives; by mid-1964 the Ghanaians were providing funding as well as training and in August Nkrumah announced in Cairo that his government would only in future support one liberation movement from each country. Sources: letter from Jacob Nyaose to

Maseru headquarters, 30 March 1964; undated memorandum from Dar es Salaam to Maseru (mid-1964); Report from Dar es Salaam to Maseru, 14 August 1964.

62 Report from Dar es Salaam to Maseru, 14 August 1964.

63 *Ibid.*

64 Pan-Africanist Congress, Dar es Salaam office, financial statement, 31 October 1963 to 31 May 1964.

65 Undated letter from Jacob Nyaose, Dar es Salaam, to Maseru headquarters [May 1964].

66 Matthew Nkoana, *Crisis in the Revolution*, Chapter 4.

67 Driver, *Patrick Duncan*, p. 244.

68 University of York, Centre for Southern African Studies (UY-CSAS), Lionel Morrison Papers, Memorandum of meeting to discuss 'revolutionary nucleus', 12 November 1967.

69 Matthew Nkoana to Potlake Leballo, London, 2 December 1966, p. 8.

70 State *vs.* Stanley Thabo Pule and two others, trial records.

71 Pan-Africanist Congress, 'Official statement of expulsion and repudiation of the call for United Nations intervention', p. 4.

72 UY-CSAS, Patrick Duncan Papers, Report of a joint meeting between OAU/ALC and PAC officials, 6 April 1967.

73 Pan-Africanist Congress, 'Official statement of expulsion . . .', p. 3.

74 Pan-Africanist Congress, Press statement on Moshi Conference, September 1967, signed by Barney Desai, Lusaka, 29 September 1967.

75 Information on the PAC/Coremo expedition derived from Michael Morris, *Southern African Terrorism* and State *vs.* Stanely Thabo Pule and two others, trial records.

76 The episode is described in Morris, *Southern African Terrorism* and in much greater detail in the trial records of State *vs.* Stanley Thabo Pule and two others.

77 Pan-Africanist Congress, *Principles of a United Front in a People's War*, London, 1972, p. 17.

78 State *vs.* Stanley Thabo Pule and two others, trial records.

79 *Ibid.*

80 This was the trial of Oscar Kambona who was accused and convicted *in absentia*.

81 State *vs.* Stanley Thabo Pule and two others, trial records.

82 In December 1973 two members of the Revolutionary Command, P. Gqobose (recently arrived from Lesotho) and Z. P. Moboko, visited Chunya camp and discussed with APLA soldiers the possibility of Leballo's expulsion if an infiltration programme was not launched.

83 *Azania Combat*, London, 1, 1975, p. 7.

84 Pan-Africanist Congress, *The Status of the Bogus Republic of South Africa*, London, 1975.

85 State *vs.* Stanley Thabo Pule and two others, trial records.

86 *Ibid.*

CHAPTER 13

Children of Soweto

This final chapter can be little more than a postscript. The principal concern of this book has been with the protest and resistance movements of the early apartheid period, a time when conditions for the rapid development of the South African economy were provided by increasingly stringent limits on the political and social aspirations of the black population. The movements we have been examining have been, characteristically, localised, fragmented and desperately short of material resources. Only exceptionally did organised and spontaneous movements cohere into significant challenges to the state, and only rarely were these challenges sustained more than momentarily.

The resistance of the 1970s provides a startling contrast in terms of scale and duration to the movements of the 1950s and early 1960s. This has reflected a fundamental crisis in South African society, in its origins both economic and political, a crisis which the authorities are apparently incapable of resolving through reform. The particular drama central to this book has seen its cast swollen by hundreds of thousands, and the intimate localised scenarios through which we have viewed earlier acts are no longer appropriate. Resistance itself has become one of the components of this crisis. But the most this chapter can present is a synopsis.

Before this, though, a tentative explanation for the relative tranquility of the 1960s is necessary. The most obvious cause of this was the suppression of the nationalist movements and the imprisonment, banning or exile of an entire generation of politicians and trade unionists. During the 1960s the police were granted unlimited powers of arrest and detention as well as increasingly lavish budgets. The police recruited an army of informers whose activities promoted a climate of fear and distrust, effectively paralysing any political initiative amongst Africans.[1] The decade also witnessed fresh restrictions on political discussion with the silencing of the radical press and the increasingly apolitical content of African commercial journalism.[2]

As well as legislation specifically intended to contain radical protest, other policies effectively served to curb any African political dissent. During the decade the government worked systematically to reverse the flow of African urbanisation and to restructure the industrial workforce into one composed principally of migrant labour. The process set in motion in the late 1950s in the western Cape was now enacted on a national scale. Over a million labour tenants and farm squatters and 400 000 city dwellers were resettled in the Bantustans, the population of which increased by 70 per cent in the 1960s. In addition, 327 000 people were brought directly under the control of the Bantustan authorities as a result of townships being incorporated within the boundaries of the reserves neighbouring them.[3] Nearly two-thirds of the country's African townships actually declined in size. Movement between the reserves and the towns was further controlled after 1968 with the completion of the rural labour bureaux system. As official regulation of people's lives became more and more severe so the prison population rose: by 1970 it was nearly twice what it had been in 1960 (outstripping an overall population growth of 25 per cent).[4] All these changes helped to break down existing networks of social solidarity and hamper the creation of new ones. They also contributed to the atmosphere of fear and insecurity which perpetuated political apathy.

Finally, and less importantly, the institutions of apartheid provided a limited degree of cooption. The administrative and political structures of the Bantustans helped to accommodate the career aspirations of a section of the African petty bourgeoisie. The expansion of segregated educational facilities and the African white-collar employment generated by the 1960s may have helped to deflect well-educated Africans from political activism. Nevertheless, by 1968 there were signs of revolt amongst one of the groups placed to enjoy whatever modest benefits apartheid in its prosperity could offer Africans: the students of the new segregated universities.

The role of African student disaffection and the political discourse arising from it in generating the conditions which gave birth to the uprisings of the mid-1970s is a controversial issue and will be discussed later. There is no question, though, that as far as young urban middle class Africans were concerned, by 1976 the often inchoate philosophy of 'Black Consciousness' was the dominant intellectual influence in their political perceptions.

The Black Consciousness movement was philosophic and introspective at first; only later did its leaders consciously attempts to popularise their ideas and evolve a political programme, and even then their activism was limited to initiating community development projects. Though drawing on the same intellectual tradition as the Africanists, they did not share the latter's passionate concern with strategic and tactical questions. The Africanists were a pressure group within a political party whereas the Black Consciousness movement's influence cannot be adequately understood if analysis is limited to its formal organisational expressions. The history of these is well documented[5] and a brief recapitulation will have to suffice here.

In the post-Sharpeville era the avowedly liberal National Union of South African Students (NUSAS) was one of the few remaining vehicles for multiracial political activity. Its following was concentrated in the four English-medium universities of Witwatersrand, Cape Town, Durban, and Rhodes (Grahamstown), the first three of which accepted black students (after 1959 only with ministerial permission). The efforts of students' representative councils at the African segregated universities of Turfloop, Ngoye and Fort Hare to affiliate to NUSAS was one of the main issues over which African students clashed with the university authorities between 1960 and 1967. Nevertheless, by 1967, many black students were disenchanted with NUSAS's leadership. There were several reasons for this. First, white student leaders had become less politically outspoken and more concerned with the preservation of academic freedoms which most black students did not in any case enjoy. Secondly, the number of African students on the segregated campuses had quadrupled since 1960; these now represented the majority of African students and NUSAS's predominantly white leadership was unable to reflect their particular concerns. Even if they had been sensitive to the needs of this constituency their organisation was in any case prohibited from operating on African campuses in 1967. Finally, there were ideological stimuli which helped to distance black students from whites, especially the American-derived Black Theology which predominated in the University Christian Movement, which from its inception in 1967 had gained a significant following on the segregated campuses. An incident in 1967 served to underline for black NUSAS members the futility of participation in white liberal institutions: at NUSAS's annual conference at Rhodes the university authorities insisted that African delegates should use segregated social facilities. During the following year, black students involved both in NUSAS and in the University Christian Movement began to discuss the establishment of an all-black movement. The South African Students' Organisation (SASO) held its inaugural conference at Turfloop in July 1969.

From its foundation SASO perceived its purpose to be an agent in the process of 'conscientisation' within the black communities. Its leaders, like their intellectual forerunners the Africanists, argued that the immediate problem in mobilising black resistance was psychological. Before one could consider the difficulties of organisation and strategy the inferiority complexes engendered by oppression and paternalism had to be overcome. Jettisoning any links between black leadership groups and predominantly white liberal institutions was essential if all traces of a dependency mentality were to be eradicated. White liberals lacked the appropriate motivation to identify fully with black political and social aspirations. More positively, blacks had to create a social identity to replace the concepts generated by white liberal notions of African integration into a western capitalist society. To this end blacks should draw on indigenous cultural traditions and critically scrutinise externally-derived ideological systems. At a less abstract level, commercial, cultural, professional and welfare institutions should be established so as to instil black self-confidence as well as lessening the material reliance of blacks on white-controlled resources. In two important respects the SASO generation differed in its analysis from the Africanists. First, while attributing the same value to group assertion as a response to oppression by a homogenously conceived white community, they were nevertheless prepared to concede there were divisions within the black community; increasingly these were conceptualised in class terms.[6] Secondly, blacks were not defined as such ethnically: from the start the Black Conciousness movement involved Indians and coloureds as well as Africans.

The organisational manifestations of this new intellectual movement were not very extensive: SASO's leaders, together with personalities drawn from several (rather conservative) African religious and educational bodies, established in 1972 a Black People's Convention (BPC). The BPC's proclaimed objectives included liberation from psychological and physical oppression and the implementation of 'Black Communalism' through economic cooperatives, literacy campaigns, health projects, cultural activity and a general workers' union, the Black Allied Workers' Union (BAWU). Despite its 41 branches the BPC did not develop into a mass organisation, probably not exceeding the membership of SASO which claimed 4 000 subscribers to its newsletters.

It is at this point that the comparison between the Black Consciousness movement and its ideological precursors becomes misleading. The Africanists had the immediate and narrow aim of altering the programme of a political organisation, and through the organisation then influencing popular political behaviour. Their success can be measured in formal organisational terms. They were a small exclusive sect; only at a late stage in their development did they attempt to transform themselves into a popular movement. The Black Consciousness movement from its start had a much larger constituency and because of the absence of an effective national political organisation worked through more informal channels of influence. Merely because its exponents and identifiable followers were relatively socially privileged and hence unrepresentative of the black community as a whole did not mean they were not popularly influential. The student advocates of Black Consciousness were to become school teachers, priests and journalists, and its basic themes were taken up in the popular press, in township cultural events, and even, though at a later stage, in African consumer-oriented advertising.

Existing academic discussions of Black Consciousness have consisted principally of intellectual appraisals of the ideas. These range from sympathetic expositions of their analytical logic[7] to scathing attacks, usually mounted from Marxist premises, on their sociological shallowness and internal inconsistencies.[8] What is lacking is a historical explanation of the emergence of the movement and a sociological investigation of the extent of its influence. Both of these are beyond the scope of this chapter. There are no scholarly biographical studies of the leading figures in the movement, an essential prerequisite for any understanding of why men like Steve Biko, Barney Pityana or Harry Nengwekulu developed intellectually when they did in the way they did. Any appreciation of the popular impact of their ideas should be informed by a detailed knowledge of the changing sociological composition of the African population in the major urban centres during the 1960s. In Johannesburg especially, the commercial centre of South Africa, one of the corollaries of economic expansion was the growth of an African clerical workforce. Primary and secondary education had contributed to a sharply rising growth in the number of people who were literate; this was reflected in the development of a tabloid mass circulation press – Johannesburg's black population by 1970 was supporting two daily newspapers. This is not to suggest that the sixties was a decade of general prosperity – poverty datum line statistics indicate an unchanging degree of urban black penury – but rather that in contrast to the 1940s, there was a considerable enlargement in the size of an audience receptive to fairly complex political ideas. An indication of this was the fashion in which the rhetoric of Black Consciousness washed over the boundaries of purely political concerns to infuse the patois of African petty-bourgeois culture with a fresh bitter assertiveness. Nowhere is this more evident than in the township literary revival of the early seventies – especially in its poetry:

> Now I'm talking about this;
> 'Shit' you hear an old woman say,
> Right there, squeezed in her little match-box
> With her fatness and gigantic life experience,
> Which makes her a child,
> 'Cause the next day she's right there,

> Right there serving tea to the woman
> Who's lying in bed at 10 a.m. sick with wealth,
> Which she's prepared to give her life for
> 'Rather than you marry my son or daughter.'[9]

Academic dissection of the intellectual components of Black Consciousness has had a tendency to underestimate the sheer emotional power of its message. More acutely than any of their predecessors, Biko and his colleagues understood the complexity of feelings engendered through subservience:

> But the type of black man we have today has lost his manhood. Reduced to an obliging shell, he looks with awe at the white power structure. . . . In the privacy of his toilet his face twists in silent condemnation of white society but brightens up in sheepish obedience as he comes out hurrying in response to his master's impatient call. . . . His heart yearns for the comfort of white society and makes him blame himself for not having been 'educated' enough to warrant such luxury.[10]

Of course it could be contended that the problems of self-identity and cultural emasculation were of relevance only to those who were most affected by 'white' cultural hegemony, that the concerns of Black Consciousness were rather precious in the light of the daily struggle for existence of working-class men and women.[11] This may have been the case but it scarcely diminishes the movement's importance. If its influence was limited to the urban intelligentsia this would have guaranteed its imprint on almost any African political assertion of the time. Distilled to a basic set of catchphrases Black Consciousness percolated down to a much broader and socially amorphous group than African intellectuals.

The obvious philosophic contributions to Black Consciousness derived from contemporary American theorists of Black Power, who with the somewhat earlier existentialist school of francophone African writers, were key elements in shaping the thinking of this new political generation. So too was Bantu Education and, conversely, the declining force of South African liberalism. A more fundamental cause of the genesis of the new movement, however, was the social development referred to above; the coming of age, despite the institutions of apartheid, of a new African petty bourgeoisie.[12]

The re-emergence of black industrial and political resistance which began with the Durban strike movement of October 1972 must be understood in the context of the difficulties which were beginning to be encountered within the South African economy. Differences between the various interpretations of these difficulties have flowed mainly from the question of whether they are endemic (or 'organic' or 'structural') to South African capitalism, or, on the other hand, whether they are capable of being resolved within the framework of capitalist relations of production. The debate need not concern us here: both Marxists and non-Marxists (including apologists for the system) appear to be in agreement that in South Africa for the foreseeable future capitalism will survive though a rising rate of coercion will be needed to cope with the accompanying political tensions.[13]

The elements in this economic crisis reflect the pattern of economic development during the 1960s, when a vast quantity of foreign capital was invested in South African manufacturing. By the 1970s local industrialists were confronted with the need for larger markets than the South African economy could provide. They were in a disadvantaged position compared with manufacturers in industrially developed countries for two reasons. First, political hostility to South Africa inhibited their efforts to convert the rest of Africa into a market for South African manufacturers. Second, to compete with European, Japanese and American products, South African exports needed to be cheaper. This would require higher levels of labour productivity, that is, a more skilled and technically competent workforce. The obvious implication of this would be higher wages (which would effectively enlarge the domestic market). Raising black wages would involve two sets of socio-political problems. The corollary of higher wages would be greater capital intensity and in consequence an increase in unemployment. More affluent black workers could stimulate anxiety and political disaffection among badly paid white groups.

Contributing to the climate of economic uncertainty were sharp movements in the gold price, when first of all South Africa, in order to raise the price of gold from its fixed convertibility to the dollar, began to restrict the gold supply, thereby leading to a sixfold increase in its price between February 1973 and December 1974. This was followed by a sharp fall in the gold price between December 1974 and August 1975, as the United States began to sell of its reserves on the private market, and a consequent economic recession in South Africa.

As growth rates slackened to a point of actual decline in 1976 the climate of insecurity was accentuated by external political developments. With the massive rise in the oil price in 1973 the relative importance of African oil producers as trading partners to Western industrial countries grew and South Africa's correspondingly diminished. More immediately alarming, South Africa's immunity from guerrilla insurgencies was substantially reduced with the collapse in 1974 of Portuguese authority in Angola and Mozambique.

Economic recession led to sudden rises in the rate of inflation in the early and mid-seventies as well as spasmodic contractions in the job market. The need for more skilled labour and a larger domestic market led to reformist impulses among more advanced sectors of the business community and in consequence raised economic and social expectations among urban Africans. This sharpened the psychological effect of price rises and unemployment. Political and economic insecurity within the white community contributed to the inability of the regime to respond effectively to black unrest. Inhibited on the one hand by the needs of big business, and on the other by the requirements of economically vulnerable but politically powerful white workers, the government could adopt neither a strategy of thoroughgoing reform nor a policy of unmitigated repression. This strategic indecisiveness on the part of the state has been one of the most significant factors which have distinguished the development of black resistance movements in the 1970s from those in the two preceding decades.[14]

The post-Sharpeville quiescence ended with a dramatic explosion of labour unrest in Durban in the first months of 1973. The statistics tell their own story: during the 1960s approximately 2 000 workers went on strike each year; the early 1970s saw a slight rise in these figures with six strikes and 5 000 strikers in 1972, and then in the first three months of 1973, 160 strikes involving 61 000 workers took place, these being concentrated in Durban but spreading to East London and the Rand later.[15] From 1973 to 1976 Durban continued to be the centre of industrial militancy, with East London and the East Rand as the two other areas most affected by strikes.[16]

Their scale, spontaneous character and degree of success made these strikes unique in South Africa's labour history. They had several distinctive features. The strikers refused to elect a leadership, thus immunising themselves from the effects of victimisation and cooption. They avoided all formally constituted representative bodies (there were in any case very few of these). They relied principally on the sharp demonstrative shock of a short withdrawal of labour to gain concessions from employers rather than entering negotiations or protracted confrontations. The workers stayed in the vicinity of their factories which may have afforded them some protection against police reprisals. The conscious aim of the strikers in almost all cases was to gain better wages.

While there is little difficulty in identifying the major cause of the strikes – a sharp upswing in the inflation rate[17] after a decade of slowly increasing African real wages – more problematical is the question of why the strike wave originated in Durban. The question has a significance which extends to any analysis of the events in Soweto three years later. Durban's importance as an industrial centre is equalled only by the East Rand–Johannesburg area; unlike the latter it has a culturally rather more homogeneous workforce. This second consideration is important in explaining the unity between migrant and legally defined 'urban' workers in Durban. On the other hand, it cannot be demonstrated that material conditions for workers were any worse in Durban than elsewhere. Because of the absence of any significant features which distinguish Durban's workers from those in other places – even their cultural and linguistic uniformity was not unique – a number of incidental factors assume an additional importance, for in combination they functioned as very powerful catalysts. These included the following: a 16 per cent rise in bus fares and rumours of an impending bus boycott (the fare rises were national in their scope); the rather atypical influence of the Bantustan leadership on the Zulu workers – for reasons which will be discussed later this leadership still retained considerable popular legitimacy, and in the first of the Durban strikes the Paramount Chief had intervened on the workers' behalf; the impact on African workers of local press publicity given to the poverty datum line as a result of the work on the Natal NUSAS 'Wages Commission'; the effect of the first strike at Coronation Brick and Tile which ended with a wage increase being granted to workers in nearby factories; and finally, the presence in each of the main industrial concentrations of a factory belonging to the Frame Textile Group which was notable for its poor wages, high rate of turnover and bad labour relations – it was the workers in these factories who led the strike movement in each area.[18] In assessing the reasons for the strikes' success in extracting wage rises from employers it should be remembered that after a decade of increasing capital intensity, wages would have been a less important component of production costs and in consequence manufacturers would have been more receptive to pressure to increase wages than in an earlier era.

From the Durban strikes an African trade union movement came to life once more. It now had its nucleus in worker advisory organisations founded by mainly white, radical students and people drawn from the African affairs section of TUCSA. In this context the General Factory Workers' Benefit Fund (formed by Natal students) and the Johannesburg-based Urban Training Project were important. The characteristics of the different groups of unions which grew out of the 1973 strikes will be examined later. What is immediately relevant here is that this generation of African unions avoided any political orientation and constituted themselves from the bottom up, factory by factory. This was in direct contrast to the broad industrial mass movement approach adopted by CNETU and SACTU in the 1940s and 1950s.

Having sketched in the main features which form the background to the Soweto uprising – that is, economic recession, a more politically assertive aspirant African petty bourgeoisie, and consecutive waves of labour unrest – we can turn to an examination of the revolt itself. The initial spark to what what was to develop into a virtual communal insurrection was provided by police over-reaction to a street procession of secondary school pupils on their way to Orlando stadium to protest against the recent insistance by the educational authorities that arithmetic and social studies be taught in Afrikaans. The demonstration had been preceded by strikes and attacks on police and teachers at several junior secondary schools in Soweto. On 13 June 1976, at a meeting of the South African Students' Movement (SASM) convened at Naledi High School, a Soweto Students' Representative Council (SSRC) was formed, composed of SASM delegates, two from each Soweto secondary school. It was this body, under the initial chairmanship of Tebello Motopayane, which planned the fateful demonstration for 16 June. On that day 15 000 children converged on Orlando West Junior Secondary School, only to be confronted by a hastily summoned and aggressive police detachment which, when tear gas had failed to disperse the students, fired into the crowd, killing two and injuring several more. The schoolchildren retreated and fanned out into the township. By midday rioting had broken out in several parts of Soweto; cars were stoned and barricades erected, arson attacks took place on administration buildings and beer halls, and two white men were attacked and killed. The rioting continued into the evening and deepened in intensity when police baton-charged homecoming crowds of commuters outside railway stations.

During the next few days, while the revolt spread to pupil and student groups in Kagiso (Krugersdorp), Thembisa (Kempton Park), the East Rand and Pretoria townships and the Universities of Witwatersrand (briefly), Turfloop, Ngoye and Natal, the pattern of attacks on police patrols and symbolically significant buildings was established in Soweto. Schools were closed by the Minister for Bantu Education on the 18th and by the beginning of July Soweto was uneasily quiet. In the interval before the formal re-opening of schools on the 26th the Afrikaans teaching medium ruling was dropped by the authorities, the first ANC leaflets in response to the riots appeared (calling on the pupils to broaden the concerns and the constituency of the revolt), and an older generation of community leaders formed the Black Parents' Association

(BPA). The BPA, drawn from professional people and churchmen, took no political initiatives during the disturbances themselves (in any case all its members were in detention by mid-August), but rather played an auxiliary role in arranging medical and legal services as well as funerals for victims of police action. Meanwhile a change of leadership had taken place in the SSRC, Motopanyane, who had fled the country, being replaced by Tsietsi Mashinini. Divorced from their natural constituency by the closure of the schools (strikes had taken the form of class-boycotts rather than pupil stay-aways from school), the SSRC leaders called for a return to schools when they reopened. Their tactical reasons for doing this could obviously not be communicated in their appeal and in consequence pupil response was divided and hesitant, the reopening being marked by a trickle of returning pupils and the first arson attacks on schools. In the next ten days fifty Transvaal schools were damaged by fire. On 3 August the police settled any doubts there may have been on the question of attending school by mounting a series of raids on school premises in an effort to root out the SSRC leadership. Thereupon the schools re-emptied and were to remain empty for the rest of the year.

The revolt now passed into its second phase when the SSRC mounted the first of several stay-at-homes. This first effort on 4 August was characterised by a greater degree of coercion than was used by the inciters of any of its successors and achieved on its first and most successful day a 60 per cent abstention from work by Africans in Johannesburg. On the same day the pupils attempted to march in protest against the detentions (also the theme of the stay-away) to Johannesburg's police headquarters, John Vorster Square, but were halted on the Soweto highway by police gunfire and turned back to Soweto, leaving three dead. The next day the revolt assumed national proportions with protests by schoolchildren and violent police response in Cape Town and the urban centres of the eastern Cape. By the end of the year the only African urban communities relatively unaffected by the disturbances were those in Natal.

Two more effective stay aways were mounted by the SSRC in Soweto, one in the week beginning on 23 August and one between 13–15 September. In the second stay-at-home, which was called jointly in the name of the SSRC and the ANC, a section of the migrant worker population of Mzimhlope Hostel in Soweto, with the toleration and even alleged encouragement of the police, raged through the streets of the township killing any young people they found in their path. Though their behaviour was not typical of that of the Johannesburg hostel population during the riots, it was in part a reflection of the insecurity relative to the permanent township population of their life. There were similar tensions between Langa hostel dwellers and school pupils in Cape Town later in the year. The third stay at home which took place after the SSRC had negotiated with Mzimhlope representatives was distinguished by the support it received from migrant workers.

After the final event of this second phase – a harshly repressed street demonstration in Johannesburg's central business area (following the example of Cape Town children the demonstrators took the train into central Johannesburg) – the revolt entered a third, less activist and more introspective stage of its development, with the campaigns against shebeens, alcohol and Christmas celebrations. This was accompanied for a brief period in October by the activities of an urban guerrilla group which exploded home-made devices at Jabulani police station and the Pelikan Nite Club (its proprietor was ignoring the alcohol boycott), as well as blowing up a section of railway line. Although the educational system continued throughout 1977 to be subject to almost total disruption, and the SSRC was still capable of forcing the resignation of the Urban Bantu Council (the highly unpopular bureaucratic successor to the urban Advisory Board), the insurrectionary flavour of the revolt had diminished. The Soweto uprising had subsided leaving in its wake at least 575 dead and 2 389 wounded (the highly conservative official estimates)[19] and a completely transformed political environment.

Since 1976 four major analyses of the revolt have appeared, each with differing emphases upon the various factors they perceived to be the causes of the revolt as well as contrasting interpretations of its development and significance. Many of these differences have flowed from the ideological premises of the writers – the liberal South African journalist, John Kane-Berman; the exiled South African revolutionaries, Baruch Hirson and Brickhill and Brooks; and the Transvaal Judge-President, Cillié. Kane-Berman's analysis was the first to be published. For him 'the single most important factor' in explaining the volatility of the townships was the influence of Black Consciousness ideology.[20] A crisis of raised expectations contributed to the rebellious mood of the African urban population: a large increase in secondary school graduates as the result of recent educational expansion, as well as steadily rising wages, led to acute frustration as school leavers were confronted by a dwindling job supply and more affluent wage-earners by an ever-worsening housing shortage.[21] In Soweto the situation was aggravated by a particularly unsympathetic township administration. In 1971 responsibility for African urban communities was transferred from municipal control to regional administration boards under the Bantu Administration Department. (This was done because the government suspected that in response to pressure from local employers municipalities were resisting migratory labour practices and industrial decentralisation.) The consequences of the assumption of control of Soweto's affairs by the West Rand Administration Board (WRAB) in 1971 were the loss of a two million Rand municipal subsidy and an attempt by the Board to make Soweto completely self-financing. The consequences of this were increased rents, decreased expenditure on housing, lodgers' fees imposed on children over eighteen living with their parents, and a noticeable deterioration in the standard of services and welfare facilities. The harshness and arrogance of WRAB's officials (who more and more frequently tended to be Afrikaans-speaking whites) contributed further to popular resentment of WRAB. The police riot of 16 June was the final provocation which elicited rebellion, first from recently politicised schoolchildren and then from their increasingly alienated parents.

Jeremy Brickhill and Alan Brooks place the main emphasis of their analysis of the causes of the revolt on the changes in the educational system. In 1970, in response to the skilled labour shortage, there began a rapid expansion of African secondary education which was to nearly treble its intake during the next five years. The effects of this expansion were especially acute in Soweto where the growth in numbers of secondary school pupils had been especially swift. The expansion of the system obviously necessitated more expenditure on it but because of the recession additional funds were not allocated. Secondary schools, especially in the junior forms, became very overcrowded. This overcrowding reached crisis-point in 1975 when, in order to further enlarge the flow of secondary school graduates, the final primary form was incorporated into the lowest secondary grade, effectively doubling the 1976 secondary school intake. To an educational system already subject to severe strains was added the doctrinaire[22] ruling on the use of Afrikaans in mathematics and social studies. This was objectionable on several grounds; few teachers were qualified to use the language, proficiency in English was popularly regarded as a prerequisite for clerical employment, and Afrikaans was unacceptable for ideological reasons.

Brickhill and Brooks's interpretation of the causes of the uprising differs from Kane-Berman's in its consideration of economic factors and political influences. They concede that some groups of African workers may have been experiencing wage improvements, but the effect of this, they argue, was undercut by huge increases in the price of basic foods and other essentials during early 1976. In addition the general decline in the economy meant that many workers were confronted with the prospect of short time or total unemployment. At the political level they attribute greater importance to the ANC's role than does Kane-Berman. By 1974, they claim, former political prisoners, stimulated perhaps by Portuguese decolonisation and the opening-up of South African frontiers to insurgents, had reformed ANC cells. Some of the SSRC members later interviewed in exile said they had belonged to such cells. Brickhill and Brooks discern no direct link between SASM and the Black Consciousness groups and imply that Black Consciousness ideology was important only in relation to the responses of older middle-class Africans to the actions of the schoolchildren. SASM itself developed from an organisational subculture of township teenager associations which the authors describe in great detail but without explaining their emergence in the first place.[23]

The main thrust of Baruch Hirson's argument is towards denying the importance of the Black Consciousness movement as an instigator of, or an influence upon, the uprising; instead, in the centre of the historical stage he places the reassertion of African working-class militancy. As with Brickhill and Brooks, Hirson's analysis emphasises the organisational autonomy of SASM from the Black Consciousness groups as well as the involvement of a few of its leaders with the ANC. Black Consciousness ideas had little impact on schoolchildren; more important in affecting their behaviour were the reorganisation of secondary schools and the threat of eventual unemployment. In the course of his book, Hirson develops a systematic critique of Black Consciousness. The historical importance of the movement, one is led to conclude, was an essentially negative one. In as much as it was influential at all, with its lack of resistance strategy and its sociological obfuscation, the movement helped to immobilise and confuse a group which might have provided the experienced leadership so badly needed during the course of the uprising.

Overshadowing the significance of Black Consciousness in contributing to the ideological climate of rebellion, Hirson argues, was the effect of the strikes of 1973 and 1974 which instilled a new feeling of self-confidence in the urban African community (which of course was augmented by the South African army's inability to defeat the MPLA in Angola during the summer of 1975–6). The strikes directly affected a much larger section of the population than any of the Black Consciousness organisations, helping to induce an appetite for resistance and confrontation. The continuation of the industrial strike movement into 1976 represented a lost historical opportunity. It was the absence of a working-class oriented political party which could have made the crucial link between the community struggle in the townships and the industrial struggle in the factories that made the 1976 uprising a revolution *manquée*.[24]

In comparison with these first three treatments, the findings of the South African government's Commissioner of Inquiry, Mr Justice Cillié, as to the causes of the uprising are intellectually otiose. The immediate causes, argues the Commissioner, lay in the field of communication: in the lack of official awareness of the extent of dissatisfaction over the Afrikaans issue and in the deficiencies in police township intelligence which prevented them from foreseeing an imminent eruption. There was widespread dissatisfaction arising from the Administration Board system, low wages, influx control, housing shortages, racial discrimination, inadequacies in public transport and so forth, and this dissatisfaction crystallised into active revolt as the result of the work of agitators. Much of this agitation was of an intimidatory character, and, as Cillié goes on to explain:

> Because of this intimidation . . . it cannot be said that the riots were an expression of the Black man's wish or that, by rioting, he was raising his voice against oppression and for a more democratic dispensation in the Republic of South Africa.[25]

The value of Cillié's massive survey lies in its descriptive detail (much of which is in flat contradiction to the report's conclusions). Over a thousand pages are devoted to a meticulous (if at times tendentious) narrative of the hourly ramifications of the uprising as it manifested itself throughout the country.

From this literature it is possible to extract a convincing analysis of why the revolt in its particular form took place when it did where it did. As we have seen, however, there are obvious points of conflict in the historiography, the most important of which concern the role of Black Consciousness. Kane-Berman's assertion that Black Consciousness was the 'single most important factor' in the origins of the uprising is left unexplained and unsubstantiated save for the somewhat tentative presumption that the SSRC was 'part of the Black Consciousness movement' and as such had lines of communication extending to SASO.[26] Conversely, Kane-Berman's understanding of the revolt accords little importance to working-class struggles at the point of production. Disregarding Cillié for the moment, the other two analyses, with their more detailed grasp of the organisational complexities of Black Consciousness and township-based political groupings, view the impact of Black Consciousness on school pupils as minimal. The weakness of both contentions is that they tend to estimate the influence of ideas in terms of formal organisational structures and affiliations. Given the fact that Black

Consciousness seems to have been especially pervasive among university students, school teachers and churchmen it would surely have been a little surprising if sentiments inspired from it were not found in schoolchildren for whom such people were an important reference group. And if one insists on narrowing the focus to a consideration of the organisations, it does not take very long to find traces of Black Consciousness influence on the SSRC and its predecessors. At the third annual conference of SASM, held in Roodepoort one month before the uprising began, the theme of the discussion was 'Reconstruction towards Self-Determination'. Lecture titles included 'Militancy on the Campuses', 'Black Theology', and 'Black Consciousness and the History of the Struggle'.[27] Both Cillié and Hirson incidentally provide powerful testimony to the importance of Black Consciousness as a motivating force in the western Cape coloured community's participation in the revolt.[28]

Hirson's argument that it was the African working class, rather than the students, who set the pace of renewed resistance in the 1970s is very difficult to evaluate. Certainly it is possible that the victories arising from strike action may have contributed to the political assertiveness of urban blacks. Nevertheless it should be remembered that in 1976 any memories of events in 1973 would have been dimmed by three years, that subsequent strikes were accorded very little press publicity, and that the strike movement as a whole developed mainly in Natal, the East Rand, the East London conurbation, not in Johannesburg. It is also relevant to point out that Soweto was not a predominantly industrial working-class community; it had a disproportion-ately large white collar/petty-bourgeois group – numbering 50 000 – and the township's population had been left virtually untouched by the revival of working-class consciousness and trade unionism that had begun elsewhere. It is likely that the bewildered and self-accusatory response of the middle-class oriented *World* newspaper was a much more generalised perception among Soweto adults than the advocates of a township-based syndicalism would have us believe:

> It may be that we have become so shell-shocked that nothing seems to touch us to the raw. . . . So many parents these days are taking very calmly the horrid fact that their sons and daughters have fled the country. If parents do not shrug their shoulders with indifference when their sons and daughters are arrested, they do something very similar. . . . They sigh wearily, they shake their heads – and they trudge off to that miserable job, travelling in those miserable trains, as if the whole world was a bed of roses.
>
> I am able to trace this attitude back some months in Soweto. Early this year when the clouds of discontent were building ominously in our schoolyards, we shook our heads and clicked our collective tongue. Then the kids boycotted classes. Still we shook our collective head lethargically and hummed our collective disquiet. Then the boycotts began to spread. The reaction was the same from the whole world of adulthood. . . .
>
> The scenario began to hot up. We were frightened. We were shocked. But all we did was despair.
>
> The lens moves to the graveyards and this time the adults are in the line of fire. What a moan there was in Soweto! What a tearing out of hair and

collective gnashing of teeth there was! And that was all.

This time they were picking up our babies right in our own homes. Oh what a clicking of tongues there was this time! So many frightened mothers and fathers dashing out in their cars to hide their children.

My language spells it out very clearly – 'Singa, magwala' (we are cowards).[29]

The other topic over which there are important differences of interpretation between the historians of the uprising concerns the quality and nature of the leadership provided by the SSRC. The most favourable evaluation is from John Kane-Berman who describes the SSRC as a 'student government' and attributes to the organisation an extraordinary degree of popular legitimacy. To substantiate this he points to the shebeen closure in October (the suppression of these illegal liquor outlets was a project which had eluded the authorities for decades) and the discipline they were able to evoke from such diverse groups as shopkeepers, taxi-drivers, professional football players, and even tsotsis. While not glossing over their tactical errors (the coercion employed in the first stay-at-home and the confused policy with regard to the sitting of examinations), Kane-Berman is at pains to stress 'an intelligence, a clear-sightedness, a reasonableness, an awareness of responsibility to the community'[30] which characterised the SSRC leadership. On the whole, one does not receive the impression that the SSRC leaders behaved in the manner of revolutionaries.

Brickhill and Brooks provide a comparably idealised treatment of the leadership, though their interpretation of its role is very different from that of Kane-Berman:

> The term 'uprising' does seem appropriate when we consider the political aims of the struggle. There were a number of distinct themes such as the call for the release of political prisoners, the campaign for the replacement of Bantu Education, the campaign against the sale of liquor, etc. In South African conditions, and taken in their totality, these specific demands cannot be satisfied short of a transfer of power – a fact which was recognised by the students every time they shouted 'Power!' or 'Amandla Ngawethu' . . . In short, and at the risk of stating the obvious, the organised mass struggles of 1976 manifested a total rejection of white domination and a revolutionary movement for a fundamental change in the balance of power.[31]

Brickhill and Brooks accord considerable importance to the ANC in influencing the perceptions of SSRC leaders and detect in their tactical choices an inherited knowledge of an older generation of resistance movements.[32] The participation of the working class of Soweto in the stay-at-homes was indicative of 'its revolutionary consciousness'[33] and the students themselves displayed a surprising sensitivity to the revolutionary implications of the situation:

> If we can get the parents on our side, we can call out a strike; if we call out a strike the economy will collapse; if the economy collapses we will have black rule in 1977.[34]

Hence Kruger, the Chief of the Police, who is aware that continued loss of profits by these factory owners will result in him losing profits and taxes that sustain him and his Police Brutes, and thus his downfall from power, being so desperate and doing all in his power to destroy our unity.[35]

The situation demands that the oppressed and exploited rally around the slogans of WORKER POWER AND PEOPLES POWER.[36]

Baruch Hirson's conclusions on the leadership the students provided are considerably less enthusiastic. Unlike the other writers he is unconvinced of the pervasiveness of the SSRC's authority and critical of its frequent presumption to be representative of the township community. Nor does he view the SSRC's linkages with the ANC to be as significant as do Brooks and Brickhill (who write from within the exile movement). He points out that the external ANC appeared to be unaware of the conflict which was brewing in early 1976 over educational issues. If the SSRC's mechanistic advocacy of stay-at-homes was a reflection of advice proffered by older activists then this was scarcely to the latter's credit; the stay-at-home appeals sometimes demonstrated a naive underestimation of the sacrifices involved as well as a misconception as to what such demonstrations could achieve. Sometimes the SSRC was out of touch with the feelings of its own immediate constituency, as was evidently the case in its call for a return to school. Hirson's final verdict is that the political perspectives of the schoolchildren were essentially narrow, that despite the form their struggle took, its content was hardly revolutionary:

There is no way of knowing how many of these students wanted radical change in May 1976. Their hopes were probably very limited: they wanted the schools to function, they hoped they would halt the introduction of Afrikaans, and they also wanted jobs when they completed their schooling. Some undoubtedly went further, and wanted better education, without the distortions and open racism of Bantu Education. But very few spoke of unsegregated schooling, and nobody seems to have raised fundamental questions about the nature of education provided in South Africa. They wanted, at most, to receive tuition that would make them equals (in achievement) to their white peers.[37]

The debate which took place in February 1977 over the question of whether the pupils should sit their examinations tends to corroborate this view. The children of Naledi High School issued this statement:

The struggle is on and we will continue fighting the Bantu Education system. But we feel we must also equip ourselves with the little that is offered. . . . The boycott of classes and the exams does not affect the oppressor. Instead he rejoices that we are defeating our own ends. The blacks ought to equip themselves educationally so as to have a better understanding and insight of the powers that be.[38]

The emergence of an avowedly reformist and yet undeniably popular leadership during the 1977 SSRC campaign against the Urban Bantu Council (see below) is another indication of the limits to the revolutionary potential of Soweto's population. In this context some of the claims made by Brickhill and Brooks are of very dubious validity: 1976 was not an 'organised mass struggle', nor is there any evidence that the participation of workers in stay-away protests was symptomatic of their 'revolutionary consciousness'.

Yet it is difficult to resist the feeling that Hirson's criticisms of the SSRC are somewhat heavy-handed. Implicit to them is the assumption that things could have been otherwise, that the potential of the situation was not exploited to the full. But to expect teenagers to behave with the political acumen of seasoned revolutionaries is as unreasonable as to state that they did. How, in any case, could things have been otherwise? At no stage in the revolt would it have been conceivable to have mounted a challenge which the forces at the disposal of the state could not have overcome. As we shall see, the effects of the uprising were to stimulate a generalisation of resistance movements amongst Africans in South Africa. It is difficult to see how its achievement could have been more significant.

One of the most important consequences of the unrest in the factories and the African townships of the early 1970s was the reassertion in government policy-making circles of pressures for reforms in the legal status and economic position of urban Africans. In immediate response to the riots, representative bodies for Transvaal's commerce and industry produced memoranda arguing in favour of improving the legal and economic security of township residents through ameliorating influx control with respect to urban Africans, improving wages and job opportunities, providing more and better housing with land-ownership rights and encouraging the development of a black middle class. In the wake of a 'Businessmen's conference on the quality of life of urban communities' an Urban Foundation was established in late 1976; since then it has chiefly occupied itself with improving the quality of African housing and in particular assisting people who wished to take advantage of the 99-year leasehold scheme introduced by the government in late 1978. At its most radical, corporate business response was politically timid: while arguing for the recognition of the permanence of certain categories of African town-dwellers, the private business sector studiously ignored the logical political implications of a cooptionist strategy – the extension of significant suffrage rights to urban Africans.

The government itself, subject to conflicting political pressures from within the white population, has been unable and, in certain instances, unwilling in principle to embrace all the consequences of a strategy of limited cooption. The constraints on its room for manoeuvre have been most evident in its reaction to the two commissions of enquiry which were set up to investigate labour relations and 'the utilisation of manpower', respectively, the Wiehahn and Riekert Commissions.

Both sets of commission recommendations, which were published in 1979, envisaged reforms as providing the means for more efficient and systematic controls. Responding to the growth of independent African trade unionism and the industrial militancy which had continued since the Durban strikes of 1973, and informed as well by the sensitivity of multinational employers to external criticism of South African labour practices, Wiehahn proposed that African trade unions should, through a system of formal registration, be incorporated into the officially sanctioned (and highly circumscribed) collective bargaining system. At present, Wiehahn argued, in certain spheres unregistered African unions enjoyed greater freedoms than registered unions; their registration would accomplish 'a more structured and orderly situation'. African members of registered trade unions, he proposed, should be accorded the same privileges as their white, Indian and coloured colleagues; in other words statutory job reservation should be phased out, artisan training programmes should be provided for Africans, and the formation and registration of a racially 'mixed' unions should be permitted. Wiehahn also elaborated a considerably expanded system of official regulation of union activity through a National Manpower Commission and recommended a formal ban on any trade union political activity or affiliation.

The Riekert proposals complemented those of Wiehahn. While Wiehahn argued in favour of the extension of an interlocking system of privilege and control to African industrial workers, the Riekert strategy aimed to isolate this group – together with the urban African middle class – from the growing numbers of the unemployed. Two sets of measures would be needed. Africans with 'Section 10'[39] rights would be granted the legal status of permanent urban residents. They would be allowed to live with their families in cities; restrictions on their movement between jobs and towns would be relaxed; employers should be encouraged to use their labour rather than that of migrant labourers; restrictions on the development of an African business class should be removed; and more and better quality family housing should be constructed in the townships. The second thrust of the Riekert proposals involved the tightening of influx control through a variety of measures which included the validation of migrant worker contracts by rural labour bureaux, the introduction of heavy fines for employers of 'illegal' labour, and the reduction of urban job opportunities for migrants through the policy of encouraging manufacturing and commercial employers to hire Africans drawn only from the permanent urban population. The willingness of urban Africans to undertake some of the more arduous and unpleasant jobs previously performed by migrants would be increased through a policy of raising the cost of rent, public transport and other servides in such a way that they could not afford to be unemployed long enough to be 'choosy' about the type of work they did. In effect Riekert's proposals were intended to provide a political solution to social tensions generated by structural unemployment (the unemployment resulting from the increasingly capital-intensive nature of industry) as well as, more directly, the revival of political resistance amongst urban Africans in 1976. The Riekert reforms, it was hoped, would create a social and geographical distance between the haves and the have-nots within the African population, reducing the susceptibility of the former group for any form of revolutionary action and eliminating the likelihood that any such action by the latter group would be effective. Only by the most cynical of criteria could the Riekert proposals concerning rural Africans be called 'reformist'.[40]

Notwithstanding their overall purpose the Riekert-Wiehahn policies have only been adopted piecemeal. Government strategy is inhibited by two constraints. First, there is the perfectly valid objection to the reforms that their cooptive aspects, far from satisfying African political aspirations, could merely increase their economic bargaining power and hence their capacity to mount political challenges to the system. Secondly, while the measures advocated by the commissions reflected the concerns of advanced sectors of business, and moreover – because of the increasingly bourgeois character of sections of the Afrikaner nationalist elite – business with very considerable direct political influence, their reformist character aroused fear and hostility from the government's traditional working-class and petty-bourgeois constituency. These two groups were, by the late 1970s, playing an increasingly unimportant economic role, and, as was demonstrated in the 1979 white mineworkers' strike, employers could afford to disregard their special interests. The price of such disregard for the Nationalist administration has been the development of internecine political feuding and the growth of a powerful extreme right populist force, the Herstigte Nasionale Party.[41]

In the case of the Wiehahn proposals, the administration has accepted their premise that because of international pressures repression was not a viable option, and in October 1979 legislation was enacted for the registration of African trade unions. Confronted with almost total antipathy from African unions the government was compelled to drop its initial prohibition on migrant workers from joining registered trade unions.[42] While the possibility of registration resulted in the appearance of major conflict within African trade unions, the new industrial order did not, as we shall see, succeed in damping down labour militancy and in some respects indeed it contributed to it.

The enactment of Wiehahn's recommendations was at least partly attributable to powerful local pressure for African trade union recognition from the major employers. No such comparable pressure has been exerted in favour of the Riekert proposals.[43] The government was swift to enact some of the more coercive suggestions made in the report – the fines on employers and the new controls imposed by labour bureaux were two of these – but the cooptive strategy in the report has been taken up only very hesitantly. While allowing for more opportunities for African businessmen within the townships, as well as opening the townships up to external investment (both measures which were accepted by the government before the commission reported), little has been done to foster a sense of security amongst the urban African population. In 1980 two bills were drawn up which actually reduced the numbers of urban Africans enjoying existing rights; these excited much opposition and were hastily withdrawn. In terms of improving housing and other features of township life, while private ventures like the Urban Foundation have been encouraged, the government itself has not greatly increased social expenditure on urban Africans save in the field of education. To have increased the African housing budget at a time of acute shortage of housing within the white population would have been politically inexpedient.

Alongside cautious (and extremely unimaginatively presented) reforms, the government has continued to pursue traditional policies. The institutions of separate development have been augmented with four independent Bantustan governments (Transkei, Bophuthatswana, Venda and Ciskei), rather more powerful Community Councils substituted for the Urban Bantu Councils, and an advisory President's Council with white, Indian and coloured representatives, but no Africans. At the same time fiercely vindictive political measures have helped to undermine the likelihood of black middle-class political quiesence: at a time when the successors to the Black Parents' Association, the Soweto Committee of Ten, produced a blueprint for Soweto's municipal status which would have been perfectly in line with the Riekert recommendations two years later,[44] its leading figures were put into gaol. Simultaneously almost every organ of black middle class political aspirations was banned.[45] Shortly afterwards one of the founders of the Black Consciousness movement, Steve Biko, was murdered while in detention.

Given the limits of the post-1976 reformist programme, have the effects of government policies on African political responses been anything other than repressive? The answer to this question must be a very qualified yes. First, and most obviously, the fact that the authorities have chosen a policy of limited accommodation of African trade unions has had very important consequences on the development of the union movement and the political struggles which have flowed out of it. Secondly, with the concession of greater powers to separate development institutions, Bantustan-based political bodies are beginning to acquire some weight in the urban political arena. Thirdly, the rhetoric of reform and the ideological debates arising from it between advocates of statism and free enterprise[46] have had an effect on local African opponents of apartheid: at least a few conceptualise their political position as a social democratic[47] rather than a revolutionary one, and this may have a complicating effect on future alignments in African opposition politics. We look shortly at three movements which represent three different strands in African politics which arise from the environment of post-1976 'reform': the new community trade union movements, Inkatha and allied organisations, and the Soweto Civic Association. But before examining these, the post-1976 history of more traditional influences on township resistance politics, that is, the externally based nationalist movements and the internal Black Consciousness movement, require comment.

In the six years which have elapsed since the Soweto uprising the ANC has re-emerged as the political group with probably the greatest degree of popular support within the townships.[48] Already in the process of re-establishing a presence inside South Africa before June 1976, Umkonto we Sizwe was able to capitalise on the political exhilaration which was generated by the disturbances themselves in mounting an at times spectacular campaign of sabotage and guerrilla warfare. The uprising was succeeded by the exodus of thousands of young men and women to Lesotho, Swaziland and Bostwana and many of these were to provide Umkonto with a new army of highly motivated and well-educated (in contrast to the recruits in the early 1960s) saboteurs. By mid-1978 South African security police chiefs estimated that approximately 4 000 refugees were undergoing insurgent training in Angola, Libya and Tanzania, most of these under ANC auspices.[49] At the same time the police reckoned that 2 500 people had already been brought to court as a result of their participation in the sabotage campaign.[50] Together with the scale and frequency of Umkonto attacks this makes it the most sustained violent rebellion in South African history and all the indications are that it will develop into a full-scale revolutionary war. A chronology of guerrilla activity made in 1981 records 112 attacks and explosions between October 1976 and May 1981.[51] In March 1978 it was reported that one explosion a week had taken place since the previous November.[52]

In contrast to the first Umkonto campaign, the targets, particularly in the 1980–1 phase, have often been of considerable strategic or economic importance. They have included the synthetic oil refinery at Sasolburg (June 1980), power stations in the eastern Transvaal (July 1981), and the Voortrekkerhoogte military base (August 1981). Police stations have been a favourite target, especially those in or near townships; Germiston, Daveyton, New Brighton, Chatsworth, Moroka, Soekmekaar and Booysens police stations were all subjected to grenade, rocket or bomb attacks between 1977 and 1980. As well as this, a number of African security policemen have been assassinated. From the events which have been reported in the press or which have emerged from trial evidence a historical pattern is beginning to become evident. 1977 to 1979 seem to have been years in which Umkonto was principally concerned with establishing its lines of communication and infiltration (which have been principally from Mozambique, and, until a clamp-down by local authority in mid-1978, Swaziland), setting up arms caches, as well as forming a cellular organisational structure in the main townships.[53] In consequence the most dramatic incidents were in the form of gun battles between guerrillas in the north-eastern border regions and the police. In most cases these resulted from police patrols intercepting guerrilla units returning from the training camps but in some instances the guerrillas themselves mounted attacks on police patrols in what was believed to be an attempt to divert attention from the flow of insurgents to the main urban centres on the Rand.[54] Umkonto groups also tried to establish rudimentary bases and support groups in the countryside of the north-eastern Transvaal: the attack on Soekmekaar police station was designed to enhance the ANC's popularity in an area recently affected by enforced resettlement.[55] Meanwhile Molotov cocktails thrown at policemen's houses and railway bombings predominated in the reports of sabotage attempts.

From 1980, it appears, the aim seems to have been to select targets whose destruction would create the maximum popular resonance, first on the Rand, and then, possibly as a result of police pressure in Soweto, in Durban. The avowed purpose of the attacks has been demonstrative; one captured guerrilla actually used the phrase 'armed propaganda'.[56] On the whole their intention seems to have been to inspire confidence amongst the dominated population rather than terror within the white community. Much of the violence has been directed at targets with a special significance for Africans; incidents which have involved the deaths of white civilians, the 1977 Goch Street warehouse shootings or the Silvertown bank siege, for example, do not appear to have been preconceived and have rather been the consequence of only superficially trained men being forced onto the defensive. In contrast with the earlier Umkonto campaign, much more emphasis has been placed on coordinating sabotage efforts with local mass struggles; as well as the Soekmekaar attack, in 1980 Soweto bombings were orchestrated with a popular campaign against rent increases. With the exception of the asassination of informers and other people regarded as collaborators (African security policemen, for example), the campaign's strategy has been guided by the principle that civilian casualties should be avoided.[57] In August 1981, however, Oliver Tambo announced that the ANC would in future attack 'officials of Apartheid' (which in fact Umkonto insurgents had never had any inhibitions about doing) and that there might arise 'combat situations' in which civilians could be killed.[58] A few days before Tambo's statement appeared in the foreign press (it was not reported inside South Africa) a bomb exploded in the main shopping centre of Port Elizabeth; unlike earlier inner-city explosions this one took place during working hours. It was seen at the time as a reprisal for the recent murder in Salisbury of the ANC representative in Zimbabwe, Joe Gqabi. Gqabi, who had played an important role in the first Umkonto campaign, was one of the Robben Island prison veterans who had been chiefly responsible for reactivating an ANC leadership in Soweto in late 1975 and establishing what ANC links existed with the SSRC. He had gone into exile after his acquittal in one of the first major trials arising from the sabotage campaign.

Apart from the effects of Umkonto's sabotage campaign, the ANC's influence on popular political perceptions has been consolidated since 1976 by the re-emergence of open political discussion within the African community.[59] Here the commercial press has played an important role: in 1980, for example, the Soweto daily newspaper, *The Post*, ran a 'Release Mandela' petition form in its columns for several months as well as helping to popularise the Freedom Charter. The Charter was taken up and adopted by several organisations including a new student association, formed in 1979, the Congress of South African Students (COSAS). COSAS stands in conscious opposition to organisations which claim to be inspired by the precepts of Black Consciousness. The revival of political radicalism amongst Indians and the leading role assumed by the resurgent Natal Indian Congress in the boycott of the South African Indian Council[60] have also served a similar function of placing the ANC at the political centre of gravity within black South African society.

Meanwhile the ANC's external organisation has been untroubled by any serious dissension. This is all the more remarkable bearing in mind the huge infusion of new recruits, many of them from a background in which the ANC's leadership had little legitimacy. The organisation was well placed to cope with this sudden expansion; it had the equipment, the financial resources, and the training facilities (located mainly in Angola) required to transform these recruits into a guerrilla force. In contrast with the 1960s, training periods have been short, extremely effective in both military and political terms, and of course the likelihood of trained insurgents going into action has been infinitely greater; all this has contributed to discipline and morale in the camps. In consequence, ideological dissent within the leadership does not seem to have had much effect on rank and file. There have been two dissident tendencies, both of which have involved dissatisfaction with the role of the SACP within the external movement. The first involved Okhela, the faction started in Paris in 1973 as a 'white consciousness' group with the apparent encouragement of Tambo, who hoped it might counter-balance the influence of communists within the ANC. With the failure of Breytenbach's expedition Okhela lost favour with the ANC establishment. The vetoing of an

Okhela scheme to circulate Afrikaans 'samidzat' literature in South Africa confirmed a growing conviction among the remaining Okhela adherents that the ANC was racist in its attitudes towards Afrikaners. Already increasingly antipathetic to the SACP, between 1976 and 1978 the Okhela group made overtures to the ANC African Nationalist faction then based in Algiers. But in 1979 Okhela collapsed in the wake of the flight of its most influential spokesman to South Africa and his subsequent admission that he had been a police informer.[61] The African Nationalists were similarly discredited by Tennyson Makiwane's return to the Transkei and his enlistment in the Transkeian foreign service. In 1980 Makiwane was assassinated. Though the Transkeians blamed the ANC it may have been significant that he had been involved in a coup d'etat conspiracy by former ANC and PAC men to overthrow the Matanzima administration.[62]

The second group of dissenters developed from the new generation of South African Marxist academics which had emerged at English universities in the early 1970s. Together with recent exiles who had been involved with the regeneration of African trade unions in South Africa they became increasingly sceptical of the SACP's capacity to create a proletarian democracy, and increasingly critical of the petty-bourgeois orientation of the ANC's exile leadership. Their criticisms were first of all centred on the work of SACTU in which some of them were involved; in particular, they disagreed with what they felt to be the dominant perception of SACTU's function – to serve as a 'signpost', directing workers to Umkonto we Sizwe.[63] With the expulsion of the principal figures in this group, Martin Legassick, Rob Petersen, David Hemson, and Paula Ensor, the ANC effectively cut itself off from a potentially creative source of intellectual stimulation. The rebels subsequently constituted themselves as a 'workers' tendency' within the ANC, but because of their isolation from rank and file ANC membership their aim of helping to transform the nationalist movement into a truly working-class organisation appears forlornly romantic.

Despite the fresh emphasis on insurgent activity the ANC's leadership has been careful not to neglect diplomacy. Here it has displayed considerable self-confidence and finesse. This is a field in which the Tambo leadership was always rather adept and in the post-Soweto years it has had to contend with several significant challenges. The first of these was posed by the emergence of a third exile force as a result of the arrival in European and African capitals of SASO, BPC and SSRC leaders. The less ideologically doctrinaire of these found little difficulty in joining the ANC but for those who subscribed fully to the tenets of Black Consciousness there were obvious objections to this. At the same time the disarray among the Pan-Africanists made them equally unacceptable. Furthermore there were substantial temptations to maintain a distance from the two exile organisations: European social democrats were keen to patronise a 'third force' free of Soviet connections and more vital than the PAC. From the mid-1970s, the International University Exchange Fund (IUEF), under the direction of Lars-Gunner Eriksson, began channelling large sums of money to the Black Consciousness movement representatives both within and outside the country. According to a South African security policeman who infiltrated the IUEF, through skilful lobbying of the various left-wing and social democrat groupings which financed the IUEF, the ANC was able to put a stop to this in 1978. Moreover the ANC succeeded in extracting an agreement from IUEF representatives that in future no South African projects would be funded without their approval.[64] By late 1980 many of the principal figures in the Black Consciousness Movement of Azania, which had been formally established the year before in London, were joining the ANC. These included Barney Pityana, one of the founders of SASO in 1969.[65]

The episode was an indication of an increasingly determined effort by the ANC to gain for itself 'sole legitimate representative' status in the view of potential allies. Here it has been aided by the faction fighting in the PAC which prevented this organisation from fully exploiting the victory of its erstwhile ally, ZANU, in the Zimbabwe elections. The ANC's guerrilla units, incidentally, were reported to be fighting alongside ZAPU-oriented forces until the ceasefire. The appointment of Joe Gqabi as the ANC representative was tactful and astute, since he, like many of the ZANU military leaders, was Chinese-trained and in addition had not been involved in any previous exile political activity.

Meanwhile, in London, Oliver Tambo arranged and attended his daughter's wedding in St Paul's Cathedral and maintained (against strong internal pressure from the left wing of his organisation) discreet links with Gatsha Buthelezi. Even when finally compelled to attack the homeland leader for his behaviour during a Kwa Mashu school boycott in 1980, Tambo was nevertheless careful not to condemn outright the Inkatha movement. With the development in South Africa of legal mass organisations[66] with a Congress orientation, the solidly middle-class respectability of the Tambo leadership has an important function in ensuring that internal support for the ANC remains as widely based as possible. The current enthusiasm for the Freedom Charter and the apparent downgrading of the more radical 'Strategy and Tactics' adopted at Morogoro may also be indicative of a realistic perception of the danger of alienating the steadily growing black middle class.[67]

Since 1976 the PAC's history has continued to be characterised by byzantine leadership intrigues and rank-and-file rebellions, the latter given new impetus as a result of the fresh infusion of independently minded refugees from Soweto. In contrast to the ANC, the PAC's activity within the country has been minimal. Between 1975 and 1977 a courageous nucleus of former Robben Island prisoners, led by Zephania Mothopeng, established a 'Coordinating Committee' in Johannesburg and a 'Planning Committee' in East London, and succeeded before their arrest in bringing within the PAC orbit various youth groups on the West Rand, establishing contact with PAC officials in Swaziland, and starting a recruiting programme. At least two groups were active in the aftermath of Mothopeng's arrest in sending recruits across the Swazi border. Once there the PAC sent them on for brief bouts of military training in Libya and China. The first trained PAC insurgents had returned to the country in 1978. Three men were arrested and subsequently convicted for possession of explosives and setting up an arms cache in Krugersdorp. The PAC's external offices have not claimed PAC responsibility for any major sabotage actions.[68]

The death of Robert Sobukwe from lung cancer while serving a banning order in Kimberley signalled the beginning of a bitter conflict over the leadership of the exile organisation. Potlake Leballo moved swiftly to assert his claim to the succession, inciting the Swazi and Botswana authorities to lock up large numbers of potentially disloyal recent PAC recruits who were reportedly critical of his performance as acting president.[69] By June 1978 Leballo was in a strong enough position to emerge triumphant from a conference which had been summoned in response to the demands of the new membership from Soweto. Leballo was confirmed as the presiding authority over the PAC. It was a short-lived victory; Leballo's ascendency was the cost of provoking the antipathy of the APLA leader Templeton Ntantala, who had considerable support in the training camps. Ntantala was expelled and founded, together with various malcontents in London, an Azanian People's Revolutionary Party. In May 1979, under pressure from his colleagues, Leballo resigned his office, to be replaced by a three-man presidential council, David Sibeko, Vus' Make, and Elias Ntloedibe. This hardly placated the leadership's internal critics; Sibeko in particular was seen as a loyal adherent of Leballo and had taken part with him in the negotiations with the Swazi authorities which resulted in the rounding-up of local PAC members. In June 1979 Sibeko was assassinated in Dar es Salaam by three men from one of the APLA training camps. Six men were finally convicted in a Tanzanian court for manslaughter; their ages ranged between 21 and 25. At the OAU summit conference in Monrovia in August 1979 Vus' Make admitted in his speech to the delegates that internecine gangsterism was draining the movement of whatever vitality it retained. In January 1981 a new chairman was elected – John Pokela, who had recently arrived in Dar es Salaam after serving a long prison sentence on Robben Island. Pokela's first action after his election was to bring back within the fold the Azanian People's Revolutionary Party. Subsequently the Pokela leadership has been accorded recognition from the Zimbabwean authorities but the PAC's chances of re-establishing itself as an effective force in South African politics seem fairly remote despite the evident integrity of its new leader.[70]

In the arena of legitimate political activity the Azanian Peoples' Organisation (AZAPO) is today the most influential vehicle for the political tradition represented outside South Africa by the PAC (though in its public statements AZAPO is careful to emphasise its organisational autonomy and non-alignment). AZAPO was founded in April 1978 at a weekend conference held in Roodepoort at the instigation of five Soweto Action Committee[71] men. The first organisation formed since the banning of the previous October, it placed itself unequivocally in the Black Consciousness camp with its motto, 'One people, one Azania'.[72] Within two weeks of its foundation branches were formed in Bloemfontein, Welkom and Kroonstadt as well as on the Rand. Two weeks later most of its national and local leadership were in detention and nothing was heard of AZAPO for over a year. Then, in September 1979, a second conference was held in Roodepoort and a new executive was elected. Like its predecessor, the new leadership was dominated by Sowetans, the president being Curtis Nkondo, chairman of the Teachers' Action Committee which had led the wave of teacher resignations after June 1976.

From its inception, AZAPO announced that it would direct its activities towards the political involvement of the black working class. With considerably more precision and sophistication than their predecessors in the

Black Consciousness movement, AZAPO spokesmen incorporated a class analysis into their policy. This was most fully developed in a paper read to an AZAPO conference in early 1981. Here it was suggested that South African society could be divided into eight classes (international, national, comprador and petty bourgeoisie, proletariat, lumpenproletariat, rich and poor peasants), two of which included both whites and blacks. Notwithstanding this there was no material basis for united class action by whites and blacks: white workers had defected to the capitalists and were appendages of that class, while the black petty bourgeoisie

. . . are subjected to the vile rigours of racism and many of their members have joined the Black liberation struggle. The leadership of the Black liberation strugle is provided largely by this class.[73]

AZAPO's formulations differed from earlier Black Consciousness analyses in two respects. First, there was the recognition that some blacks would collaborate with the authorities because it was in their class interests to do so.[74] Secondly, there was their insistence on the importance of 'trade unions as an instrument that can bring about the redistribution of power'.[75] AZAPO conceived its role as activist; as its leaders put it: 'AZAPO has taken Black Consciousness beyond the phase of Black awareness into class struggle.'[76] This would be achieved, in the view of AZAPO, by

. . . [leading] the workers in their everyday struggle . . . [campaigning and developing] community support for each strike . . . [giving] clear priority to mobilising the worker not only in the factories, but also in the ghettos . . . labour clinics and workshops in the ghettos must be developed by the branches and other organs of the liberation movement.[77]

Despite these protestations AZAPO does not appear to have developed any formal connections with significant labour organisations, nor does it seem to have a strong working-class following. The most militant and politically oriented trade union groupings are opposed to the AZAPO view that trade unions have to be exclusively black in order to be politically effective.[78] It is true that the Confederation of Unions of South Africa (CUSA), formed in September 1980 from those unions associated with the Johannesburg-based Urban Training Project, emphasises the importance of black leadership and control of any union federation. Its leading officials claim that CUSA's guiding philosophy is that of Black Consciousness.[79] Although it is difficult to generalise about the unions represented by CUSA, a point which can be made about most of them is that in the past their preferred strategy was scarcely confrontationist. Despite CUSA's Black Consciousness leanings it does not seem inclined to provide the vehicle for worker mobilisation sought by AZAPO. AZAPO does have a close relationship with the Media Workers' Association of South Africa (MWASA), a militant Black Consciousness journalists' group. AZAPO claims to have helped organise communal support for the MWASA-led strike at the Associated Newspaper offices in Johannesburg. On the whole however, the basis for cooperation between movements like AZAPO and trade unions is a very narrow one; AZAPO officials tend to be contemptuous of negotiated reforms involving bread-and-butter issues, whereas not even the most politically radical trade union can afford to dismiss the value of material improvements conceded within the system.

So in contrast to its stated strategy, AZAPO's activities have not involved the mobilisation of workers as workers. Its most sustained campaign has been in the Pietersburg area where, in September 1980, local AZAPO officials led a township bus boycott in response to a ten per cent fare increase imposed by the Lebowa Transport Company. The boycott was successful in its immediate aim; the increase was suspended after three weeks, but then the AZAPO leaders over-reached themselves by calling on the township community to continue the boycott to force the company to reduce the old fare.[80] Apart from this, AZAPO played an auxiliary role in the Soweto rents campaign[81] (see below) and on several occasions has tried ineffectually to mount boycotts of visiting black American entertainers. The limits of its influence in Soweto were demonstrated by the absence of any response whatsoever to its proposed PUTCO bus boycott in July 1981.[82] In a public opinion poll conducted by *The Star* newspaper in September, even in Johannesburg where support for AZAPO was found to be strongest, it was rated lower in popularity than both the ANC and Inkatha. Its president, Khehla Mtembu, polled a third of the support attributed to the leading figure in the Soweto Civic Association, Dr Nthato Motlana.[83] Nevertheless, though its popular following may be insignificant, as the main bearer of Black Consciousness orthodoxy its political influence within the Soweto intelligentsia should not be entirely discounted.

A considerably more formidable political challenge to the state than AZAPO is posed today by the revival of political trade unionism. Before looking at this though, we must quickly survey the development of African trade unionism from its rennaissance in the aftermath of the 1973 Durban strikes. From 1973 to 1979 African trade unions could be broken down into five separate categories. First there were the parallel unions, mentioned briefly at the end of Chapter 8. They need not detain us here. Their leading spokeswoman, Lucy Mvubelo, has been in the forefront of campaigns to promote foreign investment and for her efforts has received awards from both *The Star* and Barclays Bank. The unions themselves perform mainly benefit society functions. The parallel unions are not, by any definition, resistance movements. The second category, of political or communal unions, was filled by BAWU, never an effective force among workers.

Thirdly, there were the unions formed and guided by the Urban Training Project, which formed a Black Consultative Committee. To quote Philip Bonner, this group could be distinguished from other post-1973 African union movements by their

. . . heavy emphasis on approaches to management, sometimes even before organising workers from their factories. They appeal to management's enlightened self interest, believing that it is sometimes a failure of communication which leads to management's hostile attitude toward African trade unions. Their vision of the role of trade unions is comparable to that of the registered trade unions, emphasising a relatively specialised and bureaucratised leadership, little mobilisation of workers from below, and the benefit functions (e.g. funeral benefits) of trade unions – all of which is consistent with their strategy of emphasis on approaches to management.[84]

Some of these unions were to form the Confederation of Unions of South Africa (CUSA) in 1980.

The fourth approach to African unionism was that taken by the successor to the General Factory Workers' Benefit Fund in Durban, the Trade Union Advisory and Coordinating Council (TUACC) and an allied group on the Rand, the Industrial Aid Society (IAS), both formed in late 1973. Their strategy had four main essentials. First, TUACC-IAS unions should be built on a factory-by-factory basis, a strong shop-floor organisation being the prerequisite to any development. Secondly, together with quality of organisation, quality of leadership was seen as crucial, and an important dimension of TUACC-IAS activity was worker education with weekend training seminars for shop floor organisers. Thirdly, the shop-steward system was imported from Britain together with a strong insistence on a democratic organisational structure. Finally, these unions aimed first of all at gaining the recognition of individual employers rather than attempting to extract industry-wide agreements. The first such agreement was conceded by a British textile firm in Pinetown in 1974. These principles were carried over into the Federation of South African Trade Unions (FOSATU), formed in April 1979 by TUACC and IAS-influenced unions as well as some of the more militant members of the Consultative Committee grouping. FOSATU was from its inception non-racial in character and permitted the involvement of whites as full-time officials and organisers.[85] At the time of its formation FOSATU's affiliates had a reputation for militancy, many having been involved in strikes in 1974 to 1975 arising from disputes over workers' rights and representation.[86] FOSATU and its predecessors, despite their shop-floor militancy, have been careful to confine their concern to factory issues; the Federation has eschewed any form of political alignment.

The fifth trade union tendency, represented by the Western Province General Workers' Union (WPGWU), differed from the FOSATU group in its advocacy of an all-embracing general workers' union as opposed to individual unions for each industry. This was a reflection of the character of its constituents who were mainly unskilled African migrant workers with a high rate of job turnover among whom it would have been difficult to create stable industrial unions.

By mid-1976, 75 000 Africans belonged to 25 trade unions[87] and of these, eleven unions with a membership of 58 260 were to constitute themselves as FOSATU in 1979, making the Federation one of the largest and certainly the best-organised group of African trade unions ever to have existed in South Africa. Together with the surges of strike action out of which it developed, FOSATU could take credit for whatever internal pressure motivated the authorities to attempt to incorporate rather than suppress African trade unionism. But since 1979 a new type of unionism has emerged which threatens to rival FOSATU in influence.

Its first manifestation was in Cape Town when in April 1979 several African workers were dismissed from their employment at the Fatti's and Moni's pasta factory after refusing to resign from the African Food and Canning Workers' Union (AFCWU). The AFCWU, a former SACTU affiliate, had recently been revived in the Cape. Seventy-eight of the sacked workers' colleagues walked out and were to remain out on strike for seven months until their reinstatement by the Fatti's and Moni's management. An important ingredient in the AFCWU's eventual victory was the degree of support the union succeeded in mobilising in the African and coloured communities in the Cape. A consumer boycott of Fatti's and Moni's products had the effect of halving the company's profits in the first six months of 1979. Fatti's and Moni's had recently made large investments in capital equipment and were in no position to withstand a drop in profits. The settlement included recognition of the union and reinstatement and wage rises for the strikers. The boycott was organised on behalf of the AFCWU by township-based professional and political groupings and, most crucially, the Western Cape [African] Traders' Association.[88]

Inspired by the success of the Fatti's and Moni's boycott, from May to August 1980 the Western Cape General Workers' Union led a communal campaign, this time against Table Bay Cold Storage which had similarly tried to force workers to resign from a union, in this case the WCPGWU. As with the AFCWU, the WPGWU drew on community resources to give the workers strike pay – in three months mounting to R100 000. A red meat boycott assumed national proportions and the union also had some success in promoting an embargo on scabbing in the tightly knit African squatter communities.[89]

From these experiences a new union strategy was beginning to emerge. Both the WPGWU and the AFCWU were especially vulnerable in that their members were predominantly migrant and unskilled in an area where there was unusually heavy unemployment. Limiting their offensive against employers to within the workplace would have left them with very little bargaining power; community support was an indispensable weapon. Mobilising such support, however, inevitably brought them into contact with non-worker organisations and could also involve their struggles with wider conflicts. This was particularly so in the Cape peninsula at that time, since it coincided with a resurgence of protest by schoolchildren against inferior education. Accordingly, trade unions which relied on community support could not afford to be politically non-aligned.[90]

Following its success in Cape Town the AFCWU extended its influence to the Eastern Province. In East London it collaborated with a new general workers' union, the South African Allied Workers' Union (SAAWU). SAAWU was formed in April 1979 as the result of a split in the then almost defunct BAWU. It differed from its parent body over the question of black exclusivism, and from its foundation SAAWU's policy had been non-racial. With the establishment of an office in the centre of East London in March 1980 SAAWU's growth was phenomenal, reaching a claimed membership of 20 000 by the end of the year. SAAWU's development has been in stark contrast to the careful professionalism of that of FOSATU. Its membership was drawn from almost every form of working-class employment in East London, much of the recruitment taking place at mass meetings. Factory workforces are encouraged to elect workers' committees which then seek to enrol and broaden the union's support within the factory. When the SAAWU 'branch' was representative of 60 per cent of the workforce it would demand recognition from the employer. A spate of strikes broke out when employers refused recognition, in the wake of which SAAWU succeeded in extracting recognition agreements from various employers. In common with the WPGWU, with whom it shares many structural characteristics, SAAWU operates at a community level – most notably in the Rowntrees sweet boycott in 1980–1, organised in response to Rowntree's refusal to recognise SAAWU's authority in their factory. In East London political questions are difficult for any union to ignore as the nearby Ciskeian government, which controls the lives of many of East London's workers, does not subscribe to any cooptionist ideas with relation to trade unions. It prefers instead a straightforward policy of terror and repression.

In Port Elizabeth the first inroad into FOSATU support was made when the FOSATU-affiliated United Automobile Workers' Union (UAW) refused to support a spontaneous strike in protest against Ford's forced resignation of Thozamile Botha, the leader of the Port Elizabeth Black Civic Organisation. The UAW was already unpopular as a result of organisational inadequacies[91] and a pro-management attitude amongst its officials. Arguing that the strike was inspired by the civic organisation and did not involve worker concerns, the UAW managed to alienate most of its original membership at the Ford Cortina plant where the strike started. The strikers' committee became the nucleus for a new union, the Motor Assembly and Component Workers' Union of South Africa (MACWUSA), which by February 1981 could claim 2 100 members in three plants in Port Elizabeth. Three months later MACWUSA was reported to be attempting to build up a branch in Pretoria. Though MACWUSA differs from the other new unions in being comprised predominantly of skilled, well-educated and young workers under a mainly white collar leadership, it shares with them a concern with political issues, particularly those which are locally, immediately relevant.[92]

There is considerable rivalry and strategic disagreement between these recently consolidated groups and the first generation of post-1973 African trade unionists. It is true that to an extent the community unions have forced the less politically outspoken unionists to become more assertive politically: CUSA's inauguration was attended by a large number of Soweto politicans, including a Soweto Civic Association spokesman who informed his audience that 'everybody in Soweto is a worker. Whatever the difference in our living standards, we have that in common'.[93] CUSA has also deliberately identified itself with the Black Consciousness movement. In the wake of MACWUSA's emergence, FOSATU strategists now argue in favour of 'a deeper understanding of the interrelatedness of workplace issues and political structures'.[94] FOSATU too has resorted to the weapon of the consumer boycott with the struggle for recognition by the Chemical Workers' Industrial Union at the Colgate plant in the Transvaal.[95] Nevertheless, despite this broadening of the concerns of the more established trade unions, there remain strong differences of principle between them and the AFCWU/WPGWU/SAAWU/MACWUSA group.

The chief of these concerns the question of whether African trade unions should accept the dispensation offered by post-Wiehahn legislation and register. The CUSA group have had no difficulty in doing this (though registration probably undermines their credibility with non-collaborationist Black Consciousness groups). FOSATU, after considerable hesitation, has encouraged its affiliates to register on condition that in so doing they could maintain their non-racial constitutions. The FOSATU case rests on two basic arguments. The first is that registration will strengthen their affiliates' position *vis à vis* employers. The second is that the Wiehahn reforms involve real concessions and that these concessions are the result of workers' struggles and therefore should not be written off as merely privileged forms of subordination.[96] The new unions, on the other hand, are totally opposed to registration, conditional or otherwise, contending simply that 'registering means becoming part of the system',[97] a system in whose destruction they perceive themselves to have an important role.

Notwithstanding their intransigence the new unions themselves are a produce of the climate provided by the switch from a strategy of pure repression to one of partial reform in the government's handling of labour matters. An important factor in their current success has been the willingness of certain employers to sign recognition agreements with unregistered trade unions. In part these employers may respond to pressure from foreign investors, but they are also motivated by their lack of confidence in the ability of the state to protect them from industrial unrest. The state's reluctance to discredit its new labour regime by resorting once again to unmitigated coercion contributes to employers' nervousness.

The prospects of the new unions appear at best uncertain. With their largely unskilled membership they are particularly vulnerable at a time of economic recession; indeed their efforts to organise the unemployed so as to inhibit the dismissal and replacement of militant workers are a recognition of this weakness. Consumer boycotts can only be an effective form of pressure in the case of boycotts of staple commodities. But despite their inherent weaknesses, any analysis of contemporary African resistance must recognise the resurrection of a brand of political unionism which has been absent in South Africa for a long time – a movement which in the event of an upheaval comparable to Soweto could generate a considerably more serious crisis for the state than in 1976.

It is difficult to predict whether in such circumstances Inkatha Yenkululeko ye Sizwe would function as a liberator or a collaborator. Originally founded as a Zulu cultural organisation by the royal house in 1928, Inkatha ka Zulu was revived by Chief Gatsha Buthelezi in the early 1970s, and with the change in its name to Inkatha Yenkululuke ye Sizwe ('Freedom of the Nation')[98] in 1975 it began to structure itself as a mass organisation. Chief Buthelezi, a grandson of King Dinuzulu, the last king of an independent Zulu state, is one of the more enigmatic and attractive figures to have emerged from the milieu of homeland politics. Born in 1928, he was educated at Adams College and was a contemporary of Robert Sobukwe at Fort Hare, from which he was later expelled. He was for a short time a member of the ANC Youth League, but that phase of his political activism ended when he joined the Department of Native Administration as a clerical worker. He maintained, however, friendly contacts with the ANC leadership, who, his official biographer claims, used Buthelezi as a 'sounding board of rural opinion'.[99] Installed as a chief in 1957 with the apparent approval of Natal ANC leaders, Buthelezi was to take up his hereditary function of chief advisor to the king to become the most powerful political influence in the Natal Zulu reserves. In 1970 a Kwa Zulu Territorial Authority was established with Chief Buthelezi as its chief executive officer. Two years later Buthelezi was appointed as chief executive councillor of the Kwa Zulu legislative Assembly.

Despite his senior position within the political structure of separate development Buthelezi claims to be an opponent of apartheid and has consistently refused any overtures from Pretoria to accept an independence settlement for Kwa Zulu. The chief's biography carefully endorses almost every stage of its subject's career with evidence of sanction of the ANC and even today, after bitter mutual recriminations between Buthelezi and the Tambo leadership, Inkatha claims to be the 'custodian of the ideals of the ANC'.[100] These ideals, though, are subject to an increasingly conservative (and mystifying) interpretation.[101] The basic premise to almost all of Buthelezi's contentions is that the political machinery of apartheid provides scope for developing and increasing the degree of leverage Africans would ultimately be able to exert against the system.

In the first half of the decade a fairly plausible case could be sustained that this was what the Buthelezi administration intended to do. The intervention of the Kwa Zulu Community Affairs Councillor, Barney Dladla, in Durban industrial disputes in 1973 contrasted favourably with the behaviour of other homelands' officials when confronted with similar situations.[102] Although some early critics of Buthelezi suggested that Dladla's subsequent dismissal from his office was because of his apparent radicalism, this was denied by the Chief's supporters. Shortly after this episode the Chief travelled to Lesotho to receive an posthumous award from the Organisation of African Unity for Albert Lutuli on behalf of his widow. Buthelezi's claim to adhere to the African nationalist tradition was similarly asserted when Inkatha adopted the ANC flag and uniform in 1975. A charitable interpretation of the role of Chief Buthelezi and Inkatha in the 1976 disturbances could emphasise the efforts to placate the Mzimhlope hostel dwellers after their attacks on Soweto youth.

In 1981 it is much less easy to view the Chief and the force he represents in such a favourable light. The Inkatha movement has become almost inseparable from state structures in Kwa Zulu, with its influence on school syllabuses, its community development projects, and the interlocking of political and administrative office. Inevitably it has begun to function in an openly repressive way: the brutal treatment meted out by Inkatha vigilante groups to school boycotters in Kwa-Mashu in May–June 1980 is an especially clear example of this.[103] And despite much initial publicity, little has been heard of Inkatha's promised monitoring of employers' codes of conduct. Inkatha's leadership has a strong public commitment to free enterprise (the earlier advocacy of a degree of state control in the economy appears, for the time being, to have been dropped).[104] Despite the movement's professed belief 'in the wisdom of the ordinary black worker',[105] trade unions are perceived to need 'to have a broadly based responsibility towards the community'[106] and might, accordingly, require some form of government restriction. And despite

Buthelezi's professed commitment to a broad all-embracing black South African nationalism,[107] when forced on the defensive, he and his acolytes are apt to resort to Zulu chauvinist rhetoric.[108] The closure of the Johannesburg editorial office of the Inkatha newspaper, *The Nation*, in 1979, and its transformation from a journal oriented to a wide range of Soweto middle-class opinion to a Zulu vehicle for Buthelezi's personality cult, may also be significant in this respect.

Inkatha's apologists suggest that the activities of the movement and its leadership must be understood in the context of its long-term strategy. This, they say, involves a laborious and careful process of mass mobilisation in an efficiently-run organisation which, in order to avoid suppression at a stage when it is still vulnerable, has had to restrain itself from any form of political activism. The price for its survival is the occasional authoritarian action against misconceived and ill-timed forms of political adventurism. At some point in the future Inkatha would possess the organisational resources to mount a demonstration of its power sufficiently impressive to compel the government into negotiating a redistribution of power and resources. At one stage the form this demonstration would take was suggested by Buthelezi's frequent references to African workers' and consumers' bargaining power; now it would seem that less confrontationist tactics are envisaged.[109]

Such a strategy does provide a credible alternative to a violent transformation of South African society but has as its premise that a unitary, majoritarian form of democracy is either not attainable or not worth the cost its achievement would involve.[110] This is an option which probably would be unacceptable to most urban Africans outside Natal. Nevertheless, the Inkatha movement's influence should not be underestimated in any attempts to predict the course of future black resistance politics. It is a huge organisation, numbering at the end of 1980 about 350 000 members in nearly 1 000 branches, mostly in Natal, but with a significant following among Zulu hostel dwellers on the Reef as well.[111] A proportion of this membership might have been coerced into joining: teachers in Kwa Zulu must be Inkatha members and the government of the homeland, Inkatha is in a position to withhold resources from people or groups who do not support the movement.[112] Nevertheless it would be unwise to conceptualise Inkatha's influence purely in terms of coercion or clientage. A series of opinion polls have indicated that Inkatha and Buthelezi enjoy a genuine degree of popularity, especially in Natal.[113]

It is this last factor which makes Inkatha's future role difficult to predict. Exactly how its grass roots supporters understand the character and nature of the organisation is unknown. It is possible that given the populist rhetoric sometimes employed by the leadership, and the leadership's attempts to legitimise itself by identification with the ANC, the movement's rank and file members may neither comprehend nor assent to the increasingly conservative variety of reformism advocated by Buthelezi and his colleagues. If this is the case then their behaviour in any future eruption may be very different from the activity prescribed for them by their leaders.

Returning to the present, Inkatha, despite its increasingly conscious rivalry with and antagonism towards the ANC,[114] is likely to expand its power and influence within urban African communities. Unlike its more radical opponents it rejects a boycott strategy, and with its superb organisation is well placed to take advantage of whatever devolution of authority a reformist administration in Pretoria is prepared to concede to township Community Councils and similar bodies. It has already announced its willingness to contest the Soweto Council elections in 1982.[115] If control of the allocation of township facilities is coupled with a significant degree of external financial assistance (and this still remains an open question) then Inkatha could be considerably more effective than it is today in affecting popular political perceptions in Soweto.

There is room here for only a brief consideration of the civic leadership which has emerged in the last few years as an alternative to the Community Councils, the local bodies created by the state in 1977–8 to replace the discredited Urban Bantu Councils. In Soweto the SSRC led a successful campaign in 1977 against a rent increase imposed by the West Rand Administration Board in an ill-timed attempt to make up the revenue deficit resulting from the destruction of WRAB-controlled liquor outlets. A series of public meetings and angry demonstrations finally led to the resignation of most of the Urban Bantu Councillors who, though not responsible for the increase (they had mainly advisory functions), had nevertheless been consulted about them beforehand. Most of the Councillors, however, were to resume their positions in 1978, when a miniscule electoral poll returned them back to their old chamber in Jabulani as members of the Soweto Community Council. They now had real if limited powers: the new Council was responsible for collection of rents and deciding on increases, allocating houses and trading licences and various other matters. To compensate for the additional unpopularity such duties would bring there were the obvious opportunities for self-aggrandisement.[116] Only in late 1980, though, was a limited provision made for an expansion in community revenue when the Minister for Cooperation and Development, Dr Koornhof, announced that with the help of the private sector a programme of industrialisation in the township would begin shortly. Together with various administrative alterations, mainly involving the assumption by the Councils of more of the functions now performed by the Administration Boards (though not influx control), these developments would result in the Councils acquiring local government status equal to that of a white municipality. Meanwhile the Councils have had to make do with what resources are immediately available; in other words they have been forced to follow the same self-financing principles as the Administration Boards. In the case of the Soweto Council in 1979, confronted with a budgetary deficit of R22.7 million, its members voted in favour of a rent increase as an alternative to cutting services. A 100 per cent increase was announced, to be implemented in three stages between September 1979 and August 1980.

During the undignified process of the Council's birth a new leadership had come to fill the gap left by the departing SSRC leaders. Some days after the resignation of the Urban Councillors, the Soweto branch of the Black People's Convention called for the formation of a properly representative civic organisation reflecting popular aspirations in the township. A meeting was held on 26 June 1977 at the offices of *The World* newspaper, attended by 61 Soweto notables. These people elected a Committee of Ten. The Committee's members included four former SASO/BPC adherents, the President of the Soweto Traders' Association, and one of the leading figures in the Teacher's Action Committee. Several had been involved during the riots in the Black Parents' Association.[117] The Committee's Chairman was Dr Nthato Motlana, a prominent medical practitioner and a former ANCYL activist before his first restriction order in the early 1950s.

The Committee chose as its first project the drawing-up of a blueprint for Soweto's municipal autonomy: a plan for a fifty-man elected local authority which, as well as having revenue-raising and budgetary powers, would also be able to legislate. The basis for local prosperity would be laid through the granting of freehold land tenure to those of Soweto's inhabitants who could afford it, and an externally-financed R5 000 million development plan. The plan was that once public sanction had been given through mass meetings at which the blueprint would be introduced, the document would then form the basis of representations to Pretoria.

As was pointed out at the time by *Die Transvaaler*, 'the structure envisaged [was] not entirely beyond the bounds of current debate in Nationalist Party circles'.[118] This did not prevent the police from first banning the rallies held by the Committee in order to publicise the document, and then imprisoning its members in October 1977 as part of their efforts to contain the continuing rebellion of the schoolchildren.

Notwithstanding the reformist content of their programme, and indeed its formal similarity to the long-term aspirations of Mr David Thebahali and his fellow community councillors, the Committee of Ten are at present unlikely candidates for co-option. The more pragmatic members of the government have not been blind to the possibility of doing so; in early 1978 five of the more conservative members of the Committee were released in a successful effort to persuade Inkatha to concede a limited degree of support for the Council elections. Since their release, Dr Koornhof has on several occasions requested individuals among them to participate in his various advisory committees. The Committee members, despite such temptations, have remained true to the non-collaborationist policy central to the Black Consciousness organisations which originally sponsored the body. Because of this there is a certain amount of confusion as to whether they would accept the reforms envisaged in their blueprint if they were granted within the present dispensation.

Until September 1979 the Committee functioned as a 'spokesman' body; in the surprisingly flattering words of a profile of its members published in *The Nation*, as 'apostles of the people'. As such, it could be unashamedly élitist; in retorting to the claim that the less well-off members of the community favoured a degree of collaboration with the system, Dr Motlana was reported to have said: 'the task of the leaders . . . [is] to guide and lead the broad mass of labourers and to move ahead of their thinking and not simply reflect it'.[119] Guiding the people was mainly done through the forums provided by the liberal English press (which lionised the committee) and massive commemorative rallies often held at Soweto's Regina Mundi Cathedral. While it can be said that the Committee during this stage provided a morally attractive and sometimes emotionally satisfying form of community leadership, it should be said that to their detriment it took them a long time to start building a political organisation which would allow their local constituency to participate in their decisions rather than merely ratify them at public meetings. The first steps to organise a Soweto Civic Association (SCA) were taken in September 1979, two years after the Committee had been formed.

In 1980 the SCA looked as if it had come into its own, its 33 branches spearheading an extremely effective campaign against the proposed rent increases. Although the traditional resort of middle-class activists, the legal court case, appeared at first to predominate in the Committee's strategy (the Committee functioned as the SCA executive), the campaign developed in a more militant direction with first a rent boycott and then a stay-away from work and demonstrations coinciding with Thebahali's invitation to Dr Koornhof to visit Soweto. A ban on public meetings forced the SCA to maintain contact with its supporters through concentrating on vitalising its branch structure. In fact the rent boycott was never more than five per cent effective but the campaign had nevertheless succeeded in delaying the implementation of the new tariffs for over a year; many of the SCA leaders had not hoped to achieve more than that.[120]

In the last few months of 1980, however, the SCA appeared to have lost its momentum and it seems rather unlikely that it will enjoy the same degree of success in mobilising people against the 1982 Council elections, at least not if Inkatha throws its full organisational weight behind participation. The SCA's problem is that as a local organisation its concerns are first of all parochial and, despite its anti-collaborationist stance, essentially reformist. People cannot be kept in a constant state of political ferment over everyday problems such as housing and services unless there are concrete possibilities of remedying such problems through action. The SCA leadership, aware of the dangers of cooption, is naturally unwilling to be directly involved in the solution of bread-and-butter issues. This would not matter if it had a clear long-term political programme which involved a rather wider vision than municipal autonomy for a segregated township. It does not have this because constituted as it is as a representative body it embraces and reflects a wide range of political opinion. While the centre ground is taken up by advocacy of the Freedom Charter and calls for a national convention, on the right V. L. Kraai of the Soweto Traders' Association and Dr Motlana busy themselves with promoting the cause of black capitalism,[121] while on the left George Wauchope espouses the incantatory socialism of AZAPO. The political heterogeneity of the SCA is a telling reflection of the precarious economic position of Soweto's petty-bourgeoisie, torn as it is between the competing inducements of entrepreneurial cooperation with the Johannesburg business community and consolidating their popular power base through a populist form of nationalism. If the SCA succeeds in holding the more self-serving class aspirations of this group in check then it will have performed an important historical function.

This survey of African political responses since Soweto has for reasons of brevity and simplicity confined itself to looking at organised groups. Consequently the more spontaneous acts of resistance, the resurgence of school boycotts, the community battles over rent, housing and transport, and the explosion of industrial unrest, all of which have characterised the opening of a new decade, have entered the story only incidentally. But even from this superficial analysis it should be evident that a qualitative transformation has taken place in African political life. The complex combination of social forces present in black resistance have succeeded in igniting a conflagration which no amount of repression or incorporation will succeed in extinguishing.

Notes

1 Philip Frankel, 'South Africa: the politics of police control', *Comparative Politics*, xii, 4 (July 1980), pp. 484–5.

2 *New Age* was proscribed in 1962 and shortly afterwards *Contact* and *The Torch* ran into financial difficulties and ceased publication. After 1961 *Drum's* editorial policy became increasingly subject to commercial considerations, as did that of the tabloid *Golden City Post*, both becoming oriented to crime, sport and human interest reportage. Ownership changes also brought *The World* into line with the prevalent intellectually lightweight tone of African journalism. However, the transformation of both *The World* and *Post* into dailies with Sunday editions once again, by the end of the decade, opened up African newspapers to political dissent. The vernacular press had a very limited readership in Johannesburg.

3 Alan Baldwin, 'Mass removals and separate development', *Journal of Southern African Studies*, i, 1 (1974), pp. 215–27.

4 John Kane-Berman, *Soweto: black revolt, white reaction*, Ravan, Johannesburg, 1978, p. 83.

5 On organisations see Gail Gerhart, *Black Power in South Africa*, University of California Press, Berkeley, 1978, Chapter 8; Gessler Nkondo, *Turfloop Testimony*, Ravan, Johannesburg, 1978; B. A. Khoapa, *Black Review 1972*, Black Community Programmes, Durban, 1973; Mafika Gwala, *Black Review 1973*, Black Community Programmes, Durban, 1974; Thoko Mbanjwa, *Black Review 1974/5*, Black Community Programmes, Durban 1975. For a representative selection of Black Consciousness thought see Steve Biko, *I Write What I Like*, Heinemann, London, 1979; Hendrik Van der Merwe and David Welsh (eds), *Student Perspectives on South Africa*, David Philip, Cape Town, 1972; Hendrik Van der Merwe and Nancy Charton (eds), *African Perspectives on South Africa*, David Philip, Cape Town, 1978; Thoahlane Thoalane, *Black Renaissance*, Ravan, Johannesburg 1974; Basil Moore, *Black Theology: the South African voice*, C. Hurst and Co, London, 1973.

6 See, for example, Mafika Gwala, 'Towards the practical manifestations of Black Consciousness' in Thoahlane, *Black Renaissance*, p. 31.

7 Kane-Berman, *Soweto: black revolt, white reaction*, Chapter 8, and Gerhart, *Black Power in South Africa*.

8 Baruch Hirson, *Year of Fire, Year of Ash*, Zed Press, London, 1979, Chapters 3, 4, 6, 15 and 16.

9 Mongane Serote, 'What's in this Black "Shit"?', in Barry Feinberg (ed.), *Poets to the People*, Heinemann, London, 1980, p. 163.

10 Biko, *I Write What I Like*, p. 28.

11 Hirson, *Year of Fire, Year of Ash*, p. 284.

12 Statistical evidence drawn from the 1960 and 1970 censuses indicates that the number of Africans in Johannesburg employed in white-collar occupations grew by 180 per cent in the 1960s, from 17 270 to 48 402. As a proportion of Johannesburg's African population they increased in significance, from 2.7 per

cent to 5.9 per cent. The industrial working class in Johannesburg increased in size only negligably, by 8 per cent, outstripped by the 25 per cent expansion of Johannesburg's African population. The relative growth of numbers of African white-collar workers in other centres was similarly dramatic contrasted to the growth of the African industrial workforce. In Durban, for example, their numbers rose by 104 per cent whilst the number of industrial workers declined in absolute terms, from 63 000 to 62 000. See Republic of South Africa, *Population Census 1960*, Reports of the metropolitan areas of Durban and Johannesburg, volume 2, numbers 5 and 9, Government Printer, Pretoria, 1966, and Republic of South Africa, *Population Census 1970*, Occupation and Industry by District and Economic Region, report number 02. 05. 06., Government Printer, Pretoria, 1976.

13 See for examples: Michael Williams, *South Africa: the crisis of world capitalism and the apartheid economy*, Winstanley Publications, London. 1977, p. 18; Simon Jenkins, 'The survival ethic', *The Economist*, 19 September 1981, p. 16; Stoffel Van der Merwe, 'More repression for the sake of change', *Frontline* (Johannesburg), August 1980, p. 24.

14 The argument in this section has been drawn from R. W. Johnson, *How Long Will South Africa Survive?*, Macmillan, Johannesburg, 1977; Alex Callinicos and John Rogers, *Southern Africa after Soweto*, Pluto Press, London, 1978; John Saul and Stephen Gelb, *The Crisis in South Africa: class defense, class revolution*, Monthly Review Press, New York, 1981.

15 For strike statistics, see C. Joakimidis and A. Sitas, 'A study of strikes in the 1970s' in *Work in Progress* (Johannesburg), no. 6, November 1978, pp. 105–112.

16 A useful, though incomplete, list of strikes between 1974 and 1977 is provided by C. Joakimidis and A. Sitas in 'A study of strikes in the 1970s' (Part 2), *Work in Progress*, no. 7, March 1979, pp. 36–45.

17 David Hemson, in 'Trade unionism and the struggle for liberation in South Africa', *Capital and Class*, no. 6, 1978, p. 19, claims that between 1971 and 1973 the price of essential commodities for African workers rose by 40 per cent.

18 The most comprehensive analysis of the Durban strikes is: Institute for Industrial Education, *The Durban Strikes 1973*, IIE/Ravan Press, Durban and Johannesburg, 1976, especially Chapter 3. Also useful is L. Douwes Dekker *et al.*, 'Case studies in labour action in South Africa and Namibia' in Richard Sandbrook and Robin Cohen, *The Development of an African Working Class*, Longman, London, 1975, pp. 220–26; Baruch Hirson, *Year of Fire, Year of Ash*, pp. 133–43; David Hemson, 'Trade unionism and the struggle for liberation', pp. 18–26.

19 Republic of South Africa, *Report of the Commission of Inquiry into the Riots at Soweto and Elsewhere* (Cillié Commission Report), Government Printer, Pretoria, RP 55/1980, Volume 1, pp. 523–5.

20 Kane-Berman, *Soweto*, p. 48.

21 In 1970 an average of 13 people lived in each house in Soweto. By 1976 this figure had swollen to 17; *ibid*, p. 51.

22 Hirson, *Year of the Fire, Year of Ash*, p. 99, suggests that the Afrikaans teaching regulation was enforced in response to the labour needs of Afrikaner industrialists. The implementation of the ruling was the result of the initiative of Dr Andries Treurnicht, the Deputy Minister of Bantu Education. Treurnicht's then recent appointment reflected efforts by the Prime Minister, John Vorster, to neutralise his right-wing critics within the Nationalist Party, the most prominent of whom was Treurnicht. Treurnicht's power base is not among Afrikaner business groups (which tend to favour 'reform') but rather among the most economically vulnerable sections of the Afrikaans-speaking population. These tend to *oppose* any intrusion by Africans into the ranks of the clerical, skilled and semi-skilled workforce.

23 Alan Brooks and Jeremy Brickhill, *Whirlwind before the Storm*, International Defence and Aid Fund for Southern Africa, London, 1980.

24 See Hirson, *Year of Fire, Year of Ash*, especially pp. 142–3.

25 Cillié Commission Report, p. 626.

26 Kane-Berman, *Soweto*, p. 109.

27 Cillié Commission Report, p. 84.

28 Hirson provides an excellent analysis of the peculiar factors inherent to the Cape revolt (pp. 216–37). The Cape events are analysed in detail in Centre for Extra-Mural Studies, *History Workshop*, University of Cape Town, 1977, and movingly described by a middle-class housewife from Guguletu, Cape Town in Carol Hermer, *The Diary of Maria Tholo*, Ravan Press, Johannesburg, 1980.

29 Aggrey Klaaste writing in October in *Weekend World*, quoted by Kane-Berman, *Soweto*, p. 126. Until its suppression *The World* adopted a highly sympathetic position towards the SSRC, printing its statements and encouraging support for the student leadership.

30 Kane-Berman, *Soweto*, p. 132.

31 Brooks and Brickhill, *Whirlwind before the Storm*, pp. 151–2.

32 *Ibid*, p. 200.

33 *Ibid*, p. 238.

34 *Ibid*, p. 198. The quotation is from a discussion held by coloured schoolchildren in the western Cape.

35 *Ibid*, p. 227. Anonymous leaflet circulated in Katlehong, Germiston.

36 *Ibid*, p. 228. Leaflet produced by coloured school students in Cape Town.

37 Hirson, *Year of Fire, Year of Ash*, p. 287.

38 Kane-Berman, *Soweto*, p. 135.

39 Section 10 of the Black (Urban Areas) Act lays down the qualifications required by Africans for legal residence for more than 72 hours in any town.

40 Useful discussions of the Reports can be found in *South African Labour Bulletin* (special issue on Wiehahn), v, 2 (August 1979), and *South African Labour Bulletin* (special issue on Riekert), v, 4 (November 1979); Students' Representative Council Wages Commission, *Riekert: Don't worry, everything's okay*, University of Cape Town, 1979; Saul and Gelb, *The Crisis in South Africa*, pp. 63–83; Simon Jenkins, 'The great evasion', *The Economist*, 21 June 1980, pp. 14–22; and Steven Friedman, 'Political implications of industrial unrest in South Africa', African Studies Institute, 14 September 1981, pp. 12–19.

41 Although it captured no seats in the 1981 election the HNP succeeded in attracting 13 per cent of the vote, making heavy inroads in traditional Nationalist constituencies on the Transvaal platteland and Rand working-class constituencies. See Craig Charney, 'Towards rupture or stasis? An analysis of the 1981 South African General Election', African Studies Institute seminar paper, University of the Witwatersrand, 1981.

42 The Wiehahn Commission underestimated the proportions of unregistered trade union members who were migrants and suggested that with registration the unions themselves would exclude unskilled migrant workers from joining them. The government was unconvinced and issued a white paper which, with subsequent legislation, made migrant worker exclusion compulsory, but because of opposition from the unions and employers the prohibition was dropped by proclamation.

43 Multinational companies were anxious to legitimise their operations in South Africa in the view of public opinion in Europe and America. International labour boycotts were also a powerful incentive for the incorporation of the African labour movement in South Africa.

44 See Kane-Berman, *Soweto*, p. 210.

45 These included all the important Black Consciousness organisations as well as *The World* and the *Weekend World*.

46 Michael O'Dowd has emerged as the most fluent exponent of the free enterprise position with a weekly column in the *Sunday Times*. The theoretical basis for the opposed school is mainly developed by University of Stellenbosch economists.

47 Dr Nthato Motlana, for example, in newspaper interviews, professes admiration for the Swedish brand of social democracy.

48 See the finding of *The Star* public opinion survey, 23–24 September 1981.

49 *Rand Daily Mail*, 2 June 1978.

50 *The Star*, 17 April 1978.

51 See *Work in Progress*, Development Studies Group, University of the Witwatersrand, no. 18, 1981, pp. 22–6.

52 *Rand Daily Mail*, 10 March 1978.

53 South African Institute of Race Relations, *Annual Survey of Race Relations, 1980*, SAIRR, Johannesburg, 1981, p. 61.

54 *Sunday Tribune* (Durban), 16 April 1978.

55 See report on Treason Trial, *Work in Progress*, no. 16 (February 1981), p. 3.

56 *Ibid.*

57 In November 1980 the ANC became a signatory to Protocol One of the 1949 Geneva Convention which binds it to refraining from attacks on civilian targets as well as treating captured South African soldiers as prisoners of war. The initiative in persuading the ANC to take this step was taken by the International Red Cross.

58 *The Times* (London), 13 April 1981 and 14 April 1981.

59 See *Star* survey, cited above.

60 The South African Indian Council is a consultative body established by the government in 1964. A comprehensive analysis of the successful 1981 electoral boycott is in *Social Review*, Cape Town, no. 16 (November 1981), pp. 4–9.

61 Information on Okhela derived from: *Sunday Times* (Johannesburg), 21 January 1979, 3 February 1980, 25 October 1980; *The Citizen* (Johannesburg), 4 August 1977, 24 November 1979; *The Star*, 2 February 1978; *Daily Dispatch* (East London), 4 November 1977.

62 *Sunday Times* (Johannesburg), 31 August 1980.

63 Robert Petersen, 'Memorandum to the National Executive Committee of SACTU', London, 8 April 1979, p. 20.

64 See Ken Owen, 'War in the shadows', *Sunday Times* (Johannesburg), 19 October 1980.

65 *The Star*, 13–14 October 1980.

66 For example, as well as the Natal Indian Congress, 1981 witnessed the revival of the Federation of South African Women. See 'A song of defiance' in *The Star*, 10 August 1981.

67 This point is developed by Saul and Gelb, *The Crisis in South Africa*, p. 144.

68 Edwin Makoti claims that PAC 'strategy is that, first of all, we are preparing the people in the countryside for the struggle. This is where our main forces are concentrated'. (*Ikwezi*, no. 14 [March 1980] p. 16). If this is the case then the PAC has been uncharacteristically successful in remaining undetected. For trial evidence of PAC activity, see Glenn Moss, *Political Trials in South Africa*, Development Studies Group, Johannesburg, 1979, and *Work in Progress*, nos. 4, 7, and 8.

69 *Post* (Johannesburg), 3 June 1978 and *Rand Daily Mail*, 1 March 1980.

70 Information on PAC leadership disputes is drawn from the South African press and the columns of *Ikwezi*.

71 The Soweto Action Committee was an interim body set up in 1977 to perform the functions of the Committee of Ten, most of the members of which had been detained.

72 *Post*, 1 May 1978.

73 Khangale Mekhado, 'Black Consciousness as a driving force', *Ikwezi*, no. 16 (March 1981).
74 AZAPO policy paper, 'Further details on Black Consciousness and an emphasis on workers' position', from 1979 conference documentation.
75 Letsatsi Mosela, 'Dynamics of black thinking in Azania today', *Ikwezi*, no. 16 (March 1981).
76 AZAPO policy paper, 'On policy', from 1979 conference documentation.
77 Letsatsi Mosele, 'The challenge of labour in the 80s', 1981 AZAPO conference paper, p. 4.
78 For South African Allied Workers' Union criticism of trade unionist racial exclusivism, see *South African Labour Bulletin*, vi, 6 (March 1981), p. 27.
79 'We are here to stay', *The Star*, 25 August 1980.
80 For AZAPO's role in the Seshogo (Pietersburg) bus boycott, see *The Star*, 8 September 1980.
81 Roseinnes Phahle, 'AZAPO, Asinimali and Azikhwelwa', *Solidarity* (Official organ of the Black Consciousness Movement of Azania), London, no. 5 (1981), pp. 15–20.
82 *The Star*, 6 July 1981.
83 *Ibid*, 23 September 1981.
84 Philip Bonner, 'Black trade unions in South Africa since World War II' in Robert Price and Carl Rosberg (eds), *The Apartheid Regime*, David Philip, Cape Town, 1980, p. 187.
85 For TUACC/FOSATU strategy see Steven Friedman, 'Political implications of industrial unrest', p. 8; Philip Bonner, 'Black trade unions in South Africa', p. 188; and John Passmore 'Fosatu: perspective on a non-racial trade union' in *Reality*, Pietermaritzburg, September 1981, pp. 11–12.
86 For details see C. Joakimidis and A. Sitas, 'A study of strikes in the 1970s'.
87 Philip Bonner, 'Black trade unions in South Africa', p. 174 and p. 187.
88 For an account of the Fatti's and Moni's strike see Liz McGregor, 'The Fatti's and Moni's strike' in *South African Labour Bulletin*, c, 6 & 7 (March 1980), pp. 122–31.
89 An excellent short account of the strike is 'The meat strike' in *Social Review*, Cape Town, no. 10, September 1980, pp. 21–4.
90 The political problems arising from community involvement in trade union struggles are discussed in WPGWU, 'The Cape meat strike', *South African Labour Bulletin*, vi, 5 (December 1980), pp. 68–9, and 'Consumer boycotts: an evaluation', *Work in Progress*, no. 12, April 1980, p. 17.
91 Well over a hundred SAAUWU members are currently held in Ciskeian prisons and several of its leading figures have suffered petrol bomb attacks on their homes in Mdantsane. Homeland governments, because they have no international status to lose, feel no constraints in behaving with a degree of savagery towards their subjects which makes the South African authorities appear semi-civilised in comparison. For discussion of SAAWU see Owen Vanqa, 'Unity is Strength' in *Sunday Post*, 17 August 1980; Steven Friedman, 'Labour's siege city' in *Rand Daily Mail*, 31 October 1980; Drew Forrest, 'New style of black trade unionism may spell trouble' in *The Star*, 5 December 1980; and Tony Davis, 'SAAWU, the union that just grows and grows' in *The Star*, 27 February 1981.
92 The genesis of MACWUSA is described by Steven Friedman in 'Ford's unions: where the militants have become the moderates', *Rand Daily Mail*, 22 October 1980. For information on the Port Elizabeth Black Civic Organisation, see Carole Cooper and Linda Ensor, *PEBCO: a black mass movement*, SAIRR, Johannesburg, 1981.
93 Mr Tom Manthatha quoted in *Rand Daily Mail*, 15 September 1980.
94 Johann Maree, 'The UAW and the 1979 Port Elizabeth strikes', *South African Labour Bulletin*, vi, 2 & 3 (September 1980), p. 29.

95 See CWIU, 'Workers' struggle at Colgate', *South African Labour Bulletin*, vi, 8 (July 1981).

96 The most subtle version of this argument is to be found in Duncan Innes, Bob Fine, and Francine de Clercq, 'Trade unions and the state', *South African Labour Bulletin*, vii, 1 & 2 (September 1981), pp. 39–68.

97 *The Star*, 5 December 1980.

98 'Inkatha' is the Zulu expression for the head pad worn by women to ease the weight of heavy loads carried on the head.

99 Ben Temkin, *Gatsha Buthelezi: Zulu statesman*, Purnell, Cape Town, 1976, p. 57.

100 Gatsha Buthelezi, 'The power that has not yet been wielded', *Frontline*, Johannesburg, i, 6 (October 1980).

101 See, for example, Jordan Ngubane, 'Ubuntu-Botho', *The Condenser*, Tongaat Sugar Company, 1981, pp. 9–12. 'The ideals, strategies and priorities outlined . . . above shed light on the philosophy which Inkatha and its leader translate into action. This philosophy, it must be repeated, regards liberation at all levels generally and, in particular, on the political, economic and cultural planes, as simultaneous movement toward the creation of a society in which the person shall be equipped, enabled and seen to realise the promise of being human (ukubu ngumuntu) regardless of race, colour and sex. The inseparable precondition for successful movement to this goal are, in Inkatha's view, peaceful evolution, education for equal citizenship, the equitable distribution of land and other forms of wealth and the encouragement of foreign investments to provide employment for growing poopulation.'

102 See, for example, the behaviour of the Ciskeian authorities in 1974 as documented by Baruch Hirson, *Year of Fire, Year of Ash*, pp. 151–3.

103 'Inkatha and Natal education boycotts' in *Work in Progress*, no. 15, October 1980.

104 There is probably a calculated ambiguity to Inkatha statements on economic matters. A good description of Inkatha's early mixture of free enterprise and African communalism ideology is in 'Inkatha: centrepoint of the gathering storm', *Frontline*, i, 1 (December 1979), p. 24. See also *Sunday Times* (Johannesburg), 3 September 1978.

105 Gatsha Buthelezi, 'The power that has not yet been wielded'.

106 Quoted in Lawrence Schlemmer, 'The stirring giant: observations on Inkatha and other black political movements', in Robert Price and Carl Rosberg (eds), *The Apartheid Regime*, p. 113.

107 Exemplified in such bodies as the Black Unity Front and more recently the South African Black Alliance, which group Inkatha alongside various homeland and middle-of-the-road coloured organisations.

108 For example, during the Kwa Mashu school boycott: 'there is an anger [amongst the older Zulus directed against non-Zulu agitators] the like of which does not exist in any other group in this country'. For other examples see *Work in Progress*, no. 15, October 1980, p. 35.

109 'We believe that a grass roots-based mass organisation which is disciplined and responsible gains a respect and exerts a pressure without necessarily having to confront the system violently.' Buthelezi quoted in *The Star*, 12 August 1981.

110 See *Frontline*, i, 1 (December 1979), p. 25.

111 Schlemmer, 'The stirring giant', p. 115; *Frontline*, i, 6 (October 1980); and Philip Frankel, 'The politics of poverty: political competition in Soweto', *Canadian Journal of African Studies*, xiv, 2 (1980), p. 206, provide useful statistical information.

112 See report in *Sunday Tribune* (Durban), 26 March 1978, on the Kwa Zulu elections.

113 The most encouraging of these for Inkatha was the survey conducted by the Bergstrasse Institute during 1978 which found that Buthelezi enjoyed the support

of over forty per cent of the black urban population. See Frankel, 'The politics of poverty', p. 213.

114 Inkatha spokesmen have a tendency today to ascribe most of the external ANC leadership's faults to its manipulation by the SACP. The assumption by Jordan Ngubane in April 1980 of the role of Inkatha chief ideologue is significant in this context. Ngubane, a founder of the ANCYL, distinguished himself in the 1950s with the bitterness of his attacks on the Congress leadership, finally leaving the ANC and joining the Liberal Party.

115 *Sunday Times*, 16 November 1980.

116 See, for examples, 'Urban control – next year's model', *Social Review*, no. 11, December 1980, p. 17.

117 A useful profile of the Committee is provided in *The Nation*, Johannesburg, ii, 18 (June 1978), p. 5.

118 Quoted in 'The Committee of 10', *Work in Progress*, no. 10, November 1979, p. 7.

119 South African Institute of Race Relations, *Annual Survey of Race Relations, 1979*, SAIRR, Johannesburg, 1980, p. 48.

120 See Craig Charney, 'Soweto rents: golden political opportunity', *The Star*, 28 October 1980.

121 See, for example, 'Motlana supports Blackchain plans', *Sunday Post*, 14 May 1978.

Sources

Documents

Azanian African People's Organisation. Documents from Inaugural Conference and First Annual Congress.

Margaret Ballinger Papers, University of the Witwatersrand.

Carter and Karis microfilm collection, Southern African Research Archives Project, copy held in the University of South Africa Library.

Cooperative Africana Microfilm Collection:

Regina *versus* Robert Sobukwe and 22 others, 1960, trial transcript, NF 2399.

Proceedings of the Snyman Commission of Enquiry, 1962–1963, transcript, MF 647.

State *versus* Jeffrey Masemula and 15 others, 1963, trial transcript, MF 568.

State *versus* Pascal Ngakane, Pietrmaritzburg, 1964, trial transcript, MF 568.

Held in the University of York Library.

Patrick Duncan Papers, University of York.

Federation of South African Women Papers, University of the Witwatersrand.

Alfred Hoernlé Papers, University of the Witwatersrand.

Clements Kadalie Papers, photocopied correspondence between Clements and Alexander Kadalie, held at the African Studies Institute, University of the Witwatersrand.

Atwell Mopeli-Paulus Papers, University of the Witwatersrand.

Lionel Morrison Papers, University of York.

J. M. Nhlapo Papers, University of the Witwatersrand.

Pan-Africanist Congress, miscellaneous correspondence from a privately owned collection.

Albie Sachs Papers, Institute of Commonwealth Studies, University of London, trial records:

Regina *versus* Synod Madlebe and 31 others, 1960, AS 31/11.

State *versus* Mandla and 31 others, 1963, AS 69/8.

State *versus* Matikila and 3 others, 1962, AS 83/14.

State *versus* Xintolo, n. d., AS 83/14.

State *versus* Dudaza and 3 others, 1963, AS/70.

African Resistance Movement trial, Cape Town, 1964, AS 76/6.

Rheinallt-Jones Papers, University of the Witwatersrand.

South African Institute of Race Relations, pamphlet collection, Box File 26A (Education).

South African Institute of Race Relations (SAIRR) Papers, University of the Witwatersrand.

South African Institute of Race Relations, trial records collection:

Crown *versus* F. Adams and 29 others, 1956–1961 (Treason Trial) transcript.

State *versus* Makatezi and 20 others, SAIRR 1/1963, transcript.

Sharpeville Advisory Board minutes, Town Clerk's Office, Vereeniging.

State versus Stanley Thabo Pule and 2 others, Supreme Court, Natal Division, Case no. cc 133/1977, trial records.

University of York, Centre for Southern African Studies, South African trial transcripts:

State *versus* Nomapelisa Meji and 22 others, Butterworth, 21 August 1963, Box 1 File 2.

State *versus* Ngconcolo and 19 others, CC/9/1963, Box I File 3.

Transport Files, South African Association of Newspapers Library, Johannesburg.

Transcript of the Commission of Enquiry into the Events which occurred in the Districts of Vereeniging and Vanderbijlpark, 21 March 1960, held in the University of York Library.

Vereeniging Old Location Advisory Board minutes, Town Clerk's Office, Vereeniging.

Vereeniging Town Council Non-European Affairs Committee minutes, Town Clerk's Office, Vereeniging.

Alfred Xuma Papers, University of the Witwatersrand.

Newspapers and Periodicals

(dates indicate the volumes which were consulted)

Africa Confidential (London), 1963–1971.
Africa Perspective (Johannesburg), 1976–1981.
Africa South (Cape Town), 1956–1960.
Africa X-Ray Report (Johannesburg), 1955.
The Africanist (Soweto), 1955–1959.
Azania Combat (London), 1975–1977.
Bantu World (Johannesburg) (from 1956 *The World*), 1950–1960.
Cape Argus (Cape Town), 1960–1965.
Cape Times (Cape Town), 1959–1963.
Contact (Cape Town), 1958–1963.
Counter-Attack (Johannesburg), 1955–1959.
Drum (Johannesburg), 1952–1963.
Daily Dispatch (East London), 1946–1952.
Eastern Province Herald (Port Elizabeth), 1945–1952.
Fighting Talk (Johannesburg), 1952–1060.
The Forum (Johannesburg), 1940–1960.
Forward (Johannesburg), 1952.
Frontline (Johannesburg), 1952.
The Good Shepherd (Johannesburg), 1942–1948.
Golden City Post (Johannesburg), 1959.
The Guardian (Cape Town), later *Clarion, Peoples' World, Advance,* and *New Age,* 1947–1962.
Ikwezi (Nottingham), 1976–1981.
Ikwezi Lomso (Queenstown), 1958–1960.
Imvo Zabantsundu (Kingwilliamstown), 1943–1950.
Inkululeko (Johannesburg) 1943–1950.
Inkundla ya Bantu (Durban), 1949–1950.
Liberation (Johannesburg), 1957–1959.
The Nation (Johannesburg), 1976–1979.
The New African (London), 1962–1965.
Rand Daily Mail (Johannesburg), 1948–1960; 1978–1981.
Social Review (Cape Town), 1978–1981.
South Africa: Information and Analysis (Paris, 1962–1969.
South African Labour Bulletin (Durban), 1976–1980.
The Spark (Johannesburg), 1952.
The Star (Johannesburg), 1952–1957; 1978–1981.
Sunday Express (Johannesburg), 1978–1981.

Sunday Times (Johannesburg), 1978–1981.
The Torch (Cape Town), 1949–1961.
Vereeniging and Vanderbijlpark News, 1958–1961.
The Voice of Orlando (Soweto), 1952–1953.
Work in Progress (Johannesburg), 1977–1981.

Interviews

Frances Baard, Mabopane, 1981.
Brian Bunting, London, 1975.
Marion Friedman, London, 1976.
Peter Hjul, London, 1976.
Helen Joseph, Johannesburg, 1981.
William Letlalo, Soweto, 1979.
Don Mattera, Johannesburg, 1980.
Tommy Mohajane, York, 1975.
Dr Nthato Motlana, Soweto, 1981.
Es'kia Mphahlele, Johannesburg, 1980.
Matthew Nkoana, London, 1975.
A. B. Ngcobo, London, 1975.
Peter Rodda, London, 1975.
Albie Sachs, London, 1976.
Rose Schlacter, Johannesburg, 1981.
David Sibeko, London, 1976.
Ben Turok, London, 1975.
Randolph Vigne, London, 1975.
M. B. Yengwa, London, 1977.

Official Publications

Annual Report of the Native Affairs Commission, Pretoria:
   1927–1931, UG 26/1932.
   1939–1940, UG 42/1941.
   1946–1947, UG 15/1949.
   1948–1952, UG 36/1954.
Annual Report of the Native Affairs Department, Pretoria:
   1935–1936, UG 41/1937.
   1944–1945, UG 44/1946.
   1945–1947, UG 14/1948.
   1947–1948, UG 35/1949.
   1948–1949, UG 51/1950.
   1949–1950, UG 61/1951.
   1950–1951, UG 30/1953.
   1951–1952, UG 37/1955.
   1952–1953, UG 48/1955.
   1953–1954, UG 53/1956.
   1954–1957, UG 14/1959.
   1958–1959, UG 51/1960.
Annual Report of the South African Police Commissioner, Pretoria:
   1944, SAP 36/16/44.
   1943, SAP 36/27/43.

1946, UG 39/1947.
1947, UG 55/1948.
1948, UG 42/1949.
1950, UG 52/1950.
1951, UG 44/1952.
1952, UG 33/1953.
1953, UG 39/1954.
1954, UG 54/1955.
1955, UG 52/1956.
1956, UG 41/1958.
1957, UG 35/1959.
1958, UG 43/1960.
1959, UG 73/1960.
1960, RG 19/1961.

Annual Report of the National Transport Commission, Pretoria:
1954–1957, UG 26/1958.

Ciskeian General Council Proceedings, Kingwilliamstown, 1945–1951.

Population Census, 1946, UG 41/1954.

Population Census, 1951, UG 61/1954.

Population Census, 1960, Bureau of Statistics, Pretoria, 1966.

Population Census, 1970, Bureau of Statistics, Pretoria, 1976.

Report of the Commission of Enquiry into Acts of Violence Committed by Natives at Krugersdorp, Newlands, Randfontein and Newclare, Pretoria, UG 47/1950.

Report of the Commission of Enquiry into the Disturbances at the Witzieshoek Native Reserve, Cape Times Ltd, Parow, UG 26/1951.

Report of the Commission of Enquiry into the Riots at Soweto and Elsewhere, Pretoria, RP 55/1980.

Report of the Commission Appointed to Inquire into the Events on the 20–22nd November 1962 at Paarl, Pretoria, RP 51/1963.

Report of the Commission appointed to Inquire into the Operation of Bus Services for Non-Europeans on the Witwatersrand, Pretoria, UG 1/1944.

Report of the Witwatersrand Mine Natives' Wages Commission, Pretoria, UG 21/1944.

Report of the Select Committee on the Suppression of Communism Act, Cape Town, SC 10/1953.

Summary of the Commission of Enquiry into the Events which occurred in the Districts of Vereeniging and Vanderbijlpark, mimeo., 1960.

Verbatim Record of the Natives' Representative Council, Pretoria, 1943.

City of Johannesburg, Non-European Affairs Department, *Survey of the Western Areas of Johannesburg*, 1950.

City of Johannesburg, Non-European Affairs Department, *Report on a Sample Survey of the Native Population Residing in the Western Areas of Johannesburg*, 1951.

Unpublished dissertations

Alan Brooks, 'From class struggle to national liberation: the Communist Party of South Africa, 1940–1950', M.A. thesis, University of Sussex, 1973.

Edward Feit, 'Conflict and Communication: an analysis of the 'Western Areas' and 'Bantu Education' campaigns, Ph.D. thesis, University of Michigan, 1965.

Robert Johnson, 'Indians and Apartheid in South Africa', Ph.D. thesis, University of Massachusetts, 1973.

Moira Levy, 'Opposition to Apartheid in the Fifties: the Liberal Party and the Congress of Democrats', B.A. Honours Dissertation, University of the Witwatersrand, 1981.

Gary Longden, 'Umkonto we Sizwe and the Reasons for its Failure', B.Phil Dissertation, University of York, 1976.

E. Murphy, 'Bantu Education in South Africa', Ph.D. thesis, Connecticut, 1973.

Essop Pahad, 'The Development of Indian Political Movements in South Africa', Ph.D. Dissertation, University of Sussex, 1972.

Desirée Soudien, 'The Food and Canning Workers' Union: the Organisation of the Food and Canning Workers during the SACTU Years', B.A. Honours Dissertation, University of the Witwatersrand, 1981.

Index